D1489260

SOMETHING ABOUT THE AUTHOR®

Something about
the Author *was named
an "Outstanding
Reference Source,"*
*the highest honor given
by the American
Library Association
Reference and Adult
Services Division.*

ISSN 0276-816X

SOMETHING ABOUT THE AUTHOR®

**Facts and Pictures about Authors
and Illustrators of Books for Young People**

volume 163

THOMSON

GALE

Detroit • New York • San Francisco • San Diego • New Haven, Conn. • Waterville, Maine • London • Munich

THOMSON

GALE

Something About the Author, Volume 163

Project Editor
Maikue Vang

Editorial
Katy Balcer, Michelle Kazensky, Julie Keppen, Joshua Kondek, Lisa Kumar, Tracey Matthews, Mary Ruby, Mark Rzeszutek

Permissions
Lori Hines, Shalice Shah-Caldwell, Kim Smilay

Imaging and Multimedia
Leitha Etheridge-Sims, Lezlie Light, Dan Newell

Composition and Electronic Capture
Carolyn Roney

Manufacturing
Drew Kalasky

Product Manager
Chris Nasso

LIBRARY OF CONGRESS CATALOG CARD NUMBER 62-52046

ISBN 0-7876-8787-1
ISSN 0276-816X

Printed in the United States of America
10 9 8 7 6 5 4 3 2 1

Contents

Authors in Forthcoming Volumes

Below are some of the authors and illustrators that will be featured in upcoming volumes of *SATA*. These include new entries on the swiftly rising stars of the field, as well as completely revised and updated entries (indicated with *) on some of the most notable and best-loved creators of books for children.

Dori Hillestad Butler ▮ Starting out as a picture-book author, Butler has expanded her audience to include older readers with middle-grade novels such as *Trading Places with Tank Talbot* and *Sliding into Home*. Raised on the inspiring novels of Judy Blume and Paula Danzinger, Butler features newly minted teen characters whose positive spirit and determination help them conquer barriers and follow their dreams.

*Judith Ortiz Cofer ▮ Born in Puerto Rico, the multi-award-winning Cofer draws on her family's culture and her own memories of growing up in suburban New Jersey in her many books for young children. *The Year of Our Revolution* collects stories and poems for teen readers that focus on growing up during the turbulent 1960s, while in the middle-grade novel *Call Me Maria* a girl is emotionally torn between her family in Puerto Rico and her father's new home in New York City. In addition to her own prose and poetry, Cofer has edited several collections showcasing the writing of other Puerto-Rican authors.

Loren Coleman ▮ One of the world's leading cryptozoologists, Coleman is a respected researcher who has dedicated his career and his writing to exploring and popularizing the growing body of information regarding many of Earth's most tantalizing and mysterious creatures. His book *Cryptozoology A to Z: The Encyclopedia of Loch Monsters, Sasquatch, Chupacabras, and Other Authentic Mysteries of Nature* is popular with curious readers, and Coleman has also shared his research and his wide-ranging knowledge on radio and television.

*Niki Daly ▮ South African author-illustrator, Daly creates picture books that celebrate children's vivid imagination and their naturally optimistic view of life. Woven with African-based themes, Daly's books include *Not So Fast, Songololo* and *Jamela's Dress*, have been consistently praised as valuable contributions to a growing body of work that is inclusive of all races and ethnic groups.

Laura Geringer ▮ In addition to publishing the books of several well-known authors as the head of her own imprint at a top New York publishing company, Geringer has written several well-received novels under her pen name, L. G. Bass. In addition to producing picture-book retellings of Greek and Roman myths,

such as *Theseus: The Hero of the Maze*, she has also moved to fantasy with *Sign of the Qin*, the opening book in her ongoing "Outlaws of Moonshadow Marsh" trilogy.

Christine Petrell Kallevig ▮ An author, storyteller, and origami artist, Kallevig has woven her various creative interests into an art form she calls "storigami." In books such as *Fold-along Stories: Quick and Easy Origami Tales for Beginners* she pairs entertaining story-hour tales with directions for the origami figures that will make them come alive for young audiences.

*Sam McBratney ▮ Hailing from Northern Ireland, McBratney has penned over fifty books for young readers, producing everything from science fiction to picture books to radio plays. He gained acclaim among U.S. readers with his 400-word story *Guess How Much I Love You*, which has since been translated into dozens of languages. Known for his witty plots and warmhearted characters, McBratney also focuses on childhood emotions in the books *I'm Sorry* and *You're All My Family*, and has also proved a talented reteller of traditional folktales.

Daniel Powers ▮ Primarily known as an illustrator, Powers has also won critical acclaim for his self-illustrated picture book *Jiro's Pearl*. Borrowing from both Japanese tradition and western fairy tales, the story of a young boy, a sick grandmother, and a wise conjurer also features Powers's compelling art. As an illustrator, Powers has collaborated on books by well-known authors such as Newbery winner Jean Craighead George and Judith St. George.

Curtis Sittenfeld ▮ Sittenfeld drew on her experiences attending a prestigious New England private school in her debut novel, *Prep*. *Prep* views student life at Boston's prestigious Ault School, illustrating the cliques, social pressures, and problems that arise within a student body composed almost totally of the offspring of the so-called social elite. Narrated by Lee, a self-conscious twenty-something who reflects back on her years at Ault, Sittenfeld's novel resonates with readers attempting to negotiate their own path through adolescence.

*Margaret Weis ▮ Known to fantasy fans as the "Dragon Lady," Weis is a popular and prolific writer and game designer. She is best known for her collaborations with coauthor Tracy Hickman on the "Dragonlance" fantasy adventure series. Set in the imaginary world of Krynn, the "Dragonlance Chronicles" that serve as the core of Weis's vast saga have recently been re-released specifically for teen readers. Weis began the series while working at TSR, a gaming company whose *Dragonlance* role-playing game inspired the author's early fiction; she has since gone on to write in other genres as well, and now publishes through her own gaming company, Sovereign Press.

Introduction

Something about the Author (*SATA*) is an ongoing reference series that examines the lives and works of authors and illustrators of books for children. *SATA* includes not only well-known writers and artists but also less prominent individuals whose works are just coming to be recognized. This series is often the only readily available information source on emerging authors and illustrators. You'll find *SATA* informative and entertaining, whether you are a student, a librarian, an English teacher, a parent, or simply an adult who enjoys children's literature.

What's Inside *SATA*

SATA provides detailed information about authors and illustrators who span the full time range of children's literature, from early figures like John Newbery and L. Frank Baum to contemporary figures like Judy Blume and Richard Peck. Authors in the series represent primarily English-speaking countries, particularly the United States, Canada, and the United Kingdom. Also included, however, are authors from around the world whose works are available in English translation. The writings represented in *SATA* include those created intentionally for children and young adults as well as those written for a general audience and known to interest younger readers. These writings cover the entire spectrum of children's literature, including picture books, humor, folk and fairy tales, animal stories, mystery and adventure, science fiction and fantasy, historical fiction, poetry and nonsense verse, drama, biography, and nonfiction. Obituaries are also included in *SATA* and are intended not only as death notices but also as concise overviews of people's lives and work. Additionally, each edition features newly revised and updated entries for a selection of *SATA* listees who remain of interest to today's readers and who have been active enough to require extensive revisions of their earlier biographies.

Autobiography Feature

Beginning with Volume 103, *SATA* features two or more specially commissioned autobiographical essays in each volume. These unique essays, averaging about ten thousand words in length and illustrated with an abundance of personal photos, present an entertaining and informative first-person perspective on the lives and careers of prominent authors and illustrators profiled in *SATA*.

Two Convenient Indexes

In response to suggestions from librarians, *SATA* indexes no longer appear in every volume but are included in alternate (odd-numbered) volumes of the series, beginning with Volume 57.

SATA continues to include two indexes that cumulate with each alternate volume: the Illustrations Index, arranged by the name of the illustrator, gives the number of the volume and page where the illustrator's work appears in the current volume as well as all preceding volumes in the series; the Author Index gives the number of the volume in which a person's biographical sketch, autobiographical essay, or obituary appears in the current volume as well as all preceding volumes in the series.

These indexes also include references to authors and illustrators who appear in *Gale's Yesterday's Authors of Books for Children, Children's Literature Review,* and *Something about the Author Autobiography Series.*

Easy-to-Use Entry Format

Whether you're already familiar with the *SATA* series or just getting acquainted, you will want to be aware of the kind of information that an entry provides. In every *SATA* entry the editors attempt to give as complete a picture of the person's life and work as possible. A typical entry in *SATA* includes the following clearly labeled information sections:

PERSONAL: date and place of birth and death, parents' names and occupations, name of spouse, date of marriage, names of children, educational institutions attended, degrees received, religious and political affiliations, hobbies and other interests.

ADDRESSES: complete home, office, electronic mail, and agent addresses, whenever available.

CAREER: name of employer, position, and dates for each career post; art exhibitions; military service; memberships and offices held in professional and civic organizations.

MEMBER: professional, civic, and other association memberships and any official posts held.

AWARDS, HONORS: literary and professional awards received.

WRITINGS: title-by-title chronological bibliography of books written and/or illustrated, listed by genre when known; lists of other notable publications, such as plays, screenplays, and periodical contributions.

ADAPTATIONS: a list of films, television programs, plays, CD-ROMs, recordings, and other media presentations that have been adapted from the author's work.

WORK IN PROGRESS: description of projects in progress.

SIDELIGHTS: a biographical portrait of the author or illustrator's development, either directly from the biographee—and often written specifically for the *SATA* entry—or gathered from diaries, letters, interviews, or other published sources.

BIOGRAPHICAL AND CRITICAL SOURCES: cites sources quoted in "Sidelights" along with references for further reading.

EXTENSIVE ILLUSTRATIONS: photographs, movie stills, book illustrations, and other interesting visual materials supplement the text.

How a *SATA* Entry Is Compiled

A *SATA* entry progresses through a series of steps. If the biographee is living, the *SATA* editors try to secure information directly from him or her through a questionnaire. From the information that the biographee supplies, the editors prepare an entry, filling in any essential missing details with research and/or telephone interviews. If possible, the author or illustrator is sent a copy of the entry to check for accuracy and completeness.

If the biographee is deceased or cannot be reached by questionnaire, the *SATA* editors examine a wide variety of published sources to gather information for an entry. Biographical and bibliographic sources are consulted, as are book reviews, feature articles, published interviews, and material sometimes obtained from the biographee's family, publishers, agent, or other associates.

Entries that have not been verified by the biographees or their representatives are marked with an asterisk (*).

Contact the Editor

We encourage our readers to examine the entire *SATA* series. Please write and tell us if we can make *SATA* even more helpful to you. Give your comments and suggestions to the editor:

Editor
Something about the Author
Thomson Gale
27500 Drake Rd.
Farmington Hills MI 48331-3535

Toll-free: 800-877-GALE
Fax: 248-699-8070

Something about the Author Product Advisory Board

The editors of *Something about the Author* are dedicated to maintaining a high standard of excellence by publishing comprehensive, accurate, and highly readable entries on a wide array of writers for children and young adults. In addition to the quality of the content, the editors take pride in the graphic design of the series, which is intended to be orderly yet inviting, allowing readers to utilize the pages of *SATA* easily and with efficiency. Despite the longevity of the *SATA* print series, and the success of its format, we are mindful that the vitality of a literary reference product is dependent on its ability to serve its users over time. As literature, and attitudes about literature, constantly evolve, so do the reference needs of students, teachers, scholars, journalists, researchers, and book club members. To be certain that we continue to keep pace with the expectations of our customers, the editors of *SATA* listen carefully to their comments regarding the value, utility, and quality of the series. Librarians, who have firsthand knowledge of the needs of library users, are a valuable resource for us. The *Something about the Author* Product Advisory Board, made up of school, public, and academic librarians, is a forum to promote focused feedback about *SATA* on a regular basis. The nine-member advisory board includes the following individuals, whom the editors wish to thank for sharing their expertise:

Eva M. Davis
Youth Department Manager,
Ann Arbor District Library,
Ann Arbor, Michigan

Joan B. Eisenberg
Lower School Librarian,
Milton Academy,
Milton, Massachusetts

Francisca Goldsmith
Teen Services Librarian,
Berkeley Public Library,
Berkeley, California

Susan Dove Lempke
Children's Services Supervisor,
Niles Public Library District,
Niles, Illinois

Robyn Lupa
Head of Children's Services,
Jefferson County Public Library,
Lakewood, Colorado

Victor L. Schill
Assistant Branch Librarian/Children's Librarian,
Harris County Public Library/Fairbanks Branch,
Houston, Texas

Caryn Sipos
Community Librarian,
Three Creeks Community Library,
Vancouver, Washington

Steven Weiner
Director,
Maynard Public Library,
Maynard, Massachusetts

Acknowledgments

Grateful acknowledgment is made to the following publishers, authors, and artists whose works appear in this volume.

ADLERMAN, DANIEL (EZRA) ▮ Adlerman, Kim, illustrator. From an illustration in *Rock-a-bye Baby*, by Danny Adlerman. Text copyright © 2004 by Danny Adlerman. Illustration copyright © 2004 by Kim Adlerman. Used with permission by Charlesbridge Publishing, Inc. All rights reserved. / Adlerman, Daniel, with daughter, Rachelle, photograph by Marbeth. Reproduced by permission.

ADOFF, JAIME (LEVI) ▮ French, Martin, illustrator. From an illustration in *The Song Shoots Out of My Mouth*, by Jaime Adoff. Dutton Children's Books, 2002. Copyright © 2002 by Martin French, illustrations. Used by permission of Dutton Children's Books, A Division of Penguin Young Readers Group, A Member of Penguin Group (USA) Inc., 345 Hudson Street, New York, NY 10014. All rights reserved. / Chow, Symon, photographer. From a jacket of *Names Will Never Hurt Me*, by Jaime Adoff. Dutton Children's Books, 2004. Copyright © 2004 by Symon Chow, jacket photo. Used by permission of Dutton Children's Books, A Division of Penguin Young Readers Group, A Member of Penguin Group (USA) Inc., 345 Hudson Street, New York, NY 10014. All rights reserved.

ALLENDE, ISABEL ▮ Nielsen, Cliff, illustrator. From a jacket of *Kingdom of the Golden Dragon*, by Isabel Allende. HarperCollins Publishers, 2004. Cover art © 2004 by Cliff Nielsen. Used by permission of HarperCollins Publishers. / Pioltelli, Luca, illustrator. From a jacket of Zorro, by Isabel Allende. HarperCollins Publishers, 2005. Jacket photographs © by Luca Pioltelli. Text copyright © 2005 by Isabel Allende. The use of "Zorro" and other characters created by Johnson McCulley has been licensed and authorized by Zorro Productions, Inc. Copyright © 2005 by Zorro Productions, Inc. All rights reserved. ZORRO is a trademark owned by Zorro Productions, Inc., Berkeley, CA. Reprinted by permission of HarperCollins Publishers and Zorro Productions, Inc. / Allende, Isabel, photograph by Jakub Mosur. AP/Wide World Photos. Reproduced by permission.

ARCHAMBAULT, JOHN ▮ Chitwood, Suzanne Tanner, illustrator. From an illustration in *Boom Chicka Rock*, by John Archambault. Copyright © 2004 by Suzanne Tanner Chitwood, illustrations. Used by permission of Philomel Books, A Division of Penguin Young Readers Group, A Member of Penguin Group (USA) Inc., 345 Hudson Street, New York, NY 10014. All rights reserved.

BOELTS, MARIBETH ▮ Widener, Terry, illustrator. From *The Firefighters' Thanksgiving*, by Maribeth Boelts. Copyright © 2004 by Terry Widener, illustrations. Used by permission of G.P. Putnam's Sons, A Division of Penguin Young Readers Group, A Member of Penguin Group (USA) Inc., 345 Hudson Street, New York, NY 10014. All rights reserved.

BREDESON, CARMEN ▮ Rosing, Norbert, photographer. From a photograph in *Animals That Migrate*, by Carmen Bredeson. Franklin Watts, 2001. Photographs copyright © Animals Animals: #23 by Norbert Rosing. Reproduced by permission. / Mawson Antarctic Collection, photographer. From a photograph in *After the Last Dog Died: The True-Life, Hair-Raising Adventures of Douglas Mawson and His 1911-1914 Antarctic Expeditions*, by Carmen Bredeson. National Geographic Society, 2003. Reproduced by permission of Mawson Collection & Industrial History Collection. / Space shuttle lifting off, photograph. NASA.

BROWNE, ANTHONY (EDWARD TUDOR) ▮ Browne, Anthony, photograph by Ellen Browne. Reproduced by permission of Anthony Browne.

BYARS, BETSY (CROMER) ▮ Simont, Marc, illustrator. From an illustration in *My Brother, Ant*, by Betsy Byars. Puffin Books, 1996. Copyright © 1996 by Marc Simont, illustrations. Used by permission of Viking Penguin, A Division of Penguin Young Readers Group, A Member of Penguin Group (USA) Inc., 345 Hudson Street, New York, NY 10014. All rights reserved. / Sabin, Robert, illustrator. From a cover of *Disappearing Acts*, by Betsy Byars. Puffin Books, 1998. Copyright © 2000 by Robert Sabin, cover illustration. Used by permission of Puffin Books, A Division of Penguin Young Readers Group, A Member of Penguin Group (USA) Inc., 345 Hudson Street, New York, NY 10014. All rights reserved. / Vojnar, Kamil, illustrator. From a jacket of *Keeper of the Doves*, by Betsy Byars. Viking, 2002. Copyright © 2002 Kamil Vojnar, jacket illustration. Used by permission of Viking Children's Books, A Division of Penguin Young Readers Group, A Member of Penguin Group (USA) Inc., 345 Hudson Street, New York, NY 10014. All rights reserved. / Byars, Betsy, photograph. Reproduced by permission of Betsy Byars.

CANNON, A(NN) E(DWARDS) ▮ Sano, Kazuhiko, illustrator. From a jacket of *Charlotte's Rose*, by A. E. Cannon. Wendy Lamb Books, 2002. Jacket illustration copyright © 2002 by Kazuhiko Sano. All rights reserved. Used by permission of Random House Children's Books, a division of Random House, Inc.

CAPUCILLI, ALYSSA SATIN ▮ Rankin, Joan, illustrator. From an illustration in *Mrs. McTats and Her Houseful of Cats*, by Alyssa Satin Capucilli. Margaret K. McElderry Books, 2001. Illustrations copyright © 2001 Joan Rankin. Reprinted with the permission of Margaret K. McElderry Books, an imprint of Simon & Schuster Children's Publishing Division.

CARLE, ERIC ▮ Carle, Eric, illustrator. From an illustration in *Slowly, Slowly, Slowly, Said the Sloth*, by Eric Carle. Philomel Books 2002. Copyright © 2002 by Eric Carle. Used by permission of Philomel Books, A Division of Penguin Young Readers Group, a Member of Penguin Group (USA) Inc., 345 Hudson Street, New York, NY 10014. All rights reserved. / Carle, Eric, illustrator. From

2004. Copyright © 2004 Petr Horacek. Reproduced by permission of the publisher Candlewick Press, Inc., Cambridge, MA., on behalf of Walker Books Ltd., London.

JOCELYN, MARTHE ▌ Jocelyn, Marthe, illustrator. From an illustration in *Hannah's Collections*, by Marthe Jocelyn. Dutton Children's Books, 2000. Copyright © 2000 by Marthe Jocelyn. Used by permission of Dutton Children's Books, A Division of Penguin Young Readers Group, A Member of Penguin Group (USA) Inc., 345 Hudson Street, New York, NY 10014. All rights reserved. / Jocelyn, Marthe, illustrator. From an illustration in *Mayfly*, by Marthe Jocelyn. © 2004 by Marthe Jocelyn. Published in Canada by Tundra Books and in the United States by Tundra Books of Northern New York. / Jocelyn, Marthe, photograph. Reproduced by permission.

KUKLIN, SUSAN ▌ Kuklin, Susan, photographer. From a photograph in *Hoops with Swoopes*, by Sheryl Swoopes. Hyperion Books for Children, 2001. Copyright © 2001. Reprinted by permission of Hyperion Books For Children. / Kuklin, Susan, photographer. From a photograph in *All Aboard!: A True Train Story*, by Susan Kuklin. Orchard Books, an imprint of Scholastic, Inc., 2003. Photographs copyright © 2003 by Susan Kuklin. Reprinted by permission of Orchard Books, an imprint of Scholastic Inc. / Kuklin, Susan, photograph by Bailey H. Kuklin. Reproduced by permission of Susan Kuklin.

LAMINACK, LESTER L. ▌ Soentpiet, Chris, illustrator. From an illustration in *Saturdays and Teacakes*, by Lester L. Laminack. Peachtree Publishers, 2004. Paintings © 2004 by Chris Soentpiet. All rights reserved. Reproduced by permission.

LEONARD, ELMORE (JOHN JR.) ▌ Leonard, Elmore, photograph by Paul Sancya. AP/Wide World Photos. Reproduced by permission.

LINDBERGH, REEVE ▌ Pearson, Tracey Campbell, illustrator. From an illustration in *The Awful Aardvarks Shop for School*, by Reeve Lindbergh. Viking, 2000. Copyright © 2000 by Tracey Campbell Pearson, illustrations. Used by permission of Viking Children's Books, A Division of Penguin Young Readers Group, A Member of Penguin Group (USA) Inc., 345 Hudson Street, New York, NY 10014. All rights reserved. / Carter, Abby, illustrator. From an illustration in *My Hippie Grandmother*, by Reeve Lindbergh. Candlewick Press, 2003. Text Copyright © 2003 Reeve Lindbergh. Illustrations Copyright © 2003 Abby Carter. Reproduced by permission of the publisher Candlewick Press, Inc., Cambridge, MA. / McElmurry, Jill, illustrator. From an illustration in *Our Nest*, by Reeve Lindbergh. Candlewick Press, 2004. Text Copyright © 2004 Reeve Lindbergh. Illustrations Copyright © 2004 Jill McElmurry. Reproduced by permission of the publisher Candlewick Press, Inc., Cambridge, MA.

MASON, ADRIENNE ▌ Ogle, Nancy Gray, illustrator. From an illustration in *Bats*, by Adrienne Mason. Kids Can Press, 2003. Illustration © 2003 Nancy Gray Ogle. Used by permission of Kids Can Press Ltd., Toronto, Canada.

MCDERMOTT, GERALD (EDWARD) ▌ McDermott, Gerald, illustrator. From an illustration in *Arrow to the Sun*, adapted by Gerald McDermott. Viking, 1974. Copyright © 1974 by Gerald McDermott. Used by permission of Viking Penguin, A Division of Penguin Young Reader's Group, A Member of Penguin Group (USA) Inc., 345 Hudson Street, New York, NY 10014. All rights reserved. / McDermott, Gerald, illustrator. From *Creation*, by Gerald McDermott. Copyright © 2003 by Gerald McDermott, text and illustrations. Used by permission of Dutton Children's Books, A Division of Penguin Young Readers Group, A Member of Penguin Group (USA) Inc., 345 Hudson Street, New York, NY 10014. All rights reserved.

MCGEE, MARNI ▌ Shearing, Leonie, illustrator. From an illustration in *The Noisy Farm*, by Marni McGee. Bloomsbury, 2004. Illustrations copyright © 2004 Leonie Shearing. All rights reserved. Reproduced by permission.

MOSS, MARISSA ▌ Amelia, artist and designer. From an illustration in *Amelia's Notebook*, by Marissa Moss. Simon & Schuster, 2006. Copyright © 1995 by Marissa Moss. Reproduced by permission.

NUTT, KEN ▌ Beddows, Eric, illustrator. From a jacket of *Toes*, by Tor Seidler. Laura Geringer Books, 2004. Cover art © 2004 by Eric Beddows. Used by permission of HarperCollins Publishers. / Beddows, Eric (Ken Nutt), photograph. Reproduced by permission of Eric Beddows.

PHILBRICK, (W.) RODMAN ▌ Shannon, David, illustrator. From a cover of *Freak the Mighty*, by Rodman Philbrick. Scholastic Signature, 1993. Illustration copyright © 1993 by David Shannon. Reprinted by permission of Scholastic Inc. / Thompson, John, illustrator. From a cover of *The Fire Pony*, by Rodman Philbrick. A Scholastic Apple Signature Edition Book, 1997. Illustration copyright © 1997 by Scholastic Inc. Reprinted by permission of Scholastic Inc. / Call, Greg, illustrator. From a cover of *REM World*, by Rodman Philbrick. Scholastic Signature, 2001. Cover illustration copyright © 2001 by Greg Call. Reprinted by permission of Scholastic Inc. / Philbrick, Rodman, photograph by Lynn Harnett. Reproduced by permission of Rodman Philbrick.

RYDER, JOANNE (ROSE) ▌ Winter, Susan, illustrator. From an illustration in *Come Along, Kitten*, by Joanne Ryder. Simon & Schuster Books for Young Readers, 2003. Illustrations copyright © 2003 Susan Winter. Reprinted with the permission of Simon & Schuster Books for Young Readers, an imprint of Simon & Schuster Children's Publishing Division.

SEGAL, LORE (GROSZMANN) ▌ Kulikov, Boris, illustrator. From an illustration in *Morris the Artist*, by Lore Segal. Farrar, Straus and Giroux, 2003. Text copyright © 2003 by Lore Segal. Illustrations copyright © 2003 by Boris Kulikov. Reprinted by permission of Farrar, Straus and Giroux, LLC. / Ruzzier, Sergio, illustrator. From an illustration in *Why Mole Shouted*, by Lore Segal. Farrar, Straus and Giroux 2004. Text copyright © 2004 by Lore Segal. Illustrations copyright © 2004 by Sergio Ruzzier. Reprinted by permission of Farrar, Straus and Giroux, LLC.

SNYDER, ZILPHA KEATLEY ▌ All photographs reproduced by permission of Zilpha Keatley Snyder.

STEWART, PAUL ▌ Riddell, Chris, illustrator. From a cover of *The Edge Chronicles: Stormchaser*, by Paul Stewart. David Fickling Books, 1999. Cover illustration copyright © 2004 by Chris Riddell. Used by permission of Random House Children's Books, a division of Random House, Inc. / Riddell, Chris, illustrator. From a cover of *The Edge Chronicles: Midnight Over Sanctaphrax*, by Paul Stewart. David Fickling Books, 2000. Cover illustration copyright © 2004 by Chris Riddell. Used by permission of Random House Children's Books, a division of Random House, Inc. / Riddell, Chris, illustrator. From a cover of *The Edge Chronicles: The Curse of the Gloamglozer*, by Paul Stewart. David Fickling Books, 2001. Cover illustration copyright © 2005 by Chris Riddell. Used by permission of Random House Children's Books, a division of Random House, Inc.

TAKAHASHI, RUMIKO ▌ From a cover of *Maison Ikkoku*, by Rumiko Takahashi. MAISON IKKOKU © 1984 Rumiko TAKAHASHI/Shogakukan Inc. Reproduced by permission. / From a cover of *Ranma 1/2*, by Rumiko Takahashi. RANMA 1/2 © 1988 Rumiko TAKAHASHI/Shogakukan Inc. Reproduced by permission. / From a cover of *InuYasha*, by Rumiko Takahashi. InuYasha © 1997 Rumiko TAKAHASHI/Shogakukan Inc. Reproduced by permission.

THOMPSON, COLIN (EDWARD) ∎ Pignataro, Anna, illustrator. From an illustration in *Unknown*, by Colin Thompson. Walker & Company, 2000. Reproduced by permission. / Redlich, Ben, illustrator. From an illustration in *The Great Montefiasco*, by Colin Thompson. Star Bright Books, 2004. Illustrations copyright © 2004 Ben Redlich. All rights reserved. Reproduced by permission of Thomas C. Lothian Pty. Ltd. In the U.S. by Star Bright Books. / Thompson, Colin, photograph by Roger Beresford-Jones. Reproduced by permission of Colin Thompson.

VAIL, RACHEL ∎ Heo, Yumi, illustrator. From an illustration in *Sometimes I'm Bombaloo*, by Rachel Vail. Scholastic Press, 2002. Illustrations copyright © 2002 by Yumi Heo. Reprinted by permission of Scholastic Inc. / Vail, Rachel, photograph by Bill Harris. Reproduced by permission of Rachel Vail.

WISE, WILLIAM ∎ Benson, Patrick, illustrator. From a jacket of *Christopher Mouse: The Tale of a Small Traveler*, by William Wise. Bloomsbury Children's Books, 2004. Illustrations copyright © 2004 by Patrick Benson. Reproduced by permission.

SOMETHING ABOUT THE AUTHOR

ADLERMAN, Danny (Ezra) 1963-
(Kin Eagle, a joint pseudonym)

Personal

Born June 6, 1963, in Princeton, NJ; son of Mel (an in-
surance broker) and Gloria (a travel agent; maiden
name, Katz) Adlerman; married Kimberly Hauck (an illustrator and designer), August 10, 1991; children:
Rachelle, Joshua, Maxx. *Education:* Boston University,
B.S./B.A. *Hobbies and other interests:* Comic books,
cooking, tennis.

Addresses

Home—Metuchen, NJ. *Home and office*—Kids at Our
House, 47 Stoneham Pl., Metuchen, NJ 08840. *E-mail*—
info@dannyandkim.com.

Career

Writer, musician, and children's publishing consultant.

Member

Society of Children's Book Writers and Illustrators.

Writings

(With wife, Kimberly Adlerman, under joint pseudonym
Kin Eagle) *It's Raining, It's Pouring,* illustrated by
Rob Gilbert, Whispering Coyote Press (Danvers, MA),
1994.

Daniel Adlerman

Daniel Adlerman, *Africa Calling, Nighttime Falling,* illus-
trated by Kim Adlerman, Whispering Coyote Press
(Danvers, MA), 1996.
(With Kimberly Adlerman, under joint pseudonym Kin
Eagle) *Hey, Diddle Diddle,* illustrated by Rob Gilbert,
Whispering Coyote Press (Danvers, MA), 1997.

Enhanced by the unique collage illustrations created by wife and collaborator Kim Adlerman, **Rock-a-bye Baby** *was inspired by the classic nursery rhyme and a love of nature.*

(With Kimberly Adlerman, under joint pseudonym Kin Eagle) *Rub a Dub Dub,* illustrated by Rob Gilbert, Whispering Coyote Press (Danvers, MA), 1999.

(With Kimberly Adlerman, under joint pseudonym Kin Eagle) *Humpty Dumpty,* illustrated by Rob Gilbert, Whispering Coyote Press (Danvers, MA), 1999.

(Editor with Kim Adlerman) *Songs for America's Children,* Kids at Our House (Metuchen, NJ), 2002.

Rock-a-Bye Baby, Charlesbridge (Watertown, MA), 2004.

How Much Wood Could a Woodchuck Chuck?, illustrated by Kim Adlerman and others, Kids at Our House (Metuchen, NJ), 2006.

Sidelights

Danny Adlerman once told *Something about the Author:* "Next to my wife and children, writing and making music are the most gratifying aspects of my life. Artistically, I feel we have many phases. People cannot traverse to the next level until they have made at least a self-satisfying contribution to the area in which they started. I know I have some novels and adult nonfiction inside me, but I also know that I have not yet finished writing picture books.

"For example, I've been writing from the time I was a very young child. In fourth grade, it was poetry. In sixth and seventh grades, I was writing comedy bits and sketches with friends. Early in high school I discovered dialects. By the end of my high school career, college, and beyond, I wrote songs almost exclusively. It is hard for me to imagine tackling any of these categories un-

less I was satisfied that I had at least contributed something significant to the phase immediately preceding it.

"As for inspiration, look around you. It's everywhere. Writing picture books feels natural to me, perhaps because my life is very much like a fairy tale. In all capacities—business, life, love, family, and books—my partner is my best friend. In my estimation, it would take hard work to become uninspired!"

Biographical and Critical Sources

PERIODICALS

Kirkus Reviews, January 15, 2004, review of *Rock-A-Bye Baby,* p. 79.

Publishers Weekly, January 1, 2001, review of *Africa Calling, Nighttime Falling,* p. 94.

School Library Journal, April, 2004, Martha Topol, review of *Rock-a-Bye-Baby,* p. 127.

ONLINE

Adlermans' Home Page, http://www.dannyandkim.com (July 15, 2005).

Woodbridge Sentinel Online (Woodbridge, NJ), http://ws. gmnews.com/ (May 17 2005), Darcie Borden, "Gallery Features 3-D Kids' Book Illustrator," p. 1.

* * *

ADLERMAN, Kim
See ADLERMAN, Kimberly (Marie)

* * *

ADLERMAN, Kimberly (Marie) 1964-
(Kim Adlerman, Kin Eagle, a joint pseudonym)

Personal

Born January 5, 1964, in Niagara Falls, NY; daughter of William (a chemical engineer) and Lillian (Strozewski) Hauck; married Daniel Adlerman (a writer), August 10, 1991; children: Rachelle, Joshua, Max. *Education:* Attended Niagara County Community College; State University of New York at Buffalo, B.F.A. *Hobbies and other interests:* Tennis, gardening, baking, drawing, antiquing, "hanging out with my kids."

Addresses

Home—Metuchen, NJ. *Home and office*—Kids at Our House, 47 Stoneham Pl., Metuchen, NJ 08840. *E-mail*—info@dannyandkim.com.

Career

Graphic designer, art director, and illustrator. Book designer, Macmillan Publishing, New York, NY; owner and creative director, Kids at Our House, Metuchen, NJ.

Member

Society of Children's Book Writers and Illustrators, Toastmasters International, Metuchen ArtWorks (cooperative gallery).

Writings

(With husband, Danny Adlerman, under name Kin Eagle) *It's Raining, It's Pouring,* illustrated by Rob Gilbert, Whispering Coyote Press (Danvers, MA), 1994.

(With Danny Adlerman, under name Kin Eagle) *Hey, Diddle Diddle,* illustrated by Rob Gilbert, Whispering Coyote Press (Danvers, MA), 1997.

(With Danny Adlerman, under joint pseudonym Kin Eagle) *Rub a Dub Dub,* illustrated by Rob Gilbert, Whispering Coyote Press (Danvers, MA), 1999.

(With Danny Adlerman, under joint pseudonym Kin Eagle) *Humpty Dumpty,* illustrated by Rob Gilbert, Whispering Coyote Press (Danvers, MA), 1999.

(Editor with Danny Adlerman) *Songs for America's Children,* Kids at Our House (Metuchen, NJ), 2002.

ILLUSTRATOR

Danny Adlerman, *Africa Calling, Nighttime Falling,* Whispering Coyote Press (Danvers, MA), 1996.

Danny Adlerman, *Rock-a-Bye Baby,* Charlesbridge (Watertown, MA), 2004.

(With others) Danny Adlerman, *How Much Wood Could a Woodchuck Chuck?,* Kids at Our House (Metuchen, NJ), 2006.

Work in Progress

Illustrations for the picture book *Oh, No, Domino,* written by the artist.

Sidelights

In addition to writing with her husband, children's author Danny Adlerman, under the pseudonym Kin Eagle, Kimberly Adlerman has created illustrations for several of her husband's children's books, among them *Africa Calling, Nighttime Falling* and *Rock-a-bye Baby.* Branching out from the traditional nursery rhyme, in *Rock-a-bye Baby* Danny Adlerman relays the tale of a young child's adventures, his gentle, reassuring text complemented by wife Kimberly's collage illustrations. A *Kirkus Reviews* critic enjoyed the work, commenting that highlighting the work are the "pictures full of remarkable texture, depth, and color," and went on to note that readers will likely "appreciate the Adlermans' creative artistry."

Adlerman once told *Something about the Author:* "I've been drawing and painting for as long as I can remember. Illustrating has always been a dream of mine, but I haven't had enough confidence in myself to do something about it until recently.

"I hate to admit it, but I have horrible working habits! My husband and I have an office in our cellar, where we keep our computer, drawing table, and other office equipment. Although I can design there, it is extremely difficult for me to sketch or paint down there. Being a night person, with two small children, I find the best time to work is at night in our family room, after the kids have gone to bed.

"Some of my favorite artists include Eric Carle, Betsy Lewin, and Milton Glaser: Carle and Lewin for their simplicity. They can express so much with so little. Also, their work is often rife with humor. It's a characteristic that I not only appreciate, but find outstanding. If a visual can make me laugh out loud, even without the benefit of words, then I know it is effective.

"One of the main things I hope to achieve in illustrating children's books is to reach children—to help instill the love of books and reading that I have. Children are never too young to start reading. It's one of the reasons I like to make school appearances often. I want the opportunity to impress that message directly to as many children as possible."

Biographical and Critical Sources

PERIODICALS

Booklist, October 1, 1996, review of *Africa Calling, Nighttime Falling.*

Kirkus Reviews, January 15, 2004, review of *Rock-a-Bye Baby,* p. 79.

Publishers Weekly, January 1, 2001, review of *Africa Calling, Nighttime Falling,* p. 94.

School Library Journal, April, 2004, Martha Topol, review of *Rock-a-Bye-Baby,* p. 127.

ONLINE

Adlermans' Home Page, http://www.dannyandkim.com (July 15, 2005).

University at Buffalo Alumni Association Web site, http://www.alumni.buffalo.edu/ (September 20, 2005), "Kimberly Adlerman."

Woodbridge Sentinel Online (Woodbridge, NJ), http://ws.gmnews.com/ (May 17 2005), Darcie Borden, "Gallery Features 3-D Kids' Book Illustrator," p. 1.

*   *   *

ADOFF, Jaime (Levi)

Personal

Born in New York, NY; son of Arnold Adoff (a poet) and Virginia Hamilton (an author); married; wife's name

Mary Ann. *Education:* Central State University, B. Mus.; attended Manhattan School of Music.

Addresses

Home—Yellow Springs, OH. *Agent*—c/o Arnold Adoff, 750 Union St., Yellow Springs, OH 45487. *E-mail*—jaime@jaimeadoff.com.

Career

Writer of children and young-adult books, 1998—. Songwriter and musician in a rock band for eight years.

Awards, Honors

Lee Bennett Hopkins Poetry Award honor book designation, International Reading Association notable book designation, and New York Public Library Book for the Teen Age designation, all 2003, all for *The Song Shoots out of My Mouth: A Celebration of Music*; New York Public Library Book for the Teen Age designation, 2005, for *Names Will Never Hurt Me.*

Writings

The Song Shoots out of My Mouth: A Celebration of Music (poetry), illustrated by Martin French, Dutton (New York, NY), 2002.
Names Will Never Hurt Me (novel), Dutton (New York, NY), 2004.
Jimi and Me (novel), Jump at the Sun/Hyperion Books for Children (New York, NY), 2005.

Sidelights

Jaime Adoff is the author of such critically acclaimed works as the poetry collection *The Song Shoots out of My Mouth: A Celebration of Music* and *Names Will Never Hurt Me,* a young-adult novel. Adoff's success comes as no surprise: his father, Arnold Adoff, is an accomplished poet, biographer, and anthologist, and his mother, the late Newbery Award-winning writer Virginia Hamilton, was a highly respected author who received the Laura Ingalls Wilder Award for her contributions to children's literature. "I don't think I realized the impact my parents had on my future career until I was much older," Adoff explained on the *Embracing the Child* Web site. "As writers, both of my parents worked at home, so I got to see what they did every day. I remember watching them go into their offices in the morning with nothing but a cup of coffee. Then emerge hours later with pages of writing. To a small kid, it was like magic."

Adoff grew up in Yellow Springs, Ohio, and attended Central State University in nearby Wilberforce, studying drums and percussion and graduating with a degree in music. In 1990 he moved to New York City to attend the Manhattan School of Music, where he studied voice

Jaime Adoff draws on his love of music in the twenty-four poems included in **The Song Shoots out of My Mouth,** *which features verses about hip-hop, Latin, rock, reggae, jazz, and classical music. (Illustration by Martin French.)*

and drums. He also formed a rock band and spent eight years writing songs and performing at clubs throughout the northeast before turning his attention to writing for young adults.

Adoff draws on his passion for music in his 2002 book, *The Song Shoots out of My Mouth,* an illustrated collection of twenty-four poems that explores musical experiences from a teenager's perspective. Among the subjects of Adoff's verse are the struggles of a garage band, the intensity of an air guitarist, and the hopes of an aspiring trumpet player. In *School Library Journal,* Nina Lindsay remarked that Adoff's "free verse is highly rhythmic and demands to be performed" while also complimenting his "raplike word-play and puns." In a review for *Booklist,* Michael Cart praised "the energy underscoring Adoff's language, which invites readers to move to the rhythm of the words." The passion reflected in Adoff's verse was also noted by other critics; his "enthusiasm for his subject comes endearingly to the fore in the section of 'Backnotes,' in which he identifies the artists alluded to and includes specific selections for listening," noted a *Kirkus* reviewer in a review of *The Song Shoots out of My Mouth.*

Names Will Never Hurt Me was cited as "a powerful, complex, skillfully written novel" by *Booklist* reviewer Frances Bradburn. The work follows four teenagers—a star football player, a bullied outcast, a power-hungry snitch, and a lonely biracial girl—through an anxious, tension-filled day at Rockville High, where, one year earlier, a fellow student was killed in a school shooting. As events unfold, the lives of the four teens overlap until they are all brought together outside the principal's office. "With painfully immediate accounts of daily humiliations and power-plays, Adoff sets a time bomb ticking, but the final outcome is not quite what we expect," observed Lauren Adams in *Horn Book*. "Writing in a free-verse, almost-poetic style, Adoff pulls off a young adult page-turner with literary ease," noted *School Library Journal* contributor Angela J. Reynolds, while a *Kirkus* contributor deemed it "outstanding."

Adoff's free-verse novel *Jimi and Me* focuses on eighth-grader Keith James, who is thrust into a new school in a quiet, mid-western town far from his native Brooklyn, New York, following the violent death of his father. Feeling like an outsider because of his unusual clothes and taste in music, Keith finds solace in the music of guitar legend Jimi Hendrix. Gradually, he begins to come to terms with life in his new town, and also begins to deal with his father's responsibility in his own death in a novel that *Voice of Youth Advocates* contributor David Goodale praised as "an exceptional story about a young teen who must cope with grief, love, prejudice, and betrayal."

On the *Embracing the Child* Web site, Adoff discussed the role inspiration plays in his writing. "I begin with a very basic emotion, a feeling," he commented. "I put it down on paper. It's usually something that really needs to get out of me. Something that needs to get air. Something that needs to see the light of the page." Regardless of whether the feeling becomes a poem, a story, or a novel, Adoff is most concerned "with getting that initial feeling down on paper. That first feeling is what is trapped inside of me, screaming to get out. Wherever it goes from there, it goes."

Adoff told *Something about the Author:* "I write for the boy in the last row who never raises his hand, but has so much to say.

"I write for the girl in the front row who now has pages of poems and stories for me to read, before I've even taken my coat off.

"I write because it is the most freeing experience I know of. I can create my own world, my own universe, create my own rules, then break them if I want to.

"I would like to think that I could make a difference in a young person's life, but that is making too much of what I do. I would settle for just being a small part in getting a young person to see themselves and to see others around them. To see how we are all the same and different at the same time, and to respect an honor those differences. Showing a teen that there can be hope, that there is always hope even in the darkest hour.

"I write because I love the fact that a book doesn't care what color you are, or what religion you are or how

In this compelling 2004 novel four students at a troubled high school reflect on racism, bullying, and the course their lives have taken in the wake of a fellow student's murder one year ago.

much money your parents make. Books are for everyone and should be shared like a big slice of apple pie with two scoops of ice-cream on top.

"So what do you say?

"Let's dig in. . . ."

Biographical and Critical Sources

PERIODICALS

Booklist, January 1, 2003, Michael Cart, review of *The Song Shoots out of My Mouth: A Celebration of Music*, p. 864; April 1, 2004, Frances Bradburn, review of *Names Will Never Hurt Me*, p. 1359.

Horn Book, July-August, 2004, Lauren Adams, review of *Names Will Never Hurt Me*, p. 445.

Kirkus Reviews, October 15, 2002, review of *The Song Shoots out of My Mouth*, p. 1526; March 1, 2004, review of *Names Will Never Hurt Me*, p. 217.

Kliatt, March, 2004, Michele Winship, review of *Names Will Never Hurt Me*, p. 6.

Publishers Weekly, May 3, 2004, review of *Names Will Never Hurt Me,* p. 193.

School Library Journal, October, 2002, Nina Lindsay, review of *The Song Shoots out of My Mouth,* pp. 178-179; April, 2004, Angela J. Reynolds, review of *Names Will Never Hurt Me,* p. 148; December, 2004, Ginny Gustin, review of *The Song Shoots out of My Mouth,* p. 60; May, 2005, Jennifer Ralston, review of *Names Will Never Hurt Me,* p. 51.

Voice of Youth Advocates, October, 2005, David Goodale, review of *Jimmi and Me.*

ONLINE

Embracing the Child Web site, http://www.embracingthe child.org/ (July 15, 2005), "Jaime Adoff."

Jaime Adoff Web site, http://www.jaimeadoff.com (July 15, 2005).

* * *

ALLENDE, Isabel 1942-

Personal

Surname is pronounced "Ah-*yen*-day"; born August 2, 1942, in Lima, Peru; daughter of Tomas (a Chilean diplomat) and Francisca (Llona Barros) Allende; married Miguel Frias (an engineer), September 8, 1962 (divorced, 1987); married William Gordon (a lawyer), July 17, 1988; children: (first marriage) Paula (deceased), Nicolas; Scott (stepson). *Education:* Educated privately.

Addresses

Home—San Francisco, CA. *Agent*—Carmen Balcells, Diagonal 580, Barcelona 21, Spain.

Career

United Nations Food and Agricultural Organization, Santiago, Chile, secretary, 1959-65; *Paula* magazine, Santiago, journalist, editor, and advice columnist, 1967-74; *Mampato* magazine, Santiago, journalist, 1969-74; television interviewer for Canal 13/Canal 7 (television station), 1970-75; worked on movie newsreels, 1973-78; *El Nacional,* Caracas, Venezuela, journalist, 1974-75, columnist, 1976-83; Colegio Marroco, Caracas, administrator, 1979-82; writer. Guest teacher at Montclair State College, 1985, and University of Virginia, 1988; Gildersleeve Lecturer, Barnard College, 1988; teacher of creative writing, University of California, Berkeley, 1989.

Awards, Honors

Panorama Literario Award (Chile), 1983; Grand Prix d'Evasion (France), 1984; Author of the Year and Book of the Year awards (Germany), 1984; Point de Mire (Belgium), 1985; Colima award for best novel (Mexico), 1985; Author of the Year award (Germany), 1986; Quality Paperback Book Club New Voice Award nomination, 1986, for *The House of the Spirits; Los Angeles Times* Book Prize nomination, 1987, for *Of Love and Shadows;* XV Premio Internazionale (Italy), and Mulheres best foreign novel award (Portugal), both 1987; *Library Journal* Best Books of 1988 designation, American Book Award, Before Columbus Foundation, 1989, Freedom to Write Pen Club Award, 1991, and XLI Bancarella Literature Award (Italy), and Brandeis University Major Book Collection Award, both 1993, all for *The Stories of Eva Luna;* named Hans Christian Andersen goodwill ambassador, 2004.

Writings

FOR YOUNG ADULTS; "ALEXANDER COLD" SERIES

La Ciudad de las bestias, Rayo (New York, NY), 2002, translation by Margaret Sayers Peden published as *City of the Beasts* (young adult), HarperCollins (New York, NY), 2002.

El Reino del dragón de oro, Montena Mondadori (Barcelona, Spain), translation by Margaret Sayers Peden published as *Kingdom of the Golden Dragon,* HarperCollins (New York, NY), 2004.

El Bosque de los Pigmeos, Rayo (New York, NY), 2004, translated by Margaret Sayers Peden as *Forest of the Pygmies,* HarperCollins (New York, NY), 2005.

OTHER

Civilice a su troglodita: Los impertinentes de Isabel Allende (humor), Editorial Lord Cochran (Santiago, Chile), 1974.

La Casa de los espíritus, Plaza y Janés (Barcelona, Spain), 1982, HarperLibros (New York, NY), 1985, translation by Magda Bogin published as *The House of the Spirits,* Knopf (New York, NY), 1985.

La Gorda de porcelana (juvenile; title means "The Fat Porcelain Lady"), Alfaguara (Madrid, Spain), 1984.

De amor y de sombra, Plaza y Janés (Barcelona, Spain), 1984, HarperLibros (New York, NY), 1995, translation by Margaret Sayers Peden published as *Of Love and Shadows,* Knopf (New York, NY), 1987.

Eva Luna, translation by Margaret Sayers Peden published under same title, Knopf (New York, NY), 1988, HarperLibros (New York, NY), 1995.

Cuentos de Eva Luna, Plaza y Janés (Barcelona, Spain), 1990, HarperCollins (New York, NY), 1995, translation by Margaret Sayers Peden published as *The Stories of Eva Luna,* Atheneum (New York, NY), 1991.

El Plan infinito, Editorial Sudamericana (Buenos Aires, Argentina), 1991, translation by Margaret Sayers Peden published as *The Infinite Plan,* HarperCollins (New York, NY), 1993.

Paula (autobiography), Plaza y Janés (Barcelona, Spain), 1994, translation by Margaret Sayers Peden, HarperCollins (New York, NY), 1995.

Isabel Allende

(With others) *Salidas de madre,* Planeta (Santiago, Chile), 1996.

Afrodita: Recetas, cuentos y otros afrodisiacos, Harper-Collins (New York, NY), 1997, translation by Margaret Sayers Peden published as *Aphrodite: A Memoir of the Senses,* HarperFlamingo (New York, NY), 1998.

Hija de la fortuna (novel), Plaza y Janés (Barcelona, Spain), 1999, translation by Margaret Sayers Peden published as *Daughter of Fortune,* HarperCollins (New York, NY), 1999.

(And author of foreword) *Conversations with Isabel Allende,* edited by John Rodden, translations from the Spanish by Virginia Invernizzi and from the German and Dutch by John Rodden, University of Texas (Austin, TX), 1999, revised edition, 2004.

Retrato en sepia, Plaza y Janés (Barcelona, Spain), 2000, translation by Margaret Sayers Peden published as *Portrait in Sepia,* HarperCollins (New York, NY), 2001.

Mi país inventado, Areté (Barcelona, Spain), 2003, translation by Margaret Sayers Peden published as *My Invented Country: A Nostalgic Journey through Chile,* HarperCollins (New York, NY), 2003.

Zorro, translated by Margaret Sayers Peden, HarperCollins (New York, NY), 2005.

Author of several plays and stories for children. Contributor to *Los Libros tienen sis propios espíritus,* edited by Marcello Coddou, Universidad Veracruzana, 1986; *Paths of Resistance: The Art and Craft of the Political Novel,* edited by William Zinsser, Houghton Mifflin, 1989; and *El Amor: Grandes escritores latinoamericanos,* Ediciones Instituto Movilizador, 1991.

Adaptations

The House of the Spirits was adapted for film by Bille August, starring Meryl Streep, Jeremy Irons, Antonio Banderas, and Vanessa Redgrave, 1993. *City of the Beasts* was adapted as an audiobook, read by Blair Brown, Harper Audio, 2002. *Kingdom of the Golden Dragon* was adapted for audio, read by Brown, Harper Audio, 2004.

Sidelights

Isabel Allende is a Chilean-born novelist whose experiences as a journalist and the niece of assassinated socialist Chilean President Salvador Allende, have made politics an integral part of her life. Salvador Allende's murder in 1973 as part of a military coup had a profound effect on the novelist; "I think I have divided my life [into] before that day and after that day," she told *Publishers Weekly* interviewer Amanda Smith. "In that moment, I realized that everything was possible—that violence was a dimension that was always around you."

The world view that was shaped by this experience forms an integral part of Allende's novels for adults, which include *The House of the Spirits, Eva Luna,* and *Daughter of Fortune.*

In the mid-1990s, at the urging of her grandchildren, Allende turned to a young-adult audience and wrote the first book in the "Alexander Cold" series, about an eighteen year old who joins his travel-writer grandmother on a series of globe-hopping trips that reveal the beauty and danger of the world's most magical regions. She has also penned the historical novel *Zorro,* a "lively retelling" of the popular legend that, according to a *Publishers Weekly* reviewer, "reads as effortlessly as the [Mexican-American] hero himself might slice his trademark 'Z'"

After the fall of her uncle's democratic government in Chile, Allende and her family fled to Venezuela. Although she had been a noted journalist in Chile, she found it difficult to get a job and did not write for several years. However, after receiving word from her aged grandfather, who had remained in Chile, she put pen to paper and composed a letter to him. "My grandfather thought people died only when you forgot them," the author explained to Harriet Shapiro in *People.* "I wanted

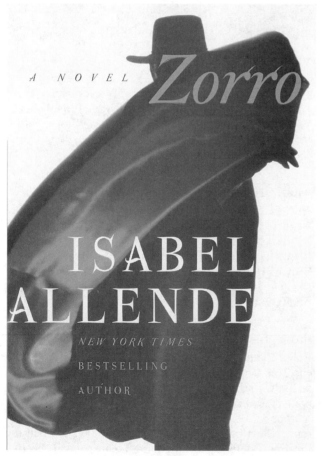

Allende becomes the first to work the mythical character Zorro—a Mexican-American Robin Hood who attempts to correct injustice—into a novel in this 2005 work.

to prove to him that I had forgotten nothing, that his spirit was going to live with us forever." Allende never sent the letter, as the old man died shortly thereafter, but the act of writing a letter to him sparked memories of her family and her country and inspired her first novel, *The House of the Spirits.*

Following three generations of the Trueba family and their domestic and political conflicts, *The House of the Spirits* was published in its original Spanish in 1982. Called "a novel of peace and reconciliation" by *New York Times Book Review* contributor Alexander Coleman, the novel introduces family patriarch Esteban Trueba, a strict conservative who exploits his workers and allows his uncompromising beliefs to distance him from his wife and children, even in the face of tremendous events. Allende's use of fantastic elements and characters led critics to classify *The House of the Spirits* as an example of "magic realism," a style popularized by Nobel Prize-winning novelist Gabriel García Márquez in *One Hundred Years of Solitude.* "Allende has her own distinctive voice, however," noted a *Publishers Weekly* reviewer; "while her prose lacks the incandescent brilliance of the master's, it has a whimsical charm, besides being clearer, more accessible and more explicit about the contemporary situation in South America." *Washington Post Book World* critic Jonathan Yardley also noted comparisons to Márquez, but concluding that Allende "is most certainly a novelist in her own right and, for a first novelist, a startlingly skillful, confident one."

Allende's adult novels have continued to explore the intersection between violence and family history. *Of Love and Shadows* begins with the switching of two identically named newborn infants, one of which grows up to become the focus of a journalist's investigation as romance and a danger-fraught search for the truth intertwine. Gene H. Bell-Villada, reviewing the novel for the *New York Times Book Review,* noted that "Allende skillfully evokes both the terrors of daily life under military rule and the subtler form of resistance in the hidden corners and 'shadows' of her title," while *Christian Science Monitor* reviewer Marjorie Agosin declared the book to be "a love story of two young people sharing the fate of their historical circumstances, meeting the challenge of discovering the truth, and determined to live their life fully, accepting their world of love and shadows." *The Tales of Eva Luna* focuses on an orphaned young woman who, as a scriptwriter, finds her world colliding with that of an Austrian filmmaker haunted by traumatic memories of World War II. *Eva Luna* is "filled with a multitude of characters and tales," recounted *Washington Post Book World* contributor Alan Ryan. A "cascade of stories tumbles out before the reader, stories vivid and passionate and human enough to engage, in their own right, all the reader's attention and sympathy."

Two of Allende's more recent novels share characters with her first novel, *The House of the Spirits. Daughter of Fortune* takes place during the California gold rush of the mid-1800s, and focuses on Eliza Somers, who spends several years disguised as a boy. Cecilia Novella remarked in *Américas* that in the novel Allende "provides us with a masterly description of that part of North America that was to become California at the height of the gold rush, painting a vivid picture of boisterous activity, chaos, avarice, unrelieved drudgery, and the broad range of lifestyles, habits and dissolute ways of those drawn there by the gleaming precious metal." A sequel of sorts, *Portrait in Sepia* finds Aurora del Valle filled with questions about the mysterious beginnings of her life. At age five she was sent to live with her grandmother, Paulina, a wealthy woman who provided Aurora with material comforts but refused to answer questions about the past. The girl's confusion lingers until adulthood, when she becomes a talented photographer. After Paulina's death, Aurora explores her own and her family's past, examining her memories as well as those of relatives. According to Teresa R. Arrington in *World Literature Today,* "The three novels represent a transnational saga that shows us how major historical events across the world can affect the lives of several generations of an extended Chilean family." In *Book,* Beth Kephart observed, "Allende's imagination is a spectacle unto itself—she infects her readers with her own colossal dreams."

City of the Beasts is the first of several novels that Allende has written for a younger audience. As she told *Booklist* interviewer Hazel Rochman, "The idea of writing for young adults wasn't mine; it was something that my three grandchildren had been asking me to do for a long time." Alexander Cold, the main character in the novel series, is modeled after Allende's grandson, Alejandro Frías, while another character, Nadia Santos, was inspired by her two granddaughters, Andrea and Nicole. In *City of the Beasts* fifteen-year-old Alexander is sent to stay with his grandmother, Kate Cold, in the Amazon while his mother receives chemotherapy in Texas. Kate, an adventurous travel writer for *International Geography,* is researching the Yeti, a mysterious creature living in the Amazon jungle. Kate and Alexander join a group of adventurers that includes a self-centered anthropologist, a government doctor, and the jungle guide Cesar Santos, who brings with him his daughter, Nadia. Soon, Alexander and Nadia soon find themselves facing a battle with a supernatural evil, but with aid from a local shaman and the invisible People of the Mist, they tap into their inner totemic powers (Alexander's is a jaguar and Nadia's is an eagle) and prevail. A *Publishers Weekly* reviewer praised Allende's coming-of-age story as an adventure tale that "moves at a rapid pace, laced with surprises and ironic twists," while in *Booklist* Hazel Rochman wrote that *City of the Beasts* "blends magical realism with grim history and contemporary politics in a way that shakes up all the usual definitions of savagery and civilization."

Like *City of the Beasts, Kingdom of the Golden Dragon* and *Forest of the Pygmies* also feature Alexander, Na-

Alexander follows feisty grandma Kate up into the mysterious Himalayas in the hopes of saving a magical statue from a band of greedy thieves who hope to benefit from the statue's power of foretelling the future. (Cover illustration by Cliff Nielsen.)

dia, and Alexander's grandmother Kate. They also feature a similar formula: an "environmentalist theme, a pinch of the grotesque, and a larger dose of magic," according to a *Publishers Weekly* contributor. In *Kingdom of the Golden Dragon* the teens—now aged sixteen—travel with Kate to the Himalayas where they hope to track down a rare statue, the Golden Dragon, which is rumored be the key to foretelling the future of the remote mountain kingdom. In this forbidding—and forbidden—land the group discovers a corporate plot to steal the statue that involves kidnaping and murder. Joined by a Buddhist monk and a band of Yeti, Alex and Nadia soon find themselves enmeshed in another battle against evil in a novel that a *Publishers Weekly* contributor praised for its "complex heroes, suspenseful tests of courage" that confront Alex and his friends, and the "mystic aura" Allende creates to "add depth and excitement" to her tale. The author "combines empathetic young characters; exciting adventures; and an intelligent, sympathetic look at cultures, customs, and creatures of a remote . . . area," added Susan L. Rogers in *School Library Journal,* noting that *Kingdom of the Golden Dragon* stands on its own as a fast-paced teen adventure.

In *Forest of the Pygmies,* the final volume of the "Alexander Cold" trilogy, Alexander is now eighteen, and on his way to Africa where he, Nadia, and Kate join an elephant-led safari. After a Catholic missionary asks for help locating some friends lost in the jungle swamps, a world of corruption is revealed: poachers deplete the wildlife while a savage ex-military tyrant who wears a necklace made from human fingers attempts to enslave both Bantu and Pygmy tribes. Into the fray come Alex and his friends, rallying the diminutive Africans and drawing on animal totems and other magic in their battle for freedom. While noting that the teens' ability to transform into their totems might confuse readers new to Allende's series, Eva Mitnick wrote in *School Library Journal* that *Forest of the Pygmies* is "a fine adventure tale" featuring the author's characteristic "lyrical" language.

In *My Invented Country: A Nostalgic Journey through Chile* Allende examines, in fictional form, her own history as it fits within her family story and the larger history of Chile as well as that of her adopted country, the United States. In *Booklist,* Donna Seaman maintained that "Allende's conjuring of her 'invented,' or imaginatively remembered, country is riveting in its frankness and compassion, and her account of why and how she became a writer is profoundly moving." In this, as in all her works, Allende examines the facts of cultural and political history and transforms those facts into something more through story and memory. While writing remains the focus of her public life, Allende's ultimate goal is more personal. As she told *San Francisco Chronicle* interviewer Heather Knight, "I'd like to be remembered by my grandchildren as a grandma who gave them unconditional love, stories, and laughter."

Biographical and Critical Sources

BOOKS

Bloom, Harold, editor, *Isabel Allende,* Chelsea House (Philadelphia, PA), 2003.
Contemporary Hispanic Biography, Volume 1, Gale (Detroit, MI), 2003.
Contemporary Literary Criticism, Gale (Detroit, MI), Volume 39, 1986, Volume 57, 1990, Volume 97, 1997.
Feal, Rosemary G., and Yvette E. Miller, editors, *Isabel Allende Today: An Anthology of Essays,* Latin American Literary Review Press (Pittsburgh, PA), 2002.
Hart, Patricia, *Narrative Magic in the Fiction of Isabel Allende,* Fairleigh Dickinson University Press (Teaneck, NJ), 1989.
Levine, Linda Gould, *Isabel Allende,* Twayne Publishers (New York, NY), 2002.
Lindsay, Claire, *Locating Latin American Women Writers: Cristina Peri Rossi, Rosario Ferré, Albalucía, and Isabel Allende,* Peter Lang (New York, NY), 2003.
Postlewate, Marisa Herrera, *How and Why I Write: Redefining Women's Writing and Experience,* Peter Lang (New York, NY), 2004.

Ramblado-Minero, Maria de la Cinta, *Isabal Allende's Writing of the Self: Trespassing the Boundaries of Fiction and Autobiography,* E. Mellen Press (Lewiston, NY), 2003.
Rojas, Sonia Riquelme, and Edna Aguirre Rehbein, editors, *Critical Approaches to Isabel Allende's Novels,* P. Lang (New York, NY), 1991.
Zapata, Celia Correas, *Isabel Allende: Life and Spirits,* translation by Margaret Sayers Peden, Arte Público Press (Houston, TX), 2002.

PERIODICALS

Américas, November-December, 1995, p. 36; September, 1999, Cecilia Novella, review of *Daughter of Fortune,* p. 61; October, 2001, Barbara Mujica, review of *Portrait in Sepia,* p. 63.
Architectural Digest, April, 1995, p. 32.
Atlanta Journal-Constitution, December 2, 2000, Greg Changnon, review of *Portrait in Sepia,* p. C4.
Book, November-December, 2001, Beth Kephart, review of *Portrait in Sepia,* p. 60.
Booklist, February 1, 1998, p. 875; August, 1999, Brad Hooper, review of *Daughter of Fortune,* p. 1984; September 1, 2001, Brad Hooper, review of *Portrait in Sepia,* p. 3; November 15, 2002, Hazel Rochman, review of *City of the Beasts,* p. 590, and interview with Allende, p. 591; April 1, 2003, Donna Seaman, review of *My Invented Country: A Nostalgic Journey through Chile,* p. 1354; February 15, 2004, Hazel Rochman, review of *Kingdom of the Golden Dragon,* p. 1050; March 15, 2005, Hazel Rochman, review of *Forest of the Pygmies,* p. 1284.
Chicago Tribune, May 19, 1985.
Christian Science Monitor, June 7, 1985; May 27, 1987.
Detroit Free Press, June 7, 1987.
Globe and Mail (Toronto, Ontario, Canada), June 24, 1985; June 27, 1987.
Guardian, November 13, 1999, Alex Clark, review of *Daughter of Fortune,* p. 10; November 30, 2002, Carol Birch, review of *City of the Beasts,* p. 33.
Horn Book, January-February, 2003, Christine M. Heppermann, review of *City of the Beasts,* p. 65.
Kirkus Reviews, October 1, 2002, review of *City of the Beasts,* p. 1462; April 1, 2003, review of *My Invented Country,* p. 514; April 1, 2004, review of *Kingdom of the Golden Dragon,* p. 323; April 15, 2005, review of *Forest of the Pygmies,* p. 467.
Kliatt, May, 2005, Paula Rohrlick, review of *Forest of the Pygmies,* p. 6.
Library Journal, August, 1999, Barbara Hoffert, review of *Daughter of Fortune,* p. 134; October 15, 2001, Barbara Hoffert, review of *Portrait in Sepia,* p. 105; June 1, 2003, Sheila Kasperek, review of *My Invented Country,* p. 118; October 15, 2003, Gloria Maxwell, review of *My Invented Country,* p. 115; March 1, 2005, Misha Stone, review of *Zorro,* p. 74.
Los Angeles Times, February 10, 1988.
Los Angeles Times Book Review, June 16, 1985; May 31, 1987.
Mother Jones, December, 1988.
Ms., May-June, 1995, p. 75.

Nation, July 20-27, 1985.

New Leader, November-December, 2001, Philip Graham, review of *Portrait in Sepia,* p. 38.

New Statesman, July 5, 1985.

Newsweek, May 13, 1985.

New York Review of Books, July 18, 1985.

New York Times, May 2, 1985; May 20, 1987; February 4, 1988.

New York Times Book Review, May 12, 1985; July 12, 1987; October 23, 1988; May 21, 1995, p. 11.

People, June 10, 1985; June 1, 1987; June 5, 1995, p. 34; April 20, 1998, p. 47.

Publishers Weekly, March 1, 1985; May 17, 1985; January 19, 1998, p. 360; August 23, 1999, review of *Daughter of Fortune* p. 41; July 16, 2001, review of *Portrait in Sepia,* p. 1142; June 24, 2002, review of *City of the Beasts,* p. 58; April 28, 2003, review of *My Invented Country,* p. 57; June 30, 2003, review of *City of the Beasts;* March 15, 2004, review of *Kingdom of the Golden Dragon,* p. 75; February 28, 2005, review of *Zorro,* p. 39.

Review of Contemporary Fiction, summer, 2000, Sophia A. McClennan, review of *Daughter of Fortune,* p. 184.

St. Louis Post-Dispatch, October 28, 2001, Jan Garden Castro, review of *Portrait in Sepia,* p. G11.

San Francisco Chronicle, October 19, 2001, Heather Knight, review of *City of the Beasts,* p. 1.

School Library Journal, December, 2002, "Isabelle Allende on Her Magical Adventures" (interview), p. 58; April, 2004, Susan L. Rogers, review of *Kingdom of the Golden Dragon,* p. 148; June, 2005, Eva Mitnick, review of *Forest of the Pygmies,* p. 147.

Sunday Telegraph (London, England), October 14, 2001, Jenny McCartney, review of *Portrait in Sepia.*

Time, May 20, 1985.

Times (London, England), July 4, 1985; July 9, 1987; March 22, 1989; March 23, 1989.

Times Literary Supplement, July 5, 1985; July 10, 1987; April 7-13, 1989.

Tribune Books (Chicago, IL), October 9, 1988.

U.S. News and World Report, November 21, 1988.

Village Voice, June 7, 1985.

Voice Literary Supplement, December, 1988.

Wall Street Journal, March 20, 1998.

Washington Post Book World, May 12, 1985; May 24, 1987; October 9, 1988; July 24, 2005, Elizabeth Ward, review of *Forest of the Pygmies,* p. 11.

World Literature Today, winter, 2002, Teresa R. Arrington, review of *Portrait in Sepia,* p. 115.

World Press Review, April, 1995, p. 47.

ONLINE

Isabel Allende Web site, http://www.isabelallende.com (July 20, 2005).*

*   *   *

ANTHONY, Barbara 1932-
(Antonia Barber)

Personal

Born December 10, 1932, in London, England; daughter of Derek (a box-office manager) and Julie (a land-scape gardener; maiden name, Jeal) Wilson; married Kenneth Charles Anthony (a structural engineering consultant), August 6, 1956 (died December, 1981); children: Jonathan Charles, Nicholas James, Gemma Thi-Phi-Yen. *Education:* University College, London, B.A. (with honors), 1955. *Hobbies and other interests:* Walking, reading, theatre, gardening.

Addresses

Home—Horne's Place Oast, Appledore, Kent TN26 2BS, England. *Agent*—David Higham Associates, 5-8 Lower John St., Golden Square, London W1R, 4HA, England.

Career

Writer, beginning 1966.

Member

British Society of Authors, Friends of the Earth, Amnesty International, Greenpeace.

Awards, Honors

Carnegie Award runner-up, for *The Ghosts,* and short-list, for *The Ring in the Rough Stuff;* Nestle Smarties Book Prize Children's Choice, Kate Greenaway Medal Commendation, and British Book Award for Illustrated Book of the Year, all for *The Mousehole Cat.*

Writings

UNDER PSEUDONYM ANTONIA BARBER

The Affair of the Rockerbye Baby, J. Cape (London, England), 1966, Delacorte (New York, NY), 1970.

The Ghosts, Farrar, Straus (New York, NY), 1969, published as *The Amazing Mr. Blunden,* Penguin (Harmondsworth, England), 1972.

The Ring in the Rough Stuff, J. Cape (London, England), 1983.

The Enchanter's Daughter, illustrated by Errol le Cain, J. Cape (London, England), 1987.

Satchelmouse and the Dinosaurs, Walker Books (London, England), 1987.

Satchelmouse and the Doll's House, Walker Books (London, England), 1987.

The Mousehole Cat, illustrated by Nicola Bayley, Macmillan (New York, NY), 1990.

Gemma the Broody Hen, illustrated by Karin Littlewood, ABC (London, England), 1992, published as *Gemma and the Baby Chick,* Scholastic (New York, NY), 1993.

(Adaptor) *Tales from Grimm,* illustrated by Margaret Chamberlain, Frances Lincoln (London, England), 1992.

Catkin, illustrated by P. J. Lynch, Candlewick Press (Cambridge, MA), 1994.

The Monkey and the Panda, illustrated by Meilo So, Macmillan Books for Young Readers (New York, NY), 1995.

Shoes of Satin, Ribbons of Silk: Tales from the Ballet, illustrated by Diz Wallis, Kingfisher (New York, NY), 1995, published as *Tales from the Ballet,* 1999.

(Reteller) *Snow White and Rose Red,* MacDonald Young (London, England), 1997.

Apollo and Daphne: Masterpieces of Greek Mythology, J. Paul Getty Museum, 1998, published as *Apollo and Daphne: Masterpieces of Mythology,* Frances Lincoln (London, England), 1998.

Noah and the Ark, Corgi (London, England), 1998.

Hidden Tales from Eastern Europe, illustrated by Paul Hess, Frances Lincoln (London, England), 2002.

The Frog Bride, Frances Lincoln (London, England), 2006.

Contributor to books, including Pamela Oldfield, editor, *Hurdy Gurdie,* Blackie & Son, 1984; and Jean Richardson, editor, *Cold Feet,* Hodder & Stoughton (London, England), 1985.

Anthony's books have been translated into Gaelic.

"DANCING SHOES" SERIES; UNDER PSEUDONYM ANTONIA BARBER

Friends and Rivals, Puffin (London, England), 1998.
Into the Spotlight, Puffin (London, England), 1998.
Lessons for Lucy, Puffin (London, England), 1998.
Out of Step, Puffin (London, England), 1998.
Making the Grade, Puffin (London, England), 1999.
Time to Dance, Puffin (London, England), 1999.
Lucy's Next Step, Puffin (London, England), 1999.
Best Foot Forward, Puffin (London, England), 1999.
Model Dancers, Puffin (London, England), 2000.
In a Spin, Puffin (London, England), 2000.
In the Wings, Puffin (London, England), 2000.
Dance to the Rescue, Puffin (London, England), 2000.
The Big Book of Dancing Shoes, Volume 1, Puffin (London, England), 2000.
The Big Book of Dancing Shoes, Volume 2, Puffin (London, England), 2001.

Adaptations

The Ghosts was adapted for film as *The Amazing Mr Blunden,* 1971, and later adapted for television by the British Broadcasting Corporation (BBC-TV); *The Ring in the Rough Stuff* was adapted for television by BBC-TV; *The Mousehole Cat* was adapted as an animated film, a concert production, music by Ian Hughes, 1995, and as a musical stage play.

Sidelights

Writing under the pen name Antonia Barber, British writer Barbara Anthony has gained widespread praise for her fanciful stories for young children as well as her retelling of traditional folklore and mythology. Beginning her writing career in the mid-1960s, Anthony has produced the award-winning novel *The Ghosts,* and the popular picture books *The Mousehole Cat* and *Gemma and the Baby Chick,* as well as story collections that include *Tales from the Ballet* and *Hidden Tales from Eastern Europe.* Noting that the seven stories in *Hidden Tales from Eastern Europe* combine tradition story elements "in unusual combinations," a *Publishers Weekly* contributor wrote that, "with economy and restraint," Anthony "renders even miraculous moments simply, allowing the luster of these stories to shine forth."

Anthony's second published book, the novel *The Ghosts,* combines suspense and the supernatural. A young brother and sister, James and Lucy Allen, are confronted by the ghosts of two children killed a hundred years earlier in a fire. The apparitions seek aid, and the Allen children are required to travel back in time in order to change the course of history. A *Horn Book* reviewer called *The Ghosts* "a good English time fantasy, filled with surprising twists and ingeniously resolved mysteries." Popular with readers, the novel was later released as the feature film *The Amazing Mr Blunden.*

Despite the success of her first two books—particularly *The Ghosts,* which was honored by the Carnegie Award committee—Anthony credits her experiences as a mother with enhancing her work as a children's writer. As she once told *Something about the Author* (SATA): "I am an example of a contemporary phenomenon: the professional woman writer who takes a few years out for the fascinating experience of raising young children. After two successful children's books, both widely published and translated, I gave up writing for a while to bring up two adopted sons, intending to return to work when they reached school age. The chance to add a baby daughter, a Vietnamese war orphan, to our family delayed me again; but [after] she . . . joined the boys in school, I . . . returned to writing full time. The marvelous years in between have been of inestimable value to me as a writer. Having seen childhood . . . from the outside as well as the inside, and knowing what it is to be a parent as well as to have parents, I have a much deeper understanding of human character and relationships."

The Mousehole Cat is one of many books Anthony has written since taking a break to raise her family. Taking place in the Cornish fishing village of Mousehole—pronounced "Mowzel"—the story follows the efforts of Mowzer, a wise old cat, to protect her human companion, fisherman Tom, when a vicious storm forces the villagers to stay indoors and food becomes scarce. Mowzer's caterwauling and soothing purr appeases the Great Storm Cat and allows Tom to cast his nets and bring food to the town. Praising the book for its "captivating" story, a *Publishers Weekly* contributor added that Anthony's text is "by turns funny, dramatic and touching" and her story's resolution "comforting." Also cited for its artwork by Nicola Bayley, *The Mousehole Cat* earned the British Book Award for Best Illustrated Book, among other honors. It has been adapted as an animated film as well as a concert production and a stage musical.

A caretaker cat also plays a starring role in Anthony's *Catkin,* which, like *The Mousehole Cat,* contains an element of fantasy. In this tale a fortune-teller seeing danger in young Carrie's future gives the girl a clever cat to watch over her. The fortune-teller's vision proves accurate, however, when Catkin is distracted by some passing butterflies and Carrie is abducted into the underworld by the Little People. In tracing Catkin's journey to free her charge, Anthony spins a tale that "rings with the . . . nostalgia of the best fairy stories and the primacy of myth," according to a reviewer for *Publishers Weekly.*

After Anthony's husband passed away in 1991, the author "joined the growing band of single parents," as she once explained to *SATA.* "Single parents do not have much time for writing, so I . . . turned for a while to shorter books for younger children." Drawing on her love of the ballet, Anthony produced twelve volumes in the "Dancing Shoes" series, a group of books inspired by her 1995 story collection *Tales from the Ballet. Tales from the Ballet* retells the story of nine popular ballets in what *Booklist* reviewer April Judge described as "crisp, dramatic, and action-packed prose." Enchanters, princes and princesses, nutcrackers, nightingales, and firebirds, together with comments about the actual ballet, all find their way into the book, which features engaging pastel illustrations by Diz Wallis.

Commenting on the inspiration for her fiction, Anthony once told *SATA:* "The question children ask me most often in their letters is: 'What made you write the book *The Ghosts?'* My answer is: J. W. Dunne's book *An Experiment with Time,* which I read when I was seventeen; T. S. Eliot's poem 'Four Quartets,' which I read when I was seventeen; a story about a real apparition, told to me by an elderly man when I was twenty-six; and an old house I visited for a furniture auction when I was thirty-two, which made all the other memories come together to make a story. The moral is: You never know what may be useful if you are a writer."

Biographical and Critical Sources

PERIODICALS

Booklist, November 15, 1995, April Judge, review of *Shoes of Satin, Ribbons of Silk: Tales from the Ballet,* p. 594; October 15, 1998, Susan Dove Lempke, review of *Apollo and Daphne: Masterpieces of Greek Mythology,* p. 409.
Publishers Weekly, August 31, 1990, review of *The Mousehole Cat,* p. 65; January 18, 1993, review of *Gemma and the Baby Chick,* p. 468; November 21, 1994, review of *Catkin,* p. 76; March 15, 2004, review of *Hidden Tales from Eastern Europe,* p. 75.

Teacher Librarian, June, 2000, Jessica Higgs, review of *Apollo and Daphne,* p. 53.
Times Literary Supplement, June 26, 1969.

ONLINE

David Higham Associates Web site, http://www.david higham.co.uk/ (June 20, 2005), "Antonia Barber."*

*   *   *

ARCHAMBAULT, John

Personal

Born in Pasadena, CA. *Education:* Attended Columbia Teacher's College; University of California, B.A., 1981; graduate study at University of California, Riverside.

Addresses

Office—PMB 488 20505 Yorba Linda Blvd., Yorba Linda, CA 92886. *E-mail*—john@johnarchambault.com.

Career

Children's book author, poet, storyteller, and musician. CD recordings with David Plummer include *Painting My World* and *Dancing on the Moon,* for Youngheart Music.

Awards, Honors

Irma Simonton Black Honor Book, Bank Street College of Education, 1985, for *The Ghost-Eye Tree;* Children's Choice designation, International Reading Association/Children's Book Council (CBC), 1986, for *The Ghost-Eye Tree,* and 1987, for *Barn Dance!;* Notable Children's Trade Book in the Field of Social Studies designation, CBC/National Council on the Social Studies, 1987, for *Knots on a Counting Rope;* Boston Globe/Horn Book Honor Book designation, 1990, for *Chicka Chicka Boom Boom; Chicka Chicka Boom Boom* was chosen to be included in the Twenty-first-Century Literature Collection.

Writings

FOR CHILDREN

Counting Sheep, illustrated by John Rombola, Holt (New York, NY), 1989.
The Birth of a Whale, illustrated by Janet Skiles, Silver Press (Parsippany, NJ), 1996.
(With David Plummer) *The Fox and the Chicken,* illustrated by Marian Young, Silver Press (Parsippany, NJ), 1996.

(With David Plummer) *Counting Chickens,* illustrated by Lisa Chauncy Guida, Silver Press (Parsippany, NJ), 1996.

Grandmother's Garden, illustrated by Raul Colon, Silver Press (Parsippany, NJ), 1997.

(With David Plummer) *I Love the Mountains: A Traditional Song,* illustrated by Susan Swan, Silver Press (Parsippany, NJ), 1998.

Chicka Chicka Rock, illustrated by Suzanne Tanner Chitwood, Philomel (New York, NY), 2004.

"LITTLE SEASHORE BOOKS" SERIES; WITH BILL MARTIN, JR.

A Harvest of Oysters, Encyclopedia Britannica Educational Corporation (Chicago, IL), 1982.

The Irritable Alligator, Encyclopedia Britannica Educational Corporation (Chicago, IL), 1982.

The Loggerhead Turtle Crawls out of the Sea, Encyclopedia Britannica Educational Corporation (Chicago, IL), 1982.

The Night-hunting Lobster, Encyclopedia Britannica Educational Corporation (Chicago, IL), 1982.

A River of Salmon, Encyclopedia Britannica Educational Corporation (Chicago, IL), 1982.

The Seafaring Seals, Encyclopedia Britannica Educational Corporation (Chicago, IL), 1982.

The Silent Wetlands Hold Back the Sea, Encyclopedia Britannica Educational Corporation (Chicago, IL), 1982.

The Singing Whale, Encyclopedia Britannica Educational Corporation (Chicago, IL), 1982.

A Skyway of Geese, Encyclopedia Britannica Educational Corporation (Chicago, IL), 1982.

The Sooty Shearwater Flies over the Sea, Encyclopedia Britannica Educational Corporation (Chicago, IL), 1982.

WITH BILL MARTIN, JR.

Knots on a Counting Rope (originally published by Martin as part of "Young Owl Books Social Studies" series, Holt (New York, NY), 1966), illustrated by Ted Rand, Holt (New York, NY), 1987.

The Ghost-Eye Tree, illustrated by Ted Rand, Holt (New York, NY), 1985.

Barn Dance!, illustrated by Ted Rand, Holt (New York, NY), 1986.

White Dynamite and Curly Kidd, illustrated by Ted Rand, Holt (New York, NY), 1986.

Here Are My Hands, illustrated by Ted Rand, Holt (New York, NY), 1987.

Up and down on the Merry-Go-Round, illustrated by Ted Rand, Holt (New York, NY), 1988.

Listen to the Rain, illustrated by James Endicott, Holt (New York, NY), 1988.

The Magic Pumpkin, illustrated by Robert J. Lee, Holt (New York, NY), 1989.

Chicka Chicka Boom Boom, illustrated by Lois Ehlert, Simon & Schuster (New York, NY), 1989.

(Compilers with Peggy Brogan) *Sounds of the Storyteller,* DLM (Allen, TX), 1991.

Words, illustrated by Lois Ehlert, Little Simon (New York, New York), 1993.

A Beautiful Feast for a Big King Cat, illustrated by Bruce Degen, HarperCollins (New York, NY), 1994.

Chicka Chicka Sticka Sticka: An ABC Sticker Book, illustrated by Lois Ehlert, Simon & Schuster (New York, NY), 1995.

Also author of poetry and educational books.

"ROCKIN' READERS" SERIES; WITH DAVID PLUMMER

Magical, Miracle Me, with photographs by Michael Jarrett, Creative Teaching Press (Huntington Beach, CA), 2001.

Anthills and Apartments, illustrated by Sally J. K. Davis, Creative Teaching Press (Huntington Beach, CA), 2001.

I'm a Can-Do Kid, with photographs by Michael Jarrett, Creative Teaching Press (Huntington Beach, CA), 2001.

Grandmother's Garden, with photographs by Michael Jarrett, Creative Teaching Press (Huntington Beach, CA), 2001.

The Fox and the Children, illustrated by Karl Edwards, Creative Teaching Press (Huntington Beach, CA), 2001.

I Love the Mountains, illustrated by Pam Thomson, Creative Teaching Press (Huntington Beach, CA), 2001.

Counting Kittens, illustrated by Priscilla Burris, Creative Teaching Press (Huntington Beach, CA), 2001.

Rhythm, Rhythm, illustrated by Jackie Urbanovic, Creative Teaching Press (Huntington Beach, CA), 2001.

Baseball Cards and Piggy Banks, illustrated by Catherine Leary, Creative Teaching Press (Huntington Beach, CA), 2001.

Rickety Rock around the Clock, illustrated by Kathi Ember, Creative Teaching Press (Huntington Beach, CA), 2001.

Electric Car, illustrated by John Manders, Creative Teaching Press (Huntington Beach, CA), 2001.

RECORDINGS

CD recordings by Archambault and Plummer include *Chicka Chicka Boom Boom and Other Coconutty Songs, Plant a Dream, Grandmother's Garden, Wonder the Ocean, Painting My World,* and *Dancing on the Moon,* all for Youngheart Music.

Adaptations

Videotapes of poems and stories have been produced by DLM Publishers.

Sidelights

John Archambault is a children's writer dedicated to making reading comfortable, stimulating, and above all, fun for young readers. He has enjoyed a productive and successful collaboration with Bill Martin, Jr., with whom he shares an interest in the art of storytelling and in creating books meant to be seen and heard, as well as read. Archambault and Martin have also combined their efforts in designing innovative ways to help children discover the sheer joy of reading. *Los Angeles Times Book Review* contributor Kristiana Gregory called the two authors "a valuable duo with much to offer" young readers. Archambault is also an accomplished songwriter and has recorded several CDs of children's tunes.

Archambault was an eager reader and writer as a child. He was particularly inspired by E. B. White's classic novel *Charlotte's Web* after being introduced to the book by his third-grade teacher. Archambault read the book cover-to-cover and it was then, as he recalled on his Web site, that he realized what he wanted to do with his life. "I told my teacher, Mrs. Williams, that I wanted to do what E. B. White does," Archambault commented. "She said, 'John, if you want to be a writer, you have to be a reader.'"

Fortunately for Archambault, his parents valued literature and encouraged reading. His professional writing career began when, as a sophomore in high school, he took a part-time job at his local newspaper, the Pasadena, California *Star.* His good work was quickly rewarded with a full-time position as a reporter, a job he maintained throughout his high-school years. Archambault carried his involvement in writing and journalism into college as the editor of his campus newspaper. While a graduate student at the University of California at Riverside, he met Martin, a children's writer and educator who had been working on books and educational techniques for children for many years. In the mid-1980s, the two men began collaborating on children's picture books designed for early readers.

The Ghost-Eye Tree was the first publication written by Archambault and Martin that features Ted Rand as illustrator; the trio have since produced several popular juvenile books. *The Ghost-Eye Tree* is the story of a boy and his sister who are sent out by their mother for a pail of milk on a dark, windy night. In order to get to the milkman's farm, the children have to go past an old oak tree that the little boy fears is haunted. On their way back, both the boy and his sister, who has been teasing him for being afraid, see the ghost of the tree and flee home.

The Ghost-Eye Tree "emphasizes the bonds of love and friendship that develop between a brother and sister as they face their fears together," according to *Washington Post Book World* contributor John Cech. Critics have praised the book for its imaginatively spooky story, its rhythmic readability, and Rand's effective illustrations. *The Ghost-Eye Tree* is "a top-notch hair-raiser," noted a reviewer for the *Bulletin of the Center for Children's Books,* the critic adding that "it's poetry, too, the kind that reaches out to grab you." *Horn Book* commentator Ann A. Flowers concluded that *The Ghost-Eye Tree* is perfect for reading aloud.

In *Barn Dance!* Archambault, Martin, and Rand again present a child's nighttime adventures. A little boy, lying awake in a sleeping farmhouse, hears the unmistakable pluck of a violin. Following his ears to the barn, he finds a scarecrow playing the fiddle and the farm animals dancing. He joins them and dances until dawn. Read aloud, this book sounds like a square dance. With upbeat words and rhythms—"a hummin' an' a-yeein' an' a-rockin' an' a-sockin,'" or "Let's begin! Grab yourself a partner and jump right in!" the authors mimic the lively music and dance.

The energy of *Barn Dance!* is more than matched by the spiritedness of the trio's *White Dynamite and Curly Kidd,* the story of a girl watching her rodeo-star father ride White Dynamite, "the meanest bull in the whole United States." Once again, the rhythm and tone of the poetry match the frenzied pace of the rodeo: "Oh! Dad's in the rocker now . . . floppin' back and forth! His head's goin' south! Bull's goin' north . . . twistin' like a corkscrew straight down the right-away. His middle name's Doomsday! U!S!A!" *Los Angeles Times Book Review* contributor Kristiana Gregory summarized that the story "is rousing as a pep rally and meant to be yelled aloud so GET READY."

Knots on a Counting Rope is one of Martin and Archambault's most popular works. In the book the coauthors tell the story of a blind Indian boy who repeatedly asks his grandfather to tell him the tale of his birth and upbringing. The grandfather tells the boy of two great blue horses that looked upon him when he was a weak newborn baby, giving him strength. The elder also relates how the blind child learned to ride his horse by memorizing trails—and even took part in a horse race. Each time he tells the story, the grandfather ties another knot in his rope, assuring his grandson that when the counting rope is filled with knots, the boy will know the story of his own birth by heart.

Los Angeles Times Book Review contributor Barbara Karlin noted that the aging grandfather in *Knots on a Counting Rope* "is telling his grandson that he will not always be there to tell the tale, even though his love for the child will last forever." The novel reflects the passing on of identity, love, and strength through the spoken word. This "dialogue between generations" observed Richard Peck in the *Los Angeles Times Book Review,* demonstrates the power of "the oral tradition, the link best forged by families."

With their more recent collaborations, Archambault and Martin dramatize familiar experiences in appealing ways. In her *Horn Book* critique of *Up and down on the Merry-Go-Round,* Ellen Fader found Archambault and Martin to be supremely successful in capturing the motion and joy of riding a carousel. The pair's *Chicka Chicka Boom Boom,* also received enthusiastic reviews. "Rap comes to alphabet books," declared *School Library Journal* critic John Philbrook of the book's "engaging rhyme" and "restless, exciting rhythms." Mary

In **Boom Chicka Rock** *one dozen fun-loving mice living in a cuckoo clock emerge, one by one, and take advantage of Max the cat's cat nap to have a birthday party. (Illustration by Susan Tanner Chitwood.)*

M. Burns, writing in *Horn Book,* called *Chicka Chicka Boom Boom* "one of the liveliest, jazziest alphabet books on record. . . . Tongue-tingling, visually stimulating. . . . Absolutely irresistible. Join in, snap your fingers, listen to the beat, let yourself go—and have fun." *Chicka Chicka Boom Boom* garnered a *Boston Globe/Horn Book* Honor Book designation in 1990. In an even more recent work, *Boom Chicka Rock,* Archambault tells the story of a group of mice prepare for a late-night birthday celebration while taking care not to wake the cat sleeping nearby. "The rollicking refrain—'Boom Chicka Rock, Chicka Rock, Chicka Boom!'—will have children moving to the rhythm," noted *School Library Journal* contributor Robin L. Gibson.

In *A Beautiful Feast for a Big King Cat* a cat catches a little mouse who has been teasing him. Unable to run to his mother like he did before, the small mouse must save himself. Using his cunning, he entices the feline to dream of a delicious feast and when the cat closes his eyes to picture the food all laid out before him, the mouse runs to safety. "Archambault and Martin's rambunctious plot and lively, rhymed verse are perfectly

complimented by the slapstick in Degen's detailed and faintly Victorian illustrations," noted a *Publishers Weekly* reviewer.

In a solo project, *The Birth of a Whale,* Archambault introduces readers to a miracle of nature: the birth of a baby humpback out in deep water. While providing some whale-related facts, Archambault's verse focuses primarily on the rhythm and grandeur of the giant mammal. In her review for *Booklist,* Lauren Peterson noted the author's poetic slant, explaining that he is "more concerned with capturing the grace and majesty of the magnificent creature than with . . . presenting information."

As the author noted on his Web site, "I have a passion for bringing words to life. I stir rhythm, rhyme, and whimsy, stringing words so that a melody is created, then kids can ride along on this musical river." In addition to his literary efforts, Archambault has teamed with David Plummer to record several children's songs for Youngheart Music; he appears on the recordings *Plant a Dream* and *Dancing on the Moon.*

Biographical and Critical Sources

PERIODICALS

Booklist, July, 1994, Deborah Abbott, review of *Beautiful Feast for a Big King Cat,* p. 1952; March 15, 1996, Lauren Peterson, review of *The Birth of a Whale,* p. 1265.
Bulletin of the Center for Children's Books, February, 1986, review of *The Ghost-Eye Tree,* p. 114.
Entertainment Weekly, May 1, 1992, Susan Stewart, review of *Chicka Chicka Boom Boom,* p. 114.
Horn Book, January-February, 1986, Ann A. Flowers, review of *The Ghost-Eye Tree,* p. 51; July-August, 1988, Ellen Fader, review of *Up and down on the Merry-Go-Round,* p. 483; January-February, 1990, Mary M. Burns, review of *Chicka Chicka Boom Boom,* p. 54.
Kirkus Reviews, June 15, 1996, p. 906; April 15, 2004, review of *Boom Chicka Rock,* p. 389.
Los Angeles Times Book Review, June 15, 1986, Kristiana Gregory, review of *White Dynamite and Curly Kidd,* p. 7; December 6, 1987, Barbara Karlin, review of *Knots on a Counting Rope,* p. 7; March 27, 1988, Richard Peck, "Birds, Deserts, Space Insects, and a Navajo Grandfather," p. 12.
Publishers Weekly, May 30, 1994, review of *A Beautiful Feast for a Big King Cat,* p. 55; March 15, 2004, review of *Boom Chicka Rock,* p. 72.
School Library Journal, November, 1989, John Philbrook, review of *Chicka Chicka Boom Boom,* p. 89; July, 1994, p. 73; March, 1996, p. 184; November, 1996, p. 76; May, 2004, Robin L. Gibson, review of *Boom Chicka Rock,* p. 100.
Washington Post Book World, November 10, 1985, John Cech, "A Palette of Picture Books," p. 19.

ONLINE

John Archambault Web site, http://www.johnarchambault. com (July 15, 2005).*

B

BARBER, Antonia
See ANTHONY, Barbara

* * *

BEDDOWS, Eric
See NUTT, Ken

* * *

BEEKE, Tiphanie

Personal

Born in England; married; children: two boys. *Education:* Royal College of Art, M.A. (illustration), 1995. *Hobbies and other interests:* Puppet making, traveling.

Addresses

Home—Hertfordshire, England. *Agent*—c/o Author Mail, HK Portfolio, Mela Bolinao, 10 East 29th St., No. 40-G, New York, NY 10016.

Career

Illustrator. Artist-in-residence at Ottawa School of Art, Ottawa, Canada, and on various expeditions. Designer of textiles and greeting cards.

Writings

SELF-ILLUSTRATED

Aesop's Fables, Bloomsbury (London, England), 1998.
Bigger Smaller, David & Charles, 1999.
Up down over Under, David & Charles, 1999.
Roar like a Lion!: A First Book about Sounds, Gullane Children's Books (London, England), 2001.
Wake up Baby Bear!: A First Book about Opposites, Gullane Children's Books (London, England), 2001.

ILLUSTRATOR

Jemma Beeke, *The Brand New Creature,* Levinson Books (London, England), 1997.
Adrian Chatfield, *Something In Common,* St. John's Extension Studies (Nottingham, England), 1998.
Deborah Bruss, *Book! Book! Book!,* Arthur A. Levine Books (New York, NY), 2001.
Ian Whybrow, *The Snow Friends,* Gullane Children's Books (London, England), 2001, published as *Wish, Change, Friend,* Margaret K. McElderry Books (New York, NY), 2002.
Ian Whybrow, *The Noisy Way to Bed,* Macmillan Children's Books (London, England), 2003, Arthur A. Levine Books (New York, NY), 2004.
Alyssa Satin Capucilli, *Only My Dad and Me,* HarperFestival (New York, NY), 2003.
Alyssa Satin Capucilli, *Only My Mom and Me,* HarperFestival (New York, NY), 2003.
Dandi Daley Mackall, *First Day,* Harcourt (San Diego, CA), 2003.
Tara Jaye Morrow, *Mommy Loves Her Baby; Daddy Loves His Baby,* HarperCollins (New York, NY), 2003.
Eileen Spinelli, *Polar Bears and Arctic Hares,* Hyperion Books for Children (New York, NY), 2003.
Anthony France, *From Me to You,* Candlewick Press (Cambridge, MA), 2004.
Falling Leaves, Gullane Children's Books (London, England), 2004.
Angela McAllister, *Brave Bitsy and the Bear,* Macmillan (London, England), 2004.
Cynthia Rylant, *The Stars Will Still Shine,* HarperCollins (New York, NY), 2005.
Mary Ann Hoberman, *I'm Going to Grandma's,* Harcourt (Orlando, FL), 2006.

Biographical and Critical Sources

PERIODICALS

Booklist, January 1, 1999, John Peters, review of *The Brand New Creature* p. 885; March 1, 2002, Ilene

Cooper, review of *Roar like a Lion!: A First Book about Sounds,* p. 1139; August, 2003, Stephanie Zvirin, review of *First Day,* p. 1994.

Horn Book, May-June, 2003, Lauren Adams, review of *Mommy Loves Her Baby/Daddy Loves His Baby,* p. 331.

Kirkus Reviews, November 15, 2001, review of *Wish, Change, Friend,* p. 1616; March 15, 2003, review of *Mommy Loves Her Baby/Daddy Loves His Baby,* p. 474.

Publishers Weekly, December 21, 1998, review of *The Brand New Creature,* p. 67; April 23, 2001, review of *Book! Book! Book!,* p. 76; November 26, 2001, review of *Wish, Change, Friend,* p. 61; March 3, 2003, review of *Family Affair,* p. 78; August 25, 2003, review of *First Day,* p. 62; March 15, 2004, review of *The Noisy Way to Bed,* p. 73.

School Library Journal, May, 2001, Grace Oliff, review of *Book! Book! Book!,* p. 110; January, 2002, Shawn Brommer, review of *Wish, Change, Friend,* p. 112; February, 2003, Jody McCoy, review of *A Treasury of Alphabets,* p. 124; May, 2003, Leslie Barban, review of *Only My Dad and Me,* p. 109; July, 2003, Marilyn Taniguchi, review of *Mommy Loves Her Baby/Daddy Loves His Baby,* p. 101; September, 2003, Lisa Gangemi Kropp, review of *First Day,* p. 184.

ONLINE

H. K. Portfolio Web site, http://www.hkportfolio.com/ (July 6, 2005), "Tiphanie Beeke."

PFD Web site, http://www.pfd.co.uk/ (July 6, 2005), "Tiphanie Beeke."*

* * *

BERGSMA, Jody Lynn

Personal

Children: Jessica, Sky. *Education:* Attended college. *Hobbies and other interests:* Riding horses.

Addresses

Home—WA. *Office*—Bergsma Gallery 1301 Fraser St. #A6, Bellingham, WA 98229. *E-mail*—bergsma@ bergsma.com.

Career

Illustrator, author, designer, and figurative painter. Bergsma Gallery, Bellingham, WA, owner, beginning 1984; contractual artist for SeaWorld.

Awards, Honors

Best Children's Book, Coalition of Visionary Retailers, and Best Children's Picture Book Award, Independent Publishers Association, both 2003, both for *Faerie.*

Writings

SELF-ILLUSTRATED

Dragon, Illumination Arts (Bellevue, WA), 1999.
The Little Wizard, Illumination Arts (Bellevue, WA), 2000.
Faerie, Gallery Press (Bellingham, WA), 2002.

ILLUSTRATOR

Sandy Kleven, *Touching,* Whatcom County Opportunity Council/Bergsma Collectibles (Bellingham, WA), 1985.
Sandy Kleven, *The Right Touch: A Read Aloud Story to Help Prevent Child Sexual Abuse,* Illumination Arts (Bellevue, WA), 1997.
David Ogden, *Dreambirds,* Illumination Arts (Bellevue, WA), 1997.
Sandra Hanken, *Sky Castle,* Illumination Arts (Bellevue, WA), 1998.

Adaptations

Characters from Bergsma's works have been adapted as plush toys, stained glass, figurines, scupture, and jewelry.

Biographical and Critical Sources

PERIODICALS

Art Business News, June, 2003, "SeaWorld Contracts Artist Jody Bergsma," p. 12.
Home Accents Today, June, 2003, "Fiesta Partners with Artist Jody Bergsma," p. 35.
School Library Journal, April, 2000, Rosalyn Pierini, review of *Dragon,* p. 90.
Skipping Stones, May-August, 1997, review of *Dreambirds,* p. 31.

ONLINE

Bergsma Gallery Web site, http://www.bergsma.com/ (March 19, 2005).

* * *

BINGHAM, Jane M(arie) 1941-

Personal

Born September 21, 1941, in Huntington, WV; daughter of Ferrell Jeff and Nora Lucille (Stephenson) Bingham. *Education:* Flint Junior College, A.A., 1961; Central Michigan University, B.A., 1964; Michigan State University, M.A., 1966, Ph.D., 1970.

Addresses

Home—Rochester, MI. *Office*—Department of Education, Oakland University, 501 O'Dowd Hall, Rochester, MI 48309-4401. *E-mail*—bingham@oakland.edu.

Career

Elementary school teacher at public schools in Flint, MI, 1961-65; Michigan State University, East Lansing, assistant instructor in education, 1965-66; Flint Junior College, Flint, instructor in children's literature, summer, 1967; Oakland University, Rochester, MI, instructor, 1969-70, assistant professor, 1970-75, associate professor of children's literature, 1975-c. 2001. Member of Friends of Flint Public Library, Detroit Public Library, Avon Township Library, Kerlan Collection at University of Minnesota, Osborne Collection at Toronto Public Library, DeGrummond Collection at University of Mississippi, and Detroit Institute of Art.

Member

International Reading Association, International Research Society for Children's Literature, Association for Childhood Education International, National Council of Teachers of English (treasurer of Children's Literature Assembly, 1973-75; chairperson, 1976-78), American Library Association (member of Laura Ingalls Wilder and Caldecott Medal awards committees; chairperson of national planning for special collections committee), Children's Literature Association (board member, 1975-78; secretary, 1975-76).

Writings

NONFICTION FOR CHILDREN

(Editor, with Fiona Chandler and Sam Taplin) *The Usborne Internet-linked Encyclopedia of World History*, Usborne, 2001.
Tiananmen Square: June 4, 1989, Raintree (Chicago, IL), 2004.
The Red Cross Movement, Raintree (Chicago, IL), 2004.
The Human Body: From Head to Toe, Heinemann Library (Chicago, IL), 2004.
A History of Fashion and Costume, Volume 1: *The Ancient World*, Facts on File (New York, NY), 2005.
Johnny Depp, Raintree (Chicago, IL), 2005.
Sikh Gurdwaras, Raintree (Chicago, IL), 2005.
Why Do Families Break Up?, Raintree (Chicago, IL), 2005.

"WHAT'S THE DEAL?" SERIES; NONFICTION FOR CHILDREN

Heroin, Heinemann Library (Chicago, IL), 2005.
Alcohol, Heinemann Library (Chicago, IL), 2005.
Marijuana, Heinemann Library (Chicago, IL), 2005.
Smoking, Heinemann Library (Chicago, IL), 2005.

"WORLD ART AND CULTURE" SERIES; NONFICTION FOR CHILDREN

Indian Art and Culture, Raintree (Chicago, IL), 2004.
African Art and Culture, Raintree (Chicago, IL), 2004.
Aboriginal Art and Culture, Raintree (Chicago, IL), 2005.

FOR ADULTS

(With Grayce Scholt) *Fifteen Centuries of Children's Literature: An Annotated Chronology of British and American Works in Historical Context*, Greenwood Press (Westport, CT), 1980.

Author of "Children's Literature: Views and Reviews," a quarterly column written with Grayce Scholt for *Michigan Reading Journal*, 1971-76. Contributor of articles and reviews to education, library, and women's studies journals. Editor of *Children's Literature in Review* and *The Three R's: Reading, Writing and Radio* (children's magazine).

Sidelights

Jane M. Bingham spent most of her adult life teaching college students about children's literature at Oakland University, collecting and studying children's books from across history and around the world, and campaigning for better materials for children to read. After she retired from that career, she began writing children's books of her own. Bingham has since authored several nonfiction books that seek to explain contemporary issues to children, including divorce, the dangers of drug abuse, and the art and culture of civilizations around the world.

In *Why Do Families Break Up?* Bingham attempts to demystify the process of divorce for middle-school students. The book begins by examining some of the reasons a couple might decide to divorce, then moves on to explain the process of coping and moving on after a family separates. *School Library Journal* contributor Sharon A. Neal described the book as "supportive [and] unbiased" and noted, "Despite the nature of the topic, the book is hopeful."

Tiananmen Square: June 4, 1989 examines the student-led protest against China's Communist rulers that occurred there, in the middle of Beijing, in the spring of 1989. On June 4 the government mobilized the army, including tanks, to disperse the demonstrators, killing several of them in the process. "The excellent illustrations and clear narrative," Elizabeth Talbot wrote in *School Library Journal*, make *Tiananmen Square* a "good introduction" to the protest and its aftermath.

Bingham is the author of three installments in the "World Art and Culture" series, examining India, Africa, and Aboriginal Australia. Each book is brief, only fifty-six pages long, and "the texts are straightforward and concise," Gillian Engberg noted in a review of *Af-*

rican Art and Culture for *Booklist*. Despite this brevity, much information is packed into each volume. Bingham opens each book with a chapter about the history of the region, from thousands of years ago to the present day, and follows with chapters about the art forms practiced in that area. These include architecture, basket-weaving, creating musical instruments, dance, and body modification (tattoos, piercings, and the like), among others. *Indian Art and Culture* also includes a chapter on one of that country's modern art forms, the "Bollywood" movie industry. As Donna Cardon noted in *School Library Journal*, "The texts not only describe the art forms and how they are created, but also explain the role that art plays in the cultures."

Bingham once wrote: "In 1981 I completed a trip which took me to American Samoa, New Zealand, Australia, Hong Kong, China, Thailand, Bangladesh, India, Kenya, South Africa, and Swaziland. I collected examples of children's books along the way and became acutely aware of the need for books and other teaching resources in many developing countries. I was especially impressed with the variety of India's and Bangladesh's children's books—in spite of the difficulties their creators often encounter in publishing and promoting them. I also found that becoming aware of and enjoying the literature from other countries enriched my appreciation of American children's books. I found myself asking over and over why we, with the plethora we have to choose from, too often opt for the mediocre rather than the 'rarest kind of best.' As educators, creators, and consumers, we all too often forget to think of children's books as real literature because we fail to apply critical literary standards. It is my hope that my teaching and writing will draw attention to the continuing need for quality books in our own country and will also encourage American students and teachers to adopt a wider, world view of children's literature."

Biographical and Critical Sources

PERIODICALS

Booklist, April 1, 2004, Gillian Engberg, review of *African Art and Culture,* p. 1373.

Oakland University Post (Oakland, MI), March 27, 2002, Ashlyn Cates, "Bingham Gives Kresge Books."

School Arts, February, 2005, Ken Marantz, review of *Indian Art and Culture,* p. 55.

School Library Journal, November, 2001, review of *The Usborne Internet-linked Encyclopedia of World History,* p. 86; February, 2004, Donna Cardon, review of *African Art and Culture,* p. 156; April, 2004, Wendy Lukehart, review of *African Art and Culture,* p. 63; June, 2004, Marilyn Ackerman, review of *The Red Cross Movement,* p. 157; October, 2004, Elizabeth Talbot, review of *Tiananmen Square: June 4, 1989,* p. 186; February, 2005, Sharon A. Neal, review of *Why Do Families Break Up?,* p. 145.*

BJÖRKMAN, Steve

Personal

Married; children: three. *Education:* Attended college.

Addresses

Home—Irvine, CA. *Office*—6 Journey #250, Aliso Viejo, CA 92656. *Agent*—Vince Kamin, 400 W. Erie, Chicago, IL 60610. *E-mail*—stevebjorkman@sbcglobal.net.

Career

Illustrator, beginning c. mid-1970s, including advertising/editorial, children's books and greeting cards. Art teacher at youth camps and for other groups.

Writings

SELF-ILLUSTRATED

Good Night, Little One, WaterBrook Press (Colorado Springs, CO), 1999.

The Flyaway Kite, WaterBrook Press (Colorado Springs, CO), 2000.

Supersnouts!, Holiday House (New York, NY), 2004.

ILLUSTRATOR

Jonathan Etra, *Aliens for Breakfast,* Random House (New York, NY), 1988.

Ellen Levine, *I Hate English!,* Scholastic (New York, NY), 1989.

Edith Baer, *This Is the Way We Go to School: A Book about Children around the World,* Scholastic (New York, NY), 1990.

Jonathan Etra and Stephanie Spinner, *Aliens for Lunch,* Random House (New York, NY), 1991.

Greg Johnson, *If I Could Ask God One Question—,* Tyndale House (Wheaton, IL), 1991.

Jean Marzollo, *In 1492,* Scholastic (New York, NY), 1991.

Todd Temple, *How to Become a Teenager Millionaire,* T. Nelson (Nashville, TN), 1991.

Susan Saunders, *Tyrone Goes to School,* Dutton Children's Books (New York, NY), 1992.

Joyce K. Ellis, editor, *The One-Minute Bible for Kids: From the New International Version of the Bible,* Garborg's (Bloomington, MN), 1993.

Ruth Belov Gross, *A Book about Your Skeleton,* Scholastic (New York, NY), 1994.

Jean Marzollo, *In 1776,* Scholastic (New York, NY), 1994.

George Shannon, *Seeds,* Houghton Mifflin (Boston, MA), 1994.

Stephanie Spinner, *Aliens for Dinner,* Random House (New York, NY), 1994.

Edith Baer, *This Is the Way We Eat Our Lunch: A Book about Children around the World,* Scholastic (New York, NY), 1995.

George Shannon, *Heart to Heart,* Houghton Mifflin (Boston, MA), 1995.

Jeff Brown, *Flat Stanley,* HarperTrophy (New York, NY), 1996.

Jeff Brown, *Invisible Stanley,* HarperTrophy (New York, NY), 1996.

Jeff Brown, *Stanley and the Magic Lamp,* new edition, HarperCollins (New York, NY), 1996.

Bobbie Katz, *Germs! Germs! Germs!,* Scholastic (New York, NY), 1996.

L. J. Sattgast, *When the World Was New,* Gold 'n' Honey Books (Sisters, OR), 1996.

Louise Borden, *Thanksgiving Is—,* Scholastic (New York, NY), 1997.

Melody Carlson, *The Ark That Noah Built,* Gold 'n' Honey Books (Sister, OR), 1997.

Melody Carlson, *A Tale of Two Houses,* Gold 'n' Honey Books (Sisters, OR), 1998.

Bobbi Katz, *Lots of Lice,* Scholastic (New York, NY), 1998.

Jennifer Rees Larcombe, *The Terrible Giant,* Crossway Books (Wheaton, IL), 1999.

Edith Tarbescu, *Bring Back My Gerbil!,* Scholastic (New York, NY), 1999.

Melody Carlson, *The Lost Lamb,* Crossway Books (Wheaton, IL), 1999.

Melody Carlson, *The Other Brother,* Crossway Books (Wheaton, IL), 1999.

Bobbi Katz, *Make Way for Tooth Decay,* Scholastic (New York, NY), 1999.

Jennifer Rees Larcombe, *The Baby in the Basket,* Crossway Books (Wheaton, IL), 1999.

Jennifer Rees Larcombe, *The Boy Who Ran Away,* Crossway Books (Wheaton, IL), 1999.

Jennifer Rees Larcombe, *The Man Who Was Not Tall Enough,* Crossway Books (Wheaton, IL), 1999.

Jennifer Rees Larcombe, *Lost in Jerusalem!,* Crossway Books (Wheaton, IL), 2000.

Jennifer Rees Larcombe, *The Walls That Fell down Flat,* Crossway Books (Wheaton, IL), 2000.

Rachel Vail, *Mama Rex and T Lose a Waffle,* Scholastic (New York, NY), 2000.

Rachel Vail, *Mama Rex and T Shop for Shoes,* Scholastic (New York, NY), 2000.

Eve Bunting, *Dear Wish Fairy,* Scholastic (New York, NY), 2000.

Melody Carlson, *Farmer Brown's Field Trip,* Crossway Books (Wheaton, IL), 2000.

Melody Carlson, *It's Not Funny, I Lost My Money,* Crossway Books (Wheaton, IL), 2000.

Jennifer Rees Larcombe, *The Best Boat Ever Built,* Crossway Books (Wheaton, IL), 2000.

Jennifer Rees Larcombe, *Danger on the Lonely Road,* Crossway Books (Wheaton, IL), 2000.

Melody Carlson, *A Treasure beyond Measure,* Crossway Books (Wheaton, IL), 2001.

Carol Wallace, *Poky,* Holiday House (New York, NY), 2005.

Renee Riva, *Izzy the Lizzy,* WaterBrook Press (Colorado Springs, CO), 2005.

Renee Riva, *Guido's Gondola,* WaterBrook Press (Colorado Springs, CO), 2005.

Stuart J. Murphy, *Same Old Hankie,* HarperCollins (New York, NY), 2005.

ILLUSTRATOR; "WEEBIE ZONE" SERIES

Stephanie Spinner and Ellen Weiss, *Gerbilities,* Harper Collins (New York, NY), 1996.

Stephanie Spinner and Ellen Weiss, *Sing, Elvis, Sing!,* Harper Collins (New York, NY), 1996.

Stephanie Spinner and Ellen Weiss, *Bright Lights, Little Gerbil,* HarperCollins (New York, NY), 1997.

Stephanie Spinner and Ellen Weiss, *Born to Be Wild,* HarperCollins (New York, NY), 1997.

Stephanie Spinner and Ellen Weiss, *The Bird Is the Word,* HarperCollins (New York, NY), 1997.

Stephanie Spinner and Ellen Weiss, *We're Off to See the Lizard,* HarperCollins (New York, NY), 1998.

Biographical and Critical Sources

PERIODICALS

Booklist, February 1, 1997, Carolyn Phelan, review of *Germs, Germs, Germs!,* p. 950.

Kirkus Reviews, February 1, 2004, review of *Supersnouts!,* p. 129.

Publishers Weekly, January 20, 2003, review of *Farm Life,* p. 80.

School Library Journal, August, 2002, Linda Beck, review of *So You Want to Be a Teenager?* p. 216; August, 2002, Nancy A. Gifford, review of *Safari Park,* p. 178; May, 2004, Marge Loch-Wouters, review of *Supersnouts!,* p. 102.

ONLINE

Steve Björkman Web site, http://www.stevebjorkman.com (July 6, 2005).*

*   *   *

BOELTS, Maribeth 1964-

Personal

Born January 19, 1964, in Waterloo, IA; daughter of Gerald Clifford (a machinist) and Dorothy Angela (a registered nurse; maiden name, Shimek) Condon; married Darwin Dale Boelts (a firefighter), August 1, 1983; children: three. *Education:* University of Northern Iowa, B.A., 1987; Hawkeye Institute of Technology, emergency medical technician certification, 1988. *Politics:* Democrat. *Religion:* Christian Reformed. *Hobbies and other interests:* Reading, exercise, spending time with husband and children.

Addresses

Home—3815 Clearview Dr., Cedar Falls, IA 50613.
E-mail—maribeth@cfu.net.

Career

Author. St. John/St. Nicholas School, Evansdale, IA, preschool teacher, 1988-91, has also worked as a substitute teacher; *Waterloo Courier*, Waterloo, IA, freelance feature writer, 1992-94.

Member

Society of Children's Book Writers and Illustrators.

Writings

FICTION

With My Mom, with My Dad, Pacific Press (Boise, ID), 1992.
Tornado, Paulist Press (Mahwah, NJ), 1993.
Grace and Joe, Albert Whitman (Morton Grove, IL), 1994.
Lullaby Babes, Albert Whitman (Morton Grove, IL), 1994.
Summer's End, illustrated by Ellen Kandoian, Houghton Mifflin (Boston, MA), 1995.
Big Daddy, Frog Wrestler, illustrated by Benrei Huang, Albert Whitman (Morton Grove, IL), 2000.
Lullaby Lullabook, illustrated by Bruce Whatley, Harper-Festival (New York, NY), 2002.
The Sloths Get a Pet, illustrated by Jan Gerardi, Random House (New York, NY), 2003.
Looking for Sleepy, illustrated by Bernadette Pons, Albert Whitman (Morton Grove, IL), 2004.
When It's the Last Day of School, illustrated by Hanako Wakiyama, Putnam (New York, NY), 2004.
The Firefighters' Thanksgiving, illustrated by Terry Widener, Putnam (New York, NY), 2004.

"LITTLE BUNNY" SERIES

Dry Days, Wet Nights, Albert Whitman (Morton Grove, IL), 1994.
Little Bunny's Preschool Countdown, illustrated by Kathy Parkinson, Albert Whitman (Morton Grove, IL), 1996.
Little Bunny's Cool Tool Set, illustrated by Kathy Parkinson, Albert Whitman (Morton Grove, IL), 1997.
Little Bunny's Pacifier Plan, illustrated by Kathy Parkinson, Albert Whitman (Morton Grove, IL), 1999.
You're a Brother, Little Bunny!, illustrated by Kathy Parkinson, Albert Whitman (Morton Grove, IL), 2001.

NONFICTION

(With husband, Darwin Boelts) *Kids to the Rescue!: First Aid Techniques for Kids*, Parenting Press (Seattle, WA), 1992, revised edition, illustrated by Marina Megale, Parenting Press (Seattle, WA), 2003.

A Kid's Guide to Staying Safe on the Streets, PowerKids Press (New York, NY), 1997.
A Kid's Guide to Staying Safe in the Water, PowerKids Press (New York, NY), 1997.
A Kid's Guide to Staying Safe on Bikes, PowerKids Press (New York, NY), 1997.
A Kid's Guide to Staying Safe at School, PowerKids Press (New York, NY), 1997.
A Kid's Guide to Staying Safe at Playgrounds, PowerKids Press (New York, NY), 1997.
A Kid's Guide to Staying Safe around Fire, PowerKids Press (New York, NY), 1997.

"HELPING KIDS HEAL" SERIES

Sometimes I'm Afraid: A Book about Fear, illustrated by Cheri Bladholm, Zonderkidz (Grand Rapids, MI), 2004.
Sarah's Grandma Goes to Heaven: A Book about Grief, illustrated by Cheri Bladholm, Zonderkidz (Grand Rapids, MI), 2004.
With My Mom, with My Dad, illustrated by Cheri Bladholm, Zonderkidz (Grand Rapids, MI), 2004.
Why Did You Bring Home a New Baby?, illustrated by Cheri Bladholm, Zonderkidz (Grand Rapids, MI), 2005.

Sidelights

Maribeth Boelts is the author of a number of works for children, including picture books such as *When It's the Last Day of School* and *Big Daddy, Frog Wrestler*, and nonfiction titles such as *Kids to the Rescue!: First Aid Techniques for Kids*, cowritten with her husband, Darwin Boelts, a firefighter. The mother of three children, Boelts often draws on her experiences as a parent for inspiration.

A former preschool teacher, Boelts once explained her decision to write children's books to *Something about the Author*: "I grew up in a family of readers, spending long hours at the Waterloo Public Library, filling my backpack every Saturday with Beverly Cleary, Laura Ingalls Wilder, and *Boy's Life* magazine (much more exciting, I thought, than anything out for girls at the time.) The writing joined the reading when I was in first grade, and from that [first] poem on, I was hooked on words. I continued to write through high school and into college, but as a twenty-year-old married college student with a newborn baby, pursuing an actual writing career seemed like a frivolous dream. I needed a job, and because I liked kids and had always liked school, teaching seemed a reasonable choice. After three years of teaching, however, I realized that the writing, like an impatient child, wouldn't wait. I quit my job, taking with me a file folder of ideas from the children I taught and the two young children I had at home. I wrote a few really bad children's stories, received a lot of rejections, did some more research, spent hours reading children's books, and then wrote some more. Eventually, I got some good news from a publisher, and that was all I needed for fuel."

The festivities of the firemen on duty during the holiday shift as a small fire station are almost derailed by twelve-alarm cooking mishaps and more serious emergencies in Maribeth Boelts' **The Firefighters' Thanksgiving.** *(Illustration by Terry Widener.)*

Shortly after publishing her debut work, Boelts was hired to write *Kids to the Rescue!,* a first aid book for children. "It was a great fit for me," Boelts stated on the Parenting Press Web site. "I took the Emergency Medical Technician certification course at my local community college and worked on *Kids to the Rescue!* with my husband, who was completing paramedic training for his new job with the fire department." Boelts has since published several other easy-to-read advice books for children, including *A Kid's Guide to Staying Safe in the Water* and *A Kid's Guide to Staying Safe on Bikes.*

Boelts's "Little Bunny" series of picture books for toddlers explores familiar family situations. In *Little Bunny's Pacifier Plan,* the title character attempts to wean himself from his source of comfort. "The situation is never defined as a problem, just a normal part of growing up," remarked Carolyn Phelan in *Booklist.* The arrival of a new sibling is the subject of *You're a Brother, Little Bunny!* Little Bunny believes he is well prepared for baby Kale, but the newborn's constant crying and smelly diapers prove to be quite a challenge. "Boelts has a good ear for the feelings of a preschooler," Phelan observed.

In *Big Daddy, Frog Wrestler,* a young frog named Curtis discovers his father had once been a champion grappler. Though Curtis is elated when his father is offered a world tour, Big Daddy quickly realizes that he prefers time with his family to life on the road. "The father-son relationship glows with affection," noted Gay Lynn Van Vleck in *School Library Journal.* An energetic class clown decides to rein in his antics in *When It's the Last Day of School,* "a story that radiates the lighter side—or anyway more rascally side—of schooling," according to a critic in *Kirkus Reviews.* James is on his best behavior, stifling burps, thanking a grumpy

lunch lady, and earning a gold star. As the last bell rings, "James literally explodes off the final page, ready for a long, hot summer of frolicking with his friends," wrote *School Library Journal* contributor Lisa Gangemi Kropp.

Boelts again used her knowledge of rescue workers in the rhyming picture book *The Firefighters' Thanksgiving.* On Thanksgiving Day, fireman Lou volunteers to cook a big meal for his coworkers, but his plans are interrupted by several calls to duty. When Lou has to be hospitalized after fighting a blaze, the grateful people he helped that day pitch in to deliver a wonderful feast to the station. A contributor in *Kirkus Reviews* called the work "a satisfying holiday story with an unusual perspective."

Biographical and Critical Sources

PERIODICALS

Booklist, April 1, 1995, Hazel Rochman, review of *Summer's End,* p. 1422; September 15, 1996, Carolyn Phelan, review of *Little Bunny's Preschool Countdown,* p. 245; September 15, 1997, April Judge, review of *Little Bunny's Cool Tool Set,* p. 239; March 1, 1999, Carolyn Phelan, review of *Little Bunny's Pacifier Plan,* p. 1218; March 1, 2000, Gillian Engberg, review of *Big Daddy, Frog Wrestler,* p. 1249; December 1, 2001, Carolyn Phelan, review of *You're a Brother, Little Bunny!,* p. 647; April 15, 2004, Carolyn Phelan, review of *When It's the Last Day of School,* p. 1445; May 15, 2004, Ilene Cooper, review of *Looking for Sleepy,* p. 1624; August, 2004, Gillian Engberg, review of *The Firefighters' Thanksgiving,* p. 1940.

Kirkus Reviews, September 15, 2001, review of *You're a Brother, Little Bunny!,* p. 1354; January 15, 2004, review of *When It's the Last Day of School,* p. 80; July 1, 2004, review of *The Firefighters' Thanksgiving,* p. 625.

Publishers Weekly, September 27, 2004, review of *The Firefighters' Thanksgiving,* p. 59.

School Library Journal, March, 2000, Gay Lynn Van Vleck, review of *Big Daddy, Frog Wrestler,* p. 189; January, 2002, Doris Gebel, review of *You're a Brother, Little Bunny!,* p. 95; April, 2004, G. Alyssa Parkinson, review of *Looking for Sleepy,* and Lisa Gangemi Kropp, review of *When It's the Last Day of School,* pp. 102-103; January, 2005, James K. Irwin, review of *The Firefighters' Thanksgiving,* p. 86.

ONLINE

Maribeth Boelts Home Page, http://maribethboelts.com (July 15, 2005).

Parenting Press Web site, http://www.parentingpress.com/ (fall, 2002), "Maribeth Boelts Launched Writing Career Three Months into Sabbatical from Teaching."

* * *

BREDESON, Carmen 1944-

Personal

Born November 3, 1944, in Norfolk, VA; daughter of Ralph (a professor and music critic) and Betty (Trader) Thibodeau; married Larry Dean Bredeson (an engineer), December 27, 1969; children: two children. *Education:* Texas A & I University, B.S., 1967; Southern Illinois University, M.S., 1981.

Addresses

Home—TX. *Agent*—agentc/o Author Mail, Children's Press, Scholastic Library Publishing, P.O. Box 1795, 90 Sherman Tpke., Danbury, CT 06816. *E-mail*—ctbkaty@aol.com.

Career

Writer. Taught high school English until 1972. Volunteered in neighborhood schools and libraries; board member, Maud Marks Friends of the Library.

Member

Society of Children's Book Writers and Illustrators, American Association of University Women, Texas Library Association, Harris County Historical Commission.

Awards, Honors

Texas Institute of Letters Best Juvenile Book Award, 2001, for *Animals That Migrate;* Society of Children's Book Writers and Illustrators Golden Kite Honor Book designation, 2004, for *After the Last Dog Died.*

Writings

NONFICTION

Jonas Salk: Discoverer of the Polio Vaccine, Enslow Publishers (Springfield, NJ), 1993.

Henry Cisneros: Building a Better America, Enslow Publishers (Springfield, NJ), 1995.

Ross Perot: Billionaire Politician, Enslow Publishers (Springfield, NJ), 1995.

Ruth Bader Ginsburg: Supreme Court Justice, Enslow Publishers (Springfield, NJ), 1995.

The Battle of the Alamo: The Fight for Texas Territory, Millbrook Press (Brookfield, CT), 1996.

American Writers of the Twentieth Century, Enslow Publishers (Springfield, NJ), 1996.

Presidential Medal of Freedom Winners, Enslow Publishers (Springfield, NJ), 1996.

The Spindletop Gusher: The Story of the Texas Oil Boom, Millbrook Press (Brookfield, CT), 1996.

Texas, Marshall Cavendish, 1997.

Gus Grissom: A Space Biography ("Countdown to Space" series), Enslow Publishers (Springfield, NJ), 1997.

Neil Armstrong: A Space Biography ("Countdown to Space" series), Enslow Publishers (Berkeley Heights, NJ), 1998.

The Moon, Franklin Watts (New York, NY), 1998.

Shannon Lucid: Space Ambassador, Millbrook Press (Brookfield, CT), 1998.

Tide Pools, Franklin Watts (New York, NY), 1999.

The Mighty Midwest Flood: Raging Rivers, Enslow Publishers (Berkeley Heights, NJ), 1999.

Fire in Oakland, California: Billion-Dollar Blaze, Enslow Publishers (Berkeley Heights, NJ), 1999.

Our Space Program, Millbrook Press (Brookfield, CT), 1999.

The Challenger Disaster: Tragic Space Flight, Enslow Publishers (Berkeley Heights, NJ), 1999.

NASA Planetary Spacecraft: Galileo, Magellan, Pathfinder, and Voyager, Enslow Publishers (Berkeley Heights, NJ), 2000.

John Glenn: Space Pioneer, Millbrook Press (Brookfield, CT), 2000.

John Glenn Returns to Orbit, Enslow Publishers (Berkeley Heights, NJ), 2000.

El Niño and La Niña: Deadly Weather, Enslow Publishers (Berkeley Heights, NJ), 2001.

Animals That Migrate, Franklin Watts (New York, NY), 2001.

Labor Day, Children's Press (New York, NY), 2001.

Looking at Maps and Globes, Children's Press (New York, NY), 2001.

Pluto, Franklin Watts (New York, NY), 2001.

Mount St. Helens Volcano: Violent Eruption, Enslow Publishers (Berkeley Heights, NJ), 2001.

(With Ralph Thibodeau) *Ten Great American Composers,* Enslow Publishers (Berkeley Heights, NJ), 2002.

George W. Bush: The 43rd President, Enslow Publishers (Berkeley Heights, NJ), 2002.

Laura Bush: First Lady, Enslow Publishers (Berkeley Heights, NJ), 2002.

Texas, Children's Press (New York, NY), 2002.

Georgia, Children's Press (New York, NY), 2002.

Florida, Children's Press (New York, NY), 2002.

Neptune, Franklin Watts (New York, NY), 2002.

After the Last Dog Died: The True-Life, Hair-raising Adventure of Douglas Mawson and His 1912 Antarctic Expedition, National Geographic (Washington, DC), 2003.

The Solar System, Children's Press (New York, NY), 2003.

The Moon, Children's Press (New York, NY), 2003.

Purim, Children's Press (New York, NY), 2003.

St. Patrick's Day, Children's Press (New York, NY), 2003.

Getting Ready for Space, Children's Press (New York, NY), 2003.

Living on a Space Shuttle, Children's Press (New York, NY), 2003.

Astronauts, Children's Press (New York, NY), 2003.

Liftoff!, Children's Press (New York, NY), 2003.

Texas, Marshall Cavendish (New York, NY), 2005.

Great White Sharks up close, Enslow (Berkeley Heights, NJ), 2006.

Giant Pandas up Close, Enslow (Berkeley Heights, NJ), 2006.

Emperor Penguins up Close, Enslow (Berkeley Heights, NJ), 2006.

Boa Constrictors up Close, Enslow (Berkeley Heights, NJ), 2006.

African Elephants up Close, Enslow (Berkeley Heights, NJ), 2006.

Several of Bredeson's science books have been translated into Spanish.

Sidelights

Carmen Bredeson has written a number of well-received nonfiction titles for young children, middle graders, and young adults. Her works on prominent twentieth-century Americans in such fields as science, politics, and the arts—men and women such as Dr. Jonas Salk, the discoverer of the polio vaccine; Supreme Court Justice Ruth Bader Ginsburg; astronaut Neil Armstrong; poet Maya Angelou; and Presidential Medal of Freedom winners Helen Keller, Caesar Chavez, and Colin Powell—have been praised for providing a wealth of information. Equally praised have been her books about historical places and events, several of which address subjects relevant to Bredeson's adopted home state of Texas. Commended for creating balanced, well-organized overviews that are considered good introductions to their topics and useful references for school reports, the author is also acknowledged for the in-depth discussions and vivid details of her books as well as for the clarity and liveliness of her writing style.

Bredeson developed a love of books as a child in Virginia. As she told *Something about the Author* (*SATA*): "I grew up in a house filled with books. They lined the shelves, covered the tables, and piled up on the floor. Members of my family often traded books across the hallway at night and read favorite passages aloud for anyone who would listen." Later, as an English major attending college in Texas, she discovered

that she "always enjoyed writing research papers. Most of my classmates complained about the assignments, but I loved being in the library, digging through books for information. Making notes and arranging the facts into logical order appealed to me. These skills served me well in graduate school while I was studying to become a school librarian. I especially enjoyed the many reference assignments we were given. Although I never worked as a librarian, the things I learned didn't go to waste."

Bredeson's first career was as a high-school English teacher. In 1972, she became a full-time mother, and as she told *SATA*, she carried the love of books she had established as a child and young adult "to my new life. I began reading to my own children when they were still tiny babies, barely able to focus their eyes. When they got bigger, we made regular visits to the library and bookstore. There was always a pile of books sitting around in our house just waiting to be read. As a former English teacher, I knew that there was no substitute for good reading skills." While raising her two children, Bredeson volunteered at local schools and libraries. Since her own town did not have a public library, she and other members of her community spent time and energy lobbying county officials to build one. Although it took ten years, their efforts were successful. As she

In **Animals That Migrate** *Carmen Bredeson presents information regarding the manner in which some creatures move to a new home in response to Earth's changing seasons.(Photograph by Norbert Rosing.)*

In **After the Last Dog Died** *Bredeson tells the story of Australian explorer Sir Douglas Mawson and his grueling expedition to the unexplored regions of the Antarctic in the early 1900s. (Photograph courtesy of National Geographic Society.)*

recalled, "When our shiny new library opened, we had accumulated $100,000 to spend on extra books, equipment, and programs." In 1990, around the time the library was built and her children were entering college, Bredeson decided to begin writing. She explained to *SATA,* "Since I love to do research, nonfiction was perfect for me. I wrote a short biography and spent the next two years sending it to publishers. I collected a big stack of rejection notices before finally getting the attention of an editor." Bredeson's first work, *Jonas Salk: Discoverer of the Polio Vaccine,* was published in 1993.

In *Jonas Salk* Bredeson describes Salk's career from his days at medical school through his development of the polio vaccine and his research on a vaccine to combat the AIDS virus. In her *Appraisal* review, Janet K. Baltzell commented that the book "is especially notable for its in-depth discussion of the polio epidemic and the social and emotional importance of Dr. Salk's work in vaccine development." Baltzell concluded that the book "should be a valuable contribution" to biographies of leaders in the scientific field. Writing in *School Library Journal,* Joyce Adams Burner praised the work as "a good overview" of Salk's life and work that would be "useful for reports" and "of interest to general science or biography readers."

In 1995, Bredeson published three biographies of well-known politicians: *Henry Cisneros: Building a Better America,* a study of the Mexican American who became a Texas mayor and Supreme Court official; *Ross Perot: Billionaire Politician,* the story of the businessman and U.S. Presidential candidate; and *Ruth Bader Ginsburg: Supreme Court Justice,* an outlining of the career of the second woman named to the U.S. Supreme Court. Writing in *Booklist* about *Ross Perot,* Mary Harris Veeder noted that Bredeson "presents a vivid detailing of her subject's early years." In her review of *Ruth Bader Ginsburg* for *Voice of Youth Advocates,* Mary Jo Peltier called the book an "informative biography" that is a "good source of current information on Ginsburg as well as a serviceable introduction to the Supreme Court." *School Library Journal* reviewer Katrina Yurenka concurred with Peltier's assessment, noting that the "brief history of the U.S. Supreme Court will help readers understand just what [Ginsburg's] position entails."

In *American Writers of the Twentieth Century* Bredeson introduces middle graders to ten major literary figures, among them Willa Cather, John Steinbeck, Toni Morrison, and Ernest Hemingway. In her review for *Booklist,* Laura Tillotson commented that Bredeson "effectively capsules each [author] in a brief but thorough description." In *The Battle of the Alamo,* one of her first works focusing on an historical event, Bredeson offers readers a "brief, readable, and well-organized introduction to the historical background surrounding this momentous battle," in the words of Phyllis Graves of *School Library Journal.* Another of the author's books related to Texas, *The Spindletop Gusher,* tells the story of the discovery of oil at Spindletop Field in Beaumont, Texas in 1901 and provides information on petroleum and the oil industry. Writing in *Review of Texas Books,* Judith Linsley called *The Spindletop Gusher* "a must for any school and library," and added that it is "an excellent basic reference on the petroleum industry for adults as well."

In more recent books Bredeson has turned to scientific topics, including biographies of astronauts Gus Grissom, Neil Armstrong, John Glenn, and Shannon Lucid. In a review of the "Countdown to Space" series, which includes *Neil Armstrong: A Space Biography* and *Gus Grissom: A Space Biography, Science Activities* contributor Jacqueline V. Mallinson commented that these "interesting little books are written in a clear understandable style that should appeal to upper elementary school children." Similarly, *Booklist* critic Susan DeRonne, reviewing *Gus Grissom,* thought the book would be most appreciated by "older reluctant readers and younger space buffs." Bredeson's writing in these two books was also praised by critics; *School Library Journal* contributor Phyllis Graves deemed *Gus Grissom* "well-written," "easy-to-read," and overall an "excellent introductory biograph[y]," while Allison Trent Bernstein, also writing in *School Library Journal,* called *Neil Armstrong* "clear, concise," and "well organized." In *Shannon Lucid: Space Ambassador* Bredeson "depicts both Lucid's accomplishments and her delightful personality," Shelley Townshend-Hudson noted in *Booklist.* The latter, as T. J. Lee commented in a *School Library Journal* review, comes through in "quotes from family members and friends'that "add personal notes and insights."

Bredeson also discusses astronauts, this time for younger children, in *Getting Ready for Space, Liftoff!,* and *Living on a Space Shuttle.* "With their large print, simple vocabulary, and few sentences per page, these books are good choices for emergent readers," Lynda Ritterman noted in *School Library Journal.* The books explain the basics of an astronaut's life, from their arduous training regimen in *Getting Ready for Space* through the challenges of eating, sleeping, and maintaining personal hygiene in a zero-gravity environment in *Living on a Space Shuttle. Liftoff!* focuses more on the technical side of space flight, showing all the work that must be done to ready the space shuttle for launch before explaining what astronauts experience during their eight-minute ride into space.

In her award-winning *After the Last Dog Died: The True-Life, Hair-raising Adventures of Douglas Mawson and His 1911-1914 Antarctic Expedition* Bredeson tells the story of a lesser-known Antarctic explorer. Mawson and two other men set out from their base camp at Cape Denison—the windiest spot on the face of the planet, although this fact was as yet unknown—to explore the continent in November 1912. One of the men, Lt. Belgrave Ninnis, fell into a crevasse and was killed. Most of the party's food also was lost in the crevasse, forcing Mawson and the other explorer, Dr. Xavier Mertz, to kill and eat their sled dogs as they attempted to make their way back to camp. Mertz also died on the way, almost certainly of Vitamin A poisoning from eating the dogs' livers, but Mawson, frost-bitten, starving, and suffering from severe Vitamin A poisoning himself, finally made it back the following February. *After the Last Dog Died* is "an enticing, attractive, and inspiring addition to adventure/exploration collections," Joel Shoemaker wrote in *School Library Journal,* while a *Kirkus Reviews* contributor concluded that Bredeson's harrowing survival tale "won't fail to give readers both chills and thrills." A *National Geographic Children's Book* reviewer also thought young readers would enjoy the book, declaring, "This spellbinding adventure will keep kids turning pages!"

"Writing nonfiction has been grand!" Bredeson once told *SATA.* "I have learned so much in the process and enjoy the challenge of each new topic. Hopefully I can transfer some of my enthusiasm for reading and learning to the students who check out my books. Someone asked me one day how I happened to start writing. I answered that I had unknowingly been preparing for it my whole life."

Biographical and Critical Sources

PERIODICALS

Appraisal, winter, 1994, Janet K. Baltzell, review of *Jonas Salk: Discoverer of the Polio Vaccine,* p. 8.

Booklist, April 15, 1995, Mary Harris Veeder, review of *Ross Perot: Billionaire Politician,* p. 1494; June, 1996, Laura Tillotson, review of *American Writers of the Twentieth Century,* p. 1706; April, 1998, Susan DeRonne, review of *Gus Grissom: A Space Biography,* p. 1315; January 1, 1999, Shelley Townshend-Hudson, review of *Shannon Lucid: Space Ambassador,* p. 862; May 1, 1999, Carolyn Phelan, review of *Tide Pools,* p. 1588; November 1, 2001, Carolyn Phelan, review of *Looking at Maps and Globes,* p. 485.

Kirkus Reviews, October 1, 2003, review of *After the Last Dog Died: The True-Life, Hair-raising Adventures of Douglas Mawson and His 1911-1914 Antarctic Expedition,* p. 1220.

Review of Texas Books, summer, 1996, Judith Linsley, review of *The Spindletop Gusher: The Story of the Texas Oil Boom.*

School Library Journal, November, 1993, Joyce Adams Burner, review of *Jonas Salk,* p. 113; May, 1995, Margaret B. Rafferty, review of *Ross Perot,* p. 112; July,

1995, Phyllis Graves, review of *Henry Cisneros: Building a Better America,* p. 83; December, 1995, Katrina Yurenka, review of *Ruth Bader Ginsburg: Supreme Court Justice,* pp. 112-113; September, 1996, Judy R. Johnston, review of *American Writers of the Twentieth Century,* p. 230; April, 1997, Phyllis Graves, review of *The Battle of the Alamo: The Fight for Texas Territory,* p. 144; June, 1997, Denise E. Agosto, review of *Texas,* p. 130; May, 1998, Phyllis Graves, review of *Gus Grissom: A Space Biography,* p. 151; July, 1998, Allison Trent Bernstein, review of *Neil Armstrong: A Space Biography,* p. 102; January, 1999, Jane Claes, review of *Shannon Lucid,* p. 111; May, 1999, John Peters, review of *Our Space Program,* p. 135; February, 2002, Cathie E. Bashaw, review of *Animals That Migrate,* p. 117; June, 2002, Eva Elisabeth VonAncken, review of *El Niño and La Niña: Deadly Weather,* p. 153; October, 2003, Lynda Ritterman, review of *Getting Ready for Space, Liftoff!,* and *Living on a Space Shuttle,* p. 144; January, 2004, Joel Shoemaker, review of *After the Last Dog Died,* p. 142.

Science Activities, summer, 1998, Jacqueline V. Mallinson, review of *Neil Armstrong* and *Gus Grissom,* p. 44.

Science Teacher, January, 2002, Sue LeBeau, review of *John Glenn Returns to Orbit: Life on the Space Shuttle,* pp. 88-89.

Voice of Youth Advocates, February, 1994, p. 390; April, 1996, Mary Jo Peltier, review of *Ruth Bader Ginsburg,* p. 47.

ONLINE

National Geographic Web site, http://www.national geographic.com/ (May 31, 2004), review of *After the Last Dog Died.*

SCBWI Houston Web Site, http://www.scbwi-houston.org/ (July 15, 2005), "Carmen Bredeson."

* * *

BROWN, Reeve Lindbergh
See LINDBERGH, Reeve

* * *

BROWNE, Anthony (Edward Tudor) 1946-

Personal

Born September 11, 1946, in Sheffield, England; son of Jack Holgate (a teacher) and Doris May (Sugden) Browne; married Jane Franklin (a violin teacher), July 26, 1980; children: Joseph, Ellen. *Education:* Leeds College of Art, B.A. (with honors), 1967. *Hobbies and other interests:* Reading, music, theater, films, swimming, tennis, squash, cricket.

Addresses

Home and office—The Chalk Garden, The Length, St. Nicholas-at-Wade, Birchington, Kent CT7 0PJ, England.

Anthony Browne

Career

Victoria University of Manchester, Manchester, England, medical artist at Royal Infirmary, 1968-70; Gordon Fraser Greeting Cards, London, England, designer, 1971-88; author and illustrator of children's books, 1975—. Writer and illustrator-in-residence, Tate Britain Gallery, London, 2001-02. Has also held two teaching positions. *Exhibitions:* Illustrations from *Alice's Adventures in Wonderland* were exhibited at Barbican Gallery, London, England, 1988; work exhibited in Mexico, 1994.

Awards, Honors

Kate Greenaway Medal commendation, British Library Association, 1982, and International Board on Books for Young People (IBBY) Award for Illustration in Great Britain, 1984, both for *Hansel and Gretel;* Kate Greenaway Medal, and Kurt Maschler/"Emil" Award, British Book Trust, 1983, *New York Times* best illustrated children's books of the year citation, 1985, *Boston Globe-Horn Book* Honor Book for illustration, 1986, Child Study Association of America Children's Books of the Year citation, 1986, *Horn Book* Honor List, 1986, and 1989, and Silver Pencil Award (Netherlands), 1989, all for *Gorilla;* Deutscher Jugendliteratur Preis (German Youth Literature Prize; with Annalena McAfee), and Notable Children's Trade Book in the Field of Social Studies, National Council for Social Studies/Children's

Book Council, both 1985, both for *The Visitors Who Came to Stay;* Parents' Choice Award, Parents' Choice Foundation, for *Piggybook,* 1987, and 1988, for *Look What I've Got!;* Kate Greenaway Medal, highly commended, 1988, Kurt Maschler/"Emil" Award, and Parents' Choice Award, both 1989, all for *Alice's Adventures in Wonderland;* Silver Pencil Award, 1989, for *The Tunnel;* Kate Greenaway Medal, 1992, for *Zoo;* silver medal, Society of Illustrators, 1995, for *King Kong;* Kurt Maschler Award, Best Books designation, *Publishers Weekly,* and Best Books designation, *School Library Journal,* all 1998, Fanfare list, *Horn Book,* and Notable Books for Children designation, American Library Association, both 1999, all for *Voices in the Park;* Hans Christian Andersen Illustration Award, 2000, for body of work.

Writings

"BEAR" SERIES; SELF-ILLUSTRATED

Bear Hunt, Hamish Hamilton (London, England), 1979, Atheneum (New York, NY), 1980.
Bear Goes to Town, Hamish Hamilton (London, England), 1982, Doubleday (New York, NY), 1989.
The Little Bear Book, Hamish Hamilton (London, England), 1988, Doubleday (New York, NY), 1989.
A Bear-y Tale, Hamish Hamilton (London, England), 1989.

"WILLY" SERIES; SELF-ILLUSTRATED

Willy the Wimp, Alfred A. Knopf (New York, NY), 1984, reprinted, Candlewick Press (Cambridge, MA), 2002.
Willy the Champ, Alfred A. Knopf (New York, NY), 1985.
Willy and Hugh, Alfred A. Knopf (New York, NY), 1991, reprinted, Candlewick Press (Cambridge, MA), 2003.
Willy the Wizard, Alfred A. Knopf (New York, NY), 1995.
Willy the Dreamer, Walker (London, England), 1997, Candlewick Press (Cambridge, MA), 1998.
Willy's Pictures, Candlewick Press (Cambridge, MA), 2000.

RETELLINGS

(Adaptor) Jacob Grimm and Wilhelm Grimm, *Hansel and Gretel,* MacRae (London, England), 1981, Franklin Watts (New York, NY), 1982.
(Story conceived by Edgar Wallace and Merian C. Cooper) *King Kong,* Turner Publishing (Atlanta, GA), 1994, published as *Anthony Browne's King Kong,* MacRae (London, England), 1994.

PICTURE BOOKS

Through the Magic Mirror, Hamish Hamilton (London, England), 1976, Greenwillow Books (New York, NY), 1977, reprinted, 1992.

A Walk in the Park, Hamish Hamilton (London, England), 1977, revised edition, Doubleday (London, England), 1990, published as *Voices in the Park,* DK Ink (New York, NY), 1998.
Look What I've Got!, MacRae (London, England), 1980, Alfred A. Knopf (New York, NY), 1988.
Gorilla, Alfred A. Knopf (New York, NY), 1983, revised edition, 1991
Piggybook, Alfred A. Knopf (New York, NY), 1986.
I Like Books, Alfred A. Knopf (New York, NY), 1989, reprinted, Candlewick Press (Cambridge, MA), 2004.
Things I Like, Alfred A. Knopf (New York, NY), 1989, reprinted, Candlewick Press (Cambridge, MA), 2004.
The Tunnel, Alfred A. Knopf (New York, NY), 1989.
Changes, Alfred A. Knopf (New York, NY), 1990.
Zoo, Alfred A. Knopf (New York, NY), 1992, reprinted, Farrar, Straus & Giroux (New York, NY), 2002.
The Big Baby: A Little Joke, MacRae (London, England), 1993, Knopf (New York, NY), 1994.
My Dad, Farrar, Straus & Giroux (New York, NY), 2001.
Animal Fair, Candlewick Press (Cambridge, MA), 2002.
The Shape Game, Farrar, Straus & Giroux (New York, NY), 2003.
Into the Forest, Candlewick Press (Cambridge, MA), 2004.
My Mom, Farrar, Straus & Giroux (New York, NY), 2005.

ILLUSTRATOR; FICTION, EXCEPT AS NOTED

Annalena McAfee, *The Visitors Who Came to Stay,* Hamish Hamilton (London, England), 1984, Viking (New York, NY), 1985.
Sally Grindley, *Knock, Knock! Who's There?,* Hamish Hamilton (London, England), 1985, Alfred A. Knopf (New York, NY), 1986.
Annalena McAfee, *Kirsty Knows Best,* Alfred A. Knopf (New York, NY), 1987.
Lewis Carroll, *Alice's Adventures in Wonderland,* Alfred A. Knopf (New York, NY), 1988.
Gwen Strauss, *Trail of Stones* (young adult poems), Alfred A. Knopf (New York, NY), 1990.
Gwen Strauss, *The Night Shimmy,* Alfred A. Knopf (New York, NY), 1992.
Ian McEwan, *The Daydreamers,* HarperCollins (New York, NY), 1994.
Janni Howker, *The Topiary Garden,* Orchard Books (New York, NY), 1995.

Browne's works have been translated into numerous languages, including Spanish, Welsh, French, Italian, German, Hebrew, Japanese, Chinese, Dutch, Finnish, Swedish, and Danish.

Adaptations
Bear Hunt was adapted as a filmstrip by Weston Woods, 1981.

Sidelights
Anthony Browne is an English author, illustrator, and reteller who is acclaimed as a gifted artist and incisive social critic whose works have helped to define the

modern picture book. Browne has been called "one of the most original and accomplished of our picture book artists" by Chris Powling in *Books for Keeps* and "one of the most highly original creators of picture books to arrive on the scene in recent years" by Amy J. Meeker in *Children's Books and Their Creators*. Celebrated for creating unconventional, often provocative works that challenge and delight both young readers and adults, Browne uses spare texts and symbolic pictures filled with surrealistic details and humorous visual puns to address serious themes about personal relationships, social conventions, human behavior, and the thin line between perception and reality. His artistic style is a highly individualistic, intensely personal approach that combines fantastic and representational imagery in a precise, meticulous technique. It is noted for its bold, rich colors; use of animals to represent humans, especially gorillas and chimpanzees; and references to popular culture, to literary characters, to his own work, and to artists such as Salvador Dali, Leonardo da Vinci, and Edvard Munch.

Browne is perhaps best known as the creator of *Gorilla*, a picture book that features a lonely girl infatuated with apes who, after receiving a toy gorilla from her often absent father, dreams that it turns into a real animal. Browne has also written and illustrated two popular series of picture books—the first about Willy, an ingenuous chimp, and the second about Bear, a jaunty teddy who averts danger with the aid of his magic pencil. In addition, he has retold the fairy tale *Hansel and Gretel* and the story of the film *King Kong* and has illustrated the works of such authors as Lewis Carroll, Janni Howker, Ian McEwan, Annalena McAfee, and Gwen Strauss in a style that features his familiar motifs.

As a writer, Browne often uses the formats of the folktale, fairy tale, and cautionary tale as the framework for stories that depict humans and anthropomorphic animals who use their imaginations and interior strength to affect their personal situations. Browne's characters face loneliness, neglect, boredom, jealousy, ridicule, and social differences with spirit and resourcefulness, and the author presents his readers with subtle messages about being true to oneself and reaching out to others. Praised for his sensitivity to the needs and concerns of children, Browne has also developed a reputation as a sharp social observer. Several of his books skewer contemporary adult behavior—especially that of males—by showing how foolishness, cruelty, and self-absorption bring out the baseness of our animal natures.

As an artist, Browne uses color and pattern to define the symbolism of his pictures, detailed, hyper-realistic paintings set against white backgrounds. His art is often credited with helping readers to view the world in a new way. In his depiction of the inner nature of things, Browne includes some details that are considered disturbing, a factor for which he has been criticized. In addition, his books are sometimes considered too clever and sophisticated for children. However, most review-

ers view Browne as a writer and artist of great talent and singular vision whose works contain emotional depth and foster powerful responses. A critic in *Kirkus Reviews* noted that Browne's picture books "comment on the human condition with perception and originality," while Jane Doonan, in *Twentieth-Century Children's Writers*, claimed that he "has given a large audience (of all ages) consistently interesting work that, at every level, contains something to be enjoyed, discovered, and considered." Writing in *Magpies*, Browne's longtime editor Julia MacRae said that he "is truly an artist who opens our minds—and our hearts."

Browne was born in Sheffield, Yorkshire, in the north of England, to pub owners Jack and Doris May Browne. In an interview in *Something about the Author* (*SATA*), Browne recalled, "Books were a huge part of our lives. We had annuals, *The Beano Annual* or *The Dandy Annual*, that sort of thing. And fairy stories, particularly *Hansel and Gretel*. I do remember *Alice in Wonderland*, which must have been read to me. Perhaps I have better recall of the Tenniel pictures than the story." When he was a child, Browne wanted to be a boxer like his father had been, and then a newspaper reporter. "I suppose what I really wanted was to be like my dad—a big, powerfully built man, and I was always a small boy," he mused.

Both Browne's father and brother Michael had artistic talent. The author recalled in *SATA* that they would draw "a British and a German soldier, for instance, with all the details of uniforms and guns. I, on the other hand, would draw battle scenes with jokes thrown in—a decapitated head speaking or a picture of an invisible man. Knights on horseback and cowboys and Indians shared the same battle. Looking back I see that my pictures took on a narrative form." On occasion, Browne would stand on a table in the tap room of his parents' pub and tell stories to the patrons. One of these tales featured a Superman-like hero called Big Dumb Tackle. Browne recalled in *SATA*, "My mother told me that in one of my stories Big Dumb Tackle went to heaven and knocked on the door of heaven and said, 'Can Jesus come out to play?' I shudder to think what the answer might have been!"

Recalling his childhood to *SATA*, Browne described himself as "a kid with terrors—people coming after me, things under the bed, in the wardrobe. . . . Looking back, I was quite the wimp." (In 1984, Browne published *Willy the Wimp*, the story of a skinny, refined young chimp who triumphs over his gorilla tormentors.) By the age of five, Browne was learning Latin at a local private school. When he was seven, Browne and his family moved to Wyke, near Bradford, a tough industrial area. This relocation proved particularly difficult for the small boy who enjoyed drawing and writing as much as rambunctious outdoor games. Throughout his school years, Browne continued drawing, mostly detailed sketches of battles based on the comic books he read. He was also learning to appreciate literature. His most memorable teacher, Browne recalled in *SATA,* "introduced me to the work of Beckett and Pinter. Encountering Beckett was a bit like discovering surrealism in painting—something at once totally unexpected and yet deeply familiar. It struck a chord, because I seemed to recognize something in it."

At age sixteen, Browne announced that he wanted to go straight from high school to art college. His family agreed. During Browne's first year as a graphic design major at Leeds College of Art, his father passed away, suffering a fatal heart attack right before his son's eyes. The author recalled in *SATA,* "It was terrible. His two previous massive heart attacks should have prepared me, but I didn't take in the significance of that." When asked by Chris Powling in *Books for Keeps* if he is, to some extent, fulfilling his father's ambition to become an artist, Browne replied, "It's not something I think about but I suppose in a way, yes. If he'd been given the opportunities I had, I'm pretty sure he'd have done something very similar." Browne's picture book *My Dad* pays loving homage to his father.

After two years as a medical artist, Browne felt that he needed to stretch his imagination, so he began creating a collection of greeting cards while working in an ad agency. He sent his cards to Gordon Fraser, a large greeting card company in London, and shortly thereafter began a long career there as a card artist. Through his company's founder, Browne was introduced to the world of children's books. He recalled in *SATA,* "I began thinking about books, because cards weren't a proper living, really." Hamish Hamilton published Browne's first book, *Through the Magic Mirror,* in 1976. A picture book in which young Toby—bored in the house—enters a fantastic world through a looking glass before returning home, *Through the Magic Mirror* is noted for introducing the stylistic touches that would later become the hallmarks of Browne's work. Writing in *Horn Book,* Aidan Chambers noted that the book "firmly announces in an uncompromising way that Browne intends to bring into children's books some of the twentieth-century art which has often been thought too difficult for children to understand."

His next work, *A Walk in the Park,* was published in 1977 in England and appeared in the United States as *Voices in the Park* in 1998, featuring different illustrations. In this picture book, working-class Smudge and her father take their dog to the park, where they meet middle-class Charles, his mother, and their pedigreed dog. The children and the dogs play together happily while the parents ignore each other. In *Twentieth-Century Children's Writers,* Jane Doonan wrote that "Smudge and Charles are accompanied by a yob and a snob, but win for themselves a spell of perfect happiness." A reviewer in *Publishers Weekly,* assessing the American edition, noted that "Browne again proves himself an artist of inventive voice and vision as he creates perhaps his most psychologically complex work to date."

In 1980, Browne married violin teacher Jane Franklin; the couple have two children, Joseph and Ellen. In 1981, Browne published his retelling of the Grimm Brothers' fairy tale *Hansel and Gretel,* a work that is often considered a creative breakthrough as well as one of the artist's most controversial titles. Rather than presenting the tale as a period piece, Browne sets his illustrations in the present day and uses them to reflect the subconscious of young children. Writing in the *Times Literary Supplement,* Tanya Harrod observed, "What . . . do we make of this contemporary stepmother's squalid dressing table with lipsticks, talcum powder and cigarette ends lovingly depicted by Anthony Browne? Is her taste for fake furs and stiletto heels the cause of the family's poverty? Why have the Social Services let them slip through the net? I really cannot envision buying any child this book." In her *Signal* review, Jane Doonan claimed, "Without question, Anthony Browne's pictures supply a piece of visual storytelling, a psychological commentary, which interprets the folktale in a positive way. . . . Browne's visual interpretation of *Hansel and Gretel* offers children a chance to recognize the nature of their deeper and truer feelings."

Two years after the publication of *Hansel and Gretel,* Browne created *Gorilla.* In this work, small Hannah longs both for a gorilla and for the attention of her father. After she dreams that her stuffed toy is transformed into a huge ape that dons her father's hat and coat and takes her to the zoo and to the movies, her real father actually takes her to the zoo. A reviewer in the *Junior Bookshelf* commented that the book's detail "will yield more each time to the reader—it is brilliantly worked out," while Kenneth Marantz commented in *Horn Book:* "Despite the fantasy, Browne has created a picture book that explores real emotions with a beautifully realized child protagonist. Using his artistic skills, he's fashioned the visual metaphors that help to transcend superficial meanings and feel the power of the more archetypal emotions that bind children to parents and people to the other animals." In her *Magpies* article, Julia MacRae wrote, "*Gorilla* speaks individually to each reader and always will."

In 1983 Browne won his first Greenaway Medal as well as Germany's Kurt Maschler Award for *Gorilla,* which also won the Silver Pencil Award from the Netherlands in 1989. The author has noted that *Gorilla* had its origin in a greeting card that he did for Gordon Fraser; the card depicted a big male gorilla holding a teddy bear. In his interview in *SATA,* Browne said, "I think the image goes back to my father, who in some ways was like a gorilla, big and potentially aggressive during his pub days." The author added, "I must confess that [*Gorilla*] has changed my life."

Following the success of *Gorilla,* Browne continued his fascination with simian characters with his series about Willy, a chimp who lives in a world dominated by gorillas. A critic in *Publishers Weekly* described Willy, who has prompted more letters from children than any of Browne's other characters, as "an earnest and endearing youngster, often lonely and sometimes bullied, but who wins out thanks to perseverance and pluck." In *Willy's Pictures,* for instance, the versatile chimp draws his own versions of great art masterpieces such as Botticelli's "Birth of Venus" and Leonardo da Vinci's "Mona Lisa." Needless to say, filtered through Willy's imagination, the masterpieces become subtly overrun with chimp-inspired imagery such as bananas and tropical foliage. The wily Willy also mixes and matches, adding elements of one great artist's work to the masterpiece of another. Browne described *Willy's Pictures* in *School Library Journal* as just one of the books he has done to encourage children "to look at paintings with a fresh eye, and see that most paintings do have a story." Speaking generally of Willy, a *Publishers Weekly* critic described him as an "ingenuous, remarkably human chimp" who "delivers a beneficial message to all youngsters."

In 1986, Browne also wrote and illustrated *Piggybook,* a picture book that is often considered among his best works. *Piggybook* features Mrs. Piggott, a harried wife and mother in a male-dominated family who is tired of doing all of the housework in addition to her other job. Her husband and sons, sloppy and demanding, infuriate Mrs. Piggott to the point that she shouts "You are pigs!" before storming out of the house. In her absence, the men become pink pigs. Before Mrs. Piggott returns and order is restored, they discover the joys of a clean home. Challenging male chauvinism and sexual stereotyping, *Piggybook* is acknowledged for its humorous but pointed examination of male and female roles. Kathleen Brachmann, writing in *School Library Journal,* called it a "wickedly feminist tale if ever there was one" and added that in "terms of cleverness and style, this one brings home the bacon." Doonan noted in the *Times Literary Supplement* that, "Both funny and disturbing, Browne achieves a fine balance between the humour of the fantastic imagery and the seriousness of his message."

In the mid-1980s, editor MacRae made the suggestion, the author once told *SATA,* "that I should break away and make a big change. She suggested a number of classics, among them *Alice's Adventures in Wonderland.* 'After Tenniel,' I thought, 'who am I to even attempt.' But the story seeped into my consciousness." Browne published his illustrated version of Lewis Carroll's book in 1988, and his pictures are noted for their imagination, detail, and humor as well as for reflecting the surreal quality of the text. However, as with *Hansel and Gretel, Alice's Adventures in Wonderland* received a mixed critical reception. Marcus Crouch in *Junior Bookshelf* called the artist's pictures "intellectually rather than emotionally satisfying" while Frances Spaulding in the *Times Literary Supplement* noted that Browne's illustrations "are freshly imagined but overloaded. In trying to dislodge Tenniel he offers intensely detailed renderings of scenes that far exceed the text." In contrast, Ann A. Flowers stated in *Horn Book,* "Browne's illus-

trations certainly add a new and suggestive dimension to *Alice's Adventures in Wonderland* and even extend the story." Bernard Ashley in *Books for Keeps* likewise called Browne's version of *Alice* "a marvelous way for Juniors to drink from the labelled bottle. . . . The Junior mind may not understand Browne's allusions all the time any more than it will understand Carroll's, but it will be somehow aware of being in the presence of an artist it will never forget."

Browne won his second Greenaway Medal for *Zoo,* a picture book in which the doltish behavior of a family of zoo visitors is juxtaposed against the dignity of the caged animals. At the end of the family's visit—in which boorish dad and his impatient sons behave insensitively—the mother, who alone feels some sympathy for the animals, says, "I don't think the zoo's really for animals. I think it's for people." Browne's illustrations reflect this sentiment—paintings on opposite pages balance the family's actions with the zoo's animals and settings. Other visitors to the zoo are pictured sporting flippers and tails beneath their clothes. Writing in *Booklist,* Stephanie Zvirin noted that "Browne is just as sly as ever. Here . . . he brings the surreal and the real together to give us a world transformed. This time, however, he challenges us to examine not only the things we take for granted, but also the way we are." Writing in *School Librarian,* Griselda Greaves commented that "Browne's propaganda is unsubtle. The suitability of much of his work for the young is questionable, because it seems to express such distaste for humanity that no redemption is possible. Those who like Browne's work will find all they have come to expect in this book, but there is nothing new here." A reviewer in *Publishers Weekly* concluded, "Browne's effectively stark, magnificently realistic illustrations of the zoo animals offer a distinct contrast to his clever renditions of the supposedly human visitors to the zoo."

Among the most personal of Browne's works is his illustrated retelling of the classic 1930s film *King Kong.* Browne bases many of his illustrations on the movie while adding several twists of his own. For example, the female lead bears a striking resemblance to Marilyn Monroe. His dramatic, dreamlike illustrations have been noted for their new mastery of crowd scenes and group movement, while his text—considered both a love story and a tragedy by critics—was described by a reviewer in *Publishers Weekly* as "appropriately cinematic." Writing in *Junior Bookshelf,* Marcus Crouch—noting the "fine production and superb art-work"—stated that whether Browne's version of *King Kong* "adds anything to the interpretation to justify his efforts is open to doubt. This is not to say that the book is anything other than a remarkable achievement." A reviewer in *Publishers Weekly* commented, "If ever a couple seemed made for each other artistically, it's the multitalented Browne and King Kong. . . . Browne's imagery reaches new heights—think *Gorilla* on steroids—with his powerful renderings of the fabled beast." MacRae concluded in *Magpies* that Browne's "dramatic pictures complemented to perfection this classic of the cinema."

Discussing the work in *Books for Keeps,* Browne acknowledged that *King Kong* pays homage to his father: "I have in the past tried to explain my fascination with gorillas by comparing them to my father. He was a big man and I was a small boy. He was strong and physical. . . . Yet he was also artistic and sensitive. . . . It's the dual nature of Kong which attracts me—the terrifying beast who is, in reality, a gentle, beautiful creature. Memories of my father's death have, for me, terrible echoes of Kong's fall from the Empire State Building." Browne called *King Kong* "the most exhausting book I've ever worked on." However, the author wrote, "I'm just beginning to consider the possibilities of *Dr. Jekyll and Mr. Hyde,* or *Tarzan,* or *Frankenstein* or . . . any suggestions?"

My Dad was also inspired by Browne's affection for his late father, and the author/illustrator felt the urge to create it after finding his father's old bathrobe on a hanger in the closet. With gentle pictures done in a bathrobe-plaid motif, *My Dad* celebrates one youngster's fearless, loving, and sometimes silly father, who can send the Big Bad Wolf packing with a simple gesture and who sings tenor with Luciano Pavarotti and Placido Domingo. "Browne has a winner here," commented Beth Tegart in *School Library Journal.* "The clever pictures have true child appeal." GraceAnne A. DeCandido, writing in *Booklist,* found the mutual affection between son and father "genuinely moving as well as funny," and a *Publishers Weekly* reviewer deemed the work "an endearing paean to patriarchs."

The same family that visits the zoo in *Zoo* takes a trip to the art museum in *The Shape Game.* This time it is Mother's birthday, and Dad and the two sons reluctantly accompany her out of a sense of duty. As the family strolls the halls of London's Tate Britain gallery, Mom encourages the boys to make up stories about the paintings—and soon enough, the various family members find themselves *inside* the art works. The day culminates with a train ride home, during which the boys sketch random shapes and turn them into recognizable pictures. The book was inspired by Browne's work as an author/illustrator-in-residence at the Tate gallery, as well as by his ongoing crusade to interest young children in fine art. *Horn Book* reviewer Roger Sutton felt that *The Shape Game* offers an "important invitation to make the connection between art and life and back again." A *Publishers Weekly* critic concluded: "This personal, playful introduction to art and drawing may well give readers a fresh take on both."

With dozens of books to his credit, Browne noted in *Publishers Weekly* that his job has gotten harder, not easier. "You're much more aware of what people expect from you. Twenty years ago I just had an idea and I did it. Now I'm a bit more conscious of what I'm doing

and the effect of what I'm doing." Asked if he is still having fun at his chosen occupation, Browne replied, "Yes, absolutely. Every bit as much as when I started."

Biographical and Critical Sources

BOOKS

Children's Literature Review, Volume 19, Gale (Detroit, MI), 1990.
Silvey, Anita, editor, *Children's Books and Their Creators,* Houghton Mifflin (Boston, MA), 1995, pp. 98-99.
Twentieth-Century Children's Writers, 4th edition, St. James Press (Detroit, MI), 1995, p. 160.

PERIODICALS

Book, July, 2001, Kathleen Odean, review of *My Dad,* p. 81.
Booklist, December 15, 1992, Stephanie Zvirin, review of *Zoo,* p. 730; September 15, 1998, Hazel Rochman, review of *Voices in the Park,* p. 234; March 1, 2001, GraceAnne A. DeCandido, review of *My Dad,* p. 1286; September 15, 2003, Gillian Engberg, review of *The Shape Game,* p. 238.
Books for Keeps, May, 1987, Chris Powling, interview with Browne, pp. 16-17; November, 1988, Bernard Ashley, review of *Alice's Adventures in Wonderland,* p. 28; November, 1994, Anthony Browne, "Capturing Kong," pp. 24-25.
Horn Book, April, 1980, Aidan Chambers, "Hughes in Flight," pp. 211-214; January-February, 1986, Kenneth Marantz, review of *Gorilla,* p. 46; March-April, 1989, Ann A. Flowers, review of *Alice's Adventures in Wonderland,* p. 208; November, 1998, Joanna Rodge Long, review of *Voices in the Park,* p. 712; September-October, 2003, Roger Sutton, review of *The Shape Game,* p. 590.
Junior Bookshelf, August, 1983, review of *Gorilla,* pp. 152-153; February, 1989, Marcus Crouch, review of *Alice's Adventures in Wonderland,* p. 19; August, 1995, Marcus Crouch, review of *King Kong,* pp. 125-126.
Kirkus Reviews, August 15, 1986, review of *Piggybook,* p. 1288.
Magpies, May, 1996, Julia MacRae, "Anthony Browne," pp. 8-10.
New York Times Book Review, May 17, 1998, Robin Tzannes, review of *Willy the Dreamer,* p. 32.
Publishers Weekly, February 15, 1993, review of *Zoo,* p. 236; November 7, 1994, review of *King Kong,* p. 76; December 18, 1995, review of *Willy the Wizard,* p. 54; June 1, 1998, review of *Voices in the Park,* p. 48; July 20, 1998, "About Our Cover Artist," p. 121; October 16, 2000, review of *Willy's Pictures,* p. 75; February 12, 2001, review of *My Dad,* p. 209; July 28, 2003, review of *The Shape Game,* p. 94.
School Librarian, February, 1993, Griselda Greaves, review of *Zoo,* p. 20.

School Library Journal, October, 1986, Kathleen Brach-
mann, review of *Piggybook,* p. 157; December, 2000,
"Anthony Browne on Writing *Willy's Pictures,*" p. 25;
April, 2001, Beth Tegart, review of *My Dad,* p. 105;
September, 2003, Wendy Lukehart, review of *The
Shape Game,* p. 196.

Signal, September, 1983, Jane Doonan, "Talking Pictures:
A New Look at 'Hansel and Gretel,'" pp. 123-131.

Times Literary Supplement, November 20, 1981, Tanya
Harrod, "Illustrating Atmosphere," p. 1360; November
28, 1986, Jane Doonan, review of *Piggybook,* p. 1345;
November 25, 1988, Frances Spaulding, "Up-to-Date
Embellishments," p. 1320.*

*   *   *

BYARS, Betsy (Cromer) 1928-

Personal

Born August 7, 1928, in Charlotte, NC; daughter of
George Guy (a cotton mill executive) and Nan (a homemaker; maiden name, Rugheimer) Cromer; married Edward Ford Byars (a professor of engineering), June 24,
1950; children: Laurie, Betsy Ann, Nan, Guy. *Education:* Attended Furman University, 1946-48; Queens
College, Charlotte, NC, B.A., 1950. *Hobbies and other
interests:* Gliding, flying airplanes, reading, traveling,
music, needlepoint, crosswords.

Addresses

Home—401 Rudder Rdg., Seneca, SC 29678-2035.

Career

Children's book author.

Awards, Honors

Book of the Year selection, Child Study Association of
America, 1968, for *The Midnight Fox,* 1969, for *Trouble
River,* 1970, for *The Summer of the Swans,* 1972, for
The House of Wings, 1973, for *The Winged Colt of Casa
Mia* and *The Eighteenth Emergency,* 1974, for *After the
Goat Man,* 1975, for *The Lace Snail,* 1976, for *The TV
Kid,* and 1980, for *The Night Swimmers;* Lewis Carroll
Shelf Award, 1970, for *The Midnight Fox;* Newbery
Medal, 1971, for *The Summer of the Swans;* Dorothy
Canfield Fisher Memorial Book Award, Vermont Con-
gress of Parents and Teachers, 1975, for *The Eighteenth
Emergency;* Woodward Park School Annual Book
Award, 1977, Child Study Children Book Award, Child
Study Children's Book Committee at Bank Street Col-
lege of Education, 1977, Hans Christian Andersen
Honor List for Promoting Concern for the Disadvan-
taged and Handicapped, 1979, Georgia Children's Book
Award, 1979, Charlie May Simon Book Award, Arkan-
sas Elementary School Council, 1980, Surrey School
Book of the Year Award, Surrey School Librarians of
Surrey, British Columbia, 1980, Mark Twain Award,

Betsy Byars

Missouri Association of School Librarians, 1980, Will-
iam Allen White Children's Book Award, Emporia State
University, 1980, Young Reader Medal, California
Reading Association, 1980, Nene Award runner up,
1981 and 1983, and Golden Archer Award, Department
of Library Science of the University of Wisconsin—
Oshkosh, 1982, all for *The Pinballs; Boston Globe—
Horn Book* fiction honor, 1980, Best Book of the Year,
School Library Journal, 1980, and American Book
Award for Children's Fiction (hardcover), 1981, all for
The Night Swimmers; International Board on Books for
Young People Award, 1982, for *The Two-Thousand-
Pound Goldfish* (in translation); Children's Choice, In-
ternational Reading Association, 1982, Tennessee Chil-
dren's Choice Book Award, Tennessee Library
Association, 1983, Sequoyah Children's Book Award,
1984, all for *The Cybil War;* Parents' Choice Award for
literature, Parents' Choice Foundation, 1982, CRAB-
bery Award, Oxon Hill Branch of Prince George's
County Library, MD, 1983, Mark Twain Award, 1985,
all for *The Animal, the Vegetable, and John D. Jones;*
Parents' Choice Award for literature, 1985, South Carolina Children's Book Award, 1987, William Allen White
Children's Book Award, Emporia State University,
1988, and Maryland Children's Book Award, 1988, all
for *Cracker Jackson;* Parents' Choice Award for litera-

ture, 1986, for *The Not-Just-Anybody Family;* Regina Medal, Catholic Library Association, 1987; Charlie May Simon Award, 1987, for *The Computer Nut;* Edgar Allan Poe Award, Mystery Writers of America, 1992, for *Wanted . . . Mud Blossom;*Notable Book selection, American Library Association, 1969, for *Trouble River,* 1972, for *The House of Wings,* 1974, for *After the Goat Man,* 1977, for *The Pinballs,* 1981, for *The Cybil War,* 1982, and for *The Two-Thousand-Pound Goldfish; The House of Wings* named to *Library Journal* Book List, 1972, and named a National Book Award finalist, 1973; *The Winged Colt of Casa Mia* and *The Eighteenth Emergency* selected outstanding books of 1973, *New York Times; After the Goat Man* named to *School Library Journal* Book List, 1974; *Horn Book* selected *The Pinballs,* 1977, and *Cracker Johnson,* 1985, to its honor list; *Good-bye Chicken Little* named outstanding book of 1979, *New York Times; The Cybil War* selected a Notable Children's Book by *School Library Journal,* 1981; *The Animal, the Vegetable, and John D. Jones* selected among the Best Children's Books of 1982 by *School Library Journal; The Two-Thousand-Pound Goldfish* selected a notable book of 1982, *New York Times.*

Writings

FOR CHILDREN

Clementine, illustrated by Charles Wilton, Houghton (Boston, MA), 1962.

The Dancing Camel, illustrated by Harold Berson, Viking (New York, NY), 1965.

Rama, the Gypsy Cat, illustrated by Peggy Bacon, Viking (New York, NY), 1966.

(And illustrator) *The Groober,* Harper (New York, NY), 1967.

The Midnight Fox, illustrated by Ann Grifalconi, Viking (New York, NY), 1968.

Trouble River, illustrated by Rocco Negri, Viking (New York, NY), 1969.

The Summer of the Swans, illustrated by Ted CoConis, Viking (New York, NY), 1970, reprinted, Puffin (New York, NY), 2004.

Go and Hush the Baby, illustrated by Emily A. McCully, Viking (New York, NY), 1971.

The House of Wings, illustrated by Daniel Schwartz, Viking (New York, NY), 1972.

The Eighteenth Emergency, illustrated by Robert Grossman, Viking (New York, NY), 1973.

The Winged Colt of Casa Mia, illustrated by Richard Cuffari, Viking, 1973.

After the Goat Man, illustrated by Ronald Himler, Viking (New York, NY), 1974.

(And illustrator) *The Lace Snail,* Viking (New York, NY), 1975.

The TV Kid, illustrated by Richard Cuffari, Viking (New York, NY), 1976.

The Pinballs, Harper (New York, NY), 1977.

The Cartoonist, illustrated by Richard Cuffari, Viking (New York, NY), 1978.

Good-bye Chicken Little, Harper (New York, NY), 1979.

The Night Swimmers, illustrated by Troy Howell, Delacorte (New York, NY), 1980.

The Cybil War, illustrated by Gail Owens, Viking (New York, NY), 1981.

The Animal, the Vegetable, and John D. Jones, illustrated by Ruth Sanderson, Delacorte (New York, NY), 1982.

The Two-Thousand-Pound Goldfish, Harper (New York, NY), 1982.

The Glory Girl, Viking (New York, NY), 1983.

The Computer Nut, illustrated with computer graphics by son, Guy Byars, Viking (New York, NY), 1984.

Cracker Jackson, Viking (New York, NY), 1985.

(Author of afterword) Margaret Sidney, *The Five Little Peppers and How They Grew,* Dell (New York, NY), 1985.

The Not-Just-Anybody Family, illustrated by Jacqueline Rogers, Delacorte (New York, NY), 1986.

The Golly Sisters Go West, illustrated by Sue Truesdell, Harper (New York, NY), 1986.

The Blossoms Meet the Vulture Lady, illustrated by Jacqueline Rogers, Delacorte (New York, NY), 1986.

The Blossoms and the Green Phantom, illustrated by Jacqueline Rogers, Delacorte (New York, NY), 1987.

(Author of preface) Margaret M. Kimmel, *For Reading out Loud,* Dell (New York, NY), 1987.

A Blossom Promise, illustrated by Jacqueline Rogers, Delacorte (New York, NY), 1987.

Beans on the Roof, illustrated by Melodye Rosales, Delacorte (New York, NY), 1988.

The Burning Questions of Bingo Brown, illustrated by Cathy Bobak, Viking (New York, NY), 1988.

Bingo Brown and the Language of Love, illustrated by Cathy Bobak, Viking (New York, NY), 1989.

Hooray for the Golly Sisters, illustrated by Sue Truesdell, Harper, 1990.

Bingo Brown, Gypsy Lover, Viking (New York, NY), 1990.

Seven Treasure Hunts, Harper (New York, NY), 1991.

Wanted . . . Mud Blossom, Delacorte (New York, NY), 1991.

The Moon and I (autobiography), J. Messner (New York, NY), 1991.

Bingo Brown's Guide to Romance, Viking (New York, NY), 1992.

Coast to Coast, Delacorte (New York, NY), 1992.

McMummy, Viking (New York, NY), 1993.

The Golly Sisters Ride Again, illustrated by Sue Truesdell, HarperCollins (New York, NY), 1994.

The Dark Stairs: A Herculeah Jones Mystery, Viking (New York, NY), 1994.

Tarot Says Beware, Viking (New York, NY), 1995.

(Compiler) *Growing up Stories,* illustrated by Robert Geary, Kingfisher (New York, NY), 1995, published as *Top Teen Stories,* Kingfisher (Boston, MA), 2004.

My Brother, Ant, illustrated by Marc Simont, Viking (New York, NY), 1996.

Tornado, HarperCollins (New York, NY), 1996.

The Joy Boys, illustrated by Frank Remkiewicz, Delacorte (New York, NY), 1996.

A Bean Birthday, Macmillan (New York, NY), 1996.

Dead Letter: A Herculeah Jones Mystery, Viking (New York, NY), 1996.

Ant Plays Bear, illustrated by Marc Simont, Viking (New York, NY), 1997.

Death's Door, Viking (New York, NY), 1997.

Disappearing Acts, Viking (New York, NY), 1998.

Me Tarzan, illustrated by Bill Cigliano, HarperCollins (New York, NY), 2000.

(With daughters Betsy Duffey and Laurie Myers) *My Dog, My Hero,* Holt (New York, NY), 2000.

Little Horse, illustrated by David McPhail, Holt (New York, NY), 2002.

Keeper of the Doves, Viking (New York, NY), 2002.

(With daughters Betsy Duffey and Laurie Myers) *The SOS File,* illustrated by Arthur Howard, Henry Holt (New York, NY), 2004.

Little Horse on His Own, illustrated by David McPhail, Henry Holt (New York, NY), 2004.

Contributor of articles to periodicals, including *Saturday Evening Post, TV Guide,* and *Look.* Writings included in anthologies *Scary Stories to Read When It's Dark,* SeaStar Books, 2000.

Author's works have been translated into several languages.

Author's manuscripts are housed at Clemson University, South Carolina.

Adaptations

The following were adapted as episodes of the *ABC Afterschool Special,* for ABC-TV: "Pssst! Hammerman's After You," adapted from *The Eighteenth Emergency,* 1973; "Sara's Summer of the Swans," adapted from *The Summer of the Swans,* 1974; "Trouble River," 1975; "The Winged Colt," adapted from *The Winged Colt of Casa Mia,* 1976; "The Pinballs," 1977; and "Daddy, I'm Their Mamma Now," adapted from *The Night Swimmers,* 1981. *The Lace Snail* was adapted as a film-strip with cassette by Viking; *The Midnight Fox, The Summer of the Swans,* and *Go and Hush the Baby* were recorded on cassette by Miller-Brody; *Sara's Summer of the Swans* was adapted for videocassette, Martin Tahse Productions, 1976; *The TV Kid* was recorded on cassette, 1977.

Sidelights

Betsy Byars is one of the most popular and prolific authors of contemporary realistic fiction for middle-school readers. Called "one of the best writers for children in the world" by critic Nancy Chambers in *Signal,* Byars had been consistently lauded for creating adventurous works that blend humor and sympathy to address the universal emotions of childhood. Concentrating on themes of maturation and relationships with family, peers, and animals, she frequently portrays the growth of respect and understanding between child and adult characters. A distinctive mixture of unsentimental pathos, humor, and fundamental optimism coupled with

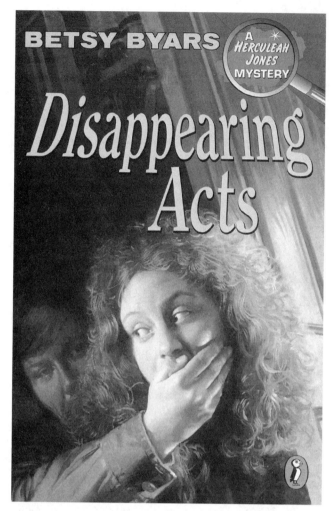

In this installment of Byars's popular "Herculeah Jones" mystery series, a best friend's long-lost father suddenly surfaces while Herculeah investigates a murder victim that has gone missing. (Cover illustration by Robert Sabin.)

an attraction to life's oddities allows her to examine successfully subjects usually considered too disturbing for young readers.

Byars came relatively late to her writing career. "In all of my school years . . . not one single teacher ever said to me, 'Perhaps you should consider becoming a writer,'" she told interviewer Elizabeth Segel in *Children's Literature in Education.* "Anyway, I didn't want to be a writer. Writing seemed boring. You sat in a room all day by yourself and typed. If I was going to be a writer at all, I was going to be a foreign correspondent like Claudette Colbert in *Arise My Love.* I would wear smashing hats, wisecrack with the guys, and have a byline known round the world."

The author married Edward Byars after graduating from college, in 1950. They had been married for five years and had two daughters when Ed decided that he needed a Ph.D. degree to continue in his career. The family packed up its belongings and moved to Illinois for the next two years. Byars soon discovered that the other wives living in her neighborhood either worked or were in school. "The highlight of my day was the arrival of the grocery truck after lunch," she later wrote in *Something about the Author Autobiography Series.* So she got herself a second-hand typewriter—"so old I had to press the keys down an inch to make a letter"—and began to write. "I thought it couldn't be as hard as people say it is. I thought probably the reason professional writers claim it's so hard is because they don't want any more competition."

Although she wrote "constantly" for the next two years, successful writing proved more difficult than she had anticipated. "My first sale was a short article to the *Saturday Evening Post* and I got seventy-five dollars for it. I was elated. I had known all along there was nothing to writing. Seven months passed before I sold a second article.

"I was learning what most other writers have learned before me—that writing is a profession in which there is an apprenticeship period, oftentimes a very long one. In that, writing is like baseball or piano playing. You have got to practice if you want to be successful."

Byars's early books, including *Clementine, The Dancing Camel, Rama, the Gypsy Cat,* and *The Groober,* received a somewhat cool reception from critics. Of her next publication Byars remarked in *Something about the Author Autobiography Series:* "The first book that turned out the way I had envisioned it was *The Midnight Fox.* . . . I look on *The Midnight Fox* as another turning point of my career. It gave me a confidence I had not had before. I knew now that I was going to be able to do some of the things I wanted to do, some of the things I had not had the courage and skill to try. For this reason, and others, it remains my favorite of my books."

With *The Midnight Fox* and *Trouble River* (which was written before *The Midnight Fox* though published after it) Byars began utilizing humor and realistic details in her stories. *Trouble River* tells the story of Dewey Martin, a twelve-year-old boy who is left alone with his grandmother on the frontier during his mother's lying-in. Dewey and his dog successfully drive off a hostile Indian, but realizing he will return, the boy takes his grandmother on his raft down Trouble River to safety. Margaret F. O'Connell of *New York Times Book Review* remarked: "Byars has a talent for plot and dialogue that makes her low-keyed story a skillful portrayal of the growing respect between a young boy and an old woman." In *The Midnight Fox,* Tom is left to spend the summer at his Aunt Millie and Uncle Fred's farm while his parents take a bicycle tour of Europe. Tom is bored and lonely until he begins searching the woods and fields around the farm for the beautiful black fox he saw one day. When the fox steals one of Aunt Millie's turkeys, however, Uncle Fred decides to hunt it down, and Tom must defy his uncle in order to rescue the animal he feels so close to.

The Summer of the Swans grew out of Byars's experiences telling stories to a Brownie troop of mentally challenged children, augmented by some additional research. In this work, Sara, an unhappy adolescent, takes her mentally challenged younger brother to see six swans that have alighted on a lake near their home. Charlie is mesmerized by the birds and goes in search of them on his own late that night, quickly becoming lost. Sara's agonized search for her brother changes her perspective on many of the things that had been making her unhappy. In *Children's Literature in Education,* I. V. Hansen described Byars's protagonist as "a character rich in teenage humour and genuine compassion."

Byars was awarded the Newbery Medal in 1971 for *The Summer of the Swans,* an experience, she wrote in *Something about the Author Autobiography Series,* that "literally changed my life overnight. Up until this time I had had a few letters from kids. Now we had to get a bigger mailbox. I got tapes, questionnaires, invitations to speak, invitations to visit schools, requests for interviews. For the first time in my life, I started feeling like an author."

Byars's next effort, the simple picture book *Go and Hush the Baby,* describes an inventive older brother's attempts to quiet his younger sibling. *The Lace Snail,* another picture book, grew out of the author's experiments with etching and was praised for its humorous dialogue.

With *The House of Wings* Byars returned to realistic fiction for young adults. In this book, Sammy is left with his grandfather, a virtual stranger, in a rundown cabin in Ohio, while his parents travel on to Detroit to try to find work there. Sammy's anger at being abandoned sends him running off into the woods followed closely by his grandfather, but the chase is brought to an abrupt end when the two discover an injured whooping crane. A relationship develops as they work together to nurse the bird back to health. In *The Eighteenth Emergency,* "Mouse" Fawley must face one of the many emergencies for which he and his friend Ezzie have prepared—the wrath of the school bully, Marv Hammerman. Mouse successfully avoids Marv until, influenced by studying medieval chivalry in his English class, he decides to do the honorable thing and face the consequences of insulting the other boy. Hansen called *The Eighteenth Emergency* "a wry, sometimes uproariously humorous story, and yet the medieval vision Mouse has slips easily into its fabric."

After the Goat Man is the story of an elderly man who returns to the cabin home he was forced to give up when the state decided to build a highway on the land, was more warmly received. Three children, the cool Ada, Harold, who is overweight and rueful, and Figgy, the old man's grandson, whose fears are overwhelming without his magic rabbit foot, come to the old man's rescue and learn something about themselves in the process. Alice Bach wrote in the *New York Times Book*

Review: "Never losing control of her material (and God knows a fat kid, an uprooted old man and a puny boy scared silly could be prime candidates for a pile of damp Kleenex in the hands of a lesser writer), Byars remains a dispassionate craftsman, weaving a sturdy homespun tale with the simple words of plain people."

In *The TV Kid* Byars's story centers on a boy who deals with the loneliness of the drifter lifestyle he and his mother have lived by watching a lot of television. He rejects the unreality of his fantasy life after it leads him to break into someone else's home and be bitten by a snake. While some reviewers criticized what they found to be a facile morality tale preaching against the evils of television, Elizabeth Segel commented in the *Dictionary of Literary Biography:* "The superior credibility of the contemporary children in [Byars's] books owes a great deal to her use of television and other manifestations of popular culture in characterization."

The Pinballs is one of Byars's most highly acclaimed works. The pinballs of the title are three children who have been abandoned or abused and have come to live one summer with the same foster parents. Together they help each other come to feel that they are not merely pinballs but have some control over their lives. As Ethel L. Heins remarked in *Horn Book,* "The stark facts about three ill-matched, abused children living in a foster home could have made an almost unbearably bitter novel; but the economically told story, liberally spiced with humor, is something of a tour de force." Writing in *School Library Journal,* Helene H. Levene called *The Pinballs* "engrossing."

In *The Cartoonist,* like *The TV Kid,* a boy seeks to escape his problems with his family. Alfie escapes to the attic to draw cartoons and locks himself in when it looks like he will have to give up his sanctuary. Of Alfie's story, Paula Fox wrote in the *Washington Post Book World:* Byars "tells it splendidly, with clarity, verve and grace."

With *Good-bye Chicken Little* Byars returns to a serious subject matter and focuses on individuality, a theme that runs through several of her more recent works. When Jimmie "Chicken" Little's Uncle Pete takes a dare to walk across a frozen river and falls through and drowns, Jimmie worries that he did not try hard enough to save him. When Jimmie's mother plans a festive Christmas party a few days later, Jimmie is offended until he realizes the she knows better than he how to honor her unique brother. Byars focuses on parental irresponsibility in *The Night Swimmers,* a story about three children who are left alone every evening while their father pursues his career singing country music. They often swim secretly in a nearby private swimming pool, until the youngest child is nearly drowned and the eldest child is finally relieved of responsibility for their welfare. Elaine Moss concluded in the *Times Literary Supplement* that, "In *The Night Swimmers* [Byars] has

written a short novel that makes the reader hold his breath, cry and laugh; not for one moment are the emotions disengaged."

Byars turned to a more lighthearted subject in *The Cybil War,* which humorously depicts the troubled friendship between fourth-grader Simon and his disloyal friend Tony, both of whom are in love with a little girl named Cybil. Some critics found these characters disappointingly ordinary after those in Byars's previous works, but Zena Sutherland wrote in the *Bulletin of the Center for Children's Books* that the text "seems deceptively simple, but has a polished fluency and spontaneity." Similarly, *The Animal, the Vegetable, and John D. Jones* is a humorous and realistic tale of a summer "family" vacation taken by two girls and their divorced father who unexpectedly invites a widowed woman and her son to join them. Critic Sutherland commented: "This doesn't have as strong a story line as some of Byars' stories, but it has the same perceptive exposition of the intricacy of ambivalent relationships."

In *The Two-Thousand-Pound Goldfish* a boy creates imaginary horror films to distract himself from the insecurity and lack of love in his own life. Marilyn Kaye of the *New York Times Book Review* remarked: "Byars' straightforward narration lets pure gut feelings come through." Byars depicts another outcast in *The Glory Girl,* which centers on Anna, the only nonmusical member of a family of gospel singers. In the story, Anna is befriended by her Uncle Newt, an ex-convict. In *The Computer Nut,* Byars joined forces with her son, Guy Byars, who provides the computer graphics that illustrate this story of a girl who gets a message from a space alien via her home computer.

With *Cracker Jackson* Byars takes on the serious subject of spousal abuse with what critics noted is a characteristic blend of realism and humor. The title character, eleven-year-old Jackson, is called Cracker only by Alma, his former babysitter, who now has a husband and small child. When the boy begins to suspect that Alma's husband, Billy Ray, is beating her, he enlists his friend Goat in a desperate rescue attempt that Lillian Gerhardt characterized in *School Library Journal* as leading to "some of the most harrowing but hilarious moments in the book." Audrey Laski, writing in the *Times Educational Supplement,* remarked of Byars: "nobody writing in America for this age range is as good." Byars reintroduces Jackson and Goat in *The Seven Treasure Hunts,* a humorous tale that critics called lighthearted for its episodic plot and adventurous action.

With *The Not-Just-Anybody Family* and its sequels Byars again addresses the importance of individuality. In *The Not-Just-Anybody Family* the reader is introduced to the poor and eccentric members of the Blossom family, who always seem to be getting into trouble. Katherine Duncan-Jones, writing in the *Times Literary Supplement,* dubbed it "a tough, entertaining American urban romance, in the best tradition of stories about children carrying more than adult responsibilities and almost magically winning the day." Like several other reviewers, Susan Kenney commented in the *New York Times Book Review* that some of the events depicted in this work would be frightening to younger readers. "Tragicomedy would be a truer description of what goes on here," Kenney wrote, but concluded: "Funny-ha-ha maybe not; well worth reading, certainly yes."

In the second volume of the "Blossom Family" series, *The Blossoms Meet the Vulture Lady,* Junior gets caught in his own coyote trap and is rescued by the dreaded Mad Mary, a woman who lives in a cave and eats road kill. "This is a lively, likable family, handled lightly but surely by an author known for her ability to write believable dialogue and present the desires of her characters with humor and understanding," wrote Sara Miller for *School Library Journal.* In *The Blossoms and the Green Phantom,* Junior Blossom is depressed by his failure to interest anyone in the flying saucer he has made. His mother takes time out from searching for her father, Pap, who has disappeared, to rally the family around the boy. In a review in *School Library Journal,* Dudley B. Carlson wrote: "This is a story about love in its many forms. Like Byars' best, it is rock-solid and full of chuckles, and it lingers in the mind."

In the fourth book about the Blossoms, *A Blossom Promise,* the family is struck by disaster on several fronts, culminating in a mild heart attack suffered by Pap. Billed as the last in the series, the book elicited much praise from critics, who commented that children would miss the Blossom family. Kristiana Gregory wrote in the *Los Angeles Times Book Review* that "This is the final, bittersweet volume in the Blossom Family Quartet, bittersweet only because the cast is so memorably quirky that you hate to say goodbye."

To appease "Blossom Family" fans, Byars published *Wanted . . . Mud Blossoms* as a fifth in the series. The story takes place one weekend when the family is plagued by the disappearance of Mad Mary, now a family friend, and the hamster entrusted to Junior by his class. In the latter case, the family dog, Mud, is suspected, and many critics praised the children's mock trial of Mud Blossom.

In *The Golly Sisters Go West* and *Hooray for the Golly Sisters* Byars introduces two women whose ignorance and exuberance lead them into and out of all sorts of adventures as they sing and dance their way westward across North America. Set up as collections of stories for young readers, the books garnered praise for their humor and accessibility. A reviewer for the *Bulletin of the Center for Children's Books* remarked that Byars makes a virtue of the simple vocabulary of books for beginning readers, "spoofing the choppy style with dialogue in which the childlike sisters echo each other." Also for young readers is *Beans on the Roof,* which introduces each character through the poem he or she composes while sitting on the roof of the house. Diane

Roback commented in *Publishers Weekly* commented: "In the simplest language and a natural, unadorned style, Byars has created an easy-to-read chapter book that is humorous and realistic."

Byars has written a series of books centering on the lovesick adventures of Bingo Brown. In the first installment, *The Burning Questions of Bingo Brown,* Bingo learns that even though his love for Melissa is returned, not everyone is so lucky, as his teacher, the suicidal Mr. Markham, proves. A reviewer for the *Bulletin of the Center for Children's Books* concluded: "This is a story that children are going to get a lot out of and love, while adults appreciate both craft and content." In *Bingo Brown and the Language of Love* Melissa has moved away, inspiring many expensive long-distance phone calls between the two. Byars's universally loved protagonist must also contend with the odd behavior of his parents and the attentions of a physically well-developed classmate. Fannie Flagg reviewed *Bingo Brown and the Language of Love* for the *New York Times Book Review,* writing: "If there is such a thing as a typical American kid, Bingo Brown is it. He is funny and bright and lovable without being precocious, and Betsy Byars has demonstrated a special creative genius in pulling off this delicate balancing act."

The adventures of Bingo continue in *Bingo Brown, Gypsy Lover,* in which Melissa tells Bingo that he resembles the hero in the romantic novel she is reading. As Christine Behrmann wrote in *School Library Journal:* "Bingo continues to grow . . . in each book, and here he progresses from slightly cocky self-preoccupation to vulnerable concern for others." This volume was followed by *Bingo Brown's Guide to Romance,* in which Bingo records his misadventures with Melissa, who is back in town, in the hope that his baby brother will be spared some of his troubles when the time comes for him to fall in love. A reviewer for the *Bulletin of the Center for Children's Books* concluded: "More episodic than cohesive, this is nevertheless keen-eyed and better-written than most series titles."

Byars is also the author of *Coast to Coast,* in which Birch convinces her grieving grandfather to take one last trip in his antique airplane before he sells it, the girl's hope being that the flight will raise his spirits in the wake of his wife's death. "The details about flying will draw readers in, as will the loving story of friendship over the generations," wrote Judy Fink in *Voice of Youth Advocates.* A reviewer for the *Bulletin of the Center for Children's Books* concluded: "It's an episodic trip, but one worth taking."

My Brother, Ant and *Ant Plays Bear* are books for early readers about a boy and his little brother Anthony, known as Ant. Although Ant does his best to annoy his big brother—scribbling on homework, making the older sibling chase "monsters' out of their room—the narrator never loses his patience. The four stories about the pair contained in *My Brother, Ant* "are full of homespun warmth and easy-going humor," commented a *Publishers Weekly* contributor. "A great story teller and a great illustrator [Marc Simont] are at their very best in this tender, funny, easy-to-read chapter book," *Booklist* reviewer Hazel Rochman declared about the same title.

Byars teamed up with her daughters, Betsy Duffey and Laurie Myers, to write *My Dog, My Hero* and *The SOS Files,* collections of short stories. In *My Dog, My Hero* the stories are designed as entries in the "My Hero" essay contest, where contestants are asked to write about why their dog is their hero. "Drama, humor, excitement, and love fuel these short, well-written stories," Ellen Mandel noted in *Booklist.* In *The SOS Files* the stories are meant to be essays written for extra credit by students in Mr. Magro's class. Each story is about a time when the student needed help, from needing medical help after crashing a go-cart to needing a rescuer after being abandoned in a dumpster as a baby. "Some tales are poignant, others are humorous," Maria B. Salvadore commented in *School Library Journal,* but as a whole "this collection will be a hit with its target audience and is perfect for encouraging reluctant readers," concluded a *Kirkus Reviews* contributor.

The four stories in **My Brother, Ant** *focus on a close sibling relationship as a caring older brother deals with nightime fears, helps compose a letter to Santa, and tolerates other little-brother hijinks.(Illustration by Marc Simont.)*

Little Horse and *Little Horse on His Own,* also for beginning readers, are fantasies about a tiny horse no bigger than a kitten. In the first title, the pint-sized horse is terrified when he loses his mother and has to fend for himself in a strange world that is full of hazards, including streams, birds, and a dog. Luckily for Little Horse, a boy comes along to take care of him. "Young horse lovers will delight in the idea of a real horse they could hold in their hands and will enjoy the small creature's adventures," Louise L. Sherman wrote in *School Library Journal,* speaking about the former title. In *Little Horse on His Own,* the tiny creature sets out to find his family, even though the world is still a very dangerous place for someone so small. The book's "brief, action-packed chapters will please horse fanciers ready to advance beyond traditional easy readers," Jennifer Mattson wrote in *Booklist.*

The middle-grade novel *Keeper of the Doves,* set during the 1890s, is told from the point of view of the youngest child in a family of five daughters. The girl, Amen McBee ("Amie' for short), is a born poet who writes her first work at the age of six. In addition to her four older sisters—Abigal, Augusta, and twins Annabella and Arabella—and her parents, the McBee household also includes Mr. Tominski, a reclusive man whom their father allows to live in the chapel on the family's estate; and Aunt Pauline and Grandmama, who help care for the girls while their fragile mother copes with her latest pregnancy. Byars's story of the joys and tragedies that come to this family over several years was widely praised by critics. Byars writes "in a prose that ripples with clarity and sweetness and an underlying evolution of spirit," declared a *Kirkus Reviews* contributor, and a *Publishers Weekly* critic concluded that "the snippets of Amie's and her family's lives add up to an exquisitely complete picture."

Byars is also the author of the highly acclaimed autobiography *The Moon and I.* Critic Roback called the writer's memoir "an appealingly idiosyncratic narrative that seamlessly weaves together the Newbery winner's life and art." Phyllis Graves, writing in *School Library Journal,* described it as "very special nonfiction that truly entertains as it informs."

Byars is often commended as a thoughtful and original writer who creates fresh, convincing characterizations, skillful portrayals of human interaction, vibrant images, and deceptively simple prose. While occasional critics find her conclusions contrived, Byars is well regarded as a compassionate explorer of the social and moral issues confronting her audience. Jennifer FitzGerald described Byars in *School Library Journal* as "preeminent among authors" with the ability to "combine unstinted awareness with a remarkable rollicking sense of humor, dispelling despair and self-pity without ignoring pain."

"I used to think, when I first started writing, that writers were like wells," Byars wrote in an essay for the *Something about the Author Autobiography Series,* "and

Taking place in 1899, Byars's 2002 novel focuses on a world in flux and a young girl's determination to discover the truth when her father's faith in an eccentric neighbor contradicts local gossip.

sooner or later we'd use up what had happened to us and our children and our friends and our dogs and cats, and there wouldn't be anything left. We'd go dry and have to quit. I imagine we would if it weren't for that elusive quality—creativity. I can't define it, but I have found from experience that the more you use it, the better it works."

Biographical and Critical Sources

BOOKS

Authors and Artists for Young Adults, Volume 19, Gale (Detroit, MI), 1997.
Beacham's Guide to Literature for Young Adults, Volume 3, Beacham Publishing (Osprey, FL), 1990.
Carpenter, Humphrey, and Mari Prichard, *The Oxford Companion to Children's Literature,* Oxford University Press (Oxford, England), 1984.
Children's Literature Review, Volume 16, Gale (Detroit, MI), 1989.

Contemporary Literary Criticism, Volume 35, Gale (Detroit, MI), 1985.
Dictionary of Literary Biography, Volume 52: *American Writers for Children since 1960: Fiction,* Gale (Detroit, MI), 1986.
Drew, Bernard A., *The One Hundred Most Popular Young Adult Authors,* Libraries Unlimited (Englewood, CO), 1996.
Hopkins, Lee Bennett, *More Books by More People,* Citation Press (New York, NY), 1974.
Kingman, Lee, editor, *Newbery and Caldecott Medal Books, 1966-1975,* Horn Book (Boston, MA), 1975.
St. James Guide to Young Adult Writers, 2nd edition, St. James Press (Detroit, MI), 1999.
Science Fiction & Fantasy Literature, 1975-1991, Gale (Detroit, MI), 1992.
Silvey, Anita, editor, *Children's Books and Their Creators,* Houghton Mifflin (Boston, MA), 1995.
Twentieth-Century Children's Writers, St. Martin's Press (New York, NY), 1978, pp. 215-217.
Twentieth-Century Young Adult Writers, St. James Press (Detroit, MI), 1994.
Usrey, Malcolm, *Betsy Byars,* Twayne (New York, NY), 1995.
Ward, Martha E., and others, *Authors of Books for Young People,* 3rd edition, Scarecrow Press (Metuchen, NJ), 1990.

PERIODICALS

Book September, 2000, Kathleen Odean, review of *Me Tarzan,* p. 86.
Booklist, January 15, 1993, Ilene Cooper, "The Booklist Interview: Betsy Byars," pp. 906-907; August, 1994, Stephanie Zvirin, review of *The Dark Stairs,* p. 2042; July, 1995, Stephanie Zvirin, review of *Tarot Says Beware,* p. 1878; January 1, 1996, Hazel Rochman, review of *My Brother,* p. 828; June 1, 1996, Ilene Cooper, review of *Dead Letter,* p. 1716; September 15, 1996, Carolyn Phelan, review of *Tornado,* p. 238, Kristi Beavin, review of *The Dark Stairs,* p. 264; March 1, 1997, Stephanie Zvirin, review of *Death's Door,* p. 1162; September 1, 1997, Hazel Rochman, review of *Ant Plays Bear,* p. 116; February 15, 1998, Barbara Baskin, review of *The Golly Sisters Ride Again,* p. 1027; March 1, 1998, Stephanie Zvirin, review of *Disappearing Acts,* p. 1134; March 1, 2000, Debra McLeod, review of *The Summer of the Swans,* p. 1255; January 1, 2001, Ellen Mandel, review of *My Dog, My Hero,* p. 954; March 15, 2002, Gillian Engberg, review of *Little Horse,* p. 1255; October 1, 2002, Ilene Cooper, review of *Keeper of the Doves,* p. 322; June 1, 2004, Shelle Rosenfeld, review of *The SOS File,* p. 1725; July, 2004, Anna Rich, review of *Keeper of the Doves,* p. 1857; September 1, 2004, Jennifer Mattson, review of *Little Horse on His Own,* p. 120.
Bulletin of the Center for Children's Books, January, 1985, review of *The Computer Nut,* p. 81; March, 1986, review of *The Not-Just-Anybody Family,* p. 123; October, 1986, review of *The Blossoms Meet the Vulture Lady,* pp. 22-23; November, 1986, review of *The Golly Sisters Go West,* p. 44; April, 1987, review of *The*

Blossoms and the Green Phantom, p. 143; November, 1987, review of *A Blossom Promise*, p. 44; November, 1988, review of *Beans on the Roof*, pp. 66-67; June, 1989, review of *Bingo Brown and the Language of Love*, p. 244; June, 1990, review of *Bingo Brown, Gypsy Lover*, p. 234; April, 1991, review of *The Seven Treasure Hunts*, pp. 185-186; March, 1992, review of *The Moon and I*, p. 77; June, 1994, review of *The Golly Sisters Ride Again*, p. 314.

Children's Literature in Education, winter, 1982, Elizabeth Segel, "Betsy Byars: An Interview."

Horn Book, August, 1971, Betsy Byars, "Newberry Award Acceptance Speech"; February, 1971, Helen L. Heins, review of *The Summer of the Swans*, pp. 53-54; September-October, 1986, Ann A. Flowers, review of *The Not-Just-Anybody Family*, p. 588; July-August, 1990, Nancy Vasilakis, review of *Bingo Brown, Gypsy Lover*, p. 453; January-February, 1991, Carolyn K. Jenks, review of *Horray for the Golly Sisters!*, p. 63; November-December, 1994, Elizabeth S. Watson, review of *Tarot Says Beware*, p. 730; November-December, 1995, Elizabeth S. Watson, review of *Tarot Says Beware*, p. 760; July-August, 1996, Hanna B. Zeiger, review of *My Brother, Ant*, pp. 459-460; November-December, 1996, Maeve Visser Knoth, review of *Tornado*, p. 732; July-August, 1997, Martha A. Parravano, review of *Ant Plays Bear*, pp. 450-452; May-June, 1998, Elizabeth S. Watson, review of *Disappearing Acts*, p. 341; May-June, 2000, review of *Me Tarzan*, p. 309; May-June, 2002, Betty Carter, review of *Little Horse*, p. 325; September-October, 2002, Joanna Rudge, review of *Keeper of the Doves*, p. 567.

Kirkus Reviews, March 15, 2002, review of *Little Horse*, p. 407; July 15, 2002, review of *Keeper of the Doves*, p. 1028; May 1, 2004, review of *The SOS File*, p. 439; August 15, 2004, review of *Little Horse on His Own*, p. 803.

New York Times, January 23, 1971.

New York Times Book Review, October 13, 1974; December 15, 1974; May 2, 1976; August 4, 1985, Mary Louise Cuneo, review of *Cracker Jackson*, p. 2; April 2, 1989, review of *The Burning Questions of Bingo Brown*, p. 26; December 15, 1991, Elizabeth Ann-Sachs, review of *Wanted . . . Mud Blossom*, p. 29.

Publishers Weekly, February 22, 1971; September 6, 1971; July 25, 1977; May 24, 1985, review of *The Glory Girl*, p. 70; June 14, 1985, Jean F. Mercier, review of *Cracker Jackson*, p. 72; October 31, 1986, review of *Cracker Jackson*, p. 65; September 25, 1987, review of *A Blossom Promise*, p. 111; April 8, 1988, Kimberly Olson Fakih and Diane Roback, review of *The Burning Question of Bingo Brown*, p. 95; May 12, 1989, Penny Kaganoff and Diane Roback, review of *Bingo Brown and the Language of Love*, p. 294; May 11, 1990, Diane Roback and Richard Donahue, review of *Bingo Brown, Gypsy Lover*, p. 260; January 25, 1991, Diane Roback and Richard Donahue, review of *Bingo Brown and the Language of Love*, p. 59; April 12, 1991, Diane Roback and Richard Donahue, review of *The Seven Treasure Hunts*, p. 58; July 19,

1991, review of *Wanted . . . Mud Blossom*, p. 56; April 20, 1992, review of *The Moon and I*, p. 58; May 18, 1992, review of *Bingo Brown's Guide to Romance*, p. 71; October 12, 1992, review of *Coast to Coast*, pp. 79-80; August 16, 1993, review of *Mc-Mummy*, p. 105; July 18, 1994, review of *The Dark Stairs*, p. 246; January 15, 1996, review of *My Brother, Ant*, p. 462; May 22, 2000, review of *Me Tarzan*, p. 93; October 16, 2000, "Putting on the Dog," p. 78; August 19, 2002, review of *Keeper of the Doves*, p. 90; February 2, 2004, review of *Keeper of the Doves*, p. 80; May 17, 2004, review of *The SOS File*, p. 50.

School Librarian, March, 1986, Betsy Byars, "Spinning Straw into Gold," pp. 6-13.

School Library Journal, May, 1985, Lillian Gerhardt, review of *Cracker Jackson*, p. 87; May, 1986, Connie C. Rockman, review of *The Not-Just-Anybody Family*, pp. 88-89; December, 1986, Nancy Palmer, review of *The Golly Sisters Go West*, p. 122; November, 1987, Amy Kellman, review of *A Blossom Promise*, pp. 103-104; May, 1988, Ellen Fader, review of *The Burning Question of Bingo Brown*, pp. 95-96; November, 1988, Trev Jones, review of *Beans on the Roof*, p. 84; July, 1989, Martha Rosen, review of *Bingo Brown and the Language of Love*, pp. 81-82; January, 1990, review of *The Two-Thousand-Pound Goldfish*, p. 56; September, 1990, Sharon McElmeel, review of *Hooray for the Golly Sisters!*, p. 194; June, 1991, Martha Rosen, review of *The Seven Treasure Hunts*, p. 74; July, 1991, review of *Wanted: Mud Blossom*, p. 72; April, 1992, review of *The Moon and I*, p. 112; September, 1994, Ellen Fader, review of *The Dark Stairs: A Herculeah Jones Mystery*, p. 214; July, 2000, Janet Gillen, review of *Me Tarzan*, p. 68; April, 2002, Louise L. Sherman, review of *Little Horse*, p. 101; October, 2002, Caroline Ward, review of *Keeper of the Doves*, p. 158; November, 2003, Carol Fazioli, review of *The Moon and I*, p. 81; June, 2004, MaryAnn Karre, review of *Keeper of the Doves*, p. 73, Maria B. Salvatore, review of *The SOS File*, p. 103; September, 2004, Marilyn Taniguchi, review of *Little Horse on His Own*, p. 154.

Times Literary Supplement, July 18, 1980, Elaine Moss, "Dreams of a Surrogate Mother," p. 806.

Tops in the News, April, 1971, pp. 240-241.

Voice of Youth Advocates, August-October, 1986, review of *The Not-Just-Anybody Family*, p. 140; December, 1986, review of *The Blossoms Meet the Vulture Lady*, p. 213; April, 1987, review of *The Blossoms and the Green Phantom*, p. 29; December, 1987, review of *A Blossom Promise*, p. 46; August, 1991, review of *Wanted . . . Mud Blossom*, p. 168.

ONLINE

Betsy Byars Home Page, http://www.betsybyars.com (July 27, 2005).

Random House Web site, http://www.randomhouse.com/ teachers/ (March 7, 2002), "Betsy Byars."*

C

CANNON, A(nn) E(dwards)

Personal

Born in Salt Lake City, UT; daughter of Patti Louise Covey and LaVell Edwards; married Ken Cannon; children: Philip, Alec, Dylan, Geoffrey, Quinton. *Education:* Brigham Young University, B.A. (English literature), M.A. (English literature). *Hobbies and other interests:* Gardening, traveling, cooking, knitting, collecting antique dolls.

Addresses

Home—Salt Lake City, UT. *Agent*—Adams Literary, 295 Greenwich St., No. 260, New York, NY 10007. *E-mail*—acannon@desnews.com.

Career

Children's book author and journalist.

Member

Authors Guild.

Awards, Honors

Delacorte Press Prize for Outstanding First Young-Adult Novel, 1988, for *Cal Cameron by Day, Spider-Man by Night;* New York City Public Library Outstanding Books for Children designation, 2002, and Utah Book Award, and PEN Award finalist, all for *Charlotte's Rose.*

Writings

NOVELS

Cal Cameron by Day, Spider-Man by Night, Delacorte (New York, NY), 1988.
The Shadow Brothers, Delacorte (New York, NY), 1990.

Amazing Gracie, Delacorte (New York, NY), 1991.
Sam's Gift, Shadow Mountain (Salt Lake City, UT), 1996.
Charlotte's Rose, Wendy Lamb Books (New York, NY), 2002.

PICTURE BOOKS

Great-Granny Rose and the Family Christmas Tree, illustrated by Jacqui Grothe, Deseret Books (Salt Lake City, UT), 1996.
I Know What You Do When I Go to School, Gibbs Smith (Salt Lake City, UT), 1996.
On the Go with Pirate Pete and Pirate Joe, illustrated by Elwood H. Smith, Viking (New York, NY), 2002.
Let the Good Times Roll with Pirate Pete and Pirate Joe, illustrated by Elwood H. Smith, Viking (New York, NY), 2004.

OTHER

What's a Mother to Do? (humor), Signature Books (Salt Lake City, UT), 1997.

Contributor to *Dialogue: A Journal of Mormon Thought, Exponent II, New Era, Parent Express, Teen,* and *This People.* Columnist for *Deseret News.*

Work in Progress

A third "Pirates" book.

Sidelights

A. E. Cannon is a writer with remarkable insights into the concerns of young people. Her fictional characters are sensitively drawn, prompting readers to identify with their anxieties and fears while applauding their successes. At the same time, commentators have noted that the problems confronting Cannon's young characters are neither trite nor overblown; issues such as independence, sibling rivalry, and even depression and suicide are thoughtfully considered in her works.

Cannon was born in Salt Lake City, Utah, and raised in Provo. Her interest in literature began when she was felled by a serious childhood illness that required her to remain in bed for the better part of a year, under strict doctor's orders not to engage in strenuous physical activity. "With nothing else to do, I was forced to discover books," Cannon recalled on her Web site. "Before I knew it, books moved into my life permanently, setting up house and lounging around in chairs and on the foot of my bed just like a crowd of favorite cousins."

After graduating from Provo High School, Cannon attended Brigham Young University, earning a bachelor's degree followed by a master's degree in English literature. She published her debut novel, *Cal Cameron by Day, Spider-Man by Night,* in 1988.

Cal Cameron by Day, Spider-Man by Night is the story of a high school football player named Cal Cameron who, despite popularity and good looks, is having a crisis of conscience. His friends seem suddenly shallow and insensitive, and even football begins to lose its appeal. In addition, Cal is troubled by problems at home: his grandfather, an ornery, despotic patriarch, adores Cal but constantly belittles both Cal's father and his older brother, making Cal's own relationship with his father and brother somewhat strained. Cal is totally lost until he meets Marti, a new girl who seemingly cares nothing about impressing others and is not afraid to speak her mind. Marti seems to have what Cal feels he is lacking, and through their friendship he gains a better understanding of himself. *School Library Journal* contributor Janet DiGianni offered a favorable assessment of *Cal Cameron by Day, Spider-Man by Night,* asserting: "This is a totally absorbing novel, with flesh and blood characters that readers will care about and stay with until the end."

A young man's coming-of-age is also the topic of Cannon's second novel, *The Shadow Brothers.* Narrated by sixteen-year-old Marcus Jenkins, *The Shadow Brothers* focuses on Marcus's relationship with his foster brother, Henry Mazzie—a Navajo who has lived with the Jenkins family since the age of seven. Henry has always been the leader of the two boys, with superior athletic and academic skills, while Marcus slipped easily and comfortably into his role as the underachieving shadow of Henry. During the brothers' junior year in high school, the appearance of another Native American student at school causes the tension level to increase. The newcomer is defiant of authority and challenges Henry both athletically and spiritually, calling him an "apple": red on the outside and white on the inside. Henry then struggles with an identity crisis that culminates in his decision to return to his tribal reservation to find his roots, leaving Marcus to learn to stand on his own merits. In *Horn Book,* Margaret A. Bush described *The Shadow Brothers* as "a sensitive account of the intricacies of brotherhood in which old dependencies must be redefined." Nina VandeWater, writing in *Voice of Youth*

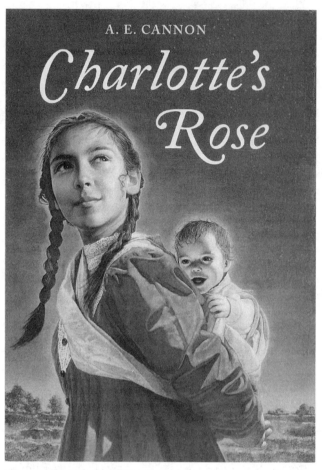

When twelve-year-old Charlotte takes on the care of a newborn infant born during a trek along the Oregon Trail, she dreads the day she and her new charge will be separated.

Advocates, added that "Cannon writes with humor, empathy, and a light touch."

In *Amazing Gracie* Cannon tackles suicide, depression, and growing up. Gracie is a pretty high-school sophomore with many friends and a close relationship with her widowed mother, Cynthia. While Cynthia remarries, she continues to struggle with debilitating depression, causing Gracie to worry about her mother's health as well as the instability created in planning her own future.

In a review of *Amazing Gracie* for *Horn Book,* Margaret A. Bush commented that, "for all of its sobering content, the story resounds with a tempered optimism; friendship is a dominant theme, treated in many facets." *Voice of Youth Advocates* contributor Marian Rafal praised Cannon's depiction of her central character, asserting: "Gracie is a strong character and readers will identify with her anxieties and fears, and will applaud her insights at novel's end." Barbara Chatton, reviewing *Amazing Gracie* for *School Library Journal,* offered an assessment that highlights a common thread running through each of Cannon's works: a young person's concerns over his or her identity. Chatton commented: "While [*Amazing Gracie*] includes a medical issue and a blended family, it is not a problem novel. Instead, it focuses on the universal desire of every young teen to be thought competent and unique."

Cannon delved into her own family background in creating the plot of *Charlotte's Rose*, "an engrossing, detailed, thoroughly real story of faith, family, and community," in the words of a *Kirkus Reviews* critic. In the work, twelve-year-old Charlotte and her widower father, both converts to the Mormon church, immigrate from Wales to America, where they seek the promised land of Zion. After arriving by cattle car in Iowa City, Charlotte and her fellow travelers begin an arduous journey during which they use pushcarts to transport their belongings across the prairies and mountains. After a young mother dies while giving birth to a baby girl, Charlotte agrees to care for the newborn, whom she names Rose. When Rose's father overcomes his grief and wishes to reclaim his daughter, Charlotte is forced to make a wrenching decision. "Charlotte herself blossoms through her sacrifice," noted a reviewer in *Publishers Weekly*, "and her maturation will likely endear her to readers." According to *School Library Journal* contributor Carol A. Edwards, *Charlotte's Rose* "offers a genuine headstrong girl in hardscrabble circumstances with a lightness of heart and a strong will to do right."

In addition to novels, Cannon has created a picture-book series for early readers. In *On the Go with Pirate Pete and Pirate Joe* she introduces a pair of buccaneer brothers who prefer to play the hornpipe and collect seashells rather than plunder and pillage. Best known for their fear of water and their stinky feet, Pirate Pete and Pirate Joe travel around in a black minivan dubbed the "Jolly Roger," accompanied by their pets, Studley the cat and Dudley the dog. When the time comes to locate an authentic pirate's parrot, the pair pass over both an operatic bird and a multilingual bird to purchase Bucko, a parrot who can say only one thing: "Yo ho!" *Let the Good Times Roll with Pirate Pete and Pirate Joe* details the further adventures of the wacky duo. This time the brothers visit the home of the Pirate Queen, who is nowhere to be found. After Pete and Joe futilely search under the queen's bed as well as in her hot tub, the royal person arrives with a seafood buffet to feed the hungry pair, who turn out to be her sons.

Reviewing *On the Go with Pirate Pete and Pirate Joe* in *School Library Journal*, Carol Schene remarked that Cannon's "compact text has just enough repetition for beginning readers, who will enjoy these charming protagonists." Reviewing the sequel, *School Library Journal* contributor Laura Scott praised Cannon's "lively, accessible text," and a contributor in *Kirkus Reviews* remarked that *Let the Good Times Roll with Pirate Pete and Pirate Joe* "won't be headed for Davy Jones's locker any time soon."

Biographical and Critical Sources

PERIODICALS

Booklist, April 1, 1988, p. 1334; October 1, 2002, Hazel Rochman, review of *Charlotte's Rose,* p. 340.
Bulletin of the Center for Children's Books, October, 1991, p. 33.
Horn Book, July-August, 1990, Margaret A. Bush, review of *The Shadow Brothers,* p. 461; January-February, 1992, Margaret A. Bush, review of *Amazing Gracie,* pp. 79-80; November-December, 2002, Christine M. Heppermann, review of *Charlotte's Rose,* p. 749.
Kirkus Reviews, May 1, 2002, review of *On the Go with Pirate Pete and Pirate Joe,* p. 650; August 15, 2002, review of *Charlotte's Rose,* p. 1220; January 15, 2004, review of *Let the Good Times Roll with Pirate Pete and Pirate Joe,* p. 81.
Kliatt, July, 2004, review of *Charlotte's Rose,* p. 14.
Publishers Weekly, June 8, 1990, Diane Roback and Richard Donahue, review of *The Shadow Brothers,* p. 56; November 22, 1991, review of *Amazing Gracie,* p. 58; September 9, 2002, review of *Charlotte's Rose,* p. 69.
School Librarian, August, 1992, p. 112.
School Library Journal, April, 1988, Janet DiGianni, review of *Cal Cameron by Day, Spider-Man by Night,* p. 111; August, 1991, Barbara Chatton, review of *Amazing Gracie,* p. 195; August, 2002, Carol Schene, review of *On the Go with Pirate Pete and Pirate Joe,* p. 148; September, 2002, Carol A. Edwards, review of *Charlotte's Rose,* p. 220; February, 2004, Laura Scott, *Let the Good Times Roll with Pirate Pete and Pirate Joe,* p. 104.
Voice of Youth Advocates, December, 1990, Nina VandeWater, review of *The Shadow Brothers,* p. 277; October, 1991, Marian Rafal, review of *Amazing Gracie,* p. 222.

ONLINE

A. E. Cannon Web site, http://www.aecannon.com (July 15, 2005).*

*   *   *

CAPUCILLI, Alyssa Satin 1957-

Personal

Born November 2, 1957, in Brooklyn, NY; married Bill Capucilli; children: Peter, Laura. *Education:* Sarah Lawrence College, B.A.

Addresses

Home—P.O. Box 605, Hastings-on-Hudson, NY 10706. *Agent*—Liza Voges, Kirchoff/Wohlberg, 866 U.N. Plaza, New York, NY 10017. *E-mail*—Alyssa@alyssacapucilli. com.

Career

Dancer, teacher, and author. Currently teaches writing at Sarah Lawrence College, Bronxville, NY.

Member

Society of Children's Book Writers and Illustrators, Authors Guild, Authors League.

Awards, Honors

American Booksellers Association Pick of the Lists designations, 1994, for *Good Morning, Pond,* 1996, for *Biscuit,* and 1997, for *Bathtime for Biscuit;* Oppenheim Toy Portfolio Gold Award winners, 2002, for *Biscuit's New Trick,* and 2004, for *Only My Dad and Me* and *Biscuit's Big Friend;* Washington Irving Children's Book Choice Award, 2004, for *Mrs. McTats and Her Houseful of Cats;* Garden State Book Award, 2005, for *Biscuit Goes to School.*

Writings

Peekaboo Bunny, illustrated by Mary Melcher, Scholastic (New York, NY), 1994.

Good Morning, Pond, illustrated by Cynthia Jabar, Hyperion (New York, NY), 1994.

Peekaboo Bunny Friends in the Snow, Scholastic (New York, NY), 1995.

Inside a Barn in the Country: A Rebus Read-along Story, illustrated by Tedd Arnold, Scholastic (New York, NY), 1995.

Wee Mouse Christmas, illustrated by Linda Birkinshaw, Random House (New York, NY), 1995.

Inside a House That Is Haunted: A Rebus Read-along Story, illustrated by Tedd Arnold, Scholastic (New York, NY), 1998.

(With Iris Hiskey Arno) *Wake up, Night,* Kidsbooks (Chicago, IL), 1998.

Inside a Zoo in the City: A Rebus Read-along Story, illustrated by Tedd Arnold, Scholastic (New York, NY), 2000.

The Potty Book for Girls, illustrated by Dorothy Stott, Barron's Educational (Hauppage, NY), 2000.

The Potty Book for Boys, illustrated by Dorothy Stott, Barron's Educational (Hauppage, NY), 2000.

Bear Hugs, illustrated by Jim Ishi, Golden Books (New York, NY), 2000.

Mrs. McTats and Her Houseful of Cats, illustrated by Joan Rankin, Margaret K. McElderry (New York, NY), 2001.

What Kind of Kiss?, illustrated by Hiroe Nakata, HarperCollins (New York, NY), 2002.

The Brightest Star, illustrated by Clare Beaton, Simon & Schuster (New York, NY), 2003.

Only My Mom and Me, illustrated by Tiphanie Beeke, HarperCollins (New York, NY), 2003.

Only My Dad and Me, illustrated by Tiphanie Beeke, HarperCollins (New York, NY), 2003.

Little Spotted Cat, illustrated by Dan Andreason, HarperCollins (New York, NY), 2005.

Capucilli's books have been translated into French, Hebrew, Afrikaans, Japanese, Spanish, Korean, Bulgarian, and Greek.

"BISCUIT" SERIES

Biscuit, illustrated by Pat Schories, HarperCollins (New York, NY), 1996.

Biscuit Finds a Friend, illustrated by Pat Schories, HarperCollins (New York, NY), 1997.

Bathtime for Biscuit, illustrated by Pat Schories, HarperCollins (New York, NY), 1997.

Hello, Biscuit!, illustrated by Pat Schories, HarperCollins (New York, NY), 1998.

Biscuit's Picnic, illustrated by Pat Schories, HarperCollins (New York, NY), 1998.

Happy Birthday, Biscuit!, illustrated by Pat Schories, HarperCollins (New York, NY), 1998.

Biscuit's New Trick: A Scratch-and-Sniff Book, illustrated by Pat Schories, HarperCollins (New York, NY), 2000.

Happy Halloween, Biscuit!, illustrated by Pat Schories, HarperCollins (New York, NY), 2000.

Happy Thanksgiving, Biscuit!, illustrated by Pat Schories, HarperCollins (New York, NY), 2000.

Happy Easter, Biscuit!, illustrated by Pat Schories, HarperCollins (New York, NY), 2000.

Happy Valentine's Day, Biscuit!, illustrated by Pat Schories, HarperCollins (New York, NY), 2000.

Time to Paint, Biscuit!, illustrated by Pat Schories, HarperCollins (New York, NY), 2001.

Merry Christmas, from Biscuit, illustrated by Pat Schories, HarperCollins (New York, NY), 2001.

Biscuit's Valentine Day, illustrated by Pat Schories, HarperCollins (New York, NY), 2001.

Biscuit's Day at the Beach, illustrated by Pat Schories, HarperCollins (New York, NY), 2001.

Biscuit Wants to Play, illustrated by Pat Schories, HarperCollins (New York, NY), 2001.

Biscuit Visits the Farm, illustrated by Pat Schories, HarperCollins (New York, NY), 2002.

Biscuit Meets the Neighbors, illustrated by Pat Schories, HarperCollins (New York, NY), 2002.

Biscuit Goes to the Park, illustrated by Pat Schories, HarperCollins (New York, NY), 2002.

Biscuit Goes to School, illustrated by Pat Schories, HarperCollins (New York, NY), 2002.

Happy Hanukkah, Biscuit, illustrated by Pat Schories, HarperCollins (New York, NY), 2002.

Biscuit's Big Friend, illustrated by Pat Schories, HarperCollins (New York, NY), 2003.

Biscuit Loves School, illustrated by Pat Schories, HarperCollins (New York, NY), 2003.

Biscuit Is Thankful, illustrated by Pat Schories, HarperCollins (New York, NY), 2003.

Biscuit and the Bunny, illustrated by Pat Schories, HarperCollins (New York, NY), 2003.

What Is Love, Biscuit?, illustrated by Pat Schories, HarperCollins (New York, NY), 2003.

Biscuit Wins a Prize, illustrated by Pat Schories, HarperCollins (New York, NY), 2004.

Biscuit Visits the Pumpkin Patch, illustrated by Pat Schories, HarperCollins (New York, NY), 2004.

Biscuit Storybook Collection, illustrated by Pat Schories, HarperCollins (New York, NY), 2004.

Biscuit Loves Mother's Day, illustrated by Pat Schories, HarperCollins (New York, NY), 2004.

Biscuit Loves Father's Day, illustrated by Pat Schories, HarperCollins (New York, NY), 2004.

Biscuit Gives a Gift, illustrated by Pat Schories, Harper-Collins (New York, NY), 2004.

Biscuit's Hanukkah, illustrated by Pat Schories and Mary O'Keefe Young, HarperCollins (New York, NY), 2005.

Biscuit's Graduation Day, illustrated by Pat Schories and Mary O'Keefe Young, HarperCollins (New York, NY), 2005.

Biscuit's Fourth of July, illustrated by Pat Schories and Mary O'Keefe Young, HarperCollins (New York, NY), 2005.

Biscuit's Birthday, illustrated by Pat Schories, HarperCollins (New York, NY), 2005.

Biscuit and the Baby, illustrated by Pat Schories, Harper-Collins (New York, NY), 2005.

Meet Biscuit!, illustrated by Pat Schories, HarperCollins (New York, NY), 2005.

Biscuit Visits the Big City, illustrated by Pat Schories, HarperCollins (New York, NY), 2006.

Biscuit's Touch-and-Feel Christmas, illustrated by Pat Schories, HarperCollins (New York, NY), 2006.

Biscuit's Snowy Day, illustrated by Pat Schories, Harper-Collins (New York, NY), 2006.

Biscuit's 100th Day of School, illustrated by Pat Schories, HarperCollins (New York, NY), 2006.

Sidelights

Alyssa Satin Capucilli is the imaginative author of books for both pre-schoolers and beginning readers. Her creations include lift-the-flap books for toddlers that feature gentle, lovable characters and easily identifiable objects as well as a series of beginning readers starring Biscuit, a rambunctious golden-haired puppy whose adventures are brought to life by illustrator Pat Schories.

Born in Brooklyn, New York, in 1957, Capucilli developed an early love of books, and looked forward to weekly trips to the library with her mother and sisters. "I could hardly wait to choose a special book from all of the books that lined the shelves," she once recalled to *Something about the Author* (*SATA*). "As a matter of fact, my sisters and I would often play library at home! We would take turns pretending to be the librarian, and we would recommend books to each other, check them out, and tell each other to 'SSSSHHH!'" Among Capucilli's favorite authors were Louisa May Alcott, author of *Little Women,* and Beverly Cleary, whose stories about Henry and his dog, Ribsy, she loved. "The funny thing was, although I loved to imagine myself as different characters in books," Capucilli added, "I never imagined that the authors who created them were real people!"

Although as a child she wrote stories, poems, and puppet shows, Capucilli never took her writing seriously until many years later. In the meantime, she focused on her love of dance, a method, she explained, of "telling stories in another way." She became a professional dancer and soon was teaching as well as performing on stage. While reading to her own two children, her love affair with children's books was rekindled, and she began to split her time between work as a dance instructor and performer and work as a writer.

Capucilli's first published book was *Peekaboo Bunny,* a lift-the-flap book published in 1994. Illustrated by Mary Melcher, the book helps small children navigate in a garden, and it was popular enough to prompt a sequel, *Peekaboo Bunny Friends in the Snow.* The connection between objects and sounds has inspired several of Capucilli's other books, including *Good Morning, Pond,* which uses repetition and rhythm to teach the names of pond-dwelling creatures, and books that tell stories using rebuses, pictures of items that, when sounded out in order, make words. One such, *Inside a Barn in the Country,* illustrated by Tedd Arnold, encourages young listeners to mimic barnyard noises and uses rebuses for the text. *Booklist* reviewer Stephanie Zvirin praised Capucilli's thoughtfully designed text as "part poetry, part puzzle game, and part tool for learning the sounds animals make." Noting that the text models itself after the familiar "This Is the House That Jack Built," a *Publishers Weekly* contributor said that "Capucilli and Arnold give their work plenty of extra bounce."

Capucilli introduces a new character to young readers in *Biscuit.* A small, soft-eared, lovable puppy the color of freshly baked, golden biscuits, Capucilli's Biscuit bounds into the life of a young girl, quickly becoming her best friend as she interprets his "Woof, Woof" to mean many things. From wanting a small snack before bedtime to being tucked in snugly under layers of blankets, the activities of Biscuit and his young owner are depicted in "oodles of contextual clues," easy-to-read sentences, and "repetitive word and phrases," according to *School Library Journal* reviewer Gale W. Sherman. "I find that inspiration for stories and characters comes from so many places: our memories, our family, our friends, our pets, our own observations and our own wonderings," Capucilli explained. "I first got the idea to write about . . . Biscuit after watching my daughter dog-sit a neighbor's huge golden retriever! But deep inside, I think that the 'Biscuit' stories are really about that puppy I always imagined I would someday have, from when I was a young girl, reading and dreaming."

Novice readers have encountered Biscuit's "Woof, Woof" in numerous other books. Illustrated by Schories, the series has even become so popular with readers that a stuffed toy puppy resembling the floppy-eared canine has become available. In *Biscuit Finds a Friend* the puppy noses a small duckling out from under the porch of his family's house, and the two become fast friends. Cooper deemed the story "just right" for beginning readers. In *Bathtime for Biscuit* the task of getting the pup into hot water is made easier through a variety of antics, and Capucilli tells her story in a way that "makes this a good choice for the youngest readers and listeners alike," in the opinion of *School Library Journal* contributor Sharon R. Pearce.

Biscuit celebrates his first birthday with his many new friends in *Happy Birthday, Biscuit!,* offering equal appeal to "librarians who find it difficult to sustain a squirmy toddler's interest," according to Lauren Peterson's *Booklist* appraisal. In *Biscuit's New Trick* the young dog learns how to fetch a ball. Biscuit is so eager to play that his owner can't stop him from chasing the ball even when it rolls into a sloppy mud puddle. *School Library Journal* reviewer Janie Schomberg noted that the tale "provides plenty of repetition for new readers." *Biscuit's Valentine's Day,* a lift-the-flap book, describes the pup's busy day chewing on ribbon and playing with balloons. Youngsters "will enjoy the simple action," wrote *Booklist* critic Ilene Cooper.

In *Happy Hanukkah, Biscuit!,* another lift-the-flap holiday book, the puppy attends a Hanukkah celebration with his owner. While the party guests spin the dreidel and make beeswax candles, Biscuit causes all sorts of mischief. A contributor in *Kirkus Reviews* deemed the work "a pleasant addition to the Biscuit canon." The playful pup tackles the ABCs in *Biscuit Goes to School,* a story "that will capture the attention of the newest reader," observed Cooper. When his owner leaves the house one morning, the curious Biscuit follows along and eventually makes his way into her school building. Capucilli's "hallmark combination of questions and statements, liberally interspersed with Biscuit's jovial barks, executed in the most basic language—is at once familiar and encouraging" to children, remarked a *Kirkus Reviews* critic.

Capucilli has created several other picture books featuring genial, engaging creatures. In *What Kind of Kiss?* a bear cub seeks the answer to his questions about smooching. He learns that Mama enjoys a "rise-and-shine" kiss to start the day and Papa enjoys a "shaving cream" kiss. The cub questions other creatures, including a puppy and a bird, about their favorite kisses. At day's end, the cub makes a list of his favorites, ending

Alyssa Satin Capucilli's sense of fun comes to the fore as a single-cat family expands its feline quota exponentially in **Mrs. McTats and Her Houseful of Cats.** *(Illustration by Joan Rankin.)*

with a good-night kiss. *Booklist* reviewer Connie Fletcher called *What Kind of Kiss?* "a satisfying snuggle of a book," and a *Kirkus Reviews* critic deemed the work "a warm and cozy depiction of the contented bliss of a well-loved child."

Only My Dad and Me describes the outdoor adventures of a young rabbit and his father. According to *School Library Journal* contributor Leslie Barban, "children will delight in discovering what the cozy twosome" have planned.

Furry felines are the subject of Capucilli's popular works *Mrs. McTats and Her Houseful of Cats* and *Little Spotted Cat.* In the former, Mrs. McTats lives happily with her gray cat, Abner, but when two more cats, Basil and Curly, come scratching at her door, she invites them to stay. Surprisingly, more and more cats keep arriving, in alphabetical order, until the house is bursting with twenty-five in all. Mrs. McTats can't help feeling that something is missing, however, until a puppy named Zoom shows up to set things right. The author has created "a picture of cozy domesticity while incorporating a subtle lesson in letters and numbers," observed a *Publishers Weekly* reviewer.

A kitten refuses his mother's call to take a nap in *Little Spotted Cat.* Tangling with yarn and hopping along with a grasshopper prove far more appealing to the little cat, who knows he should obey his mother but just can't stop himself from playing. In the words of *Booklist* critic Jennifer Mattson, young readers of Capucilli's tale will "recognize . . . their own reluctance to miss out on fun."

Biographical and Critical Sources

PERIODICALS

Booklist, January 15, 1995, Stephanie Zvirin, review of *Inside a Barn in the Country,* p. 935; August, 1996, Ilene Cooper, review of *Biscuit,* p. 1910; May 1, 1997, Ilene Cooper, review of *Biscuit Finds a Friend,* p. 1503; November 1, 1998, p. 506; June 1, 1999, Lauren Peterson, review of *Happy Birthday, Biscuit!,* p. 1838; December 15, 2000, Carolyn Phelan, review of *Inside a Zoo in the City: A Rebus Read-along Story,* p. 824; February 15, 2001, Ilene Cooper, review of *Biscuit's Valentine's Day,* p. 1139; September 1, 2001, Susan Dove Lempke, review of *Mrs. McTats and Her Houseful of Cats,* p. 113; November 1, 2001, Hazel Rochman, review of *Biscuit Wants to Play,* pp. 485-486; April 1, 2002, Connie Fletcher, review of *What Kind of Kiss?,* pp. 1331-1332; August, 2002, Ilene Cooper, review of *Biscuit Goes to School,* p. 1969; July, 2003, Stephanie Zvirin, review of *Biscuit's Big Friend,* p. 1899; March 15, 2005, Jennifer Mattson, review of *The Spotted Cat,* p. 1298.

Kirkus Reviews, November 15, 2001, review of *What Kind of Kiss?,* p. 1610; June 15, 2002, review of *Biscuit Goes to School,* p. 877; November 1, 2002, review of *Happy Hanukkah, Biscuit!,* p. 1616; March 15, 2005, review of *The Spotted Cat,* p. 248.

Publishers Weekly, January 3, 1994, p. 82; March 27, 1995, review of *Inside a Barn in the Country,* p. 84; May 28, 2001, review of *Mrs. Mctats and Her Houseful of Cats,* p. 87; September 22, 2003, review of *The Brightest Star,* p. 69.

School Library Journal, November, 1994, pp. 72-73; April, 1995, p. 98; July, 1996, Gale W. Sherman, review of *Biscuit,* p. 57; June, 1997, p. 85; September, 1998, p. 165; October, 1998, Sharon R. Pearce, review of *Bathtime for Biscuit,* p. 87; June, 1999, p. 91; June, 2000, Janie Schomberg, review of *Biscuit's New Trick,* p. 102; September, 2000, Jane Marino, review of *The Potty Book for Girls* and *The Potty Book for Boys,* p. 186; August, 2001, Caroline Ward, review of *Mrs. McTats and Her Houseful of Cats,* p. 144; December, 2001, Karen J. Tannenbaum, review of *What Kind of Kiss?,* pp. 91-92; May, 2002, Shauna Yusko, review of *Bathtime for Biscuit,* p. 7; October, 2002, Ilene Abramson, review of *Happy Hanukkah, Biscuit!,* p. 58; May, 2003, Leslie Barban, review of *Only My Dad and Me,* p. 109; October, 2003, Susan Patron, review of *The Brightest Star,* p. 61.

ONLINE

Alyssa Satin Capucilli Web site, http://www.alyssacapucilli. com (July 15, 2005).

*   *   *

CARLE, Eric 1929-

Personal

Born June 25, 1929, in Syracuse, NY; son of Erich W. (a civil servant) and Johanna (Oelschläger) Carle; married Dorothea Wohlenberg, June, 1954 (divorced, 1964); married Barbara Morrison, June, 1973; children: (first marriage) Cirsten, Rolf. *Education:* Graduated from Akademie der bildenden Künste (Stuttgart, Germany), 1950.

Addresses

Home—P.O. Box 485, Northampton, MA 01060.

Career

U.S. Information Center, Stuttgart, Germany, poster designer, 1950-52; *New York Times,* New York, NY, graphic designer, 1952-56; L. W. Frohlich & Co., New York, NY, art director, 1956-63; freelance writer, illustrator, and designer, 1963—. Guest instructor, Pratt Institute, 1964. *Military service:* U.S. Army, 1952-54.

Member

Authors Guild.

Eric Carle

Awards, Honors

New York Times Ten Best Illustrated Books of the Year selection, 1969, for *The Very Hungry Caterpillar,* and Outstanding Children's Books of the Year selection, 1974, for *My Very First Library;* Deutscher Jugendpreis, for *1, 2, 3 to the Zoo!* and *The Very Hungry Caterpillar,* both 1970, and 1972, for *Do You Want to Be My Friend?;* first prize for picture books, International Children's Book Fair, 1970, for *1, 2, 3 to the Zoo!,* 1972, for *Do You Want to Be My Friend?,* and for *Papa, Please Get the Moon for Me;* Children's Book of the Year awards, Child Study Association, 1977, for *Do You Want to Be My Friend?, The Very Busy Spider,* and *The Very Lonely Firefly;* American Institute of Graphic Arts (AIGA) awards, both 1970, for *Pancakes, Pancakes* and *The Very Hungry Caterpillar;* Grand Prix des Treize selection, 1972, for *The Very Hungry Caterpillar,* and for *Do You Want to Be My Friend?* and *Have You Seen My Cat?,* both 1973; Nakamori Reader's Prize, 1975, for *The Very Hungry Caterpillar;* AIGA certificate of excellence, 1981, for *The Honeybee and the Robber;* silver medal from the city of Milan, Italy, awarded 1989 for *The Very Quiet Cricket;* Heinrich-Wolgast prize, German Education and Science Union, 1996, for *My Apron;* Medallion award, University of Southern Mississippi, 1997; medallion from DeGrumond Collection, University of Southern Mississippi, 1997; best book award, 1997, for *From Head to Toe,* and platinum book award, 1999, for *You Can Make a Collage,* both from Oppenheim Toy Portfolio; Regina Medal, Catholic Library Association, 1999; Outstanding Friend of Children award, Pittsburgh Children's Mu-

seum, 1999; Literary Lights for Children award, Boston Public Library, 2000; Japan Picture Book Awards translation winner, 2000, for *Hello, Red Fox;* Officer's Cross, Order of Merit of the Federal Republic of Germany, 2001; Laura Ingalls Wilder Award, American Library Association, 2003. Also recipient of numerous other awards, including awards from New York Art Directors Show, New York Type Directors Show, Society of Illustrators Show, Best Book Jacket of the Year Show, and Carnegie Award for Excellence in Video for Children. Notable citations, including Child Study Association citation, 1970, for *Pancakes, Pancakes;* American Library Association (ALA) notable book, for *The Very Busy Spider,* and 1971, for *Do You Want to Be My Friend?;* 100 Titles for Reading and Sharing selection, for *The Very Quiet Cricket,* and Gift List selections, 1971, for *Do You Want to Be My Friend?,* and 1972, for *Secret Birthday Message,* all from New York Public Library; ALA notable book, for *The Very Busy Spider,* and 1971, for *Do You Want to Be My Friend?;* Brooklyn Museum of Art citation, 1973, for *The Very Hungry Caterpillar;* Outstanding Science Trade Book for Children designation, for *A House for Hermit Crab;* National Children's Trade Book in the Field of Social Studies designation, 1977, for *The Grouchy Ladybug;* Children's Choices award, Children's Book Council, for *The Very Lonely Firefly,* 1984, for *Brown Bear, Brown Bear* (both with International Reading Association) and 1987, for *Papa, Please Get the Moon for Me;* Parents Choice award, 1986, for *Papa, Please Get the Moon for Me,* and 1988, for *The Mixed-up Chameleon* (paperback); Jane Addams Children's Book Honorary Award, 1987, for *All in a Day; Booklist* Children's Editor's Choice designation, for *Animals, Animals,* and Best Books of the '80s choice, for *The Very Busy Spider,* both 1989; *Parenting* magazine certificate of excellence, 1989, for *Animals, Animals;* California Children's Book and Video award, 1990, for *The Very Quiet Cricket* (picture book category); *Redbook* top ten children's books of the year, 1989, for *Animals, Animals,* and 1990, for *The Very Quiet Cricket; Parents* magazine Best Kid's Books award, 1989, for *Animals, Animals,* and 1995, for *The Very Lonely Firefly;* Buckeye Children's Book Award, Ohio Council of the International Reading Association, 1993, for *The Very Quiet Cricket;* Association of Booksellers Children Bookseller's Choices award, 1995, for *The Very Hungry Caterpillar* board book; David McCord Children's Literature citation, Framingham State College/Nobscot Reading Council of the International Reading Association, 1995; *The Very Lonely Firefly* named a Kansas City Reading Circle selection, 1996; National Parenting Publications award, 1998, for *You Can Make a Collage;* Bank Street College Best Books award, 1998, for *Hello, Red Fox;* numerous titles selected for American Bookseller's Pick of the List. Additional awards for *The Very Busy Spider* include Library of Congress Advisory Committee recommended title; Best Books for Children selection, R. R. Bowker and Co.; Children's Editor's choice, *Booklist; Horn Book* Fanfair title; California Reading Initiative title. *The Very Hungry Caterpillar* named

Book of the Year by the California Reading Initiative, and named among England's best books, 1971. *Papa, Please Get the Moon for Me* was awarded the gold medal during the Bratslavia Biennial of Illustration. Recipient of honorary degrees from College of Our Lady the Elms, Chicopee, MA, and Niagara University, Niagara, NY.

Writings

SELF-ILLUSTRATED

The Say-with-Me ABC Book, Holt (New York, NY), 1967.

1, 2, 3 to the Zoo, World Publishing (Cleveland, OH), 1968.

The Very Hungry Caterpillar, World Publishing (Cleveland, OH), 1969, Philomel (New York, NY), 1996.

Pancakes, Pancakes, Knopf (New York, NY), 1970, Aladdin (New York, NY), 2005.

The Tiny Seed, Crowell (New York, NY), 1970, published as *The Tiny Seed and the Giant Flower,* Nelson (London, England), 1970.

Do You Want to Be My Friend?, Crowell (New York, NY), 1971.

The Secret Birthday Message, Crowell (New York, NY), 1972.

The Very Long Tail (folding book), Crowell (New York, NY), 1972.

The Very Long Train (folding book), Crowell (New York, NY), 1972.

Walter the Baker: An Old Story Retold and Illustrated by Eric Carle, Knopf (New York, NY), 1972.

The Rooster Who Set Out to See the World, F. Watts (New York, NY), 1972, published as *Rooster's Off to See the World,* Picture Book Studio (Natick, MA), 1987.

Have You Seen My Cat?, F. Watts (New York, NY), 1973.

All about Arthur (an Absolutely Absurd Ape), F. Watts (New York, NY), 1974.

My Very First Library, Crowell (New York, NY), 1974.

The Mixed-up Chameleon, Crowell (New York, NY), 1975.

Eric Carle's Storybook: Seven Tales by the Brothers Grimm, F. Watts (New York, NY), 1976.

The Grouchy Ladybug, Crowell (New York, NY), 1977, published as *The Bad-tempered Ladybird,* Hamish Hamilton (London, England), 1977.

(Reteller) *Seven Stories by Hans Christian Andersen,* F. Watts (New York, NY), 1978.

Watch Out! A Giant!, Philomel (New York, NY), 1978.

Twelve Tales from Aesop: Retold and Illustrated, Philomel (New York, NY), 1980.

The Honeybee and the Robber: A Moving Picture Book, Philomel (New York, NY), 1981.

Catch the Ball, Philomel (New York, NY), 1982, Scholastic (New York, NY), 1982.

Let's Paint a Rainbow, Philomel (New York, NY), 1982, Scholastic (New York, NY), 1982.

What's for Lunch?, Philomel (New York, NY), 1982, Scholastic (New York, NY), 1982.

The Very Busy Spider, Philomel (New York, NY), 1985.

All around Us, Picture Book Studio (Natick, MA), 1986.

Papa, Please Get the Moon for Me, Picture Book Studio (Natick, MA), 1986.

A House for Hermit Crab, Picture Book Studio (Natick, MA), 1987.

Eric Carle's Treasury of Classic Stories for Children, Orchard Books (New York, NY), 1988.

Eric Carle's Animals, Animals, edited by Laura Whipple, Philomel (New York, NY), 1989.

The Very Quiet Cricket, Philomel (New York, NY), 1990.

Eric Carle's Dragons, Dragons (also see below), edited by Laura Whipple, Philomel (New York, NY), 1991.

Draw Me a Star, Philomel (New York, NY), 1992.

Today Is Monday, Philomel (New York, NY), 1993.

My Apron: A Story from My Childhood, Philomel (New York, NY), 1994.

The Very Lonely Firefly, Philomel (New York, NY), 1995.

I See a Song, Crowell (New York, NY), 1973, Scholastic (New York, NY), 1996.

Little Cloud, Philomel (New York, NY), 1996.

The Art of Eric Carle, Philomel (New York, NY), 1996.

The Very Special World of Eric Carle, Penguin Putnam (New York, NY), 1996.

From Head to Toe, HarperCollins (New York, NY), 1997.

Flora and the Tiger: Nineteen Very Short Stories from My Life, Philomel (New York, NY), 1997.

Hello, Red Fox, Simon & Schuster (New York, NY), 1998.

You Can Make a Collage, Klutz (Palo Alto, CA), 1998.

The Eric Carle Library, HarperCollins (New York, NY), 1998.

The Very Clumsy Click Beetle, Putnam (New York, NY), 1999.

Does a Kangaroo Have a Mother, Too?, HarperCollins (New York, NY), 2000.

Dream Snow, Putnam (New York, NY), 2000.

"Slowly, Slowly, Slowly," Said the Sloth, Philomel (New York, NY), 2002.

(With Kazuo Iwamura) *Where Are You Going? To See My Friend!,* Orchard Books (New York, NY), 2003.

Mister Seahorse, Philomel (New York, NY), 2004.

Eric Carle's Dragons, Dragons and Other Creatures That Never Were, edited by Laura Whipple, Puffin (New York, NY), 2004.

Ten Little Rubber Ducks, HarperCollins (New York, NY), 2005.

"MY VERY FIRST LIBRARY" SERIES; SELF-ILLUSTRATED

My Very First Book of Colors, Crowell (New York, NY), 1974, Philomel (New York, NY), 2005.

My Very First Book of Numbers, Crowell (New York, NY), 1974.

My Very First Book of Shapes, Crowell (New York, NY), 1974, Philomel (New York, NY), 2005.

My Very First Book of Words, Crowell (New York, NY), 1974.

My Very First Book of Food, Crowell (New York, NY), 1986.

My Very First Book of Growth, Crowell (New York, NY), 1986.

My Very First Book of Heads and Tails, Crowell (New York, NY), 1986.

My Very First Book of Homes, Crowell (New York, NY), 1986.

My Very First Book of Motion, Crowell (New York, NY), 1986.

My Very First Book of Sounds, Crowell (New York, NY), 1986.

My Very First Book of Tools, Crowell (New York, NY), 1986.

My Very First Book of Touch, Crowell (New York, NY), 1986.

ILLUSTRATOR

Sune Engelbrektson, *Gravity at Work and Play,* Holt (New York, NY), 1963.

Sune Engelbrektson, *The Sun Is a Star,* Holt (New York, NY), 1963.

Bill Martin, Jr., *If You Can Count to Ten,* Holt (New York, NY), 1964.

Aesop's Fables for Modern Readers, Pauper Press, 1965.

Louise Bachelder, editor, *Nature Thoughts,* Pauper Press, 1965.

Lila Perl, *Red-Flannel Hash and Shoo-Fly Pie: America's Regional Foods and Festivals,* World Publishers, 1965.

Samm S. Baker, *Indoor and Outdoor Grow-It Book,* Random House, 1966.

Louise Bachelder, editor, *On Friendship,* Pauper Press, 1966.

Bill Martin, Jr., *Brown Bear, Brown Bear, What Do You See?,* Holt (New York, NY), 1967, reprinted, 1992.

Carl H. Voss, *In Search of Meaning: Living Religions of the World,* World Publishers, 1968.

Nora Roberts Wainer, *The Whale in a Jail,* Funk, 1968.

William Knowlton, *The Boastful Fisherman,* Knopf (New York, NY), 1970.

Bill Martin, Jr., *A Ghost Story,* Holt (New York, NY), 1970.

Eleanor O. Heady, *Tales of the Nimipoo from the Land of the Nez Pierce Indians,* World Publishing 1970.

Aileen Fisher, *Feathered Ones and Furry,* Crowell (New York, NY), 1971.

George Mendoza, *The Scarecrow Clock,* Holt (New York, NY), 1971.

Vanishing Animals (posters), F. Watts (New York, NY), 1972.

Aileen Fisher, *Do Bears Have Mothers Too?,* Crowell (New York, NY), 1973, published as *Animals and Their Babies,* Hamish Hamilton (London, England), 1974.

Isaac Bashevis Singer, *Why Noah Chose the Dove,* translated by Elizabeth Shub, Farrar, Straus, 1974.

Norma Green, reteller, *The Hole in the Dike,* Crowell (New York, NY), 1975.

Norton Juster, *Otter Nonsense,* Philomel (New York, NY), 1982.

Hans Baumann, *Chip Has Many Brothers,* Philomel (New York, NY), 1983.

Richard Buckley, *The Foolish Tortoise,* Picture Book Studio (Natick, MA), 1985.

Richard Buckley, *The Greedy Python,* Picture Book Studio (Natick, MA), 1985.

Alice McLerran, *The Mountain That Loved a Bird,* Picture Book Studio (Natick, MA), 1985.

Mitsumasa Anno, *All in a Day,* Dowaya (Tokyo, Japan), 1986.

Arnold Sundgaard, *The Lamb and the Butterfly,* Orchard Books (New York, NY), 1988.

Bill Martin, Jr., *Polar Bear, Polar Bear, What Do You Hear?,* Holt (New York, NY), 1991.

Peter Martins, *Tributes,* Morrow, 1998.

Glassman, Peter, editor, *Oz: The Hundredth Anniversary Celebration,* HarperCollins (New York, NY), 2000.

Bill Martin, Jr., *Panda Bear, Panda Bear, What Do You See?,* Holt (New York, NY), 2003.

Sidelights

Eric Carle "is one of the most beloved illustrators of children's books," according to *Booklist* writer Ilene Cooper. The author/illustrator of over seventy books, most of them bestsellers and many award-winners, Carle has had his work translated into more than thirty languages with sales in the millions. Known as a pioneer of the novelty book, Carle has developed innovative picture books for very young readers which include pages that grow larger as a ladybug meets ever larger animals, which have holes in them bored by a ravenous caterpillar, or which contain computer chips that provide the chirping of a cricket and the flashing lights of a firefly—books which bridge the gap between touchable book and readable toy. As Ethel Heins noted in *Horn Book,* "Almost from the start [Carle] has worked in collage—brilliantly painted tissue paper, cut and layered for nuances in color and texture."

Even as a child, Carle was fascinated by drawing, and he shared his playfully artistic approach to picture books with his earliest published work. His third book, 1969's *The Very Hungry Caterpillar,* is still in print around the world and as popular as ever. Carle blends simple, primary-colored cut-paper art depicting mostly small animals and insects with direct and repetitive text, a winning formula for his legion of very young readers.

"Until I was six years old I lived in Syracuse, New York, where I went to kindergarten. I remember happy days with large sheets of paper, bright colors and wide brushes!" the author once told *Something about the Author* (*SATA*). Just after Carle started first grade, his family moved to Stuttgart, Germany, his father's original home. Carle grew up in Hitler's Germany, a country gearing for war. His strict schooling was counterpoised with encouragement from an art teacher who praised the young boy's drawings. He also quickly made friends and was made to feel secure in the warm circle of a large extended family. When war came in 1939, Carle's world changed. His father was absent from the family for eight years, first in the German army and then in a Soviet prisoner of war camp. Along with other children his age, Carle was a loyal German citizen, following news of the war and each of Hitler's victories. When the fortunes of war began to change, he and his family spent many nights in their local air-raid shelter. Finally he was removed to the country to be safe from the bombing raids.

Even in the midst of war, Carle was able to learn about art. As he explained in his acceptance speech for the 2003 Laura Ingalls Wilder Award, "In high school my art teacher, Herr Krauss, who also believed in my talent, secretly introduced me, an unsophisticated boy of about twelve, to the beauty of abstract, modern, and expressionistic art. This was actually a very risky thing to do during the Nazi years, as Hitler had declared these kinds of art to be 'degenerate.' It was 'verboten'—forbidden—to be practiced by artists and forbidden to be shown. Herr Krauss was a dedicated and courageous teacher. I will always remember him as a shining example of what an educator can be."

With the end of the war, Germany slowly recovered. Carle's father returned to his family in 1947; Carle entered the fine arts academy and was soon designing posters for the American information center in Stuttgart. Finally, in 1952, Carle felt confident enough in his art to take his portfolio and return to the United States. Soon after arriving, however, he was drafted into the U.S. Army and was stationed back in Stuttgart. There he met his first wife. After Carle's discharge the couple moved back to New York; they eventually had two children together, but separated in 1964. During this time, Carle worked as a designer and art director. In 1963 he quit his full-time company job to begin working as a freelance artist. As he related in his *Something about the Author Autobiography Series* (SAAS) essay, "I had come to the conclusion that I didn't want to sit in meetings, write memos, entertain clients, and catch commuter trains. I simply wanted to create pictures."

Carle first became interested in children's literature when he was asked to do illustrations for a book by Bill Martin, Jr. "I found Bill's approach to the world of the preschool and first grade child very stimulating; it reawakened in me struggles of my own childhood," Carle commented to Delores R. Klingberg in *Language Arts*. Remembering his difficult early schooldays in Germany, Carle added that the conflicts from that time "remained hidden until the opportunity and insight presented themselves. Through my work with Bill Martin, an unfinished area of my own growing up had been touched."

"I didn't realize it clearly then, but my life was beginning to move onto its true course," Carle noted in his *SAAS* essay. "The long, dark time of growing up in wartime Germany, the cruelly enforced discipline of my school years there, the dutifully performed work at my jobs in advertising—all these were finally losing their rigid grip on me. The child inside me—who had been so suddenly and sharply uprooted and repressed—was beginning to come joyfully back to life."

"It was then that I met Ann Beneduce (then editor with World), and with her kind help and understanding I created my first two books: *1, 2, 3 to the Zoo* and *The Very*

Hungry Caterpillar," Carle once recalled to *SATA*. "A mixture of negative and positive influences had led to a fruitful expression." Both of Carle's first books contain bold, collage pictures and feature many different animals. The author recalled in a *Books for Keeps* essay that his early years with his father taught him about nature. "We used to go for long walks in the countryside together, and he would peel back tree bark to show me what was underneath it, lift rocks to reveal the insects. As a result, I have an abiding love and affection for small, insignificant animals."

1, 2, 3 to the Zoo was published in 1968 and follows several animals on their train trip to live in a zoo, with a tiny mouse observing each car. The book is full of "superb paintings of animals, bold, lively, handsome, spreading over big double-spread pages," Adele McRae wrote in the *Christian Science Monitor* that "His elephant is all magnificent power, his giraffes a precision of delicacy, his monkeys a tangle of liveliness. This is a book to grow with its owner. The tiny mouse lurking in every picture may remain invisible to the smallest reader and, as the title implies, the book is waiting to teach the art of counting."

Carle's award-winning *The Very Hungry Caterpillar* was published in 1969. "I was just playfully punching holes in a stack of paper," the author told Molly McQuade of *Publishers Weekly*, "and I thought to myself, 'This could've been done by a bookworm.' From that came a caterpillar." *The Very Hungry Caterpillar* "tells the story of a caterpillar's life-cycle, from egg to butterfly," as John A. Cunliffe described it in *Children's Book Review*. The caterpillar "eats through a great many things on the way—one apple on Monday, two pears on Tuesday, and so on, to a list of ten exotic items on Saturday." Cunliffe went on to note "the book's delight, and originality, lie in the way in which these cumulative items are shown. . . . The text is brief and simple, and has a satisfying cumulative effect that neatly matches the pictures, which are large and bold, in brilliant colours and crisp forms set against the white page, mainly achieved by the use of collage."

Not only does *The Very Hungry Caterpillar* contain brightly colored shapes designed to appeal to young children, it also has holes in the pages that match the path of the caterpillar. As Carle explained in *Books for Your Children*, the holes in *The Very Hungry Caterpillar* "are a bridge from toy to book, from plaything, from the touching to understanding. . . . In the very young child the thought travels mightily fast from fingertips to brain. This book has many layers. There is fun, nonsense, colour, surprise. There is learning, but if the child ignores the learning part, let him, it's OK. Someday he'll hit upon it by himself. That is the way we learn." Carle's approach in *The Very Hungry Caterpillar* has proved so popular that the book has sold millions of copies and been translated into over thirty languages.

Do You Want to Be My Friend? is another innovative picture book filled with bright and colorful animals. The only words in the story are the title question "Do you want to be my friend?" spoken by a lonely mouse, and a joyful "yes" from the new friend he finally discovers. Calling it "a perfect picture book for a small child," *Washington Post Book World* contributor Polly Goodwin added that *Do You Want to Be My Friend?* "offers a splendid opportunity for a pre-reader, with a little initial help, to create his own story based on the brilliantly colored, wonderfully expressive pictures." *The Rooster Who Set out to See the World*—later published as *Rooster's Off to See the World*—is another "brilliantly colored picture story that does double duty as a counting book," Lillian N. Gerhardt said in *Library Journal*. The story follows a rooster who decides to travel and see the world. As he travels, he adds friends in twos, threes, fours, and fives. "The sums are presented pictorially in the corners of the page," Marcus Crouch noted in *Junior Bookshelf*, but this does not detract from Carle's "exquisitely drawn coloured pictures. Mr. Carle is still the best of all artists for the very young," Crouch concluded.

Carle introduced another innovation in his 1977 book *The Grouchy Ladybug:* the pages grow in size as larger and larger animals appear on them. The story follows a bad-tempered ladybug as she challenges different creatures, starting with other insects and ending with the whale whose cutout tail slaps her back to her home leaf. While Carle presents such instructive concepts as time and size, "this book is chiefly a pleasure to read and to look at," Caroline Moorhead wrote in the *Times Educational Supplement,* "with its cross and good-natured ladybirds. . .and its deep-toned illustrations of animals."

The Very Busy Spider follows a spider that spends her day spinning a web, which grows larger with each page. Although she is interrupted by a number of farm animals, the spider continues her work until the web is finished and she catches the fly that has been bothering the other animals. Because the web and fly are raised above the page so that they can be felt, the book "is obviously of value to the visually handicapped," as Julia Eccleshare commented in the *Times Literary Supplement.* Denise M. Wilms agreed, writing in *Booklist* "this good-looking picture book has just the ingredients" to become an "instant classic."

More of these "Very" insect books have followed. *The Very Quiet Cricket* tells the tale of a cricket who wants to find someone to talk to. He desperately wants to be able to rub his wings together and make a sound to return the greetings of other insects, and finally, after much labor, he gets his wish. The cricket's sound is reproduced via a battery-aided computer chip on the final page of the book. "Carle has created yet another celebration of nature," declared Starr LaTronica in a *School Library Journal* review of the book. LaTronica further noted, "Typical of Carle's style, the language is simple,

with rhythm, repetition, and alliteration to delight young listeners. Painted collage illustrations are lavish and expressive." A *Books for Keeps* reviewer called the same book "perfect," remarking that "the lyrical text illustrated in Carle's individual and immediately recognisable style, moves to a moment of pure astonishment that touches every young reader."

The Very Lonely Firefly presents another lovable insect in search of love, a firefly that goes out into the night in search of others like itself. In its quest for illuminated buddies, it mistakes headlights, fireworks, even a flashlight for other fireflies before it finally finds its own kind on the final page of the book, with battery-powered twinkling lights. Roger Sutton, writing in *Bulletin of the Center for Children's Books,* noted that "toddlers will appreciate the predictability and rhythm of the text and the bold shapes of the firefly and other figures set against the streaky blue-black sky." Reviewing this supposed final book in the series, Christina Dorr concluded in *School Library Journal,* "This is a compelling accomplishment that will leave readers and listeners alike wishing Carle would turn the quartet into a quintet. A guaranteed winner as a read-aloud or read-alone." In the event Dorr, and thousands of young fans, were rewarded with a fifth entrant in the series in 1999, *The Very Clumsy Click Beetle,* about this peculiar insect which must learn to jump in the air in order to move once it has fallen on its back. Julie Corsaro called the book a "winning addition to Carle's oeuvre," in a *Booklist* review.

Carle has produced another series of books that deal with numbers, letters of the alphabet, tools, and a plethora of other activities and subjects for the very young. The "My Very First Book" series is designed in a "Dutch-door" style, each page split in half with separate illustrations on top and bottom halves so that the young reader can mix and match images. Again, such images are designed from brilliantly vibrant bits of collage tissue paper. Additionally, Carle has also written his own versions of familiar children's works, such as Grimm's fairy tales, Aesop's fables, and Hans Christian Andersen's stories. Reviewing *Eric Carle's Treasury of Classic Stories for Children,* a compilation of his retellings, LaTronica noted in *School Library Journal* "Carle's distinctive style of bright watercolor and collage illustration provides an excellent complement to the lively text."

Poems for young readers—from haiku to Kipling—were adapted for two popular picture books for the young reader, *Eric Carle's Animals, Animals* and *Eric Carle's Dragons, Dragons,* which was later expanded into *Eric Carle's Dragons, Dragons, and Other Creatures that Never Were.* Susan Schuller, reviewing the first named in *School Library Journal,* observed, "Carle's distinctive tissue paper collages bring brilliance and verve to this excellent anthology of poems which conveys the wonder and diversity of the animal world." Betsy Hearne commented in the *Bulletin of the Center for Children's Books* that *Eric Carle's Animals, Animals* provided a "splendid showcase for Carle's dramatic double image." Reviewing *Eric Carle's Dragons, Dragons,* a contributor to *Kirkus Reviews* called it a "well-chosen, gorgeously illustrated collection of poetry."

Carle has also produced many stand-alone titles that both delight and educate very young readers. *Today Is Monday* takes the young reader on a song-journey through the days of the week and the foods eaten every day. "Lovely to look at; delightful to know," concluded Trevor Dickinson in a *Books for Keeps* review. In *Little Cloud,* Carle tells of the "whimsical world of everchanging shapes in the sky," according to Kathy Mitchell in *School Library Journal.* The cloud in mention delights in changing its shape into a lamb or airplane or shark, finally joining the others in one large rain cloud. "Children will enjoy the simple text and the colorful illustrations," Mitchell concluded. Dickinson, reviewing *Little Cloud* in the *School Librarian,* felt that the book was a "delight in its own artistic right," and would "encourage close and interested observation of the wider world."

Carle's 1997 *From Head to Toe* presents animals and multiethnic children demonstrating various body movements. "Keeping both text and graphics to a minimum, Carle proves once again just how effective simplicity can be," wrote a reviewer for *Publishers Weekly.* The same contributor concluded that children will "eagerly clap, stomp, kick and wriggle their way through these pages from start to finish." *Booklist*'s Cooper observed, "Carle's signature strong collages are put to good use in this book about movement." In *Hello, Red Fox,* "Carle asks readers to engage in optical illusions to view his illustrations for a story that becomes an unforgettable lesson in complementary colors," according to a *Kirkus Reviews* critic. After staring at a picture of the fox in green, for ten seconds, the reader then shifts focus to a pure white facing page and the fox appears in red as an after image. A reviewer for *Publishers Weekly* felt that Carle once again proved the old adage that "Less is more" with a "straightforward, repetitive text and minimalist cut-paper art." *Booklist*'s Linda Perkins commented that this "playful starting point for science discussions at home or at school" would be "sure to intrigue children."

Carle has used his childhood in Germany for several other books, including his award-winning *Draw Me a Star,* the autobiographical *My Apron: A Story from My Childhood,* and his only book for older readers, *Flora and Tiger: Nineteen Very Short Stories from My Life.* In *Draw Me a Star,* he harks back to memories of his German grandmother and links it to a dream that parallels the story of Creation. A reviewer for *Books for Keeps* called this a "splendid book for its colour, its richness and its potential for thought vond imagination." *School Library Journal*'s Eve Larkin thought *Draw Me a Star* was an "inspired book in every sense of the word." *My*

Readers discover in **Mister Seahorse** *that a father seahorse's role as nurturer of his young is a task shared by males of other ocean-dwelling species.*

Apron: A Story from My Childhood tells of a young boy whose aunt makes him an apron so that he can help his uncle plaster the chimney. In the original edition of this novelty book, a child-size apron was included for young readers. *Flora and Tiger: Nineteen Very Short Stories from My Life* presents "spare autobiographical vignettes that take place from [Carle's] childhood to the present," according to *Booklist* contributor Hazel Rochman. Jane Claes noted in *School Library Journal* that these "sketches are sometimes moving, sometimes funny, and sometimes uplifting" and are a "super addition to any study of Carle or his work."

Such work continues into the new millennium. With *Does a Kangaroo Have a Mother, Too?,* Carle asks this question about ten other animals, to show that all animals have mothers. The side of the other parent is presented in *Mister Seahorse,* which focuses on fish fathers who take care of their young. The story follows Mister Seahorse as he carries his young through the family's aquatic neighborhood; each time he sees another father fish, he stops to praise the finned parent for the good job he is doing taking care of his young. A *Publishers Weekly* critic noted that with this book, "Carle adds to his rich cache of endearing animal characters while delivering some intriguing information about several underwater species." According to *Booklist* reviewer Julie Cummins, "The vivid, multicolored fish and translucent scenery perfectly evoke the watery backdrop." Many fish appear camouflaged in the book, so that although Mister Seahorse does not notice them on his travels, readers are sure to spot them in the illustrations. While these hidden fish are not part of the story, "they introduce a greater variety of sea life and are sure to be a hit with children," assured Piper L. Nyman, writing in *School Library Journal.*

In *Dream Snow* Carle produced a counting story for the holiday season. Featuring a farmer who dresses like Santa Claus, the story reveals the different animals on the farm, each of which is given a number for a name. Each page has a plastic overlay printed with snow to show snow covering the various animals and aspects of the farm as the farmer gives the animals their presents. Gillian Engberg of *Booklist* noted that the book contains "Carle's signature bright, textured collages." Another of Carle's animal books shows the value of taking your time in *"Slowly, Slowly, Slowly," Said the Sloth.* The book includes a preface by zoologist Jane Goodall and tells the story of a sloth who is mocked by other creatures for taking his time. "Colorful endpapers name

In both collage illustrations and gentle text, Carle illustrates the benefits of a less-hectic existence in **"Slowly, Slowly, Slowly," Said the Sloth.**

all of the animals introduced in Carle's signature collage illustrations," pointed out a reviewer for *Publishers Weekly.* A critic for *Kirkus Reviews* noted, "Despite the fact that hardly anything happens, this depiction of a day in the life of a sloth is never boring," and added that Carle's jungle "teems with life." Mary Elam, writing in *School Library Journal,* noted that "The artwork alone places this book as a treasured addition for all libraries."

In a joint effort with Japanese artist Kazuo Iwamura, the two artists created the bilingual book *Where Are You Going? To See My Friend!* The book reads from left to right in English for the first half of the book, then reads from right to left in transliterated Japanese from the back half of the book. Each half features animals and a child, drawn in each artist's signature style, who are all going to visit a friend, and the characters from both sides of the book meet in the center. Andrea Tarr, writing in *School Library Journal,* called *Where Are You Going? To See My Friend!* "an irresistible, spirited ode to friendship." A contributor to *Kirkus Reviews* considered the work to be "a unique venture between two friends, who happen to be famous artists." Jennifer M. Brabander, writing for *Horn Book,* commented, "Well-designed pages feature lots of white space that attractively showcases both Carle's bold collage art and Iwamura's delicate watercolors." Although the two artists have very different styles, "the artists' work merges without jarring contrast" in the center according to John Peters, writing for *Booklist.* A reviewer for *Christian Century* summed the book up as "a bilingual tour de force about friendship."

Carle and Bill Martin, Jr., teamed up for a third bear book in 2003 with *Panda Bear, Panda Bear, What Do You See?* In *Brown Bear, Brown Bear, What Do You See?*, the text focuses on neighborhood animals in North America, ending with a group of children identifying animals in their back yard. Teachers and parents wrote letters to Holt, the publisher, begging for another book of the same style, and the pair collaborated on *Polar Bear, Polar Bear, What Do You Hear?,* which takes place at a zoo and describes the sounds that various zoo animals make. As of 2004, these two titles combined have sold more than ten million copies and have been translated into thirty languages. Again, another collaboration was requested, and it took time—nearly eleven years—for just the right topic to come up. Laura Godwin, vice president of Holt, explained to Lodge, "no one wanted to do a sequel just to do a sequel. A third book had to be something that stood on its own and had its own voice." Because the first book focused on sight and the second book focused on hearing, it took some time to come up with a third theme. When Martin decided to focus on the movement of animals, the book started to come together. The focus changed from North American animals and zoo animals to endangered species, and the environmental theme carries through to the book's ending, in which a child reports that he sees the animals "all wild and free—that's what I see!" Carle told Lodge that he had to do the illustrations twice. "After completing the first version, I realized that something wasn't right, so I started over." His second set of illustrations feature painted backgrounds for each of the animals, helping young readers to visualize the threatened animals in their natural habitats. Critics praised *Panda Bear, Panda Bear, What Do You See?*; GraceAnne A. DeCandido considered it "a fine read-aloud with a subtle, yet clear, message."

In *Ten Little Rubber Ducks* Carle creates a counting adventure based on a true story of bath toys falling off of a container ship. The ducks of the title are swept overboard, and each ends up in a different part of the world, encountering animals including dolphins, seals, and, for the tenth lucky duck, a family of wild ducks. The tenth duck is adopted into the wild-duck family, although he continues to squeak when his duck family quacks. "This book makes a wonderful read-aloud for storytimes or one-on-one sharing," praised Linda Staskus in *School Library Journal,* concluding, "It's a definite 10." A *Kirkus Reviews* contributor predicted that "Audiences of one or many will enjoy it," while a critic for *Publishers Weekly* noted that when Carle combines his "characteristically jewel-toned collage art with a breezy text," it makes for "a ducky tale indeed."

On November 22, 2002, Carle celebrated picture book art in a new way when the Eric Carle Museum of Picture Book Art opened in Amherst, Massachusetts. Founded in part by Carle and his wife, Barbara Carle, the museum offers exhibisions and programming that encourage inquiry, foster an appreciation for the visual arts, and engage, delight, and inspire children and their families. When asked by Holly J. Morris of *U.S. News and World Report* when he started planning the museum, Carle answered it had taken him about seven years. "I always compare it to a fairy tale," Carle explained; "there's always the number seven in fairy tales. It probably started off as an idle remark, 'Wouldn't it be nice to have a picture book museum?'" Having visited the Japanese museum dedicated to picture book artist Chihiro Iwasaki, Carle modeled much of the Eric Carle Museum after its Japanese predecessor. In its three galleries, the museum has rotated exhibits of the works of picture book artists from around the world, including Maurice Sendak, Margaret Wise Brown, Mitsumasa Anno, William Steig, Beatrix Potter, Chris Van Allsburg, Steven Kellogg, Tomie de Paola, Arthur Rackham, and Leo Lionni. The museum has also featured picture book art completed by middle-school students. Along with the galleries, there are also workshops for both young and old to practice their own picture book art. Speaking to Luann Toth of *School Library Journal,* Carle said, "Our hope is that this museum will be a celebration of creativity, a place for learning and enjoyment, and a salute to picture book art from around the world."

Reviewing *Does a Kangaroo Have a Mother, Too?* in *Booklist,* Tim Arnold noted, "Almost no author/

illustrator over the past thirty years has played a more prominent role in the literary lives of preschoolers than Eric Carle." Arnold further commented, "His large, inviting graphic animals have consistently delighted and taught children during early stages of development. This latest effort is no exception." Whatever their topic, all of Carle's works are educational tools that interest children with their bold, imaginative drawings and whimsical presentations. "We underestimate children," Carle said in a 1982 *Early Years* interview. "They have tremendous capacities for learning." The author/illustrator's belief in the inquisitiveness of the child has not altered over the years. In his Web page, Carle responds to frequently asked questions about himself. Under "hobbies" he notes, "I would have to say my work is my hobby. And my hobby is my work. Even when I'm not working in my studio, I might be thinking about future books. I will probably never retire from creating books."

Carle devotes a multi-layered artistic sensibility to this "hobby." As he explained on his Web site, "I want to show [my readers] that learning is really both fascinating and fun." In his acceptance speech for the 2003 Laura Ingalls Wilder Medal, Carle told listeners, "Not so long ago, a child told me, 'You are a good picture writer.' I think that is a very good description of what I do. I like being a picture writer. Someone else has said that my books are 'literature for the not-yet and just-about-to-be reader.' I like that description, too. Literature!" As Donnarae MacCann and Olga Richard claimed in the *Wilson Library Bulletin,* "Carle is like a half dozen creative people rolled into one." Because of Carle's skill in writing for pre-schoolers, his "innovativeness and artistic discipline," and his ability to turn a book into a toy, the critics concluded, "a child reared on such books will blossom into a confirmed bibliophile."

Biographical and Critical Sources

BOOKS

Children's Literature Review, Volume 10, Gale (Detroit, MI), 1986.

Martin, Bill, Jr., *Panda Bear, Panda Bear, What Do You See?,* Holt (New York, NY), 2003.

Norby, Shirley, and Gregory Ryan, editors, *Famous Children's Authors,* Denison, 1988.

Pendergast, Sara, and Tom Pendergast, editors, *St. James Guide to Children's Writers,* 5th edition, St. James Press (Detroit, MI), 1999.

Silvey, Anita, editor, *Children's Books and Their Creators,* Houghton Mifflin, 1995.

Something about the Author Autobiography Series, Volume 6, Gale (Detroit, MI), 1988.

PERIODICALS

Art Business News, January, 2003, "Eric Carle Museum of Picture Book Art," p. 64.

Booklist, June 1, 1985, Denise M. Wilms, review of *The Very Busy Spider,* p. 1398; September 15, 1996, Ilene Cooper, review of *The Art of Eric Carle,* p. 253; April 15, 1997, Ilene Cooper, review of *From Head to Toe,* p. 1431; December 15, 1997, Hazel Rochman, review of *Flora and Tiger,* p. 692; April, 1998, Linda Perkins, review of *Hello, Red Fox,* p. 1329; October 1, 1999, Julie Corsaro, review of *The Very Clumsy Click Beetle,* p. 360; January 1, 2000, Tim Arnold, review of *Does a Kangaroo Have a Mother, Too?,* p. 930; September 1, 2000, Gillian Engberg, review of *Dream Snow,* p. 130; January 1, 2001, Isabel Schon, review of the Spanish translation of *Polar Bear, Polar Bear, What Do You Hear?* p. 973; January 1, 2003, John Peters, review of *Where Are You Going? To See My Friend!,* p. 894; July, 2003, GraceAnne A. DeCandido, review of *Panda Bear, Panda Bear, What Do You See?* p. 1897; April 1, 2004, Julie Cummins, review of *Mister Seahorse,* p. 1365.

Books for Keeps, May, 1985, Eric Carle, "Authorgraph No. 2: Eric Carle," pp. 14-15; November, 1987, p. 4; May, 1994, Trevor Dickinson, review of *Today Is Monday,* p. 33; March, 1995, p. 25; July, 1995, review of *Draw Me a Star,* p. 6; December, 1996, p. 82; January, 1997, p. 18; March, 1997, p. 7; June, 1997, p. 352; November, 1997, review of *The Very Quiet Cricket,* pp. 5-6; January, 1998, p. 156.

Books for Your Children, Spring, 1978, Eric Carle, "From Hungry Caterpillars to Bad Tempered Ladybirds," p. 7.

Bulletin of the Center for Children's Books, October, 1989, Betsy Hearne, review of *Eric Carle's Animals, Animals,* p. 47; November, 1990, p. 56; July-August, 1995 Roger Sutton, review of *The Very Lonely Firefly,* pp. 379-380.

Children's Book Review, February, 1971, John A. Cunliffe, review of *The Very Hungry Caterpillar,* p. 14.

Christian Century, December 13, 2003, review of *Where Are You Going? To See My Friend!,* p. 25.

Christian Science Monitor, May 1, 1969, Adele McRae, "Crayoned Morality Plays," p. B2.

Early Years, April, 1982, "Eric Carle's Children's Books Are to Touch," p. 23.

Horn Book, March-April, 1997, Ethel Heins, review of *The Art of Eric Carle,* pp. 215-16; May-June, 2003, Jennifer M. Brabander, review of *Where Are You Going? To See My Friend!,* p. 326; July-August, 2003, Eric Carle, "Wilder Medal Acceptance," pp. 421-425.

Junior Bookshelf, October, 1972, Marcus Crouch, review of *The Rooster Who Set Out to See the World,* pp. 301-302; January, 1994, p. 14; June, 1994, p. 93; October, 1995, p. 167.

Kirkus Reviews, July 1, 1989, p. 988; July 15, 1991, review of *Eric Carle's Dragons, Dragons,* p. 940; June 1, 1995, p. 778; August 1, 1996, p. 1159; April 1, 1997, p. 551; February 1, 1998, review of *Hello, Red Fox,* p. 194; August 1, 2002, review of *"Slowly, Slowly, Slowly," Said the Sloth,* p. 1123; March 15, 2003, review of *Where Are You Going? To See My Friend!,* p. 460; April 15, 2004, review of *Mister Seahorse,* p. 391; January 1, 2005, review of *Ten Little Rubber Ducks,* p. 49.

Language Arts, April, 1977, Delores R. Klingberg, "Eric Carle," p. 447.

Library Journal, June 15, 1973, Lillian N. Gerhardt, review of *The Rooster Who Set Out to See the World,* pp. 1992-93.

Los Angeles Times Book Review, April 11, 1999, p. 6.

Magpies, July, 1996, p. 26.

Publishers Weekly, September 29, 1989, Molly McQuade, "Ballyhooing Birthdays: Four Children's Classics and How They Grew," pp. 28-29; February 17, 1997, review of *From Head to Toe,* p. 219; January 26, 1998, review of *Hello, Red Fox,* p. 91; October 18, 1999, p. 86; January 10, 2000, p. 66; September 25, 2000, Elizabeth Devereaux, review of *Dream Snow,* p. 67; June 11, 2001, review of *Hello, Red Fox,* p. 87; July 1, 2002, review of *"Slowly, Slowly, Slowly," Said the Sloth,* p. 77; July 7, 2003, Sally Lodge, "A Bear of a Project for Martin & Carle," pp. 20-21; November 10, 2003, review of *Where Are You Going? To See My Friend!,* p. 35; March 15, 2004, review of *Mister Seahorse,* p. 74; January 24, 2005, review of *10 Little Rubber Ducks,* p. 242.

School Arts, May, 1999, p. 18; April, 2003, Jane Sutley, "Art History à' la Eric Carle," pp. 32-33.

School Librarian, August, 1997, p. 130; November, 1997, Trevor Dickinson, review of *Little Cloud,* p. 184; autumn, 1998, p. 129.

School Library Journal, April, 1988, Starr LaTronica, review of *Eric Carle's Treasury of Classic Stories for Children,* p. 94; November, 1989, Susan Schuller, review of *Eric Carle's Animals, Animals,* p. 101; December, 1990, Star LaTronica, review of *The Very Quiet Cricket,* p. 72; October, 1992, Eve Larkin, review of *Draw Me a Star,* p. 80; November, 1992, p. 133; April, 1993, p. 109; November, 1994, p. 73; February, 1995, p. 126; August, 1995, Christina Dorr, review of *The Very Lonely Firefly,* pp. 120-121; May, 1996, Kathy Mitchell, review of *Little Cloud,* p. 85; December, 1996, p. 46; April, 1997, p. 120; February, 1998, Jane Claes, review of *Flora and Tiger,* p. 113; July, 1998, p. 71; November, 1999, p. 112; October, 2000, review of *Dream Snow,* p. 57; September, 2002, Mary Elam, review of *"Slowly, Slowly, Slowly," Said the Sloth,* p. 181; January, 2003, Luann Toth, "A Museum Grows in Amherst," p. 17; March, 2003, Andrea Tarr, review of *Where Are You Going? To See My Friend!,* p. 216; May, 2004, Piper L. Nyman, review of *Mister Seahorse,* p. 102; January, 2005, Linda Staskus, review of *Ten Little Rubber Ducks,* p. 88.

Times Educational Supplement, February 3, 1978, Caroline Moorhead, "Animal/Animal, Animal/Human," p. 45.

Times Literary Supplement, March 29, 1985, Julia Eccleshare, "Following the Thread," p. 351.

U.S. News and World Report, November 18, 2002, Holly J. Morris, "The Very Busy Artist," p. 14.

Washington Post Book World, May 9, 1971, Polly Goodwin, review of *Do You Want to Be My Friend?,* section II, p. 4.

Wilson Library Bulletin, January, 1989, Donnarae MacCann and Olga Richard, "Picture Books for Children," pp. 90-91.

ONLINE

Eric Carle Museum of Picture Book Art Web site, http://www.picturebookart.org/ (July 31, 2005).
Eric Carle: Picture Writer (video), Searchlight Films, 1993.*
Official Eric Carle Web Site, http://www.eric-carle.com (July 31, 2005).

* * *

CATALANO, Dominic 1956-

Personal

Born January 9, 1956, in Syracuse, NY; son of Dominic (a blue-collar manager) and Virginia Mayer (a blue-collar worker; maiden name, Strong) Catalano; married Virginia Hullings (a doctoral candidate in human development), April 15, 1989; children: Sara Elizabeth, Grant Haskell (stepson). *Education:* State University of New York at Buffalo, B.S., 1978; State University of New York at Oswego, M.A., 1988; Syracuse University, M.F.A., 1991. *Hobbies and other interests:* Reading, camping, canoeing, cooking, woodworking, toy making.

Addresses

Home—106 Terrace Drive, Syracuse, NY 13219. *E-mail*—catalano.15@osu.edu.

Career

Children's book illustrator and author. Cat Graphics Design and Illustration, Syracuse, NY, owner, artist, and creative director, 1978—; art and music teacher for various schools in New York State, 1978-87; *Herald Journal* and *Post Standard* (newspapers), Syracuse, art director and graphic artist, 1982-86; Cazenovia College, Cazenovia, NY, design, drawing, and illustration teacher, 1988—; State College of New York at Oswego, Syracuse, assistant professor of illustration, 1989-91; Onondaga County Board of Cooperative Educational Services, Syracuse, graphic design teacher, 1991-93. *Exhibitions:* Society of Illustrators Original Art Show, 1992; Tyler Gallery of the State University of New York at Oswego; New York State Fair; Everson Museum of Art, Syracuse, NY; and Limestone Gallery, Fayetteville, NY.

Member

National Wildlife Federation, Nature Conservancy.

Awards, Honors

First prize in graphics, New York State Fair; second prize, Everson Museum WCNY Art Invitational.

Writings

SELF-ILLUSTRATED

Wolf Plays Alone, Philomel (New York, NY), 1992.

Dominic Catalano

The Highland Minstrel Players Proudly Present Frog Went a-Courting: A Musical Play in Six Acts, Boyds Mills Press (Honesdale, PA), 1998.
Santa and the Three Bears Boyds Mills Press (Honesdale, PA), 2000.
Mr. Basset Plays Boyds Mills Press (Honesdale, PA), 2003.
Hush!: A Fantasy in Verse, Gingham Dog Press (Columbus, OH), 2004.

ILLUSTRATOR

Arnold Sungaard, *The Bear Who Loved Puccini,* Philomel (New York, NY), 1992.
Nancy W. Carlstrom, *Rise and Shine,* HarperCollins (New York, NY), 1993.
Eric L. Houck, Jr., *Rabbit Surprise,* Crown (New York, NY), 1993.
Roni Schotter, *Monsieur Cochon,* Philomel (New York, NY), 1993.
Roni Schotter, *That Extraordinary Pig of Paris,* Philomel (New York, NY), 1994.
Larry Dane Brimner, *Merry Christmas, Old Armadillo,* Boyds Mills (Honesdale, PA), 1995.
Christine San Jose, *Sleeping Beauty,* Boyds Mills Press (Honesdale, PA), 1997.
Marilyn J. Woody, *Basil Bear Takes a Trip,* Gold 'n' Honey (Sisters, OR), 1998.

Marilyn J. Woody, *Basil Bear Goes to Church,* Multnomah (Sisters, OR), 1998.

Joan Elizabeth Goodman, *Bernard's Nap,* Boyds Mills Press (Honesdale, PA), 1999.

Marilyn J. Woody, *Basil Bear Learns to Tell Time,* Gold 'n' Honey (Sisters, OR), 1999.

Joan Elizabeth Goodman, *Bernard's Bath,* Boyds Mills Press (Honesdale, PA), 2000.

Hazel Hutchins, *The Wide World of Suzie Mallard,* Ducks Unlimited (Memphis, TN), 2000.

Tobi Tobias, *The Ballerina Cat,* Browndeer (San Diego, CA), 2000.

Patricia L. Barnes-Svarney, *A House for Wanda Wood Duck,* Ducks Unlimited (Memphis, TN), 2001.

Joan Elizabeth Goodman, *Bernard Goes to School,* Boyds Mills Press (Honesdale, PA), 2001.

Dandi Daley Mackall, *A Tree for Christmas,* Concordia Publishing House (Saint Louis, MO), 2004.

Miriam Aroner, *Clink, Clank, Clunk,* Boyds Mills Press (Honesdale, PA), 2005.

Sidelights

In addition to writing and illustrating several books for young readers, Dominic Catalano has illustrated more than a dozen children's books for other authors, among them the popular "Bernard" series written by Joan Elizabeth Goodman and the "Basil Bear" series by Marilyn J. Woody. Catalan's picture-book debut was as the illustrator to Arnold Sungaard's *The Bear Who Loved Puccini,* about which a reviewer for *Publishers Weekly* wrote that the artist's "muted pastel illustrations echo the understated wit of this upbeat tale." Catalano's illustrations for *Rabbit Surprise,* by Eric L. Houck, Jr., have also been well received due to their sense of fun; "Youngsters will relish the abundant humor of Catalano's illustrations," maintained a reviewer for *Publishers Weekly.*

Catalano's illustrations for Goodman's "Bernard" books counts among his best-known work. Bernard is a young elephant who happens to have many things in common with young children, such as not being sleepy at nap time in *Bernard's Nap,* the first installment of the series. Catalano's illustrations for *Bernard's Bath* focus on tubby time, and were equally as well received, *Booklist* critic Lauren Peterson describing them as "bursting with all the fun and activity one would expect from a

Based on the traditional song "Hush Little Baby," the humorous **Hush!** *finds a father hooked on telling a nighttime story while his sleepy-eyed daughter just wants quiet.*

A wealthy Basset hound realizes that something is missing from his lackluster life in Catalano's entertaining self-illustrated picture book **Mr. Basset Plays.**

tub full of elephants." A reviewer for *Publishers Weekly* also mentioned that "there's much sly visual enjoyment" within Catalano's work for the series.

Catalano made his debut as an author/illustrator with *Wolf Plays Alone,* a book about a wolf who wants to play his horn one night but keeps getting interrupted. A reviewer for *Publishers Weekly* summed it up as a "sweet, though unexceptional, read-aloud." In his second book, *The Highland Minstrel Players Proudly Present Frog Went a-Courting: A Musical Play in Six Acts,* Catalano sets his stage adaptation of the familiar American folk song in Scotland. A reviewer for *Publishers Weekly* wrote that "A simple arrangement of the song, complete with guitar chords, sounds the closing notes to this buoyant musical." Similarly, *Santa and the Three Bears* presents a variation on the classic Goldilocks tale, with Mama, Papa, and Baby Bear wandering into Santa's workshop. A contributor to *School Library Journal* dubbed the volume useful during the holiday season as "an additional title for storytime."

Mr. Basset Plays is a story about a rich businessdog who learns the value of friendship and play. Leslie Barban, writing for *School Library Journal,* wrote that "Large, bold illustrations fill the pages with color, bringing these well dressed characters to life with personality

and humor," while a *Kirkus* contributor deemed the volume "a good choice for sharing with friends." Catalano has also written the self-illustrated bedtime story *Hush!: A Fantasy in Verse,* about a child waking from a bad dream who is comforted by her father. Kathleen Simonetta summed up the book in *School Library Journal* as "an interesting and fun take on the rhyme."

"As a junior high school student," Catalano once reminisced to *Something about the Author* (SATA), "I 'rediscovered' picture books. The class, a creative writing course, was taught by a man who just sparkled when he read to us. *Where the Wild Things Are* by Maurice Sendak was a motivational read and each of us wrote our own stories à la Max's adventure. I illustrated mine as well. Needless to say I was bitten by the bug."

Catalano divides his life among his three joys: art, music, and teaching. He teaches illustration at Columbus College of Art and Design and lives in nearby Bexley, Ohio with his wife and stepson. "I feel so lucky to be writing and illustrating children's books now," he noted to *SATA.* "This is an exciting time in books, and a very competitive one. I know my most valuable trait will be my persistence. I believe in myself—one has to! I know I have a contribution to make to our children. In some ways I just can't believe it's all happened! If my junior high teacher could see me now."

Biographical and Critical Sources

PERIODICALS

Booklist, February 1, 1996, review of *Bernard's Bath,* p. 938; October 15, 1997, Julie Corsaro, review of *Sleeping Beauty,* p. 410; October 15, 1998, Helen Rosenberg, review of *Frog Went a-Courting,* p. 424; September 1, 2000, Hazel Rocman, review of *Santa and the Three Bears,* p. 131.

Kirkus Reviews, March 15, 2003, review of *Mr. Basset Plays,* p. 461.

Publishers Weekly, June 15, 1992, review of *The Bear Who Loved Puccini,* p. 101; August 31, 1992, review of *Wolf Plays Alone,* p. 79; August 3, 1998, review of *Frog Went a-Courting,* p. 84; January 17, 2000, review of *Bernard's Bath,* p. 58; September 25, 3000, review of *Santa and the Three Bears,* p. 68.

School Library Journal, October, 1998, Jane Marino, review of *Frog Went a-Courting,* p. 122; October, 2000, review of *Santa and the Three Bears,* p. 58; March, 2003, review of *Mr. Basset Plays,* p. 179; January, 2004, review of *Hush!: A Fantasy in Verse,* p. 95.

ONLINE

Dominic Catalano Home Page, http://www.author-illustr-source.com/dominiccatalano (August 15, 2004).*

*   *   *

CAZET, Denys 1938-

Personal

Born March 22, 1938, in Oakland, CA; son of Alex Denys (in finance and banking) and Yvonne (Aye) Cazet; married Carol Hesselschwerdt, August 8, 1958 (divorced), married Donna Maurer, 1982; children: Craig, Robert, Scott, Michelle. *Education:* St. Mary's College, Moraga, CA, B.A., 1960; attended Fresno State College (now California State University, Fresno), 1960-61; San Francisco State College (now San Francisco State University), teaching credential, 1961; attended University of California, Berkeley, 1962; Sonoma State College (now California State College, Sonoma), M.A., 1971; Pacific Union College, librarian credential, 1974.

Addresses

Home—1300 Ink Grade Rd., Pope Valley, CA 94567.

Career

Author and illustrator. Worked as a gardener, writer, mail carrier, warehouse worker, cable line worker, cook, stock clerk, and process server, 1955-60; taught school in Corcoran, CA, and in St. Helena, CA, 1960-75; writer, 1973—; Elementary School, St. Helena, librarian and media specialist, 1975-85; University of California, Davis, extension classes, member of faculty, 1976-78; St. Helena School District Media Centers, St. Helena, director, 1979-81; California College of Arts and Crafts, instructor, 1985-86. Founder of Parhelion & Co. (printers and designers of educational materials), 1972-73.

Awards, Honors

California Young Reader award, 1992, for *Never Spit on Your Shoes.*

Writings

SELF-ILLUSTRATED

Requiem for a Frog, Sonoma State College (Sonoma, CA), 1971.

The Non-Coloring Book: A Drawing Book for Mind Stretching and Fantasy Building, Chandler & Sharp, 1973.

The Duck with Squeaky Feet, Bradbury Press (Scarsdale, NY), 1980.

Mud Baths for Everyone, Bradbury Press (Scarsdale, NY), 1981.

You Make the Angels Cry, Bradbury Press (Scarsdale, NY), 1983.

Lucky Me, Bradbury Press (Scarsdale, NY), 1983.

Big Shoe, Little Shoe, Bradbury Press (Scarsdale, NY), 1984.

Christmas Moon, Bradbury Press (Scarsdale, NY), 1984.

Saturday, Bradbury Press (Scarsdale, NY), 1985.

December 24th, Bradbury Press (New York, NY), 1986.

Frosted Glass, Bradbury Press (New York, NY), 1987.

A Fish in His Pocket, Orchard Books (New York, NY), 1987.

Mother Night, Bradbury Press (New York, NY), 1987.

Sunday, Bradbury Press (New York, NY), 1988.

Great-Uncle Felix, Orchard Books (New York, NY), 1988.

Good Morning, Maxine!, Bradbury Press (New York, NY), 1989.

Daydreams, Orchard Books (New York, NY), 1990.

Never Spit on Your Shoes, Orchard Books (New York, NY), 1990.

I'm Not Sleepy, Orchard Books (New York, NY), 1992.

Are There Any Questions?, Orchard Books (New York, NY), 1992.

Born in the Gravy, Orchard Books (New York, NY), 1993.

Nothing at All!, Orchard Books (New York, NY), 1994.

Dancing, music by Craig Bond, Orchard Books (New York, NY), 1995.

Night Lights: Twenty-four Poems to Sleep On, Orchard Books (New York, NY), 1997.

Minnie and Moo Go to the Moon, Dorling Kindersley (New York, NY), 1998.

Minnie and Moo Go Dancing, Dorling Kindersley (New York, NY), 1998.

Minnie and Moo Go to Paris, Dorling Kindersley (New York, NY), 1999.

Minnie and Moo Save the Earth, Dorling Kindersley (New York, NY), 1999.

Minnie and Moo and the Musk of Zorro, Dorling Kindersley (New York, NY), 2000.

Minnie and Moo and the Thanksgiving Tree, Dorling Kindersley (New York, NY), 2000.

Never Poke a Squid, Orchard Books (New York, NY), 2000.

Minnie and Moo Meet Frankenswine, HarperCollins (New York, NY), 2001.

Minnie and Moo and the Potato from Planet X, Harper-Collins (New York, NY), 2002.

Minnie and Moo: The Night before Christmas, HarperCollins (New York, NY), 2002.

Minnie and Moo: The Night of the Living Bed, HarperCollins (New York, NY), 2003.

Minnie and Moo and the Seven Wonders, Atheneum (New York, NY), 2003.

Minnie and Moo: Will You Be My Valentine?, HarperCollins (New York, NY), 2003.

Elvis the Rooster Almost Goes to Heaven, HarperCollins (New York, NY), 2003.

Elvis the Rooster and the Magic Words, HarperCollins (New York, NY), 2004.

Minnie and Moo: The Attack of the Easter Bunnies, HarperCollins (New York, NY), 2004.

Halloween Pie, Atheneum (New York, NY), 2005.

Minnie and Moo: The Case of the Missing Jelly Donut, HarperCollins (New York, NY), 2005.

The Octopus, HarperCollins (New York, NY), 2005.

The Perfect Pumpkin Pie, Atheneum (New York, NY), 2005.

A Snout for Chocolate, HarperCollins (New York, NY), 2006.

Minnie and Moo, Wanted Dead or Alive, HarperCollins (New York, NY), 2006.

ILLUSTRATOR

Dan Elish, *The Great Squirrel Uprising,* Orchard Books (New York, NY), 1992.

Donna Maurer, *Annie, Bea, and Chi Chi Dolores: A School Day Alphabet,* Orchard Books (New York, NY), 1993.

Leah Komaiko, *Where Can Daniel Be?,* Orchard Books (New York, NY), 1994.

Sidelights

"Every moment in a writer's life exerts some influence on his work," author and illustrator Denys Cazet once commented to *Something about the Author* (SATA). With such whimsical works as *The Duck with Squeaky Feet, A Fish in His Pocket,* and the "Minnie and Moo" series to his credit, Cazet has become well known in the world of children's picture books. A prolific author and illustrator, he has more than thirty-five self-illustrated storybooks to his credit, and he is respected for his ability to give "dignity to a child's need to feel special," according to *School Library Journal* contributor Leda Schubert. Cazet is also noted for creating unique beginning readers; in a review of *The Octopus,* *Horn Book* contributor Betty Carter noted the author's "short, declarative sentences, snappy dialogue," and an "ambitious" and "original story" that features a structure "not usually found in books for the youngest of readers." Also commenting on Cazet's tall tale—narrated by a grandfather who recalls the time a host of sea creatures were swept by a bad storm through the sewers and up out of the bathtub drain—will appeal to young readers due to its "humor, action, and compasion."

Born in Oakland, California, in 1938, Cazet was raised in what he has described as a "traditional 'first American' French family [with] . . . a strange mix of features—European with a touch of American." Each member of his large family was an individualist, which, Cazet recalled, "made for impossible personality situations. . . . They were a lively and noisy cast of characters." The most lively times were those spent around the table, during meals that were followed by card playing and discussions that evolved into arguments ranging from "current political conflicts to how many layers of custard in a proper Napoleon." No sooner had one meal been completed, but the table was being set for another. "Family functions were like participating in a Renaissance fair held in the middle of a Barnum and Bailey freak show," Cazet added. "Everyone had a position to maintain and a point to get across. The intellectuals got theirs across by dismissing everyone else's arguments as so much rubbish, and those less endowed, by not knowing the difference. Stories were told with great gusto, laughter, and animation. Each version became more elaborate than the last. Children walked and talked with adults. They were treated with care, respect, and above all, were listened to. For a child, it was like being at the bottom of the funnel of love."

Some of Cazet's picture books reflect these close relationships between the generations, especially between children and grandparents or other elderly relatives. For example, *December 24th* is a holiday story with a difference, as Grandpa Rabbit's doting grandchildren, Emily and Louise, stump him the day before Christmas by having him guess what holiday it is (it turns out that Grandpa was born on Christmas Eve, so it is also his birthday). Leslie Chamberlin observed in *School Library Journal* that there is "more than enough love to go around in this warm, vibrant and charming family story." In *Great-Uncle Felix,* a young rhino named Sam eagerly awaits the arrival of the dapper Great-Uncle Felix. While Sam worries that his small social blunders will make his uncle think less of him, Felix quickly reassures the youngster that Sam holds a special place in his heart precisely *because* he is who he is. A *Publishers Weekly* critic called *Great-Uncle Felix* "a quiet and satisfying evocation of intergenerational love and mutual respect."

Sunday, with its pen-and-ink drawings and text simplified for more inexperienced readers, recounts Barney's Sundays spent with his grandparents. Grandpa Spaniel-son (yes, the family is a dog family), a war veteran, proudly wears his medals to church; later the group participates in the church pancake breakfast and a game of Bingo. When Grandpa attempts to help fix a neighbor's clothes dryer, chaos ensues before everyone goes home to a quiet dinner and stories. While maintaining that the plot of *Sunday* is subdued, *Booklist* reviewer Denise Wilms added that "there is a strong sense of family warmth" in the story. A *Kirkus Reviews* critic called the book "a friendly look at the comedy in some familiar activities."

If a human baby has a babysitter, then Louie, a young rabbit, has bunnysitters, and in *Big Shoe, Little Shoe,* his most favorite of all bunnysitters are his grandma and grandpa. While the three usually spend relaxing days together playing checkers, this day is different: Grandpa has to make an important delivery at 4:00 and must watch the clock. Louie is not allowed to go but must stay and clean his room; Grandpa tells the disappointed bunny that only those who wear the big shoes are allowed on this trip. Louie, who would rather his grandfather stay at home, hatches on a clever plan—to hide the older man's big shoes so he cannot leave the house either. A *Publishers Weekly* commentator called *Big Shoe, Little Shoe* "a merry story, spiced by fun, colorful art." *School Library Journal* correspondent Diane S. Rogoff found the book "nicely told, without becoming cloying."

In *Frosted Glass,* Cazet uses pencil and watercolor to paint a portrait of a budding artist who is unaware that there is more to talent than being able to draw shapes exactly the same way the teacher does. Young Gregory, a pup struggling through art lessons at school, tries hard to concentrate on his lessons, but his vivid imagination turns flower vases into rocket ships soaring into space. Fortunately, his wise and supportive teacher recognizes the youngster's talent, in a story useful for sparking "a discussion on creativity and imagination," according to *Booklist* reviewer Denise Wilms. A *Publishers Weekly* critic also praised *Frosted Glass,* calling it "an affirmation of friendship and childhood creativity." Writing in *Bulletin of the Center for Children's Books,* Betsy Hearne dubbed the work "insightful and entertaining," and added: "The art keeps the quiet story perking along in perfect harmony with its leading character."

Childhood is full of new experiences, and children are sometimes faced with strange situations that cause anxiety or confusion. Cazet addresses several of these situations in such books as *A Fish in His Pocket, Are There Any Questions?,* and *You Make the Angels Cry.* In *A Fish in His Pocket,* illustrated in brown-toned watercolor and pencil, Russell the bear cub drops his math book into a pond on the way to school; when he fishes it out, he discovers that a small fish became caught within its pages and died. Feeling responsible for the fish's death and confused about what to do, he ponders on it all day, even discussing the matter with his teacher before finally deciding to make a paper boat in which

the ex-fish can fittingly sail into the sunset. David Gale, in an appraisal for *School Library Journal,* praised the volume as "a respectful and amusing book that celebrates the renewal of life," while in the *Bulletin of the Center for Children's Books,* Betsy Hearne commented that Russell's "childlike behavior will strike sympathetic chords" with youngsters concerned about the results of their own mishaps. A *Kirkus Reviews* critic pronounced *A Fish in His Pocket* a "fine exploration of a sensitive subject."

Are There Any Questions? is the title of Cazet's story about school field trips, events that can strike both excitement and terror into young scholars—sometimes simultaneously. In his humorous story, readers meet Arnie, who goes with his class to the local aquarium to see everything from snakes and turtles to piranhas, squid, and alligators. There is a lot of confusion about permission slips, who sits with whom on the bus, and who brought what for lunch, and "children will enjoy recognizing themselves and their friends in Arnie's class," in the opinion of *School Library Journal* contributor Nancy Seiner. "Cazet accurately portrays a primary-grade field trip," noted *Booklist* correspondent Karen Hutt, and his "homey illustrations hilariously fill in details Arnie leaves out," according to a *Kirkus Reviews* critic.

While most of Cazet's books feature animal characters that have been given the mental and physical characteristics of civilized human beings, some of his works also feature actual humans. Readers meet young Alex and his dad in a series of two books, beginning with *I'm Not Sleepy.* The title tells the story: Alex will try any trick to keep from going to sleep, despite his dad's efforts to tire him out with tales of high adventure and daring do, all starring his young son. Both language and illustrations alternate between Alex's realistic bedroom and the dreamlike tropical jungles and mysterious shadows of the storyteller's world. "This is Cazet at his best," hailed Luann Toth in her *School Library Journal* review. "He has taken an age-old theme and given it fresh, humorous enchantment." A *Publishers Weekly* critic predicted that "families will embrace this warm, wry and reassuring celebration of father and son in a familiar ritual."

Alex and his dad appear again in *Dancing,* as the arrival of a new baby breaks the quiet of their evening hours together. Although frustrated at first and afraid that he has lost his father's devotion, Alex is eventually reassured that his dad will always be there for him; a dance in the moonlight cements their strong relationship. "Luminous watercolors," as a *Kirkus Reviews* commentator attested, illustrate a story with a musical score that "works both as a lesson about sibling rivalry and as a lullaby."

The nighttime setting of *I'm Not Sleepy* and *Dancing* is revisited in the poetry collection *Night Lights: Twenty-four Poems to Sleep On* as well as in the lyrical story

Enhanced by splashy watercolor illustrations, Denys Cazet recounts the efforts of two bovine buddies to save a flock of turkeys from an unpleasant fate in **Minnie and Moo and the Thanksgiving Tree.**

Mother Night. School Library Journal contributor Angela J. Reynolds appraised the former as a collection that deserves "a place in the plethora of bedtime books, where it will spice up those sleepy poems and give children a fun place to dream." In *Mother Night* Cazet gently depicts a variety of bedtime rituals, undertaken by bears, foxes, birds, and field mice. As the new day approaches, the animals rise to greet the sun, reminding young listeners that a new day can only be reached after "good nights" are said. "Cazet succeeds best with his impressionistic watercolor renditions of the night sky and nighttime landscapes," wrote *School Library Journal* contributor Ruth K. MacDonald, who described the result as "solemn and elegant."

Cazet's books continue to range in theme from such gentle, reassuring stories to tales comprised of total nonsense, complete with appropriately silly illustrations. In *The Duck with Squeaky Feet,* "especially for the whimsically minded," as Barbara Elleman remarked in *Booklist,* foolishness reigns among the animal kingdom, as a stage-struck duck with new shoes brings down the

house amid a menagerie of other whimsical animals. And in *Nothing at All!,* what *Bulletin of the Center for Children's Books* reviewer Betsy Hearne characterized as "upbeat barnyard buffoonery" follows the announcement, via megaphone, "Cock-a-doodle-dooooo! Good morning to you!," by a farm's resident rooster. Pairs of animals greet the day in a swinging verse story that features animal sounds and provides young readers with "a colorful cast, a lively scarecrow rap, and a surprise ending," according to *Booklist* critic Kathryn Broderick.

A visit to his mother-in-law's house in the Napa Valley inspired a whole new direction in Cazet's work. Driving in the car with his young family, he saw a herd of cows in a pasture. Usually the cows in the herd all faced the same direction, but on this particular occasion, two of them were standing at a remove from the herd, facing in the opposite direction. From that observation Cazet devised Minnie and Moo, a pair of bovine friends whose behavior is unconventional indeed. In a series of easy-to-read chapter books aimed at early independent readers, Cazet has devised all sorts of antics for the pair, from adventures tied to holidays to episodes of travel mix-ups, and even to encounters with space aliens. Throughout all the books, Minnie and Moo preserve their close friendship and often blunder into pranks that save the day.

In *Minnie and Moo and the Thanksgiving Tree,* for instance, the cows take pity on the turkeys in their barnyard and help the feathered gobblers hide in a big tree. This event causes a general panic, as the chickens and pigs fear they may be expected to substitute for the turkeys. Before long, *all* the farm animals are hiding in the tree, just as the farmer's wife fills the table with vegetarian dishes. Of course, the animals start to lose their grip on the branches and find themselves falling onto the table. In her *Booklist* review of the title, Ilene Cooper commented upon the amount of hilarity Cazet is able to stuff into an easy reader, concluding that the book is "a cornucopia of fun."

Other holidays are skewered in *Minnie and Moo: Will You Be My Valentine?* and *Minnie and Moo: The Attack*

When Elvis realized that the sun rises without his morning crow, he falls into a funk that only his faithful friends can cure in **Elvis the Rooster Almost Goes to Heaven.**

of the Easter Bunnies. In the first book, the bovines decide to play Cupid, causing ruffled feathers everywhere when they fail to get their love notes to the proper recipients, while in *The Attack of the Easter Bunnies* they go in search of a replacement egg-hider when their farmer announces that he is too old to play Easter Bunny for his grandchildren's egg hunt. Minnie and Moo save Christmas for their farm family in *Minnie and Moo: The Night before Christmas.* Inspired by the Clement C. Moore poem, the cows create their own sleigh, lumber to the farmhouse roof, and create havoc as they mis-deliver the farmer's holiday gifts. In *Minnie and Moo Go to Paris,* the duo think they are touring the world, when all they are actually doing is visiting the landmarks in their own community. Whatever their pranks, Minnie and Moo are designed to delight not only the beginning reader, but also the adult who may be helping that reader to get started. Cooper, in a *Booklist* review, called the quirky cows "a jaunty duo that . . . elicits giggles at a glance."

Elvis the rooster makes cameo appearances in the "Minnie and Moo" series, but with *Elvis the Rooster Almost Goes to Heaven* and *Elvis the Rooster and the Magic Words* he takes on star status. All set to perform his important job of ushering in the daylight, Elvis chokes on a bug just as the sun peeks over the horizon in the first book. Realizing that day came without his help, Elvis sinks into despair and takes to his bed. It falls to the other residents of the chicken house to restore Elvis's confidence and joy of living. In *Elvis the Rooster and the Magic Words* the rooster's lack of manners cause his fellow chicken-coop dwellers to ignore demands made without a "please" attached. Some reviewers particularly liked Cazet's illustrations of Elvis, whose cockscomb is distinctly rockabilly. A *Publishers Weekly* critic praised the book for "packing plenty of pluck and cluck, and careening from the slapstick to the droll."

In addition to the books he writes himself, Cazet has also contributed illustrations to the works of other authors, including Donna Maurer and Leah Komaiko. While most of the characters in Cazet's illustrations are animals, he admits: "the truth is, they are all based on the wonderful people who influenced my life. They gave me much, and I try not to forget them. By putting them in my books, I hope to make them live forever." Speaking specifically of Minnie and Moo to J. Loudon Bennett in New York's *Rochester Democrat and Chronicle,* Cazet said: "All I want to do is tell a good story about two really close friends, and when I do that I seem to have the ability to pull together what makes for good friendships."

Biographical and Critical Sources

PERIODICALS

Booklist, February 1, 1981, Barbara Elleman, review of *The Duck with the Squeaky Feet,* p. 751; April 15, 1987, Denise Wilms, review of *Frosted Glass,* pp.

1283-1284; April 15, 1988, Denise Wilms, review of *Sunday,* pp. 1426-1428; August, 1992, Karen Hutt, review of *Are There Any Questions?,* pp. 2016-2017; March 1, 1994, Kathryn Broderick, review of *Nothing at All,* p. 1268; September 15, 1995, Lauren Peterson, review of *Dancing,* p. 175; July, 1998, Ilene Cooper, review of *Minnie and Moo Go Dancing,* p. 1891; December 1, 1999, Ilene Cooper, review of *Minnie and Moo Go to Paris,* p. 715; September 1, 2000, Ilene Cooper, review of *Minnie and Moo and the Thanksgiving Tree,* p. 127; January 1, 2003, Ilene Cooper, review of *Minnie and Moo: Will You Be My Valentine?,* p. 904; January 1, 2005, Jennifer Mattson, review of *The Octopus,* p. 868.

Bulletin of the Center for Children's Books, May, 1987, Betsy Hearne, review of *Frosted Glass,* p. 163; January, 1988, Betsy Hearne, review of *A Fish in His Pocket,* p. 84; July-August, 1994, Betsy Hearne, review of *Nothing at All,* pp. 351-352; September, 1998, review of *Minnie and Moo Go Dancing,* p. 10; October, 1999, review of *Minnie and Moo Go to Paris,* p. 715.

Horn Book, September-October, 1998, Martha V. Parravano, review of *Minnie and Moo Go to the Moon,* p. 604; January-February, 2005, Betty Carter, review of *The Octopus,* p. 89.

Kirkus Reviews, July 1, 1987, review of *A Fish in His Pocket,* p. 988; March 1, 1988, review of *Sunday,* p. 360; July 1, 1992, review of *Are There Any Questions?,* p. 847; July 15, 1995, review of *Dancing,* p. 1021; January 1, 2004, review of *The Attack of the Easter Bunnies,* p. 34; April 1, 2004, review of *Elvis the Rooster and the Magic Words,* p. 326.

Publishers Weekly, February 10, 1984, review of *Big Shoe, Little Shoe,* p. 194; March 13, 1987, review of *Frosted Glass,* p. 82; December 25, 1987, review of *Great-Uncle Felix,* p. 73; March 9, 1992, review of *I'm Not Sleepy,* p. 55; March 17, 2003, review of *Elvis the Rooster Almost Goes to Heaven,* p. 77.

Rochester Democratic and Chronicle, June 25, 2003, J. Loudon Bennett, "Minnie and Moo Message Is Secondary."

School Library Journal, August, 1984, Diane S. Rogoff, review of *Big Shoe, Little Shoe,* pp. 57-58; December, 1986, Leslie Chamberlin, review of *December 24th,* p. 82; December, 1987, David Gale, review of *A Fish in His Pocket,* p. 72; March, 1988, Leda Schubert, review of *Great-Uncle Felix,* p. 160; January, 1990, Ruth K. MacDonald, review of *Mother Night,* p. 78; February, 1992, Luann Toth, review of *I'm Not Sleepy,* p. 72; September, 1992, Nancy Seiner, review of *Are There Any Questions?,* p. 200; May, 1997, Angela J. Reynolds, review of *Night Lights: Twenty-four Poems to Sleep On,* p. 99; September, 2000, Holly Belli, review of *Never Poke a Squid,* p. 186; March, 2004, Marilyn Taniguchi, review of *The Attack of the Easter Bunnies,* p. 154; June, 2004, Melinda Piehler, review of *Elvis the Rooster and the Magic Words,* p. 104; September, 2004, Shauna Yusko, review of *Minie and Moo: The Night before Christmas,* p. 78; January, 2005, Laura Scott, review of *The Octopus,* p. 88.

ONLINE

HarperCollins Web site, http://www.harperchildrens.com/ (July 15, 2005), "Denys Cazet."*

* * *

CHISHOLM, P. F.
See FINNEY, Patricia

* * *

CORRIGAN, Eireann 1977-

Personal

Born 1977, in NJ. *Education:* Sarah Lawrence College, B.A.; New York University, M.A.

Addresses

Home—NJ. *Agent*—c/o Author Mail, Scholastic, Inc., 557 Broadway, New York, NY 10012.

Career

Writer.

Writings

You Remind Me of You: A Poetry Memoir, Scholastic (New York, NY), 2002.
Splintering (verse novel), Scholastic (New York, NY), 2004.

Sidelights

New Jersey native Eireann Corrigan began writing poetry as a child, and when her older brother left home to attend high school in Germany, she spent hours writing him verse letters. Her first published work, *You Remind Me of You: A Poetry Memoir,* draws from that childhood habit, and teh book's free-verse ponderings regarding the author's relationship to a friend "swirl . . . with emotion and pain," according to *Kliatt* contributor Rebecca Rabinowitz. Corrigan's young-adult novel *Splintering,* also written in verse, was described by a *Publishers Weekly* critic as "gripping."

In *Splintering,* fifteen-year-old Paulina and her older brother Jeremy are visiting their married sister Mimi when a crazed drug addict breaks into Mimi's apartment and threatens their lives. After the attack the three siblings are left to reflect on the haunting incident, each through a series of poems. In Corrigan's free-verse text each of the characters must deal with the troublesome event in their own way, and the feelings of each indi-

In her 2004 verse novel, Corrigan focuses on a typical American family and the aftershock caused by a random act of violence that reveals hidden fears, acts of courage, and human vulnerability.

vidual tap into deep-seated emotions and bring up unique memories from the past. A *Kirkus Reviews* critic stated that *Splintering* is both "effective and affecting," and the novel's "culminating event brings the strands and family together in a satisfying denouement."

In an interview in *ThisIsPush.com,* Corrigan described what poetry means to her, noting: "Poetry demands a certain kind of emotional honesty. Oftentimes, I'm not even sure how I feel about something until I sit down and try to write about it. I don't mean everyday kind of questions like, 'Is there enough milk in the fridge?' I mean questions about things like regret and resolve, grief, or that whole love thing."

Biographical and Critical Sources

PERIODICALS

Kirkus Reviews, April 1, 2004, review of *Splinter,* p. 327.

Kliatt, September, 2002, Rebecca Rabinowitz, review of *You Remind Me of You: A Poetry Memoir,* p. 32; March, 2004, Claire Rosser, review of *Splintering,* p. 9.

Publishers Weekly, March 4, 2002, review of *You Remind Me of You,* p. 81; April 19, 2004, review of *Splintering,* p. 62.

School Library Journal, August, 2002, Susan Riley, review of *You Remind Me of You,* p. 204; July, 2004, Ginny Gustin, review of *Splintering,* p. 102.

ONLINE

ThisIsPush.com, http://www.thisispush.com/ (July 6, 2005), interview with Corrigan.

*   *   *

CREW, Gary 1947-

Personal

Born September 23, 1947, in Brisbane, Queensland, Australia; son of Eric (a steam engine driver) and Phyllis (a milliner; maiden name, Winch) Crew; married Christine Joy Willis (a teacher), April 4, 1970; children: Rachel, Sarah, Joel. *Education:* Attended Queensland Institute of Technology; University of Queensland, Diploma (civil engineering drafting), 1970, B.A., 1979, M.A., 1984.

Addresses

Home—P.O. Box 440, Maleny, Queensland, 4552, Australia. *Agent*—c/o Author Mail, Lothian Books, 11 Munro St., Port Melbourne, Victoria 3207, Australia.

Career

Writer for children and young adults, 1985—. Mc Donald, Wagner, and Priddle, Brisbane, Queensland, Australia, senior draftsman and drafting consultant, 1962-72; Everton Park State High School, Brisbane, English teacher, 1974-78; Mitchelton State High School, Brisbane, English teacher, 1978-81; Aspley High School, Brisbane, subject master in English, 1982; Albany Creek High School, Brisbane, subject master in English and head of English Department, 1983-88; Queensland University of Technology, creative writing lecturer, 1989—; Thomas Lothian (South Melbourne, Victoria, Australia), editor, 1990—. Lecturer, University of the Sunshine Coast.

Member

Australian Society of Authors, Queensland Writers Centre (chair).

Awards, Honors

Book of the Year Award for Older Readers, Children's Book Council of Australia (CCBA), 1991, for *Strange Objects,* and 1994, for *Angel's Gate;* Alan Marshall Prize for Children's Literature, and New South Wales Premier's Award, both 1991, both for *Strange Objects;*

shortlist, Edgar Allan Poe Award, Mystery Writers of America, 1992, for *Strange Objects,* and 1995, for *Angel's Gate; Lucy's Bay* shortlisted for CCBA picture book of the year, 1993; National Children's Book of the Year citation, 1994, for *Angel's Gate;* Book of the Year Award for Picture Books, CCBA, 1994, for *First Light,* and 1995, for *The Watertower;* Bilby Children's Choice Award, 1995, for *The Watertower;* Ned Kelly Award for Crime Writing, 1996, for *The Well; The Blue Feather* shortlisted for West Australian Premier's Award, 1997; CCBC Notable Book designation, 1997, for *Tagged;* CCBA Picture Book of the Year shortlist, 2000, for *Memorial.*

Writings

FICTION

The Inner Circle, Heinemann Octopus (Melbourne, Victoria, Australia), 1985.

The House of Tomorrow, Heinemann Octopus (Melbourne, Victoria, Australia), 1988.

Strange Objects, Heinemann Octopus (Melbourne, Victoria, Australia), 1990, Simon & Schuster (New York, NY), 1993.

No Such Country: A Book of Antipodean Hours, Heinemann Octopus (Melbourne, Victoria, Australia), 1991, Simon & Schuster (New York, NY), 1994.

Angel's Gate, Heinemann Octopus (Melbourne, Victoria, Australia), 1993, Simon & Schuster (New York, NY), 1995.

Inventing Anthony West, University of Queensland Press, 1994.

(With Michael O'Hara) *The Blue Feather,* Heinemann Octopus (Melbourne, Victoria, Australia), 1997.

Mama's Babies, 1998.

The Force of Evil, Lothian (South Melbourne, Victoria, Australia), 1998.

Gothic Hospital, Lothian (South Melbourne, Victoria, Australia), 2001.

The Diviner's Son, Pan (Sydney, New South Wales, Australia), 2002.

(With Declan Lee) *Automaton,* Lothian (South Melbourne, Victoria, Australia), 2004.

The Plague of Quentaris, Lothian (South Melbourne, Victoria, Australia), 2005.

Me and My Dog, Lothian (South Melbourne, Victoria, Australia), 2005.

The Lace Maker's Daughter, Pan (Sydney, New South Wales, Australia), 2005.

The Mystery of the Eilean Mor (mystery), illustrated by Jeremy Geddes, Lothian (South Melbourne, Victoria, Australia), 2005.

Sam Silverthorne: Quest, Hodder (Sydney, New South Wales, Australia), 2005.

PICTURE BOOKS

Tracks, illustrated by Gregory Rogers, Lothian (South Melbourne, Victoria, Australia), 1992, and Gareth Stevens (New York, NY), 1996.

Lucy's Bay, illustrated by Gregory Rogers, Jam Roll Press, 1993.

The Figures of Julian Ashcroft, illustrated by Hans De-Haas, Jam Roll Press, 1993.

First Light, illustrated by Peter Gouldthorpe, Lothian (South Melbourne, Victoria, Australia), 1993, Gareth Stevens (New York, NY), 1996.

Gulliver in the South Seas, illustrated by John Burge, Lothian (South Melbourne, Victoria, Australia), 1994.

The Watertower, illustrated by Steven Woolman, ERA Publishers (Adelaide, South Australia, Australia), 1994, Crocodile Books (New York, NY), 1998.

The Lost Diamonds of Killicrankie, illustrated by Peter Gouldthorpe, Lothian (South Melbourne, Victoria, Australia), 1995.

Caleb, illustrated by Steven Woolman, ERA Publishers (Adelaide, South Australia, Australia), 1996.

Bright Star, illustrated by Anne Spudvilas, Lothian (South Melbourne, Victoria, Australia), Kane Miller, 1997.

Tagged, illustrated by Steven Woolman, ERA Publishers (Adelaide, South Australia, Australia), 1997.

The Viewer, illustrated by Shaun Tan, Lothian (South Melbourne, Victoria, Australia), 1997.

Troy Thompson's Excellent Poetry Book, illustrated by Craig Smith, Lothian (South Melbourne, Victoria, Australia), 1998.

Memorial, illustrated by Shaun Tan, Lothian (South Melbourne, Victoria, Australia), 1999.

(With Annmarie Scott) *In My Father's Room,* Hodder (Sydney, New South Wales, Australia), 2000.

Beneath the Surface, Hodder (Sydney, New South Wales, Australia), 2004.

The Lantern, illustrated by Bruce Whatley, Hodder (Sydney, New South Wales, Australia), 2005.

The Mystery of Eileen Mor, illustrated by Jeremy Geddes, Lothian (South Melbourne, Victoria, Australia), 2005.

"AFTER DARK" SERIES; FICTION

The Windmill, Franklin Watts (London, England), 1998.

The Fort, Franklin Watts (London, England), 1998.

The Barn, Franklin Watts (London, England), 1999.

The Bent-back Bridge, Franklin Watts (London, England), 1999.

The Well, Franklin Watts (London, England), 1999.

NONFICTION

(With Mark Wilson) *The Castaways of the Charles Eaton,* Lothian (South Melbourne, Victoria, Australia), 2002.

(With Robert Ingpen) *In the Wake of the Mary Celeste,* Lothian (South Melbourne, Victoria, Australia), 2004.

Young Murphy: A Boy's Adventures (picture book biography), illustrated by Mark Wilson, Lothian (South Melbourne, Victoria, Australia), 2005.

Pig on the Titanic: A True Story, illustrated by Bruce Whatley, HarperCollins (New York, NY), 2005.

"EXTINCT" SERIES; NONFICTION; WITH MARK WILSON

I Saw Nothing: The Extinction of the Thylacine, Lothian (South Melbourne, Victoria, Australia), 2003.

I Said Nothing: The Extinction of the Paradise Parrot,
Lothian (South Melbourne, Victoria, Australia), 2003.

I Did Nothing: The Extinction of the Gastric-Brooding
Frog, Lothian (South Melbourne, Victoria, Australia),
2004.

OTHER

Contributor of short stories to anthologies, including
Hair Raising, edited by Penny Matthews, Omnibus,
1992; *The Blue Dress,* edited by Libby Hathorn, Heinemann, 1992; *The Lottery,* edited by Lucy Sussex, Omnibus, 1994; *Family,* edited by Agnes Nieuwenhuizen,
Reed, 1994; *Crossing,* edited by Agnes Nieuwenhuizen
and Tessa Duder, Reed, 1995; *Nightmares in Paradise,*
edited by R. Sheahan, Queensland University Press,
1995; and *Celebrate,* edited by M. Hillel and A. Hanzl,
Viking, 1996. Compiling editor, *Dark House,* Reed,
1995, and *Crew's 13,* ABC Books, 1997. Contributor to
books, including *At Least They're Reading! Proceed-*
ings of the First National Conference of the Children's
Book Council of Australia, Thorpe, 1992; *The Second*
Authors and Illustrators Scrapbook, Omnibus Books,
1992; and *The Phone Book,* Random House, 1995. Contributor to periodicals, including *Age, Australian Au-*
thor, Imago, Magpies, Reading Time, Viewpoint, and
World Literature Written in English.

Adaptations

The story "Sleeping over at Lola's" was adapted as a
radio play by the Australian Broadcasting Corporation.

Sidelights

The novels of Australian writer Gary Crew have received critical acclaim for achieving two qualities that
are difficult to combine; they have been declared intricate and enriching examples of literary writing, and
they are also accessible to young readers. "His novels
epitomize young adult literature in Australia to date,"
wrote Maurice Saxby in *The Proof of the Pudding.*
"They successfully combine popular appeal with intellectual, emotional, psychological and spiritual substance." Crew's books often explore the history of Australia, but he finds that it is his own personal history
that often drives his fiction. "Perhaps more than other
mortals, it is the writer of children's fiction who suffers
most from the desire to return to the past," he wrote in
an essay in *Magpies.* "I know I cannot entirely abandon
my own past. Once I would have longed to; I would
have given anything to at least redress, at best forget,
the forces that shaped me—but, as I grow older, and
more confident in my art, I am not so certain. . . . A
writer who cannot remember must produce lean fare.
And surely, a children's writer who cannot remember is
no writer at all."

Crew's past begins in Brisbane, Australia, where he
was born in 1947. In his *Magpies* essay, Crew recalled
that he "spent most of my childhood with the local kids
racing around the neighbourhood," but there was also a
sadder aspect to the author's early years. Crew began to
suffer from poor health as a youngster, describing himself in a speech published in *Australian Author* as "a
sickly, puny child." As a result, his rambunctious adventures soon gave way to calmer pursuits. "My mother
says that I was a very quiet child, and my earliest
memories suggest that she is right," Crew once told
Something about the Author (SATA). "I was always happiest by myself, reading, drawing, or making models. I
never did like crowds or noise." Crew's illness also
forced him to spend a lot of time in hospitals or con-
fined to the house, but this experience later benefited
his writing in at least two ways. It first allowed him
much time to read. In *Magpies,* Crew recalled that he
and his sister read "anything," and this interest in books
continued into adulthood, providing him with a solid
literary background.

A second benefit of Crew's illness was that it brought
him in closer contact with an influential setting that
would later be featured in one of his books. "A significant period of my childhood had been spent at my great-
grandmother's house in Ipswich, to the west of Brisbane," Crew related in *Australian Author.* "My great-
grandmother was bedridden in this house; my widowed
grandmother cared for her. Because I was always sick,
there seemed to be some logic in packing me off to join
them." Recalling the location in *The Second Authors*
and Illustrators Scrapbook, Crew wrote that "this house
was wonderful, with verandas all around, and a great
big mango tree growing right up against it. We could
climb over the rail and drop onto the branches of the
mango. This house gave me the main idea for my second novel, *The House of Tomorrow.*" In that novel,
Crew writes of Danny, a teenage boy who has difficulty
coping with the increased pressures in his life. Searching for a means to order and understand the world
around him, Danny finds solace in the house that is
modeled on the home in Ipswich. As the author explained it in *Australian Author:* "In *The House of To-*
morrow my great-grandmother's house reestablished a
sense of place and belonging in a young boy's life."

Crew's stays in Ipswich had other benefits, as well.
"My first public attempts at writing were letters sent
from my great-grandmother's house to my parents," he
wrote in *The Second Authors and Illustrators Scrap-*
book, and writing and drawing later became important
elements in his life. "Until I went to high school, I
never seemed to be especially good at anything," Crew
once admitted in SATA, "but at fifteen years old, I realized that I could write and draw—but that was about all
I could do well!"

Despite his desire to continue his studies, Crew's drawing abilities and his family's economic status soon led
him in another direction. "My parents had very little
money, so I left school at sixteen to become a cadet
draftsman, working for a firm of engineers. I hated this,
and at twenty-one I returned to college to matriculate
by studying at night; then I went to university. All this

time I was earning a living as a draftsman, but had decided to be a teacher of English because I loved books so much." Crew soon proved his abilities as a student, and he valued the opportunity to continue his delayed education. "I don't think anyone was ever more comfortable at uni[versity] than I was," he told *Scan* interviewer Niki Kallenberger, "It was most wonderful! I would have done all the assignments on the sheets! It was a feeling of being totally at home and I was a changed person."

It was not until after he became a high school English teacher that Crew began writing fiction, and then only at the urging of his wife. "Christine cut out a piece from the paper advertising a short story contest which I entered virtually as a joke," he told Kallenberger. The story placed in the contest and later won a best short story of the year contest. Crew then turned to novels for young adults and drew inspiration from the students in his English classes. "I guess my first novels came out of my experience as a high school teacher," he once told *SATA*. "I saw so many teenagers who were confused and unhappy—about themselves and the world around them." His first book, *The Inner Circle,* focuses on the relationship between a black teenager named Joe, and a white teen named Tony, who form a bond despite their racial differences. Saxby, analyzing the novel in *The Proof of the Pudding,* found that *The Inner Circle* is "above all, a well-told story incorporating many of the concerns of today's teenagers. The theme of personal and racial reintegration and harmony is inherent in the plot and reinforced through symbolism." The book has enjoyed great popularity in Australia, and English and Canadian editions have also been published. Crew has been pleased by the book's success but believes the work contains several flaws. "I'm not a fool in regard to approaching the book critically myself and I know the book's got phenomenal weaknesses," he told Kallenberger. "But I also see it as being a remarkable publishing oddity because it's so accessible to kids and its use in the classroom continues to astound me."

Crew's enjoyment of academic study—and research in particular—has influenced his fiction-writing process. He is not an author who sits at a desk and waits for inspiration to visit him; instead, Crew actively seeks out information about a subject and collects the materials in a journal. As he told Kallenberger, a typical journal contains "clippings, drawings, scrappy notes I write to myself. I just keep it all in a carton and throw in anything, even books, that's broadly relevant. . . . It all goes in there and if it's a rainy day I'll look at it." Crew has also conducted computer searches to gain information on subjects, and he often employs his artistic skills in preparation for writing a book. "I think that drawing people and places before I write about them prevents me from having writer's block, and allows me to write smoothly without interruptions," he related in *The Second Authors and Illustrators Scrapbook.* "These jottings are quick and rough but they mean a great deal

to me when I come to write the episode they represent; they serve as mental reminders."

Crew's explorations of Australian history began with his third novel, the award winning *Strange Objects.* The novel's hero, Stephen Messenger, is a sixteen year old who discovers a leather-bound journal and other mysterious objects in a cave. The relics are believed to have belonged to two survivors from the *Batavia,* a ship that wrecked off the coast of Australia in 1629. These relics provide Messenger with a direct link to his country's earliest European inhabitants, and they provide Crew with a means of addressing the relationship between the Europeans and the aboriginal peoples who were the original inhabitants of the Australian continent. As is the case in several of Crew's books, *Strange Objects* forces readers to consider some unpleasant aspects of the European conquest of the island and is often critical of the colonists who settled in Australia. Commenting on *Strange Objects* in *Reading Time,* Crew wrote that the book is "intended to challenge the reader to examine what has happened in our past, to reassess what forces shaped this nation—and the effect the white invasion has had on the original inhabitants of this country."

Crew finds that, like many other things, his interest in the past stems from his childhood. In his speech accepting the Book of the Year Award from the Children's Book Council of Australia for *Strange Objects,* Crew explained the influence of his early years. "The origins of *Strange Objects* are founded deep in my memory," he stated in the speech, later published in *Reading Time.* "During the never-ending sunshine of my childhood in the 50's, my parents would regularly take me and my sister Annita to the Queensland Museum. . . . Here we were able to stare goggle-eyed and open-mouthed at mummies stolen-away from the Torres Strait Islands, bamboo headhunters' knives complete with notches from every head taken and other so-called 'cannibal' artifacts. . . . When I had been made wiser by my studies, I began to understand the colonist's fear of the Indigene [or aborigines] as The Other, and to appreciate fully the fantastical and ever-changing phenomenon we call 'history.'"

Crew has further explored the legacy of Australia's past in his novel *No Such Country,* which takes place in the fictional setting of New Canaan and concerns the fate of the White Father, a priest who enjoys great power in the village. Joan Zahnleiter, writing about the book in *Magpies,* noted that "the Father uses his knowledge of a particularly evil event in the past of New Canaan to blackmail superstitious fisherfolk into accepting him as the Messiah who controls their lives with his great book." Zahnleiter also found that "the book has deeply religious concepts embedded in it so that a working knowledge of the Bible enriches the reading of it. However it is a story which works well for the reader without that knowledge."

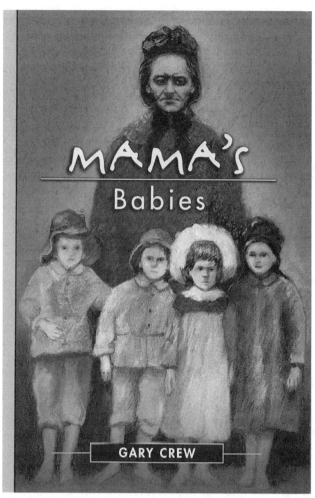

When twelve-year-old Sarah realizes that Mama Pratchett's young charges are dying at an alarming rate, she begins to suspect foul play in Gary Crew's historical novel, based on actual accounts from 1890s Australia. (Cover illustration by Danuta K. Frydrych.)

As the editor of Lothian Books' "After Dark" series as well as the author of some of the titles in the series, Crew is no stranger to terrifying tales of gothic horror. Sometimes these stories come from history, such as *Mama's Babies.* Using actual nineteenth-century cases of women who would take on additional children for cash, only to later "dispose" of these children when they could, Crew tells the story of Sarah, the oldest adoptive child of Mama Pratchett. It seems as though each time a child has a mysterious accident, is hospitalized, or disappears, a new baby is brought into the family. When Sarah is forced to feed one of the younger children "medicine" that seems to make the child worse, she begins to develop suspicions about Mama Pratchett's behavior—but not soon enough to save the child. It is only with the help of her friend Will that Sarah is able to gain the courage to bring her suspicions to the authorities.

"Although the author wisely prepares readers for the horrific events well in advance, this gripping story isn't for the fainthearted," warned Kay Weisman in *Booklist,* adding in her review of *Mama's Babies* that horror lovers will be unable to put the book down. Sarah Applegate, writing for *Kliatt,* noted, "The story is disjointed and disconcerting but also morbidly fascinating to read." Kathryn A. Childs, in *Book Report,* found that the novel "will intrigue young adult readers who enjoy historical fiction as well as a good mystery."

Crews has also penned more traditional gothic horror stories, including *Gothic Hospital.* Narrated by the disturbed Johnny Doolan, a patient at a hospital situated in a dark castle on a mountain run by a mad doctor. Unlike most of the other children, who have lost their parents, Johnny's father is still alive, and Johnny has dreams that his father is being tortured somewhere inside the hospital. According to David Carroll, who reviewed the book for *Tabula-Rasa Online, Gothic Hospital* is "a mature, challenging, and ultimately fascinating work, and very much recommended."

In addition to his novels, Crew has published story books for young children such as *Tracks* and *Lucy's Bay,* both including illustrations by Gregory Rogers. In *Tracks,* a young boy ventures into the strange, nighttime world of the jungle, making many unusual and beautiful discoveries. *Lucy's Bay* concerns a boy, Sam, whose sister drowns while he is taking care of her. Several years later, Sam returns to the scene of the tragedy in an attempt to come to terms with his feelings of sadness and guilt. A *Reading Time* review found *Lucy's Bay* to be "a beautiful piece of descriptive writing which places in perspective Sam's grief for his sister against the ceaseless rhythm of nature."

Crew is a consummate explorer who keeps a journal of ideas and "artifacts" to remind him of experiences and thoughts. He has drawn upon personal experiences, as well as fantasies born from reality to write children's stories. Some ideas, such as the fishing trip in *First Light,* come from his own life. Others, including the story presented in *The Watertower,* may have begun by remembering a childhood prank, and grew as the imagination took hold. The plot begins in a small town where two boys sneak a swim in an old watertower on a hot summer day. When one boy's pants blow away, the other leaves to get another pair. When he returns, his friend has a crazed, vacant stare and a strange new marking on his hand. Crew teamed up with illustrator Steve Woolman to enhance the mystery visually, making it "a genuinely eerie picture book, which is constructed as a kind of puzzle," according to a *Kirkus Reviews* critic. *School Library Journal* reviewer Patricia Lothrop-Green called *The Watertower* a "Twilight Zone-type picture book for older children . . . in which text and illustrations work inseparably to create a strange but compelling whole."

Crew also builds themes around ideas from criminology, science, and history as in *The Lost Diamonds of Killiecrankie.* Sometimes contemporary themes are woven into historically based fiction. *Bright Star* takes place in rural Australia in 1871. A school girl becomes frustrated because she does not have the same freedom as boys to choose what she studies. She dreams of learning astronomy rather than needlepoint, the curriculum usually offered to girls. An encounter with astronomer John Tebbutt, who lived in New South Wales and discovered "the Great Comet of 1861," along with her mother's support, helps her realize that she must choose her own destiny. Even though *Booklist* reviewer Carolyn Phelan found the girl's "longing for freedom romanticized," she added that "the differences between the treatment of girls and boys in the 1800s are clearly set out, and picture books dealing with the history of astronomy are few."

Troy Thompson's Excellent Poetry Book features the poetry of fictional student Troy Thompson, a sixth grader competing in a poetry contest for his teacher, Ms. Kranke. Thompson's poetry covers silly topics, including gym locker rooms and talk show hosts, as well as serious issues, including the death of his father. The forms of poetry included in the book range from haiku to ballads to limericks, and the layout is designed to look like a student's notebook, as all of the poems are either handwritten, or typed and appear to be pasted into the notebook. "The title is complete with silliness and serious topics," noted Shawn Brommer, reviewing the title for *School Library Journal.*

Crew has worked with artist Shaun Tan to produce two surreal tales, one about a dystopian future and the other about the nature of memory. In *The Viewer* Tristan discovers a strange box that contains a mask-like device which reveals visions of the past, including evil acts committed by humankind. Tristan watches scenes of war, torture, and slavery on his first day with the viewer, and when he returns to look through it on the second day, he finds that the pictures have changed into depictions of horrible possibilities for the future. On the third day when his mother goes to wake him for school, Tristan has disappeared, and the mysterious box is locked on his desk. Donna Ratterree called *The Viewer* an "eerie and disturbing story, while a critic for *Publishers Weekly* noted, "The audience can almost feel the power that the mask exudes in this unsettling walk through history."

Tan and Crew's second collaboration, *Memorial,* tells the story of a young boy who wants to save a living memorial, an overgrown tree that was planted the day that his great-grandfather came home from World War I. Though the boy loses his battle to stop the tree from being cut down, his great-grandfather teaches him that the important part to carry with him is the memory, and that by fighting against the city council, his acts—and the tree he was unable to save—will also be remembered. "Crew's words are simple and powerful and will resonate with both young and older readers," appraised Joanne de Groot in *Resource Links,* while Ellen Fader, writing for *School Library Journal,* considered the book "undeniably a powerful package."

The story of the U.S.S. *Titanic* provided the plot for Crew's 2005 picture book *Pig on the Titanic: A True Story.* Edith Rosenbaum, a passenger on the *Titanic*'s ill-fated voyage, had a wonderful mechanical pig that played music. When Rosenbaum tried to give up her seat on a life boat, a member of the ship's crew mistook the pig she clutched in her arms for a baby, and forced the woman onto the boat. Told from the perspective of the marvelous machine, Maxine the musical pig, the book expresses her delight at being able to keep up the spirits of the children sharing the life boat with Rosenbaum. "Crew deftly captures the drama of that night," proclaimed Grace Oliff in her *School Library Journal* review. A critic for *Kirkus Reviews* commented that the book "lends the historical catastrophe immediacy . . . while downplaying its horrific aspects." A *Publishers Weekly* reviewer noted, "families and classrooms familiar with the *Titanic*'s story will be thrilled to find a book that tells the tale from a childlike perspective."

Set in a small Australian town, **The Watertower** *focuses on a malevolent presence that invades the local citizenry and threatens the friendship of Steve and Bubba. (Illustration by Steven Woolman.)*

Crew believes that his personal experiences continue to play a large role in his books. "As a writer, I am not done with looking inward," he explained in *Australian Author.* "There is much for me still to find in my house of fiction; in those fantastical inner rooms of childhood from which, I imagine, some choose never to emerge." In each book he writes, he has definite aims regarding his young audience. "My main objective in writing is to open the minds of my readers," Crew once explained to

Crew brings to light a true story about a musical pig named Maxine who helped calm a boatload of young refugees from a sinking ocean liner in **Pig on the Titanic.** *(Illustration by Bruce Whatley.)*

SATA, "to say 'the world can be a wonderful place—its possibilities are open to you and your imagination.'"

Biographical and Critical Sources

BOOKS

At Least They're Reading! Proceedings of the First National Conference of The Children's Book Council of Australia, 1992, Thorpe, 1992.

McKenna, Bernard, and Sharyn Peare, *Strange Journeys: The Works of Gary Crew,* Hodder, 1998.

Saxby, Maurice, *The Proof of the Pudding,* Ashton, 1993.

The Second Authors and Illustrators Scrapbook, Omnibus Books (London, England), 1992.

PERIODICALS

Australian Author, autumn, 1992, Gary Crew, "The Architecture of Memory," pp. 24-27.

Booklist, June 1, 1993, p. 1812; May 1, 1994, p. 1594; October 1, 1995, p. 303; August, 2002, Kay Weisman, review of *Mama's Babies,* p. 1948.

Book Report, November-December, 2002, Kathryn A. Childs, review of *Mama's Babies,* p. 45.

Horn Book, September-October, 1994, p. 596; March-April, 1996, p. 205; May, 1998, p. 330.

Kirkus Reviews, June 15, 1994, p. 842; August 15, 1995, p. 1186; January 1, 1998, review of *The Watertower,* p. 55; April 1, 2002, review of *Mama's Babies,* p. 489; March 1, 2005, review of *Pig on the Titanic: A True Story,* p. 285.

Kliatt, September, 2002, Sarah Applegate, review of *Mama's Babies,* p. 16.

Magpies, May, 1991, p. 22; July, 1991, p. 37; September, 1991, Joan Zahnleiter, "Know the Author: Gary Crew," pp. 17-19; March, 1992, p. 34; July, 1992, Gary Crew, "New Directions in Fiction," pp. 5-8; March, 1996, p. 12; October 15, 1997, Carolyn Phelan, review of *Bright Star,* p. 412; November, 1997, p. 21; May, 1998, p. 37; May, 2005, review of *The Plague of Quentaris,* p. 36.

Papers: Explorations in Children's Literature, August, 1990, pp. 51-58; April, 1992, pp. 18-26.

Reading Time, Volume 35, number 3, 1991, Gary Crew, essay on *Strange Objects,* pp. 11-12; Volume 35, number 4, 1991, Gary Crew, "Awards: The Children's Book Council of Australia Awards 1991 Acceptance Speeches," pp. 4-5; May, 1992, review of *Lucy's Bay,* p. 20.

Resource Links, October, 2004, Joanne de Groot, review of *Memorial,* p. 3.

Scan, November, 1990, Niki Kallenberger, interview with Crew, pp. 9-11.

School Librarian, spring, 2005, Joan Hamilton Jones, review of *I Did Nothing: The Extinction of the Gastric-Brooding Frog,* p. 44.

School Library Journal, May, 1993, p. 124; July, 1994, p. 116; October, 1995, p. 152; February, 1998, p. 79; March, 1998, Patricia Lothrop-Green, review of *The Watertower,* p. 168; June, 2002, Mary R. Hofmann, review of *Mama's Babies,* p. 136; January, 2004, Shawn Brommer, review of *Troy Thompson's Excellent Poetry Book,* p. 128; March, 2004, Donna Ratterree, review of *The Viewer,* p. 204; December, 2004, Ellen Fader, review of *Memorial,* p. 144; May, 2005, Grace Oliff, review of *Pig on the Titanic,* p. 80.

Voice of Youth Advocates, August 1993, p. 162; April, 1994, p. 19; April, 1996, p. 25.

ONLINE

Tabula-Rasa Online, http://www.tabula-rasa.info/ (July 31, 2005), David Carroll, review of *Gothic Hospital.*

*　　　*　　　*

CROWTHER, Robert 1948-

Personal

Born May 25, 1948, in Leeds, England; son of Jack (a "commercial traveler") and Lavinia (Nutter) Crowther; married; wife's name Jill, August 22, 1970 (divorced, 1984); married Nancy Kellogg, July 15, 2000; children: Victoria Dobbin, Kate McMahon. *Education:* Norwich

School of Art, diploma in art and design, 1970; Royal College of Art, M.A., 1973. *Politics:* "Liberal Democrat." *Religion:* Church of England (Anglican). *Hobbies and other interests:* Fine art, reading, cycling, following soccer.

Addresses
Home and office—Alphabet Cottage, 38 Station Rd., Great Massingham, King's Lynn PE32 2HW, England. *E-mail*—crowtherpopsup@tiscali.co.uk.

Career
Freelance designer, 1973-87, including work with Madame Tussaud's Group, London, England. Part-time teacher at Oxford Polytechnic, Leicester Polytechnic, Exeter College of Art, and Norwich School of Art. Freelance author and illustrator.

Member
Federation of Children's Book Groups, British Society of Authors.

Awards, Honors
Runner-up for Mother Goose Award for best newcomer to children's illustration, 1978; runner up for *Parents* magazine award for best novelty book, 1997; honorable mention at Bologna-Ragazzi Awards, 2000, for *Deep down under Ground.*

Writings

SELF-ILLUSTRATED

The Most Amazing Hide-and-Seek Alphabet Book, Viking Kestrel (London, England), 1978.
The Most Amazing Hide-and-Seek Counting Book, Viking Kestrel (London, England), 1981.
Pop Goes the Weasel, Walker Books (London, England), 1987.
Pop-up Machines, Walker Books (London, England), 1988.
Who Lives on the Farm?, Walker Books (London, England), 1989.
How Many Babies Live on the Farm?, Walker Books (London, England), 1990.
All the Fun of the Fair, Walker Books (London, England), 1991.
Who Lives in the Garden?, Candlewick Press (Cambridge, MA), 1992.
Who Lives in the Country?, Candlewick Press (Cambridge, MA), 1992.
Little Red Car, Candlewick Press (Cambridge, MA), 1992.
A Night to Remember, Candlewick Press (Cambridge, MA), 1992.
Animal Rap!, Candlewick Press (Cambridge, MA), 1993.
Animal Snap!, Candlewick Press (Cambridge, MA), 1993.

Little Red Car to the Rescue, Candlewick Press (Cambridge, MA), 1994.
Robert Crowther's Pop-up Animal Alphabet, Candlewick Press (Cambridge, MA), 1994.
The Most Amazing Night Book, Penguin Books (New York, NY), 1995.
Robert Crowther's Pop-up Olympics: Amazing Facts and Record Breakers, Walker (London, England), 1995.
Tractors and Trucks, Candlewick Press (Cambridge, MA), 1996.
Dump Trucks and Diggers, Candlewick Press (Cambridge, MA), 1996.
My Oxford Pop-up Surprise ABC, Oxford University Press (New York, NY), 1996.
My Oxford Pop-up Surprise One Two Three, Oxford University Press (New York, NY), 1996.
Deep down under Ground, Candlewick Press (Cambridge, MA), 1998.
Robert Crowther's Most Amazing Hide-and-Seek Alphabet Book, Candlewick Press (Cambridge, MA), 1999.
Robert Crowther's Most Amazing Hide-and-Seek Numbers Book, Candlewick Press (Cambridge, MA), 1999.
Robert Crowther's Amazing Pop-up House of Inventions: Hundreds of Fabulous Facts about Where You Live, Candlewick Press (Cambridge, MA), 2000.
Football!, Walker (London, England), 2001, published as *Soccer: Facts and Stats; The World Cup and Superstars and Games with Pop-Ups,* Candlewick Press (Cambridge, MA), 2001.
Colors, Candlewick Press (Cambridge, MA), 2001.
Shapes, Candlewick Press (Cambridge, MA), 2002.
Let's Cook!, Candlewick Press (Cambridge, MA), 2004.
Opposites, Candlewick Press (Cambridge, MA), 2005.

Sidelights
Highly praised paper engineer and author Robert Crowther has enjoyed drawing ever since he was taught by his father how to trace the Three Little Pigs. Among his many works are a series of intriguing pop-up books that includes *Pop-up Olympics: Amazing Facts and Record Breakers* and *Incredible Animal Alphabet.*

Crowther's work in *Pop-up Olympics* was lauded by a *Publishers Weekly* critic who commented that "Crowther rustles up an impressive number of Olympics-related facts and figures"; his text and illustrations reflect "genuine enthusiasm," the critic added, "and he aims high, squeezing in as much trivia and activity as will fit on a page." In a review of *Incredible Animal Alphabet,* another of Crowther's engineered pop-up books, another *Publishers Weekly* critic stated that ""P" should stand for playful in this clever compendium of concealed critters. . . . In a crowded field, this book definitely jumps out."

"My primary motivation is to make books that will encourage reluctant readers," Crowther once commented. "At art college, the work of Seymour Chwast influenced the way my style developed. These days, talking to the children I meet in schools and libraries influences the sort of subjects I choose to make as pop-up books.

"The creative process behind a pop-up book involves, first, coming up with a suitable theme. Then I make individual black-and-white working 'roughs' of mechanics suitable for the book. The best of these ideas are then designed into a rough dummy of the complete book, colored with felt-tip pens. After the rough is approved by the publisher, I do the art work in black line and watercolor. The mechanical pieces (usually about one hundred separate bits) are painted separately from the backgrounds.

"Mostly the subjects I've chosen have been colorful and packed with action. For example, I've used fairgrounds, building sites, and the Olympics. Otherwise I've chosen educational themes, such as alphabets or numbers."

Discussing his art, Crowther more recently noted to *Something about the Author:* "I'm attempting to alter my style of illustration in order to give my upcoming titles a different visual look. Instead of using a black outline for the drawings and coloring in with watercolor, I am now using cut paper in a precise way. I have just finished illustrating a pop-up train book which contains 9,500 separate pieces of cut paper. These pieces are cut from pre-painted sheets of watercolor.

"After twenty-five years spent illustrating pop-up and flap books I feel it is time to try something fresh. My recent book *Let's Cook,* published in 2004, uses photographs rather than drawings to give a super-real feel to the images."

Biographical and Critical Sources

PERIODICALS

Booklist, December 1, 2000, Ilene Cooper, review of *Amazing Pop-up House of Inventions,* p. 728.

Publishers Weekly, May 11, 1992, review of *All the Fun of the Fair: A Pop-Up Book,* p. 72; September 20, 1993, review of *Animal Snap!,* p. 70; September 20, 1993, review of *Animal Rap!,* p. 70; May 20, 1995, review of *Incredible Animal Alphabet,* p. 59; August 7, 1995, review of *The Most Amazing Night Book,* p. 459; April 1, 1996, review of *Pop-up Olympics: Amazing Facts and Record Breakers,* p. 77; August 16, 1999, "Up with Pop-ups," p. 87; October 30, 2000, review of *The Scientific Method,* p. 78; January 10, 2005, review of *Snow Day Fun,* p. 58.

School Library Journal, July, 2001, Joy Fleishhacker, review of *Colors,* p. 93; March, 2004, Andrew Medlar, review of *Pop-up Olympics,* p. 68.

ONLINE

Walker Books Web site, http://www.walkerbooks.co.uk/ (August 15, 2005), "Robert Crowther."

D

DANTZ, William R.
See PHILBRICK, (W.) Rodman

*   *   *

DICAMILLO, Kate 1964-

Personal
Born March 25, 1964, in Merion, PA; daughter of Adolph Louis (an orthodontist) and Betty Lee (a teacher; maiden name, Gouff) DiCamillo. *Education:* University of Florida, B.A., 1987.

Addresses
Home—2403 West 42nd St., No. 3, Minneapolis, MN 55410.

Career
Writer. Bookman (book distributor), St. Louis Park, MN, former bookstore clerk.

Awards, Honors
McKnight artist fellowship for writers, 1998; Newbery Honor Book award, and Hedgie Award, Hedgehogbooks.com, both 2000, and Dorothy Canfield Fisher Children's Book Award, 2002, all for *Because of Winn-Dixie;* finalist, National Book Award, for *Tiger Rising*; Newbery Medal, 2003, for *The Tale of Despereaux.*

Writings

Because of Winn-Dixie, Candlewick Press (Cambridge, MA), 2000.
The Tiger Rising, Candlewick Press (Cambridge, MA), 2001.
The Tale of Despereaux: Being the Story of a Mouse, a Princess, Some Soup, and a Spool of Thread, illustrated by Timothy Basil Ering, Candlewick Press (Cambridge, MA), 2003.

Kate DiCamillo

Mercy Watson to the Rescue, illustrated by Chris van Dusen, Candlewick Press (Cambridge, MA), 2005.
Mercy Watson Goes for a Ride, illustrated by Chris van Dusen, Candlewick Press (Cambridge, MA), 2006.
The Mysterious Journey of Edward Tulane, illustrated by Bagram Ibatoulline, Candlewick Press (Cambridge, MA), 2006.

Contributor of short fiction to periodicals, including *Jack and Jill, Alaska Quarterly Review, Greensboro Review, Nebraska Review,* and *Spider.*

Adaptations

Several of author's books have been adapted as audio books; *Because of Winn-Dixie* was adapted for film, 2005.

Sidelights

Kate DiCamillo is "short. And loud," as she admitted on her Web site. Though she had trained to become an author throughout her education, prior to 2000 she had only published a few adult short stories in magazines. She worked in Minneapolis for The Bookman, a book distributor, in the children's department. It was during this time in Minneapolis, while she was missing the warm weather of Florida where she had spent much of her life, that DiCamillo began her first novel. Jennifer M. Brown, who interviewed the author for *Publishers Weekly,* reported, "This is what happened: she was just about to go to sleep when the book's narrator, India Opal Buloni, spoke to her, saying, 'I have a dog named Winn-Dixie.' DiCamillo says that after hearing that voice, 'the story told itself.'" From that moment, DiCamillo never stopped listening, and from India Opal Buloni in *Because of Winn-Dixie* to the mouse Despereaux in *The Tale of Despereaux,* each of her narrators has given voice to a new story, different from the last. *Because of Winn-Dixie* was named a Newbery Honor Book after its publication, and three years later, *The Tale of Despereaux* was awarded with the prestigious Newbery Medal.

Because of Winn-Dixie is the tale of a girl and her dog— only the dog in this case is Winn-Dixie, a stray mutt, a smelly, ugly dog who seems to have plenty of love to give. India Opal is in need of some of that love; she and her father just moved to Naomi, Florida, after her mother died, and she has been having trouble fitting in. "Rarely does salvation come in the form of a creature with as much personality as Winn-Dixie," wrote a *Horn Book* reviewer. Somehow, Winn-Dixie manages to open doors in her life that she had not even seen. "Readers will connect with India's love for her pet and her open-minded, free-spirited efforts to make friends and build a community," assured Gillian Engberg in her *Booklist* review. Helen Foster James, writing for *School Library Journal,* asked if libraries really need another girl-and-her-dog book, then answered her own question: "Absolutely, if the protagonist is as spirited and endearing as Opal and the dog as loveable and charming as Winn-Dixie." A critic for *Publishers Weekly* noted that DiCamillo's "bittersweet tale of contemporary life in a Southern town will hold readers rapt," while Kathleen Odean wrote in *Book* that *Because of Winn-Dixie* is "a short, heartfelt book."

It took DiCamillo some time to get *Because of Winn-Dixie* to a publisher. She continued to work at The Bookman until she ran into a sales rep for Candlewick Press. "I told her, 'I love everything that Candlewick does, but I can't get in the door because I don't have an agent, and I've never been published, and they won't

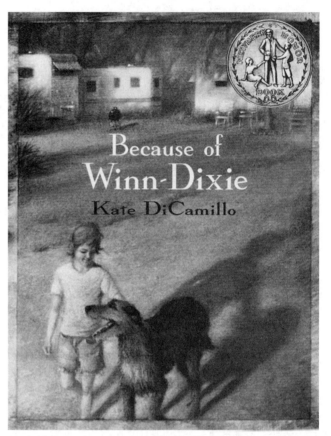

The love of a scruffy dog helps a shy ten-year-old girl gain the self-confidence to question her world and assert her rightful place in it. (Cover illustration by Chris Sheban.)

look at unsolicited manuscripts,'" DiCamillo explained to Kathleen T. Horning in an interview for *School Library Journal.* The sales rep responded, "If you give me a manuscript, I'll get it to an editor." From there, it wasn't long until DiCamillo became a published children's author. "So that's how it happened," she explained, "great good fortune."

DiCamillo's second novel, *The Tiger Rising,* is aimed at a young-adult audience, but contains a similar setting to *Because of Winn-Dixie.* Rob and his father move to a small town in Florida, and Rob cannot figure out how to fit in. Rob has been dealing with pain for a long time, however, and he is good at keeping his emotions to himself. He manages to get a job with his father's boss, Beauchamp, the boy taking care of a caged wild tiger Beauchamp keeps at an abandoned gas station. Ultimately, Rob meets Sistine, another new kid at school who is as openly angry at the world as Rob is secretive about his feelings, and things begin to change in Rob's life. Rob and Sistine come to believe they must free the tiger in order to liberate themselves.

The Tiger Rising "has a certain mythic quality" according to a reviewer in *Horn Book.* A critic for *Publishers Weekly* noted that, with her second novel, "DiCamillo demonstrates her versatility by treating themes similar to those of her first novel with a completely different approach," while *School Library Journal* reviewer Kit Vaughan cpraised the "slender story" as "lush with haunting characters and spare descriptions, conjuring up vivid images." Claire Rosser, writing in *Kliatt,* complimented DiCamillo's text as "spare, poetic, [and] moving," while GraceAnne A. DeCandido, in a *Booklist* review, wrote that the author's "gorgeous language wastes not a single word."

In 2003, DiCamillo took a new path in her writing, released something entirely different with more than a little trepidation. In the acceptance speech for her Newbery Medal, she explained, "Four years ago, when he was eight years old, my friend Luke Bailey asked me to write the story of an unlikely hero. I was afraid to tell the story he wanted told: afraid because I didn't know what I was doing; afraid because it was unlike anything I had written before; afraid, I guess, because the story was so intent on taking me into the depths of my own heart. But Luke wanted the story. I had promised him. And so, terrified and unwilling, I wrote *The Tale of Despereaux.*" DiCamillo needn't have worried; the book was well received by critics and readers and earned her the Newbery Medal. The story, which has the subtitle *Being the Story of a Mouse, a Princess, Some Soup, and a Spool of Thread,* tells of Despereaux Tilling, a mouse more interested in reading books than eating them, who falls in love with a human princess. It also tells of a villainous rat, Roscuro, who longs to live in the light, and Miggery Sow, a serving girl who believes that someday she will become a princess. When Roscuro and Miggery kidnap the princess, it is up to Despereaux, small even for a mouse, to come to her rescue.

Narrated in a style that encourages reading aloud, *The Tale of Despereaux* contains "all the ingredients of an old-fashioned drama," according to a critic for *Kirkus Reviews.* Peter D. Sieruta, writing in *Horn Book,* noted that "DiCamillo tells an engaging tale. . . . Many readers will be enchanted by this story of mice and princesses, brave deeds, . . . and forgiveness." Miriam Lang Budin, writing in *School Library Journal,* considered the book to be "a charming story of unlikely heroes whose destinies entwine to bring about a joyful resolution." Kathleen T. Horning wrote in *School Library Journal* that the book "contains a cast of quirky characters that would have made Dickens proud," while a *Publishers Weekly* critic, imitating the narrator's style, wrote, "I must tell you, you are in for a treat."

DiCamillo is also the author of a series of early chapter books about a pet pig named Mercy Watson, who has "personality a-plenty" according to a reviewer for *Publishers Weekly.* In the first book, *Mercy Watson to the Rescue,* Mercy manages to make her owners' bed start to fall through the floor of their room while they are on it; afraid to move, they cheer for Mercy as she leaves the room, convinced that she is going to find a way to rescue them. After a series of chaotic events, the neighbors eventually call the fire department, and when Mercy's owners are rescued, they give the pig all the credit.

A *Publishers Weekly* critic felt that with *Mercy Watson to the Rescue,* DiCamillo "once again displays her versatility with this jaunty debut to an early chapter-book series."

DiCamillo once told *Something about the Author:* "I was a sickly child. My body happily played host to all of the usual childhood maladies (mumps and measles, chickenpox twice, and ear infections), plus a few exotic extras: inexplicable skin diseases, chronic pinkeye, and, most dreaded of all, pneumonia, recurring every winter for the first five years of my life. I mention this because, at the time, it seemed like such a senseless and unfair kind of thing to me, to be sick so often, to miss so much school, to be inside scratching or sneezing or coughing when everybody else was outside playing.

"Now, looking back, I can see all that illness for what it was: a gift that shaped me and made me what I am. I was alone a lot. I learned to rely on my imagination for

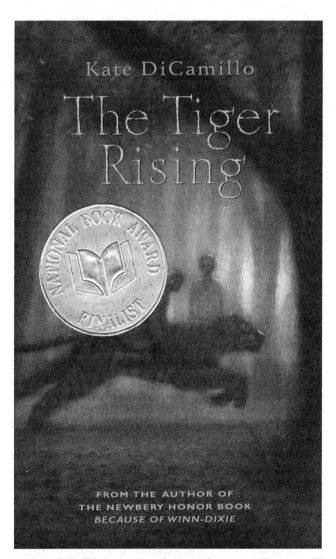

DeCamillo tells an emotional story about a twelve-year-old boy's efforts to come to terms with his sadness over his mother's death in this 2001 novel. (Cover illustration by Chris Sheban.)

entertainment. Because I was always on the lookout for the next needle, the next tongue depressor, I learned to watch and listen and gauge the behavior of those around me. I became an imaginative observer.

"Also, I suffered from chronic pneumonia at a time when geographical cures were still being prescribed. I was born near Philadelphia and, after my fifth winter in an oxygen tent, the doctor gave my parents this advice: take her to a warmer climate. We moved to central Florida. There I absorbed the speech patterns and cadences and nuances of life in a small southern town. I did not know it at the time, but Florida (and pneumonia) gave me a great gift: a voice in which to tell my stories.

"When I look back on childhood, I remember one moment with great clarity. I was three years old and in the hospital with pneumonia, and my father came to visit me. He arrived in a black overcoat that smelled of the cold outdoors, and he brought me a gift. It was a little, red net bag. Inside it there was a wooden village: wooden church, house, chicken, tree, farmer. It was as if he had flung the net bag out into the bright world and captured the essential elements and shrunk them down and brought them to me.

"He opened the bag and said, 'Hold out your hands.' I held out my hands. 'No,' he said, 'like this. Like you are going to drink from them.' I did as he said, and he poured the wooden figures, piece by piece, into my waiting hands. Then he told me a story about the chicken and the farmer and the house and the church. Something opened up inside me. There was the weight of the wooden figures in my hands, the smell of my father's overcoat, the whole great world hiding, waiting in the purple dusk outside my hospital room. And there was the story—the story.

"I think of that moment often. It was another gift of my illness. When I write, I sometimes stop and cup my hands, as if I am drinking water. I try, I want desperately to capture the world, to hold it for a moment in my hands."

Biographical and Critical Sources

PERIODICALS

Book, May, 2001, Kathleen Odean, review of *Because of Winn-Dixie,* p. 80; November-December, 2003, review of *The Tale of Despereaux,* p. 67.

Booklist, May 1, 2000, Gillian Engberg, review of *Because of Winn-Dixie,* p. 1665; June 1, 2001, GraceAnne A. DeCandido, review of *The Tiger Rising,* p. 1882, Patricia Austin, review of *Because of Winn-Dixie,* p. 1906; October 15, 2001, Lolly Gepson, review of audio book *The Tiger Rising,* p. 428; January 1, 2004, review of *The Tale of Despereaux,* p. 780; March 1, 2004, Patricia Austin, review of *The Tale of Despereaux* (audiobook), p. 1212.

Horn Book, July, 2000, review of *Because of Winn-Dixie,* p. 455; May, 2001, review of *The Tiger Rising,* p. 321, Kristi Beavin, review of *Because of Winn-Dixie* (audiobook), p. 359; September-October, 2003, Peter D. Sieruta, review of *The Tale of Despereaux,* p. 609; May-June, 2004, Kristi Elle Jemtegaard, review of *The Tale of Despereaux* (audiobook), p. 349; July-August, 2004, Kate DiCamillo, "Newbery Medal Acceptance Speech," pp. 395-400, Jane Resh Thomas, "Kate DiCamillo," pp. 401-404.

Kirkus Reviews, July 15, 2003, review of *The Tale of Despereaux,* p. 962.

Kliatt, November, 2002, Claire Rosser, review of *The Tiger Rising,* p. 18.

Publishers Weekly, February 21, 2000, review of *Because of Winn-Dixie,* p. 88; June 26, 2000, Jennifer M. Brown, "Kate DiCamillo," p. 30; January 15, 2001, review of *The Tiger Rising,* p. 77; April 9, 2001, review of *Because of Winn-Dixie* (audiobook), p. 28; July 9, 2001, review of *The Tiger Rising* (audiobook), p. 22; June 16, 2003, review of *The Tale of Despereaux,* p. 71; June 20, 2005, review of *Mercy Watson to the Rescue,* p. 77.

School Library Journal, June, 2000, Helen Foster, review of *Because of Winn-Dixie,* p. 143; March, 2001, Kit Vaughan, review of *The Tiger Rising,* p. 246; June, 2001, Lori Craft, review of *Because of Winn-Dixie* (audiobook), p. 74; August, 2001, Emily Herman, review of *The Tiger Rising* (audiobook), p. 90; August, 2003, Miriam Lang Budin, review of *The Tale of Despereaux,* p. 126; March, 2004, Barbara Wysocki, review of *The Tale of Despereaux* (audiobook), p. 88; April, 2004, Kathleen T. Horning, "The Tale of DiCamillo," pp. 44-48, review of *The Tale of Despereaux,* p. S28; April, 2005, "A Winn-Winn Situation," p. S7.

ONLINE

Kate DiCamillo Home Page, http://www.katedicamillo.com (July 31, 2005).*

E

EAGLE, Kin
    See ADLERMAN, Danny (Ezra)

    *   *   *

EAGLE, Kin
    See ADLERMAN, Kimberly (Marie)

    *   *   *

EGIELSKI, Richard 1952-

Personal

Born July 16, 1952, in Queens, NY; son of Joseph Frank (a police lieutenant) and Caroline (an executive secretary) Egielski; married Denise Saldutti (an illustrator), May 8, 1977. *Education:* Attended Pratt Institute, 1970-71; Parsons School of Design, graduated 1974. *Hobbies and other interests:* Playing the mandolin.

Addresses

Home—7 West 14th St., New York, NY 10011.

Career

Illustrator, 1973—. *Exhibitions:* "Illustrators 16," 1974, and "Illustrators 18," 1976, Society of Illustrators, New York, NY.

Member

Awards, Honors

The Porcelain Pagoda was included in American Institute of Graphic Arts Book Show, 1976; Children's Book of the Year citation, Child Study Association of America, 1976, for *The Letter, the Witch, and the Ring;* certificate of merit, Society of Illustrators, 1978, 1981, 1984, 1985; best books citation, *School Library Journal,* 1980, for *Louis the Fish;* plaque from Biennale of Illustrations Bratislava, 1985, for *It Happened in Pinsk;* Parents' Choice Picture Book Award, 1985, for *Amy's Eyes,* and 1989, for *The Tub People;* Caldecott Medal, American Library Association, 1987, for *Hey, Al;* Best Illustrated Book designation, *New York Times,* 1998, for *Jazper.*

Writings

SELF-ILLUSTRATED

Buz, HarperCollins (New York, NY), 1995.
The Gingerbread Boy, HarperCollins (New York, NY), 1997.
Jazper, HarperCollins (New York, NY), 1998.
Three Magic Balls, Laura Geringer Books (New York, NY), 2000.
Slim and Jim, Laura Geringer Books (New York, NY), 2001.
Saint Francis and the Wolf, Laura Geringer Books (New York, NY), 2005.

ILLUSTRATOR

Moonguitars (reader), Houghton Mifflin (Boston, MA), 1974.
F. N. Monjo, *The Porcelain Pagoda,* Viking (New York, NY), 1976.
John Bellairs, *The Letter, the Witch, and the Ring,* Dial Books (New York, NY), 1976, reprinted, Puffin Books (New York, NY), 1993.
Arthur Yorinks, *Sid and Sol,* Farrar, Straus & Giroux (New York, NY), 1977.
Miriam Chaikin, *I Should Worry, I Should Care,* Harper-Collins (New York, NY), 1979.
Arthur Yorinks, *Louis the Fish,* Farrar, Straus & Giroux (New York, NY), 1980.
Miriam Chaikin, *Finders Weepers,* HarperCollins (New York, NY), 1980.

Isabel Langis Cusack, *Mr. Wheatfield's Loft,* Holt (New York, NY), 1981.

Miriam Chaikin, *Getting Even,* HarperCollins (New York, NY), 1982.

Jim Aylesworth, *Mary's Mirror,* Holt (New York, NY), 1982.

Arthur Yorinks, *It Happened in Pinsk,* Farrar, Straus & Giroux (New York, NY), 1983.

Miriam Chaikin, *Lower! Higher! You're a Liar!,* HarperCollins (New York, NY), 1984.

Gelett Burgess, *The Little Father,* Farrar, Straus & Giroux (New York, NY), 1985.

Richard Kennedy, *Amy's Eyes,* HarperCollins (New York, NY), 1985.

Arthur Yorinks, *Hey, Al,* Farrar, Straus & Giroux (New York, NY), 1986.

Arthur Yorinks, *Bravo, Minski,* Farrar, Straus & Giroux (New York, NY), 1988.

Miriam Chaikin, *Friends Forever,* HarperCollins (New York, NY), 1988.

Pam Conrad, *The Tub People,* HarperCollins (New York, NY), 1989.

Arthur Yorinks, *Oh, Brother,* Farrar, Straus & Giroux (New York, NY), 1989.

Arthur Yorinks, *Ugh,* Farrar, Straus & Giroux (New York, NY), 1990.

William J. Brooke, *A Telling of the Tales: Five Stories,* HarperCollins (New York, NY), 1990.

Arthur Yorinks, *Christmas in July,* HarperCollins (New York, NY), 1991.

Pam Conrad, *The Lost Sailor,* HarperCollins (New York, NY), 1992.

Pam Conrad, *The Tub Grandfather,* HarperCollins (New York, NY), 1993.

Pam Conrad, *Call Me Ahnighito,* HarperCollins (New York, NY), 1995.

Bill Martin, Jr., *Fire! Fire! Said Mrs. McGuire,* Harcourt, Brace (New York, NY), 1996.

William Wise, *Perfect Pancakes, If You Please,* Dial Books (New York, NY), 1997.

Alan Arkin, *One Present from Flekman's,* HarperCollins (New York, NY), 1999.

Pam Conrad, *The Tub People's Christmas,* HarperCollins (New York, NY), 1999.

Douglas Kaine McKelvey, *Locust Pocus: A Book to Bug You,* Philomel Books (New York, NY), 2001.

Margie Palatini, *The Web Files,* Hyperion Books (New York, NY), 2001.

Margaret Wise Brown, *The Fierce Yellow Pumpkin,* HarperCollins (New York, NY), 2003.

Rosemary Wells, *The Small World of Binky Braverman,* Viking (New York, NY), 2003.

Adaptations

The Tub People was adapted for audio cassette.

Sidelights

Author and illustrator Richard Egielski is a master of "idiosyncratic and highly personal picture books," according to Anne Quirk in *Children's Books and Their Creators.* In collaboration with writers such as Arthur

Yorinks and Pam Conrad, as well as in his own self-illustrated picture books, this American illustrator "has created some of the most quirky and original children's books of recent decades," Quirk noted. The winner of the 1987 Caldecott Medal, Egielski—though noted for the sometimes surreal nature of his content—presents illustrations with sharp lines and vivid colors; illustrations that enhance the text rather than simply amplify it. "I love to interpret text," Egielski once told *Something about the Author* (*SATA*). "A good illustrator is never a slave to text. The text rarely tells him what to do, but, rather, what his choices are. I only illustrate texts I truly believe in." In award-winning books such as *Hey, Al,* done in collaboration with Yorinks, and *The Tub People,* with Conrad, as well as in his own creations such as *Buz, Jazper,* and *Slim and Jim,* Egielski has demonstrated, in the words of Quirk, the "singular vision, emotional urgency, and technical mastery of an artist at the top of his form."

Born in Queens, New York, in 1952, Egielski grew up in Maspeth, Queens, the son of a police lieutenant. "They called me 'the artist of the family,'" he once recalled to *SATA,* "but it seemed that there was one in every family. It didn't necessarily mean you were good at drawing, just that you enjoyed doing it." Egielski's earliest influences were comic books and movies. He retained his love for both and later looked back at his earliest cartoon sketches to realize that, as picture books had originally given rise to cartoons, the opposite hap-

Richard Egielski won the Caldecott Medal for his illustrations for Arthur Yorinks's* Hey, Al, *about a lonely janitor and his dog who are wisked away to a perfect world.

pened for him: he started with cartoons and moved to picture books. "I wasn't aware of picture books until I was old enough to consider them 'baby books,'" he explained. In his opinion, books were not an essential ingredient of his childhood; a child of the 1950s, he grew up in what he recalls as a visual universe.

Catholic school was the bane of Egielski's early life, an institution that "felt like a concentration camp" to him. "All those things you hear about: nuns throwing erasers at students; rapping kids' knuckles with rulers, is all true," he told *SATA*. When it came time for high school, Egielski did research, in the hopes of going to a public school, and an interest in freedom, rather than art, led him to apply to New York's High School of Art and Design. Once accepted there, his love for line and design became firmly established. "At the end of four years, I'd resolved to become a painter because I'd discovered such artists as Rembrandt and Goya, whose work made a deep impression on me," Egielski recalled. "They are the most illustrative of painters."

Upon graduation Egielski attended the Pratt Institute for a year. The painting program there was heavily influenced by abstract expressionism and Egielski "felt like a dinosaur doing representational work," although that was where his heart was. He was attracted to narrative artists such as nineenth-century N. C. Wyeth, and ultimately determined that illustration was a better match for his interests than fine art. The son of a middle-class family, he was practical about his career choices, opting for a field that generates a marketable product. In 1971 he transferred to Parsons School of Design, planning to become a commercial illustrator, and his student work appeared in several magazines before his direction changed after taking a class in picture books taught by Maurice Sendak. For Egielski, Sendak was that wonderful find, a real teacher. "An important teacher is one who exposes you to something new, and points out a direction you otherwise might have missed," Egielski explained. "In introducing me to the art of the picture books, Maurice Sendak became a crucial influence. The quality of his work is a continuing inspiration." Another important influence came about as a result of Egielski's years at Parsons. He met the illustrator Denise Saldutti, whom he married in 1977.

Graduating from Parsons in 1974, Egielski met with skeptical looks from editors when he submitted his portfolio, and was told his work is too strange and sophisticated for children's books. Once again Sendak came to his aid, introducing Egielski to young writer Arthur Yorinks, whose books were badly in need of a sympathetic illustrator. Yorinks and Egielski ultimately formed a collaborative bond, working together on eight titles, including the Caldecott Medal-winning *Hey, Al.* Unlike some authors and illustrators who work separately, these two worked closely on each project. Their first book together, *Sid and Sol,* was published in 1977, and over the next fourteen years they produced seven more titles.

Yorinks's texts often draw inspiration from classic writers such as Gogol and Kafka. *Louis the Fish,* for example, was suggested by Kafka's *The Metamorphosis,* in which a man is turned into a large insect. The award-winning *Hey, Al* tells the story of a janitor and his dog who live in a cramped apartment and dream of a tropical island with plenty of room. When a tropical bird offers them the opportunity of living on such an island, they eagerly take it. Egielski's drawings for this book range from cramped and pinched illustrations of the apartment with legs going out of the frame, emphasizing the tiny space, to large and animated tropical animals that emphasize the exotic quality of the island. "Every aspect of the picture book as an art form is utilized to create an unforgettable partnership of pictures and words," noted Kay Vandergrift in *School Library Journal.* "Egielski takes us from the real world to a world of fantasy and back. . . . Shifts in framing techniques as well as in palette deftly mirror and expand the pattern of the text." Another Egielski-Yorinks title, *Oh, Brother,* tells the "uproarious misadventures" of twin brothers, according to a *School Library Journal* commentator, as they travel from a home for lost boys to England, arguing all the while. The reviewer called the book a "playful look at brotherly love," and remarked in particular on the "jolly good humor bursting from the illustrations."

Egielski has also teamed up with other authors to create books of distinction. Illustrating for Pam Conrad, he has published award winners such as *The Tub People* and its sequel, *The Tub Grandfather,* as well as *The Lost Sailor* and *Call Me Ahnighito.* Egielski created a cast of little wooden figures who inhabit the bathroom for *The Tub People;* in its sequel the Tub People move out to a cozier room where they discover the long-lost Tub Grandfather of the title. There is a sentimental reunion as the grandmother dances across the carpet with her newly rediscovered husband; the Egielski-illustrated depiction of this is "almost heartachingly tender," according to Quirk in *Children's Books and Their Creators.* Carolyn Phelan remarked in *Booklist* that while this sequel may not have "the innate child appeal" of its predecessor, the reader should not "underestimate the charm or the power of Egielski's large-scale watercolor illustrations to bring the tub toys and this picture book to life." Joy Fleishhacker, reviewing the same title in *School Library Journal,* commented that Egielski "constructs a variety of moods through a clever use of perspective and the careful positioning of the figures in each scene."

In *The Lost Sailor* Egielski joins Conrad to tell the story of a shipwrecked mariner. Ann A. Flowers, writing in *Horn Book,* found the artist's work "clear, simple" and "almost stylized," while a *Publishers Weekly* contributor noted that Egielski's watercolors "pack more dramatic punch and, especially in his depictions of the solitary figure on the lush abandoned island, contain more food for the imagination." A further joint effort with Conrad, *Call Me Ahnighito* is the story of a mete-

Egielski's illustrations for Marge Palatini's **The Web Files** *play up the story's debt to the 1960s television series* **Dragnet.**

orite that landed in the Arctic, told in the first person by the meteorite itself. "Egielski's interpretations of the Arctic are magnificent," noted Elizabeth S. Watson in *Horn Book,* the critic going on to praise the "provocative pictures of the frozen landscape, yellow northern light, and icy waters" that capture "the cold isolation that the voice describes." Carolyn Phelan, a reviewer for *Booklist,* concluded that Egielski "achieves subtle and exceptionally beautiful effects with color, texture, and light," while a critic for *Publishers Weekly* enthused that "Egielski's familiar art takes on a majestic quality" in this book.

Other collaborative efforts have included working with Bill Martin, Jr., on *Fire! Fire! Said Mrs. McGuire,* and with William Wise on *Perfect Pancakes, If You Please.* The former title provides "slapstick humor and fast-paced action" in a rhyming story, according to a *Publishers Weekly* contributor. Originally published in 1970, the new edition, featuring Egielski's illustrations, is "bigger, brighter, and more original in concept," according to Carolyn Phelan in *Booklist.* A critic for *Publishers Weekly* concluded that "Egielski's rumble-tumble stage business and inventive subplots combine with Martin's comic puns and rhythmic verve to make this picture book a five alarm delight." Wise's text about a king who offers his daughter's hand to the man who can make perfect pancakes is also adroitly accompanied by Egielski's "robust, richly colored illustrations" which "capture the comedy well," according to *Booklist* re-

viewer Stephanie Zvirin. In creating illustrations for Margaret Wise Brown's previously unpublished story *The Fierce Yellow Pumpkin,* Egielski turns out one of the "season's holiday standouts," according to a *Publishers Weekly* reviewer, the critic dubbing the illustrator's "nostalgic" illustrations in warm gold tones "a polished presentation."

Egielski, who works primarily in watercolors and who once said that he would never try to write his own picture books, has discovered that one should never say "never." *Buz, The Gingerbread Boy, Jazper, Slim and Jim, Three Magic Balls,* and *Saint Francis and the Wolf* are all picture books written and illustrated by Egielski. In *Buz* a boy eats a bug with his breakfast; the ensuing story follows the bug through the boy's digestive system and as pills ordered by the doctor attempt to track the insect down. Writing in *School Library Journal,* Wendy Lukehart commented that Egielski "makes effective use of double-page close-ups, interior and exterior perspectives, and page layout to build suspense and heightened dramatic impact." A *Publishers Weekly* reviewer called this debut solo book a "droll adventure," and concluded that "this book is . . . great fun to read and to look at."

Egielski adapted the nursery rhyme *The Gingerbread Boy* for his next solo effort. In this story, he gives the tale a big-city twist, with the Gingerbread Boy getting loose in New York City and being chased by rats, construction workers, and even a mounted policeman. Judith Constantinides, in *School Library Journal,* felt that "Egielski's retelling is straightforward," and his illustrations "adroitly evoke the city setting while giving a solid three-dimensionality and unique individuality to the Gingerbread Boy and his pursuers." Constantinides concluded that this "clever confection makes a fine addition to folklore collections." Ann A. Flowers, reviewing *The Gingerbread Boy* for *Horn Book,* dubbed Egielski's work "a smooth and sophisticated version of the famous tale," while Hazel Rochman noted in a *Booklist* review that "the combination of wild farce and luscious paintings make for great storytelling and a celebration of the city."

Returning to a bug motif for *Jazper,* Egielski created a Pinocchio-like boy insect in his eponymous hero. Jazper and his dad live in a rented eggshell while their more affluent neighbors inhabit full-size cans and cereal boxes. When Jazper's dad loses his job, the boy sets out to earn some money by house-sitting. Then the trouble begins, as Jazper runs afoul of five very strange moths. A *New York Times* Best Illustrated Book for 1998, *Jazper* is "sure to appeal to youngsters growing up on surreal dollops of Dr. Seuss, William Joyce, Daniel Kirk, William Steig, and earlier Egielski," predicted *School Library Journal* contributor John Sigwald.

Three Magic Balls also makes use of the city skyline, this time in a fantastic caper involving magic run amok. Rudy is at work in his uncle's toy store when an old woman brings in three odd-looking balls and sells them, along with a golden whistle. When Rudy finds himself alone in the shop, he begins to experiment with the balls, and they quickly turn into giant, round, fun-seeking men who can also perform miracles. Only when the action seems ready to veer out of hand does Rudy remember the whistle and its role in keeping the magic balls in line. A *Publishers Weekly* reviewer commended the book for its "old-fashioned enchantment," adding that Egielski "approaches the art and narration with boundless energy." In *School Library Journal,* Lauralyn Persson noted that Egielski's "artwork is great," and concluded: "The figures have the look of real substance, and the action has the look of real motion, both wonderful things to accomplish on a flat page."

Slim and Jim weaves a tale of tolerance and friendship around two urban rodents. Slim is a rat who, down on his luck, is lured into crime by a cat named Buster. Jim, a mouse, has been pampered but has a good heart. When Slim rescues Jim from drowning, the two take refuge in Jim's house, where they joyfully play yo-yo together. All seems to be well until Slim is once again kidnapped by the cat—and Jim must go to his rescue. Joanna Rudge Long maintained in *Horn Book* that Egielski's "timeless cityscape and comically expressive animals are all delightfully engaging." *Booklist* contributor Ilene Cooper noted that, in contrast to many picture books, "this has a real story, with adventure, friendship, dastardly deeds—and yo yos!"

Although he originally aspired to create museum-quality fine art, Egielski has no regrets about the course his career has taken. "I like the whole idea of creating picture books within the standard thirty-two page format," he once told *SATA.* "It's not unlike the sonnet form, in which the poet has so many lines in which to express himself. I don't feel at all constricted by this. On the contrary, the 'rules' of the form seem to set me free. I'm always discovering new things I can do. The picture book is an art form unto itself." He concluded: "My illustration is my fine art. I have absolutely no reason to wish to liberate or wean myself from dependence upon text. It is through my illustrations that I express myself most deeply and fully."

Biographical and Critical Sources

BOOKS

Silvey, Anita, editor, *Children's Books and Their Creators,* Houghton Mifflin (Boston, MA), 1995, pp. 219-220.

PERIODICALS

Booklist, October 15, 1993, Carolyn Phelan, review of *The Tub Grandfather,* p. 451; May 1, 1995, Carolyn Phelan, review of *Call Me Ahnighito,* p. 1579; March 15, 1996, Carolyn Phelan, review of *Fire! Fire! Said Mrs. McGuire,* p. 1266; December 1, 1996, Stephanie Zvirin, review of *Perfect Pancakes, If You Please,* p. 670; October 15, 1997, Hazel Rochman, review of *The Gingerbread Boy,* p. 409; September 15, 1998, Michael Cart, review of *Jazper,* p. 171; September 1, 1999, Hazel Rochman, review of *The Tub People,* p. 147; September 1, 2000, Ilene Cooper, review of *Three Magic Balls,* p. 121; May 1, 2001, Ilene Cooper, review of *The Web Files,* p. 1690; May 1, 2002, Ilene Cooper, review of *Slim and Jim,* p. 1520; September 1, 2003, Carolyn Phelan, review of *The Fierce Yellow Pumpkin,* p. 133; September 15, 2004, Karin Snelson, review of *Liberty's Journey,* p. 247.

Bulletin of the Center for Children's Books, February, 1998, review of *The Gingerbread Boy,* p. 198; November, 1998, review of *Jazper,* p. 94; September, 2000, review of *Three Magic Balls,* p. 121; September, 2002, review of *Slim and Jim,* p. 14.

Horn Book, July-August, 1987, Arthur Yorinks, "Richard Egielski," pp. 436-438; March-April, 1993, Ann A. Flowers, review of *The Lost Sailor,* p. 194; July-August, 1995, Elizabeth S. Watson, review of *Call Me Ahnighito,* p. 448; September-October, 1997, Ann A. Flowers, review of *The Gingerbread Boy,* p. 587; May, 2001, review of *The Web Files,* p. 314; July-August, 2002, Joanna Rudge Long, review of *Slim and Jim,* p. 445.

Kirkus Reviews, July 1, 2003, review of *The Fierce Yellow Pumpkin,* p. 907.

Publishers Weekly, June 29, 1992, review of *The Lost Sailor,* p. 63; May 15, 1995, review of *Call Me Ahnighito,* p. 73; July 17, 1995, review of *Buz,* p. 229; March 18, 1996, review of *Fire! Fire! Said Mrs. McGuire,* p. 68; August 3, 1998, review of *Jazper,* p. 84; February 22, 1999, review of *Buz,* p. 97; July 31, 2000, review of *Three Magic Balls,* p. 93; May 6, 2002, review of *Slim and Jim,* p. 56; August 4, 2003, review of *The Fierce Yellow Pumpkin,* p. 77; August 18, 2003, review of *The Small World of Binky Braverman,* p. 78.

School Library Journal, March, 1987, Kay Vandergrift, pp. 78-80; March, 1994, Joy Fleishhacker, review of *The Tub Grandfather,* p. 192; September, 1995, Wendy Lukehart, review of *Buz,* p. 175; September, 1997, Judith Constantinides, review of *The Gingerbread Boy,* p. 180; January, 1998, review of *Oh, Brother,* p. 43; September, 1998, John Sigwald, review of *Jazper,* pp. 171-172; May, 1999, Rosalyn Pierini, review of *One Present from Fleckman's,* p. 79; September, 2000, review of *Three Magic Balls,* p. 194; August, 2003, James K. Irwin, review of *The Fierce Yellow Pumpkin,* p. 123.*

*   *   *

ELLIOTT, David 1952-

Personal

Born 1952; married; children: Eli. *Education:* School of International Training, M.A.

Addresses

Home—NH. *Office*—Department of Humanities, Colby-Sawyer College, 541 Main St., New London, NH 03257. *E-mail*—delliott@colby-sawyer.edu.

Career

Colby-Sawyer College, New London, NH, instructor and director of English language and American culture program.

Writings

An Alphabet of Rotten Kids, illustrated by Oscar de Mejo, Philomel (New York, NY), 1991.

The Cool Crazy Crickets, illustrated by Paul Meisel, Candlewick Press (Cambridge, MA), 2000.

The Cool Crazy Crickets to the Rescue, illustrated by Paul Meisel, Candlewick Press (Cambridge, MA), 2001.

The Transmogrification of Roscoe Wizzle, Candlewick Press (Cambridge, MA), 2001.

Hazel Nutt, Mad Scientist, illustrated by True Kelley, Holiday House (New York, NY), 2003.

And Here's to You!, illustrated by Randy Cecil, Candlewick Press (Cambridge, MA), 2004.

Evangeline Mudd and the Golden-haired Apes of the Ikkinasti Jungle, illustrated by Andréa Wesson, Candlewick Press (Cambridge, MA), 2004.

Hazel Nutt, Alien Hunter, illustrated by True Kelley, Holiday House (New York, NY), 2004.

Elliott's titles have been translated into German and Italian.

Work in Progress

Evangeline Mudd and the Great Mink Escapade, a sequel to *Evangeline Mudd and the Golden-haired Apes of the Ikkinasti Jungle,* and *Herculese Smith and the Wuv Bunnies from Outers Pace.*

Sidelights

David Elliott, an instructor at Colby-Sawyer College in New Hampshire, stumbled into his second career as a children's-book author while at a party. In a conversation with a woman named Amy Ehrlich, he began to discuss ideas for an alphabet book, unaware that Ehrlich was a retired editor from Dial Books. She got him in contact with some other editors, and not long after, Elliott was the author of *An Alphabet of Rotten Kids.* The title introduces readers to twenty-six naughty children, and, according to some reviewers, the humor is reminiscent of Edward Gorey's macabre alphabet book *The Gashlycrumb Tinies.* "The humor is silly enough to appeal to kids," commented a reviewer for *Publishers Weekly.* Not all parents appreciated the humor, however, and Elliott's first book was banned in at least one U.S. city on moral grounds. Elliott was disappointed in the

A ten-year-old fast-food addict finds that his unhealthy diet changes more than his weight in David Elliott's humorous 2001 novel. (Cover illustration by Vladimir Radunsky.)

book himself; he was surprised that the illustrator had depicted the children as all one race. "I joke that the book should have been banned because it's so bad," he told an interviewer for the Colby-Sawyer College Web site.

The disappointment of his first book did not deter Elliott from further writing, and in 2000, a multi-racial group of kid heroes hit the scene with *The Cool Crazy Crickets.* In the book four friends decide to form a club, and over the course of the story, decide the club's name, find their clubhouse, vote on a mascot, and put together a reason for their club's existence. *The Cool Crazy Crickets* contains "Quick-paced dialogue, brief sentences and a generous smattering of art," according to a *Publishers Weekly* reviewer, who noted that these qualities will make the book appeal to young readers bridging from picture books to chapter books. *Booklist* reviewer John Peters called the book a "light, good-humored tale."

The friends return in *The Cool Crazy Crickets to the Rescue,* in which all four club members are looking for ways to earn money. Through responsibilities like babysitting, pet-sitting, and building a lemonade stand, they begin to bring in some money and discuss how they will spend it. Then a sickly cat moves into their clubhouse, and they quickly discover the best way to spend their money: taking their new charge to take her to the vet. Roxanne Burg, reviewing the obook for *School Library Journal,* called *The Cool Crazy Crickets to the Rescue,* "An easygoing tale about summer days."

Fast food, science-fiction, and Franz Kafka mix in Elliott's *The Transmogrification of Roscoe Wizzle,* in which the title character begins to turn into a bug after eating too much food from the ominous restaurant Gussy's. When Roscoe begins to investigate, he discovers that Gussy's may also be the reason that several children from his town have been going missing. Soon it is up to him and vegetarian friend Kinshasa to solve the mystery. A *Publishers Weekly* reviewer noted that Elliott combines "sassy first-person narration and snappy dialogue" to create a story skewed "a few thoroughly enjoyable degrees off normal." Eva Mitnick, writing in *School Library Journal* felt that "The wacky plot and quirky details . . . will appeal to young and reluctant readers," while a *Publishers Weekly* critic praised the audiobook version, noting that "Elliott spins Roscoe's adventures into a breezy funny whodunit with a happy ending."

Elliott introduces Hazel Nutt in *Hazel Nutt, Mad Scientist,* a story based on old horror movies and puns. Hazel Nutt is determined to cross a vampire with an opera singer; when she brings her creation to life, she calls it "Dracula-la-la." The townspeople are not thrilled with having a mad scientist in their neighborhood, so they approach with torches, ready to drive her out. Instead, Nutt invites them to a concert where Dracula-la-la is accompanied by a living piano named "Frankenstein-way." "Children with a good sense of humor should appreciate this book," recommended Kristin de Lacoste in her review for *School Library Journal,* while a reviewer for *Publishers Weekly* quipped that "the transmosterfied piano is a hoot."

Hazel Nutt goes through a career change for her next adventure, *Hazel Nutt, Alien Hunter.* When Nutt and her crew land their spaceship directly on top of the leader of planet Wutt, much confusion ensues, from an Abbott-and-Costellolike discussion about the planet's name to Hazel giving the aliens a ladder. When the ship leaves, the Wuttite leader is miraculously revived. "Elliott's story is nonsensical goofiness," noted a *Kirkus Reviews* contributor, while Lisa Gangemi recommended that *Hazel Nutt, Alien Hunter* "will be a hit with younger fans" of other goofy authors, including Dav Pilkey (author of *Captain Underpants*) and Jon Scieszka (author of the "Timewarp Trio" series).

A young girl raised by primatologists is the heroine of *Evangeline Mudd and the Golden-haired Apes of the Ikkinasti Jungle.* Evangeline's parents raised her as the golden-haired apes raise their young, and the result is that the girl can use her toes to eat, swing from tree to tree, and complete other daring tasks. When Evangeline is eight years old, her parents leave on a research trip. She stays with her mink rancher uncle, a man who is unkind to animals and the environment and is also possibly plotting against Evangeline's parents! When Dr. Aphrodite Pikkaflee comes to find Evangeline to tell her that her parents have vanished, it is up to Evangeline and her new friend to save the day. The "madcap adventures will appeal to kids with a taste for silliness," noted a *Publishers Weekly* critic, while B. Allison Gray wrote in *School Library Journal* that in *Evangeline Mudd and the Golden-haired Apes of the Ikkinasti Jungle* "Everything is sorted out neatly, but not facilely, in the end."

Although most of his books are beginning readers, Elliott has also penned the picture book *And Here's to*

When her spaceship flattens the ruler of Planet Wutt, the ship's captain finds some heavy-duty apologizing in **Hazel Nutt Alien Hunter.** *(Illustration by True Kelley.)*

You! In rhyming text, he raises a toast to creatures of land and sea, from birds to bugs to fish to humans. Andrea Tarr deemed the book "a powerful package," while a critic for *Kirkus Reviews* noted that the work "will have young readers and listeners calling for another round."

While Elliott's books are lighthearted and zany, their genesis is not necessarily instantaneous; sometimes takes months for an idea to arrange itself as a story. However, Elliott continues to be inspired, and has plans to write a sequel to Evangeline's first adventures, as well as dream up adventures of a new character, Hercules Smith, who discovers a spaceship in his back yard. When not writing, he continues to teach and is the director of Colby Sawyer's English language and American culture program.

Biographical and Critical Sources

PERIODICALS

Booklist, September 15, 2000, John Peters, review of *The Cool Crazy Crickets,* p. 240; October 15, 2003, Todd Morning, review of *Hazel Nutt, Mad Scientist,* p. 418.
Children's Bookwatch, October, 2004, review of *Hazel Nutt, Alien Hunter.*
Kirkus Reviews, February 1, 2004, review of *Evangeline Mudd and the Golden-haired Apes of the Ikkinasti Jungle,* p. 132; March 15, 2004, review of *And Here's to You!* p. 268; August 15, 2004, review of *Hazel Nutt, Alien Hunter,* p. 805.
People, August 26, 1991, review of *An Alphabet of Rotten Kids!* p. 31.
Publishers Weekly, May 24, 1991, review of *An Alphabet of Rotten Kids!* p. 58; June 25, 2000, review of *The Cool Crazy Crickets,* p. 75; May 7, 2001, review of *The Transmogrification of Roscoe Wizzle,* p. 247; July 9, 2001, p. 21; October 13, 2003, review of *Hazel Nutt, Mad Scientist,* p. 77; March 15, 2004, review of *Evangeline Mudd and the Golden-haired Apes of the Ikkinasti Jungle,* p. 75.
School Library Journal, August, 2000, Kate McLean, review of *The Cool Crazy Crickets,* p. 154; June, 2001, Eva Mitnick, review of *The Transmogrification of Roscoe Wizzle,* p. 112; July, 2001, Roxanne Burg, review of *The Cool Crazy Crickets to the Rescue!,* p. 75; March, 2004, Kristin de Lacoste, review of *Hazel Nutt, Mad Scientist,* p. 156, B. Allison Gray, review of *Evangeline Mudd and the Golden-haired Apes of the Ikkinasti Jungle,* p. 156; May, 2004, Andrea Tarr, review of *And Here's to You!,* p. 109; October, 2004, Lisa Gangemi, review of *Hazel Nutt, Alien Hunter,* p. 112.

ONLINE

Colby-Sawyer College Web site, http://www.colby-sawyer.edu/ (July 29, 2005), "David Elliott."*

F

FEINSTEIN, John 1956-

Personal

Surname pronounced "Fine-steen"; born July 28, 1956, in New York, NY; son of Martin (an opera director) and Berwile (a college professor; maiden name, Richman) Feinstein; married; wife's name, Mary Clare; children: Daniel. *Education:* Duke University, B.A., 1977 (one source says 1978). *Politics:* Democrat. *Religion:* Jewish.

Addresses

Home—9200 Town Gate Lane, Bethesda, MD 20817. *Agent*—c/o Esther Newburg, ICM, 40 West 57th St., New York, NY 10019.

Career

Washington Post, Washington, DC, sportswriter, beginning 1977; special contributor to *Sports Illustrated.* Commentator for National Public Radio and ESPN.

Member

U.S. Basketball Writer's Association, U.S. Tennis Writer's Association (vice president), National Sportscasters and Sportswriters Association, Newspaper Guild.

Awards, Honors

Awards from U.S. Basketball Writer's Association, 1981, 1982, 1983, 1984, 1985; National Sportscasters and Sportswriters Association, best sports stories awards, 1982, 1985, 1986, D.C. Writer of the Year award, 1985; best event coverage award, Associated Press Sports Editors, 1985.

Writings

A Season on the Brink: A Year with Bob Knight and the Indiana Hoosiers, Macmillan (New York, NY), 1986.

A Season Inside: One Year in College Basketball, Villard Books (New York, NY), 1988.

Forever's Team, Villard Books (New York, NY), 1990.

Hard Courts: Real Life on the Professional Tennis Tours, Villard Books (New York, NY), 1991.

Running Mates (mystery novel), Villard Books (New York, NY), 1992.

Play Ball: The Life and Troubled Times of Major League Baseball, Villard Books (New York, NY), 1993.

A Good Walk Spoiled: Days and Nights on the PGA Tour, Little, Brown (Boston, MA), 1995.

Winter Games (mystery novel), Little, Brown (Boston, MA), 1995.

A Civil War, Army vs. Navy: A Year inside College Football's Purest Rivalry, Little, Brown (Boston, MA), 1996.

(Editor) *The Best American Sports Writing 1996,* Houghton (Boston, MA), 1997.

A March to Madness: The View from the Floor in the Atlantic Coast Conference, Little, Brown (Boston, MA), 1998, with new afterword, 1999.

The First Coming: Tiger Woods, Master or Martyr?, Ballantine (New York, NY), 1998.

The Majors: In Pursuit of Golf's Holy Grail, Little, Brown (Boston, MA), 1999.

The Last Amateurs: Playing for Glory and Honor in Division 1 Basketball's Least-known League, Little, Brown (Boston, MA), 2000.

The Punch: One Night, Two Lives, and the Fight That Changed Basketball Forever, Little, Brown (Boston, MA), 2002.

Open: Inside the Ropes at Bethpage Black, Little, Brown (Boston, MA), 2003.

Caddy for Life: The Bruce Edwards Story, Little, Brown (New York, NY), 2004.

(With Red Auerbach) *Let Me Tell You a Story: A Lifetime in the Game,* Little, Brown (New York, NY), 2004.

Last Shot: A Final Four Mystery (young-adult novel), Knopf (New York, NY), 2005.

Contributor to periodicals, including *Sporting News, Basketball Times, Outlook,* and *Eastern Basketball.*

Adaptations

A Good Walk Spoiled: Days and Nights on the PGA Tour was adapted as an audiobook, Time Warner AudioBooks, 1998. *A Season on the Brink* was filmed as a made-for-TV movie starring Brian Dennehy, ESPN, 2002. *Last Shot* was adapted as an audiobook, narrated by the author.

Work in Progress

A sequel to *Last Shot.*

Sidelights

John Feinstein is an award-winning sportswriter who gained national attention with his 1986 best seller, *A Season on the Brink: A Year with Bob Knight and the Indiana Hoosiers.* The book recounts Indiana University's 1985-1986 basketball season, from the first organizational meetings to the team's surprising loss to Cleveland State University in the first round of the National Collegiate Athletic Association (N.C.A.A.) basketball tournament. Feinstein wrote the book after enjoying unusually close access to coach Bobby Knight and his team's practices, meetings, and game-time huddles during an entire season. (Many reporters have tried unsuccessfully to get the kind of intimate coverage Feinstein was allowed.) When *A Season on the Brink* was published, it quickly sold out of its initial printing of seventeen thousand copies and appeared on the New York Times best-seller list, where it was number one for seventeen weeks. Impressive sales of *A Season on the Brink* reflect the widespread interest in Indiana's legendary basketball coach. Kim Gagne wrote in the Atlanta *Journal and Constitution* that "Feinstein offers an insider's perspective that brings the reader to an appreciation of both the genius and the madness of the coach."

Feinstein has written two other books on college basketball. *A Season Inside: One Year in College Basketball* details the 1987-1988 basketball season, during which Feinstein saw 104 games. He recounts the highs and lows of that season and provides an inside look at such prominent university coaches as Dean Smith of North Carolina, John Thompson of Georgetown, and Larry Brown of Kansas, the school that won the 1988 N.C.A.A. championship. According to *Washington Post* contributor Robert D. Novak, in the book "Feinstein has attempted a tour de force and pretty well pulled it off. He has managed to convey the excitement, intrigue, confrontation, hysteria and sheer intoxication of college basketball." Feinstein's other college basketball book, *Forever's Team,* is his most personal: it concerns the 1978-1979 basketball team from Duke University, his alma mater.

In *Hard Courts: Real Life on the Professional Tennis Tours* Feinstein demystifies the glamour surrounding the world of professional tennis. He spent a year on the pro tennis circuit, getting to know the famous and not-so-famous players, their families, and their agents. More

The moving story of the man who dedicated his career to caddying top golfer Tom Watson until he became stricken with Lou Gehrig's disease is the focus of this 2004 book.

than one hundred interviews form the text, which presents professional tennis in a distinctly unflattering light. As Julie Cart wrote in the *New York Times,* Feinstein shows he has "rare insight into the professional tennis tour. *Hard Courts* peels back layer after layer of surface gloss and undeniable glamour to expose the machinations of players' agents, the power of television and the wheeling and dealing of unscrupulous promoters. The picture is not pretty." Feinstein takes a similar approach in *A Good Walk Spoiled: Days and Nights on the PGA Tour,* spending a year on the PGA tour to learn what life is like for golf insiders. He found golf a stark contrast to many other professional sports; golfers generally really do play by the rules, live quiet lives, and go to bed early. Michael Bamberger state in the *New York Times Book Review* that Feinstein "has proved himself to be a dependable, thorough and honest reporter." The author revisited the golf world several years later with *The Majors: In Pursuit of Golf's Holy Grail.*

According to a *Kirkus Reviews* contributor, Feinstein "revisits an important National Basketball Association incident and ably dramatizes how it changed the participants and the league forever" in *The Punch: One Night,*

Two Lives, and the Fight that Changed Basketball Forever. Retelling the story of Los Angeles Lakers forward Kermit Washington, who punched and broke the jaw of Houston Rocket All-Star Rudy Tomjanovich during a fight on the basketball court, Feinstein explains how the incident, which left Washington suspended and struggling to regain his reputation and brought Tomjanovich close to death, played out in both players' careers. Neither was able to recapture the promising status of his pre-fight career.

In a completely different sports story, Feinstein retells the life of Bruce Edwards, professional caddy for legendary golfer Tom Watson, in *Caddy for Life: The Bruce Edwards Story.* Edwards served as a caddy for Watson for over forty years, and his life story reveals aspects of the golf industry known only to insiders. Edwards was diagnosed with Lou Gehrig's disease in 2003, and Feinstein covers the caddy's struggle with the disease. "This book will thoroughly entertain golf fans," promised a critic for *Publishers Weekly.* Larry R. Little, writing in *School Library Journal,* commented that readers will appreciate the "unique insight into a caddy's dedicated life on the P. G. A. tour."

In addition to his nonfiction work, Feinstein has also penned two mysteries. *Running Mates* is a political thriller involving the assassination of Maryland's governor. An investigative reporter looking into the case discovers a surprising alliance between a right-wing extremist and a radical feminist who may have had the governor killed so that his female lieutenant-governor can rise to power. A *Publishers Weekly* reviewer voiced praise for *Running Mates,* stating: "A strong, surprising resolution caps this thriller that delivers on its promise despite its protagonist's occasionally larger-than-life heroism and incredible luck."

In *Winter Games,* Feinstein's second mystery, a burned-out reporter returns to his hometown seeking peace and quiet, but discovers that the place is in an uproar because of a superstar on the high-school basketball team. The recruiting frenzy surrounding the young sports figure leads to the death of an assistant coach. *Winter Games* is, in the opinion of a Publishers Weekly commentator, a "dark portrayal of murder and rampant corruption on the college courts."

Feinstein combines his love of mystery novels and his expertise in sportswriting in his first novel for teens, *Last Shot: A Final Four Mystery.* Teen writers Steven Thomas and Susan Carol Anderson, both aspiring journalists, have won an award in a sportswriting competition, and are being allowed to cover the NCAA Final Four game alongside professional journalists. The two begin as rivals, but when they uncover a blackmail plot against one of the players, the pair become a team, working to uncover the mystery and get the scoop, "ultimately weaseling themselves into the bad guys' lair in classic Hardy Boys' fashion," as Bill Ott pointed out in *Booklist.* "This story . . . breaks new ground for teens,

focusing primarily on the influential role of media in promoting college basketball," noted Gerry Larson, reviewing the book for *School Library Journal.* According to a *Kirkus Reviews* critic, "Feinstein uses simple prose, lively dialogue, and authentic details" to bring the Final Four game to life for his readers. A *Publishers Weekly* critic praised the mystery aspect, noting that "the author's plotting entails some fancy footwork that will keep readers on their toes." With experience as a commentator for National Public Radio, Feinstein performed the audiobook version of *Last Shot* himself.

On the *Random House Canada Web site,* an interviewer asked Feinstein why he decided to write teen fiction. "Mostly I was inspired to write this by having a ten-year-old son who is a huge basketball fan," the sportswriter/novelist explained. "It is tough for him to read my 'grown-up' stuff on basketball—though he tried—so I wanted to write something he could read that would give him a sense of the sport and, I hoped, entertain him at the same time."

THE PUNCH
ONE NIGHT, TWO LIVES, AND THE FIGHT THAT CHANGED BASKETBALL FOREVER

"THE BEST WRITER OF SPORTS BOOKS IN AMERICA TODAY." –BOSTON GLOBE

JOHN FEINSTEIN
AUTHOR OF *THE LAST AMATEURS* AND *A GOOD WALK SPOILED*

Sports commentator Feinstein focuses on the violence that broke out on the basketball court during a 1977 match-up between the Houston Rockets and the Los Angeles Lakers. (Cover photograph by Photodisc.)

Biographical and Critical Sources

PERIODICALS

Booklist, March 15, 1992, Mary Carroll, review of *Running Mates,* p. 1340; April 1, 1993, Wes Lukowsky, review of *Play Ball: The Life and Troubled Times of Major League Baseball,* p. 1386; May 15, 1995, Bill Ott, review of *A Good Walk Spoiled: Days and Nights on the PGA Tour,* p. 1626; November 1, 1995, Wes Lukowsky, review of *Winter Games,* p. 457; October 1, 1996, Bill Ott, review of *The Best American Sports Writing,* 1996, p. 316; November 15, 1996, Wes Lukowsky, review of *A Civil War, Army vs. Navy: A Year inside College Football's Purest Rivalry,* p. 565; November 15, 1997, Wes Lukowsky, review of *A March to Madness: The View from the Floor in the Atlantic Coast Conference,* p. 522; September 1, 1998, Bill Ott, review of *A March to Madness,* p. 55; March 1, 1999, Bill Ott, review of *The Majors: In Pursuit of Golf's Holy Grail,* p. 1100; September 15, 2000, Wes Lukowsky, review of *The Last Amateurs: Playing for Glory and Honor in Division I, Basketball's Least-known League,* p. 186; July, 2002, Wes Lukowsky, review of *The Punch: One Night, Two Lives, and the Fight That Changed Basketball Forever,* p. 1794; May 1, 2003, Bill Ott, review of *Open: Inside the Ropes at Bethpage Black,* p. 1506; April 15, 2004, Gilbert Taylor, review of *Caddy for Life: The Bruce Edwards Story,* p. 1402; February 1, 2005, Bill Ott, review of *Last Shot: A Final Four Mystery,* p. 954.

Book Week, January 18, 1998, review of *A March to Madness,* p. 6.

Business Week, April 5, 1993, David Greising, review of *Play Ball: The Life and Troubled Times of Major League Baseball,* p. 8.

Chicago Tribune, November 16, 1986.

Christian Science Monitor, August 23, 1991, Gregory M. Lamb, review of *Hard Courts: Real Life on the Professional Tennis Tours,* p. 12; April 23, 1993, Charles Fountain, review of *Play Ball,* p. 11; October 4, 1995, Keith Henderson, review of *A Good Walk Spoiled,* p. 15; December 6, 1996, Ross Atkin, review of *A Civil War, Army vs. Navy,* p. 13.

Commentary, September, 1993, Jay P. Lefkowitz, review of *Play Ball,* p. 61.

Economist, February 15, 1997, review of *The Best American Sports Writing 1996,* p. 15.

Globe & Mail (Toronto, Ontario, Canada), April 10, 1999, review of *The Majors,* p. D11.

Horn Book,.

Journal and Constitution, (Atlanta, GA), March 1, 1987.

Kirkus Reviews, November 15, 1997, review of *A March to Madness,* p. 1683; March 15, 1999, review of *The Majors,* p. 426; September 15, 2002, review of *The Punch,* p. 1363; January 1, 2005, review of *Last Shot,* p. 51.

Kliatt, September, 1997, review of *A Good Walk Spoiled,* p. 7.

Knight-Ridder/Tribune News Service, August 2, 1999, Ed Sherman, review of *The Majors,* p. K6030; December 10, 2000, Ed Sherman, "Sports Books by Cramer, Feinstein Tell Intriguing Stories," p. K2566.

Library Journal, May 1, 1993, Albert Spencer, review of *Play Ball,* p. 92; May 15, 1995, Terry Madden, review of *A Good Walk Spoiled,* p. 76; November 1, 1995, Rex E. Klett, review of *Winter Games,* p. 109; October 1, 1996, review of *A Civil War, Army vs. Navy,* p. 87; January, 1998, William O. Scheeren, review of *A March to Madness,* p. 109; April 15, 1999, Peter Ward, review of *The Majors,* p. 105; June 15, 2000, Ray Vignovich, review of *The Majors* (audio version), p. 138; December 10, 2000, Ed Sherman, review of *The Last Amateurs,* p. K2566; November 1, 2002, Jim Burns, review of *The Punch,* p. 97; April 15, 2004, Larry R. Little, review of *Caddy for Life,* p. 93.

Library Media Connection, April-May, 2005, Ruth Cox Clark, review of *Last Shot,* p. 77.

New York Times, August 25, 1991, Julie Cart, review of *Hard Courts;* December 22, 1991, Michael Kornfeld, review of *Hard Courts;* February 11, 1996, Charley Rosen, review of *Winter Games;* December 24, 1997, Richard Bernstein, review of *A March to Madness;* December 12, 2000, Michiko Kakutani, review of *The Last Amateurs,* p. B7.

New York Times Book Review, January 22, 1989; January 7, 1990; May 10, 1992, Marilyn Stasio, review of *Running Mates,* p. 23; April 4, 1993, Roger Noll, review of *Play Ball,* p. 24; June 11, 1995, Michael Bamberger, review of *A Good Walk Spoiled,* February 11, 1996, Charley Rosen, review of *Winter Games,* p. 22; November 3, 1996, Michael Lichtenstein, review of *A Civil War, Army vs. Navy,* p. 18; March 22, 1998, David Davis, review of *A March to Madness,* p. 16; February 28, 1999, review of *A March to Madness,* p. 24; May 2, 1999, Dave Anderson, review of *The Majors,* p. 16.

People, June 19, 1995, Tony Chiu, review of *A Good Walk Spoiled,* p. 36; March 16, 1998, Alex Tresniowski, review of *A March to Madness,* p. 34.

Publishers Weekly, March 2, 1992, review of *Running Mates,* p. 52; April 24, 1995, review of *A Good Walk Spoiled,* p. 52; September 25, 1995, review of *Winter Games,* p. 46; September 16, 1996, review of *A Civil War, Army vs. Navy,* p. 61; October 14, 1996, review of *The Best American Sports Writing 1996,* p. 78; December 1, 1997, review of *A March to Madness,* p. 38; March 22, 1998, David Davis, review of *A March to Madness,* p. 16; March 29, 1999, review of *The Majors,* p. 76; October 23, 2000, review of *The Last Amateurs,* p. 71; April 28, 2003, review of *Open,* p. 60; April 5, 2004, review of *Caddy for Life,* p. 58; April 19, 2004, Daisy Maryles, "Remembering the Caddy," p. 18; January 24, 2005, review of *Last Shot,* p. 244; March 14, 2005, review of *Last Shot* (audio book), p. 26.

School Library Journal, January, 1992, Dino Vretos, review of *Hard Courts,* p. 145; August, 1993, Judy Sokoll, review of *Play Ball,* p. 206; January, 2005, Gerry Larson, review of *Last Shot,* p. 128.

Sporting News, February 16, 1987; July 3, 1995, Steve Gietschier, review of *A Good Walk Spoiled,* p. 7; November 18, 1996, Steve Gietschier, review of *A Civil War, Army vs. Navy,* p. 8.

Sports Illustrated, November 19, 1986; October 14, 1991, Ron Fimrite, review of *Hard Courts,* p. 8; February 23, 1998, Charles Hirshberg, review of *A March to Madness,* p. 27A; March 22, 1999, Walter Bingham, review of *The Majors,* p. R26; November 13, 2000, Charles Hirshberg, review of *The Last Amateur,* p. R16..

Time, September 2, 1991, John Skow, *Hard Courts,* p. 69.

Voice of Youth Advocates, April, 1998, review of *Winter Games,* p. 41.

Wall Street Journal, April 23, 1993, Frederick C. Klein, review of *Play Ball,* p. A12; July 26, 1995, Frederick C. Klein, *A Good Walk Spoiled,* p. A10; April 9, 1999, review of *The Majors,* p. W10; November 10, 2000, Larry Platt, review of *The Last Amateurs,* p. W8.

Washington Monthly, December, 2000, David Plotz, review of *The Last Amateurs,* p. 52.

Washington Post, November 28, 1988; January 26, 1990.

Washington Post Book World, November 23, 1986.

ONLINE

Golf California Web site, http://www.golfcalifornia.com/ (December 29, 2000), Mike Dalecki, review of *The Majors.*

Random House Canada Web site, http://www.random house.ca/ (July 29, 2005) interview with Feinstein.*

*   *   *

FINNEY, Patricia 1958-
(P. F. Chisholm)

Personal

Born May 12, 1958, in London, England; daughter of Jarlath John (an attorney) and Daisy (an attorney; maiden name, Veszy) Finney; married; children: three. *Education:* Wadham College, Oxford, B.A. (with honors), 1980. *Politics:* "Right-wing." *Religion:* Roman Catholic. *Hobbies and other interests:* Science, karate, embroidery, folk music.

Addresses

Home—Spain. *Agent*—McIntosh & Otis, Inc., 475 Fifth Ave., New York, NY 10017. *E-mail*—patricia@patricia-finney.co.uk.

Career

Writer, 1977—.

Awards, Honors

David Higham Award, David Higham Associates Literary Agency, 1977, for *A Shadow of Gulls;* Edgar Allan Poe Award nomination, Mystery Writers of America, 2005, for *Assassin.*

Writings

FOR CHILDREN

I, Jack, illustrated by Peter Bailey, Corgi Yearling (London, England), 2000, HarperCollins (New York, NY), 2004.

Jack and Police Dog Rebel, illustrated by Peter Bailey, Corgi Yearling (London, England), 2002.

"LADY GRACE MYSTERIES"; HISTORICAL FICTION; FOR YOUNG ADULTS

Assassin, Delacorte Press (New York, NY), 2004.

Betrayal, Delacorte Press (New York, NY), 2004.

Deception, Delacorte Press (New York, NY), 2005.

"DAVID BECKET AND SIMON AMES" SERIES; HISTORICAL FICTION; FOR ADULTS

Firedrake's Eye, St. Martin's (New York, NY), 1992.

Unicorn's Blood, Picador (New York, NY), 1998.

Gloriana's Torch, St. Martin's Press (New York, NY), 2003.

"SIR ROBERT CAREY MYSTERIES"; AS P. F. CHISHOLM; FOR ADULTS

A Famine of Horses, Hodder and Stoughton (London, England), 1994.

A Season of Knives, Hodder and Stoughton (London, England), 1995.

A Surfeit of Guns, Hodder and Stoughton (London, England), 1996.

A Plague of Angels, Hodder and Stoughton (London, England), 1998, with introduction by Diana Gabaldon, Poisoned Pen Press (Scottsdale, AZ), 2000.

OTHER

A Shadow of Gulls ("Lugh Mac Romain" series; historical fiction), Putnam (New York, NY), 1977.

The Flood (radio play), broadcast by British Broadcasting Corporation (BBC) Radio, 1977.

The Crow Goddess ("Lugh Mac Romain" series; historical fiction), Putnam (New York, NY), 1978.

Author of television preview column for London *Evening Standard;* author of unproduced screenplay *Saint Bridget.* Contributor of articles and stories to magazines and newspapers.

Work in Progress

Jack and Old Chap, a sequel to *Jack and Police Dog Rebel;* "Reykiki," a fantasy trilogy for children; *Pushing a Pea up Your Nose,* a contemporary love story; *The Durable Fire,* an historical novel; *Queen's Shade,* a film script; and *A Quarrell of Lawyers,* a sequel to *A Plague of Angels.*

Sidelights

British-born writer Patricia Finney was only seventeen years old when she completed her first novel, *A Shadow of Gulls*. Set in second-century Ireland, the book is based on the Ulster cycle of Celtic hero tales. The hero of the story is Lugh the Harper, a warrior who participates in many bloody battles. In *The Crow Goddess* Finney continues the saga of Lugh the Harper and his adventures in ancient Ireland.

Finney has continued to write historical fiction, for both adults and young adults. Her adult series include the "David Becket and Simon Ames" series, about a pair of spies in the service of Queen Elizabeth I; and—under the pseudonym P. F. Chisholm—the "Sir Robert Carey Mysteries," based on an actual, historical figure who lived in England in the late sixteenth century. Finney's young-adult series, the "Lady Grace Mysteries" are set in the same time period. Their protagonist, Lady Grace Cavendish, is a teenaged maid of honor to Queen Elizabeth I. The books are all written as entries in Lady Grace's journal, called a "day-booke" in the story's Renaissance parlance. In the first book in the series, *Assassin,* the queen arranges several suitors for the orphaned Lady Grace, and the girl must choose between them. Immediately after she does, at a regal St. Valentine's Day ball, one of the men Grace has rejected is found stabbed to death, and the man she chose is accused of being the murderer. Lady Grace believes that the man, Lord Robert Radcliffe, has been wrongly accused, and she is determined to investigate and exonerate him. "Action makes the story a page-turner," Cheri Dobbs wrote in *School Library Journal,* "but Lady Grace's wit and personality are what readers will really enjoy." *BookLoons.com* contributor J. A. Kaszuba Locke also praised the tale, calling it "a sparkling combination of mystery and history, with surprising sidesteps, excellent momentum, and likable characters."

Lady Grace and her fellow sleuths Masou (a court acrobat and juggler) and Ellie (a laundry maid) return to investigate more strange happenings in *Betrayal* and *Conspiracy.* In the former title Lady Sarah Bartelmy, a maid of honor to the queen, disappears. She has eloped with Captain Francis Drake, according to a letter to the queen that is seemingly from Lady Sarah, but Lady Grace is suspicious. Disguised as a young man, she goes with Masou to Drake's ship to investigate and the two sleuths accidentally become stowaways. "Packed with grand adventure and frequent plot twists," according to a reviewer for *LookingGlassReview.com, Betrayal* "will delight those who relish tales of great deeds, foiled plots, and seafaring exploits."

Conspiracy takes place during the summer months, as Queen Elizabeth and her entourage travel throughout England visiting the manors of various nobles. Her majesty nearly falls victim to several potentially fatal accidents on this "progress," as the journey is called, and Lady Grace suspects a conspiracy against the controversial monarch. A reviewer for *Kidsreads.com*

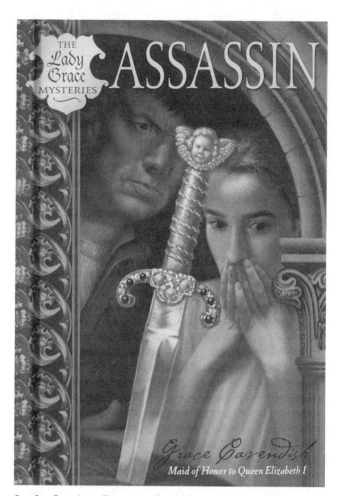

In the first installment in Patricia Finney's "Lady Grace" series a thirteen-year-old maid of honor to the queen works to solve a murder mystery in order to save her future husband. (Cover illustration by Daniel Craig.)

dubbed *Conspiracy* "not only a terrific read but also a fascinating and fun history lesson" due to Finney's inclusion of many details about life in the Elizabethan court.

Finney's novels about a big yellow Lab named Jack are in a very different vein from her other works. The first book in this series, *I, Jack,* concerns the mutt's puppy love for Petra, a neighboring dog, and the difficulties the pair face when Petra has puppies. The book is written in Jack's voice, and the dog's "limited understanding of the human world and his funny names for things provide some droll humor," commented a *Kirkus Reviews* contributor. "Jack's sincere attempts to make sense of what people are telling him are particularly funny," wrote *School Library Journal* reviewer James K. Irwin. As *Booklist* contributor Michael Cart noted, additional amusement appears in the form of "acid commentary" provided by three cats and transcribed in the book's footnotes.

Finney once commented: "I write because I enjoy doing it. When it stops being fun I'll stop writing. I believe that writing is half talent, half skill—a writer should be able to turn her hand to anything that interests her. I particularly disagree with the idea that in order to be considered 'good' fiction must be 'highbrow' and literary. All the great writers have been bestsellers in their way, from Homer to Shakespeare to Dickens.

"As far as my future writing career is concerned, I would very much like to write screenplays. I intend to keep on writing historical novels but would also like to try my hand at publishing light nonfiction, science fiction, children's books, and history.

"To expand on my politics, I am a feminist, and am against all forms of totalitarian or authoritarian thought or government. As socialism and Communism seem to me at the moment greater threats to freedom than fascism or Nazism, I am right-wing."

Biographical and Critical Sources

PERIODICALS

Best Sellers, October, 1977, review of *A Shadow of Gulls,* p. 196.

Booklist, December 15, 2003, Michael Cart, review of *I, Jack,* p. 750.

Books and Bookmen, November, 1978, review of *The Crow Goddess,* p. 64.

Kirkus Reviews, September 15, 2003, review of *Gloriana's Torch,* p. 1144; January 15, 2004, review of *I, Jack,* p. 82.

Library Journal, January, 1998, Nancy Pearl, review of *Unicorn's Blood,* p. 139; October 1, 2003, Nancy Pearl, review of *Gloriana's Torch,* p. 116.

Listener, April 14, 1977.

Observer (London, England) June 5, 1977, review of *A Shadow of Gulls,* p. 29; September 3, 1978, review of *The Crow Goddess,* p. 26.

People, September 26, 1977.

Publishers Weekly, April 27, 1992, review of *Firedrake's Eye,* p. 253; November 24, 1997, review of *Unicorn's Blood,* p. 51; October 27, 2003, review of *Gloriana's Torch,* p. 44; February 23, 2004, review of *I, Jack,* p. 77; November 1, 2004, review of *Assassin,* p. 63.

School Library Journal, May, 2004, James K. Irwin, review of *I, Jack,* p. 147; October, 2004, Cheri Dobbs, review of *Assassin,* p. 158.

Times Literary Supplement, April 15, 1977, review of *A Shadow of Gulls,* p. 451.

ONLINE

BookLoons.com, http://www.bookloons.com/ (July 25, 2005), J. A. Kaszuba Locke, reviews of *Assassin, Betrayal,* and *Conspiracy;* Wesley Williamson, review of *Unicorn's Blood.*

Fantastic Fiction Web site, http://www.fantasticfiction.co.uk/ (July 6, 2005), "Patricia Finney."

Kidsreads.com, http://www.kidsreads.com/ (July 28, 2005), Shannon McKenna, review of "Lady Grace Mysteries"; reviews of *Assassin, Betrayal,* and *Conspiracy.*

LookingGlassReview.com, http://www.lookingglassreview.com/ (July 28, 2005), reviews of *Assassin, Betrayal,* and *Conspiracy.**

MysteryGuide.com, http://www.mysteryguide.com/ (July 25, 2005), review of *Firedrake's Eye.*

National Association for the Teaching of English Web site, http://www.nate.org.uk/ (July 28, 2005), Leanne Wood, review of *Assassin.*

Patricia Finney Home Page, http://www.patricia-finney.co.uk (July 6, 2005),

Shots: The Crime and Mystery Magazine Online, http://www.shotsmag.co.uk/ (July 25, 2005), Maureen Carlyle, review of *Gloriana's Torch.*

*   *   *

FRITZ, Jean (Guttery) 1915-

Personal

Born November 16, 1915, in Hankow, China; moved to United States c. 1928; daughter of Arthur Minton (a minister and YMCA missionary) and Myrtle (Chaney) Guttery; married Michael Fritz, November 1, 1941; children: David, Andrea. *Education:* Wheaton College, A.B., 1937; attended Columbia University. *Hobbies and other interests:* Reading, traveling.

Addresses

Home—50 Bellewood Ave., Dobbs Ferry, NY 10522. *Agent*—Gina MacCoby Literary Agency, 1123 Broadway, Ste. 1010, New York, NY 10010. *E-mail*—jfritz60@aol.com.

Career

Writer of historical biographies and novels for young people. Silver Burdett Co., New York, NY, research assistant, 1937-41; Dobbs Ferry Library, Dobbs Ferry, NY, children's librarian, 1955-57; Jean Fritz Writers' Workshops, Katonah, NY, founder and instructor, 1962-70; Board of Co-operative Educational Service, Westchester County, NY, teacher, 1971-73; Appalachian State University, Boone, NC, faculty member, summer, 1980-82. Lecturer.

Awards, Honors

New York Times Outstanding Book of the Year citations, 1973, for *And Then What Happened, Paul Revere?,* 1974, for *Why Don't You Get a Horse, Sam Adams?,* 1975, for *Where Was Patrick Henry on the 29th of May?,* 1976, for *What's the Big Idea, Ben Franklin?,* 1981, for *Traitor: The Case of Benedict Arnold,* and 1982, for *Homesick: My Own Story; Boston Globe/Horn Book* honor book citations, 1974, for *And Then What Happened, Paul Revere?,* 1976, for *Will You Sign*

Jean Fritz

Here, John Hancock?, and 1980, for *Stonewall;* named outstanding Pennsylvania author, Pennsylvania School Library Association, 1978; Honor Award for Nonfiction, Children's Book Guild, 1978, and 1979, for "body of her creative writing"; American Book Award nomination, 1980, for *Where Do You Think You're Going, Christopher Columbus?,* and 1981, for *Traitor: The Case of Benedict Arnold;* LL.D., Washington and Jefferson College, 1982, Wheaton College, 1987; Child Study Award, and Christopher Award, both 1982; Newbery Honor Book Award, American Book Award, and *Boston Globe/Horn Book* honor book designation, all 1983, all for *Homesick: My Own Story; Boston Globe/ Horn Book* Nonfiction Award, 1984, for *The Double Life of Pocahontas,* and 1990, for *The Great Little Madison;* Regina Award, 1985; Laura Ingalls Wilder Award, 1986; Orbis Pictus Award, National Council of English Teachers, 1989, for *The Great Little Madison;* Knickerbocker Award for Juvenile Literature, 1992; National Humanities Medal, National Endowment for the Humanities, 2003. Many of Fritz's books have been named notable books by the American Library Association.

Writings

FOR CHILDREN

Bunny Hopwell's First Spring, illustrated by Rachel Dixon, Wonder (New York, NY), 1954.

Help Mr. Willy Nilly, illustrated by Jean Tamburine, Treasure (New York, NY), 1954.

Fish Head, illustrated by Marc Simont, Coward (New York, NY), 1954.

Hurrah for Jonathan!, illustrated by Violet La Mont, A. Whitman (Racine, WI), 1955.

121 Pudding Street, illustrated by Sofia, Coward (New York, NY), 1955.

Growing Up, illustrated by Elizabeth Webbe, Rand McNally (Chicago, IL), 1956.

The Late Spring, illustrated by Erik Blegvad, Coward (New York, NY), 1957.

The Cabin Faced West, illustrated by Feodor Rojankovsky, Coward (New York, NY), 1958.

(With Tom Clute) *Champion Dog, Prince Tom,* illustrated by Ernest Hart, Coward (New York, NY), 1958.

The Animals of Doctor Schweitzer, illustrated by Douglas Howland, Coward (New York, NY), 1958.

How to Read a Rabbit, illustrated by Leonard Shortall, Coward (New York, NY), 1959.

Brady, illustrated by Lynd Ward, Coward (New York, NY), 1960.

Tap, Tap Lion, 1, 2, 3, illustrated by Leonard Shortall, Coward (New York, NY), 1962.

San Francisco, illustrated by Emil Weiss, Rand McNally (Chicago, IL), 1962.

I, Adam, illustrated by Peter Burchard, Coward (New York, NY), 1963.

Magic to Burn, illustrated by Beth Krush and Joe Krush, Coward (New York, NY), 1964.

Surprise Party (reader), illustrated by George Wiggins, Initial Teaching Alphabet Publications, 1965.

The Train (reader), illustrated by Jean Simpson, Grosset (New York, NY), 1965.

Early Thunder, illustrated by Lynd Ward, Coward (New York, NY), 1967.

George Washington's Breakfast, illustrated by Paul Galdone, Coward (New York, NY), 1969.

And Then What Happened, Paul Revere?, illustrated by Margot Tomes, Coward (New York, NY), 1973.

Why Don't You Get a Horse, Sam Adams?, illustrated by Trina Schart Hyman, Coward (New York, NY), 1974.

Where Was Patrick Henry on the 29th of May?, illustrated by Margot Tomes, Coward (New York, NY), 1975.

Who's That Stopping on Plymouth Rock?, illustrated by J. B. Handelsman, Coward (New York, NY), 1975.

Will You Sign Here, John Hancock?, illustrated by Trina Schart Hyman, Coward (New York, NY), 1976.

What's the Big Idea, Ben Franklin?, illustrated by Margot Tomes, Coward (New York, NY), 1976.

The Secret Diary of Jeb and Abigail: Growing up in America, 1776-1783, illustrated by Kenneth Bald and Neil Boyle, Reader's Digest Association (Pleasantville, NY), 1976.

Can't You Make Them Behave, King George?, illustrated by Tomie de Paola, Coward (New York, NY), 1977.

Brendan the Navigator, illustrated by Enrico Arno, Coward (New York, NY), 1979.

Stonewall, illustrated by Stephen Gammell, Putnam (New York, NY), 1979.

Where Do You Think You're Going, Christopher Columbus?, illustrated by Margot Tomes, Putnam (New York, NY), 1980.

The Man Who Loved Books, illustrated by Trina Schart Hyman, Putnam (New York, NY), 1981.

Traitor: The Case of Benedict Arnold, illustrated with engravings and prints, Putnam (New York, NY), 1981.

Back to Early Cape Cod, Acorn, 1981.

The Good Giants and the Bad Pukwudgies (folktale), illustrated by Tomie de Paola, Putnam (New York, NY), 1982.

Homesick: My Own Story, illustrated by Margot Tomes, Putnam (New York, NY), 1982, reprinted, Paperstar, 1999.

The Double Life of Pocahontas, illustrated by Ed Young, Putnam (New York, NY), 1983.

China Homecoming, illustrated with photographs by Mike Fritz, Putnam (New York, NY), 1985.

Make Way for Sam Houston!, illustrated by Elise Primavera, Putnam (New York, NY), 1986.

Shh! We're Writing the Constitution, illustrated by Tomie de Paola, Putnam (New York, NY), 1987.

China's Long March: 6,000 Miles of Danger, illustrated by Yang Zhr Cheng, Putnam (New York, NY), 1988.

The Great Little Madison, Putnam (New York, NY), 1989.

Bully for You, Teddy Roosevelt!, illustrated by Mike Wimmer, Putnam (New York, NY), 1991.

George Washington's Mother, illustrated by DyAnne DiSalvo-Ryan, Putnam (New York, NY), 1992.

(With others) *The World in 1492*, illustrated by Stefano Vitale, Holt (New York, NY), 1992.

Surprising Myself, photographs by Andrea Fritz Pfleger, Owen (Katonah, NY), 1992.

The Great Adventure of Christopher Columbus: A Pop-up Book, illustrated by Tomie de Paola, Putnam & Grosset (New York, NY), 1992.

Just a Few Words, Mr. Lincoln: The Story of the Gettysburg Address, illustrated by Charles Robinson, Grosset & Dunlap (New York, NY), 1993.

Around the World in a Hundred Years: From Henry the Navigator to Magellan, illustrated by Anthony Bacon Venti, Putnam (New York, NY), 1994.

Harriet Beecher Stowe and the Beecher Preachers, illustrated with engravings and prints, Putnam (New York, NY), 1994.

You Want Women to Vote, Lizzie Stanton?, illustrated by DyAnne DiSalvo-Ryan, Putnam (New York, NY), 1995.

Why Not, Lafayette?, illustrated by Ronald Himler, Putnam (New York, NY), 1999.

Leonardo's Horse, illustrated by Hudson Talbott, Putnam (New York, NY), 2001.

The Lost Colony of Roanoke, illustrated by Hudson Talbott, Putnam (New York, NY), 2004.

OTHER

Cast for a Revolution: Some American Friends and Enemies, 1728-1814 (adult biography), Houghton-Mifflin (Boston, MA), 1972.

Contributor to books, including William Zinsser, editor, *Worlds of Childhood: The Art and Craft of Writing for Children*, Houghton-Mifflin, 1990; author of introduction to *Flaming Arrows, The Perilous Road,* and *The Buffalo Knife*, by William O. Steele, Harcourt, 2004. Book reviewer, *San Francisco Chronicle*, 1941-43, and *New York Times*, beginning 1970. Contributor of short stories to periodicals, including *Seventeen, Redbook,* and *New Yorker.*

Fritz's papers are housed in a permanent collection in the Children's Literature Collection at the University of Oregon, Eugene, and included in the Kerlan Collection at the University of Minnesota, and in a collection at the University of Southern Mississippi.

Sidelights

Jean Fritz is a highly regarded author of historical biographies for young people. As *Horn Book* contributor Mary M. Burns stated, "No one is better than Jean Fritz at making history interesting as well as comprehensible. She has the ability to define a theme, support it with facts, and transform a collection of data into a synthesis that reads like an adventure story." Fritz has written biographies of many heroes of the American Revolution, including George Washington, Paul Revere, Samuel Adams, and John Hancock, as well as other significant figures in history before and after this much-studied era, such as Christopher Columbus, Pocahontas, Elizabeth Cady Stanton, and Harriet Beecher Stowe. Fritz has won numerous awards for this work, and critics highlight her ability to bring alive complex events and people from the past through the use of humor and the inclusion of personal details that are usually left out of historical accounts.

As a child growing up in China as the daughter of missionaries, Fritz turned to writing as a "private place, where no one could come," as she recalled in a *Publishers Weekly* interview. She kept a journal into which she copied passages from books and poems written by others; later, "it became a place for her to articulate her feelings about people and life. Years later she drew upon it in her writings for children," according to O. Mell Busbin in the *Dictionary of Literary Biography*. Living in China as an American focused much of Fritz's fantasy life on the land of her parents' birth, which they spoke of frequently and with much feeling. "I think it is because I was so far away that I developed a homesickness that made me want to embrace not just a given part of America at a given time but the whole of it," Fritz wrote in an article for *Horn Book*. "No one is more patriotic than the one separated from his country; no one is as eager to find roots as the person who has been uprooted."

Fritz is credited with producing biographies that are consistently well-crafted, realistic, thoroughly researched, and often witty accounts of the characters who have shaped and influenced history. For example, in her *Language Arts* review of *Traitor: The Case of*

Benedict Arnold, Ruth M. Stein noted that Fritz's "books exemplify criteria for good biographies—accuracy, interest, relevance to our times, and insight into the person, the period and contemporaries. . . . However cozy the style and informal the writing, the scholarship is solid, yet unobtrusive." Georgess McHargue remarked in the *New York Times Book Review* that "Fritz has what amounts to perfect pitch when writing history or biography for young people."

Fritz's talent for bringing historical figures to life is a major source of her popularity with readers and critics alike. As Busbin stated in the *Dictionary of Literary Biography:* "In her biographies Fritz attempts to get at the truth of the individual through his likes, dislikes, worries, joys, successes, failures. . . . Through her humorous style she paints a full, believable picture of each individual, using specific, exact language and precise detail." "I like being a detective, a treasure hunter, an eavesdropper," Fritz revealed to Richard Ammon in a profile for *Language Arts.* "I look for personalities whose lives make good stories. I like complicated

★ "A remarkable blend of truth and storytelling."
—*Booklist* (starred review)

JEAN FRITZ
HOMESICK
My Own Story

Illustrated by Margot Tomes

In this 1982 work Fritz recounts memories from her own childhood in China where, during the 1920s, Caucasian foreigners were increasingly endangered. (Cover illustration by Margot Tomes.)

people, persons who possessed contradictions or who have interesting quirks."

Fritz began her career as a writer in the 1950s by publishing children's picture books such as *Bunny Hopwell's First Spring* and *Help Mr. Willy Nilly.* She soon branched out into historical narratives and gained a reputation as a stellar biographer of American heroes with titles published in the 1960s and 1970s, such as *Why Don't You Get a Horse, Sam Adams?, Who's That Stopping on Plymouth Rock?,* and *Can't You Make Them Behave, King George?* In the 1980s, Fritz continued to publish biographies on pivotal figures in American history, but moved beyond the core group around George Washington and the signers of the American Constitution with titles such as *Where Do You Think You're Going, Christopher Columbus?, The Double Life of Pocahontas,* and *Make Way for Sam Houston!* Like her earlier biographies, these more recent works take on subjects often written about before by others. However, reviewers compare Fritz's accounts favorably to those written by others, for she is unfailingly clear, interesting, and accessible.

The 1990s often found Fritz venturing beyond the shores of the United States in her quest for biographical material. In 1992 she contributed to *The World in 1492,* a compendium of six essays that offers a worldwide glimpse of human history five hundred years ago from the perspective of six different geographic locations. Though the depth of information offered is necessarily limited, reviewers noted, the scarcity of books offering world history to students in middle school makes the contribution invaluable. "The cumulative effect presents a global pattern of currents and undercurrents making up the swirling ocean of human existence 500 years ago," Patricia Manning commented in *School Library Journal.*

Around the World in a Hundred Years: From Henry the Navigator to Magellan also focuses on the fifteenth century. Here Fritz presents a series of European explorers whose conquest of the world beyond the shores of Europe helped make more accurate maps available for the first time, and also reaped untold profits for the Spanish and Portuguese monarchies through the enslavement of native peoples. Critics noted that Fritz does not shy away from telling unflattering truths about characters often hailed as heroes in the annals of history, and that her characteristic wit is also ever-present. "Those [students] seeking a broader picture will find this an intriguing view of the age of exploration," predicted Carolyn Phelan in *Booklist.*

Fritz returned to the time of the American Revolution with *George Washington's Mother,* a humorous biography of the mother of the first president of the United States that "depicts Mary Ball Washington as a manipulative and stubborn worrywart," according to Gale W. Sherman in *School Library Journal.* Geared for a younger audience than most of Fritz's historical narratives, *George Washington's Mother* was perceived by reviewers as intended to teach younger children something about early American history through anecdotes that emphasize how even important people are sometimes embarrassed by the behavior of their mothers.

Also intended for early-grade readers is Fritz's *Just a Few Words, Mr. Lincoln: The Story of the Gettysburg Address.* In this short history, Fritz concisely explains the causes of the American Civil War and relates the story of the battle of Gettysburg, where 23,000 Union soldiers died. The author refutes the legend that has Lincoln writing his famous speech on the train ride to Gettysburg, and includes the text of the speech at the end of the book. Though carefully designed and written with a younger audience in mind, *Just a Few Words, Mr. Lincoln,* like Fritz's books for older children, "informally yet ably conveys the significance of Lincoln's eloquent speech," according to a reviewer for *Publishers Weekly.*

In *Harriet Beecher Stowe and the Beecher Preachers,* Fritz returns readers to the U.S. Civil War era by focusing on the woman whom Lincoln credited with starting the war to end slavery through the publication of her protest novel, *Uncle Tom's Cabin.* Fritz describes Stowe's childhood as one of nine children born to a fire-and-brimstone preacher who was disappointed that his child was born a girl. "With her usual respect for young readers, Fritz explores not only a life, but also a family, an era, and vitally important social movements," remarked Sally Margolis in *School Library Journal.* Fritz notes that while Harriet Beecher Stowe was punished as a child for seeking creative expression in writing, as an adult it was the profits from Stowe's writing that supported her husband and six children. "How she managed to write at all, given the circumstances under which she struggled, is the central conflict in a biography which reads like a novel," according to Mary M. Burns in *Horn Book. Harriet Beecher Stowe and the Beecher Preachers* is often compared to two other biographies of the author of *Uncle Tom's Cabin* published near-contemporaneously. *Bulletin of the Center for Children Books* reviewer Deborah Stevenson favored Fritz's version for several reasons: "the portrayals here are livelier, . . . and the style is informative but conversational and unintimidating, qualities that make it more suitable for preteens than [the other books]."

In *You Want Women to Vote, Lizzie Stanton?* Fritz celebrates another female hero of the nineteenth century. Like Stowe, Stanton was born to a father who wished she had been born a boy, and she spent much of her life chasing her father's approval. Like Beecher Stowe, Stanton was also able to balance the acute demands of motherhood and housekeeping with the demands of her political conscience, finding the time to help organize and lead the American suffrage movement, and in the process, becoming the "Grand Old Woman of America," as Mary M. Burns noted in her review for *Horn Book.* Some reviewers claimed that Fritz manages to tell the story of Stanton's life in such an entertaining manner that students may want to read it for the story rather than for the history. Indeed, in *You Want Women to Vote, Lizzie Stanton?* Stanton "comes alive for middle

In **Why Not, Lafayette?** *Fritz presents the biography of the eighteenth-century French aristocrat who fought on behalf of democracy in both the American Revolution and in other French territories. (Illustration by Ronald Himler.)*

graders in a narrative with almost novelistic pacing, a dose of humor, and an affectionate point of view," proclaimed a critic for *Kirkus Reviews.*

Fritz offers a different perspective on the American Revolution in *Why Not, Lafayette?,* a portrait of the French nobleman who was inspired by the colonists' bid for freedom to fight alongside Washington and other Republican heroes of the war against Britain. The author portrays her protagonist as stifled by the boredom of his life in Paris, electrified by news of the colonists' struggle, on fire with admiration for General Washington, and a lifelong idealist in pursuit of republicanism. Fritz follows Lafayette from the years that made him a hero in the eyes of a new country, to the tricky years of the French Revolution, and his triumphal tour of the United States in his later life. As usual, Fritz relies on the effective inclusion of personal details to draw the reader into the reality of the life being studied. "Readers will be stirred even at this distance by Lafayette's accomplishments," predicted a contributor to *Kirkus Reviews.* Though reviewers disagreed about the degree to which Fritz is successful in portraying the important players in both the French and American revolutionary scenes, a reviewer for *Publishers Weekly* came down on the affirmative side of the question and concluded that *Why Not, Lafayette?* is "lively, vigorous and just plain fun to read."

Fritz goes beyond the borders of the United States to find a topic for *Leonardo's Horse,* which presents the five-hundred-year-long story of one piece of art designed by the famous Renaissance artist Leonardo da Vinci. In the late fifteenth century, the duke of Milan commissioned da Vinci to create for him a gigantic statue of a bronze horse. Da Vinci agreed, and got as far as making a full-size clay model of the proposed twenty-four-foot-high statue. Then the French army invaded, and their archers used the model for target practice. With the model thus destroyed, the statue was never completed. Hundreds of years later an American named Charles Dent heard about the statue, saw some of da Vinci's sketches for it, and decided to complete the project as a present from the United States to Italy. In *Leonardo's Horse* Fritz weaves in information about the life and other major works created by da Vinci, forming what *Booklist* critic Carolyn Phelan described as an "absorbing text [that] is both a lively introduction to Leonardo and a tribute to Dent." Plus, noted a *Kirkus Reviews* critic, "the contemporary process by which the horse was created and cast is described with enough detail to fascinate but not to bore."

Fritz received her inspiration to write *Leonardo's Horse* from an unusual source. A foundry near Fritz's upstate New York home had received the contract to cast the statue, and before the horse went to its permanent home in Milan, Italy, it was on view at the foundry. Fritz discovered this by accident while searching for a fun weekend activity for her and a friend, and they decided to go see the horse. As soon as they drove within view of the horse "I said, 'Oh my gosh, that belongs in a book,'" Fritz told *Publishers Weekly* interviewer Heather Vogel Frederick. She found one of the men in charge of the horse's creation and asked to write a story about it, but he was skeptical. "He said, 'Well, I'll send my children to school tomorrow to see if they have any of your books at the library,'" she continued. "They came back with about thirty, so I guess he decided I'd be all right."

The Lost Colony of Roanoke examines one of the great mysteries of American history: what happened to this colony, the first English colony in what would become the United States? Fritz first traces the history of the colony's founding and the brief years of its known existence. Famed English explorer Sir Walter Raleigh tried twice to plant a colony on the island of Roanoke, located off the coast of what later became North Carolina, but both times supplies and food ran low. Twice some of the Englishmen returned to their home country for more provisions, and both times those who were left behind disappeared, with no trace remaining when the next expedition arrived. Fritz searches for clues to these disappearances in Roanoke's known history, and finds some in the settlers' hostile attitude towards the Native American inhabitants of the area. "Lively storytelling . . . archaeological details, and a survey of theories make this a fascinating volume," wrote a *Kirkus Re-*

Leonardo's Horse **focuses on two dreamers: Leonardo da Vinci and American sculptor Charles Dent who made real da Vinci's centuries-old dream of creating a giant bronze horse for the city of Milan.** *(Illustration by Hudson Talbott.)*

views contributor. "Fritz has scored again," Ann Welton declared in *School Library Journal,* "making history breathe while showing both historians and archaeologists at their reconstructive best."

Fritz once shared her thoughts on the perennial popularity of biographies: "I think young people of almost any age or ability read biographies for the same reason that adults do—or would if they could find what they want. We all seek insight into the human condition, and it is helpful to find familiar threads running through the lives of others, however famous. We need to know more people in all circumstances and times so we can pursue our private, never-to-be-fulfilled quest to find out what life is all about. In actual experience we are able to see so few lives in the round and to follow them closely from beginning to end. I, for one, need to possess a certain number of relatively whole lives in the long span of history."

Fritz has summed up her feelings on writing about the past in this manner: "My interest in writing about American history stemmed originally, I think, from a subconscious desire to find roots. I lived in China until I was thirteen, hearing constant talk about 'home' (meaning America), but since I had never been 'home,'

I felt like a girl without a country. I have put down roots quite firmly by now, but in the process I have discovered the joys of research and am probably hooked. I eavesdrop on the past to satisfy my own curiosity, but if I can surprise children into believing history, I will be happy, especially if they find, as I do, that truth is stranger (and often funnier) than fiction."

Biographical and Critical Sources

BOOKS

Children's Literature Review, Gale (Detroit, MI), Volume 2, 1976, Volume 14, 1988.

Dictionary of Literary Biography, Volume 52: *American Writers for Children since 1960: Fiction,* Gale (Detroit, MI), 1986.

Hostetler, Elizabeth Ann Rumer, *Jean Fritz: A Critical Biography,* University of Toledo (Toledo, OH), 1981.

Norton, Donna E., *Through the Eyes of a Child: An Introduction to Children's Literature,* 2nd edition, Merrill (Columbus, OH), 1987.

Something about the Author Autobiography Series, Volume 2, Gale (Detroit, MI), 1986.

PERIODICALS

Booklist, November 1, 1992, Carolyn Phelan, review of *The World in 1492,* p. 506; October 1, 1993, Kay Weisman, review of *Just a Few Words, Mr. Lincoln,* p. 347; May 15, 1994, Carolyn Phelan, review of *Around the World in a Hundred Years,* p. 1676; September 15, 1999, Randy Meyer, review of *Why Not, Lafayette?,* p. 253; April 15, 2000, Sue-Ellen Beauregard, review of *Who's That Stepping on Plymouth Rock?,* p. 1558; October 15, 2001, Carolyn Phelan, review of *Leonardo's Horse,* p. 394; April 1, 2004, Carolyn Phelan, review of *The Lost Colony of Roanoke,* p. 1362.

Bulletin of the Center for Children's Books, March, 1961; March, 1974; November, 1975, Zena Sutherland, review of *Where Was Patrick Henry on the 29th of May?,* p. 44; July-August, 1982; June, 1994, Betsy Hearne, review of *Around the World in a Hundred Years,* p. 319; October, 1994, Deborah Stevenson, review of *Harriet Beecher Stowe and the Beecher Preachers,* p. 45; October, 1995, Elizabeth Bush, review of *You Want Women to Vote, Lizzie Stanton?,* pp. 53-54; December, 1999, Elizabeth Bush, review of *Why Not, Lafayette?,* p. 128.

Catholic Library World, July-August, 1985.

Early Years, February, 1982.

Five Owls, May-June, 1987; May-June, 1994, Mary Bahr Fritts, review of *Around the World in a Hundred Years,* p. 108.

Horn Book, October, 1967; January-February, 1985; July-August, 1986; March-April, 1993, Anita Silvey, review of *The World in 1492,* p. 226; July-August, 1994, Mary M. Burns, review of *Around the World in a Hundred Years,* p. 471; September-October, 1994, Mary M. Burns, review of *Harriet Beecher Stowe and the*

Beecher Preachers, pp. 606-607; January-February, 1996, Mary M. Burns, review of *You Want Women to Vote, Lizzie Stanton?,* pp. 89-90; November, 1999, Margaret A. Bush, review of *Why Not, Lafayette?,* p. 756; March-April, 2004, "National Humanities Medal," p. 221; May-June, 2004, Betty Carter, review of *The Lost Colony of Roanoke,* p. 344.

Instructor, April, 2002, Judy Freeman, review of *Leonardo's Horse,* p. 19.

Kirkus Reviews, August 1, 1995, review of *You Want Women to Vote, Lizzie Stanton?,* p. 1109; October 1, 1999, review of *Why Not, Lafayette?,* p. 1579; September 15, 2001, review of *Leonardo's Horse,* p. 1357; April 1, 2004, review of *The Lost Colony of Roanoke,* p. 329.

Language Arts, February, 1977; April, 1980; September, 1982, Ruth M. Stein, review of *Traitor: The Case of Benedict Arnold,* p. 605; March, 1983, Richard Ammon, "Profile: Jean Fritz," pp. 365-369; September, 1994, Miriam Martinez and Marcia F. Nash, review of *George Washington's Mother,* pp. 371-372.

Los Angeles Times Book Review, July 25, 1982, Barbara Karlin, review of *And Then What Happened, Paul Revere?, What's the Big Idea, Ben Franklin?,* and *Where Was Patrick Henry on the 29th of May?,* p. 9.

New Yorker, December 6, 1982, Faith McNulty, review of *Homesick: My Own Story.*

New York Times Book Review, November 9, 1980, Georgess McHargue, "Early Explorers," pp. 60-61; November 14, 1982, James A. Michener, "China Childhood," pp. 41, 57.

Publishers Weekly, July 24, 1981; October 26, 1992, review of *The World in 1492,* p. 73; September 20, 1993, review of *Just a Few Words, Mr. Lincoln,* p. 72; September 20, 1999, review of *Why Not, Lafayette?,* p. 89, review of *Homesick: My Own Story,* p. 90; March 26, 2001, review of *Why Not, Lafayette?,* p. 95; October 22, 2001, Heather Vogel Frederick, interview with Fritz, p. 25; May 17, 2004, review of *The Lost Colony of Roanoke,* p. 52.

San Francisco Chronicle, April 3, 1985.

School Library Journal, November, 1967; October, 1992, Gale W. Sherman, review of *George Washington's Mother,* p. 103; November, 1992, Patricia Manning, review of *The World in 1492,* p. 115; October, 1993, Leda Schubert, review of *Just a Few Words, Mr. Lincoln,* p. 118; September, 1994, Sally Margolis, review of *Harriet Beecher Stowe and the Beecher Preachers,* p. 227; September, 1995, Rebecca O'Connell, review of *You Want Women to Vote, Lizzie Stanton?,* p. 208; September, 2001, Anne Chapman Callaghan, review of *Leonardo's Horse,* p. 214; November, 2003, Carol Fazioli, review of *Homesick,* p. 82; January, 2004, Joy Fleishhacker, review of *Around the World in a Hundred Years: From Henry the Navigator to Magellan,* p. 79; May, 2004, Ann Welton, review of *The Lost Colony of Roanoke,* p. 167; October, 2004, review of *The Lost Colony of Roanoke,* p. S31.

Top of the News, June, 1976.

Voice of Youth Advocates, August, 1994, Joanne Johnson, review of *Harriet Beecher Stowe and the Beecher Preachers,* p. 166.

ONLINE

Scholastic Web site, http://www.scholastic.com/ (July 6, 2005), interview with Fritz.*

G

GARRISON, Barbara 1931-

Personal

Born August 22, 1931, in London, England; daughter of Murray (a film executive) and Dorothy (Littman) Silverstone; married Michael Garrison, June 17, 1955 (deceased, 1965); children: Brian Steven. *Education:* Wellesley College, B.A., 1953; Columbia University Teachers College, M.A., 1956.

Addresses

Home—12 East 87th St., New York, NY 10028. *E-mail*—Barbara@barbaragarrison.com.

Career

Artist, illustrator, and art teacher. Spence School, New York, NY, art instructor, 1963-69; art teacher at Harriet Beecher Stowe School, 1969-70, and Nightingale-Bamford School, New York, NY, beginning 1970. Art included on UNICEF greeting cards. *Exhibitions:* Work exhibited in the United States and abroad, including at Community Church Gallery, New York, NY; Cove Gallery, Wellfleet, MA; Every Picture Tells a Story, Los Angeles, CA; Pratt Graphics Center, New York, NY; Atlantic Gallery and Long Island University, Brooklyn, NY; Watermill Gallery, Watermill, NY; The Gallery, Fort Wayne, IN; Fine Arts Gallery, Ardmore, PA; Graphics 1 and Graphics 2, Boston, MA; 2nd Street Gallery, Charleston, VA; Maine Coast Artists Gallery, Rockport; State University of New York at Alfred; Purdue University, West Lafayette, IN; Temple University, Philadelphia, PA; Haruko Ishii, Tokyo; Galerie Naif, Tokyo; and the Bieniale of Illustration, Bratislava, 2000. Work included in permanent collections at New York Public Library, Butler Institute of American Art, Georgia Museum of Art, Skirball Museum, Museum of American Illustration, University of Southern Mississippi De-Grummond Collection, and Slater Memorial Museum. Print Collection.

Member

National Association of Women Artists, Artist Equity of New York.

Awards, Honors

John Carl Giogri Memorial Prize, and Walter Giger Memorial Prize, National Association of Women Artists Exhibition, 1974; Doris Kemp Purchase Prize, National Arts Club, 1975; second highest merit award for graphics, Miniature Art Society of New Jersey, 1975; Purchase Prize, Arena '75 (Binghamton, NY), 1975; Bicentennial Award, and Silver Medal, National Arts Club Graphics Exhibition, 1976; Bicentennial Award, Miniature Art Society of New Jersey, 1976; Central Savings Bank Award, New York Outdoor Art Fair, 1976; second prize, Gracie Square Art Show, New York, NY; second prize, Art in the Aisles, Church of Heavenly Rest, New York, NY, 1977; numerous other awards

Illustrator

Jane Yolen, *The Sultan's Perfect Tree,* Parents' Magazine Press (New York, NY), 1977.

Michael Patrick Hearn, *Breakfast, Books, and Dreams: A Day in Verse,* F. Warne (New York, NY), 1981.

Gladys Scheffrin-Falk, *Another Celebrated Dancing Bear,* Scribner's (New York, NY), 1991.

Marc Harshman, *Only One,* Cobblehill Books (New York, NY), 1993.

Maida Silverman, *My First Book of Jewish Holidays,* Dial Books for Young Readers (New York, NY), 1994.

Amy Littlesugar, *Josiah True and the Art Maker,* Simon and Schuster Books for Young Readers (New York, NY), 1995.

May Garelick, *Look at the Moon,* Mondo (Greenvale, NY), 1996.

Laurence P. Pringle, *One Room School,* Boyds Mills Press (Honesdale, PA), 1998.

Johanna Hurwitz, *Dear Emma,* HarperCollins (New York, NY), 2002.

Mark Taylor, *The Frog House,* Dutton Children's Books (New York, NY), 2004.

Work has appeared in magazines and newspapers.

Biographical and Critical Sources

PERIODICALS

Booklist, July, 1995, Janice Del Negro, review of *Josiah True and the Art Maker,* p. 1884.
Publishers Weekly, September 19, 1994, review of *My First Book of Jewish Holidays,* p. 68; March 15, 2004, review of *The Frog House,* p. 74.

ONLINE

Barbara Garrison Web site, http://www.barbaragarrison. com (March 19, 2005).
Boyds Mills Press Web site, http://www.boydsmillspress. com/ (March 19, 2005), "Barbara Garrison."*

*   *   *

GEESLIN, Campbell 1925-

Personal

Born December 5, 1925, in Goldthwaite, TX; son of Edward (an engineer) and Margaret Lee (Gaddis) Geeslin; married Marilyn Low (a teacher of English as a second language), 1951; children: Seth, Meg Melillo, Ned. *Education:* Columbia College, A.B., 1949; University of Texas, M.A., 1950.

Addresses

Home—209 Davis Ave., White Plains, NY 10605. *Agent*—Robert Lescher, 47 E. 19th St., New York, NY 10003.

Career

Houston Post, Houston, TX, began as reporter, became assistant managing editor, 1950-64; worked for Gannett Newspapers in Cocoa Beach, FL, White Plains, NY, and Rochester, NY, 1964-68; *This Week,* New York, NY, managing editor, 1968-71; *Parade,* New York, NY, managing editor, 1970-71; New York Times Syndicate, New York, NY, editor, 1971-73; *Cue,* New York, NY, editor, 1973-75; *People,* New York, NY, senior editor, 1975-78; *Life,* New York, NY, text editor, 1978-89. Trustee, White Plains Public Library. *Military service:* U.S. Navy, 1943-46.

Awards, Honors

Parents Foundation award, and Comstock Book Award for Best Picture Book, 2004, both for *Elena's Serenade.*

Writings

The Bonner Boys: A Novel about Texas, Simon & Schuster (New York, NY), 1981.

In Rosa's Mexico, illustrated by Andrea Arroyo, Knopf (New York, NY), 1996.
On Ramón's Farm: Five Tales of Mexico, illustrated by Petra Mathers, Atheneum (New York, NY), 1998.
Big Ears: Growing up in West Texas (autobiography), White Pine Press (White Plains, NY), 1998.
How Nanita Learned to Make Flan (also see below), illustrated by Petra Mathers, Atheneum (New York, NY), 1999.
Elena's Serenade, illustrated by Ana Juan, Atheneum (New York, NY), 2004.

Author of libretto for *How Nanita Learned to Make Flan,* music by Enrique Gonzalez-Medina, produced in Cincinnati, OH, 2000. Columnist for *Authors Guild Bulletin.*

Author's works have been translated into Japanese and Korean.

Adaptations

Elena's serenade was optioned for an animated film produced in Japan, and was adapted for CD-ROM.

Work in Progress

Clara and Señor Frog, forthcoming, 2007.

Sidelights

Campbell Geeslin published his first book shortly before his retirement from the world of print journalism, where he had worked for more than three decades as a reporter and editor. Although Geeslin and his family were centered for many years in and around New York City, the author retains vivid memories of his youth in rural west Texas in the 1930s, and the vacations he and his family took to an even more exotic locale—across the border into Mexico. Geeslin draws on his familiarity with the Texas-Mexico border area in his writing, which includes picture books such as *Elena's Serenade* and *How Nanita Learned to Make Flan.*

Geeslin's first book, *The Bonner Boys: A Novel about Texas,* was written primarily for adult readers. A saga of five brothers who come of age on a West Texas ranch in the 1930s, the novel follows the siblings through the decisive experiences of World War II and its aftermath, as each must weigh a wide array of choices as he ponders his future. One brother becomes a musician, another an entrepreneur of questionable conduct, the third a journalist, and the last two begin careers as corporate executive and attorney. The brothers' lives are contrasted when they eventually return to the Texas capital of Austin for a reunion and a visit with their aged mother. A *Publishers Weekly* critic dubbed *The Bonner Boys* "a warm and satisfying novel" that solidly evokes life in the American Southwest of the 1930s.

Geeslin moved from novels to picture books in the mid-1990s. As he once told *Something about the Author* (*SATA*): "After I retired from a job as an editor at *Life* magazine, I wrote and hand-printed from woodcuts an illustrated story for my twin granddaughters. An editor at Knopf wanted to buy the story, *In Rosa's Mexico,* but hired a professional illustrator to do the pictures." The book was published in 1996 with illustrations by Andrea Arroyo."

Written for beginning readers, *In Rosa's Mexico* presents three tales centered on a Mexican girl and her encounters with fabled characters from Mexican folklore. In the first story, "Rosa and El Gallo," Rosa is distressed when ash from a nearby volcano ruins the local

Campbell Geeslin spins a tale about new shoes that whisk a young girl away on a magical adventure in How Nanita Learned to Make Flan. *(Illustration by Petra Mathers.)*

In Elena's Serenade *a young girl makes a long journey in the hopes of proving to her father that she has the skill to become a talented glass blower. (Illustration by Ana Juan.)*

violet crop because she sells these flowers at the market to earn money for her impoverished family. When the hungry family decides to cook their rooster for food, the bird begins to cough up lovely violet petals in an effort to save himself. Rosa now has something to sell at the market, and she earns enough money to feed her family and postpone the clever rooster's demise. In the book's second tale, when Rosa's beloved burro becomes sick, she rides up to the night sky and retrieves a remedy from "las estrellas"; the burro recovers and now wears the mark of heaven on his head. The final story centers on Rosa and her discovery of a missing wedding ring that had been stolen by a fox. Her honest actions save El Lobo, the wolf, who rewards her with a magic pillow.

Geeslin narrates all the stories included in *In Rosa's Mexico* in a limited vocabulary that incorporates many Spanish terms. Arroyo's drawings provide easy clues to these words' meaning for non-Spanish speakers, and a glossary of Spanish words precedes the text as well. *New York Times Book Review* contributor Kathleen Krull termed the language and action in *In Rosa's Mexico* somewhat "idiosyncratic," adding that the spare prose works very well for the bilingual, magical-themed format. A *Publishers Weekly* contributor noted that Geeslin crafts a "simply stated yet musical text." Praising Arroyo's illustrations, Janice M. Del Negro asserted in the *Bulletin of the Center for Children's Books* that the book's pictures reveal "a place and time more magical than mundane."

Other books by Geeslin have continued to focus on children living in Mexico, and all contain a bilingual text, created with the help of the author's wife, a Spanish teacher. *On Ramon's Farm: Five Tales of Mexico* follows a day in the life of a young boy as he goes about his farm chores. As he cleans up the barnyard and

feeds its varied residents, Ramon is entertained by the friendly animals, and in return he creates poems about them. In *Elena's Serenade* a young girl hopes to become a glass-blower like her father, but when he disapproves of such a life for his daughter, she takes her glass-blowing pipe and runs away, disguised as a boy. On the way to the city, Elena gains a special skill—she can produce sweet music as well as beautiful glass from her pipe—and when she returns home her father learns to appreciate his daughter's special creative talent. In *School Library Journal,* Tracy Bell praised *Elena's Serenade* as "a fascinating adventure that explores issues of gender roles, self-confidence, and the workings of an artist's heart," while a *Publishers Weekly* critic wrote that Geeslin presents young readers with a "magical-realist fable with a girl-power message."

Biographical and Critical Sources

PERIODICALS

Booklist, May 1, 1981, p. 1186; November 15, 1996, p. 594; March 1, 2004, Jennifer Mattson, review of *Elena's Serenade,* p. 1194.

Bulletin of the Center for Children's Books, January, 1997, Janice M. Del Negro, review of *In Rosa's Mexico,* p. 169.

Kirkus Reviews, January 15, 2004, review of *Elena's Serenade,* p. 82.

New York Times Book Review, May 11, 1997, Kathleen Krull, review of *In Rosa's Mexico,* p. 24.

Publishers Weekly, February 20, 1981, review of *The Bonner Boys,* pp. 90-91; November 18, 1996, review of *In Rosa's Mexico,* p. 74; October 12, 1998, p. 75; January 26, 2004, review of *Elena's Serenade,* p. 253.

School Library Journal, December, 1996, p. 92; March, 2004, Tracy Bell, review of *Elena's Serenade,* p. 158.

H

HAJDUSIEWICZ, Babs Bell

Personal

Married; children: two. *Education:* Indiana State University, B.S. (elementary education), 1965; Indiana State University, M.S. (elementary education, special education), 1969; Indiana State University, School Administration Specialist certification (special education), 1971. *Hobbies and other interests:* Children, travel, American antiques.

Addresses

Home—Atlanta, GA. *Agent*—c/o Author Mail, Reading Realm, P.O. Box 76732, Atlanta, GA 30358-1732. *E-mail*—bbha@wt.net.

Career

Educator and author. Elementary school teacher in Great Neck, NY, 1967-68, and Terre Haute, IN, 1965-67; teacher of special-needs students, Brazil, IN, 1968-72; director of special education services Putnam-West Hendricks Cooperative, Greencastle, IN, 1972-73, and Northville, MI, 1973-75; parenting education instructor, Rocky River, OH, 1981-82; Eastern Michigan University, Ypsilanti, special-education instructor and liaison 1978-80; Cleveland State University, Cleveland, OH, special-education instructor and liaison, 1981-83; Westshore Montessori Association, Cleveland, administrative consultant, 1983-84; Pee Wee Poetry, founder and director, 1979-89; Booking the Future: Reader to Reader, founder and director, 1993; freelance writer, beginning 1986; education consultant, beginning 1987.

Member

International Reading Association, National Association for Education of Young Children, Society of Children's Books Writers and Illustrators, Georgia Area Society of Children's Book Writers and Illustrators, Georgia Reading Association, Atlanta Area Reading Association.

Writings

You Have a Friend, Dainty Dinosaur, Modern Curriculum Press (Cleveland, OH), 1988.

You Are Here, Dainty Dinosaur, Modern Curriculum Press (Cleveland, OH), 1988.

Why, Dainty Dinosaur?, Modern Curriculum Press (Cleveland, OH), 1988.

Who Did This, Dainty Dinosaur?, Modern Curriculum Press (Cleveland, OH), 1988.

Where Is It, Dainty Dinosaur?, Modern Curriculum Press (Cleveland, OH), 1988.

When Will I, Dainty Dinosaur?, Modern Curriculum Press (Cleveland, OH), 1988.

What Is It, Dainty Dinosaur?, Modern Curriculum Press (Cleveland, OH), 1988.

Up and down, Dainty Dinosaur, Modern Curriculum Press (Cleveland, OH), 1988.

Two Homes for Dainty Dinosaur, Modern Curriculum Press (Cleveland, OH), 1988.

It Will Be Fun, Dainty Dinosaur, Modern Curriculum Press (Cleveland, OH), 1988.

How Can I, Dainty Dinosaur?, Modern Curriculum Press (Cleveland, OH), 1988.

Help from Dainty Dinosaur, Modern Curriculum Press (Cleveland, OH), 1988.

Poetry Works!, Modern Curriculum Press (Cleveland, OH), 1991.

Poetry Works! The Second Stanza, Modern Curriculum Press (Cleveland, OH), 1992.

Poetry Works! The First Verse, Modern Curriculum Press (Cleveland, OH), 1993.

Busy People, Celebration Press (Parsippany, NJ), 1993.

Jacks and More Jacks, Scott Foresman (Parsippany, NJ), 1994.

Mary Carter Smith, African-American Storyteller, PReading Realm (Atlanta, GA), 1995.

Don't Go out in Your Underwear: Poems, Pearson Learning (Parsippany, NJ), 1997.

Words, Words, Words, Good Year Books (Tucson, AZ), 1997.

Words and More Words, Good Year Books (Tucson, AZ), 1997.

Phonics through Poetry: Teaching Phoenemic Awareness Using Poetry, Good Year Books (Tucson, AZ), 1999.
More! Phonics through Poetry: Teaching Phoenemic Awareness Using Poetry, Good Year Books (Tucson, AZ), 1999.
The Bridge Is Up!, HarperCollins (New York, NY), 2004.

Contributor of poetry to periodicals, including *Hopscotch* and *Humpty Dumpty;* contributor to *Plays;* author of numerous reading curriculum books and materials.

Work in Progress

The Bridge Is Up! and *Sputter! Sputter! Sput!,* both for HarperCollins; *Oral language* and *Wow! Words,* both for Good Year Books.

Biographical and Critical Sources

PERIODICALS

Booklist, March 1, 1996, Susan Dove Lempke, review of *Mary Carter Smith: African-American Storyteller,* p. 1176; May 1, 2004, Carolyn Phelan, review of *The Bridge Is Up!*

ONLINE

Babs Bell Hajdusiewicz Home Page, http://www.ilikeme.com (July 6, 2005).
Writers Net, http://www.writers.net/ (July 6, 2005), "Babs Bell Hajdusiewicz."

*   *   *

HARLEE, J. V.
See LEESE, Jennifer L.B.

*   *   *

HAYDEN, Torey L(ynn) 1951-

Personal

Born May 21, 1951 in Livingston, MT; daughter of Joyce Jansen (a secretary); married, 1982; children: one daughter. *Education:* Whitman College, B.A. (biology and chemistry), 1972; Eastern Montana College, M.S. (special education), 1973; doctoral study at University of Minnesota, 1975-79. *Hobbies and other interests:* Opera, classical theatre, classical music, ancient history, archaeology, farming, cosmology, physics.

Addresses

Home—Northern Wales, United Kingdom. *Agent*—P. Ginsberg, Curtis Brown Associates, Inc., 10 Astor Place, New York, NY 10003.

Torey L. Hayden

Career

Writer and educator. Has worked as a special-education teacher for the emotionally disturbed, a university lecturer, a graduate lecturer, a research coordinator, a child psychologist, and a child-abuse consultant. Former archaeological site supervisor; sheep breeder.

Awards, Honors

Christopher Award, 1981, for *One Child;* New York Times Public Library Books for the Teen Age selection, 1981, for *One Child,* and 1982, for *Somebody Else's Kids;* American Library Association Best Young-Adult Book selection, and *School Library Journal* Best Young-Adult Book selection, both 1983, both for *Murphy's Boy.*

Writings

One Child (nonfiction), Putnam (New York, NY), 1980.
Somebody Else's Kids (nonfiction), Putnam (New York, NY), 1981.
Murphy's Boy (nonfiction), Putnam (New York, NY), 1983.
The Sunflower Forest (fiction), Putnam (New York, NY), 1984.
Just Another Kid (nonfiction), Putnam (New York, NY), 1988.
Ghost Girl (nonfiction), Putnam (New York, NY), 1991.
The Tiger's Child (nonfiction), Scribner (New York, NY), 1995.
The Mechanical Cat (fiction), 1999.
Beautiful Child (nonfiction), HarperCollins Publishers (New York, NY), 2002.
The Very Worst Thing (fiction), HarperCollins Publishers (New York, NY), 2003.

Twilight Children: Three Voices No One Heard until a Therapist Listened (nonfiction), William Morrow (New York, NY), 2005.

Contributor to professional journals.

Adaptations

Murphy's Boy was adapted as a television movie titled *Trapped in Silence,* starring Marsha Mason, 1986; *One Child, Somebody Else's Kids,* and *Murphy's Boy* were adapted to audio cassette for the visually impaired.

Sidelights

Author and child advocate Torey L. Hayden described herself in an interview posted on her home page as "very active, very curious, and inclined to get into everything just to find out what it was like" as a child. "Also, I liked being different, so I didn't mind making a fool of myself. I liked being alone a lot because I had an extraordinary fantasy life." Hayden's vivid imagination has helped inspire several of her books for young readers, among them her fiction books *The Mechanical Cat* and *The Very Worst Thing.* In addition, her advocacy efforts have inspired works such as *Twilight Children: Three Voices No One Heard until a Therapist Listened.* An account of Hayden's experience in a juvenile psychiatric crisis unit, the book was praised by *School Library Journal* reviewer Lynn Nutwell for presenting, with "compelling grace and compassion," a realistic and "valuable perspective" on the crisis intervention field that would be valuable to "students considering career options."

Born in 1951 in Montana, Hayden was a fan of the original *Star Trek* television series, and as an adult she developed a keen interest in computers, learning how to both repair and build them. If she had not grown up to be a teacher and author, Hayden explained in her interview that she "would . . . have been an astrophysicist or a cosmologist."

As a teacher, much of Hayden's inspiration as an author has come from her work with young people, particularly students she has known and helped. In *Ghost Girl* she focuses on eight-year-old Jadie Ekdahl, a troubled girl who, when Hayden meets her, is electively mute: she is able to talk, but chooses not to. "Jadie might as well have been a ghost," Hayden wrote in the book; she talked to no one, and no one talked to her. To make matters worse, she had unusual behaviors, such as always walking hunched over, and drawing strange markings on her papers. Hayden has a special interest in children with elective mutism, and with her skills and knowledge she is finally able to convince Jadie to start talking. When the girl reveals horrifying stories of abuse and possible involvement in a satanic cult, Hayden is unsure of whether the girl's stories are true or new manifestations of serious psychological problems. After deciding to contact the authorities, Hayden's concerns are found to be justified, and Jadie is rescued from a terrible situation.

A reviewer in *Books* called *Ghost Girl* "fascinating," and Genevieve Stuttaford, writing in *Publishers Weekly,* remarked that "ultimately Jadie's is a success story, and a testament to the powers of caring and commitment." Also praising Hayden's book, a *Kirkus Reviews* critic observed that *Ghost Girl* is "Suspenseful, compelling, and offering welcome insights into troubled children and how a gifted and compassionate professional treats them."

In *One Child* Hayden describes the day-to-day occurrences in her classroom of emotionally disturbed children, "kids with whom nobody else wants to deal," as Bonnie J. Dodge described them in a review for *English Journal.* Included are a shy boy who speaks only to repeat weather forecasts; a child so abused by his parents that the beatings have caused brain damage; and Sheila, a violent, autistic, electively mute girl with a genius-level IQ. "The reader is left with a profound sense of respect and admiration for the courage, patience, and most of all, the love it takes to be such a special teacher," Dodge remarked.

As a sequel of sorts to *One Child, The Tiger's Child* picks up Sheila's story, following her through her teenage and adult years as Hayden continues to help the autistic genius adjust to the changing world around her. Sheila's early story is more fully told: she was pushed out of a car and abandoned on the side of the road by her mother at age four; her drug-addict father abused her; and she once set fire to a younger boy. When Hayden encounters Sheila in a clinical setting after a span of several years, the emotionally troubled girl is a fourteen-year-old punk rocker, sexually precocious, but still desperately in need of help. After a few months the two develop a shaky friendship outside of the professional arena. Hayden watches as Sheila ages and matures further; eventually, she graduates from high school and finds a job that offers her a stability and contentment she never had before. A *Publishers Weekly* reviewer called *The Tiger's Child* "an inspirational testament to the healing power of love," and remarked that "this authentic tearjerker resonates with drama." Nancy E. Zuwiyya, writing in *Library Journal,* observed that Hayden's "book is not only interesting as a biography of a seriously disturbed child but as a portrayal of a working psychologist." Readers "learn about the limitations on therapy and the slow, often painful process of healing," wrote Claire Rosser in *Kliatt,* while a *Kirkus* critic called *The Tiger's Child* "An effective chronicle of a relationship full of potholes that nonetheless brings both student and teacher further along the road to maturity."

Beautiful Child follows Hayden through another academic year with another class of "fascinating, difficult, and immensely appealing" special-needs children, wrote Francine Prose in *O.* The students include a boy with Tourette's syndrome, a girl who spouts sophisticated elliptical poetry when under stress, and a set of twins with the telltale signs of fetal alcohol syndrome. The "beautiful child" of the title is seven-year-old Wanda Fox, an "unwashed, smelly, drastically neglected girl," Prose noted, who is so steadfastly mute and disinterested that she is almost catatonic. Hayden wonders if Wanda is also deaf, or developmentally disabled in some way. "Though Hayden seems almost endless resourceful, dedicated, resilient, and patient, none of the tried-and-tested techniques developed in her career with special-needs children—singing, games, behavior modification, even physical force—succeed" with this child, Prose added. Hayden's narrative describing her experiences with these children "takes on a timeless quality," observed a *Kirkus Reviews* critic. "As well as representing all special-needs children, the students come into focus as individuals about whom the reader cares deeply." Throughout the book, Hayden "shares her own thoughts, worries, and strained relationship with a mismatched classroom aide, creating a rich tapestry of the dynamics of a group of special needs youngsters and the adults who try to help them," commented a *Publishers Weekly* reviewer, while David Carr, writing in *Booklist,* concluded that *Beautiful Child* "ultimately shows this kind of teaching to be the tireless embrace of the vulnerable by the devoted."

Hayden takes a break from her real-world experience to write the novel *The Very Worst Thing.* The only stable part of twelve-year-old David's life is his sister. Bounced from one foster home to another, David repeatedly finds himself the "new kid," ridiculed because of his stutter and academic problems. Worse, his sister is in juvenile hall. In a rage over his situation, David destroys an owl's nest, but regrets his action almost immediately. He takes the single remaining egg from the nest and raises the owl that hatches from it. When the owl ultimately declines in health due to being held in captivity, David learns about "losing something you love," according to a *Kirkus Reviews* critic. Calling Hayden's protagonist "a believable child with many obstacles to mount," the critic called *The Very Worst Thing* "a well-wrought problem novel for the younger set." While Faith Brautigam wrote in *School Library Journal* that "The hatching and development of the owl keep the story moving and help to compensate for some of the plot details that seem tacked on," she ultimately conceded David's story is "adequately told."

Hayden once told *Something about the Author:* "I don't remember when I first became interested in writing. It seems like it has been something that has been with me, been a part of me, for as long as I have memories, but I have a very clear recollection of when the magic of writing took hold. I was eight, a none-too-enthusiastic third-grader in Miss Webb's class. . . . I was supposed to be at my desk doing my reading workbook, but I wrote instead on the back of an old math paper. Miss Webb came down the aisle unexpectedly, caught me, and confiscated the story.

"That wasn't a particularly traumatic event. In fact, I forgot all about it until some days later when she was

cleaning out her desk and found the story, which she returned to me. . . . Among all the memories of my childhood, that particular moment is one of the clearest. I remember the exhilaration of reading that story and finding it every bit as exciting to me as the day I wrote it. For the first time I discovered that, like a camera, words can capture the complexity, the beauty, the subtlety of life so precisely that one can return to them the next day, the next week, or years later and feel the experience they have created as powerfully as the moment it happened. That to me is magic of the first order.

"Writing remains an affair of the heart for me. . . . [and] each time I sit down to the typewriter to start a new book, I write it for me. I *love* the process of writing, the nudge and jiggle of words until that ripe moment when *snap!* the emotional photograph is taken and all the complex beauty of being human is captured.

"How did I come to write the books I did? In the case of the five nonfiction books, I think it was simply a desire to share my experiences, to open up to others a

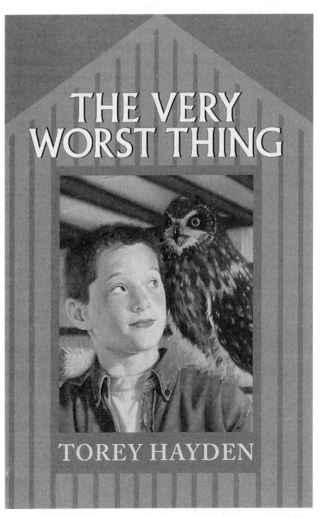

Together with his new foster mother, eleven-year-old David gains a sense of security and self-confidence as he helps to hatch and raise a baby owl. (Cover illustration by Michele Amatrula.)

world that most people do not encounter firsthand and, if I'm honest, to open minds. All the stories told in these books are true; all the characters in them exist. They did the hard part by living; I did the easy part by writing about it."

On her home page, Hayden offered the following advice to young writers: "Know that only you can write your own story. No one else can teach you how. They can teach you the mechanics of writing, like grammar and punctuation, but only you will have your particular style. So, while it is all right to read lots of books to see how other authors write or to take creative writing classes or listen to writers speak, let your own style develop."

Biographical and Critical Sources

PERIODICALS

Booklist, August, 2002, David Carr, review of *Beautiful Child,* p. 1896.
Books, March, 1992, review of *Ghost Girl,* p. 20.
English Journal, September, 1993, Bonnie J. Dodge, review of *One Child,* p. 96.
Kirkus Reviews, March 15, 1991, review of *Ghost Girl,* p. 377; January 1, 1995, review of *The Tiger's Child,* p. 47; May 15, 2002, review of *Beautiful Child,* p. 717; May 15, 2003, review of *The Very Worst Thing,* p. 751.
Kliatt, July, 1996, Claire Rosser, review of *The Tiger's Child,* p. 27.
Library Journal, March 15, 1984; January 15, 1995, Nancy E. Zuwiyya, review of *The Tiger's Child,* p. 122; July, 2002, Terry Christner, review of *Beautiful Child,* p. 94.
Los Angeles Times, April 24, 1980.
Los Angeles Times Book Review, May 26, 1991, review of *Ghost Girl,* p. 8.
New York Times Book Review, May 4, 1980; April 26, 1981; March 6, 1988.
O, June, 2002, Francine Prose, review of *Beautiful Child,* p. 73.
Publishers Weekly, March 22, 1991, review of *Ghost Girl,* p. 66; January 16, 1995, review of *The Tiger's Child,* p. 448; May 13, 2002, review of *Beautiful Child,* p. 58.
School Library Journal, October, 2003, Faith Brautigam, review of *The Very Worst Thing,* p. 166; July, 2005, Lynn Nutwell, review of *Twilight Children,* p. 133.
Voice of Youth Advocates, February, 1991, Pam Spencer, review of *Just Another Kid,* pp. 347-348.
Washington Post, May 8, 1981; July 6, 1984; April 19, 1988.
Washington Post Book World, August 15, 1982.
Wilson Library Bulletin, February, 1985.

ONLINE

Torey Hayden Home Page, http://www.torey-hayden.com (July 15, 2005).*

HODGE, Deborah 1954-

Personal

Born November 6, 1954, in Moose Jaw, Saskatchewan, Canada; daughter of John Lyndon (a writer, editor, and broadcaster) and Marion Joyce (a nursing instructor; maiden name, Baker) Grove; married David Hodge (a businessman); children: Emily, Michael, Helen. *Education:* Simon Fraser University, B.A. (psychology), 1977, graduated from Professional Development Program (teacher training), 1978.

Addresses

Home—Vancouver, British Columbia, Canada. *Agent*—officec/o Author Mail, Kids Can Press, 29 Birch Ave., Toronto, Ontario, Canada M4V 1E2. *E-mail*—dhodge@shaw.ca.

Career

Author and educator. Elementary school teacher in Armstrong and Golden school districts, British Columbia, Canada, 1978-91; British Columbia Ministry of Education, writer, editor, and instructional designer of elementary-school curriculum, 1991-99; children's author, 1994—.

Member

Canadian Children's Book Centre, Children's Writers and Illustrators of British Columbia, Vancouver Children's Literature Roundtable, Canadian Society of Children's Authors, Illustrators, and Performers.

Awards, Honors

Parents' Choice designation, Parents Choice Foundation, 1997, *Bears, Wild Cats, Wild Dogs,* and *Whales;* Pick of the Lists fall selection, *American Bookseller,* both 1997, both for *Bears, Wild Cats, Wild Dogs,* and *Whales;* Parents' Guide to Children's Media award for Outstanding Activity Book, 1997 and 2000, both for *Simple Machines;* Best Books for Children designation, *Science Books and Films,* 1998, for *Bears,* and 1999, for *Deer, Moose, Elk, and Caribou;* Red Cedar Book Award shortlist, 2000, for *Beavers,* and 2003, for *Eagles* and *The Kid's Book of Canada's Railway and How the CPR Was Built;* Silver Birch Award shortlist, 2000, and Information Book Award, Children's Literature Roundtable of Canada, 2001, both for *The Kids Book of Canada's Railway and How the CPR Was Built.*

Writings

NONFICTION FOR CHILDREN

Bears: Polar Bears, Black Bears, and Grizzly Bears, illustrated by Pat Stephens, Kids Can Press (Toronto, Ontario, Canada), 1996, Kids Can Press (New York, NY), 1997.

Deborah Hodge

Wild Cats: Cougars, Bobcats, and Lynx, illustrated by Nancy Gray Ogle, Kids Can Press (Toronto, Ontario, Canada), 1996, Kids Can Press (New York, NY), 1997.

Wild Dogs: Foxes, Wolves, and Coyotes, illustrated by Pat Stephens, Kids Can Press (New York, NY), 1996.

Whales: Killer Whales, Blue Whales, and More, illustrated by Pat Stephens, Kids Can Press (New York, NY), 1996.

Simple Machines ("Starting with Science" series), photographs by Ray Bourdeau, Kids Can Press (New York, NY), 1996.

Deer, Moose, Elk, and Caribou, illustrated by Pat Stephens, Kids Can Press (New York, NY), 1998.

Beavers, illustrated by Pat Stephens, Kids Can Press (New York, NY), 1998.

The Kids Book of Canada's Railway and How the CPR Was Built, illustrated by John Mantha, Kids Can Press (New York, NY), 2000.

Eagles, illustrated by Nancy Gray Ogle, Kids Can Press (New York, NY), 2000.

Salmon, illustrated by Nancy Gray Ogle, Kids Can Press (New York, NY), 2002.

Bees, illustrated by Julian Mulock, Kids Can Press (New York, NY), 2004.

Ants, illustrated by Julian Mulock, Kids Can Press (New York, NY), 2004.

FICTION FOR CHILDREN

Emma's Story, illustrated by Song Nan Zhang, Tundra Books (Plattsburgh, NY), 2003.

Work in Progress

The Kid's Book of Coming to Canada, illustrated by John Mantha, for Kids Can Press, 2006; the fiction book *Lily and the Mixed-up Letters,* illustrated by France Brassard, for Tundra Books, 2007.

Sidelights

Canadian writer Deborah Hodge spent over a dozen years as an elementary school teacher before leaving the classroom to write and edit curriculum for the British Columbia Ministry of Education from 1991 to 1999. During this time she pondered the lack of interesting nonfiction books available to beginning readers. As a teacher she had often observed her primary-aged students looking for (and not finding) books that were easy enough for them to read, but still compelling information on topics that fascinated them. With this in mind, Hodge decided to write her own manuscript, creating a book that was both readable and interesting for young students, and featured a topic (bears) she knew children loved. Her first book, *Bears: Polar Bears, Black Bears, and Grizzly Bears,* appeared in 1996. Praising the award-winning volumes that have followed, Wendy Flood, a contributor to *Resource Links,* reported that "simple text and realistic, detailed illustrations make them excellent for research projects for young children."

Born in Moose Jaw, Saskatchewan, Hodge grew up in Burnaby, British Columbia, and studied psychology at Simon Fraser University. Her later experience as an elementary school teacher provided her with insight into the mind of young readers; as she once explained to *Something about the Author (SATA)*: "They're fascinated by very big, very fast, or very fierce animals. They want answers to such questions as how long are a grizzly bear's claws, or how much does a blue whale eat?" In attempting to answer such questions, Hodge has produced a series of eight books, the "Kids Can Press Wildlife" series, focusing on the North American animals children are most drawn to. In *Bears, Salmon,* and *Wild Cats: Cougars, Bobcats, and Lynx,* as well as her other titles, Hodge covers topics such as food, habitat, and birth, presenting enough facts to interest readers without overwhelming them. As Jonathan Webb claimed in *Quill & Quire,* Hodge's books "fulfill, reliably and attractively, the modest objective they set themselves."

Other titles in Hodge's wildlife series include *Wild Dogs: Foxes, Wolves, and Coyotes, Whales: Killer Whales, Blue Whales, and More,* and *Eagles.* These volumes follow the same basic, easy-to-read format and include a large typeface, naturalistic drawings, and cutaway diagrams. They also contain interesting animal trivia boxes on each page. Fred Boer, reviewing both *Wild Dogs* and *Whales* for *Quill & Quire*, wrote that "Both books are well organized, with a glossary and an index." Judy Diamond, writing in *Science Books and Film,* deemed Hodge's works effective for an early elementary school readership and praised the material as clearly presented. Diamond concluded that, "Overall the information presented is accurate and complete," making each volume "a useful tool for school reports on its topics."

Beavers was praised by a contributor to *Kirkus Reviews* as having "concise, clearly organized facts corralled into brief, dual-page chapters." Dave Jenkinson, a contributor to *Canadian Review of Materials,* described this book as "a superb example of a well-written information book for pre-readers which will also appeal to students in the early elementary grades." Citing *Salmon* as "a graceful work about . . . remarkable creatures," Jean Pollock added in *School Library Journal* that Hodge relays information on salmon from both coasts of North America in "a relaxed, informative style." *Deer, Moose, Elk, and Caribou,* which focuses on members of the deer family, was praised by Robert G. Hoehn in *Science Activities* as containing a "potpourri of information . . . guaranteed to pique the interest" of both children and adult readers.

Hodge explores the world of science in the "Starting with Science" series published by Kids Can Press.

Part of a series published for the Denver Museum of Nature and Science, **Ants** *contains ant-related facts, ant-related activities, and a wealth of ant lore. (Illustration by Julie Mulock.)*

Simple Machines contains a presentation of thirteen attractive and interactive experiments, accompanied by clear and detailed directions in an easy-to-follow format which encourages children's participation. According to critics, the book has much visual appeal and lists all the materials needed along with their methodology and an explanation of the principles engaged. Safety precautions are also addressed in the text or illustrated in sidebars, and further details about each activity are listed in the appendix. Maureen Garvie, reviewing *Simple Machines* for *Quill & Quire,* noted that "The book reflects energy, esthetics, community, and curiosity. . . . With the aid of kitchen equipment and minimal supervision, science is no longer a fusty world of stained test-tubes, wire coils, and rotten-egg smells."

Ants and *Bees* are part of an insect series for young children that Hodge wrote in collaboration with the Denver Museum of Nature and Science. Both books feature photographs provided by the museum. *Ants* was dubbed a "straightforward, pleasing" example of science-based children's nonfiction by a *Kirkus* reviewer, while in *School Library Journal* Karey Wehner praised the book for its "abundant illustrations" and "clearly written" introductory text. Gillian Richardson, writing in *Canadian Review of Materials,* called the books "a great starter series that will capture a beginning reader's interest with its appealing presentation."

Hodge, whose grandparents worked for the Canadian Pacific Railway (CPR), turns her attention from nature to the history of Canada's first transcontinental railway in *The Kids Book of Canada's Railway and How the CPR Was Built.* She recounts the quest to follow the builders of the United States' Transcontinental Railway and stretch a single track of rail across Canada from the eastern regions to the Pacific. From information about William van Horne's planning of the railway, the Chinese and European immigrant laborers who blasted through mountains and tackled difficult terrain, and the types of trains eventually used on the railway, Hodge also discusses the railway's impact on Canada's Metis and Aboriginal peoples. Writing in *Quill & Quire,* Gwyneth Evans suggested that "The building of the Canadian Pacific Railway is an incredible story, and this informative new book . . . does quite a good job of presenting it."

Hodge has continued to add to her growing list of nonfiction titles, and has even ventured into fiction with the picture book *Emma's Story,* a tale if international adoption, about a young Chinese girl who begins to question why she looks different than the rest of her fair-skinned Caucasian family. As Hodge once explained to *SATA:* "Every day when I wake up I have more ideas for books I want to write. Although I'm not teaching any more, I still feel like I'm talking to my students whenever I write a book. I love the challenge of trying to create something that young readers will find interesting."

Hodge focuses on the special love that parents and other family members feel toward an adopted child in **Emma's Story.** *(Illustration by Son Nang Zhang.)*

Biographical and Critical Sources

PERIODICALS

Booklist, September 15, 1997, Carolyn Phelan, review of *Bears* and *Wild Cats,* p. 238; April 15, 1998, Carolyn Phelan, review of *Starting with Science: Simple Machines,* p. 448; January 1, 1999, April Judge, review of *Deer, Moose, Elk, and Caribou* and *Beavers,* p. 865; November 1, 2000, Gillian Engberg, review of *Eagles;* April 1, 2004, Stephanie Zvirin, review of *Ants* and *Bees,* p. 1385.

Canadian Review of Materials, August 11, 2000, Dave Jenkinson, review of *Beavers;* June, 2003, Gail Hamilton, review of *Emma's Story;* March, 2004, Gillian Richardson, review of *Ants* and *Bees.*

Kirkus Reviews, October 1, 1998, review of *Beavers,* p. 1459; April 1, 2004, review of *Ants,* p. 331.

Publishers Weekly, November 3, 2003, review of *Emma's Story,* p. 74.

Quill & Quire, March, 1996, Jonathan Webb, "Charismatic Cats and Winsome Bears," p. 73; December, 1996, Maureen Garvie, review of *Starting with Science: Simple Machines,* p. 39; January, 1997, Fred Boer, review of *Wild Dogs, Whales,* and *Living Things,* p. 38; September 1, 2000, Gwyneth Evans, review of *The Kids Book of Canada's Railway and How the CPR Was Built.*

Resource Links, October, 1998; October, 2003, Isobel Lang, review of *Emma's Story,* p. 5.

School Library Journal, November, 1997, Lisa Wu Stowe, review of *Wild Dogs* and *Whales,* pp. 108-109; July, 1998, Kathryn Kosiorek, review of *Simple Machines,* p. 88; July, 2002, Jean Pollock, review of *Salmon,* p. 107; November, 2003, Rosalyn Pierini, review of *Emma's Story,* p. 96; June, 2004, Karey Wehner, review of *Ants,* p. 128.

Science Activities, spring, 1999, Robert G. Hoehn, review of *Deer, Moose, Elk, and Caribou,* p. 39.

Science Books and Films, December, 1997, Judy Diamond, review of *Wild Dogs* and *Whales,* p. 275.

ONLINE

Canadian Society of Children's Authors, Illustrators, and Performers Web site, http://www.canscaip.org/ (July 6, 2005), "Deborah Hodge."

Children's Writers and Illustrators of British Columbia Web site, http://www.cwill.bc.ca/ (September 17, 2005), "Deborah Hodge."

* * *

HOLM, Jennifer L. 1968(?)- (Holm and Hamel)

Personal

Born c. 1968, in CA; daughter of William W. (a pediatrician) and Beverly A. (a pediatric nurse) Holm; married Jonathan Hamel (a computer programmer and writer), 1999; children: Will. *Education:* Dickinson College, B.A., 1990.

Addresses

Home—MD. *Agent*—c/o Jill Grinberg, Anderson Grinberg Literary Management, 244 Fifth Ave, New York, NY 10001. *E-mail*—author@jenniferholm.com.

Career

Broadcast producer and writer. Ogilvy and Mather (advertising agency), New York, NY, producer of television commercials, music videos, and promotional materials, 1990-c. 2001.

Awards, Honors

Parents' Choice Silver award, and Best Books of the Year designation, *Publishers Weekly,* both 1999, Newbery Honor Award, Notable Book designation, American Library Association (ALA), and Notable Children's Trade Book in the Field of Social Studies designation, National Council for the Social Studies, all 2000, and Utah Book Award, and Dorothy Canfield Fisher Children's Book Award master list inclusion, both 2000-01, all for *Our Only May Amelia;* Parent's Guide to Children's Media Award, ALA Best Book for Young Adults citation, and Book Sense 76 Pick, all for *Boston Jane: An Adventure.*

Writings

FOR CHILDREN

Our Only May Amelia, HarperCollins (New York, NY), 1999.

Boston Jane: An Adventure, HarperCollins (New York, NY), 2001.

Boston Jane: Wilderness Days, HarperCollins (New York, NY), 2002.

The Creek (horror; for young adults), HarperCollins (New York, NY), 2003.

Boston Jane: The Claim, HarperCollins (New York, NY), 2004.

Baby Mouse: Queen of the World! (picture book), illustrated by Matthew Holm, Random House (New York, NY), 2005.

Baby Mouse: Our Hero! (graphic novel), illustrated by Matthew Holm, Random House (New York, NY), 2005.

"STINK FILES" SERIES; WITH JONATHAN HAMEL UNDER JOINT PSEUDONYM HOLM AND HAMEL

The Postman Always Brings Mice, illustrated by Brad Weinman, HarperCollins (New York, NY), 2004.

To Scratch a Thief, illustrated by Brad Weinman, HarperCollins (New York, NY), 2004.

You Only Have Nine Lives, illustrated by Brad Weinman, HarperCollins (New York, NY), 2005.

Adaptations

Our Only May Amelia was adapted for the stage and performed at the Seattle Children's Theatre, 2002.

Work in Progress

Eighth Graders Are Stupid (graphic novel), for Atheneum, 2007.

Sidelights

Children's book author Jennifer L. Holm has always loved reading. "One of our neighbors said recently that his clearest memory of me as a child was watching me rake the lawn one-handed while I read a book with the other!," she admitted on her home page. Beginning her career penning *Boston Jane: An Adventure* and other works of historical fiction for middle-grade readers, Holm has also collaborated with her husband, Jonathan Hamel, to create the well-received "Stink Files" series featuring a feline version of James Bond.

While attending Dickinson College, Holm studied international relations, and in an effort to lighten the intellectual load, during her senior year she decided to audit a class in writing short stories. Her interest in writing was again sparked several years later, when Holm received an unusual Christmas present: a typed copy of a diary her great-aunt, Alice Amelia Holm, had kept as a teenager. One of Holm's aunts had found the diary among her grandmother's things, transcribed it, and sent copies to family members.

Alice Amelia Holm lived in rural Washington state in the early 1900s. While her life was a far cry from the suburban, 1970s upbringing Holm herself enjoyed, Holm realized that the teen's diary "wasn't any different from what I could have written when I was that age," as she told *Publishers Weekly* interviewer Ingrid Roper. "It got me thinking what it would be like to grow up as I did with brothers but out in the middle of nowhere in a wilderness at a very exciting time."

Holm's first book, *Our Only May Amelia,* grew out of these thoughts. Like Holm, May Amelia is the only girl in a family full of boys; May has six brothers to Holm's four. May Amelia is the first girl to be born in a fledgling village along Washington's Nasel River. At age twelve she is—like Holm at that age—quite a tomboy, much to the despair of those who are trying to raise her to be a proper young lady. May's fictitious diary reveals much about turn-of-the-twentieth century pioneer life, including the dangers from wild animals and the hard work that went into performing basic household chores. Despite all the hardships, the girl's "mischievous spirit adds many amusing moments," Barbara Wysocki noted in *School Library Journal.* The young narrator also paints vivid portraits of her numerous family and neighbors in her diary: Holm has an "uncanny ability to give each of the siblings—and a wide range of adults—a distinctive character while maintaining May Amelia's spunky narrative voice," noted a *Publishers Weekly* critic.

Holm describes the lives of pioneers living in Washington state during the 1850s in her next three books, which form the "Boston Jane" trilogy. Jane's mother died when she was young, and her father let her run wild for many years. Then, at age eleven, Jane took the advice of William, one of her father's apprentices, and enrolled at Miss Hepplewhite's Young Ladies Academy to learn proper etiquette. In the first volume of the series, *An Adventure,* Jane is aged fifteen. William, who has in the interim moved to Washington Territory, writes and asks her to come to Washington and marry him. Jane agrees, but quickly finds that her finishing-school lessons have not prepared her for the experience. *Booklist* reviewer Kay Weisman praised Holm's "strong characterizations [and] meticulous attention to historical details," and *School Library Journal* contributor Janet Hilbun wrote that "the author's portrayal of pioneer/Chinook relationships is sympathetic."

Holm's first book to be set in modern times is *The Creek.* Described by *Booklist* contributor Stephanie Zvirin as a mystery containing the "trappings of a creepy thriller that push[es] the story well beyond the wan child-plays-detective stuff so prevalent in youth mysteries," *The Creek* follows the return of delinquent teen Caleb Devlin to a Philadelphia suburb. Twelve-year-old Penny and the group of neighborhood boys she plays with are convinced that Caleb is behind certain chilling occurrences that now take place, among them the disappearances of many family pets. The children decide to investigate, not fully realizing how dangerous this choice could be. "The thriller aspects . . . are on tar-

Abandoned by her fiancée after traveling to the primitive Washington Territory, a young woman learns to survive in the sometimes forbidding wilderness of the Pacific Northwest. (Cover illustration by John Thompson.)

get," wrote a *Kirkus Reviews* critic, adding that, through her plot, Holm is successful in "ratcheting up the tension with leisurely precision."

In the "Stink Files" books, Holm collaborates with husband Hamel in a series of books about a British super-spy-cat that tragically winds up living with an average American family in New Jersey. In *The Postman Always Brings Mice* James Edward Bristlefur is trying to cope with the indignity of being renamed "Mr. Stink" while hoping to escape his new pet guardians and continue his investigation into who assassinated his former owner. Slowly, however, the cat comes to care for his new keeper, fifth-grader Aaron. Seeing that Aaron is having trouble with a bully at school, Bristlefur hires a posse of mice and sets out to take care of the bully once and for all. The "resourceful, self-assured Stink makes a beguiling narrator," wrote a *Kirkus Reviews* contributor, while Elaine E. Knight noted in *School Library Journal* the book's "upper-class, James Bond-style narration provides a humorous contrast to the Jersey accent of the local dogs and mice and the everyday American English of the humans."

Biographical and Critical Sources

PERIODICALS

Booklist, September 1, 1999, Susan Dove Lempke, review of *Our Only May Amelia;* February 1, 2001, Lolly Gepson, review of *Our Only May Amelia,* p. 1063; September 1, 2001, Kay Weisman, review of *Boston Jane: An Adventure,* p. 109; July, 2002, Barbara Baskin, review of *An Adventure,* p. 1866; September 1, 2002, Kay Weisman, review of *Boston Jane: Wilderness Days,* p. 123; August, 2003, Stephanie Zvirin, review of *The Creek,* p. 1973; March 1, 2004, Kay Weisman, review of *Boston Jane: The Claim,* p. 1203; May 1, 2004, Stephanie Zvirin, review of *The Postman Always Brings Mice,* p. 1498.

California Kids, September, 2003, Patricia M. Newman, "Who Wrote That?: Featuring Jennifer Holm."

Horn Book, January, 2001, Kristi Beavin, review of *Our Only May Amelia,* p. 121; September-October, 2001, Anita L. Burkam, review of *An Adventure,* p. 584; September-October, 2002, Anita L. Burkam, review of *Wilderness Days,* p. 574.

Kirkus Reviews, June 1, 2003, review of *The Creek,* p. 805; January 15, 2004, review of *The Claim,* p. 83; May 15, 2004, review of *The Postman Always Brings Mice,* p. 492.

Kliatt, July, 2004, Joni Spurrier, review of *Wilderness Days,* p. 19; November, 2004, Stephanie Squicciarini, review of *The Creek,* p. 18.

Publishers Weekly, June 14, 1999, review of *Our Only May Amelia,* p. 71; June 28, 1999, Ingrid Roper, "Jennifer Holm," p. 28; November 1, 1999, review of *Our Only May Amelia,* p. 58; September 3, 2001, review of *An Adventure,* p. 88; September 16, 2002, review of *An Adventure,* p. 71; July 7, 2003, review of *The Creek,* p. 73.

School Library Journal, June, 1999, Cindy Darling Codell, review of *Our Only May Amelia,* p. 130; November, 2000, Barbara Wysocki, review of *Our Only May Amelia,* p. 78; August, 2001, Janet Hilbun, review of *An Adventure,* p. 183; January, 2002, Francisca Goldsmith, review of *An Adventure,* p. 78; October, 2002, Carolyn Janssen, review of *Wilderness Days,* p. 164; July, 2003, Douglas P. Davey, review of *The Creek,* p. 131; May, 2004, Jean Gaffney, review of *The Claim,* p. 150; June, 2004, Elaine E. Knight, review of *The Postman Always Brings Mice,* p. 110.

ONLINE

Dickinson, http://www.dickinson.edu/magazine/ (September 22, 2005), Sherri Kimmel, "Novel Dickinsonia: Prodigious Producer Jennifer Holm '90 Keeps the Printing Press Humming with a Book a Year."

Jennifer Holm Home Page, http://www.jenniferholm.com (July 19, 2005).

*   *   *

HOLM AND HAMEL
See HOLM, Jennifer L.

HORÁCEK, Petr

Personal

Born in Czech Republic; married; wife's name Claire; children: Tereza, Cecilia. *Education:* Prague Academy of Fine Art, graduate. *Hobbies and other interests:* Drawing, walking, skiing, tennis, music.

Addresses

Home—England. *Agent*—c/o Author Mail, Walker Books, 87 Vauxhall Walk, London SE11 5HJ, England. *E-mail*—petrhoracek@hotmail.co.uk.

Career

Author and illustrator.

Awards, Honors

Books for Children Newcomer Award, 2001, for *Strawberries Are Red* and *What Is Black and White?*

Writings

SELF-ILLUSTRATED

Strawberries Are Red, Candlewick Press (Cambridge, MA), 2001.

What Is Black and White?, Candlewick Press (Cambridge, MA), 2001.

Flip's Day, Candlewick Press (Cambridge, MA), 2002.

Flip's Snowman, Candlewick Press (Cambridge, MA), 2002.

When the Moon Smiled, Candlewick Press (Cambridge, MA), 2004.

Run, Mouse, Run!, Candlewick Press (Cambridge, MA), 2005.

Bird, Fly High, Candlewick Press (Cambridge, MA), 2005.

A New House for Mouse, Candlewick Press (Cambridge, MA), 2005.

Sidelights

Czech-born author and illustrator Petr Horácek studied for six years at the Academy of Fine Art in Prague before turning to a career in children's books. Living and working in England, he is the author of the self-illustrated picture books *When the Moon Smiled, Bird, Fly High,* and *A New House for Mouse.* In 2001 he won the *Books for Children* Newcomer Award for *Strawberries Are Red* and *What Is Black and White?*

When the Moon Smiled is a bedtime counting book featuring ever-increasing quantities of animals to illustrate basic number. Each spread features a different set of creatures that either go to sleep at night or become active in the darkness. A *Kirkus Reviews* critic commented

In Petr Horácek's novel picture book, **A New House for Mouse** *a tiny mouse finds she needs a bigger home when she tries to bring a big, shiny apple into her snug, cozy nest.*

that Horácek's book "should provide quick bedtime quietude, as intended," while Gillian Engberg wrote in *Booklist* that *When the Moon Smiled* will serve as a "satisfying bedtime book" that "offers a cozy, appealing counting exercise from a talented artist."

In *A New House for Mouse* Horácek once again offers children a clever storyline. In this book, a tiny mouse happens upon a large apple outside her small dwelling. Excited by her find, she sets out to find a home that is large enough to accomodate both her and her gigantic meal. When every suitably sized hole she comes across is already occupied by one critter or another, the little mouse must find a more imaginative solution to her problem. Kitty Flynn, writing in *Horn Book,* commented that Horácek's "color-rich, heavily textured watercolor and cut-paper collages add much to the simple story," making *A New House for Mouse* a book that will "quickly satisfy story-hour cravings."

Biographical and Critical Sources

PERIODICALS

Booklist, May 1, 2004, Gillian Engberg, review of *When the Moon Smiled: A Bedtime Counting Book,* p. 1563; December 1, 2004, Gillian Engberg, review of *A New House for Mouse,* p. 659.
Horn Book, January-February, 2005, Kitty Flynn, review of *A New House for Mouse,* p. 77.
Kirkus Reviews, January 15, 2004, review of *When the Moon Smiled,* p. 84.
Publishers Weekly, January 10, 2005, review of *A New House for Mouse,* p. 54.

ONLINE

Walker Books Web site, http://www.walkerbooks.co.uk/ (July 6, 2005), "Petr Horácek."

*   *   *

HOUSTON, James A(rchibald) 1921-2005

OBITUARY NOTICE—See index for *SATA* sketch: Born June 12, 1921, in Toronto, Ontario, Canada; died of complications following a heart attack April 17, 2005, in New London, CT. Artist and author. Houston, whose main subject as an artist was the Inuit of the Hudson Bay area, made a dramatic contribution to the art community by bringing the craftsmanship of Eskimo art to the world's attention. After attending Ontario Art College for two years and studying art in Paris, he served in the Canadian Army during World War II as part of the Toronto Scottish Regiment. With the war over, he returned home but after a few years grew restless. Chartering a small plane, he flew to an Inuit village and knew he had found a subject for his art. He began drawing the natives, often giving his work to the villagers. Pleasantly surprised when one Inuit gave him a small sculpture in exchange for his gift, he learned that the piece was a recent work, and not one of the antique sculptures archaeologist were already familiar with. Realizing the art community would be interested in his discovery, Houston proposed to the Inuit that they sell their artwork, a scheme that would greatly help a local economy devastated by the decline in the fur trade. Setting up the West Baffin Eskimo Cooperative, Houston's idea took off, and many Inuit artisans have made a comfortable living selling their sculptures and other works of art. Houston remained in the Inuit village for fourteen years before taking a job with Steuben Glass in New York City in 1962. He worked as a master designer there until his death. In addition to his Eskimo-inspired glass sculpture and prints, Houston also wrote and illustrated children's books and wrote novels and nonfiction inspired by his Arctic experiences, many of which were award winners. Among his children's titles are *Tikta'liktak: An Eskimo Legend* (1965), *The White Archer: An Eskimo Legend* (1967), *Long Claws: An Arctic Adventure* (1981), and *Whiteout* (1988). His novels include *Ghost Fox* (1977) and *The Ice Master: A Novel of the Arctic* (1997).

OBITUARIES AND OTHER SOURCES:

PERIODICALS

Los Angeles Times, April 25, 2005, p. B9.
New York Times, April 22, 2005, p. C14.
Washington Post, April 21, 2005, p. B5.

J

JOCELYN, Marthe 1956-

Personal

Born 1956, in Toronto, Ontario, Canada; married Tom Slaughter (an artist); children: Hannah, Nell.

Addresses

Home—552 Broadway, New York, NY 10012; (summers) 233 Water St., Stratford, Ontario, Canada N5A 3C7. *E-mail*—marthe@marthejocelyn.com.

Career

Writer. Jesse Design (toy and clothing design firm), owner for fifteen years; worked variously as a cookie seller, waitress, sailor, and photo stylist.

Awards, Honors

Canadian Governor General's Award finalist, for *Hannah's Collections;* Book of the Year for Children shortlist, Canadian Library Association, 2005, for *Mable Riley;* Norma Fleck Award shortlist, 2005, for *A Home for Foundlings.*

Writings

Marthe Jocelyn

EARLY CHAPTER BOOKS

The Invisible Day, illustrated by Abby Carter, Dutton (New York, NY), 1997.

The Invisible Harry, illustrated by Abby Carter, Dutton (New York, NY), 1998.

The Invisible Enemy, illustrated by Abby Carter, Dutton (New York, NY), 2002.

SELF-ILLUSTRATED PICTURE BOOKS

Hannah and the Seven Dresses, Dutton (New York, NY), 1999.

Hannah's Collections, Dutton (New York, NY), 2000.

A Day with Nellie, Tundra Books (Plattsburgh, NY), 2002.

Mayfly, Tundra Books (Plattsburgh, NY), 2004.

PICTURE BOOKS; ILLUSTRATED BY HUSBAND, TOM SLAUGHTER

One Some Many, Tundra Books (Toronto, Ontario, Canada), 2004.

Over Under, Tundra Books (Plattsburgh, NY), 2005.

ABC x 3: English, Español, Français, Tundra Books (Plattsburgh, NY), 2005.

OTHER

Earthly Astonishments (young-adult fiction), Dutton (New York, NY), 2000.

Mable Riley: A Reliable Record of Humdrum, Peril, and Romance (young-adult fiction), Candlewick Press (Cambridge, MA), 2004.

A Home for Foundlings (nonfiction), Tundra Books (Plattsburgh, NY), 2005.

Secrets (short stories), Tundra Books (Plattsburgh, NY), 2005.

Contributor of short stories to anthologies, including *On Her Way: Stories and Poems about Growing up Girl.*

Sidelights

Marthe Jocelyn came to writing relatively late in life, after working at a variety of other occupations. Raised in Toronto, Ontario, Canada, and spending summers in nearby Stratford, where her family has lived for generations, Jocelyn left Canada in tenth grade to attend boarding school in Great Britain. "That gave me a taste of something so different that I wanted to keep exploring the world," she recalled on the *Red Cedar Awards* Web site. She has gone on to live in many different places and sampled many different jobs, even selling cookies, before settling down in New York City and opening her own company designing children's toys and clothing. While raising her two daughters, and reading children's books to them, Jocelyn was inspired to try her hand at adding "children's book author and illustrator" to her resume.

Jocelyn's first book, *The Invisible Day,* centers on ten-year-old Billie, who is frustrated by the lack of privacy while sharing a tiny studio apartment with her mother, a librarian at Billie's school. When Billie discovers a jar of powder that turns her invisible, she finally gets to experience life out from under her mother's eyes. Calling *The Invisible Day* "a fun book," Mary Thomas added in *Canadian Review of Materials* that the novel boasts "a strong female protagonist and an interesting, without being harrowing, storyline." A *Publishers Weekly* critic also praised the book, predicting that Jocelyn's "whimsical, high-spirited novel" will be "a sure-fire crowd-pleaser."

Jocelyn followed her first book with two related ones, *The Invisible Harry,* in which Billie uses the invisibility powder to try to adopt a puppy without her mother finding out, and *The Invisible Enemy,* about what happens when a mean classmate steals some of Billie's powder out of her backpack. As Jocelyn explained, *The Invisible Harry* was inspired by her younger daughter, Nell, who begged to be allowed to have a pet even though Jocelyn declared it unfair to coop a dog up in their small New York apartment. In fact, Jocelyn has never had a pet dog, so "I had to learn about puppies from watching them on the street or following them around the park," she recalled on the *Red Cedar Awards* Web site. "That was fun research."

Mable Riley: A Reliable Record of Humdrum, Peril, and Romance was inspired by a diary kept by Jocelyn's grandmother, Mable Rose. The author discovered the diary while poking around in the attic of a house her family has owned in Stratford for over a century. Most of the journal was filled with dry recollections, but "hidden on the back pages were a few lines of dreadful romantic poetry," Jocelyn noted on *Kidsreads.com.* "Just enough to reveal a character to me, a yearning and curious girl, at odds with the docility expected of her. That's when Mable Riley was born."

Like the real-life Mable Rose, the fictional Mable Riley records her experiences as a teacher in a turn-of-the-twentieth-century one-room school near Stratford, where she sometimes entertains herself by writing about love. Along the way, Mable Riley also gets caught up in the budding suffragist and labor movements through her eccentric, feminist neighbor, Mrs. Rattle. Although Jocelyn's book clearly has a message, it "is never strident," commented *Booklist* contributor Hazel Rochman, "because the funny, poignant diary entries show family and neighbors without reverence." *Horn Book* contributor Anita L. Burkam wrote that "the book's social issues

In her colorful collage illustrations, Jocelyn brings to life the lazy, hazy, crazy days of summer vacation in her 2004 picture book Mayfly.

Counting, organizing, sorting, and saving: these are the skills readers learn in Jocelyn's colorful picture book **Hannah's Collections.**

are given a realistic shades-of-gray treatment, the diary format is handled adroitly, and the diarist herself is engaging and many-faceted."

The nonfiction book *A Home for Foundlings* also has roots in Jocelyn's ancestors' experiences; in this case, those of her grandfather. As a child he lived in London's Foundling Hospital, a place where women who became pregnant and could not afford to support their babies abandoned them. However, the hospital had limited resources, and many of the "rescued" foundlings still perished. Jocelyn records the appalling conditions of the foundling home through brief biographies of several actual residents, as well as through her archival finds, such as photographs and official documents. Including detailed information helps "create drama in this history," Hazel Rochman commented in *Booklist,* while Lori Walker concluded in *Canadian Review of Materials* that *A Home for Foundlings* "provides a rich opportunity to explore poverty and the plight of children throughout the ages and the continents."

Jocelyn is also the author of several self-illustrated picture books for young listeners, including *Hannah and the Seven Dresses* and *Mayfly,* that are illustrated with unique mixed-media collages. For *Hannah and the Seven Dresses,* about a little girl who cannot decide what to wear on her birthday, Jocelyn created not only dresses but entire rooms out of scraps of fabric. "Wall-

paper, carpets, accoutrements, and Hannah herself all have an eye-popping three-dimensional quality," Ilene Cooper noted in *Booklist. Mayfly,* a simple story about children spending time at their family's summer cabin, features spreads that *Resource Links* reviewer Carolyn Cutt called "whimsical . . . bright, colorful and imaginative." *School Library Journal* contributor Shelley B. Sutherland further commented that the author's "interesting multidimensional collages . . . capture the exuberance of the narrative."

Biographical and Critical Sources

PERIODICALS

Booklinks, March, 2005, Gwenyth Swain, review of *Mable Riley,* p. 16.
Booklist, January 1, 1998, Hazel Rochman, review of *Invisible Day,* p. 813; November 15, 1998, Ilene Cooper, review of *The Invisible Harry,* p. 590; July, 1999, Ilene Cooper, review of *Hannah and the Seven Dresses,* p. 1951; September 15, 2000, Denise Wilms, review of *Hannah's Collections,* p. 236; June 1, 2002, Gillian Engberg, review of *The Invisible Enemy,* p. 1723; December 1, 2002, Ilene Cooper, review of *A Day with Nellie,* p. 675; March 1, 2004, Hazel Rochman, review of *Mable Riley: A Reliable Record of Humdrum, Peril, and Romance,* p. 1201; April 1, 2004, Carolyn Phelan, review of *One Some Many,* p. 1366; August, 2004, Carolyn Phelan, review of *Mayfly,* p. 1943; March 1, 2005, Hazel Rochman, review of *A Home for Foundlings,* p. 1151.
Canadian Review of Materials, March 27, 1998, Mary Thomas, review of *The Invisible Day;* March 3, 2000, Jo-Anne Mary Benson, review of *The Invisible Day;* February 4, 2005, Lori Walker, review of *A Home for Foundlings.*
Horn Book, May-June, 2004, Anita L. Burkam, review of *Mable Riley,* p. 329.
Kirkus Reviews, September 15, 2002, review of *A Day with Nellie,* p. 1392; February 15, 2004, review of *Mable Riley,* p. 180; June 15, 2004, review of *One Some Many,* p. 578; March 1, 2005, review of *Over Under,* p. 288.
Publishers Weekly, October 27, 1997, review of *The Invisible Day,* p. 76; June 21, 1999, review of *Hannah and the Seven Dresses,* p. 66; February 28, 2000, review of *Earthly Astonishments,* p. 80; February 23, 2004, review of *Mable Riley,* p. 77.
Resource Links, June, 1998, review of *Invisible Day,* p. 7; February, 1999, review of *Invisible Harry,* p. 9; October, 1999, review of *Hannah and the Seven Dresses,* p. 4; October, 2000, review of *Hannah's Collections,* pp. 2-3; April, 2002, Joanne de Groof, review of *The Invisible Enemy,* p. 23; April, 2004, Carolyn Cutt, review of *Mayfly,* p. 4; April, 2005, Gail de Vos, review of *Over Under,* p. 4.
School Library Journal, April, 2000, Carrie Schadle, review of *Earthly Astonishments,* p. 138; October, 2000, Meghan R. Malone, review of *Hannah's Collections,*

p. 128; May, 2002, Alison Grant, review of *The Invisible Enemy,* p. 154; January, 2003, Be Astengo, review of *A Day with Nellie,* p. 97; March, 2004, Kimberly Monaghan, review of *Mable Riley,* p. 213; May, 2004, Shelley B. Sutherland, review of *Mayfly,* p. 116; June, 2004, Rachel G. Payne, review of *One Some Many,* p. 128.

Teaching Children Mathematics, March, 2000, Betsy J. Liebmann, review of *Hannah and the Seven Dresses,* p. 470.

Voice of Youth Advocates, June, 2005, review of *A Home for Foundlings,* p. 159.

ONLINE

BookLoons.com, http://www.bookloons.com/ (July 26, 2005), Hilary Williamson, review of *One Some Many.*

Kidsreads.com, http://www.kidsreads.com/ (July 26, 2005), "Marthe Jocelyn."

Marthe Jocelyn Home Page, http://www.marthejocelyn. com (July 6, 2005).

Red Cedar Awards Web site, http://redcedar.swifty.com/ (October 28, 2002), "Marthe Jocelyn."

*   *   *

JOHANSSON, Philip

Personal

Male. *Education:* University of Vermont, B.S. (wildlife and fisheries biology); University of California, Berkeley, M.A. (zoology).

Addresses

Home—VT. *Office*—Earthwatch Institute, P.O. Box 75, Maynard, MA 01754-0075. *E-mail*—philipjo@sover. net.

Career

Biologist and nature writer. Earthwatch Institute, managing editor of *EarthWatch Journal.*

Member

National Association of Science Writers.

Awards, Honors

Science Books and Films Best Books for Children selection, 2004, for *The Tropical Rain Forest* and *The Temperate Forest;* National Science Teachers Association/Children's Book Council Outstanding Science Trade Book selection, 2005, for *The Temperate Forest.*

Writings

NONFICTION

Heart Disease, Enslow Publishers (Springfield, NJ), 1998.

Carpal Tunnel Syndrome and Other Repetitive Strain Injuries, Enslow Publishers (Berkeley Heights, NJ), 1999.

Contributor to periodicals, including *New Scientist, Sierra, AMC Outdoors,* and *Boston Globe;* contributor to *Science and Spirit* Web site.

"WEB OF LIFE" SERIES; NONFICTION

The Dry Desert, Enslow Publishers (Berkeley Heights, NJ), 2004.

The Forested Taiga, Enslow Publishers (Berkeley Heights, NJ), 2004.

The Frozen Tundra, Enslow Publishers (Berkeley Heights, NJ), 2004.

The Temperate Forest, Enslow Publishers (Berkeley Heights, NJ), 2004.

The Tropical Rain Forest, Enslow Publishers (Berkeley Heights, NJ), 2004.

The Wide Open Grasslands, Enslow Publishers (Berkeley Heights, NJ), 2004.

Sidelights

Science and nature writer Philip Johansson is the managing editor of the *Earthwatch Journal,* a publication of the globally focused Earthwatch Institute. A passionate environmental researcher and trained biologist, Johansson utilizes his expertise in covering the institute's trips and adventures into the great outdoors. He has also drawn on his scientific background to create the multi-volume "Web of Life" books for elementary-grade readers, as well as several other nonfiction titles.

The "Web of Life" series, which includes *The Forested Taiga, The Frozen Tundra,* and *The Wide Open Grasslands,* discusses the plants and animals found in each of several biomes—a unique ecological community—and how the delicate balance is maintained with regard to that biome's food and energy flow. Johansson uses an organized format, and grounds each chapter with information from a scientific specialist with a related area of expertise. Praising the author for creating an easy-to-understand text, Kathy Piehl wrote in *School Library Journal* that Johansson's "presentations are interesting enough [to] hold the attention of those exploring the topics out of personal interest."

In his award-winning volume *The Temperate Forest* Johansson brings to life one of the most diverse biomes on Earth, an environment familiar to the residents of much of North America. In *The Frozen Tundra* readers are given an in-depth look into what the author calls a "frozen desert": the arid plains located in the arctic and sub-arctic regions as well as above the tree-line in more southern lands. Johansson providers a detailed map of Earth's tundra regions, along with numerous full-color photos. Carolyn Phelan, writing in *Booklist,* noted that *The Frozen Tundra* provides "good, simple discussions of the flow of energy from the sun and soil to plants, then on to herbivores, carnivores and omnivores, decomposers, and back into the soil."

Biographical and Critical Sources

PERIODICALS

Booklist, April 1, 2004, Carolyn Phelan, review of *The Frozen Tundra,* p. 1374.

School Library Journal, August, 2004, Kathy Piehl, review of *The Forested Taiga: A Web of Life,* p. 110.

ONLINE

Philip Johansson Home Page, http://nasw.org/users/philipjo (March 19, 2005).*

*   *   *

JORDAN, Chris
See PHILBRICK, (W.) Rodman

K

KUKLIN, Susan 1941-

Personal

Born September 6, 1941, in Philadelphia, PA; daughter of Albert E. (a builder) and Bertha (Gussman) Greenbaum; married Bailey H. Kuklin (a professor of law), July 7, 1973. *Education:* New York University, B.S., 1963, M.A., 1966. *Hobbies and other interests:* Dance, traveling, gardening (in pots on a roof terrace), reading (especially Chinese and Japanese fiction and the classics), visiting museums, theater concerts, opera.

Addresses

Home—New York, NY. *Agent*—c/o Author Mail, Putnam Publishers, 200 Madison Ave., New York, NY 10016.

Career

Photographer and writer. New York City Public Schools, New York, NY, English teacher, 1965-74; New York City Board of Education, curriculum developer, 1970-74; University of Tennessee, Knoxville, teacher of film studies, 1974-76; photojournalist, 1974—. Member of executive committee, Works Ballet Company. *Exhibitions:* Photographs exhibited at Lincoln Center Library, 1973; Lever House, New York, NY, 1986; and at other group shows in and around New York City.

Member

International PEN, Authors Guild, Authors League of America, Society of Children's Book Writers and Illustrators.

Awards, Honors

Outstanding Science Trade Book for Children designation, National Science Teachers Association, 1980, for *The Story of Nim;* Notable Children's Trade Book in the Field of Social Studies designation, National Council for the Social Studies (NCSS)/ Children's Book

Susan Kuklin

Council, 1984, for *Mine for a Year; Thinking Big* named a Best Book of the Year by *School Library Journal* and International Board on Books for Young People, both 1986, and among Child Study Association of America's Children's Books of the Year, 1987; *Reaching for Dreams* named a Best Book of 1987 by American Library Association (ALA) and New York Public Library; best children's book award, San Francisco *Chronicle,* Words Project for AIDS' Names Project award, and Association of Children's Librarians of Northern California Best Book designation, all 1989, all for *Fighting Back;* Best Book for Reluctant Young-Adult Readers designation, and Best of the Year designation, New York Public Library, both 1993, and best nonfiction book designation, *Hungry Mind,* 1994, all for *Speaking Out: Teenagers Take on Race, Sex, and Identity;* ALA Best Books designation, Best Book for Reluctant Young-Adult Readers, Best of the Year designation,

New York Public Library, and Suicide Prevention Award, New Jersey Survivors of Suicide Conference, all 1994, all for *After a Suicide: Young People Speak Up;* Book of the Year designation, *Choice,* 1996, Christopher Award, 1997, and *Voice of Youth Advocates* nonfiction honor list inclusion, all for *Irrepressible Spirit: Conversations with Human Rights Activists;* Carter G. Woodson award, NCSS Outstanding Merit Book award, and Pick of the List, American Book Sellers, all for *How My Family Lives in America;* Best Book designations, New York Public Library, and *Parent's Guide to Children's Media,* both 2003, both for *All Aboard!*

Writings

AND PHOTOGRAPHER; FOR YOUNG PEOPLE

Mine for a Year, Coward (New York, NY), 1984.
Thinking Big: The Story of a Young Dwarf, Lothrop (New York, NY), 1986.
Reaching for Dreams: A Ballet from Rehearsal to Opening Night, Lothrop (New York, NY), 1987.
When I See My Doctor, Bradbury Press (New York, NY), 1988.
When I See My Dentist, Bradbury Press (New York, NY), 1988.
Taking My Cat to the Vet, Bradbury Press (New York, NY), 1988.
Taking My Dog to the Vet, Bradbury Press (New York, NY), 1988.
Fighting Back: What Some People Are Doing about AIDS, Putnam (New York, NY), 1988.
Going to My Ballet Class, Bradbury Press (New York, NY), 1989.
Going to My Nursery School, Bradbury Press (New York, NY), 1990.
What Do I Do Now: Talking about Teenage Pregnancy, Putnam (New York, NY), 1991.
Going to My Gymnastics Class, Bradbury Press (New York, NY), 1991.
How My Family Lives in America, Simon & Schuster (New York, NY), 1992.
Speaking Out: Teenagers Take on Race, Sex, and Identity, Putnam (New York, NY), 1993.
Fighting Fires, Simon & Schuster (New York, NY), 1993.
After a Suicide: Young People Speak Up, Putnam (New York, NY), 1994.
From Head to Toe: How a Doll Is Made, Hyperion (New York, NY), 1994.
Kodomo: Children of Japan, Putnam (New York, NY), 1995.
Irrepressible Spirit: Conversations with Human Rights Activists, Putnam (New York, NY), 1996.
Fireworks: The Science, the Art, and the Magic, Hyperion (New York, NY), 1996.
Dance Hyperion (New York, NY), 1998.
Iqbal Masih and the Crusaders against Child Slavery, Holt (New York, NY), 1998.
Hoops with Swoopes, Hyperion (New York, NY), 2001.

The Harlem Nutcracker, Hyperion (New York, NY), 2001.
Trial: The Inside Story, Holt (New York, NY), 2001.
From Wall to Wall, Putnam (New York, NY), 2002.
All Aboard!: A True Train Story, Orchard (New York, NY), 2003.

Contributor of photographs and essays to periodicals, including *Time, Newsweek, Psychology Today, New York, New York Times, Pegasus, Us, Der Spiegel, Science, Dance, Discovery, Cricket, Woman, Junior Scholastic, Viva, Family Weekly,* and *Planned Parenthood Review.*

PHOTOGRAPHER

Herbert Terrace, *Nim,* Simon & Schuster (New York, NY), 1979.
(With Herbert Terrace) Anna Michel, *The Story of Nim, a Chimp Who Learned Language,* Knopf (New York, NY), 1979.
Paul Thompson, *The Hitchhikers,* Franklin Watts (New York, NY), 1980.
Linda Atkinson, *Hit and Run,* Franklin Watts (New York, NY), 1981.
Gene DeWesse, *Nightmares in Space,* Franklin Watts (New York, NY), 1981.

Contributor of photographs to books, including *How Animals Behave,* National Geographic Society Books (Washington, DC), 1984; Terry Miller, *Greenwich Village and How It Got That Way,* Crown (New York, NY), 1990; and Robert Lacy, editor, *Balanchine's Ballerinas,* Simon & Schuster (New York, NY), 1984.

Sidelights

Susan Kuklin has blended her skill as a photographer with her penchant for dramatic story-telling to produce a number of books for teen readers, many of which tackle controversial and difficult subjects. Kuklin's focus has ranged from teen pregnancy to suicide, from dwarfism to AIDS, and from prejudice to the fight for human rights. In award-winning titles such as *Fighting Back: What Some People Are Doing about AIDS* and *Thinking Big,* Kuklin explores the human drama behind the statistics, making such subjects at once readable and informative. The author/photographer's love of dance and theater has also found expression in her published work, and her series of books for younger readers help children confront potentially scary situations, from a first visit to the dentist to their first day at nursery school.

Kuklin came to children's books in a roundabout manner: through dance and theater, and then to photography and writing. Growing up in Philadelphia, she was introduced to "art, theater, and books," as she once told *Something about the Author (SATA).* "Going to the opera, ballet, or theater with my family was my idea of a wonderful time. At night my grandmother would read to me Russian fables and short stories, and I spent a great deal of time at the public library."

Kuklin especially loved dance and decided she wanted to become a dancer, though by the time she was a teenager such enthusiasm had evolved from direct participation to "audience appreciation." Yet the performing arts still held her interest, and she found a new dream: becoming an actress. To that end, she spent summers as an apprentice at Philadelphia's Playhouse in the Park and Joseph Papp's New York Shakespeare Festival, working in minor roles or backstage and rubbing shoulders with real actors such as Jessica Tandy and Geraldine Page.

While attending New York University, Kuklin majored in drama and took acting classes at the Herbert Berghof Studio. In graduate school her desire for an on-stage career was replaced by an interest in directing. "While acting taught me how to interpret a part, directing forced me to look at the big picture which included a visual application of the art," Kuklin later recalled. "I learned about framing, position, lighting, movement, etc. These fundamentals later became intrinsic aspects of my approach to photography and nonfiction writing." Such a career was still several years in the future, however; shortly after graduating from college, Kuklin supplemented her meager acting income by teaching English and helping with curriculum development in the New York City schools. She liked to stress drama in her curriculum, and was particularly pleased with how her pupils—mainly inner-city kids—responded to the plays of William Shakespeare. During these years she also became an inveterate traveler; she also took up photography as a way to record some of these trips.

Kuklin married in 1973 and moved to Knoxville, Tennessee, when her law-professor husband was offered a position there. She also taught at the University of Tennessee in the film studies department. During her two years in Knoxville, and inspired by travels in Appalachia, she began to take her photography seriously. Working with Planned Parenthood, Kuklin produced a photo essay titled "Appalachian Families." Slowly, editors began to take notice of her work, and she won commissions. To hone her skills she studied photography—not only composition but also printing and other darkroom techniques.

Once back in New York Kuklin won a children's book contract, taking photographs for the story of a chimpanzee who was taught language. Work on *The Story of Nim: The Chimpanzee Who Learned Language* was "a far cry from Appalachia," as Kuklin recalled, noting that she learned basic sign language before she was introduced to her chimp subject. What resulted was a popular and award-winning account of a fascinating study in communication between the chimp and human animal species.

For her next project, Kuklin created a photographic essay documenting the production of a new ballet by noted choreographer George Balanchine. With the success of 1987's *Reaching for Dreams: A Ballet from Re-*

hearsal to Opening Night, assignments from major magazines began coming her way. During this time, she missed delving into a subject in greater depth, something her work on children's books had allowed her. Kuklin returned to children's books with her first authored and illustrated title, *Mine for a Year.* In this story, she focuses on a seeing-eye-dog-in-training and its human trainer, a foster child named George who, as part of a 4-H program, works with the puppy for a year. Interestingly, George himself suffers from failing eyesight and might one day need a dog like Doug, the puppy he is helping to train. "As a photographer, sight, obviously, is essential," Kuklin noted. "What would it be like not to have sight?" *Mine for a Year* answers this question, and was praised as containing "great" human interest appeal by a *Booklist* reviewer. A reviewer for the *Bulletin of the Center for Children's Books* was "impressed by the candor and directness of the text," which follows the 4-H Club's dog-training program.

Kuklin tells the story of eight-year-old dwarf Jaime Osborn in *Thinking Big.* She worked closely with Jaime and her family, focusing on all the things the Osborns want readers to learn about being a dwarf. *Thinking Big* does a "good job of providing information simply," according to a *Bulletin of the Center for Children's Books* writer. Readers will come to understand that "having a disability doesn't make another child different in any but a physical sense." Elizabeth S. Watson, writing in *Horn Book,* commented on the "well integrated" text and photos, and noted that the book should be "a real addition" to the limited resources available for children with such special needs. Margaret C. Howell concluded in *School Library Journal* that *Thinking Big* is a "positive book that should be of interest to libraries as it covers a subject about which little has been written."

With *Reaching for Dreams* Kuklin indulges her love of the dance once again, this time creating a book-length study of how a dance production is staged. She followed the rehearsals of the Alvin Ailey American Dance Theater in preparation for a new ballet. "All my books are important to me," Kuklin explained to *SATA,* adding that *Reaching for Dreams* "is especially from the heart." Many reviewers agreed. Margrett J. McFadden called the book "delightful" in her *Voice of Youth Advocates* review, concluding that "Students (or browsers) at any age will enjoy the pictures and commentary."

Kuklin again focuses on the dance while teaming up with choreographer Donald Byrd for *The Harlem Nutcracker.* As she explained on her Web site, in contrast to the "traditional Nutcracker by E. T. A. Hoffmann, . . . Byrd's Nutcracker is black, not white. The music is Ellington, not Tchaikovsky. The choreography is jazz dancing, not classical ballet." Although, according to a *Publishers Weekly* contributor, the work "meanders and the photos are uncharacteristically grainy," a *Kirkus* reviewer wrote that the photographs "capture both the expressive movement of the dancers and their subtle emotions." "This powerful story is not just an-

Durango & Silverton's narrow-gauge steam engines continue to ride the rails through Colorado's Rocky Mountains, a vestige of the past Kuklin documents in **All Aboard!: A True Train Story.**

other retold fairy tale," the reviewer concluded of *The Harlem Nutcracker;* "it stands on its own, dancing in the reader's imagination." She also teamed up with dancer and choreographer Bill T. Jones to produce *Dance.* Combining simple text and beautiful photos, the book captures "all the movement, joy, and pulsating energy of dance," according to a *Horn Book* contributor, while Glenn Griffin commented in *Dance* that "Kuklin's photographs of Jones illustrate the text with fine insight and powerful images," creating a volume that Griffin dubbed "a delight."

Though many of Kuklin's books are aimed at middle- and high-school readers, she has also written and illustrated several books with younger readers in mind. "By combining photojournalism techniques with medium format photography, actual experiences of a young child going to the doctor, the dentist, etc., are portrayed," Kuklin explained of these books to *SATA. When I See My Doctor* and *When I See My Dentist* won praise from a *Booklist* critic as being "notable for their realistic approaches, relatively detailed texts, and attractive formats." Other titles directed toward a young readership include *Going to My Ballet Class,* which was praised as "A handsome book on a subject seldom approached at the beginning level" by Carolyn Phelan in *Booklist.* Nancy Vasilakis, writing in *Horn Book,* described as a "welcome addition" Kuklin's inclusion of an afterword

for parents on how to choose a ballet school for their children, noting that it offers "sound and detailed practical advice."

In 2003, Kuklin traveled through the Colorado Rockies to photograph and write about Durango and Silverton Narrow-Gauge steam engines. Describing her book *All Aboard! A True Train Story,* she told *SATA* that "To write about these old gals, I rode the narrow rails, taping their chugga-chuggs, hisses, and whoos." These same sounds echo in the text of the book. Writing in *Booklist,* Lauren Peterson noted in particular the author's inclusion of "some great descriptive words, which will introduce children to the concept of onomatopoeia—as well as basic train vocabulary." "While young readers may be enthralled by the sight of a steam locomotive in action, older picture book readers may be less satisfied," countered a *Publishers Weekly* contributor, while Melinda Piehler stated in *School Library Journal* that "Young train enthusiasts will love this rifle."

From trains and fireworks, Kuklin has ranged in her subjects to walls; as Kuklin noted for *SATA,* such books were great fun to do, as they are "a departure from my other work and give me an opportunity to stretch." *From Wall to Wall* covers a variety of wall styles and function from around the world. Dealing with physical as well as emotional walls, Kuklin delves into the meaning of the barricades fashioned by humans. As a *Kirkus Re-*

views contributor noted of the book, "Kuklin's thoughtful exploration of these human-made creations is sure to inspire discussion."

Kuklin features the WNBA Houston Comets' basketball star Sheryl Swoopes in her 2001 photo essay, *Hoops with Swoopes.* The book introduces young readers to the sport of basketball, and as Ilene Cooper wrote in *Booklist,* Kuklin "captures the energy and enthusiasm of women's basketball in general and of Swoopes in particular." A reviewer for *Publishers Weekly* maintained that, through her book, Kuklin "delivers a potent message about female strength and self-esteem," although a *Horn Book* contributor noted that because the photographer depicts "Swoopes alone, away from competition," the work does not capture "the drama of contact that's a vital part of the game."

Although she has received many awards for her books, Kuklin has been particularly cited for addressing hard-hitting books on controversial topics facing teens. *Fighting Back: What Some People Are Doing about AIDS* is a "moving portrayal of a dedicated team of trained volunteers," according to a *Kirkus Reviews* contributor. Beverly Robertson, writing in *Voice of Youth Advocates,* commented that the book "is an emotionally wrenching story that is accessible to teens because it is about individuals, not numbers." Kuklin employs a similar investigative and interview approach in creating *What Do I Do Now?* in which she interviews teens from a variety of socioeconomic backgrounds to explore the impact pregnancy had on their lives. Laura L. Lent, writing in *Voice of Youth Advocates,* concluded that this "is a book that simply must be read to gain an understanding of the problem."

Race matters and prejudice are the subject of Kuklin's *Speaking Out,* which was the result of a year's worth of student interviews at a racially and culturally diverse high school in New York. Teen suicide is the focus of *After a Suicide,* for which the author interviewed young people who either attempted suicide themselves, or were deeply affected by the suicide of someone close to them. Libby K. White noted in *School Library Journal* that while many books on teen suicide discuss the effects on survivors, "Kuklin's is the only one that considers their predicament so thoroughly, sympathetically, and intelligently." William R. Mollineaux, writing in *Voice of Youth Advocates,* concluded that *After a Suicide* "merits its greatest praise for being a suicide deterrent, for I believe that any reader contemplating suicide will reconsider this final act."

Kuklin investigates human rights issues in *An Irrepressible Spirit,* which contains the personal testimonies of men and women who experienced human rights abuses. Additionally, the book presents accounts of human-rights workers and comments from representatives of the Human Rights Watch. Tracey Kroll, in *School Library Journal,* commented that Kuklin's work "will stir strong emotions and raise awareness." Equally hard-

hitting, *Iqbal Masih and the Crusaders against Child Slavery* delves into the issue of child slavery. As *Booklist* reviewer Hazel Rochman noted, the 1998 volume "is as much a call to action as an account of child slavery and the struggle against it." Drawing on the first-hand accounts of child laborers in several countries, Kuklin reveals the courageous work done by child advocates worldwide, framing the larger picture within the life story of Iqbal Masih, a young Pakistani boy who escaped slavery to become a leading voice in the international fight against child slavery until his murder at age twelve. A *Horn Book* reviewer concluded that "The honesty, documentation, and timeliness of the unfinished story of both child slavery and the killing of Iqbal Masih are riveting."

Focusing on the U.S. judicial system, Kuklin describes for readers a New York City kidnaping trial involving illegal Chinese immigrants in *Trial: The Inside Story.* In this detailed work, she covers not only the crime itself, but also the lengthy trial process as it slowly unfolds in most U.S. courts. *School Library Journal* contributor Ann Brouse concluded that the volume's "excellent organization and wealth of relevant and useful supplementary material create a revealing document," although *Booklist* contributor Randy Meyer added that *Trial* requires "a close reading to grasp all the legal maneuvering fully."

More than entertaining readers, Kuklin views as her primary role the raising of awareness among her young

In **Hoops with Swoops** *Kuklin focuses on the life and career of popular WNBA basketball player Sheryl Swoops, a member of the Houston Comets and league MVP.*

readers. "Although the topics we all explore are quite different, a common thread is always present: the urge for self-expression," she once commented to *SATA*. "In effect, my subjects reveal themselves, warts and all, as a way to begin a conversation." Throughout her body of work, as critics have noted, Kuklin never loses sight of the human subject, despite sometimes complex themes or topics. "When I get right down to it," she once said, "my books revolve around one rudimentary question: how do ordinary people deal with unusual, sometimes extraordinary, situations? I simply report my subject's choices and values, trying hard not to add editorial comments. For a person who loves sappy, happy endings, letting my subject 'go' can be trying. So far, I've been lucky. My subjects have come through wonderfully."

Biographical and Critical Sources

PERIODICALS

Booklist, September 1, 1984, review of *Mine for a Year,* p. 67; September 15, 1989, Carolyn Phelan, review of *Going to My Ballet Class,* p. 185; May 1, 1988, review of *When I See My Doctor* and *When I See My Dentist,* p. 1525; June 1, 1996, Stephanie Zvirin, review of *Fireworks: The Science, the Art, and the Magic,* p. 1710; November 1, 1998, Hazel Rochman, review of *Iqbal Masih and the Crusaders against Child Slavery,* p. 481; December 15, 2000, Randy Meyer, review of *Trial: The Inside Story,* p. 806; June 1, 2001, Ilene Cooper, review of *Hoops with Swoopes,* p. 1885; February 1, 2004, Lauren Peterson, review of *All Aboard! A True Train Story,* p. 980.

Bulletin of the Center for Children's Books, July-August, 1984, review of *Mine for a Year,* p. 207; May, 1986, review of *Thinking Big,* p. 170; April, 1987, pp. 149-150; March, 1989, p. 174; November, 1991, p. 66; April, 1992, pp. 212-213; October, 1993, p. 49; January, 1995, p. 170; April, 1995, p. 279; September, 1996, p. 19.

Dance, August, 1999, Glenn Griffin, review of *Dance,* p. 40.

Horn Book, September, 1984, p. 607; July-August, 1986, Elizabeth S. Watson, review of *Thinking Big,* p. 466; January, 1989, p. 91; September-October, 1989, Nancy Vasilakis, review of *Going to My Ballet Class,* p. 639; January, 1999, review of *Iqbal Masih and the Crusaders against Child Slavery,* p. 81; January, 2000, review of *Dance,* p. 44; May, 2001, review of *Hoops with Swoopes,* p. 348.

Kirkus Reviews, December 15, 1988, review of *Fighting Back: What Some People Are Doing about AIDS,* p. 1813; September 1, 2001, review of *The Harlem Nutcracker,* p. 1286; March 15, 2002, review of *From Wall to Wall,* p. 416.

New York Times Book Review, July 1, 1984, p. 23; January 22, 1989, p. 29.

Publishers Weekly, July 2, 2001, review of *Dance,* p. 78; September 24, 2001, review of *The Harlem Nutcracker,* p. 54; December 22, 2003, review of *All Aboard!,* p. 60.

School Library Journal, October, 1984, p. 158; May, 1987, p. 114; August, 1988, p. 89; October, 1988, p. 133; December, 1988, p. 99; February, 1989, p. 106; September, 1989, p. 241; November, 1990, p. 104; December, 1991, p. 111; March, 1992, p. 231; July, 1993, p. 108; September, 1993, p. 225; August, 1995, p. 148; April, 1996, p. 146; August, 1986, Margaret C. Howell, review of *Thinking Big,* pp. 83-84; April, 1996, Tracey Kroll, review of *Irrepressible Spirits,* p. 162; December, 1994, Libby K. White, review of *After a Suicide,* pp. 135-136; January, 2001, Ann G. Brouse, review of *Trial,* p. 148; August, 2001, Blair Christolon, review of *Hoops with Swoopes,* p. 170; December 2003, Melinda Piehler, review of *All Aboard!,* p. 136.

Voice of Youth Advocates, August, 1991, Laura L. Lent, review of *What Do I Do Now?,* p. 190; December, 1987, Margrett J. McFadden, review of *Reaching for Dreams,* p. 250; February, 1995, William R. Mollineaux, review of *After a Suicide,* pp. 359-360; April, 1989, Beverly Robertson, review of *Fighting Back: What Some People Are Doing about AIDS,* p. 59.

ONLINE

Susan Kuklin Web site, http://susankuklin.com (September 21, 2005).*

L

LAMINACK, Lester L. 1956-

Personal

Born July 11, 1956, in Flint, MI; son of Jimmy R. (a welder) and Mary Jo (Thompson) Laminack; married Glenda Jo Anthony (an employee at Department of Social Services), November 28 1974; children: Zachary Seth. *Education:* Jacksonville State University, B.S., 1977, M.S., 1978; Auburn University, Ed.D., 1983. *Religion:* Methodist. *Hobbies and other interests:* Travel, playing the saxophone, reading children's books and southern fiction.

Addresses

Agent—c/o Author Mail, Peachtree Publishers, 1700 Chattahoochee Avenue, Atlanta, GA 30318-2112. *E-mail*—laminack@wcu.edu.

Career

Cleburn County Elementary School, first-grade teacher, 1977-81, reading teacher, 1981-82; Western Carolina University Cullohwee, NC, professor, 1982-2004; author literacy education consultant, Sylva, NC; writer.

Member

International Reading Association, National Council of Teachers of English, Authors Guild, Authors League.

Awards, Honors

Botner Superior Teaching Award, Western Carolina University College of Education and Psychology, 1989; Chancellor's Distinguished Teaching Award, Western Carolina University, 1991; Fassler Award, Association for the Care of Children's Health, for *The Sunsets of Miss Olivia Wiggins.*

Writings

Learning with Zachary, Scholastic (New York, NY), 1991.

(With Katie Wood) *Spelling in Use,* National Council of Teachers of English (Urbana, IL), 1996.

Trevor's Wiggly-Wobbly Tooth, illustrated by Kathi Garry McCord, Peachtree Publishers (Atlanta, GA), 1998.

The Sunsets of Miss Olivia Wiggins, illustrated by Constance R. Bergum, Peachtree Publishers (Atlanta, GA), 1998.

Volunteers Working with Young Readers, National Council of Teachers of English (Urbana, IL), 1998.

(With Katie Wood) *The Writing Workshop: Working through the Hard Parts (And They're All Hard Parts),* National Council of Teachers of English (Urbana, IL), 2001.

Saturdays and Teacakes, illustrated by Chris Soentpiet, Peachtree Publishers (Atlanta, GA), 2004.

Jake's 100th Day of School, illustrated by Judy Love, Peachtree Publishers (Atlanta, GA), 2006.

Work in Progress

Learning under the Influence of Language and Literature, with Reba Wadsworth, for Heinemann.

Sidelights

Lester Laminack retired in 2005 after a long career in education to pursue his passion for writing, researching, and consulting. An award-winning teacher and educator, Laminack is the author of numerous books for young children, among them *Saturdays and Teacakes* and *The Sunsets of Miss Olivia Wiggins,* and has also produced several guides for teachers.

In *Saturdays and Teacakes* Laminack celebrates a young boy's relationship with his grandmother and their Saturday tradition of baking teacakes together. Linda L. Walkins, writing in *School Library Journal,* praised Laminack's descriptive text as well as illustrator Chris Soentpiet's "brilliant watercolor paintings [that] glow with light and idyllically capture the world of yesterday." A *Publishers Weekly* critic wrote that Laminack brings readers on "a sweet trip down memory lane in this ode to his grandmother," while a *Kirkus Reviews* critic noted that the author "crafted this as a tribute to a childhood tradition." "While not all of us had his childhood," the critic added, the book's "nostalgic look back offers us the childhood may of us wish we'd had."

In *The Sunsets of Miss Olivia Wiggins* Laminack once again visits the theme of close-knit family, this time through the story of Miss Olivia Wiggins, who is in a nursing home. When her daughter and great-grandson Troy come to visit her, the elderly woman acts as if she does not know they are there. However, as Troy begins to hum a tune, Miss Olivia is suddenly flooded by recollections of her children, as well as by other fond memories. "Realistic watercolors flow gently between present and past in this tender depiction of a life well lived," stated Susan Dove Lempke in a review for *Booklist.*

Laminack told *Something about the Author:* "I have always loved to write. I kept notebooks of stories and riddles in the fourth grade. I began writing for children in the 1990s after years of teaching. I hope that children see themselves and their families in these books. I want them to realize that everyone has a story to tell and that every life is worthy.

"I keep a writer's notebook with me at all times. I am always tuned in to the world around me and make notes about those things that strike me. I find ideas for stories in everyday events. *Saturdays and Teacakes* began with

the smell of cookies baking in the local grocery store." I routinely read through my notebooks and on occasion I find a little nugget that can serve as the beginning of a new story.

"When a story begins I move to my computer and save every version until the final draft is ready for my editor. I write any time of day. I don't have a special time when writing seems to work. I prefer to write in my office at home, however, I do work on books when I'm on airplanes, in hotel rooms, dining alone or sitting in an airport waiting for a plane. I write most any place.

"I wrote *The Sunsets of Miss Olivia Wiggins* as a bridge to understanding what happens as our bodies and minds begin to fail us. I wanted children to understand that their love and the love that binds families has tremendous power.

"I wrote *Trevor's Wiggly-Wobbly Tooth* because I taught first grade and I remember what a big—huge—event it is to loose a tooth. I also remember those children who were last. The book should make us all chuckle and remember.

"I wrote *Saturdays and Teacakes* to honor my maternal grandmother and my mom. I had a very special bond with my grandmother; she made me feel so very special, so very real and worthy. I wanted children to know that everyone deserves to be loved and cherished. I wanted adults to remember those feelings and to recog-

A boy's weekly bicycle trip to his grandmother's house are captured in Lester L. Laminack's nostalgic picture book **Saturdays and Teacakes.** *(Illustration by Chris Soentpiet.)*

nize the importance of making childhood that special time in life. I wanted to remind us all that children are to be cherished and nurtured if we expect them to cherish and love others as they grow up.

"The four children's authors I most admire are Mem Fox, Patricia MacLachlan, Tony Johnson, and Cynthia Rylant. For those who want to write: Stop wishing, start writing. Don't say 'one day when. . .' Just pick up a pen and open a notebook and start taking note of what you notice. Let your brain get in the habit of noticing the world. Read, read, read, read, read, read. . . . If you want to write read everything that is anything near what you hope to achieve. Fill your head with the sounds of it."

Biographical and Critical Sources

PERIODICALS

Booklist, May 1, 1998, Susan Dove Lempke, review of *The Sunsets of Miss Olivia Wiggins,* p. 1521; April 1, 2004, Hazel Rochman, review of *Saturdays and Teacakes,* p. 1369.
Children's Digest, June, 2002.
Horn Book, fall, 1998, review of *The Sunsets of Miss Olivia Wiggins,* p. 297; spring, 1999, review of *Trevor's Wiggly-Wobbly Tooth,* p. 34.
Kirkus Reviews, February 15, 2004, review of *Saturdays and Teacakes,* p. 181.
Publishers Weekly, March 30, 1998, review of *The Sunsets of Miss Olivia Wiggins,* p. 82; February 23, 2004, review of *Saturdays and Teacakes,* p. 251.
Radical Teacher, summer, 2004, Wendy Weisenberg, review of *The Writing Workshop: Working through the Hard Parts (And They're All Hard Parts),* p. 40.
School Library Journal, July, 1998, Martha Topol, review of *The Sunsets of Miss Olivia Wiggins,* p. 79; February, 1999, Farida Shapiro, review of *Trevor's Wiggly-Wobbly Tooth;* April, 2004, Linda L. Walkins, review of *Saturdays and Teacakes,* p. 118.
Teacher Librarian, May, 1999, review of *Volunteers Working with Young Readers,* p. 41.

ONLINE

Heinemann Web site, http://www.heinemann.com/ (July 6, 2005), "Lester Laminack."
Lester Laminack Home Page, http://www.lesterlaminack. com (October 15, 2005).

*   *   *

LANAGAN, Margo 1960-

Personal

Born 1960, in Newcastle, New South Wales, Australia; children: two sons. *Education:* Studied history at universities in Perth and Sydney.

Addresses

Home—Sydney, Australia. *Agent*—c/o Author Mail, Allen & Unwin, 83 Alexander St., Crows Nest, New South Wales 2065, Australia.

Career

Freelance book editor, technical writer, and author.

Writings

WildGame, Allen & Unwin (North Sydney, New South Wales, Australia), 1991.
The Tankermen, Allen & Unwin (North Sydney, New South Wales, Australia), 1992.
The Best Thing, Allen & Unwin (St. Leonards, New South Wales, Australia), 1995.
Touching Earth Lightly, Allen & Unwin (St. Leonards, New South Wales, Australia), 1996.
Walking through Albert, Allen & Unwin (St. Leonards, New South Wales, Australia), 1998.
White Time (short stories), Allen & Unwin (St. Leonards, New South Wales, Australia), 2000.
Black Juice (short stories), Allen & Unwin (St. Leonards, New South Wales, Australia), 2004, Eos (New York, NY) 2005.
Treasure Hunters of Quentaris, Lothian Books (South Melbourne, New South Wales, Australia), 2004.

Sidelights

In addition to writing for children, author Margo Lanagan has worked as a freelance book editor as well as a technical writer. Growing up in the Hunter Valley and Melbourne, Australia, she traveled extensively, in addition to studying history at universities in both Perth and Sydney. The insight and experiences gained from both her travels and her education have provided the inspiration for Lanagan's children's books and short stories such as *Black Juice.* Praised for containing "memorable characters a-plenty" by a *Kirkus Reviews* critic, the collection of ten tales is a companion volume to her fantasy fiction collection *White Time.* "Inspiration is pretty much everywhere," Lanagan noted in an essay on the *Allen & Unwin Web site.* "I get it from reading both good and bad writing, from watching and listening to people, from landscapes and cityscapes, from wildlife documentaries and building sites and classrooms and music. My problem is not finding ideas but finding time to pin a few of them down to a page."

"I write because it's my way of making sense of the world," she added. "I've always loved reading, both to escape from real life and to make life more real, and I like doing both in my writing too, writing straight realistic and fantasy stories."

Lanagan features children and teens as central characters in her books "because I'm interested in what it's like to piece together the world, to make connections and realize things for the first time. And there's a lot more room for adventure in children's and teenagers' lives, before they make the decisions that will set them on their path in adulthood."

Biographical and Critical Sources

PERIODICALS

Kirkus Reviews, February 1, 2005, review of *Black Juice,* p. 178.

ONLINE

Aussie Reviews Online, http://www.aussiereviews.com/ (March 19, 2005), Sally Murphy, review of *Black Juice.*
SFSite.com, http://www.sfsite.com/ (August, 2003), Trent Walters, interview with Lanagan.

*   *   *

LEESE, Jennifer L.B. 1970-
(J. V. Harlee, a joint pseudonym)

Personal

Born January 27, 1970; married; husband's name Thom; children: Nicholas, Cameron, Jordan. *Hobbies and other interests:* Spending time with family.

Addresses

Home—MD. *Agent*—c/o Author Mail, Heinemann Library, 100 North La Salle, Ste. 1200, Chicago, IL 60602. *E-mail*—AStoryWeaver@aol.com.

Career

Freelance writer and copyeditor. *Picket News,* managing editor and feature writer.

Member

World Romance Writers, Society of Children's Book Writers and Illustrators, EPIC, EPPRO, Potomac Writer's Guild, Parent-Teacher Association (local vice president).

Writings

Uniquely Maryland, Heinemann Library (Chicago, IL), 2004.

Also author of e-books *Two Spots Bakery* (and print), illustrated by Thom Leese, Publish America; *Jordie's School Day Adventure,* illustrated by Kym Jones, *I Am*

Me!, illustrated by Cynthia Iannaccone, *Bows for Pigel's Nose,* illustrated by Sonal Panse, and "Sounds I Can Hear" series (six volumes), all for Writers Exchange E-Publishing; *Notes on the Windowsill,* Zumaya Publications; *911: The Day America Cried;* and *Crafty Friends.* Co-author, with Valerie Hardin under joint pseudonym J. V. Harlee, of *Gargoyle Tears* (e-book; young-adult mystery), Tarbutton Press. Contributor to periodicals, including *Picket News, Whispers Online Magazine for Women, Simpler Living, Partners,* and *Livebrighter.* Contributor to poetry to publications of Webseed Publishing.

Sidelights

Jennifer L. B. Leese told *Something about the Author:* "I began writing when I was ten years old. I've always had an interest in writing fiction. As I grew older, writing sat on the back burner until my first born was four years old, which was in 1995. His father brought home a rhinocerous beetle for him to keep overnight—that was it—I started writing again. My first published children's e-book was titled 'Beetle Bug Adventures' by Wordbeams Publishing. I plan to rewrite this particular story, adding more detail, and adventures for the two mischievous little bugs, Poppy and Hue.

"I have broadened the genre from children's to include young-adult fantasy, nonfiction stories for children, periodicals, and my favorite paranormal ghostly mainstream fiction. Last year I finished my second ghostly novel titled *The Room in the House on Eleanor Street* and just began *The Carleigh House.* I'm looking for agents and publishers for both novels.

"Writing is something I must do . . . it keeps me sane and allows me to constructively file the many 'new' stories that pop into my head every singel day."

Biographical and Critical Sources

PERIODICALS

Booklist, April 1, 2004, Kay Weisman, review of *Uniquely Maryland,* p. 1380.

ONLINE

Jennifer L. B. Leese Home Page, http://www.geocities.com/ladyjiraff/ (July 6, 2005).
Writers Exchange E-Publishing Web site, http://www.writers-exchange.com/ (July 6, 2005).

*   *   *

LEONARD, Elmore (John Jr.) 1925-

Personal

Born October 11, 1925, in New Orleans, LA; son of Elmore John (an automotive executive) and Flora Amelia (Rive) Leonard; married Beverly Cline, July 30,

Elmore Leonard

1949 (divorced May 24, 1977); married Joan Shepard, September 15, 1979 (died January 13, 1993); married Christine Kent, August 19, 1993; children: (first marriage) Jane Jones, Peter, Christopher, William, Katherine Dudley. *Education:* University of Detroit, Ph.B., 1950. *Religion:* Roman Catholic.

Addresses

Home—MI. *Agent*—Michael Siegel, Michael Siegel & Associates, 11532 Thurston Circle, Los Angeles, CA 90049.

Career

Writer, 1967—. Campbell-Ewald Advertising Agency, Detroit, MI, copywriter, 1950-61; freelance copywriter and author of educational and industrial films, 1961-63; head of Elmore Leonard Advertising Company, 1963-66. Producer of film *Tishomingo Blues,* 2002. *Military service:* U.S. Naval Reserve, 1943-46.

Member

Writers Guild of America West, Authors League of America, Authors Guild.

Awards, Honors

Hombre named one of the twenty-five best western novels of all time by Western Writers of America, 1977; Edgar Allan Poe Award, Mystery Writers of America, 1984, for *LaBrava;* Michigan Foundation of the Arts Award, 1985; Hammett Prize, International Association of Crime Writers, 1991, for *Maximum Bob;* Mystery Writers of America Grand Master Award, 1992; Honorary Ph.D., Florida Atlantic University, 1996, University of Detroit Mercy, 1997, and University of Michigan, 2000.

Writings

FOR CHILDREN

A Coyote's in the House, HarperEntertainment (New York, NY), 2004.

WESTERNS

The Bounty Hunters (also see below), Houghton (Boston, MA), 1953.
The Law at Randado (also see below), Houghton (Boston, MA), 1955.
Escape from Five Shadows (also see below), Houghton (Boston, MA), 1956.
Last Stand at Saber River (also see below), Dell (New York, NY), 1957, published as *Lawless River,* R. Hale (London, England), 1959, published as *Stand on the Saber,* Corgi (London, England), 1960.
Hombre (also see below), Ballantine (New York, NY), 1961.
Valdez Is Coming (also see below), Gold Medal (New York, NY), 1970.
Forty Lashes less One (also see below), Bantam (New York, NY), 1972.
Gunsights (also see below), Bantam (New York, NY), 1979.
The Tonto Woman and Other Western Stories, Delacorte (New York, NY), 1998.
Elmore Leonard's Western Roundup #1 (contains *The Bounty Hunters, Forty Lashes less One,* and *Gunsights*), Delta (New York, NY), 1998.
Elmore Leonard's Western Roundup #2 (contains *Escape from Five Shadows, Last Stand at Saber River,* and *The Law at Randado*), Delta (New York, NY), 1998.
Elmore Leonard's Western Roundup #3 (contains *Valdez Is Coming* and *Hombre*), Delta (New York, NY), 1999.
The Complete Western Novels of Elmore Leonard, Morrow (New York, NY), 2004.

CRIME NOVELS

The Big Bounce, Gold Medal (New York, NY), 1969, revised edition, Armchair Detective, 1989.
The Moonshine War (also see below), Doubleday (New York, NY), 1969.

Mr. Majestyk (also see below), Dell (New York, NY), 1974.

Fifty-two Pick-up (also see below), Delacorte (New York, NY), 1974.

Swag (also see below), Delacorte (New York, NY), 1976, published as *Ryan's Rules,* Dell (New York, NY), 1976.

Unknown Man, No. 89, Delacorte (New York, NY), 1977.

The Hunted (also see below), Dell (New York, NY), 1977.

The Switch, Bantam (New York, NY), 1978.

City Primeval: High Noon in Detroit (also see below), Arbor House (New York, NY), 1980.

Gold Coast (also see below), Bantam (New York, NY), 1980, revised edition, 1985.

Split Images (also see below), Arbor House (New York, NY), 1981.

Cat Chaser (also see below), Arbor House (New York, NY), 1982.

Stick (also see below), Arbor House (New York, NY), 1983.

LaBrava (also see below), Arbor House (New York, NY), 1983.

Glitz, Arbor House (New York, NY), 1985.

Elmore Leonard's Dutch Treat (contains *The Hunted, Swag,* and *Mr. Majestyk*), introduction by George F. Will, Arbor House (New York, NY), 1985.

Elmore Leonard's Double Dutch Treat (contains *City Primeval: High Noon in Detroit, The Moonshine War,* and *Gold Coast*), introduction by Bob Greene, Arbor House (New York, NY), 1986.

Bandits, Arbor House (New York, NY), 1987.

Touch, Arbor House (New York, NY), 1987.

Freaky Deaky, Morrow (New York, NY), 1988.

Killshot, Morrow (New York, NY), 1989.

Get Shorty, Delacorte (New York, NY), 1990.

Maximum Bob, Delacorte (New York, NY), 1991.

Rum Punch, Delacorte (New York, NY), 1992.

Three Complete Novels (contains *LaBrava, Cat Chaser,* and *Split Images*), Wings Books (New York, NY), 1992.

Pronto, Delacorte (New York, NY), 1993.

Riding the Rap, Delacorte (New York, NY), 1995.

Out of Sight, Delacorte (New York, NY), 1996.

Cuba Libre, Delacorte (New York, NY), 1998.

Be Cool (sequel to *Get Shorty*), Delacorte (New York, NY), 1999.

Pagan Babies, Delacorte (New York, NY), 2000.

Tishomingo Blues, Morrow (New York, NY), 2002.

Mr. Paradise, Morrow (New York, NY), 2004.

The Hot Kid, Morrow (New York, NY), 2005.

SCREENPLAYS

The Moonshine War (based on Leonard's novel of the same title), Metro-Goldwyn-Mayer, 1970.

Joe Kidd, Universal, 1972.

Mr. Majestyk (based on Leonard's novel of the same title), United Artists, 1974.

High Noon, Part 2: The Return of Will Kane, Columbia Broadcasting System, 1980.

(With Joseph C. Stinson) *Stick* (based on Leonard's novel of the same title), Universal, 1985.

(With John Steppling) *52 Pick-up* (based on Leonard's novel of the same title), Cannon Group, 1986.

(With Fred Walton) *The Rosary Murders* (based on the novel by William X. Kienzle), New Line Cinema, 1987.

Desperado, National Broadcasting Corporation, 1988.

(With Joe Borrelli) *Cat Chaser* (based on Leonard's novel of the same title), Viacom, 1989.

(With Quentin Tarantino) *Jackie Brown* (based on Leonard's novel *Rum Punch*), Miramax, 1997.

Also author of filmscripts for Encyclopedia Britannica Films, including *Settlement of the Mississippi Valley, Boy of Spain, Frontier Boy,* and *Julius Caesar,* and of a recruiting film for the Franciscans.

OTHER

When the Women Come out to Dance (short fiction), William Morrow (New York, NY), 2002.

Contributor to books, including *The Courage to Change: Personal Conversations about Alcoholism,* edited by Dennis Wholey, Houghton (Boston, MA), 1984. Contributor of stories and novelettes to *Dime Western, Argosy, Saturday Evening Post, Zane Grey's Western Magazine,* and other publications.

Adaptations

The novelette *3:10 to Yuma* was filmed by Columbia Pictures, 1957; the story "The Tall T" was filmed by Columbia, 1957; *Hombre* was filmed by Twentieth Century-Fox, 1967; *The Big Bounce* was filmed by Warner Bros., 1969, and 2004; *Valdez Is Coming* was filmed by United Artists, 1970; *Glitz* was filmed for television by NBC; *Get Shorty* was filmed by Metro-Goldwyn-Mayer (MGM)/United Artists, 1995; *Touch* was filmed by Lumiere, 1996; *Rum Punch* was adapted for film by Quentin Tarantino as *Jackie Brown,* 1997; *Out of Sight,* directed by Steven Soderbergh, screenplay by Scott Frank, was filmed by Universal, 1998; *Karen Sisco* (based on characters from *Out of Sight*) was developed for television by ABC, 2003; screen rights to the novella *Tenkiller* were purchased by Paramount, 2002; *Be Cool* was filmed by MGM, 2005; *Tishomingo Blues* was adapted for film in 2005; *Killshot* was adapted for film in 2006. Many of Leonard's novels have been adapted as audiobooks, including *Mr. Paradise,* and *A Coyote's in the House,* both Harper Audio, 2004.

Work in Progress

A sequel to *The Hot Kid.*

Sidelights

A popular crime novelist who has seen several of his novels become feature films, Elmore Leonard carries on the tradition of the pulp novelists of the early twentieth century. Considered among the best authors writing modern crime fiction, he has earned particular praise for his dark humor and for a prose style that reflects the gritty realities of modern life. While his fame rests on such best-selling novels as *Get Shorty, Tishomingo Blues,* and *Mr. Paradise,* Leonard started his career penning genre Westerns; he has also authored screenplay adaptations of his novels and has tackled a new format—children's books—with the 2004 novel *A Coyote's in the House.*

Born in Louisiana, Leonard has lived in Detroit, Michigan for most of his life, and graduated from the University of Detroit in 1950. He began his writing career a few years later and, realizing where the strongest market was, began penning western stories for pulp magazines. His first sale was the novelette *Apache Agent,* for which *Argosy* magazine paid ninety dollars. Moving to longer works, he published five western novels while also working full time as an advertising copywriter. While copywriting did not appeal to the young author, as Bill Dunn noted in *Publishers Weekly,* "it allowed him precious time and a steady paycheck to experiment with fiction, which he did in the early morning before going off to work." Leonard told Dunn: "Sometimes I would write a little fiction at work, too. I would write in my desk drawer and close the drawer if somebody came in."

By the early 1960s western genre fiction was on the decline, and Leonard found the market for his fiction drying up. For several years he devoted his time to freelance copywriting, working frequently for the company that manufactured Hurst gear shifters, a popular feature in hot rod cars. He also wrote scripts for industrial films for Detroit-area companies and educational films for Encyclopedia Britannica at one thousand dollars apiece. This all ended in 1965, when his agent sold the film rights to Leonard's novel *Hombre* for ten thousand dollars.

Once again with enough of a financial cushion to take the risk with fiction, Leonard returned to writing novels, this time working in the mystery-suspense genre, and his urban detectives approached their task with the same grim determination and glib wisecracking as had his gunfighters. The typical Leonard novel, Michael Kernan explained in the *Washington Post,* is distinguished by "guns, a killing or two or three, fights and chases and sex. Tight, clean prose, ear-perfect, whip-smart dialogue. And, just beneath the surface, an acute sense of the ridiculous." Leonard's books are often peopled by anxious, lower-class characters hoping to make some quick money in a big heist or quickie scam. Inevitably, they "fall into crime," as Tucker explained, "because it's an easier way to make money than that tedious nine-to-five." George Stade, writing in the *New York Times Book Review,* called Leonard's villains "treacherous and tricky, smart enough to outsmart themselves, driven, audacious and outrageous, capable of anything, paranoid . . . and rousing fun."

Working in a new genre, Leonard had a slow start; his first crime novel, *The Big Bounce,* was rejected by some eighty-four publishers and film producers before being released as a paperback original by Gold Medal in 1969. Over a decade later *Stick* signaled that its author had made it to bestselling writer status. One of Leonard's best-known novels is *Get Shorty,* about Chili Palmer, a Miami loan shark who travels to Hollywood in pursuit of a man but who becomes entangled with a third-rate film producer, a washed-up actress, and several cocaine dealers. Palmer returns in *Be Cool* as Chili helps the career of a struggling young singer in the hopes that there is a good film plot in it, but finds himself up against the young woman'g previous manager, the Russian mob, and a gang of rappers. In the novel *Maximum Bob* a Florida judge—his nickname reflects his fondness for the electric chair—attempts to drive his wife away so that he can pursue a more interesting woman. In *Out of Sight* twenty-nine-year-old U.S. Marshall Karen Sisco runs into escaping convict Jack Foley. Romance ensues in a quirky, convoluted plot that involves Foley's raid on the home of an ex-junk bond trader who supposedly has millions of dollars hidden inside. Set in Cuba around the time of the Spanish-American War, *Cuba Libre* combines adventure, history, and romance in the story of Ben Tyler, a bank-robbing vigilante who only robs banks that contain the money of folks who owe him money.

The veteran crime novelist's "knack for creating intriguing, strong characters is evident in his first children's book," according to *School Library Journal* reviewer Ellen Fader. *A Coyote's in the House,* designed for middle-grade readers, follows jive-talking, gang-leading coyote Antwan, as he meets up with two canine residents of posh Hollywood Hills: German shepherd Buddy, a creaky-legged former film star, and champion poodle Miss Betty. Buddy has had enough of the good life, and talks Antwan into changing places so that the older dog can enjoy a more eventful life on the streets. Taken in by Buddy's owners, who believe Antwan to be a stray dog, the newly named "Timmy" settles down in his ritzy new digs in an enjoyable proximity to the fetching Miss Betty, helping friend Buddy regain his former confidence in the process. Praising Leonard's "quirky characters; snappy dialogue; short, visual scenes; and tight plotting," *Horn Book* reviewer Betty Carter dubbed *A Coyote's in the House* a "blue-ribbon, canine version" of *The Prince and the Pauper,* nineteenth-century American humorist Mark Twain's classic novel about trading identities and social class. Noting that the novel's main strength is the pithy dialogue among the dogs, Bill Ott concluded in a *Booklist* review that while some of Leonard's dry humor might fall under the radar of younger readers, the book reveals that the author "can mix comedy and reality as nimbly for a younger audience as he does for adults."

Interestingly, although he has spent much of his career penning long fiction, Leonard found novels intimidating as a child. As he once noted, he now tries to spare his readers the same situation by working "to leave out the boring parts" in his books. A disciplined author, Leonard writes every day of the week, longhand, sitting at a desk in the corner of his living room.

Biographical and Critical Sources

BOOKS

Contemporary Literary Criticism, Gale (Detroit, MI), Volume 28, 1984, Volume 34, 1985, Volume 71, 1992.
Dictionary of Literary Biography, Volume 173, *American Novelists since World War II,* Gale (Detroit, MI), 1996.
Geherin, David, *Elmore Leonard,* Continuum (New York, NY), 1989.

PERIODICALS

American Film, December, 1984.
Armchair Detective, winter, 1986; spring, 1986; winter, 1989.
Atlantic Monthly, June, 1998, Francis X. Rocca, review of *Cuba Libre,* p. 111.
Book, March-April, 2002, Rob Brookman, interview with Leonard, p. 28.
Booklist, November 1, 1998, David Pitt, review of *Be Cool,* p. 452; December 1, 2001, Bill Ott, review of *Tishomingo Blues,* p. 604; November 1, 2002, Keir Graff, review of *When the Women Come out to Dance,* p. 452; November 15, 2003, Bill Ott, review of *Mr. Paradise,* p. 548; May 15, 2004, Bill Ott, review of *A Coyote's in the House,* p. 1621; March 15, 2005, Keir Graff, review of *The Hot Kid,* p. 1246.
Boston Globe, July 30, 1992, p. 80; November 14, 1993, p. 7.
Chicago Tribune, February 4, 1981; April 8, 1983; December 8, 1983; February 7, 1985.
Christian Science Monitor, November 4, 1983; March 12, 1997.
Commentary, May, 1985, pp. 64, 66-67.
Detroiter, June, 1974, Gay Rubin, interview with Leonard.
Detroit News, February 23, 1982; October 23, 1983.
Economist (US), June 19, 1999, review of *Be Cool,* p. 4; October 14, 2000, "New Thrillers-Hit Men," p. 106; February 23, 2002, review of *Tishomingo Blues.*
Entertainment Weekly, September 22, 2000, Bruce Fretts, review of *Pagan Babies,* p. 68; January 9, 2004, Rebecca Ascher-Walsh, review of *Mr. Paradise,* p. 84.
Esquire, April, 1987, pp. 169-174.
Film Comment, March-April, 1998, Patrick McGilligan, "Get Dutch," p. 43.
Globe and Mail (Toronto, Ontario, Canada), December 14, 1985.
Horn Book, September-October, 2004, Betty Carter, review of *A Coyote's in the House,* p. 589.
Kirkus Reviews, November 15, 1997, p. 1665; November 15, 2001, review of *Tishomingo Blues,* p. 1571; October 15, 2002, review of *When the Women Come out to Dance,* p. 1497; November 1, 2003, review of *Mr. Paradise,* p. 1290; May 15, 2004, review of *A Coyote's in the House,* p. 494.
Kliatt, May, 2004, Paula Rohrlick, review of *A Coyote's in the House,* p. 10.
Library Journal, January, 2002, Karen Anderson, review of *Tishomingo Blues,* p. 153; April 15, 2005, Thomas L. Kilpatrick, review of *The Hot Kid,* p. 74.
Los Angeles Times, June 28, 1984; May 4, 1988; January 26, 1998.
Los Angeles Times Book Review, February 27, 1983; December 4, 1983; January 13, 1985; August 30, 1987, pp. 2, 8; April 23, 1989, p. 14; July 29, 1990, p. 9; August 4, 1991, pp. 2, 9; October 24, 1994, p. 8; May 14, 1995, p. 1.
Maclean's, January 19, 1987; March 16, 1998, Brian Bethune, review of *Cuba Libre,* p. 63; March 29, 1999, Anthony Wilson-Smith, "The Master of Crime: Elmore Leonard's 35th Novel Shows Him at the Top of His Form," p. 70.
Nation, December 4, 1995, Annie Gottlieb, review of *Out of Sight,* p. 724.
New Republic, November 13, 1995, p. 32; January 26, 1998.
New Statesman & Society, October 11, 1991; November 13, 1992.
Newsweek, March 22, 1982; July 11, 1983; November 14, 1983; April 22, 1985, pp. 62-64, 67.
New Yorker, September 3, 1990, pp. 106-7; October 23, 1995, p. 96; September 30, 1996; January 12, 1998; January 26, 1998; February 11, 2002, review of *Tishomingo Blues,* p. 86.
New York Times, June 11, 1982; April 28, 1983; October 7, 1983; October 29, 1983; April 26, 1985; May 2, 1988; July 25, 1991, p. C18; September 23, 1993, p. C18; May 11, 1995; February 15, 1996; August 15, 1996; January 18, 1997; February 14, 1997; June 7, 1997; December 24, 1997; January 22, 1998, Christopher Lehmann-Haupt, "Viva la Genre! Elmore Leonard Visits Old Havana"; February 11, 1999, Christopher Lehmann-Haupt, "Get Musical: Chili Palmer's Latest Movie Idea"; September 7, 2000, Janet Maslin, "'New Elmore Leonard?' 'Yeah. You Know. Punks.'"
New York Times Book Review, May 22, 1977; September 5, 1982; March 6, 1983; December 27, 1983; February 10, 1985, p. 7; January 4, 1987, p. 7; July 29, 1990, pp. 1, 28; July 28, 1991, p. 8; August 16, 1992, p. 13; October 17, 1993, p. 39; May 14, 1995, p. 7; September 8, 1996; January 22, 1998; February 8, 1998; September 20, 1998, Charles Salzberg, review of *The Tonto Woman,* p. 24; February 21, 1999, Kinky Friedman, "The Palmer Method," p. 10; September 17, 2000, Bruce DeSilva, "Turned Collar."
New York Times Magazine, November 16, 1997.
People, January 26, 2004, Steve Dougherty, review of *Mr. Paradise,* p. 43.
Publishers Weekly, February 25, 1983; June 15, 1990, p. 55; June 10, 1996, p. 84; November 16, 1998, review of *Be Cool,* p. 52; December 10, 2001, review of *Tishomingo Blues,* p. 48; January 21, 2002, interview with Leonard, p. 52; November 24, 2003, review of *Mr. Paradise,* p. 42; May 17, 2004, review of *A*

Coyote's in the House, p. 51; March 28, 2005, review of *The Hot Kid,* p. 55.
School Library Journal, Ellen Fader, review of *A Coyote's in the House,* p. 171.
Time, May 28, 1984, pp. 84, 86; February 24, 1997; August 18, 1997; January 12, 1998; June 20, 2005, Philip Elmer-DeWitt, interview with Leonard, p. 6.
Times Literary Supplement, December 5, 1986, p. 1370; November 30, 1990, p. 1287; September 27, 1991, p. 24; October 30, 1992, p. 21; November 5, 1993, p. 20.
Tribune Books (Chicago, IL), April 10, 1983; October 30, 1983; April 9, 1989, pp. 1, 4; May 21, 1995, p. 5.
Village Voice, February 23, 1982, Ken Tucker.
Wall Street Journal, January 29, 1998.
Washington Post, October 6, 1980; February 6, 1985.
Washington Post Book World, February 7, 1982; July 4, 1982; February 20, 1983; November 13, 1983; December 28, 1986, p. 3; August 23, 1987, pp. 1-2; May 1, 1988; July 14, 1991, pp. 1-2; July 19, 1992, p. 2.

ONLINE

Elmore Leonard Home Page, http://www.elmoreleonard.com (July 25, 2005).
Mr. Showbiz, http://mrshowbiz.go.com/ (October 19, 2000), Rick Schultz, interview with Leonard.
Salon.com, http://www.salon.com/ (September 28, 1999), Sean Elder, interview with Leonard.*

* * *

LINDBERGH, Reeve 1945-
(Reeve Lindbergh Brown)

Personal

Born 1945; daughter of Charles A. (an aviator) and Anne (an author; maiden name, Morrow) Lindbergh; married Richard Brown (a photographer and teacher; divorced); married Nathanial Tripp (a writer); children: (first marriage) Elizabeth, Susannah, Jonathan; (second marriage) Benjamin. *Education:* Attended Radcliff College.

Addresses

Home—Bartlet, VT. *Agent*—c/o Simon and Schuster, 1230 Avenue of the Americas, New York, NY 10020.

Career

Writer; formerly an educator in Vermont. Charles A. and Anne Morrow Lindbergh Foundation, member of board, 1977—, vice president, 1986-95, president, 1995-2004, honorary chairman, 2004—.

Awards, Honors

Redbook magazine award, 1987, for *The Midnight Farm,* and 1990, for *Benjamin's Barn.*

Writings

FOR CHILDREN

The Midnight Farm, illustrated by Susan Jeffers, Dial (New York, NY), 1987.
Benjamin's Barn, illustrated by Susan Jeffers, Dial (New York, NY), 1990.
The Day the Goose Got Loose, illustrated by Steven Kellogg, Dial (New York, NY), 1990.
Johnny Appleseed: A Poem, illustrated by Kathy Jakobsen, Joy Street (Boston, MA), 1990.
A View from the Air: Charles Lindbergh's Earth and Sky, photographs by Richard Brown, Viking (New York, NY), 1992.
Grandfather's Lovesong, illustrated by Rachel Isadora, Viking (New York, NY), 1993.
There's a Cow in the Road!, illustrated by Tracey Campbell Pearson, Dial (New York, NY), 1993.
If I'd Known Then What I Know Now, illustrated by Kimberly Bulcken Root, Viking (New York, NY), 1994.
What Is the Sun?, illustrated by Stephen Lambert, Candlewick (Cambridge, MA), 1994.
Nobody Owns the Sky: The Story of "Brave Bessie" Coleman, illustrated by Pamela Paparone, Candlewick (Cambridge, MA), 1996.
The Awful Aardvarks Go to School, illustrated by Tracey Campbell Pearson, Viking (New York, NY), 1997.
The Circle of Days, illustrated by Cathie Felstead, Candlewick (Cambridge, MA), 1997.
North Country Spring, illustrated by Liz Sivertson, Houghton Mifflin (Boston, MA), 1997.
(Compiler) *In Every Tiny Grain of Sand: A Child's Book of Prayers and Praise,* illustrated by Christine Davenier, Candlewick (Cambridge, MA), 2000.
The Awful Aardvarks Shop for School, illustrated by Tracey Campbell Pearson, Viking (New York, NY), 2000.
(Adapter) *On Morning Wings* (adapted from Psalm 139), illustrated by Holly Meade, Candlewick Press (Cambridge, MA), 2002.
My Hippie Grandmother, illustrated by Abby Carter, Candlewick Press (Cambridge, MA), 2003.
Our Nest, illustrated by Jill McElmurry, Candlewick (Cambridge, MA), 2004.
The Visit, illustrated by Wendy Halperin, Dial (New York, NY), 2004.

OTHER

(Under name Reeve Lindbergh Brown) *Moving to the Country* (novel), Doubleday (New York, NY), 1983.
The View from the Kingdom: A New England Album (essays), photographs by Richard Brown, introduction by Noel Perrin, Harcourt Brace Jovanovich (San Diego, CA), 1987.
The Names of the Mountains (novel), Simon and Schuster (New York, NY), 1992.
John's Apples (poems), illustrated by John Wilde, Perishable Press (Mt. Horeb, WI), 1995.

Under a Wing (memoir), Simon and Schuster (New York, NY), 1998.

No More Words: A Journal of My Mother, Anne Morrow Lindbergh, Simon and Schuster (New York, NY), 2001.

Some of Lindbergh's works have been translated into Spanish.

Adaptations

Johnny Appleseed was adapted as a videotape, Weston Woods/Scholastic, 2000.

Sidelights

Children's author, novelist, and poet Reeve Lindbergh is the daughter of world-renowned aviator Charles Lindbergh and his wife, the talented writer Anne Morrow Lindbergh. In 1927, Charles Lindbergh flew the first solo transatlantic flight, traveling from New York City to Paris, France. Growing up in a home with famous parents subjected the Lindbergh children to much media attention, though the elder Lindberghs shielded the family from public scrutiny as best they could.

Despite the fame accorded the family, both through the accomplishments of her parents and the notoriety surrounding the kidnapping of one of her siblings as an infant, Reeve Lindbergh and her siblings grew up to lead private lives. Lindbergh and her first husband, Richard Brown, moved from Cambridge, Massachusetts to Vermont, where they both taught school and had three children. In 1983 she published her autobiographical novel *Moving to the Country,* which follows a couple who move with their two daughters from a Massachusetts suburb to rural Vermont. The couple's marriage is strained as they adapt to a much different life in the country and seemingly indifferent neighbors. While Nancy loses a baby, Tom worries about the security of his job, but the pair eventually overcome these internal and external obstacles and gain the favor of the townspeople as well. A *Publishers Weekly* reviewer called *Moving to the Country* "comforting, hopeful, sensitively written, an honest and believable portrayal of marriage, change, and putting down roots."

In *The Names of the Mountains* Lindbergh reveals what life as a Lindbergh was like after the death of her father through her fictional family headed by aviator Cal Linley and his wife Alicia. Paula Chin wrote in *People* that Lindbergh hoped the book would "dispel previous notions about their family and the tragedies that have beset it." The story is told through the eyes of Cress Linley, youngest daughter of the couple, who spends a weekend with her siblings and their elderly mother Alicia, now suffering from memory loss. In real life, the Lindbergh children were caring for their own mother, age eighty-six at the time of the book's publication, and Anne Morrow Lindbergh was suffering from similar memory lapses and strokes. *Library Journal* reviewer

Jan Blodgett wrote that Lindbergh "gently and perceptively unfolds this complex family history."

Under a Wing: A Memoir recounts Lindbergh's life as a child growing up in Darien, Connecticut. "This gentle memoir shows a unique and uniquely poignant family life," wrote a *Publishers Weekly* reviewer. Charles was a loving but stern father who would not allow his children to drink soda or eat candy, marshmallow fluff, or grape jelly. He favored discussion over television and protected his family with a set of hard-and-fast rules. "There were only two ways of doing things—Father's way and the wrong way," Lindbergh notes in her book. Geoffrey C. Ward wrote in the *New York Times Book Review* that *Under a Wing* "beautifully recaptures the determinedly ordered life her father insisted his family lead in their Connecticut home after the war."

When her son John died of encephalitis in 1985, at the young age of twenty months, Lindbergh began writing children's books. "I wrote my first children's book the day my son died," she told Philadelphia *CityPaper.net* interviewer Neil Gladstone. "I was waiting for my family to come and meet me and I just sat there and started to write this little lullaby for Johnny."

Her first published book for children, *The Midnight Farm,* is a counting book. Unable to sleep, a young child is led by his mother on a walk around their farm where they observe the activities of the animals as night descends. Eventually the child grows tired and peacefully slips into slumber. *Times Literary Supplement* reviewer Jane Doonan called *The Midnight Farm* "a gentle progression from disturbed waking to sleeping worlds." "This warm, loving story will comfort any child afraid of the dark," wrote noted children's author Eve Bunting in the *Los Angeles Times Book Review.*

Lindbergh continues her animal theme in *Benjamin's Barn.* A young boy carries his teddy bear into a big, red barn, to find not only the usual farm animals, but also jungle and prehistoric creatures, pirate ships, a princess, and even a brass band. "The rhyming text has a comforting circular flow, well-suited to Benjamin's flight of fancy and . . . return to reality," wrote Anna DeWind in *School Library Journal.*

Lindbergh turns to American folk hero John Chapman in *Johnny Appleseed: A Poem,* and retells how Chapman traveled from the East Coast to the Midwest, planting apple seeds for future generations to enjoy. "This work shows him as a gentle, religious man on a mission, a lover of the land," wrote a *Publishers Weekly* reviewer. *Horn Book* reviewer Mary M. Burns called *Johnny Appleseed* "a splendid production." The book also features a map tracing Chapman's journey from Massachusetts to Indiana.

Lindbergh expresses her father's love of the natural world in *A View from the Air: Charles Lindbergh's Earth and Sky.* A long poem, her text is accompanied by photographs taken by Richard Brown, who flew with Charles Lindbergh over northern New England during the early 1970s. *Booklist* reviewer Deborah Abbott wrote that the verses "capture the pilot's awe and respect for the natural beauty of our land."

Lindbergh views the grandparent-grandchild relationship in a different way in *My Hippie Grandmother.* The book's narrator is a little girl who deeply loves her unconventional, flower-child grandmother, just as the grandmother loves her. Odes to her grandma are written in "bouncy and exuberant rhyme," noted a *Kirkus Reviews* critic who declared the book "a sheer delight." "Totally groovy—and in its own impish way, an eloquent rejoinder to these more buttoned-down times," concluded a *Publishers Weekly* reviewer.

In *There's a Cow in the Road!* a little girl rushes to get ready for school. Looking through her Vermont farmhouse window, she spots a cow that is soon joined by other barnyard animals until a crowd of creatures assembles. By the time the girl and the other children board the school bus, a goat, sheep, horse, pig, and goose have gathered to see them off. "The story has warmth and vitality and a sense of community," wrote Hazel Rochman in *Booklist.* A *Publishers Weekly* reviewer noticed that the details and action in the book's illustrations are not always described in the text, resulting in "a great deal of kid-pleasing, between-the-lines action." A contributor to *Kirkus Reviews* called *There's a Cow in the Road!* "a joyous, comical pacesetter for a busy morning."

A man's inept do-it-yourself projects in building and maintaining a farm are the focus of *If I'd Known Then What I Know Now.* Sally R. Dow wrote in *School Library Journal* that the book's "tall-tale humor . . . will appeal to all those 'just learning how.'" In *What Is the Sun?* a young boy questions his grandmother, and each answer leads to another question. Patricia Crawford noted in *Language Arts* that the text demonstrates the "comfort" provided to young children "through their interactions with a caring, older adult."

Nobody Owns the Sky: The Story of "Brave Bessie" Coleman is an account of how Bessie Coleman became the first African-American aviator in the world. Coleman was denied entrance to flying schools in the United States and instead obtained her pilot's license in France. She worked as a stunt pilot in the United States and Europe during the 1920s before dying in a plane accident in Jacksonville, Florida, in 1926. A critic for *Kirkus Reviews* called the work a "homage to a brave and dedicated aviation pioneer," while a *Publishers Weekly* reviewer noted that Lindbergh "chooses the elements likeliest to inspire a young audience." *Washington Post Book World* reviewer John Cech called *Nobody Owns the Sky* "an important book for the little ones who might think they can't and for those who are learning that they can."

A *Publishers Weekly* reviewer called Lindbergh's *The Awful Aardvarks Go to School* a "witty, giddy alphabet book." The aardvarks terrorize the animals that attend the school, angering anteaters, eating ants, bullying a bunny, and tossing turtles. A contributor to *Kirkus Reviews* noted that the aardvarks "are more gleeful than rude," while in *School Library Journal* a critic called *The Awful Aardvarks Go to School* "a flying success."

In *The Circle of Days* Lindbergh adapts Francis of Assisi's *Canticle of the Sun,* written in 1225. *School Library Journal* reviewer Patricia Lothrop-Green called it a book "for the eye, if not the ear." "The gentle, rhyming text follows the form of a prayer in praise of brother sun, sister moon, and mother earth and in gratitude to the Lord for providing such wondrous gifts," observed a *Publishers Weekly* reviewer. Janice M. Del Negro wrote in the *Bulletin of the Center for Children's Books* that in *The Circle of Days,* the historic text "is granted glowing life." *On Morning Wings,* another inspirational title, presents Lindbergh's adaptation of Psalm 139. The book is "rhythmic, rhyming, and above all reassuring," Carolyn Phelan wrote in *Booklist,* the critic adding that "Lindbergh writes convincingly from the child's point of view."

Lindbergh uses rhyming couplets in describing how spring unfolds in New England in *North Country Spring.* The book features a glossary of the fourteen animals in-

In **My Hippie Grandmother** *a young child enjoys spending time with a woman whose back-to-nature lifestyle provides many opportunities for time together. (Illustration by Abby Carter.)*

Featuring engaging illustrations by Tracey Campbell Pearson, Reeve Lindberg's The Awful Aardvarks Shop for School *finds a rambunctious family invading a local shopping mall.*

cluded in the text. Kay Weisman wrote in *Booklist* that junior high students will find the book to be "a springboard for writing seasonal poetry." "Lindbergh's ebullient verse is a triumph song of spring's melting, sensory flush," wrote a *Publishers Weekly* reviewer.

Our Nest also takes a grateful look at nature, as Lindbergh describes a variety of animals who snuggle securely into the nests the world provides them. Some of the nests are man-made, including the bed a child snuggles in and the laundry basket that holds a cat and her kittens, and some are metaphorical: the ocean secure in the planet's hollows, and Earth itself nested in space. *School Library Journal* reviewer Roxanne Burg noted the book's dual message: "on one level, the book describes how all things in nature are interconnected . . .; on another, it celebrates a mother's love for her child." "Bedtime reads lie thick upon the ground," noted a *Kirkus Reviews* contributor, but *Our Nest*'s "comforting message, flowing text, warm sentiment, and jewel-like art" make the book stand out from the crowd. *Booklist* contributor Jennifer Mattson also recommended *Our Nest,* writing that "a honey of a poem . . . and a sweetly optimistic message distinguish this soothing bedtime book."

In *The Visit* sisters Beth and Jill visit their aunt and uncle's farm, and revel in exploring the barns and surrounding fields and meadows, as well as eating Aunt Laura's home cooking. Although nightfall finds the girls somewhat homesick, by relying on each other they soon feel better. "The obvious affection the relatives feel for one another will warm the audience," Ilene Cooper noted in *Booklist.* "These cheerful girl adventures—and the delightful territory they cover—may well have readers longing for a similar, simple getaway," maintained a *Publishers Weekly* contributor, while *School Library*

Journal reviewer Angela J. Reynolds also found an educational aspect to the tale. "This idyllic country vacation is great for extending the vocabulary of young listeners," she concluded, predicting that readers "will pore over the drawings."

Biographical and Critical Sources

BOOKS

Lindbergh, Reeve, *There's a Cow in the Road!,* Dial (New York, NY), 1993.
Lindbergh, Reeve, *Under a Wing: A Memoir,* Simon and Schuster (New York, NY), 1998.

PERIODICALS

Booklist, September 1, 1987, review of *The Midnight Farm,* p. 65; March 1, 1989, review of *The Midnight Farm,* p. 1200; April 15, 1990, review of *Benjamin's Barn,* p. 1634; September 1, 1990, review of *Johnny Appleseed,* p. 58; September 15, 1990, review of *The Day the Goose Got Loose,* p. 171; November 15, 1991, review of *The Day the Goose Got Loose,* p. 633; August, 1992, Deborah Abbott, review of *A View from the Air: Charles Lindbergh's Earth and Sky,* p. 2015; November 15, 1992, review of *The Names of the Mountains,* p. 579; January 15, 1993, review of *Grandfather's Lovesong,* p. 915; July, 1993, Hazel Rochman, review of *There's a Cow in the Road!,* p. 1975; January 1, 1997, Carolyn Phelan, review of *Nobody Owns the Sky,* p. 869; May 15, 1997, Kay Weisman, review of *North Country Spring,* p. 1580; October 15, 1997, Ilene Cooper, review of *The Awful Aardvarks Go to School,* p. 402; April 1, 1998, review of *The Circle of Days,* p. 1325; September 15, 2001, Elsa Gaztambide, review of *No More Words: A Journal of My Mother,* p. 180; September 15, 2002, Carolyn Phelan, review of *On Morning Wings,* p. 233; March 1, 2003, Carolyn Phelan, review of *My Hippie Grandmother,* p. 1203; April 15, 2004, Jennifer Mattson, review of *Our Nest,* p. 1441; February 15, 2005, Ilene Cooper, review of *The Visit,* p. 1085.
Books, December, 1987, review of *The Midnight Farm,* p. 24.
Bulletin of the Center for Children's Books, April, 1998, Janice M. Del Negro, review of *The Circle of Days,* p. 286.
Children's Book Review Service, November, 1987, review of *The Midnight Farm,* p. 26; August, 1990, p. 160; October, 1990, p. 20; November, 1990, review of *The Day the Goose Got Loose,* p. 26; October, 1992, review of *View from the Air,* p. 20; February, 1997, review of *Nobody Owns the Sky,* p. 76; May, 1997, review of *North Country Spring,* p. 111.
Children's Book Watch, April, 1991, review of *The Day the Goose Got Loose,* p. 1; May, 1993, review of *Grandfather's Lovesong,* p. 3; January, 1997, review of *Nobody Owns the Sky,* p. 5.
Christian Science Monitor, November 6, 1987, review of *The Midnight Farm,* p. B6; January 4, 1993, Merle Rubin, review of *The Names of the Mountains,* p. 12.

*In **Our Nest** Lindbergh illustrates the universal rule that all things—from stars and boats to birds and even small children— have a place called home. (Illustration by Jill McElmurry.)*

Horn Book, September-October, 1990, Mary M. Burns, review of *Johnny Appleseed,* p. 593; November, 1990, Carolyn K. Jenks, review of *The Day the Goose Got Loose,* p. 729, pp. 774-775.

Junior Bookshelf, April, 1988, review of *The Midnight Farm,* p. 84; June, 1991, review of *Johnny Appleseed,* p. 95; August, 1993, review of *Grandfather's Lovesong,* p. 129.

Kirkus Reviews, September 1, 1987, review of *The Midnight Farm,* p. 1323; July 1, 1990, review of *The Day the Goose Got Loose,* p. 933; September 1, 1992, review of *View from the Air,* p. 1140; October 1, 1992, review of *The Names of the Mountains,* p. 1208; July 1, 1993, review of *There's a Cow in the Road!;* November 1, 1996, review of *Nobody Owns the Sky;* February 15, 1997, review of *North Country Spring,* p. 302; September 15, 1997, review of *The Awful Aardvarks Go to School;* August 15, 2001, review of *No More Words,* p. 1194; June 15, 2002, review of *On Morning Wings,* p. 884; January 1, 2003, review of *My Hippie Grandmother,* p. 63; April 1, 2004, review of *Our Nest,* p. 332; February 15, 2005, review of *The Visit,* p. 232.

Kliatt, September, 1996, review of *View from the Air,* p. 24.

Language Arts, September, 1996, Patricia Crawford, review of *What Is the Sun?,* p. 354.

Library Journal, November 15, 1992, Jan Blodgett, review of *The Names of Mountains,* p. 102; October 1, 1998, Ronald Ray Ratliff, review of *Under a Wing,* p. 104; October 15, 2001, Judith Janes, review of *No More Words,* p. 86.

Los Angeles Times Book Review, November 22, 1987, Eve Bunting, review of *The Midnight Farm,* p. 6.

Maclean's, November 9, 1998, Anthony Wilson-Smith, "A Hero's Highs and Lows: Two Books Shed Light on Fame's Toll on the First Media Superstar," p. 86.

Magpies, September, 1991, review of *Benjamin's Barn,* p. 28; March, 1997, review of *Nobody Owns the Sky,* p. 23.

New York Times Book Review, January 1, 1984, Diane Cole, review of *Moving to the Country,* pp. 20-22; December 13, 1987, Maxine Kumin, review of *The View from the Kingdom,* p. 29; April 3, 1988, review of *The Midnight Farm,* p. 16; December 2, 1990, review of *Johnny Appleseed,* p. 38; March 7, 1993, Ellen Chesler, review of *The Names of the Mountains,* p. 12; May 16, 1993, Walter Goodman, review of *Grandfather's Lovesong,* p. 31; November 14, 1993, Kathleen Krull, review of *There's a Cow in the Road!,* p. 58; May 11, 1997, review of *North Country Spring,* p. 24; September 27, 1998, Geoffrey C. Ward, review of *Under a Wing,* pp. 14-15.

People, January 25, 1993, Paula Chin, review of *The Names of Mountains,* p. 63; September 28, 1998, Bruce Frankel, review of *Under a Wing,* p. 157.

Publishers Weekly, July 22, 1983, review of *Moving to the Country,* p. 118; July 10, 1987, review of *The Midnight Farm,* p. 66; June 8, 1990, review of *Benjamin's Barn,* p. 52; July 13, 1990, review of *Johnny Appleseed: A Poem,* p. 54. July 13, 1992, review of *The Day the Goose Got Loose,* p. 53; October 12, 1992, review of *The Names of the Mountains,* p. 65; April 19, 1993, review of *Grandfather's Lovesong,* p. 59; June 21, 1993, review of *There's a Cow in the Road!,* p. 103; May 9, 1994, review of *What Is the Sun?,* p. 71; January 29, 1996, review of *What Is the Sun?,* p. 101; June 17, 1996, review of *If I'd Known Then What I Know Now,* p. 67; November 18, 1996, review of *Nobody Owns the Sky,* p. 74; March 24, 1997, review of *North Country Spring,* p. 82; August 25, 1997, review of *The Awful Aardvarks Go to School;* January

19, 1998, review of *Nobody Owns the Sky,* p. 380; March 23, 1998, review of *The Circle of Days,* p. 95; August 24, 1998, review of *Under a Wing,* p. 38; July 22, 2002, review of *The Awful Aardvarks Shop for School,* p. 182; December 23, 2002, review of *My Hippie Grandmother,* p. 70; March 22, 2004, review of *Our Nest,* p. 84; March 14, 2005, review of *The Visit,* p. 66.

School Library Journal, October, 1987, Leda Schubert, review of *The Midnight Farm,* p. 115; June, 1990, Anna DeWind, review of *Benjamin's Barn,* p. 103; August, 1990, p. 122; September, 1990, Anne Price, review of *The Day the Goose Got Loose,* p. 206; September, 1992, John Peters, review of *View from the Air,* p. 222; April, 1993, Leda Schubert, review of *Grandfather's Lovesong,* p. 100; July, 1994, Sally R. Dow, review of *If I'd Known Then What I Know Now,* p. 79; August, 1994, Marianne Saccardi, review of *What Is the Sun?,* p. 140; November, 1996, Jerry D. Flack, review of *Nobody Owns the Sky,* p. 98; February, 1997, p. 113; April, 1997, Heide Piehler, review of *North Country Spring,* p. 113; December, 1997, review of *The Awful Aardvarks Go to School*; April, 1998, Patricia Lothrop-Green, review of *The Circle of Days,* p. 119; March,

2001, Linda R. Skeele, review of *Johnny Appleseed,* p. 77; December, 2002, Marian Drabkin, review of *On Morning Wings,* p. 126; April, 2003, Judith Constantinides, review of *My Hippie Grandmother,* p. 132; May, 2004, Roxanne Burg, review of *Our Nest,* p. 117; March, 2005, Angela J. Reynolds, review of *The Visit,* p. 175.

Times Literary Supplement, November 20, 1987, Jane Doonan, review of *The Midnight Farm,* p. 1284.

Washington Post Book World, December 8, 1996, John Cech, review of *Nobody Owns the Sky,* p. 23.

ONLINE

Charles A. and Anne Morrow Lindbergh Foundation Web site, http://www.lindberghfoundation.org/ (July 6, 2005), "Reeve Lindbergh."

CityPaper.net (Philadelphia, PA), http://www.citypaper.net/ (November 12, 1998), Neil Gladstone, interview with Lindbergh.

DCPilots Web site, http://www.cookstudios.com/dcpilots/ (July 6, 2005), Jeff Cook, "Reeve Lindbergh at CGS/ College Park Airport Museum."*

M

MASON, Adrienne 1962-

Personal

Born December 23, 1962, in Nanaimo, British Columbia, Canada; daughter of David (an archivist) and Louise (a teacher; maiden name Heal) Mason; married Bob Hansen (a national park ranger) April 7, 1990; children: Ava, Patrice. *Education:* University of Victoria, B.S. (biology), 1988.

Addresses

Home—P.O. Box 386, Tofino, British Columbia V0R 2Z0, Canada. *E-mail*—amason@island.net.

Career

Freelance writer and editor, beginning 1991. Raincoast Communications, Tofino, British Columbia, Canada, hiking guide and biologist; Bamfield Marine Science Centre, Bamfield, British Columbia, public education coordinator. Consulting biologist, beginning 1994.

Member

Federation of British Columbia Writers, Canadian Society of Children's Authors, Illustrators, and Performers, Writer's Union of Canada.

Awards, Honors

Science in Society Award, 1995, and Red Cedar Book Award shortlist, Silver Birch Award shortlist, and Canadian Children's Book Centre (CCBC) Choice, all 1996-97, all for *Oceans;* Parents' Choice designation, Parents' Choice Foundation, 1998, and CCBC Choice, 1999, both for *Mealworms: Raise Them, Watch Them, See Them Change;* Science in Society Book Award, Canadian Science Writers' Association, 1997, and Parents' Choice designation, Parents' Choice Foundation, 1998, both for *Living Things;* Science in Society Book Award, 1999, for *The Nature of Spiders: Consummate Killers;* CCBC Choice, and Red Cedar Award shortlist, both for *The World of Marine Mammals;* Science in Society Book Award shortlist, and Ontario Library Association Best Bets designation, both 2003, and CCBC Choice, 2004, all for *Otters;* Science in Society Book Award shortlist, 2004, for *Bats.*

Writings

NONFICTION

The Green Classroom, Pembroke Publishers, 1991.
Oceans: Looking at Beaches and Coral Reefs, Tides and Currents, Sea Mammals and Fish, Seaweeds and Other Ocean Wonders, Kids Can Press (Toronto, Ontario, Canada), 1995.
Living Things, Kids Can Press (Toronto, Ontario, Canada), 1997.
Mealworms: Raise Them, Watch Them, See Them Change, Kids Can Press (Toronto, Ontario, Canada), 1998.
The Nature of Spiders: Consummate Killers, Greystone Books/Douglas & McIntyre (Toronto, Ontario, Canada), 1999, published as *The World of the Spider,* Sierra Club Books (San Francisco, CA), 1999.
Whales, Dolphins, and Porpoises, Altitude Publishing (Canmore, Alberta, Canada), 1999.
The World of Mammals, illustrated by Garth Buzzard, Orca Book Publishers (Custer, WA), 1999.
Bats, illustrated by Nancy Gray Ogle, Kids Can Press (Toronto, Ontario, Canada), 2003.
Otters, illustrated by Nancy Gray Ogle, Kids Can Press (Toronto, Ontario, Canada), 2003.
West Coast Adventures: Shipwrecks, Lighthouses, and Rescues along Canada's West Coast, Altitude Publishing (Canmore, Alberta, Canada), 2003.
Tales from the West Coast: Smugglers, Sea Monsters, and Other Stories, Altitude Publishing (Canmore, Alberta, Canada), 2003.
Owls, Kids Can Press (Toronto, Ontario, Canada), 2004.
Snakes, Kids Can Press (Toronto, Ontario, Canada), 2005.
Move It!: Forces Motion and You, Kids Can Press (Toronto, Ontario, Canada), 2005.
Touch It!: Materials, Matter, and You, Kids Can Press (Toronto, Ontario, Canada), 2005.

Contributor to periodicals, including *National Geographic Kids, Georgia Straight, Canadian Wildlife, Waters, Beautiful British Columbia, Wild, Nature Canada, Canadian Geographic, Owl, Ranger Rick, Prime Areas, Northwest Parks and Wildlife, Canadian Living, Boys' Life,* and *Yes.* Former columnist.

"LU AND CLANCY" SERIES; FICTION

Lu and Clancy's Secret Codes, illustrated by Pat Cuples, Kids Can Press (Toronto, Ontario, Canada), 1999.
Lu and Clancy's Spy Stuff, illustrated by Pat Cuples, Kids Can Press (Toronto, Ontario, Canada), 2000.
Lu and Clancy's Carnival Caper, illustrated by Pat Cuples, Kids Can Press (Toronto, Ontario, Canada), 2002.
Lu and Clancy Sound Off, illustrated by Pat Cuples, Kids Can Press (Toronto, Ontario, Canada), 2002.

Work in Progress

Build It!: Structures, Systems, and You, and *Change It!: Solids, Liquids, Gases, and You,* both for Kids Can Press, 2006.

Sidelights

Canadian biologist and writer Adrienne Mason is the author of a number of books that reflect her interest in the coastal region of the Pacific Northwest. In books that include *Otters, Tales from the West Coast: Smugglers, Sea Monsters, and Other Stories,* and *The World of Marine Mammals,* she introduces budding biologists to creatures ranging from small sea otters to giant whales, as well as the folklore that has grown up around these coastal creatures' habitat. In a *Resource Links* review of *The World of Marine Mammals,* a critic noted that Mason "writes with a deft hand," and presents a "well-organized [and] easy-to-follow" text that is "authoritative" due to the author's inclusion of interviews with scientists working in the field.

In addition to nonfiction, Mason has also combined learning and fun in her "Lu and Clancy" books, which find a pair of frisky pups hot on the trail of the answers to a host of science puzzles. In *Lu and Clancy's Spy Stuff,* for example, the sleuthing canines learn how to create booby traps, disguise themselves, and mix up some invisible ink, all important talents for secret agents. *Lu and Clancy Sound Off* finds the pair joining two younger dogs on a hiking trip where a strange noise in the woods and one dog's disappearance sets the stage for another mystery to be solved. Each book in the series contains several science activities, as well as a detailed explanation of the how and why behind the dogs' discoveries. Praising *Lu and Clancy Sound Off, Resource Links* contributor Linda Ludka described the book as "a fun storybook for beginning readers," while another reviewer for the same periodical described *Lu and Clancy's Secret Codes* as "informative and interesting" due to the "intriguing" facts on cryptography that Mason presents.

Children learn the truth behind such myths as the belief that bats are blind in Adrienne Mason's aptly titled and informative Bats. *(Illustration by Nancy Gray Ogle.)*

Mason told *Something about the Author:* "I started writing in earnest in 1990, when I started doing some freelance writing and newspaper columns. I published my first book in 1991. I have learned the craft of writing over the years by reading a lot, taking the occasional course, chatting with other writers, and, of course, learning from my mistakes (and successes)!

"I primarily write nonfiction, or information, books. This is a good genre for me because, as someone once said, 'I'm only interested in everything!' I have long lists of ideas and files full of newspaper clippings (even cassettes of interviews I've heard on the radio) with the stories of interesting people doing interesting things. Ideas will come to me at the strangest times. Perhaps when I am driving or hiking or having a shower. When my mind relaxes good ideas seem to come.

"When I am working on a project or getting an outline together I start to keep a file on the subject and then I research, research, research. In some ways this is my favorite part. Searching out all of the interesting tidbits is like being a detective. Once I get my ideas together I make a very detailed outline, usually one that tells me everything that will be on each page. This is a very important step as it keeps me on track when I'm writing.

"If you are interested in writing I'd suggest that you keep a journal. You don't have to write in it every day or even write at all—draw pictures, cut out pictures, copy out poems that you like, stick in photographs, doodle, whatever! You'll be amazed at what you find in these notebooks when you go back through them.

"I live in a very small town on Vancouver Island, on Canada's west coast. It is very beautiful here and there are lots of long, sandy beaches to explore. I have two lovely young daughters who explore with me and also sometimes help me with my books. I enjoy reading, cooking, gardening, hiking, and camping. I love to make collages of natural objects I find on our outdoor adventures and love to dance flamenco!"

Biographical and Critical Sources

PERIODICALS

Booklist, June 1, 1998, Carolyn Phelan, review of *Mealworms: Raise Them, Watch Them, See Them Change,* p. 1758; January 1, 2000, Nancy Bent, review of *The World of the Spider,* p. 848.

Kirkus Reviews, March 1, 2003, review of *Otters,* p. 391.

Resource Links, February, 2000, review of *Lu and Clancy's Secret Codes,* pp. 21-22; April, 2000, review of *The World of Marine Mammals,* p. 22; October, 2002, Linda Ludka, review of *Lu and Clancy Sound Off,* p. 6; April, 2003, Linda Berezowski, review of *Otters,* p. 26; October, 2003, Karen McKinnon, review of *Bats,* p. 25.

School Library Journal, August, 2001, Kathy M. Newby, review of *Lu and Clancy's Spy Stuff,* p. 167; February, 2003, Blair Christolon, review of *Lu and Clancy Sound Off,* p. 136; May, 2003, Cathie Bashaw Morton, review of *Otters,* p. 139.

Sierra, July, 1999, review of *The World of the Spider,* p. 75.

Teacher Librarian, March-April, 1999, review of *Mealworms: Raise Them, Watch Them, See Them Change,* p. 23.

ONLINE

Canadian Society of Children's Authors, Illustrators, and Performers Web site, http://www.canscaip.org/ (July 6, 2005), "Adrienne Mason."

Red Cedar Awards Web site, http://redcedar.swifty.com/ (July 6, 2005), "Adrienne Mason."*

*   *   *

MAYO, Gretchen Will 1936-

Personal

Born April 13, 1936, in Dayton, OH; daughter of John F. (a sales promotion executive) and Julia Dolan (an English teacher; maiden name, Schumacher) Will; married Thomas J. Mayo (a marketing director), 1963; children: Megan, Molly, Ann. *Education:* Marquette University, B.S. (journalism), 1958; University of Dayton, teaching certificate (elementary education), 1959; attended Milwaukee Institute of Art and Design, 1982-84, 200-06; Vermont College, M.F.A., 2000. *Religion:* Episcopalian. *Hobbies and other interests:* Traveling, hiking, reading, wildlife, movies, plays, winter in the north.

Addresses

Home—5213 Lakefield Rd., Cedarburg, WI 53012. *E-mail*—gwmayo@hotmail.com.

Career

Teacher, 1958-63; Community Newspapers, Milwaukee, WI, reporter, 1966-70; artist, 1970-88. Teacher of college-level workshops on developing children's books and of elementary and secondary school workshops and programs on writing and illustrating; speaker/consultant for Chase/Pheifer/Puerling, Milwaukee, educational consultants. Teacher and writing coach for adults, beginning 1988.

Member

Society of Children's Book Writers and Illustrators, Authors Guild, Authors League of America, Friends of the Cooperative Children's Book Center, Chicago Children's Reading Round Table, Cedarburg Artists Guild (member of board).

Awards, Honors

Outstanding Science Trade Book citation, and Chicago Book Clinic Award for Outstanding Art in a Children's Book, both 1979, both for *The Kangaroo;* New Jersey Author's Award, New Jersey Institute of Technology, 1981, for *I Hate My Name;* Notable Children's Trade Book in the Field of Social Studies citation, Original Children's Book Art Award, New York Master Eagel Gallery, and Cooperative Children's Book Center (CCBC) Choice, all 1987, all for *Star Tales: North American Indian Stories;* Notable Children's Trade Book in the Field of Social Studies citation, Original Children's Book Art Award, New York Society of Illustrators exhibit, and CCBC Choice, all 1989, all for *Earthmaker's Tales: North American Indian Stories about Earth Happenings;* Outstanding Citizen award, Pi Lambda Theta, 1993; CCBC Choice, 1993, and International Reading Association/Children's Book Council Children's Choice Award, selected among Twenty-five Best in Multicultural Books, *Boston Globe,* and Outstanding Achievement in Children's Literature by a Wisconsin author/illustrator citation, Wisconsin Library Association, all 1994, all for *Meet Tricky Coyote!* and *That Tricky Coyote!*

Writings

RETELLER; SELF-ILLUSTRATED

Star Tales: North American Indian Stories, Walker (New York, NY), 1987, published in two volumes as *Star Tales* and *More Star Tales,* 1990.

Earthmaker's Tales: North American Indian Stories about Earth Happenings, Walker (New York, NY), 1989, published in two volumes as *Earthmaker's Tales* and *More Earthmaker's Tales,* 1990.

Meet Tricky Coyote!, Walker (New York, NY), 1993.

That Tricky Coyote!, Walker (New York, NY), 1993.

Here Comes Tricky Rabbit!, Walker (New York, NY), 1994, published with *Big Trouble for Tricky Rabbit!,* 1996.

Big Trouble for Tricky Rabbit!, Walker (New York, NY), 1994, published with *Here Comes Tricky Rabbit!,* 1996.

"WHERE DOES OUR FOOD COME FROM?" SERIES; NONFICTION

Frozen Vegetables, Weekly Reader Learning Library (Milwaukee, WI), 2004.

Applesauce, Weekly Reader Learning Library (Milwaukee, WI), 2004.

Cereal, Weekly Reader Learning Library (Milwaukee, WI), 2004.

Pasta, Weekly Reader Learning Library (Milwaukee, WI), 2004.

Milk, Weekly Reader Learning Library (Milwaukee, WI), 2004.

Orange Juice, Weekly Reader Learning Library (Milwaukee, WI), 2004.

"TRAILBLAZERS OF THE MODERN WORLD" SERIES; NONFICTION

The Wright Brothers (biography), World Almanac Library (Milwaukee, WI), 2004.

Frank Lloyd Wright (biography), World Almanac Library (Milwaukee, WI), 2004.

ILLUSTRATOR

Paula Hogan, *The Kangaroo* (part of the "Life Cycle" series), Raintree (Austin, TX), 1979.

Eva Grant, *I Hate My Name,* Raintree (Austin, TX), 1980.

Barbara Steiner, *Whale Brother,* Walker (New York, NY), 1988.

Cary Siter, *Moon of Falling Leaves,* Franklin Watts (New York, NY), 1988.

Barbara Joosse, *Anna, the One and Only,* HarperCollins (New York, NY), 1988.

Susan Rowen Masters, *The Secret Life of Hubie Hartzel,* HarperCollins (New York, NY), 1990.

Barbara Joosse, *Anna and the Cat Lady* (sequel to *Anna, the One and Only*), HarperCollins (New York, NY), 1992.

Also illustrator of Laura Greene's *Help: Getting to Know about Needing and Giving,* Human Sciences; has illustrated textbooks for Silver Burdett, Ginn, Scott Foresman, and Scholastic.

Adaptations

Earthmaker's Tales was recorded for Talking Books for the Blind, 1992.

Sidelights

After spending her early career as an elementary school teacher and journalist, Gretchen Will Mayo turned her attention to art after her husband gave her a set of acrylic paints to help her relax while raising her three young daughters. Teaching herself to paint, she soon realized that art was her passion. She first began exhibiting paintings, then lithography, and in the late 1970s she moved into illustration, creating art to pair with children's book texts by authors such as Paula Hogan and Barbara Joosse. By the mid-1980s Mayo had decided to combine her artistic talent with the expertise gained from her years working with young people as a teacher, and in 1987 she published *Star Tales: North American Indian Stories.* This first collection of folk tales inspired her to create several others, and Mayo has since gone on to produce both novels and several nonfiction works for younger readers. "The timeless connection to universal experiences and feelings has always drawn me to culture stories and myths," Mayo once explained to *Something about the Author.* "I especially love those belonging to the American Indians, rooted in a land which I, too, call 'home,' springing from an oral storytelling tradition which I greatly admire."

Star Tales came about after Mayo searched in vain for a collection of Native American tales about the night sky. "When my children were quite young, I wanted to tell them stories about the stars, as my father had done for me," she once noted. "I searched unsuccessfully for respectfully told American Indian star stories to read to them, stories which had risen out of this land rather than places which were oceans away. It astounded me that in this country children could look at the night sky and recite stories about the constellations from other nations all over the globe. But in libraries and bookstores we found no collections of American Indian stories about the stars for them to read—none written specifically for children." To fill this void, Mayo researched Native legends and created both the book's text and illustrations. Uncovering a wealth of folklore, she has gone on to produce several more self-illustrated volumes, among them *Earthmaker's Tales, That Tricky Coyote!, Here Comes Tricky Rabbit!,* and *Big Trouble for Tricky Rabbit!* Noting that the stories in *That Tricky Coyote!* "have been expertly gathered and retold," a *Publishers Weekly* contributor added that all of the five trickster tales are "superb choices for reading aloud." Reviewing *Here Comes Tricky Rabbit!* in *Booklist,*

Carolyn Phelan had special praise for Mayo's illustrations, acrylic paintings done in muted earth tones that showcase the author/illustrator's "distinctive use of line."

Reflecting on the skills required in adapting stories from another culture for American readers, Mayo noted that the storyteller "needs to be sensitive and painstakingly responsible. If you are working outside of your own culture and living in a different frame of reference, you can be misled by the wording of old narrations or translations of stories. These translations usually don't illuminate the rich texture of detail and tradition underlying the story. In the case of traditional American Indian stories, many of them were recorded for the first time by non-Indians. I spent years gathering stories and researching the stories behind the stories of each of my books. I avoided retelling stories that I saw to be sacred, those held to be holy in the same manner as I regard my Bible stories. I surrounded the stories I wrote with introductions and afterwords—any information I could gather about the history of each story or about those who had narrated and recorded them. This information was often very hard to find."

While beginning her writing career adapting Native American tales, Mayo has more recently moved into juvenile fiction and nonfiction for *Cricket* and *Highlights for Children* magazines as well as the book market. She has produced juvenile biographies of architect Frank Lloyd Wright and the high-flying Wright brothers Orville and Wilbur, as well as several titles in Weekly Reader's "Where Does Our Food Come From?" series. Containing titles such as *Orange Juice, Pasta,* and *Frozen Vegetables,* the well-illustrated series answers basic questions about the source of edibles that many children encounter for the first time on supermarket shelves. Information on growing, packaging, transporting, and recipe preparation are discussed, as well as nutrition and the position of each particular food within the conventional food pyramid. Designed for children in the early elementary grades, Mayo's books are light on text, with only three or four short sentences per page. With their small, square shape, volumes such as *Milk* and *Pasta* will likely "attract readers for reports as well as young browsers," according to *Booklist* contributor Hazel Rochman.

Mayo, who was raised in the American Midwest, now makes her home in rural Wisconsin with her husband. "I grew up in southern Ohio," she once related, "where I swam in the streams, made mud slides, and searched for arrowheads and fossils along with dozens of cousins, my three brothers and our 'little' sister." Despite her active, outdoorsy childhood, Mayo also developed a love of reading and writing, as well as a talent for art. "When I was in the second grade, I invented a comic strip about the wild adventures of 'Harold and Wanda.' I sat on the school steps each morning with my friends and drew pictures of those two rascals. They broke all the rules that I wished I could break. While I drew, I pretended that I was right there with Harold and Wanda. That's how I learned what fun it could be to fit words together with pictures."

Mayo taps into that same creative mind set when she illustrate a picture-book text. "I imagine myself within the setting of the story along with the characters," she explained. "I imagine what they must see or feel. Those thoughts, running through my mind like a movie, influence the colors I choose and the style of my art. For this reason, my illustrations for one book may look quite different from another one. Since I began illustrating the hard way—without any real training—I'm always learning new techniques as I work. The excitement of finding a color or shape or medium that is just right usually follows a time of risk-taking and trial. Truly, creativity is a process, not an event."

Mayo's interest in stretching creatively has more recently led her to attain her master's in fine arts degree with a focus on writing novels for children and young adults. "The plots in my novels generally center on a young woman's need to find and follow her unique path in an adult-controlled world that is a powerful force against her interests and well-being," Mayo explained. "I'm curious about the ways young women use the vision and determination with which we're all born to some degree to significantly shape their lives. Furthermore, in my stories a young person's natural wish to belong is often in conflict with her dreams for herself. I've come to realize that all of my stories are about my own inner struggle. Thus, my girlhood need to find a balance between my interactions with people and my work toward my dreams continues even today. But I'm a visual artist as well as an author, so my dreams for myself include painting and exhibiting my art."

In addition to writing, Mayo studies oil painting at the Milwaukee Institute of Art and Design. "Oils are new for me and with them I've become a fan of plein air painting, a fancy name for painting outdoors. I've found oil colors, their buttery consistency and slower drying time are perfectly suited to painting on location. I'm allowed to enjoy two passions at once; enjoying the outdoors and painting what I see with the hope of sharing that vision."

Biographical and Critical Sources

PERIODICALS

Booklist, September 1, 1993, p. 66; August, 1994, Carolyn Phelan, review of *Here Comes Tricky Rabbit!,* p. 2046; April 1, 2004, Hazel Rochman, review of *Pasta* and *Milk,* p. 1385.
Bulletin of the Center for Children's Books, May, 1993, p. 290.
Kirkus Reviews, May 15, 1994, p. 703.
Publishers Weekly, May 31, 1993, review of *Meet Tricky Coyote!* and *That Tricky Coyote!,* p. 55.

School Library Journal, September, 1993, p. 225; July, 1994, p. 96; July, 2004, Michael Giller, review of *Frank Lloyd Wright,* p. 118.

* * *

McDERMOTT, Gerald (Edward) 1941-

Personal

Born January 31, 1941, in Detroit, MI. *Education:* Pratt Institute of Design, B.F.A., 1964.

Addresses

Agent—c/o Author Mail, Children's Book Division, Harcourt Publishers, Inc., 525 B St., Ste. 1900, San Diego, CA 92101-4495. *E-mail*—zomo2000@earthlink.net.

Career

Illustrator, author, and filmmaker. Graphic designer for public television station, New York, NY, 1962. Producer and designer of original films, including *The Stonecutter, Anansi the Spider, The Magic Tree, Sun Flight,* and *Arrow to the Sun.* Primary education program director, Joseph Campbell Foundation. *Exhibitions:* Films and artwork exhibited at San Francisco Film Festival, 1966; American Film Festival (France), 1971; Everson Museum (Syracuse, NY), 1975; Children's Museum, Indianapolis, IN, 1979; and Whitney Museum (New York, NY), 1980.

Member

AOSA National Advocacy Council (charter member)

Awards, Honors

Blue Ribbon, Educational Film Library Association, 1969; Silver Lion, Venice International Film Festival, 1970; American Film Festival Blue Ribbon, 1970, for *Anansi the Spider* (film); Caldecott Honor Book, 1973, for *Anansi the Spider: A Tale from the Ashanti;* Honor Book citation, *Boston Globe/Horn Book,* 1973, for *The Magic Tree: A Tale from the Congo;* Caldecott Medal, 1975, for *Arrow to the Sun: A Pueblo Indian Tale; Boston Globe/Horn Book*Honor Book citation, and Caldecott Honor Book, both 1993, both for *Raven: A Trickster Tale from the Pacific Northwest.*

Writings

RETELLER OF FOLKTALES; SELF-ILLUSTRATED

Anansi the Spider: A Tale from the Ashanti, Henry Holt (New York, NY), 1972.
The Magic Tree: A Tale from the Congo, Henry Holt (New York, NY), 1973, reprinted, 1994.

Arrow to the Sun: A Pueblo Indian Tale, Viking (New York, NY), 1974.
The Stonecutter: A Japanese Folk Tale, Viking (New York, NY), 1975.
The Voyage of Osiris: A Myth of Ancient Egypt, Dutton (New York, NY), 1977.
The Knight of the Lion, Four Winds Press (New York, NY), 1978.
Papagayo the Mischief Maker, Dutton (New York, NY), 1978, reprinted, Harcourt Brace Jovanovich (San Diego, CA), 1992.
Sun Flight, Four Winds Press (New York, NY), 1980.
Daughter of Earth: A Roman Myth, Delacorte Press (New York, NY), 1984.
Daniel O'Rourke: An Irish Tale, Viking Kestrel (New York, NY), 1986.
Jabuti the Tortoise: A Trickster Tale from the Amazon, Harcourt Brace Jovanovich (San Diego, CA), 1990.
Tim O'Toole and the Wee Folk: An Irish Tale, Viking (New York, NY), 1990.
Musicians of the Sun, Delacorte Press (New York, NY), 1991.
Zomo the Rabbit: A Trickster Tale from West Africa, Harcourt Brace Jovanovich (San Diego, CA), 1992.
Raven: A Trickster Tale from the Pacific Northwest, Harcourt Brace Jovanovich (San Diego, CA), 1993.
Coyote: A Trickster Tale from the American Southwest, Harcourt Brace Jovanovich (San Diego, CA), 1994.
Musicians of the Sun, Blue Sky Press (New York, NY), 1994.
The Light of the World: The Story of the Nativity, Simon & Schuster (New York, NY), 1998.
The Fox and the Stork, Harcourt Brace Jovanovich (San Diego, CA), 1999.
Creation, Dutton (New York, NY), 2003.

ILLUSTRATOR

Marianna Mayer, *Carlo Collodi's The Adventures of Pinocchio,* Four Winds Press (New York, NY), 1981.
Marianna Mayer, *Aladdin and the Enchanted Lamp,* Macmillan (New York, NY), 1985.
Marianna Mayer, *Alley Oop!,* Henry Holt (New York, NY), 1985.
Marianna Mayer, *The Brambleberrys Animal Book of Big and Small Shapes,* Bell Books (Honesdale, PA), 1987.
Marianna Mayer, *The Brambleberrys Animal Alphabet,* Bell Books (Honesdale, PA), 1991.
Marianna Mayer, *The Brambleberrys Animal Book of Colors,* Bell Books (Honesdale, PA), 1991.
Marianna Mayer, *The Brambleberrys Animal Book of Counting,* Bell Books (Honesdale, PA), 1991.
Marianna Mayer, *Marcel the Pastry Chef,* Bantam (New York, NY), 1991.

Sidelights

An acclaimed picture book artist, Gerald McDermott is motivated by an elemental interest in myth. Through films and books, McDermott has re-told classic folk tales from many different cultures, introducing new generations to the power of myths and trickster tales.

Although he began his career as an award-winning producer and director of animated films in the 1960s, McDermott is best known for his innovative picture books that have earned him prestigious awards such as the Caldecott Medal. Blending modern design techniques, vibrant colors, primitive art traditions, and straightforward narratives, McDermott's books aim to depict archetypal folk symbols that elicit universal understanding.

McDermott believes picture books deserve high artistic standards. "A picture book of artistic integrity will often be the only place where a child can expand his imagination and direct his gaze toward beauty," he remarked in his Caldecott Medal acceptance speech, as printed in *Horn Book.* "In form and content, the picture book can become an essential element in the child's evolving aesthetic consciousness, and the artist creating a picture book has an opportunity—and a special responsibility—to nurture the development of his young audience's visual perception."

McDermott was born in Detroit, Michigan, and his parents enrolled him at the age of four in classes at the Detroit Institute of Arts. "Every Saturday, from early childhood through early adolescence, was spent in those halls," he recalled in *Horn Book.* "I virtually lived in the museum, drawing and painting and coming to know the works of that great collection. I've kept a brush in my hand ever since." McDermott also became interested in films and at the age of nine became an actor on *Storyland,* a local radio program dramatizing folk tales and legends. "Working with professional actors and learning how music and sound effects are integrated in a dramatic context were indispensable experiences for a future filmmaker," he noted in *Horn Book.* In school McDermott focused his early studies on art and graphic design at Detroit's Cass Technical High School, which offered a special curriculum in Bauhaus principles of design. While in high school, he also experimented with making his own films and gained work experience creating background art for a television animation studio.

After graduating, McDermott received a Scholastic Publications national scholarship to attend the Pratt Institute in New York City. He also began work as a graphic designer for New York's public television station, Channel 13, and was granted independent credit by Pratt to pursue filmmaking. "I began to experiment with animated films," he stated in *Horn Book.* "My principal goal was to design films that were highly stylized in color and form. I also hoped to touch upon themes not dealt with in conventional cartoons. Instinctively, I turned to folklore as a source for thematic material." McDermott chose the Japanese folktale "The Stonecutter" and developed a method that became his filmmaking trademark. After designing a storyboard, McDermott drew a thousand frames, each synchronized painstakingly to the notes of a specially composed musical score. *The Stonecutter,* as McDermott explained in

Horn Book, is based on "an ancient fable of a man's foolish longing for power—a tale of wishes and dreams that can be understood on many levels. . . . The story contains in microcosm the basic theme of self-transformation that was consciously developed in my later work. While my approach to the graphic design of [*The Stonecutter*] . . . was unconventional, traditional animation techniques were used to set the designs in motion."

In 1965, after completing *The Stonecutter,* McDermott met Joseph Campbell, author of *The Hero with a Thousand Faces* and later featured in the Public Broadcasting System (PBS) series, *The Power of Myth.* McDermott became profoundly influenced by Campbell's theories of mythology's role in world cultures, and of his view that it functions "to supply the symbols that carry the human spirit forward, 'to waken and give guidance to the energies of life,'" as McDermott explained in *Horn Book.* With Campbell as his consultant, McDermott began making films that explore the theme of heroic quest in various cultures. From Africa McDermott found material for his next films, *Anansi the Spider* and *The Magic Tree,* and from the Pueblo Indians of the American Southwest, *Arrow to the Sun.* Each tale embodies Campbell's depiction of the classic heroic quest, as restated by McDermott in *Horn Book:* "A hero ventures forth from the world of common day into a region of supernatural wonder: fabulous forces are there encountered and a decisive victory is won: the hero comes back from this mysterious adventure with the power to bestow boons on his fellow man."

In the late 1960s, McDermott moved to southern France and visited the studios of European filmmakers. Before leaving, however, he was offered a multi-volume book contract by American editor George Nicholson to adapt his films into picture books. While in France, McDermott first focused his energies on producing a book version of his film *Anansi the Spider.* The change of medium posed some initial problems for McDermott, as he explained in *Horn Book.* "There was no longer a captive audience in a darkened room, its gaze fixed upon hypnotic flickering shadows. Gone were the music and sound effects and the ability to guide the viewer through a flow of images with a carefully planned progression. Now the reader was in control. The reader could begin at the end of the book or linger for ten minutes over a page or perhaps merely glance at half a dozen others. As an artist, I was challenged to resolve these problems."

His success was apparent in 1973, when his book version of *Anansi the Spider* was runner-up for the Caldecott Medal. Featuring montage-type illustrations in bold colors, along with Ashanti-inspired art and language patterns, *Anansi the Spider* tells the story of a father spider saved from a series of misadventures by his six more responsible sons. "Within each body of the six sons, an abstract symbol represents the individual's particular skill," noted Linda Kauffman Peterson in *New-*

bery and Caldecott Medal and Honor Books. "Amid geometric landscapes of magenta, turquoise, emerald, and red, the black figures, readily visible, rock across the pages on angular legs." McDermott followed *Anansi* with a book adaptation of *The Magic Tree: A Tale from the Congo,* and established himself as an innovative, highly stylized illustrator of children's books. "Like the similarly spectacular *Anansi the Spider,*" noted a *Kirkus Reviews* contributor, *The Magic Tree* "is adapted from an animated film and it's difficult not to hear the pulsing jazz music that seems to be visualized on these dynamic, semi-abstract pages, which are distinctly African in patterns and motifs but just as distinctly cinematic in their vibrant color and kinetic energy."

In 1974, McDermott embarked upon his first simultaneous film and book project, *Arrow to the Sun,* which

went on to receive the Caldecott Medal. The book adapts the popular legend of a Pueblo Indian boy who journeys to the heavens in pursuit of his cultural heritage. Using limited text and featuring stylized depictions of important Indian symbols—corn, rainbows, and the sun—*Arrow to the Sun* was an important step in McDermott's own search of the "hero-quest" in world mythologies. "This theme finds its fullest expressions in my book and in my film of *Arrow to the Sun*—with a significant difference," he commented in *Horn Book.* "In previous works, the circle was broken. Through some weakness or failing, or perhaps sheer foolishness, the protagonist fails in his search. . . . In this Pueblo Indian tale, however, the circle is complete, and the questing hero successfully finishes his journey."

McDermott's other adaptations of folktales from around the world include a book version of *The Stonecutter;*

In his 1975 Caldecott Medal-winning Arrow to the Sun *McDermott tells a story about the cycle of life and death that is framed by the beliefs of the Pueblo people.*

Based on both Genesis and the Hebrew Bible, McDermott presents a story of the Creation that features his characteristic boldly hued illustrations.(Illustration from Creation.)

The Voyage of Osiris, concerning the death and afterlife of an ancient Egyptian god; *Sun Flight,* which retells the ancient Greek myth of Daedalus and Icarus; *Daughter of the Earth,* which retells the Roman myth about the origins of spring; *Knight of the Lion,* a black-and-white illustrated adaptation of a King Arthur legend; and two tales from Ireland, *Daniel O'Rourke* and *Tim O'Toole and the Wee Folk.* The illustrations in the 1992 work *Zomo the Rabbit,* a trickster tale adapted from African myth, "masterfully integrate a variety of styles the artist has used in the past," Marilyn Iarusso stated in *School Library Journal.* The critic also lauded the "great good humor" used to create an entertaining story.

Coyote is a favorite trickster character in Native American lore. In *Coyote: A Trickster Tale from the American Southwest* McDermott tells of Coyote's wish to be the greatest of his kind. A flock of crows suggest he join them in flight, with perhaps predictable results: the vain beast falls into the dust. *Booklist* correspondent Hazel Rochman found the work "great for storytelling: kids will love the slapstick action and the bright, comic art about this gawky fool." A *Publishers Weekly* reviewer likewise deemed the book "a splendid take, perfectly paced for an amusing read-aloud." *Jabuti the Tortoise: A Trickster Tale from the Amazon* introduces another character who suffers for his vanity. Jabuti plays beautiful music on his flute, and most of the forest creatures enjoy his songs. Vulture is jealous, however, and decides to play a trick on the tortoise. Offering Jabuti a ride on his back, Vulture says he will take Jabuti to heaven to play for God. In mid-air, the Vulture tosses Jabuti, whose shell is shattered on a rock. The birds of the rain forest work together to restore Jabuti's shell,

each receiving rewards of bright feathers. Teri Markson, writing in *School Library Journal,* declared the book "a worthy addition to the artist's impressive series of trickster tales."

More recently McDermott has turned his attention to creation myths. *Musicians of the Sun* offers an Aztec version of the beginnings of the earth. Sun, in this telling, keeps prisoner the musicians, Red, Yellow, Blue, and Green, leaving the earth smothered in darkness. The colors are freed when Wind and Sun engage in a battle and Wind emerges victorious, showering the people of earth with color and music. A *Publishers Weekly* critic praised *Musicians of the Sun* as "an imposing visual interpretation of legend," concluding that McDermott's "sumptuous paintings . . . command this splendid volume." Hazel Rochman in *Booklist* likewise concluded that children "will love [the book] for the clash of battle and the triumph of joy."

Creation is McDermott's re-telling of the origin of earth according to the Book of Genesis. Using first-person narration done in poetic meter, he describes how God wrought changes to the heavens and earth, culminating in the creation of humankind. In her review of *Creation* for *School Library Journal,* Margaret Bush wrote: "Sumptuous, rhythmic, and mystical, this book is arresting and evocative." A *Publishers Weekly* correspondent similarly stated: "Masterfully executed, this will kindle and fuel much thought."

Given the themes he pursues, McDermott's works appeal to adult readers as well as young audiences. "My life and work are inseparably bound up together," he explained to David E. White in *Language Arts.* "If an artist puts himself into his work in the fullest sense—his emotions, his intellect, the symbols from his own psyche—then the work will touch others because it springs directly from the artist's own inner life." McDermott is primary education program director for the Joseph Campbell Foundation.

Biographical and Critical Sources

BOOKS

Children's Literature Review, Volume 9, Gale (Detroit, MI), 1985.

Peterson, Linda Kauffman, *Newbery and Caldecott Medal and Honor Books: An Annotated Bibliography,* G. K. Hall (Boston, MA), 1982, p. 358.

St. James Guide to Children's Writers, 5th edition, St. James Press (Detroit, MI), 1999.

Stott, Jon C., *Gerald McDermott and You,* Libraries Unlimited (Westport, CT), 2004.

PERIODICALS

Booklist, August, 1994, review of *Coyote,* p. 2041; November 1, 1997, Hazel Rochman, review of *Musicians of the Sun,* p. 467; September 15, 2001, Carolyn Phelan, review of *Jabuti the Tortoise: A Trickster Tale from the Amazon,* p. 228; September 1, 2003, Abby Nolan, review of *Creation,* p. 123.

Bulletin of the Center for Children's Books, November, 2003, Deborah Stevenson, review of *Creation,* p. 91.

Five Owls, spring, 2004, Kara Fondse van Drie, review of *Creation,* p. 84.

Horn Book, April, 1975, Gerald McDermott, "On the Rainbow Trail," pp. 123-131; August, 1975, "Caldecott Award Acceptance," pp. 349-354; July-August, 1993, Margaret A. Bush, review of *Raven: A Trickster Tale from the Pacific Northwest,* p. 470; September-October, 2003, Joanna Rudge Long, review of *Creation,* p. 632.

Kirkus Reviews, October 15, 1972, review of *The Magic Tree: A Tale from the Congo,* p. 1187.

Language Arts, March, 1982, David E. White, "Profile: Gerald McDermott," pp. 273-279.

Publishers Weekly, September 19, 1994, review of *Coyote,* p. 70; September 29, 1997, review of *Musicians of the Sun,* p. 88; August 6, 2001, review of *Jabuti the Tortoise,* p. 88; August 4, 2003, review of *Creation,* p. 76.

School Library Journal, November, 1992, Marilyn Iarusso, review of *Zomo the Rabbit: A Trickster Tale from West Afrtica,* pp. 84-85; November, 1994, Marilyn Iarusso, review of *Coyote,* p. 99; December, 1997, Pam Gosner, review of *Musicians of the Sun,* p. 111; September, 2001, Teri Markson, review of *Jabuti the Tortoise,* p. 218; September, 2003, Margaret Bush, review of *Creation,* p. 234; April, 2004, review of *Creation,* p. 20.

ONLINE

Gerald McDermott Home Page, http://www.gerald mcdermott.com (July 15, 2005).

McGEE, Marni

Personal

Born in New Orleans, LA; daughter of a minister; married Sears McGee, 1966; children: Elizabeth, Claude. *Education:* Attended Agnes Scott College; University of North Carolina, Chapel Hill, B.A. (English; with highest honors); Yale Divinity School, M.A.R. *Hobbies and other interests:* Traveling, beach walks, reading, theatre, opera and chamber music.

Addresses

Home—CA. *Agent*—Nancy Gallt, 273 Charlton Ave., South Orange, NY 07079.

Career

Author, educator, and editor. American School, London, England, teacher c. 1967-69; freelance writer and editor, 1974-94; full-time writer for children, beginning 1994.

Writings

The Quiet Farmer, illustrated by Lynne Dennis, Atheneum/Macmillan International (New York, NY), 1991.

Diego Columbus, Adventures on the High Seas, illustrations by Jim Hsieh, Fleming H. Revell (New York, NY), 1992.

Forest Child, illustrated by A. Scott Banfill, Green Tiger Press (New York, NY), 1994.

Jack Takes the Cake, illustrated by Dana Regan, Troll Communications (Metuchen, NJ), 1998.

The Colt and the King, illustrated by John Winch, Holiday House (New York, NY), 2002.

Sleepy Me, illustrated by Sam Williams, Simon & Schuster Books for Young Readers (New York, NY), 2001.

Wake up, Me!, illustrated by Sam Williams, Simon & Schuster Books for Young Readers (New York, NY), 2002.

The Noisy Farm, illustrated by Leonie Shearing, Bloomsbury Children's Books (New York, NY), 2004.

(With Ronald J. Mellor) *The Ancient Roman World,* Oxford University Press (New York, NY), 2004.

(With Amanda H. Podany) *The Ancient Near Eastern World,* Oxford University Press (New York, NY), 2005.

While Angels Watch, Good Books, 2006.

Winston the BookWolf, Walker (New York, NY), 2006.

Contributor to *Cricket;* contributor to anthologies edited by Myra Cohn Livingston.

Work in Progress

National Geographic Explores: Greece, forthcoming, 2006; *Silly Goose* and *Naomi's Gift,* both 2007.

Sidelights

Children's book author and poet Marni McGee began writing in 1974 to entertain her own children, and as the number of stories grew, family and friends began to urge her to submit her manuscripts for publication. Ranging from picture books to middle-grade fiction and poetry for all ages, her books include *The Noisy Farm, Wake up, Me!,* and *The Colt and the King,* the last a re-telling of the story of Palm Sunday from the point of view of the young donkey who carried Jesus into Jerusalem. The book was described as "reverent in tone, restrained in execution, and thoughtfully designed," by *Horn Book* contributor Mary M. Burns.

In *The Noisy Farm,* a book inspired by the author's grandfather, McGee utilizes onomatopoeia to introduce toddlers to life on a farm. As the farmer goes about his daily routine he cares for each of his animals, and McGee's text highlights the different noises that each creature makes. Maryann H. Owen, writing in *School Library Journal,* called the book "a pleasant introduction to farm life," while a *Kirkus Reveiws* critic praised *The Noisy Farm* as "a warm-hearted story that hints at the importance of symbiosis—and has a jolly good time doing it."

In *Sleepy Me* and *Wake up, Me!* McGee creates a pair of books that highlights the start and finish of a typical toddler day. Featuring an energetic young boy, both books feature a curly-haired toddler whose happy home and loving parents create a reassuring, upbeat mood. In *Sleepy Me* he is put to bed by his father, McGee's re-

In The Noisy Farm *Marni McGee creates a boisterous read-aloud by including a host of animal sounds in her barnyard tale. (Illustration by Leonie Shearing.)*

petitive rhyming prose making the book "a soothing choice for nighttime reading," according to a *Publishers Weekly* critic. In the companion volume, *Wake up, Me!,* a child narrates his daily routine with a jaunty rhyme. Wanda Meyers-Hines wrote in *School Library Journal* that the up-to-date family interactions and affectionate family life make *Wake up, Me!* "a fine choice for one-on-one sharing, for toddler storytimes, and for beginning readers."

In addition, she has produced two highly praised volumes in Oxford University Press's "World in Ancient Times" series: *The Ancient Roman World* and *The Ancient Near Eastern World.* Praising *The Ancient Roman World,* which McGee coauthored with University of California professor Ronald J. Mellor, *School Library Journal* contributor David Pauli praised the in-depth coverage of Roman history as well as "lively writing" enlivened by quotes from the ancients. In *Booklist* Ilene Cooper also enjoyed the work, writing that it is "more readable, more complete, and more attractive" than other histories of its kind.

A popular speaker at schools, McGee shares her stories with students from third grade and up, talking about the creative writing process. "Writing provides a crucial outlet for me," the author explained to *Something about the Author.* "Like dancing, it clarifies the words that stumble on the tongue and reveal the hidden thought . . . the secret knowing. . . . Writing for children is the highest honor and privilege I can imagine. Children are worth the very best we can give them. I want nothing more than to give them my best in the hope that I might make a difference in some child's life."

Biographical and Critical Sources

PERIODICALS

Booklist, April 1, 2002, Kathy Broderick, review of *The Colt an the King,* p. 1334; June 1, 2002, Carolyn Phelan, review of *Wake up, Me!,* p. 1742; April 1, 2004, Ilene Cooper, review of *The Ancient Roman World,* p. 1372.

Horn Book, March-April, 2002, Mary M. Burns, review of *The Colt and the King,* p. 202.

Kirkus Reviews, March 1, 2002, review of *Wake up, Me!,* p. 340; March 1, 2002, review of *The Colt and the King,* p. 340; April 1, 2004, review of *The Ancient Roman World,* p. 334; May 15, 2004, review of *The Noisy Farm,* p. 495.

Publishers Weekly, May 7, 2001, review of *Sleepy Me,* p. 245; February 18, 2002, review of *The Colt and the King,* p. 65.

School Library Journal, June, 2001, Martha Topol, review of *Sleepy Me,* p. 126; May, 2002, Wanda Meyers-Hines, review of *Wake up, Me!,* p. 122; July, 2004, David Pauli, review of *the Ancient Roman World,* p. 126; October, 2004, Maryann H. Owen, review of *The Noisy Farm,* p. 122.

ONLINE

Bloomsbury Press Web site, http://www.bloomsbury.com/ (July 6, 2005), "Marni McGee."

Marni McGee Home Page, http://www.marnimcgee.com (July 6, 2005).

PFD Web site, http://www.pfd.co.uk/ (July 6, 2005), "Marni McGee."

* * *

MOSS, Marissa 1959-

Personal

Born September 29, 1959; daughter of Robert (a engineer) and Harriet Moss; married Harvey Stahl (a professor); children: Simon, Elias, Asa. *Education:* University of California, Berkeley, B.A. (art history); attended California College of Arts and Crafts.

Addresses

Home—Berkeley, CA. *Agent*—c/o Author Mail, Tricycle Press, P.O. Box 7123, Berkeley, CA 94707.

Career

Author and illustrator.

Member

Authors Guild, PEN West, Society of Children's Book Writers and Illustrators, Screenwriters Guild.

Awards, Honors

Parent Council Outstanding Award for informational book, 2000, for *My Notebook (with Help from Amelia);* Parent's Guide to Children's Media Award, 2001, and Children's Choice Award, 2002, both for *Oh Boy, Amelia!*

Writings

SELF-ILLUSTRATED PICTURE BOOKS

Who Was It?, Houghton (Boston, MA), 1989.
Regina's Big Mistake, Houghton (Boston, MA), 1990.
Want to Play?, Houghton (Boston, MA), 1990.
After-School Monster, Lothrop (New York, NY), 1991.
Knick Knack Paddywack, Houghton (Boston, MA), 1992.
But Not Kate, Lothrop (New York, NY), 1992.
In America, Dutton (New York, NY), 1994.
Mel's Diner, BridgeWater Books (Mahwah, NJ), 1994.
The Ugly Menorah, Farrar, Straus (New York, NY), 1996.
Galen: My Life in Imperial Rome ("Ancient World Journal" series), Harcourt (San Diego, CA), 2002.

Max's Logbook, Scholastic (New York, NY), 2003.
Max's Mystical Notebook, Scholastic (New York, NY), 2004.

"AMELIA'S NOTEBOOK" SERIES; SELF-ILLUSTRATED

Amelia's Notebook, Tricycle Press (Berkeley, CA), 1995.
Amelia Writes Again, Tricycle Press (Berkeley, CA), 1996.
My Notebook (with Help from Amelia), Tricycle Press (Berkeley, CA), 1997.
Amelia Hits the Road, Tricycle Press (Berkeley, CA), 1997.
Amelia Takes Command, Tricycle Press (Berkeley, CA), 1998.
Dr. Amelia's Boredom Survival Guide, Pleasant Company (Middleton, WI) 1999.
The All-New Amelia, Pleasant Company (Middleton, WI), 1999.
Luv Amelia, Luv Nadia, Pleasant Company (Middleton, WI), 1999.
Amelia's Family Ties, Pleasant Company (Middleton, WI), 2000.
Amelia's Easy-as-Pie Drawing Guide, Pleasant Company (Middleton, WI), 2000.
Amelia Works It Out, Pleasant Company (Middleton, WI), 2000.
Madame Amelia Tells All: (Except Fortunes and Predictions), Pleasant Company (Middleton, WI), 2001.
Oh Boy, Amelia!, Pleasant Company (Middleton, WI), 2001.
Amelia Lends a Hand, Pleasant Company (Middleton, WI), 2002.
Amelia's Best Year Ever: Favorite Amelia Stories from American Girl Magazine, Pleasant Company (Middleton, WI), 2003.
Amelia's Sixth-Grade Notebook, Simon & Schuster (New York, NY), 2004.
Amelia's Most Unforgettable Embarrassing Moments, Simon & Schuster (New York, NY), 2005.
Amelia's Book of Notes and Note Passing, Simon & Schuster (New York, NY), 2006.

FOR CHILDREN

True Heart, illustrated by Chris F. Payne, Harcourt (San Diego, CA), 1998.
Rachel's Journal: The Story of a Pioneer Girl ("Young American Voices" series), Harcourt (San Diego, CA), 1998.
Emma's Journal: The Story of a Colonial Girl ("Young American Voices" series), Harcourt (San Diego, CA), 1999.
Hannah's Journal: The Story of an Immigrant Girl ("Young American Voices" series), Harcourt (San Diego, CA), 2000.
Rose's Journal: The Story of a Girl in the Great Depression ("Young American Voices" series), Harcourt (San Diego, CA), 2001.
Brave Harriet: The First Woman to Fly the English Channel, illustrated by C. F. Payne, Harcourt (San Diego, CA), 2001.
Mighty Jackie: The Strike-out Queen, illustrated by C. F. Payne, Harcourt (San Diego, CA), 2002.

ILLUSTRATOR

Catherine Gray, *One, Two, Three, and Four—No More?,* Houghton (Boston, MA), 1988.

Dr. Hickey, adapter, *Mother Goose and More: Classic Rhymes with Added Lines,* Additions Press (Oakland, CA), 1990.

Bruce Coville, *The Lapsnatcher,* BridgeWater Books (Mahwah, NJ), 1997.

David M. Schwartz, *G Is for Googol: A Math Alphabet Book,* Tricycle Press (Berkeley, CA), 1998.

Sidelights

Author and illustrator Marissa Moss has produced several popular picture books, as well as a series of beginning readers featuring a young writer named Amelia. Beginning with *Amelia's Notebook,* Moss follows her eponymous heroine through a series of daily adventures in the fourth grade: the young protagonist changes schools, makes new friends, and copes with an annoying older sister. Moss has captured the imagination of primary graders with the adventures of her spunky character, and has tempted them with the opportunity to "read the secrets a peer records in her journal," according to *Publishers Weekly* writer Sally Lodge. Hand-lettered and bound in a manner that resembles a black-and-white school composition book, *Amelia's Notebook* and its companion volumes, including *Amelia Hits the Road* and *Amelia's Most Unforgettable Embarrassing Moments,* are "chock-full of personal asides and tiny spot drawings" and contain a story-line that "rings true with third-grade authenticity," according to *School Library Journal* contributor Carolyn Noah.

Born in 1959, Moss earned a degree in art history from the University of California at Berkeley. She once told *Something about the Author* (SATA): "I could say I never thought I'd be a writer, only an illustrator and writing was forced upon me by a lack of other writers' stories to illustrate. Or I could say I always wanted to be a writer, but I never thought it was really possible. As a voracious reader, it seemed too much of a grown-up thing to do, and I'd never be mature enough to do it. Or I could say I've been writing and illustrating children's books since I was nine. It just took me longer than most to get published. All these stories are true, each in their own way."

Moss began her career as a picture-book illustrator working with author Catherine Gray, as well as creating art to pair with her own simple texts. One of her first published efforts as both writer and illustrator, *Who Was It?,* depicts young Isabelle's quandary after she breaks the cookie jar while attempting to sneak a between-meals snack. Praising Moss's watercolor illustrations, *Booklist* reviewer Denise Wilms also noted that the book's "moral about telling the truth is delivered with wry, quiet humor." In *Regina's Big Mistake,* a young artist's frustration with her own lack of ability compared to that of the rest of her classmates is counter-acted by a sensitive art teacher, as Regina is shown how to "draw around" a lumpy sun, transforming it into a moon. Readers "will enjoy the solace of having another child struggling to achieve, and succeeding," maintained Zena Sutherland in the *Bulletin of the Center for Children's Books. School Library Journal* contributor Ruth Semrau noted that "Moss's crayon cartoons are exactly what is needed to depict the artistic endeavors of very young children."

In *After-School Monster* Luisa returns home from school one day to find a sharp-toothed creature waiting in her kitchen. Although scared, she stands up to the monster, turning the tables on the creature and evicting him from her house before her mom gets home. While noting that the theme could frighten very small children contemplating being left alone, a *Junior Bookshelf* contributor praised Moss's "striking" full-page illustrations, which feature "an imaginative use of changing sizes." And in an equally imaginative picture book offering, Moss updates the traditional nursery rhyme "Knick Knack Paddywack" with what Sheilamae O'Hara of *Booklist* described as "rollicking, irreverent verse" and "colorful, action-filled" pictures. The author-illustrator's "use of language will tickle all but the tongue tied," added Jody McCoy in an appraisal of *Knick Knack Paddywack* for *School Library Journal.*

"The character of Amelia came to me when I opened a black and white mottled composition book and started to write and draw the way I remembered I wrote and drew when I was nine," Moss once recalled to about the beginnings of her popular "Amelia's Notebook" series. "By that age I was already a pretty good artist, winner of drugstore coloring contests and determined to grow up to be another Leonardo da Vinci." The age of nine was also significant for Moss because that was when she became confident enough to send her first illustrated children's book to a publisher. "I don't remember the title, but the story involved an owl's tea party and was in rhymed couplets—bad rhyme I'm sure, as I never got a response from the publisher whose name I mercifully don't recall." Lacking encouragement, Moss left writing for several years, although she continued to tell stories.

The power of storytelling is one of the key themes Moss endeavors to express through her young protagonist, Amelia. "When you write or tell about something," she explained, "you have a kind of control over it, you shape the events, you sort them through, you emphasize some aspects, omit others. . . . Besides the flights of pure fancy, the imaginative leaps that storytelling allows, it was this sense of control, of finding order and meaning that mattered most to me as a child."

In the "Amelia" books, the spunky young chronicler dives into activities in a new school after leaving her old friends behind during a family move. "Amelia is droll and funny and not too sophisticated for her years," noted *Booklist* reviewer Stephanie Zvirin, who added

In her popular "Amelia's Notebook" series Marissa Moss focuses on a spunky nine-year-old diarist and her upbeat attitude toward to a move to a new school.

that the diarist has a more emotional side too, missing her old friends and full of childhood aspirations about her future. In *Amelia Writes Again,* the heroine has turned ten and has begun a new notebook. In doodles, sketches, and snippets of thoughts, she comments on such things as a fire at school and her inability to pay attention during math class. Everything Moss includes in Amelia's notebooks is true, "or," as Moss will tell the groups of students she visits, "is based on the truth. Names have all been changed, because my older sister is mad enough at me already, and some details are altered to make for a better story. So, yes, there really was a fire in my school, but the idea of putting treasures in the newly poured pavement didn't occur to me at the time." Moss wishes it had; instead, she was able to let Amelia do so in *Amelia Writes Again.*

Moss enjoys writing in Amelia's voice because it allows her a flexibility that conventional picture book writing does not. "I can go back and forth between different kinds of writing—the pure invention of storytelling, the thoughtful searching of describing people and events, and the explorations Amelia takes when she writes about noses or numbers, things she notices and writes down to figure out what it is that she's noticing. In the same way that I can go from describing a new teacher to making a story about clouds, Amelia allows me to move freely between words and pictures. I can draw as Amelia draws or I can use *tromp l'oeil* for the objects she tapes into her notebook. I can play with the

art as much as I play with the text. The notebook format allows me to leap from words to images and this free flowing back and forth is how I work best. It reflects the way I think—sometimes visually, sometimes verbally—with the pictures not there just to illustrate the text, but to replace it, telling their own story. Often the art allows me a kind of graphic shorthand, a way of conveying what I mean that is much more immediate than words. Kids often ask me which comes first, the words or the pictures. With Amelia, it can be either, and I love that fluidity."

In addition to Amelia's notebooks, Moss has created a series focusing on young writers from different historical periods. "Like Amelia's notebooks, the pages . . . seem like real notebook pages," Moss explained to *SATA,* "with drawings and inserted objects on every page," although Moss's protagonist will be from a past era. The first book in the series, *Rachel's Journal: The Story of a Pioneer Girl,* allows readers to accompany a family to California in 1850 along the Oregon Trail. Unlike the "Amelia" books, which are drawn from the author's own memories, Moss spent many hours doing research, reading histories, exploring library archives, and pouring over the actual letters and diaries of people who traversed the United States by covered wagon. "It was, for the most part, riveting reading and I was impressed with what an enormous undertaking, what a leap of faith it was for pioneers to come" to the West coast, Moss noted. "It was a dangerous trip. Indians, river crossings, storms, and especially sickness were all feared. But I was struck by the difference between how men and women viewed the journey and how children saw it. To kids, it was a great adventure, troublesome at times, tedious and terrifying at others, but ultimately exciting. These children showed tremendous courage and strength of character, and I tried to capture some of that, as well as the exhilaration of travelling into the unknown, in Rachel's journal."

Moss has completed several other works in the "Young American Voices" series published by Minnesota's Pleasant Company, among them *Emma's Journal: The Story of a Colonial Girl, Hannah's Journal: The Story of an Immigrant Girl,* and *Rose's Journal: The Story of a Girl in the Great Depression. Hannah's Journal* concerns a ten-year-old Lithuanian girl who immigrates to the United States in 1901. Reviewing the work in *School Library Journal,* Jane Marino remarked that "Moss does give her readers a real sense of the time in which the protagonist lived." *Rose's Journal* is set on a Kansas farm in 1935. *School Library Journal* contributor Roxanne Burg stated that "there is quite a bit of historical information packed into this short book."

As the writer delves even further into the past, a twelve-year-old slave becomes her subject in the self-illustrated *Galen: My Life in Imperial Rome,* the first book in Harcourt's "Ancient World Journal" series. Moss blends fact and fiction in her account of Galen's life, as the boy lives and works in the home of Emperor Augustus. According to a reviewer in *Publishers Weekly,* Moss provides "a clear, intriguing portrait of ancient Roman life," and *Booklist* contributor GraceAnne A. DeCandido wrote, "This delightful book is rich in detail."

Moss looks at U.S. aviator Harriet Quimby in *Brave Harriet: The First Woman to Fly the English Channel.* Quimby, the first woman to become a licensed pilot, flew from England to France on April 16, 1912. Her historic solo flight was overshadowed by another event that occurred the same day: the sinking of the luxury ocean liner *Titanic.* Quimby's "contemplation of the glory that might have been . . . is sensitively portrayed," wrote *School Library Journal* reviewer Ann Chapman Callaghan.

Mighty Jackie: The Strike-out Queen tells the true story of Jackie Mitchell, a seventeen year old who pitched for the Chattanooga Lookouts, a minor-league baseball team. Moss describes how Mitchell received coaching and encouragement at a young age from both her father and Dazzy Vance, a major-league pitcher. In 1931, the Lookouts played an exhibition game against the New York Yankees, who were then led by superstars Babe Ruth and Lou Gehrig, and Mitchell made baseball history by striking out the legendary duo. "Moss relays the details . . . with the blow-by-blow breathless of a sportscaster and the confidence of a seasoned storyteller," wrote a critic in *Publishers Weekly,* and *School*

Library Journal contributor Grace Oliff observed that "The narrative captures the tension and excitement, and has the air of an experience remembered."

In addition to taking on other teen biographies and other writing projects, Moss continues to expand her "Amelia's Notebook" series. In *Amelia Works It Out* the adventurous heroine tries to start her own business so she can buy a pair of expensive glow-in-the-dark shoes, while in *Oh Boy, Amelia!* she takes a life-skills class and discovers that she is handy with tools. Critics have praised Moss's books for leading younger readers into the art of journal writing, a result about which their author couldn't be happier. "The many letters I get from kids show that, inspired by Amelia, they, too, are discovering the magic of writing," she told *SATA.* "When readers respond to Amelia by starting their own journals, I feel I've gotten the highest compliment possible—I've made writing cool."

Biographical and Critical Sources

PERIODICALS

Booklist, November 1, 1989, Denise Wilms, review of *Who Was It?,* p. 555; March 1, 1992, p. 1287; July, 1992, Sheilamae O'Hara, review of *Knick Knack Paddywack,* p. 1941; October 1, 1994, p. 333; April 1, 1995, Stephanie Zvirin, review of *Amelia's Notebook,* p. 1391; June 1, 1997, p. 1716; November 15, 1997, p. 561; November 1, 1999, Carolyn Phelan, review of *The All-New Amelia* and *Luv Amelia, Luv Nadia,* p. 530; February 15, 2000, Carolyn Phelan, review of *Amelia's Family Ties,* p. 1113; September 1, 2000, Carolyn Phelan, review of *Amelia Works It Out,* p. 115; October 1, 2000, Carolyn Phelan, review of *Hannah's Journal: The Story of an Immigrant Girl,* p. 340; July, 2001, Carolyn Phelan, review of *Brave Harriet: The First Woman to Fly the English Channel,* p. 2009; August, 2001, Susan Dove Lempke, review of *Madame Amelia Tells All,* p. 2121; January 1, 2002, Carolyn Phelan, review of *Oh Boy, Amelia!,* p. 859; March 1, 2002, Ilene Cooper, review of *Brave Harriet,* p. 1146; April 1, 2002, Stephanie Zvirin, "Top Ten Biographies for Youth," p. 1340; December 15, 2002, GraceAnne A. DeCandido, review of *Galen: My Life in Imperial Rome,* p. 760; October 15, 2003, Todd Morning, review of *Max's Logbook,* p. 412; January 1, 2004, GraceAnne A. DeCandido, review of *Mighty Jackie: The Strike-out Queen,* p. 868.

Bulletin of the Center for Children's Books, October, 1990, Zena Sutherland, review of *Regina's Big Mistake,* p. 40; November, 1996, p. 108.

Junior Bookshelf, review of *After-School Monster,* April, 1993, p. 62.

Kirkus Reviews, August 15, 1989, p. 1248; August 15, 1990, p. 1171; July 1, 1991, p. 865; July 1, 1996, p. 972; September 15, 2002, review of *Galen,* p. 1396; January 15, 2004, review of *Mighty Jackie,* p. 87.

Publishers Weekly, June 14, 1991, p. 57; September 30, 1996, p. 87; June 16, 1997, p. 61; July 28, 1997, p. 77; August 31, 1998, Sally Lodge, "Journaling Back through Time with Marissa Moss," p. 20; April 9, 2001, review of *Amelia's Moving Pictures* (video review), p. 29; July 16, 2001, review of *Brave Harriet,* p. 180; March 18, 2002, pp. 105-106; October 21, 2002, review of *Galen,* p. 76; July 14, 2003, review of *Max's Logbook,* p. 76; January 19, 2004, review of *Mighty Jackie,* p. 76.

Reading Today, April, 2001, Lynne T. Burke, review of "Amelia" series, p. 32; August, 2001, Lynne T. Burke, review of *Amelia Works It Out,* p. 30.

School Library Journal, January, 1991, Ruth Semrau, review of *Regina's Big Mistake,* p. 79; June, 1992, Jody McCoy, review of *Knick Knack Paddywack,* p. 100; December, 1994, p. 79; July, 1995, Carolyn Noah, review of *Amelia's Notebook,* p. 79; July, 1997, p. 60; November, 1997, p. 95; October, 1999, Lisa Gangemi Krapp, review of *The All-New Amelia,* p. 121; December, 1999, Susan Hepler, review of *Emma's Journal: The Story of a Colonial Girl,* p. 108; June, 2000, Holly Belli, *Amelia's Family Ties,* p. 122; September, 2000, Wendy S. Carroll, review of *Amelia Works It Out,* p. 206; November, 2000, Jane Marino, review of *Hannah's Journal,* p. 129; July, 2001, Leslie S. Hilverding, review of *Madame Amelia Tells All,* p. 86; September, 2001, Ann Chapman Callaghan, review of *Brave Harriet,* p. 220; October, 2001, Debbie Stewart, review of *Oh Boy, Amelia!,* p. 126; December, 2001, Roxanne Burg, review of *Rose's Journal: The Story of a Girl in the Great Depression,* p. 108; October, 2002, Lynda S. Poling, review of *Galen,* pp. 168-169; October, 2003, Elaine Lesh Morgan, review of *Max's Logbook,* p. 132; February, 2004, Grace Oliff, review of *Mighty Jackie,* pp. 134-135; May, 2005, Jennifer Ralston, review of *Amelia Takes Command,* p. 50.

ONLINE

Harcourt Books Web site, http://www.harcourtbooks.com/ (June 1, 2004), interview with Moss.*

N

NUTT, Ken 1951(?)-
(Eric Beddows)

Personal
Born November 29, 1951 (one source says 1956), in Woodstock, Ontario, Canada. *Education:* Attended York University (Toronto, Ontario, Canada), 1970-72.

Addresses
Home—Stratford, Ontario, Canada. *Agent*—c/o Author Mail, Laura Geringer Books, 1350 Avenue of the Americas New York, NY 10019.

Career
Illustrator. The Gallery, Stratford, Ontario, Canada, educator and installer and lighter of exhibitions for nine years. *Exhibitions:* Included in exhibitions at Vancouver Art Gallery, Vancouver, British Columbia, Canada, 1988-90; The Gallery, Stratford, Ontario, Canada, 1990; and Woodstock Art Gallery, Woodstock, Ontario, Canada, 1997. Work represented in permanent collections, including Osborn Collection, Toronto, Ontario, and National Library of Canada, Ottawa.

Awards, Honors
Children's Book of the Year citation, International Order of the Daughters of the Empire (IODE), 1983, Amelia Frances Howard-Gibbon Award, Canadian Association of Children's Librarians (CACL), and Ruth Schwartz Children's Book Award, Ontario Arts Council, both 1984, all for *Zoom at Sea;* Amelia Frances Howard-Gibbon Award, 1986, for *Zoom Away;* runner-up, Book of the Year for Children, Canadian Library Association, 1987, and Honor List for Illustration in Canada citation, International Board on Books for Young People, 1988, both for *The Emperor's Panda;* Honor Book, *Boston Globe/Horn Book* Illustration Award, 1988, for *Joyful Noise;* Children's Book of the Year citation, IODE, 1988, runner-up, Amelia Frances Howard-Gibbon Award, CACL, and Elizabeth Mrazik-

Ken Nutt

Cleaver Picture Book Award, Canadian Children's Book Centre, both 1989, all for *Night Cars;* Notable Books citation, American Library Association, 1992, for *Who Shrank My Grandfather's House?;* Governor General's Literary Award for Illustration, Canada Council, 1996, for *The Rooster's Gift.* Recipient of grants for book illustration from Ontario Arts Council, 1981, 1985.

Illustrator
Tim Wynne-Jones, *Zoom at Sea,* Douglas & McIntyre (Toronto, Ontario, Canada), 1983, HarperCollins (New York, NY), 1993.

Tim Wynne-Jones, *Zoom Away,* Douglas & McIntyre (Toronto, Ontario, Canada), 1985, HarperCollins (New York, NY), 1993.

Paul Fleischman, *I Am Phoenix: Poems for Two Voices,* Harper & Row (New York, NY), 1985.

UNDER NAME ERIC BEDDOWS

David Day, *The Emperor's Panda,* Dodd, Mead (New York, NY), 1986.

Dennis Hasley, *The Cave of Snores,* Harper & Row (New York, NY), 1987.

Paul Fleischman, *Joyful Noise: Poems for Two Voices,* Harper & Row (New York, NY), 1988.

Teddy Jam, *Night Cars,* Douglas & McIntyre (Toronto, Ontario, Canada), 1988, Orchard Books (New York, NY), 1989.

Paul Fleischman, *Shadow Play,* Harper & Row (New York, NY), 1990.

Barbara Juster Esbensen, *Who Shrank My Grandmother's House? Poems of Discovery,* HarperCollins (New York, NY), 1992.

Chris Van Allsburg, *Four Strange Stories,* Houghton Mifflin Canada (Markham, Ontario, Canada), 1992.

Tim Wynne-Jones, *Zoom Upstream,* Douglas & McIntyre (Toronto, Ontario, Canada), 1992, HarperCollins (New York, NY), 1994.

Pam Conrad, *The Rooster's Gift,* HarperCollins (New York, NY), 1996.

Ursula K. LeGuin, *Changing Planes* (short stories for adults), Harcourt (Orlando, FL), 2003.

Tor Seidler, *Toes,* Laura Geringer Books (New York, NY), 2004.

OTHER

(With Glen Elliott) *Ken Nutt, Drawings* [and] *Glen Elliott, Sculpture* (exhibition catalog), The Gallery (Stratford, Ontario, Canada), 1980.

Ken Nutt: The One-Man Group Show, Woodstock Art Gallery (Woodstock, Ontario, Canada), 1997.

Sidelights

Ken Nutt is a fine artist and an award-winning Canadian illustrator of children's books. He most frequently illustrates under the name Eric Beddows, which combines his middle name and his mother's maiden name. Nutt is known for his black-and-white pencil drawings, which demonstrate "a strong handling of light and shadow, composition and form," according to Julie Corsaro in *Booklist.* Nutt has also opted for a full and brilliant palette in more recent works such as *The Rooster's Gift,* which earned him the Governor General's Award for Illustration from the Canada Council in 1996.

Nutt was born in a small town in the Canadian province of Ontario. He first came into contact with the great works of children's book illustrators through the encyclopedias his parents bought at the local grocery, one volume per week. In these volumes he discovered the

work of Gustave Doré, Arthur Rackham, Rockwell Kent, and William Blake. Nutt found his place in the social hierarchy of school by drawing campaign posters for student-body elections and helping plan the decorations for school dances. After graduating from high school, he attended Toronto's York University for two years, studying painting and drawing, then decided to start his career in the field of art. When friend and writer Tim Wynne-Jones asked him to illustrate a children's book, Nutt realized that he had never even considered the possibility of book illustration. "Oddly," he reported in *Seventh Book of Junior Authors and Illustrators,* "for all my love of the great illustrators of the past, I had never thought of drawing pictures for a book myself."

That situation changed drastically after the success of *Zoom at Sea,* the first book for which Nutt provided pictures. In this story, the playful cat, Zoom, short for Wynne-Jones's family cat Montezuma, won the hearts of critics and, most importantly, young readers. His adventures with his friend Maria, who transforms her home into an ocean so as to fulfill Zoom's sea-loving fantasy, are perfectly complemented by Nutt's pencil drawings, according to numerous reviewers. Award committees added to the favorable response, and Nutt's career as an illustrator looked promising.

Nutt collaborated with Wynne-Jones on all three of the "Zoom" titles, which include *Zoom Away* and *Zoom Upstream.* With *Zoom Away* the feline and Maria go searching for the elusive Uncle Roy at the North Pole—the transformed attic of Maria's house. Mary Lou Budd, writing in *School Library Journal,* noted that the story "captures and keeps the readers' attention from beginning to end with its action-packed narrative and accompanying pencil illustrations." Budd also noted that Nutt's method of shadowing his back-and-white pictures "gives each one a photographic look."

With the final title in the series, *Zoom Upstream,* the fearless feline follows a mysterious trail through a bookshelf to join friend Maria on another search for the illusive Uncle Roy, this time in ancient Egypt. Ilene Cooper wrote in *Booklist* that "Beddows' wonderful pencil illustrations detail the ensuing adventure," going on to call the pictures "wildly imaginative and full of minute particulars." A meticulous researcher, Nutt actually went to Egypt for the last title and spent a great deal of time making his way through tombs and the insides of pyramids. Hhe did his first rough sketches for *Zoom Upstream* while floating down the Nile.

Another fruitful collaboration for Nutt has been with writer Paul Fleischman, with whom he has teamed up on two prize-winning books of poems for children: *I Am Phoenix: Poems for Two Voices,* about birds, and the Newbery Medal-winning *Joyful Noise: Poems for Two Voices,* a book of verses which describe the characteristics of a variety of insects. Nutt has also illustrated Fleischman's *Shadow Play,* about a visit to a county fair by a brother and sister who become entranced by a shadow-puppet-theater presentation of "Beauty and the Beast."

Other noteworthy titles Nutt has illustrated under the name Beddows include *The Emperor's Panda,* about a poor young shepherd boy, Kung, who becomes the emperor of China with the help of the magical Master Panda, and the collection of poems, *Who Shrank My Grandmother's House? Poems of Discovery.* In 1996, Nutt illustrated Pam Conrad's *The Rooster's Gift,* an effort that earned him the prestigious Governor General's Literary Award for Illustration. In Conrad's story, the gift in question is the rising of the sun, for which the crowing rooster takes credit. However, one day, oversleeping, Rooster is surprised and dismayed to discover the sun has risen without his call. In *Publishers Weekly,* a reviewer noted that "Beddows eschews his characteristic black-and-white drawings in favor of dazzling full-color paintings," while Martha V. Parravano, writing in *Horn Book,* commented that "Beddows depicts, in curving lines and soft colors, the changing seasons in the pastoral landscapes rolling out below the chicken coop."

Tor Siedler's story of a foundling kitten that finds a new home with a struggling musician is brought to life through Nutt's detailed drawings.

Michael Cart concluded his *Booklist* review of *The Rooster's Gift* by praising "Beddows' gently humorous treatment of character . . . and impressive command of color and light."

After this great success, Nutt abandoned illustrating for several years. His work was not seen alongside the text of a story again until 2003, when he provided sketches for best-selling science-fiction author Ursula K. Le-Guin's adult short-story collection *Changing Planes.* The next year he lent his artwork to *Toes,* a novel for middle-grades readers by Tor Seidler. The title character is a cat who got his name because he has seven toes on each foot rather than the usual five; Nutt's "small, black-and-white sketches of the cat in different poses begin each chapter," Susan Patron noted in *School Library Journal.*

While as Eric Beddows Nutt has become well known as the illustrator of children's and adult books, he also works as a figurative painter under his real name. As he explained in the *Seventh Book of Junior Authors and Illustrators,* his interests range beyond book illustration. "I like math and physics and building mathematical models," he noted. Another favorite pastime for the illustrator is paleontology and the collection of fossils, with a specialty in invertebrates. However, "no dinosaurs," he added of his collection, noting that one day he would like to illustrate a fossil book with not one dinosaur featured.

Biographical and Critical Sources

BOOKS

Sally Holmes Holtze, editor, *Seventh Book of Junior Authors and Illustrators,* H. W. Wilson (New York, NY), 1996.

PERIODICALS

Booklist, January 1, 1994, Julie Corsaro, review of *Zoom Away,* p. 834; June 1, 1994, Ilene Cooper, review of *Zoom Upstream,* p. 1846; September 15, 1996, Michael Cart, review of *The Rooster's Gift,* pp. 245-246; June 1, 2004, Michael Cart, review of *Toes,* p. 1729.
Children's Book Watch, June, 1993, p. 1.
Emergency Librarian, May-June, 1993, Dave Jenkinson, "Eric Beddows: Award Winning Illustrator," pp. 68-71.
Horn Book, November-December, 1996, Martha V. Parravano, review of *The Rooster's Gift,* pp. 721-722.
Kirkus Reviews, May 15, 2004, review of *Toes,* p. 497.
Library Journal, April 1, 2003, Devon Thomas, review of *Changing Planes,* p. 133.
Publishers Weekly, September 9, 1996, review of *The Rooster's Gift,* pp. 82-83; May 17, 2004, review of *Toes,* p. 51.

Quill and Quire, October, 1985.

School Library Journal, February, 1994, Mary Lou Budd, review of *Zoom Away,* pp. 92-93; August, 1994, Steven Engelfried, review of *Zoom Upstream,* p. 148; December, 1994, Sally Margolis, review of *Teller of Tales,* p. 104; July, 2004, Susan Patron, review of *Toes,* p. 112.

ONLINE

Canadian Children's Book Centre Web site, http:// collections.ic.gc.ca/ (July 27, 2005), "Eric Beddows."

Groundwood Books Web site, http://www.groundwood books.com/ (July 27, 2005), "Eric Beddows."*

P

PARTRIDGE, Benjamin W(aring), Jr. 1915-2005

OBITUARY NOTICE— See index for *SATA* sketch: Born March 9, 1915, in Huntington, WV; died of pneumonia April 12, 2005, in Takoma Park, MD. Naval officer, lawyer, and author. Partridge was a veteran and former attorney for the U.S. Navy who later became an active environmentalist. Graduating from the University of Florida in 1937, he was a deputy commissioner in Florida before enlisting in the U.S. Navy at the beginning of World War II. During the war, he commanded small combat ships in both the European and Pacific theaters. After the war, he earned his law degree at the University of Miami in 1948. When the United States entered the Korean conflict he returned to active duty as a ship's commander. From 1950 until 1968, Partridge was a law specialist for the navy. He then retired from the military and became actively interested in environmental issues. From 1971 until 1974 he was director of state planning in Vermont and chair of the Vermont Environmental Board, specializing in land use and helping to write state law on the subject. He later did similar work for the state of Alaska from 1976 to 1977. His last job was as a consultant for the North Slope Borough of Barrow, Alaska, from 1978 to 1985. In addition to this work, Partridge collaborated on several children's books with his wife, Cora Cheney. Among these are *China Sea Roundup* (1958), *Underseas* (1961), and *Crown of the World: A View of the Inner Arctic* (1979).

OBITUARIES AND OTHER SOURCES:

PERIODICALS

Washington Post, May 7, 2005, p. B7.

ONLINE

JuneauEmpire.com, http://juneauempire.com/ (April 19, 2005).

PHILBRICK, W. R.
See PHILBRICK, (W.) Rodman

* * *

PHILBRICK, (W.) Rodman 1951-
(William R. Dantz, Chris Jordan, W. R. Philbrick)

Personal

Born 1951, in Boston, MA; married Lynn Harnett (a novelist and journalist). *Hobbies and other interests:* Fishing.

Addresses

Home and office—P.O. Box 4149, Portsmouth, NH 03802-4149. *E-mail*—Philbrick@earthlink.net.

Career

Writer, 1987—. Formerly worked as a longshoreman and boat builder.

Awards, Honors

Best Novel award, Private Eye Writers of America, 1993, for *Brothers and Sinners;* Judy Lopez Memorial award honor book, 1994, Nebraska Golden Sower Award, Wyoming Soaring Eagle Award, 1997, California Young Readers Award, Arizona Young Readers Award, Maryland Children's Middle School Book Award, Charlotte Award, New York State Reading Association, Best Young-Adult Book of the Year and Recommended Book for the Young-Adult Reluctant Reader designations, both American Library Association (ALA), all for *Freak the Mighty;* Best Science-Fiction selection, *Voice of Youth Advocates,* 2000, and Best Young-Adult Book of the Year selection, ALA, 2001, both for *The Last Book in the Universe.*

Rodman Philbrick

Writings

NOVELS; FOR YOUNG ADULTS

Freak the Mighty, Blue Sky Press (New York, NY), 1993, published as *The Mighty,* Scholastic (New York, NY), 1997.
The Fire Pony, Scholastic (New York, NY), 1996.
Max the Mighty, Scholastic (New York, NY), 1998.
(With wife, Lynn Harnett) *Abduction,* Scholastic (New York, NY), 1998.
REM World: Where Nothing Is Real and Everything Is about to Disappear, Scholastic (New York, NY), 2000.
The Last Book in the Universe, Scholastic (New York, NY), 2000.
The Journal of Douglas Allen Deeds: The Donner Party Expedition (historical fiction), Scholastic (New York, NY), 2001.
The Young Man and the Sea, Blue Sky Press (New York, NY), 2004.

Philbrick also adapted *Freak the Mighty* as one-and two-act plays.

"HOUSE ON CHERRY STREET" SERIES; FOR YOUNG ADULTS

(With Lynn Harnett) *The Haunting,* Scholastic (New York, NY), 1995.
(With Lynn Harnett) *The Horror,* Scholastic (New York, NY), 1995.
(With Lynn Harnett) *The Final Nightmare,* Scholastic (New York, NY), 1995.

"VISITORS" SERIES; FOR YOUNG ADULTS

(With Lynn Harnett) *Strange Invaders,* Scholastic (New York, NY), 1997.
(With Lynn Harnett) *Things,* Scholastic (New York, NY), 1997.
(With Lynn Harnett) *Brain Stealers,* Scholastic (New York, NY), 1997.

"WEREWOLF CHRONICLES" SERIES; FOR YOUNG ADULTS

Night Creature, Scholastic (New York, NY), 1996.
Children of the Wolf, Scholastic (New York, NY), 1996.
The Wereing, Scholastic (New York, NY), 1996.

FOR ADULTS

Brothers and Sinners, Dutton (New York, NY), 1993.
Dark Matter, Xlibris (Philadelphia, PA), 2000.
Coffins, Forge (New York, NY), 2002.

MYSTERY NOVELS; UNDER PSEUDONYM W. R. PHILBRICK; FOR ADULTS

Shooting Star, St. Martin's Press (New York, NY), 1982.
Slow Dancer: A Connie Kale Investigation, St. Martin's Press (New York, NY), 1984.
Shadow Kills: A J. D. Hawkins Mystery, Beaufort (New York, NY), 1985.
Ice for the Eskimo: A J. D. Hawkins Mystery, Beaufort (New York, NY), 1986.
The Neon Flamingo: A T. D. Stash Crime Adventure, New American Library (New York, NY), 1987.
The Crystal Blue Persuasion: A T. D. Stash Crime Adventure, New American Library (New York, NY), 1988.
Tough Enough: A T. D. Stash Crime Adventure, New American Library (New York, NY), 1989.
Paint It Black: A J. D. Hawkins Mystery, St. Martin's Press (New York, NY), 1989.
The Big Chip, illustrated by Bruce Jensen, Microsoft Press (Redmond, WA), 1990.
Walk on the Water: A J. D. Hawkins Mystery, St. Martin's Press (New York, NY), 1991.

UNDER PSEUDONYM WILLIAM R. DANTZ

Pulse, Avon (New York, NY), 1990.
The Seventh Sleeper, Morrow (New York, NY), 1991.
Hunger, Tor (New York, NY), 1992.
Nine Levels Down, Forge (New York, NY), 1999.

Author of unproduced screenplays *The Fire Pony, Stop Time,* and *Nine Levels Down,* based on his novels.

Adaptations

The motion picture *The Mighty* was adapted from Philbrick's novel *Freak the Mighty* and produced by Miramax, 1998.

Work in Progress

The True Tales of Homer Figg, a young-adult novel set during the U.S. Civil War; *Taken,* an adult thriller to be published in 2006 under the pseudonym Chris Jordan.

Sidelights

Rodman Philbrick, a screenwriter as well as a novelist, started his career as an author of adult thrillers before shifting his interest to young-adult fiction. Gaining national accolades for his debut novel for teen readers, *Freak the Mighty,* Philbrick has gone on to lead a double life, continuing to pen adult mysteries while also adding to the body of fiction available to younger readers, sometimes in collaboration with his wife, journalist and author Lynn Harnett. Among Philbrick's novels for teens are *The Fire Pony, The Last Book in the Universe,* and *The Young Man and the Sea,* while his works for adults include *Dark Matter* and *Brothers and Sinners,* the latter a winner of the Private Eye Writers of America's best novel award in 1993.

Born in Boston, Massachusetts, Philbrick grew up close to the New England coast, where one of his hobbies, fishing, is a prominent regional industry. Although he had completed a novel-length work by the time he was in high school, adulthood for Philbrick meant focusing on the day-to-day necessities of earning a living. Drawing his livelihood from the sea in traditional New England fashion, he worked as both a longshoreman and a boat builder, but still found enough time to complete several novels. Unfortunately those works were not accepted for publication. In 1982, however, the author made his literary debut with *Shooting Star,* published under the name W. R. Philbrick.

Philbrick's *Slow Dancer,* the first of two novels featuring female sleuth Connie Kale, was released two years later, and by 1987 the writer had left his other occupations behind to devote himself to novel-writing full time. Working out the twists and turns of plots to mysteries and detective novels now became his stock in trade, with some of his work published under the pseudonym William R. Dantz. The prolific Philbrick would write more than a dozen mystery novels for adults before moving into the young-adult market in the early 1990s.

The move from adult whodunits to teen fiction happened, as Philbrick recalled, "more or less by accident." It was inspired by a boy from his own neighborhood, the novelist once explained. "I used to see two kids walking down the street near our apartment. One of them was a big guy and he sometimes carried the small kid on his shoulders. Later my wife and I became friends with the small boy's mother. We discovered that the small boy had Morquio Syndrome, which meant he would never grow to be more than three feet tall. He was extraordinarily bright, had a love for words and books, and an interest in sci-fi and Arthurian legends. About a year after his tragic death, I got an idea for a

Philbrick's 1993 novel about the power of friendship captivated readers with its unusual and inspiring tale and was eventually adapted as a feature film. (Cover illustration by David Shannon.)

story inspired by his very special personality. The story is fiction, but I never would have written it if I hadn't known the boy himself."

Inspired by the imagination and courage of his young neighbor, Philbrick penned *Freak the Mighty,* an award-winning work that has been translated into numerous languages and is read in classrooms throughout the world. The novel is described by *School Library Journal* contributor Libby K. White as "a wonderful story of triumph over imperfection, shame, and loss." In the book middle-school narrator Maxwell Kane feels doubly cursed. Not only is he clumsy, big boned, and condemned to an academic life of torment as a learning-disabled kid, but his dad is in prison for killing Maxwell's mom and the whole town knows about it. A loner, he spends much of his time in his room in the basement of his grandparents' house. Then something happens to change the dull despair of each passing day: a new boy moves in next door whom Max recognizes from his day-care days. The new boy, Kevin, is wheelchair-bound due to a birth defect that has prevented him from growing physically; however, he has an imagination and an energy that allow him to soar mentally. Soon Max and "Freak"—Kevin's name for himself—are the best of friends. With Kevin sitting astride Max's broad shoulders, the two dub their joint self "Freak the Mighty," channeling the one's strength and the other's intelligence to confront the taunting of other children and get out and explore the world. Caught up in the legend of King Arthur and his noble knights, the two boys search for causes to battle, one of which proves scary: "Killer" Kane returns and kidnaps Max, who escapes only with Kevin's help. Sadly, the effects of Morquio Syndrome begin to overtake Kevin, and he finally dies. Left to continue on his own, Max "is left with the memory of an extraordinary relationship," as well as a heightened sense of his own worth and a more optimistic outlook on his future, according to White.

The winner of numerous awards, *Freak the Mighty* has been lauded by reviewers for its sensitivity and ability to appeal to more reluctant readers. *Bulletin of the Center for Children's Books* reviewer Deborah Stevenson praised Philbrick's novel as "a sentimental story written with energy and goofy humor instead of sentimentality," while *Horn Book,* contributor Nancy Vasilakis called the novel "a fascinating excursion into the lives of people whose freakishness proves to be a thin cover for their very human existence." Stephanie Zvirin, meanwhile, labeled it "both riveting and poignant, with solid characters, brisk pacing, and even a little humor to carry us along" in her *Booklist* review.

In addition to inspiring a feature film, *Freak the Mighty* also sparked a sequel, *Max the Mighty,* which was published in 1998. Reuniting with narrator Max Kane now that he is on his own, readers are introduced to Max's new friend, Rachel, a pre-teen who has escaped so far into her hobby of reading that fellow students now refer to her as the "Worm." What prompts Rachel's reading is her need to mentally escape from the abusive household in which she has found herself since her Mom's remarriage. Unfortunately, books cannot save her from her unstable stepdad, dubbed the "Undertaker" because of his creepy demeanor. The much older Max, now aged fourteen, eventually agrees to help Rachel run away and find her real father. On their way to Chivalry, Montana, in search of Rachel's real dad, the pair encounter a colorful cast of characters ranging from wild dogs to con artists, and have numerous adventures, all the while trying to elude both the Undertaker, who follows in pursuit, and the police, who are hunting Max in response to the kidnapping charges filed by Rachel's stepfather.

Noting that the ending of *Max the Mighty* is filled with "surprises" and is "more upbeat" than Philbrick's previous YA novel, a *Publishers Weekly* reviewer called the book a "rip-roaring, heartwarming escapade." Although Nancy Vasilakis noted that several of the story's zany characters "sometimes threaten to stretch the reader's sense of reality to its limits," she concluded in her *Horn Book* review that Max and Rachel "grab our attention and engage your heart."

Fire Pony also uses Montana as its setting and features a young man as its narrator. In the story, half-brothers Joe and Roy Dilly are on their own, having fled from ranch to ranch after the habits of arsonist Joe put an end to job after job. Now Joe has found work at the Bar None Ranch, where the owner, Nick Jessup, raises Arabian horses. The older of the two brothers, Joe has a talent for both blacksmithing and saddle-breaking horses and soon becomes a prized employee. Meanwhile, eleven-year-old Roy, while remaining concerned that his older brother's fascination with fire will ultimately force the two to go on the run again, begins to settle in at the ranch. Trying to follow in Joe's footsteps, he attempts to break a palomino filly named Lady Luck, which Jessup has promised to Roy if he is successful. Ultimately, Roy rides Lady Luck to glory at a rodeo, despite the efforts of another man named Mullins to thwart the boy's success and get the horse for himself. Older brother Joe, angered at Mullins, first accosts the man, then goes into a hay field and sets a fire which quickly grows out of control and ultimately threatens the life of Roy and Lady Luck.

Noting the complex personalities of the two brothers, *Horn Book* contributor Martha V. Parravano commented

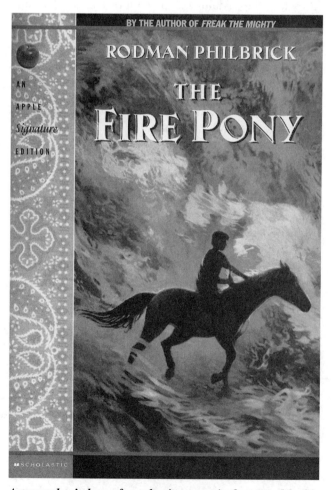

A young boy's love of a palomino pony is threatened by his older brother's compulsion for setting destructive fires in this 1997 novel. (Cover illustration by John Thompson.)

that Philbrick's portrait of "the scarred but spirited Roy is near flawless"; likewise, Joe is "loving and funny and talented even as he is scary and unpredictable and disturbed." Praising Joe's rescue effort as the high point of the novel, *School Library Journal* contributor Christina Linz noted that *The Fire Pony* "has plenty of action and suspense and is a good choice for reluctant readers."

"The idea for *The Fire Pony* came while Lynn and I were driving across the Southwest," Philbrick once explained. "I loved the landscape, and when we got to California the state was suffering from a rash of fires. The two ideas combined into a story about a boy and his older brother, who is not only a talented farrier, but a sometimes arsonist. The idea from that part may have been inspired by my love of Faulkner, in particular his story 'The Barn Burner.'"

While *The Fire Pony, Freak the Mighty,* and its sequel are very "issue-oriented" novels—learning disabilities, single parenting, and family violence are just a few of the subjects covered—Philbrick's more recent books for younger readers, particularly those written with his wife, Lynn Harnett, are fun reads which also contain a salting of typical teen concerns in their plots. Because of the fast-paced action and the relatively simple vocabulary in such books as *The Haunting, Abduction,* and *Children of the Wolf,* they have been praised for their ability to motivate even reluctant readers to turn the page and see what happens next. Part of their success may be credited to Philbrick and Harnett's ability to devise a system of working together that seems to work well. As Philbrick explained, "Lynn and I discuss story ideas. Then I write an outline and Lynn does all the heavy lifting, writing the first draft of the chapters. After more discussion we polish up a finished draft."

"I don't have any 'lessons' in mind when I write about adolescent kids," Philbrick explained in response to a question regarding his opinion on the importance of inserting a "message" in books for young adult readers. "Most of what I write, and the first person 'voice' I use, comes out of my own memories of being that age. The books Lynn Harnett and I collaborate on are intended to be easy-reading mass market paperbacks. My own work might be considered slightly more 'serious,' but, I hope, still entertaining enough to hold a reader's attention. For the most part I find that all young readers really want is a good story, of whatever type." However, Philbrick also expressed delight that the techniques he uses in creating his adult mysteries—"how to keep a reader turning pages to find out what happens next," for example—have been of value in his YA projects.

Philbrick returned to solo projects with *The Last Book in the Universe* and *REM World: Where Nothing Is Real and Everything Is about to Disappear.* In the latter novel ten-year-old Arthur Woodbury has a weight problem that makes him the object of his classmates' jokes. He buys a weight-loss device from the REM World Products company, which promises that the contraption

"A FAST AND FURIOUS JOURNEY" — *BOOKLIST*

A new weight-loss product promises to slim Arthur down while he sleeps, but when he neglects to follow the directions the teen unleashes an evil that might destroy the universe. (Cover illustration by Greg Call.)

will help him slim down while he sleeps. However, Arthur does not follow the instructions for the new gadget properly, and is instead transported to REM world, with little hope of getting back home. Arthur's arrival in REM world also disrupts the laws of the magical universe, placing its existence in jeopardy. In order to save the REM universe and return to his own world, Arthur embarks on a series of adventures involving a diverse group of fantastic creatures. With the help of these beings, Arthur is able to accomplish his twin goals, and in the process loses weight and develops courage. A *Publishers Weekly* reviewer praised the novel, noting that its "imaginative characters" make it a "fun and fast-paced read." *School Library Journal* reviewer Nina Lindsay found the plot a bit thin, but praised the book for its "action-packed, cliff-hanging chapters."

The Last Book in the Universe is a science-fiction novel set in a dystopic future, where civilization as we know it has been destroyed by a major earthquake. A few people have created a new, better, isolated society called "Eden"; the unlucky remainder face deadly pollution and rule by brutal gangs. Many of those who live in the

"Urbs," as the non-Eden part of the world is known, escape from reality through virtual-reality movies inserted directly into their brains via mind probes. The book's protagonist, Spaz, does not have this option—his epilepsy (the source of his nickname) prevents him from using them. A reluctant gang member, Spaz ends up befriending an old man named Ryter whom the teen was sent to rob, and together the two set out on a quest to save Spaz's critically ill foster sister, Bean. Their party picks up several other members along the way, including Lanaya, a resident of Eden; and Little Face, an orphan.

"Philbrick has created some memorable characters in this fast-paced adventure," Debbie Carton declared in *Booklist,* adding that *The Last Book in the Universe* "will leave readers musing over humanity's future." *School Library Journal* reviewer Louise L. Sherman also noted the "strong and provocative messages" in the book, while *Kliatt* contributor Paula Rohrlick thought that "Spaz's adventures and moral dilemmas in a strange and scary setting, vividly told from his viewpoint, make this an absorbing story with some depth to it." A *Publishers Weekly* critic praised other aspects of *The Last Book in the Universe,* noting that "Philbrick's creation of a futuristic dialect, combined with striking descriptions of a postmodern civilization, will convincingly transport readers to Spaz's world."

Philbrick branched out into historical fiction with *The Journal of Douglas Allen Deeds: The Donner Party Expedition.* While Douglas Allen Deeds was an actual member of the Donner Party, the infamous group of pioneers who were stranded in the Sierra Nevada mountains during the winter of 1846-47, the diary Philbrick creates for the fifteen-year-old orphan is fictionalized. Philbrick relates the well-known calamities that struck the party, including illness, starvation, and eventually cannibalism, but he also "show[s] the changes in people brought about by incredible hardships," Lana Mills wrote in *School Library Journal.* The author generally "shows the action rather than merely telling about it," Kay Weisman commented in *Booklist,* with the exception of the incidents of cannibalism—Deeds, disgusted at the thought, heads off into the forest so that he will not have to watch while the others "take advantage of what has been provided."

The Young Man and the Sea is "a rousing sea adventure with plenty of heart," Peter D. Sieruta declared in *Horn Book.* The young man of the title is Skiff Beaman, a twelve-year-old resident of the Maine coast. Skiff's mother has recently died, and his father, formerly a fisherman, now spends all of his time watching TV and drinking, while his neglected boat finally sinks next to the dock. Skiff makes raising and repairing the *Mary Rose* his mission, but fixing the waterlogged engine will cost over 5,000 dollars. The quickest way to make that much money is by catching just one of the massive, prized bluefin tuna that live in the ocean off Maine, so Skiff sets off in a tiny boat, seeking one of the 900-pound fish.

Skiff's hunting of the tuna is related "in a 70-plus-page action sequence that inspires awe for both man and nature," noted a *Publishers Weekly* reviewer. Philbrick's "excellent maritime bildungsroman has all of the makings of a juvenile classic," Jeffrey Hastings wrote in *School Library Journal,* citing the novel's "wide-open adventure, heart-pounding suspense, and just the right amount of tear-jerking pathos."

The Young Man and the Sea has clear parallels to early twentieth-century writer Ernest Hemingway's classic *The Old Man and the Sea,* including its spare language and reliance on inner dialogue. "I haven't read the Hemingway story since I was in high school," Philbrick told *Journal of Adolescent and Adult Literacy* interviewer James Blasingame, "but obviously it made a big impression."

As a writer, Philbrick remains constantly busy, reserving his mornings for his craft, and rewarding himself with a chance to go fishing in the afternoon. A voracious reader for many years, he counts among his favorite authors suspense novelist Elmore Leonard, as well as writers Mark Twain and Joseph Conrad. Perhaps because of his roots in the seafaring culture of the New England shoreline, Philbrick also enjoys the sea-going fiction of Patrick O'Brien. He and his wife divide their time between their home in Maine and the Florida Keys.

Biographical and Critical Sources

BOOKS

Philbrick, Rodman, *The Journal of Douglas Allen Deeds: The Donner Party Expedition,* Scholastic (New York, NY), 2001.

PERIODICALS

ALAN Review, winter, 1999; winter, 2001, Rodman Philbrick, "Listening to Kids in America," pp. 13 16.
Booklist, December 15, 1993, Stephanie Zvirin, review of *Freak the Mighty,* p. 748; June 1, 1998, Susan Dove Lempke, review of *Max the Mighty,* pp. 1749-1750; December 15, 1998, Ilene Cooper, review of *Freak the Mighty,* p. 751; May 1, 2000, review of *REM World: Where Nothing Is Real and Everything Is about to Disappear,* p. 1670; November 15, 2000, Debbie Carton, review of *The Last Book in the Universe,* p. 636; August, 2001, Anna Rich, review of *The Last Book in the Universe,* p. 2142; January 1, 2002, Kay Weisman, review of *The Journal of Douglas Alan Deeds: The Donner Party Expedition,* p. 859; March 15, 2005, Patricia Austin, review of *The Young Man and the Sea,* p. 1313.
Bulletin of the Center for Children's Books, January, 1994, Deborah Stevenson, review of *Freak the Mighty,* p. 165; July-August, 1996, p. 383; April, 1998, Debo-

rah Stevenson, review of *Max the Mighty,* p. 291; March, 2004, Elizabeth Bush, review of *The Young Man and the Sea,* p. 291.

Childhood Education, winter, 2000, Barbara F. Backer, review of *REM World,* p. 109.

Horn Book, January-February, 1994, Nancy Vasilakis, review of *Freak the Mighty,* p. 74; July-August, 1996, Martha V. Parravano, review of *The Fire Pony,* p. 464; July-August, 1998, Nancy Vasilakis, review of *Max the Mighty,* p. 495. review of *Freak the Mighty,* p. 165; March-April, 2004, Peter D. Sieruta, review of *The Young Man and the Sea,* p. 187.

Journal of Adolescent and Adult Literacy, March, 2004, James Blasingame, interview with Philbrick, p. 518.

Kirkus Reviews, February 15, 1998, review of *Max the Mighty,* p. 272; January 15, 2004, review of *The Young Man and the Sea,* p. 87.

Kliatt, March, 1999, review of *Abduction,* p. 26; May, 2002, Paula Rohrlick, review of *The Last Book in the Universe,* p. 29; January, 2004, Claire Rosser, review of *The Young Man and the Sea,* p. 12.

New Yorker, December 13, 1993, pp. 115-116.

Publishers Weekly, January 26, 1998, review of *Max the Mighty,* p. 91; March 27, 2000, review of *REM World,* p. 81; November 27, 2000, review of *The Last Book in the Universe,* p. 77; January 14, 2002, review of *Coffins,* p. 46; February 16, 2004, review of *The Young Man and the Sea,* p. 173.

School Library Journal, December, 1993, Libby K. White, review of *Freak the Mighty,* p. 137; September, 1996, Christina Linz, review of *The Fire Pony,* p. 206; April, 1998, Marilyn Payne Phillips, review of *Max the Mighty,* p. 136; July, 1998, Brian E. Wilson, review of *Freak the Mighty,* p. 56; May, 2000, Nina Lindsay, review of *REM World,* p. 175; November, 2000, Susan L. Rogers, review of *The Last Book in the Universe,* p. 160; July, 2001, Louise L. Sherman, review of *The Last Book in the Universe,* p. 60; December, 2001, Lana Miles, review of *The Journal of Douglas Allen Deeds,* p. 142; February, 2004, Jeffrey Hastings, review of *The Young Man and the Sea,* p. 152; October, 2004, review of *The Young Man and the Sea,* p. 54; April, 2005, Larry Cooperman, review of *The Young Man and the Sea,* p. 76.

Voice of Youth Advocates, April, 1994, p. 30; October, 1996, p. 212; June, 1998, p. 124.

ONLINE

Rodman Philbrick Web site, http://www.rodmanphilbrick.com (July 6, 2005).

SeacoastNH.com, http://www.seacoastnh.com/ (1999), interview with Philbrick.

TeensPoint.org, http://www.teenspoint.org/ (May 17, 2005), Scott Phillips, "Rodman Philbrick: The Writing Life."

*   *   *

POW, Tom 1950-

Personal

Born May 25, 1950, in Edinburgh, Scotland; son of Tom (an artist) and Agnes Fyffe (a teacher; maiden name, Black) Pow; married Juliette Mary Cross Smith (a drama teacher), September 4, 1990; children: Cameron, Jenny. *Education:* University of St. Andrews, M.A. (with honors), 1972; attended Aberdeen College of Education, 1972-73.

Addresses

Home—Springfield, 29 Rosemount St., Dumfries DG2 7AF, Scotland. *Office*—University of Glasgow, Crichton Campus, Room 225, Rutherford Building, Dumfries DG1 4ZL, Scotland. *E-mail*—t.pow@crichton.gla.ac.uk.

Career

Educator and author. Dumfries Academy, Dumfries, Scotland, assistant principal and English teacher; writer. *In Verse* (television program), interviewer; Dumfries and Galloway Arts Festival, co-founder; Cacafeugo Press, co-founder. Glasgow University, Crichton Campus, Dumfries, senior lecturer and head of creative and cultural studies, 2000—. Writer-in-residence, Edinburgh International Book Festival, 2001-03

Member

Scotch Malt Whiskey Association.

Awards, Honors

Scottish Arts Council Book Award, 1987, for *Rough Seas,* and 2004, for *Landscapes and Legacies;* Scottish Arts Council writer's bursary, 1988, 1997, 2003; Saltire Society Scottish Book of the Year Award, and Scottish Arts Council Book Award, both 1990, both for *The Moth Trap;* TESS Educational Publications Award, 1995, for *Shouting It Out: Stories from Contemporary Scotland;* Scottish Arts Council Children's Book of the Year Award, 2001, for *Who Is the World For?;* Hawthornden fellowship, 2002.

Writings

An Edinburgh Portrait (poetry), privately printed (Dumfries, Scotland), 1984.

The Moth Trap (poetry), illustrated by Jonathan Gibbs, Canongate (Edinburgh, Scotland), 1990.

In the Palace of Serpents: An Experience of Peru, Canongate (Edinburgh, Scotland), 1992.

National Poetry Day, 6 October 1994, Readiscovery (Edinburgh, Scotland), 1994.

(Editor) *Shouting It Out: Stories from Contemporary Scotland,* Hodder & Stoughton (London, England), 1995.

Red Letter Day (poetry), Bloodaxe Books (Newcastle upon Tyne, England), 1996.

Landscapes: A Sequence of Poems, illustrated by Hugh Bryden, Cacafuego Press (Dumfries, Scotland), 1999.

(Author of introduction) Donald MacIntosh, *Travels in Galloway,* Neil Wilson (Glasgow, Scotland), 1999.

Who Is the World For?, illustrated by Robert Ingpen, Candlewick Press (Cambridge, MA), 2000.

Callum's Big Day, illustrated by Mairi Hedderwick, Inyx (Aberdour, Fife, Scotland), 2001.

Landscapes and Legacies, Iynx (Aberdour, Fife, Scotland), 2003.

Scabbit Isle (stories), Corgi (London, England), 2003.

Tell Me One Thing, Dad, illustrated by Ian Andrew, Candlewick Press (Cambridge, MA), 2004.

The Pack (young-adult novel), Definitions (London, England)2004.

Author's works have been translated into several languages, including Italian, German, Chinese, Japanese, and Welsh.

Sidelights

Scottish writer Tom Pow has distinguished himself as a poet and playwright, in addition to being a senior lecturer in English at the University of Glasgow. Pow, whose work has been honored with awards and fellowships, has also turned his focus to children's books in 1997. As he explained on *ContemporaryWriters.com:* "Poetry has been, since the age of eighteen, how I explore what it means for me to be alive. It is my way of being in the world. However, if poetry has given me my most intense experience of language, I have also enjoyed the different challenges of a range of other genres—from picture books to art books." Pow's titles for younger readers include *Tell Me One Thing, Dad* and *Who Is the World For?*

In *Tell Me One Thing, Dad* Pow explores the love between a parent and child. As young Molly prepares for bed one evening she asks her father a series of questions about various creatures and their love for their offspring. "The familiar picture-book emotion—the love a parent feels for a child—gets new life in this wonderfully illustrated offering," commented Ilene Cooper in *Booklist.* A *Publishers Weekly* critic also enjoyed the book, stating that "The magical rapport between fathers and their young daughters takes wonderful form in Pow's text, . . . and the lighthearted imagination of [Ian] Andrew's crisply outlined, muted-tone watercolors."

In *Who Is the World For?* a young boy's father explains that Earth was created not just for one species, but for all. Once again set against soft, double-page watercolor illustrations, Pow's text presents young children with a thought-provoking work: a "gentle ode" reflecting "the understanding that nature is . . . a resource to respect, not exploit," according to Lynne T. Burke in a review for *Reading Today.* Shelley Townsend-Hudson noted in *Booklist* that Robert Ingpen's "naturalistic illustrations have a texture and glowing golden light that are ideal for this lovely poem, which asks us to slow down, ponder the imagery, and savor time together." A *Publishers Weekly* critic also enjoyed Pow's book, commenting that "the visual cadence of Ingpen's artwork reflects the graceful nuances of the text" and dubbing *Who Is the World For?* "a lovely book with a subtle environmental message."

Biographical and Critical Sources

PERIODICALS

Booklist, December 15, 2000, Shelley Townsend-Hudson, review of *Who Is the World For?,* p. 829; April 1, 2004, Ilene Cooper, review of *Tell Me One Thing, Dad,* p. 1365.

Publishers Weekly, October 30, 2000, review of *Who Is the World For?,* p. 75; May 3, 2004, review of *Tell Me One Thing, Dad,* p. 190.

Reading Today, June, 2001, Lynne T. Burke review of *Who Is the World For?,* p. 32.

School Library Journal, January, 2001, Wendy Lukehart, review of *Who Is the World For?,* p. 107; June, 2004, Jane Barrer, review of *Tell Me One Thing, Dad,* p. 116.

ONLINE

Contemporary Writers Web site, http://www.contemporary-writers.com/(July 6, 2005), "Tom Pow."

University of Glasgow Web site, http://www.cc.gla.ac.uk/ (July 6, 2005).

R

RACZKA, Bob 1963-

Personal

Born August 24, 1963, in Chicago, IL; married June 6, 1987; wife's name Amy (a home economist); children: Robert, Carl, Emma. *Education:* University of Illinois at Urbana/Champaign, B.F.A., 1985.

Addresses

Home—488 Longfellow Ave., Glen Ellyn, IL 60137. *E-mail*—bob.raczka@ogilvy.com.

Career

Writer. Bish Creative Display, Northfield, IL, designer, 1985-87; Sears & Roebuck, Chicago, IL, copywriter, 1987; Hoffman York & Compton, Milwaukee, WI, copywriter, 1987-91; Ogilvy Chicago, Chicago, IL, creative director and writer, beginning 1991.

Member

Society of Children's Book Writers and Illustrators.

Writings

No One Saw: Ordinary Things through the Eyes of an Artist, Millbrook Press (Brookfield, CT), 2002.
More than Meets the Eye: Seeing Art with All Five Senses, Millbrook Press (Brookfield, CT), 2003.
Art Is . . . , Millbrook Press (Brookfield, CT), 2003.
Here's Looking at Me: How Artists See Themselves, Millbrook Press (Minneapolis, MN), 2006.
Unlikely Pairs: Fun with Famous Works of Art, Millbrook Press (Minneapolis, MN), 2005.

Work in Progress

3-D ABC: A Sculptural Alphabet, for Millbrook Press, 2006. *Where in the World: Around the Globe in Fourteen Works of Art,* for Millbrook Press, 2007.

Sidelights

Having established his career as a copywriter and creative director at a Chicago-based advertising agency, Bob Raczka now shares his enthusiasm for fine art through books and talks with younger children. In *More than Meets the Eye: Seeing Art with All Five Senses,* for example, he "stimulates an awareness of the breadth and diversity of art," according to Lynda Ritterman in *School Library Journal.* In the book Raczka encourages children to experience a work of art with all their senses, thereby gaining exposure to the many dimensions of creativity contained in a single work. He also pairs brief biographies of the artists with each work discussed, to provide a fuller context for study. Carolyn Phelan, reviewing *More than Meets the Eye* for *Booklist,* commented that "Raczka's short, rhyming text gives structure to the book, but the color reproductions of well-chosen, vivid paintings steal the show" in a book containing "a simple concept, beautifully executed."

Raczka's *No One Saw: Ordinary Things through the Eyes of an Artist* also focuses on art, this time explaining what each of a number of individual artists are known for. *Booklist* reviewer Gillian Engberg enjoyed the book, commenting that Raczka "gets to the heart of what artists do: create unique perspectives of the world." *School Library Journal* reviewer Rosalyn Pierini also found the book unique, writing that in *No One Saw* "the singularity of artistic vision is celebrated in [Raczka's] . . . gentle text."

Raczka told *Something about the Author:* "I have always been a creative person. As a child I loved to draw and make models, and I took numerous art and writing classes in school. I studied art and advertising in college and ended up becoming an advertising writer. However, after ten years in advertising I needed a more personally fulfilling creative outlet, so I decided to try writing children's books, a field that had always impressed me with its literary and artistic talent. It took me five years to sell my first manuscript, but in the process I also found my niche: creating books that help kids to better appreciate art.

"Writing books for children is the most rewarding thing I have ever done, and I hope to build upon the small success I've had so far."

Biographical and Critical Sources

PERIODICALS

Booklist, January 1, 2002, Gillian Engberg, review of *No One Saw: Ordinary Things through the Eyes of an Artist,* p. 861; November 1, 2003, Carolyn Phelan, review of *More than Meets the Eye: Seeing Art with All Five Senses,* p. 513.

Kirkus Reviews, November 1, 2003, review of *More than Meets the Eye,* p. 1313.

School Arts, February, 2003, Ken Marantz, review of *No One Saw,* p. 58.

School Library Journal, January, 2002, Rosalyn Pierini, review of *No One Saw,* p. 123; October, 2003, Laurie Edwards, review of *Art Is . . . ,* p. 156; January, 2004, Lynda Ritterman, review of *More than Meets the Eye,* p. 121.

ONLINE

Society of Children's Book Authors and Illustrators Illinois Web site, http://www.scbwi-illinois.org/ (July 6, 2005), "Bob Raczca."

* * *

RYDER, Joanne (Rose) 1946-

Personal

Born September 16, 1946, in Lake Hiawatha, NJ; daughter of Raymond (a chemist) and Dorothy (a homemaker; maiden name, McGaffney) Ryder; married Laurence Yep (an author). *Education:* Marquette University, B.A. (journalism), 1968; graduate study at University of Chicago, 1968-69. *Hobbies and other interests:* "Travel, gardening and flower arranging, reading and listening to poetry, working and playing with puppets, and hiking through woods and parks and by the sea."

Addresses

Home—Pacific Grove, CA. *Agent*—c/o William Morrow, 1350 Avenue of the Americas, New York, NY 10019.

Career

Harper and Row Publishers, Inc., New York, NY, editor of children's books, 1970-80; full-time writer, 1980—. Lecturer at schools and conferences. Docent at San Francisco Zoo.

Member

Society of Children's Book Writers and Illustrators, California Academy of Sciences, San Francisco Zoological Society.

Awards, Honors

Children's Book Showcase selection, 1977, for *Simon Underground;* New Jersey Author's Award, New Jersey Institute of Technology, 1978, for *Fireflies,* and 1980, for *Fog in the Meadow* and *Snail in the Woods;* Outstanding Science Trade Book of the Year designation, National Science Teachers Association (NSTA), 1979, and Children's Choice Book honor, Children's Book Council/International Reading Association, 1980, both for *Fog in the Meadow;* Parents Choice designation, *Parents'* magazine, and New York Academy of Sciences Children's Science Book Award in younger category, both 1982, and Golden Sower Award nomination, Nebraska Library Association, 1984, all for *The Snail's Spell;* Outstanding Book of the Year designation, National Council of Teachers of English, and Outstanding Science Trade Book of the Year designation, NSTA, both 1985, and Outstanding Book of the Year designation, Bank Street School, all for *Inside Turtle's Shell, and Other Poems of the Field;* Outstanding Science Trade Book designation, NSTA, and Children's Book Medal, Commonwealth Club of Northern California, both 1988, both for *Step into the Night;* Outstanding Science Trade Book designation, NSTA, 1989, for *Where Butterflies Grow;* Eva L. Gordon Award for Excellence in Writing for Children, American Nature Study Society, 1995, for body of work; Favorite Book Contest winner, Aspen School (Los Alamos, NM), 1996, for *The Bear on the Moon;* Black-eyed Susan Award nomination, Maryland Education Media Organization, 1996, for *Without Words;* Pick of the Lists designation, American Booksellers Association, 1997, for *Night Gliders;* Henry Bergh Award for Children's Poetry, American Society for the Prevention of Cruelty to Animals, 2000, for *Each Living Thing;* Best Book citation, *Parents'* magazine, 2004, for *Won't You Be My Kissaroo?*

Writings

FOR CHILDREN

Simon Underground, illustrated by John Schoenherr, Harper (New York, NY), 1976.

A Wet and Sandy Day, illustrated by Donald Carrick, Harper (New York, NY), 1977.

Fireflies, illustrated by Don Bolognese, Harper (New York, NY), 1977.

Fog in the Meadow, illustrated by Gail Owens, Harper (New York, NY), 1979.

(With Harold S. Feinberg) *Snail in the Woods,* illustrated by Jo Polseno, Harper (New York, NY), 1979.

The Spider's Dance, illustrated by Robert Blake, Harper (New York, NY), 1981.

Beach Party, illustrated by Diane Stanley, Frederick Warne (New York, NY), 1982.

The Snail's Spell, illustrated by Lynne Cherry, Frederick Warne (New York, NY), 1982.

The Incredible Space Machines, illustrated by Gerry Daly, Random House (New York, NY), 1982.

C-3PO's Book about Robots, illustrated by John Gampert, Random House (New York, NY), 1983.

The Evening Walk, illustrated by Julie Durrell, Western Publishing (Racine, WI), 1985.

Inside Turtle's Shell, and Other Poems of the Field, illustrated by Susan Bonners, Macmillan (New York, NY), 1985.

The Night Flight, illustrated by Amy Schwartz, Four Winds Press (New York, NY), 1985.

Old Friends, New Friends, illustrated by Jane Chambless-Rigie, Western Publishing (Racine, WI), 1986.

Animals in the Woods, illustrated by Lisa Bonforte, Western Publishing (Racine, WI), 1987, published as *Animals in the Wild,* 1989.

Chipmunk Song, illustrated by Lynne Cherry, Lodestar, 1987.

My Little Golden Book about Cats, illustrated by Dora Leder, Western Publishing (Racine, WI), 1988.

Puppies Are Special Friends, illustrated by James Spence, Western Publishing (Racine, WI), 1988.

Under the Moon: Just Right for 3's and 4's, illustrated by Cheryl Harness, Random House (New York, NY), 1989.

Where Butterflies Grow, illustrated by Lynne Cherry, Lodestar, 1989.

The Bear on the Moon, illustrated by Carol Lacey, Morrow (New York, NY), 1991.

Hello, Tree!, illustrated by Michael Hays, Lodestar, 1991.

When the Woods Hum, illustrated by Catherine Stock, Morrow (New York, NY), 1991.

Dancers in the Garden, illustrations by Judith Lopez, Sierra Club (San Francisco, CA), 1992.

Turtle Time, illustrated by Julie Downing, Knopf (New York, NY), 1992.

The Goodbye Walk, illustrated by Deborah Haeffele, Lodestar, 1993.

One Small Fish, illustrated by Carol Schwartz, Morrow (New York, NY), 1993.

My Father's Hands, illustrated by Mark Graham, Morrow (New York, NY), 1994.

A House by the Sea, illustrated by Melissa Sweet, Morrow (New York, NY), 1994.

Without Words (poems), photographs by Barbara Sonneborn, Sierra Club Books for Children (San Francisco, CA), 1995.

Bears out There, illustrated by Jo Ellen McAllister-Stammen, Atheneum (New York, NY), 1995.

Night Gliders, illustrated by Melissa Bay Mathias, Bridge-Water Books (Mahwah, NJ), 1996.

Earthdance, illustrated by Norman Gorbaty, Holt (New York, NY), 1996.

Winter White, illustrated by Carol Lacey, Morrow (New York, NY), 1996.

Pondwater Faces, illustrated by Susan Ford, Chronicle Books (San Francisco, CA), 1997.

Rainbow Wings, illustrated by Victor Lee, Morrow (New York, NY), 2000.

Each Living Thing, illustrated by Ashley Wolff, Harcourt, 2000.

Fawn in the Grass, illustrated by Keiko Narahashi, Holt (New York, NY), 2000.

The Waterfall's Gift, illustrated by Richard Jesse Watson, Sierra Club (San Francisco, CA), 2000.

Little Panda: The World Welcomes Hua Mei at the San Diego Zoo, Simon and Schuster (New York, NY), 2001.

A Fawn in the Grass, illustrated by Keiko Narahashi, Henry Holt (New York, NY), 2001.

Mouse Tail Moon, illustrated by Maggie Kneen, Henry Holt (New York, NY), 2002.

Big Bear Ball, illustrated by Steven Kellogg, HarperCollins (New York, NY), 2002.

Wild Birds, illustrated by Susan Estelle Kwas, HarperCollins (New York, NY), 2003.

Come along, Kitten, illustrated by Susan Winter, Simon and Schuster (New York, NY), 2003.

Won't You Be My Kissaroo?, illustrated by Melissa Sweet, Harcourt (Orlando, FL), 2004.

My Mother's Voice, illustrated by Peter Catalanotto, HarperCollins (New York, NY), 2006.

"NIGHT AND MORNING" SERIES; ILLUSTRATED BY DENNIS NOLAN

Step into the Night, Four Winds Press (New York, NY), 1988.

Mockingbird Morning, Four Winds Press (New York, NY), 1989.

Under Your Feet, Four Winds Press (New York, NY), 1990.

"JUST FOR A DAY" SERIES; ILLUSTRATED BY MICHAEL ROTHMAN

White Bear, Ice Bear, Morrow (New York, NY), 1989.
Catching the Wind, Morrow (New York, NY), 1989.
Lizard in the Sun, Morrow (New York, NY), 1990.
Winter Whale, Morrow (New York, NY), 1991.
Sea Elf, Morrow (New York, NY), 1993.
Jaguar in the Rain Forest, Morrow (New York, NY), 1996.
Shark in the Sea, Morrow (New York, NY), 1997.
Tyrannosaurus Time, Morrow (New York, NY), 1999.

"FIRST GRADE IS THE BEST" SERIES; ILLUSTRATED BY BETSY LEWIN

Hello, First Grade, Troll Associates (Mahwah, NJ), 1993.
First-Grade Ladybugs, Troll Associates (Mahwah, NJ), 1993.
First-Grade Valentines, Troll Associates (Mahwah, NJ), 1993.
First-Grade Elves, Troll Associates (Mahwah, NJ), 1994.

PICTURE-BOOK ADAPTATIONS

Hardie Gramatky, *Little Toot,* illustrated by Larry Ross, Platt, 1988.

Charles Dickens, *A Christmas Carol,* illustrated by John O'Brien, Platt, 1989.

Felix Salten, *Walt Disney's Bambi,* Disney Press (New York, NY), 1993.

Felix Salten, *Walt Disney's Bambi's Forest: A Year in the Life of the Forest,* illustrated by David Pacheco and Jesse Clay, Disney Press (New York, NY), 1994.

OTHER

Contributor to periodicals.

Ryder's papers are housed in a permanent collection at the Cooperative Children's Book Center, School of Education, University of Wisconsin, Madison.

Sidelights

Joanne Ryder creates picture books for readers in the primary grades that are praised for combining poetry, fantasy, and science in a particularly original and appealing manner. A prolific, popular writer, she introduces young readers to the life cycles and habits of a variety of creatures, ranging from insects and birds to dinosaurs and whales, through the context of imaginary play. Ryder invites her audience to become the creatures that she profiles by identifying with her young male and female protagonists, who imagine what it would be like to be an animal, bird, or insect. In her works, she allows her readers, to whom she often refers in the second person, to transform themselves and to take on new points of view.

Ryder describes the sensory experiences of her subjects as well as their needs for food, self-preservation, hibernation, and—discreetly—sex. She presents this factual material in lyrical, descriptive language filled with images and sounds, adjectives, and alliteration; according to John R. Pancella of *Appraisal,* these words and phrases are "much more eloquent than those usually found in children's picture books." Through this process, Ryder challenges youngsters to see the world from an unusual perspective while heightening their awareness of, and appreciation for, the natural world. Many of Ryder's works of this type are included in the "Just for a Day" series published by William Morrow. Several of her books include author's notes that provide more detailed scientific information on their subjects.

Ryder has also created a series of quiet, impressionistic picture books that portray young children observing the wonders of nature; the "First Grade Is the Best!" fiction series featuring a cheerful group of children and their teacher, Miss Lee, that includes some subtle lessons on nature; two pourquoi tales with polar bears as their main characters; several "Golden Books" for preschoolers; a book about robots based around C-3PO from the film *Star Wars;* and picture-book adaptations of such classic stories as *Bambi, Little Toot,* and *A Christmas Carol.* Ryder has worked with such notable illustrators as John Schoenherr, Donald Carrick, Diane Stanley,

Lynne Cherry, Don Bolognese, Any Schwartz, Betsy Lewin, Dennis Nolan, Michael Rothman, and Ashley Wolff, and her works are often noted for their union of text and illustration.

Thematically, Ryder celebrates her subjects, promoting respect for nature while representing the interconnectedness of humans and other living creatures. The author underscores her works with a message to preserve the Earth and its inhabitants. In addition, her works demonstrate that the love of nature can be passed from generation to generation. Ryder has been praised for writing informative and attractive books that prove children can be introduced to and inspired by science if it is presented in a distinctive, interesting, and compelling way. She is also acknowledged for the quality of her factual information as well as for the expressiveness and accessibility of her language. While receiving some criticism for anthropomorphicized animal characters, making some scientific omissions, including some overly abstract concepts, and for the pared-down quality of her adaptations, most observers praise Ryder for creating fascinating explorations of nature that stretch children's imaginations while providing them with solid information.

Several reviewers have also noted that Ryder's works are useful complements to science classes and are good for reading aloud and for stimulating children to do further research. Writing in the *St. James Guide to Children's Writers,* Christine Doyle Stott called Ryder "a leading writer of nature books for children," adding, "One of the remarkable things about all her work, and a reason for her consistent popularity, is her extraordinary use of language that is at once simple, poetic, and vividly descriptive." Stott concluded that Ryder's work "stands among the finest nature books of the last twenty years. The scientific accuracy of detail and the beauty of language for which her books are known ensures their welcome in the science and language arts sections as well as on the home bookshelf."

Born in Lake Hiawatha, New Jersey, Ryder was attracted to nature from an early age. Her birthplace was, as the author once described it in an interview with *Something about the Author* (SATA), "a small, rural town." For her parents, who were both born and bred in New York City, Lake Hiawatha was, according to Ryder, "'the country'—very different from the crowded city they knew. For me, it was a wonderful place to explore, full of treasures to discover. There were just a few houses on our street, but there were woods all around. . . . I loved living there and playing outdoors. There were always animals around to observe and encounter." Ryder wrote in *Sixth Book of Junior Authors and Illustrators,* "When I visit schools, children often ask me why I like to write about animals. Perhaps it's because I was an only child, and when I was young in rural New Jersey, there weren't many other children living nearby. But there were animals everywhere. . . . So they became my first friends." She once recalled to

SATA: "One of my earliest memories is trying to follow a butterfly darting across the road and being scolded by a neighbor for running into the street." Growing up, Ryder had an assortment of pets, including chickens, hamsters, ducks, rabbits, and fish.

Ryder's parents were also fascinated by nature and by living in the country—"probably," their daughter surmised, "because they had spent all their lives in the city." Her mother Dorothy taught Joanne "to watch sunsets and to take time to stop and enjoy special moments in nature." Dorothy Ryder once stopped her chores to sit for hours and observe a hundred tiny birds, migrating spring warblers that had stopped to rest in a nearby tree. "My mother loved nature's grand displays—sunsets, ocean walks, spring trees all in bloom," Ryder recalled.

In contrast to her mother, Ryder's father Raymond Ryder, a chemist, "liked to pick things up and examine them. He was the one who introduced me to nature up close and made the discoveries we shared very personal ones." Raymond Ryder also liked to tend his garden, and he would often call his daughter to come and see the interesting things in it. Ryder remembered that if her father "could catch it, he would cup the tiny creature in his hands and wait until I ran to him. Then he would open his fingers and show me whatever it was he had found—a beetle, a snail, a fuzzy caterpillar. Then gently he would let me hold it, and I could feel it move, wiggle, or crawl—even breathe—as I held it in my hand." She continued, "My father's excitement was easy to catch. As he pointed out amazing features of each animal, I could see that, even though it had a few more legs or less legs than I was used to; it was rather marvelous. So tiny, hidden animals became very much a part of my world, as real to me as the people I knew."

Ryder and her father sometimes went for walks in the woods or to a nearby waterfall. She wrote in the *Sixth Book of Junior Authors and Illustrators:* "We would always bring back armloads of treasures—rocks and leaves and, sometimes, even a wandering box turtle." Walking with her father, Ryder once recalled to *SATA,* it "felt natural for me to feel comfortable and part of the world around me." "My father helped me find the magic in the natural world and appreciate what it might be like to be another creature, someone wonderfully different," she commented on the *HarperChildrens Web site.* In my books, I try to share with my readers the experience of being 'shape changers.' We imagine together how it would feel to be someone new—a huge, furry polar bear running on an ice-covered sea, a lean lizard changing colors in the hot sun, . . . a jaguar prowling in a lush tropical rain forest, and a great white shark gliding towards its prey."

In 1991 Ryder published *When the Woods Hum,* a semi-autobiographical picture book about how a father introduces his daughter to the periodical cicadas, insects that appear once every seventeen years; at the end of the

story, the protagonist, now a grown woman, introduces the cicadas to her son. In 1994 she produced *My Father's Hands,* a picture book based on her close relationship with her father and on how he opened the natural world to her.

When Ryder was almost five years old, the family moved to Brooklyn, New York, to the same apartment building where Ryder's mother had grown up. At first, it "was a bit of a shock for me to live where there were so many people all around. But the city seemed also to be a magical land, full of special places for me." Ryder enjoyed going to the park and to museums; in addition, the city provided lots of opportunities for her to use her imagination. She noted in *SATA:* "Every day on my way to school, I passed an old stone lion. I believed he could understand my thoughts, and I would tell him secrets. He was one of my first friends in the city. I also began to have lovely dreams at night in which I could fly over the tall trees outside my home." Ryder was later to use her childhood memories as the basis for her picture book *Night Flight.*

When she was almost seven, Ryder moved to the city of New Hyde Park on Long Island. At about that time, she learned to read, and began to enjoy books, "especially adventures about dogs and cats," as she noted on the *HarperChildrens* Web site. Soon she was writing her own animal stories and, when she was about eight, poetry. Ryder once told *SATA,* "Though I've always had trouble spelling words correctly, my parents and teachers encouraged me to keep on writing even when I made mistakes. I liked playing with words and making them up. I wrote about animals and everyday things—and also about imaginary people and creatures." Ryder became a voracious reader, borrowing multiple titles from her local library. "Reading so much," she noted, "made it easier for me to write. Since I enjoyed imagining other author's worlds, it seemed natural for me to create stories and worlds of my own."

By age ten, Ryder, who had first considered becoming a veterinarian, began to think seriously about being a writer. She started writing her first book, the fantasy "The Marvelous Adventures of Georgus Amaryllis the Third," when she was eleven. Although the manuscript was never finished, Ryder told *SATA,* "Maybe someday, I'll go back to it and see how it might end."

In high school, Ryder edited the school newspaper. After graduating, she enrolled at Marquette University in Wisconsin, where she studied journalism and edited the college literary magazine. She wrote on the *Harper-Childrens Web site* that, as a journalist, "I learned to do research and discover facts. Sometimes a book idea comes from an amazing animal fact I've found." At Marquette, Ryder met Laurence Yep, an aspiring author who has become a well-respected writer of books for children and young people; the couple were later married.

After receiving her bachelor's degree in journalism in 1968, Ryder studied library science at the University of Chicago for a year before moving to New York City to spend ten years working at Harper and Row as an editor of children's books. "During the day, I worked on other people's books," Ryder recalled. "Then at night, I worked on my own stories."

In 1976 she produced her first picture book. *Simon Underground* describes the activities of the mole Simon from fall to spring, taking young readers into Simon's subterranean world and describing his instincts and sensations. Writing in the *St. James Guide to Children's Writers,* Christine Doyle Stott stated that *Simon Underground* "exquisitely combines scientific accuracy with poetic expression. Young readers not only learn abstract facts about a mole, they are brought into such close contact with the details of its life that they must actively consider what it feels like, smells like, looks like, sounds like, to be a mole."

In 1985 Ryder produced her first book of verse, *Inside Turtle's Shell, and Other Poems of the Field.* She imagines a day in a field and pond from dawn to evening, and profiles the creatures that inhabit each place in short poems focusing on their essential qualities. The poems also form a picture of two turtles, one who has turned one hundred years old, and one who has recently been born, facts that the reader learns gradually. As the author once told *SATA,* "When I was six, I got a delightful birthday present, a big box turtle named Myrtle. She was my inspiration for the old turtle in *Inside Turtle's Shell.*"

Writing in *School Library Journal,* Ruth M. McConnell noted, "With pithy delicacy touched with humor, the author of picture books and prize nature writing here distills her perceptions of nature into a series of free-verse vignettes with the punch of haiku." Noting the "quiet beauty" of the poems, Carolyn Phelan concluded in *Booklist* that Ryder "offers a collection of poetry concise, precise, and immediate." Zena Sutherland, writing in the *Bulletin of the Center for Children's Books,* added that Ryder's poems "have a quiet tenderness and empathy" before concluding that most of the poems "are brief, some almost as compressed as haiku; most have delicate imagery; all are evocative."

Ryder's autobiographical picture book *Night Flight* is based on a dream from the author's childhood. In the book Anna plays in the city park near her home during the day. She enjoys riding Alexander, the stone lion, and hopes that the skittish goldfish in the pond will take bread from her hand. At night, Anna dreams that she is flying over the rooftops to the park. She rides Alexander, now running free, and becomes friends with the goldfish and pigeons. Anna goes to the park the next day; this time, the goldfish eat from her hands as she calls them by name.

Writing in *Booklist,* Ilene Cooper stated that "Ryder's lyrical text, which paints its own word pictures, meets its match with [Amy] Schwartz's vibrant, brilliantly colored illustrations." Anne E. Mulherkar of *School Library Journal* noted, "Schwartz and Ryder, each gifted artists in their own right, stretch their capabilities and children's imaginations in *Night Flight.*"

In 1995 Ryder produced a second volume of poetry, *Without Words.* With photographs by Barbara Sonneborn, the book illustrates the bonds humans share with animals. Author and photographer depict children and adults touching, holding, and playing with such animals as tigers, snakes, dolphins, chimpanzees, and elephants. A reviewer in the *Horn Book Guide* noted that "Ryder's lyrical poems convey the strength of the emotional bond between humans and beasts," while a critic in *School Library Journal* added that the author's "expressive poems are at the same time simple and thought-provoking."

Ryder's other fictional tales for children include *Big Bear Ball, Come Along, Kitten,* and *Won't You Be My Kissaroo? Big Bear Ball,* geared for pre-school and early elementary children, shows a forest full of bears throwing a wild party to celebrate the full moon. At first their loud antics annoy the other woodland creatures, who are trying to sleep, but eventually the neighboring creatures decide to get out of bed and join in the fun. "Ryder's light-footed rhymes set the celebratory pace," Ellen Mandel noted in *Booklist,* and the festive atmosphere is reflected in illustrator Steven Kellogg's brightly colored watercolors. "This team has outdone itself," Wanda Meyers-Hines declared in *School Library Journal,* dubbing *Big Bear Ball* "An absolute must for every library."

Come Along, Kitten is a quieter title, also written in simple rhymes designed for very young children. The book features a young, headstrong kitten who goes out to explore the world under the protection of a big, older dog. The kitten chases bumblebees and crickets and spies on mice, all with the encouragement of its canine guardian. "Preschoolers will identify with the curious kitten" and its need for both freedom and security, Lauren Peterson commented in *Booklist,* and Sandra Kitain similarly concluded in *School Library Journal* that *Come Along, Kitten* "will have broad appeal with the preschool set."

Won't You Be My Kissaroo? focuses on the loving care adults give to children. Like *Come Along, Kitten, Won't You Be My Kissaroo?* is written in Ryder's trademark "tender rhyming couplets," as a *Publishers Weekly* critic described them. In this title, a young lamb wakes up on its birthday to special birthday kisses and a question from its mother: "Won't you be my kissaroo?" As the day progresses, the lamb sees many other young animals, including a puppy and a bear cub, getting kisses from their own parents. *Won't You Be My Kissaroo?* is "a feel-good choice for sharing one-on-one or with a group," Kathy Krasniewicz commented in *School Library Journal.*

A tiny kitten's exploration of her new garden world is the subject of the engaging **Come Along, Little Kitten,** *featuring gentle pencil drawings by Susan Winter.*

Many of Ryder's books are notable for teaching children about the natural world, particularly the many animals that inhabit it. In some of these books, including *The Snail's Spell* and *The Chipmunk's Song,* her child protagonists become small enough to accompany animals and observe their behavior first-hand. The first of her "Just for a Day" books, *White Bear, Ice Bear,* takes this concept a step further: in this and subsequent works in the series, the main characters actually become animals. Published in 1989, *White Bear, Ice Bear* features a boy who transforms into a polar bear in an Arctic landscape. The author defines the adaptive characteristics that allow the bear to survive in this beautiful but brutal environment: heavy fur, protective coloration, strong claws, padded soles, and an advanced sense of smell. The bear also tracks a seal for food, but it gets away before the kill. At the end of the book, the boy returns to his normal state after he smells his supper.

Writing in *Booklist,* Carolyn Phelan commented that in *White Bear, Ice Bear* "Ryder shifts points of view so smoothly that the boy's transformations seem quite

natural. . . . Through imaginative writing and artwork [by Michael Rothman], the book . . . leads readers into deeper sympathy for their fellow creatures." Calling the book "the first of a projected series that one hopes will live up to the standards set here," Patricia Manning of *School Library Journal* noted that the book "is rich, empathic, and eye-pleasing," while Anne Rose of *Appraisal* concluded that *White Bear, Ice Bear* is "challenging while remaining inviting for younger readers."

In subsequent volumes of the "Just for a Day" series, Ryder continues the formula of having her young boy and girl characters shape-shift into various species of creatures; the author outlines the habits of such animals as a goose, a lizard, a whale, and a jaguar. With the publication of *A Shark in the Sea* in 1997, Ryder brought a new dimension to her series: whereas before she had only hinted at the predatory habits of her animal subjects, here she described them clearly. In this work, in which a boy dives into the ocean off the California coast and imagines himself to be a great white shark, the author includes an episode where the shark hunts and kills a young seal; it also fights off a competitor shark that tries to steal its prey.

Writing in *School Library Journal,* Helen Rosenberg stated, "The part where the great white kills a young seal is rather bloody. . . . But is at the same time realistic." Elizabeth Bush commented in the *Bulletin of the Center for Children's Books* that "the particulars of the hunt . . . should sate most shark lovers' bloodlust. A good deal of information about shark physiology and hunting method is conveyed in the intense, pulsing free verse." Writing in *Booklist,* Carolyn Phelan concluded, "Ryder captures the feeling of 'otherness,' a different environment, a different kind of body for a different way of moving, and a different way of survival. Although the story may sound slightly sensational, the treatment remains matter-of-fact."

In *Tyrannosaurus Time* two children uncover a fossil and, suddenly find themselves looking at a prehistoric world through the eyes of a T-Rex. Set in a landscape that will become the western United States, the story builds in drama as the dinosaur searches for food and kills a triceratops; in the process, readers learn about the habitat of the beast and are presented with scientific information on theories about why dinosaurs became extinct. Ellen Mandel, writing in *Booklist,* praised Ryder's "lyrical, even mystical prose. . . . Melding poetic intensity with gripping visualization of the action, the book offers a memorable depiction of prehistoric life." Although a *Kirkus Reviews* critic warned that "not all children will be ready for the gory conclusion," the writer concluded, "For readers already familiar with such realistic aspects of the dinosaurs' lives, this volume is a must-have." Reviewers have generally commended Ryder's approach in the "Just for a Day" series; for example, Carolyn Phelan, reviewing *Lizard in the Sun* for *Booklist,* called the series "consciousness-expanding."

As well as being respected as a writer, Ryder is acknowledged as a conservationist. Two of her works, *Earthdance* and *Each Living Thing,* stand as significant examples of why she has achieved this reputation. *Earthdance* is a poem that asks young readers to imagine that they are the Earth, which is personified through strong physical imagery. Ryder asks her audience to see themselves turning in space, feeling things growing and oceans shifting, and she suggests that, when taken together, the people, animals, seas, rivers, mountains, and forests of the Earth form a brightly colored quilt.

A *Kirkus Reviews* contributor commented that in *Earthdance* Ryder beckons readers "to join in a cosmic appreciation of the earth and all it holds" by combining "powerful, pulsing graphics [by Norman Gorbaty] and a valuable, almost incantatory, message." A reviewer in the *Horn Book Guide* noted that Ryder's "ecological message is clear but not heavy-handed," while Lisa Mahoney wrote in the *Bulletin of the Center for Chil-*

dren's Books that the author's "strong verbs, internal rhyme, and alliteration add force and music to her poetry."

Each Living Thing depicts a group of multicultural children who observe life in seven different habitats, including a park and the seashore, over the course of a day. In this work, which has as its theme the importance of respecting nature, Ryder asks children to be aware of animals and their needs and to take care of them—or to just let them be. She shows how animals fit into our surroundings while discouraging the notion that some animals (alligators, bats, bees, bears, snakes, and spiders, among others) are our enemies. Writing in *School Library Journal,* Susan Marie Pitard called *Each Living Thing* a "remarkable marriage of spare, poetic text and luminous, detailed paintings" by Ashley Wolff. Raising concerns about the environment in an engaging manner, Pitard deemed the book a "wonderful choice for sharing . . . [and] for learning to honor each living thing."

Ryder again encouraged her audience to explore their natural surroundings with 2000's *A Fawn in the Grass.* Her text, which consists of an extended poem, focuses on a young child's solitary walk through a meadow and recounts the animals he encounters along his way. While the little boy passes through this natural environment, he leaves its inhabitants undisturbed during his travels—thus the fawn of the title is there when he enters the meadow and, due to his respect for the surroundings, the fawn is there when the child come back. "Though never stated explicitly," a *Publishers Weekly* reviewer summarized, "[Ryder's] book underscores the message that nature is full of beauty, grace, and unexpected pleasures." Similarly, *Booklist* critic Hazel Rochman felt that Ryder successfully presents a "child's-eye view of the amazing natural world, the things you can see when you are quiet, still, alone, and very close."

Mouse Tail Moon and *Wild Birds* teach children about specific animals that they are likely to encounter—field mice in the former title and common North American birds, including geese, robins, finches, blue jays, sparrows, and starlings, in the latter. *Mouse Tail Moon* contains eighteen brief poems written from the perspective of a white tail mouse as it goes about a typical night of searching for food and avoiding foxes, cats, and other predators. "Teachers in the early elementary grades will find this book useful both as poetry and as literature that effectively integrates interesting factual information," commented a *Kirkus Reviews* contributor. *Booklist* reviewer Carolyn Phelan also praised the book as poetry, noting its "natural rhythms and unforced rhymes."

Little Panda: The World Welcomes Hua Mei at the San Diego Zoo focuses on a specific animal, a panda cub who was born at the San Diego Zoo in 1999. This tiny cub, named Hua Mei, was the first panda to be born in captivity and survive for more than a few days. Ryder combines photographs taken by the zoo with a "brief, almost haiku-like text," as Ilene Cooper described it in *Booklist.* In addition to this simple text, suitable for younger readers, Ryder also provides more detailed, scientific explanations of the panda's early life in smaller type. The resulting text is "first-rate," Lolly Robinson commented in *Horn Book,* but never the less "is upstaged by photographs showing the endearing baby" in action. *Little Panda* "is an engaging book [that] will complement any curriculum about animal extinction and environmental responsibility," Tina Hudak concluded in *School Library Journal.*

Ryder, who now lives in Pacific Grove, California, enjoys visiting schools and sharing her experiences as a writer. For preschoolers and first graders, she uses animal puppets to help illustrate her concepts of changing shape. For older students, she utilizes a personal slide show about her life as an author. She has also written and talked about her career. "My language is poetic, full of images, sounds, and sensations to help readers slip into a new skin, a new shape," she added, concluding: "My father helped me discover the wonders hidden all around me, and in my books I try to share my own discoveries with children." In *SATA,* Ryder also once commented that, "For a person who enjoys thinking in images and writing poems, writing picture books is a good life and a joyful way to make a living."

Biographical and Critical Sources

BOOKS

Children's Literature Review, Volume 37, Gale (Detroit, MI), 1996.
St. James Guide to Children's Writers, 5th edition, edited by Tom Pendergast and Sara Pendergast, St. James Press (Detroit, MI), 1999.
Sixth Book of Junior Authors and Illustrators, edited by Sally Holmes Holtze, H. W. Wilson (New York, NY), 1989.

PERIODICALS

Appraisal, summer, 1990, John R. Pancella, review of *Where Butterflies Grow,* p. 48; autumn, 1989, Anne Rose, review of *White Bear, Ice Bear,* p. 57.
Booklist, April 15, 1985, Carolyn Phelan, review of *Inside Turtle's Shell,* p. 1200; November 1, 1985, Ilene Cooper, review of *Night Flight,* pp. 413-414; March 15, 1989, Carolyn Phelan, review of *White Bear, Ice Bear,* p. 1304; March 1, 1990, Carolyn Phelan, review of *Lizard in the Sun,* p. 1348; March 1, 1997, Carolyn Phelan, review of *Shark in the Sea,* p. 1173; September 1, 1999, Ellen Mandel, review of *Tyrannosaurus Time,* p. 142; April 15, 2000, p. 1553; May 1, 2000, Susan Dove Lempke, review of *Rainbow Wings,* p. 1679; March 1, 2001, Hazel Rochman, review of *A Fawn in the Grass,* p. 1288; April 15, 2001, Ilene Cooper, review of *Little Panda: The World Welcomes Hua Mei at the San Diego Zoo,* p. 1562; May 1, 2002, Ellen Mandel, review of *Big Bear Tall,* p. 1536; January 1, 2003, Carolyn Phelan, review of *Mouse Tail Moon,* p. 900; September 1, 2003, Lauren Peterson, review of *Come Along, Kitten,* p. 130; June 1, 2004, Lauren Peterson, review of *Won't You Be My Kissaroo?,* p. 1748.
Bulletin of the Center for Children's Books, June, 1985, Zena Sutherland, review of *Inside Turtle's Shell,* p. 194; July, 1996, Lisa Mahoney, review of *Earthdance,* p. 385; April, 1997, Elizabeth Bush, review of *Shark in the Sea,* p. 295.
Childhood Education, spring, 2002, review of *Little Panda,* p. 172.
Horn Book, May, 2001, Lolly Robinson, review of *Little Panda,* p. 351.
Horn Book Guide, fall, 1995, review of *Without Words,* p. 379; fall, 1996, review of *Earthdance,* p. 368.
Kirkus Reviews, April 1, 1996, review of *Earthdance,* p. 536; July 1, 1999, review of *Tyrannosaurus Time,* p. 1058; October 1, 2002, review of *Mouse Tail Moon,* p. 1479; February 1, 2003, review of *Wild Birds,* p. 238.
Publishers Weekly, March 27, 2000, p. 79; March 19, 2001, reviews of *A Fawn in the Grass,* p. 98 and *The San Diego Panda,* p. 102; April 29, 2002, review of *Big Bear Ball,* p. 68; December 16, 2002, review of *Wild Birds,* p. 65; July 7, 2003, review of *Come Along, Kitten,* p. 70; May 17, 2004, review of *Won't You Be My Kissaroo?,* p. 49.
School Library Journal, April, 1985, Ruth M. McConnell, review of *Inside Turtle's Shell,* p. 82; November, 1985, Anne E. Mulherkar, review of *Night Flight,* p. 77; April, 1989, Patricia Manning, review of *White Bear, Ice Bear,* p. 90; June, 1995, review of *Without Words,* p. 104; April, 1997, Helen Rosenberg, review of *Shark in the Sea,* p. 116; September, 1999, p. 203; April, 2000, Susan Marie Pitard, review of *Each Living Thing,* p. 113; May, 2000, Joy Fleischhacker, review of *Rainbow Wings,* p. 153; May, 2001, Ellen A. Greever, review of *A Fawn in the Grass,* p. 134; July, 2001, Tina Hudak, review of *Little Panda,* p. 98; August, 2001, Holly T. Sneeringer, review of *The Waterfall's Gift,* p. 160; June, 2002, Wanda Meyers-Hines, review of *Big Bear Ball,* p. 110; February, 2003, Dona Ratterree, review of *Mouse Tail Moon,* p. 137; March, 2003, Susan Scheps, review of *Wild Birds,* p. 206; July, 2003, Sandra Kitain, review of *Come Along, Kitten,* p. 105; June, 2004, Kathy Krasniewicz, review of *Won't You Be My Kissaroo?,* p. 119.
Sierra, May, 2001, review of *The Waterfall's Gift,* p. 83.

ONLINE

Balkin Buddies Web site, http://www.balkinbuddies.com/ (July 6, 2005), "Joanne Ryder."
HarperChildrens Web site, http://www.harperchildren's. com (November 28, 2000), (July 6, 2005), "Joanne Ryder."
Penguin/Putnam Web site, http://www.penguin/putnam. com/ (November 27, 2000), "Joanne Ryder."*

S

SAYLES, Elizabeth 1956-

Personal

Born January 6, 1956, in Brooklyn, NY; daughter of William (a book packager) and Shirley Leah (an editor; maiden name, Weinstein) Sayles; married Matthew Justin Dow (a musician), September 5, 1993; children: Jessica Frances. *Education:* Attended Philadelphia College of Art (now University of the Arts), 1974-77, and School of Visual Arts (New York, NY). *Religion:* Jewish.

Addresses

Home—318 Fulle Drive, Valley Cottage, NY 10989. *Agent*—Cornell and McCarthy, LLC, 2-D Cross Highway, Westport, CT 06880. *E-mail*—saydow@earthlink.net.

Career

Children's book illustrator. Graphic artist with design studio in New York, NY; School of Visual Arts, New York, NY, adjunct professor of illustration. *Exhibitions:* Society of Illustrators, New York, NY; Columbus Museum of Art, Columbus, OH; Edward Hopper Art Gallery, Nyack, NY; Every Picture Tells a Story Gallery, Los Angeles, CA; Chemers Gallery, Orange County, CA; New York Public Library, New York, NY; Rockland Center for the Arts, West Nyack, NY.

Member

Illustrators' Partnership of America.

Awards, Honors

Best Book designation, *Parents'* magazine, 1995, for *Not in the House, Newton!;* Book of the Month designation, American Booksellers Association, 1995, for *The Sleeping Porch;* Best Books for Reading and Sharing citation, New York Public Library, 1999, for *Five Little Kittens.*

Writings

(And illustrator) *The Goldfish Yawned* (picture book), Henry Holt (New York, NY), 2005.

ILLUSTRATOR

Chuck Thurman, *A Time for Remembering,* Simon and Schuster (New York, NY), 1989.

Pegi Deitz Shea, *Bungalow Fungalow,* Clarion (New York, NY), 1991.

Janice May Udry, *What Mary Jo Shared,* Scholastic (New York, NY), 1991.

Louise Borden, *Albie the Lifeguard,* Scholastic (New York, NY), 1993.

Susan Tews, *Nettie's Gift,* Clarion (New York, NY), 1993.

Connie K. Heckert, *Dribbles,* Clarion (New York, NY), 1993.

Libba Moore Gray, *The Little Black Truck,* Simon and Schuster (New York, NY), 1994.

Mary Pope Osborne, *Molly and the Prince,* Knopf (New York, NY), 1994.

Karen Ackerman, *The Night Crossing,* Knopf (New York, NY), 1994.

Karen Ackerman, *The Sleeping Porch,* Morrow (New York, NY), 1995.

Judith Heide Gilliland, *Not in the House, Newton!,* Clarion (New York, NY), 1995.

Kathi Appelt, *The Thunderherd,* Morrow (New York, NY), 1996.

Tom Paxton, *The Marvelous Toy,* Morrow (New York, NY), 1996.

Pam Conrad, *This Mess,* Hyperion (New York, NY), 1998.

Mary McKenna Siddals, *Millions of Snowflakes,* Clarion (New York, NY), 1998.

Nancy Jewell, *Five Little Kittens,* Clarion (New York, NY), 1999.

Pat Mora, *The Rainbow Tulip,* Viking (New York, NY), 1999.

Mary McKenna Siddals, *Morning Song,* Henry Holt (New York, NY), 2001.

Caron Lee Cohen, *Martin and the Giant Lions,* Clarion (New York, NY), 2002.

Mary Bryant Bailey, *Jeoffry's Christmas,* Farrar Straus (New York, NY), 2002.

Terri Cohlene, *Won't Papa Be Surprised!,* HarperCollins (New York, NY), 2003.

Mary Bryant Bailey, *Jeoffry's Halloween,* Farrar Straus (New York, NY), 2003.

Billy Crystal, *I Already Know I Love You,* HarperCollins (New York, NY), 2004.

Sayles's illustrations have also appeared on dust jackets for recorded media and in magazines and newspapers articles.

Sidelights

Elizabeth Sayles left a successful career in graphic design—with clients including the Whitney Museum of American Art, UNICEF, and Arista Records—to turn her artistic hand to illustration, specializing in children's book illustration and book jackets and blending her artwork subtly with story text. Noted for her warm and somewhat soft-focus pastels, Sayles has illustrated over a score of children's books, several of them award winners, and in 2005 also created her own text, producing the self-illustrated picture book *The Goldfish Yawned.*

Born in Brooklyn, New York, in 1956, Sayles grew up in Nyack, New York, in a family that encouraged her early artistic endeavors. "I come from a 'book' family," Sayles once told *Something about the Author* (SATA). "My father, a designer and illustrator; and my mother, a writer and editor, produced books together. My father also worked for a children's-book publisher and brought lots of books home. He set up drawing tables for my brother and me right next to his in our attic. So, I always drew. My favorite illustrator then and now was Garth Williams."

Perspective was always an element Sayles enjoyed playing with, even as a child. During her later training at the Philadelphia College of Art, she began learning about other artists, and one of her favorites, Edward Hopper, was actually born in Sayles's home town. Sayles also enjoyed the art of American muralist Thomas Hart Benton, and Benton's work has been a strong influence in her books, especially in *The Little Black Truck,* a story set in the 1920s and 1930s. In college Sayles was also introduced to pastels, and she has continued to use them for her artwork.

"After college," Sayles explained, "I did a few different jobs before establishing a *design* studio which I had for about ten years before mustering the courage to concentrate solely on illustration. For a short while I did both design and illustration, but happily the illustration jobs took over." At one point Sayles set up as a freelance illustrator in her hometown of Nyack, moving into the very house where Hopper had lived. "His use of light and shadow has always had a big influence on me," she explained.

Sayles's picture book debut came in 1989 with *A Time for Remembering.* Written by Chuck Thurman, the book focuses on a boy and his dying grandfather. Patricia Pearl, writing in *School Library Journal,* praised Sayles's "double-page spreads of soft, hazy, warmly colored illustrations of the grandfather and the boy at the hospital and during happier times."

More of Sayles's signature "soft" artwork is served up in *Bungalow Fungalow,* written by Pegi Deitz Shea. This book finds a young boy visiting his grandparents' seaside bungalow. As Ellen Fader observed in *Horn Book,* "Sayles's art is full of the pale, sandy color of the beach; softly focused drawings shimmer with intense heat." Also reviewing the book, *School Library Journal* contributor Andrew W. Hunter noted that Sayles's illustrations "are realistic yet impressionistic in style, and capture the boy's enjoyment."

In 1993, three books illustrated by Sayles were published: *Albie the Lifeguard, Nettie's Gift,* and *Dribbles.* In *Dribbles* the title character, an old cat, dies, leaving three housemate cats behind. Virginia E. Jeschelnig observed in *School Library Journal* that "Sayles's rich pastel illustrations, with their subtle, painterly compositions, are the ideal accompaniment to [Jeschelnig's] . . . thoughtful text." A reviewer for *Publishers Weekly* concluded that "Sayles's full-page pastels, in soft ambers and creams, offer a gentle, cat's-eye view of friendship, love and loss; her illustrations of the three bereaved cats gazing out the window is particularly moving."

For *Nettie's Gift,* by Susan Tews, Sayles created fall landscapes that were widely praised. Writing in *Booklist,* Kay Weisman noted that the book's illustrator "makes effective use of browns and oranges in the quiet autumnal story," and went on to comment that "her artwork—with its indistinct faces and fuzzy, faraway look—lends a tranquil atmosphere to this mood piece." A *Publishers Weekly* contributor concluded a review of the book by stating that Sayles's "autumn pastel illustrations lure readers into a wistful late-afternoon light where sharp edges are blurred and fading forms catch bits of sun in luminous patches."

Sayles's work for the *The Little Black Truck* by Libba Moore Gray, which is set in an idyllic, rural past, was also appreciated by many critics. "The pictures," noted Mary Harris Veeder in *Booklist,* "in which landscapes almost always dominate, are soft-edged images that blanket rural life and the little black truck with an aura of affection." Writing in *School Library Journal,* Cynthia K. Richey compared Sayles's "impressionistic, full-color illustrations" with their "soft, sculptural shapes and rounded use of line" to the work of *Jumanji* creator Chris Van Allsburg.

Not in the House, Newton! tells the story of a young boy and a magical crayon. *Booklist* reviewer Susan Dove Lempke called Sayles's illustrations for this book "cozy and intimate," while a *Kirkus Reviews* contributor commented that the illustrator's "softened pastels create the right mood for the adventure." Her pastel illustrations for *The Sleeping Porch,* a story about a close-knit family and their new home, are "rich in hues of purple and orange [and] convey the warmth and closeness the family shares," noted *Booklist* reviewer Kay Weisman. Jane Marino commented in *School Library Journal* that "Sayles's appealing pastel illustrations are dominated by various shades of purple that serve as warm backgrounds for the comforting glow of the porch's light."

In her many illustration projects, Sayles has depicted a variety of images ranging from thunderstorms to snowflakes to mysterious toys and secret Father's Day presents. Her illustrations for Kathi Appelt's *The Thunderherd* were dubbed "dreamy pastel paintings" by *Booklist* reviewer Kay Weisman, while her artwork for Mary McKenna Siddals's *Millions of Snowflakes* was called "evocative" by Kathy Piehl in *School Library Journal.* Illustrating the lyrics of a popular folk song by Tom Paxton published in book form as *The Marvelous Toy,* Sayles "creates a satisfying unique 'marvelous toy'," according to Lisa Dennis in *School Library Journal,* citing illustrations with a "combination of cozy charm and unpredictable whimsy." Sayles's drawings for *Won't Papa Be Surprised!* "are joyful and warm," Martha Topol commented in *School Library Journal,* "with a smooth and soothing flow of color and action." These "soft, dreamy pastels," wrote a *Kirkus Reviews* contributor, "perfectly complement the [book's] gentle and reassuring theme."

Sayles has also illustrated two books by Mary Bryant Bailey about a kind-hearted cat named Jeoffry. In *Jeoffry's Christmas* "the cat is drawn with plenty of personality and an almost human expression," Mara Alpert commented in *School Library Journal,* while Wanda Meyers-Hines, also writing in *School Library Journal,* praised the book's "painterly artwork done in soft, autumn-hued pastels" that appears in *Jeoffry's Halloween.* Sayles's work also appears in *I Already Know I Love You,* a book written by actor Billy Crystal and addressed to the comedian's unborn grandchild. A *Publishers Weekly* critic noted that while Crystal's text is found lacking, there is merit in Sayles's "softly focused, emotion-filled pastels."

Sayles has worked with a score of different authors, creating her subtle pictorial effects to work in tandem with text. However, as she told Melissa Myers in the Rockland County, New York *Journal News,* "the pictures are the most important. The illustrator can definitely make or break the story." Sayles is picky when it comes to choosing manuscripts to illustrate: "I look for good stories," she told Myers. "When I read them I get pictures in my mind. Children's books do not have a lot of words, but every word is important." Having a child has also been a strong influence on Sayles's art. As she

told Myers, "I have one daughter who critiques my work and inspires me now. I can see the work differently."

"I am very disciplined when I work," Sayles once explained to *SATA.* "I am in my studio from about ten a.m. to five p.m. Monday through Friday unless I have a meeting or have to go to the library for research or whatever. I work with pastel on paper, but before doing a final painting I do lots of sketches which must be approved by the editor and art director. A children's picture book—from the time I get the manuscript through thumbnail sketches, final sketches, and final art—can take a couple of years, but probably just three months of actual work."

Biographical and Critical Sources

PERIODICALS

Booklist, February 15, 1993, Hazel Rochman, review of *Albie the Lifeguard,* p. 1066; March 1, 1993, Kay Weisman, review of *Nettie's Gift,* p. 1239; March 15, 1994, Hazel Rochman, review of *The Night Crossing,* p. 1346; June 1, 1994, Mary Harris Veeder, review of *The Little Black Truck,* p. 1837; March 1, 1995, Kay Weisman, review of *The Sleeping Porch,* p. 1246; December 15, 1995, Susan Dove Lempke, review of *Not in the House, Newton!,* p. 708; May 15, 1996, Kay Weisman, review of *The Thunderherd,* p. 1590; April 15, 1998, Stephanie Zvirin, review of *The Mess,* p. 1450; April 14, 2002, Ilene Cooper, review of *Martin and the Giant Lion,* p. 1407.

Horn Book, July-August, 1991, Ellen Fader, review of *Bungalow Fungalow,* p. 473; July-August, 1993, Hanna B. Zeiger, review of *Nettie's Gift,* p. 431.

Journal News, November 29, 1998, Melissa Myers, "Hopper House Book Fair Points Spotlight on Local Authors."

Kirkus Reviews, October 15, 1995, review of *Not in the House, Newton!;* March 15, 2003, review of *Won't Papa Be Surprised!,* p. 463

Publishers Weekly, March 15, 1993, review of *Nettie's Gift,* p. 87; May 24, 1993, review of *Albie the Lifeguard,* p. 87; August 9, 1993, review of *Dribbles,* p. 478; April 11, 1994, review of *The Little Black Truck,* p. 64; April 25, 1994, review of *The Night Crossing,* p. 79; August 15, 1994, review of *Molly and the Prince,* p. 94; August 12, 1996, review of *The Marvelous Toy,* p. 83; April 20, 1998, review of *This Mess,* p. 65; December 3, 2001, review of *Morning Song,* p. 58; March 15, 2004, review of *I Already Know I Love You,* p. 72.

School Library Journal, January, 1990, Patricia Pearl, review of *A Time for Remembering,* pp. 90-91; June, 1991, Andrew W. Hunter, review of *Bungalow Fungalow,* p. 98; June, 1993, Liza Bliss, review of *Albie the Lifeguard,* p. 70, Ann Stell, review of *Nettie's Gift,* p. 90; November, 1993, Virginia E. Jeschelnig, review of *Dribbles,* p. 82; July, 1994, Louise L. Sherman, review of *The Night Crossing,* p. 100; August, 1994, Cynthia K. Richey, review of *The Little Black Truck,* pp. 131-132; September, 1994, Heide Piehler, review of *Molly and the Prince,* p. 190; May, 1995, Jane Marino, review of *The Sleeping Porch,* p. 81; January, 1996, Ronald Jobe, review of *Not in the House, Newton!,* pp. 83-84; August, 1996, Carol Schene, review of *The Thunderherd,* p. 115, Lisa Dennis, review of *The Marvelous Toy,* pp. 127-128; April, 1998, Lisa Dennis, review of *This Mess,* p. 97; September, 1998, Kathy Piehl, review of *Millions of Snowflakes,* p. 182; December, 2001, Sally R. Dow, review of *Morning Song,* p. 111; October, 2002, Mara Alpert, review of *Jeoffry's Christmas,* p. 56; July, 2003, Martha Topol, review of *Won't Papa Be Surprised!,* p. 88; September, 2003, Wanda Meyers-Hines, review of *Jeoffry's Halloween,* p. 168.

ONLINE

Elizabeth Sayles Home Page, http://www.elizabethsayles. com (July 15, 2005).
HarperChildrens Web site, http://www.harperchildrens. com/ (July 6, 2005), "Elizabeth Sayles."

*   *   *

SEGAL, Lore (Groszmann) 1928-

Personal

Born March 8, 1928, in Vienna, Austria; daughter of Ignatz (an accountant) and Franzi (Stern) Groszmann; married David Isaac Segal (an editor), November 3, 1961 (died, 1970); children: Beatrice, Jacob. *Education:* Bedford College, London, B.A. (with honors), 1948. *Religion:* Jewish.

Addresses

Home—New York, NY. *Agent*—c/o Lynn Nesbit, ICM, 40 West 57th St., New York, NY 10019.

Career

Writer. Teacher in Dominican Republic, 1948-51; Columbia University, New York, NY, professor of creative writing, 1969-78; University of Illinois at Chicago Circle, Chicago, professor of English, beginning 1978; Ohio State University, Columbus, professor of English until 1996, professor emeritus, 2004—. Visiting professor at Bennington College, 1973, Princeton University, 1974, and Sarah Lawrence College, 1975-76; lecturer at Bryn Mawr College, 2001-02. Member, Wyman Institute for Holocaust Studies' Arts and Letters Council. Appeared in films *My Knees Were Jumping: Remembering the Kindertransports,* 1998, and *Into the Arms of Strangers: Stories of the Kindertransport,* Warner Bros., 2000.

Awards, Honors

Guggenheim fellowship in creative writing, 1965-66; National Council of the Arts and Humanities grant, 1967-68; Creative Artists Public Service Program grant, 1972-73; Children's Spring Book Festival first prize, *Book World,* and American Library Association Notable Book designation, both 1970, both for *Tell Me a Mitzie; All the Way Home* and *The Juniper Tree, and Other Tales from Grimm* included in Children's Book Showcase, 1974; Notable Book designation, *New York Times,* 1985, for *The Story of Mrs. Lovewright and Purrless, Her Cat,* and 1987, for *The Book of Adam to Moses;* American Academy of Arts and Letters Award, 1985, for *Her First American.*

Writings

FOR CHILDREN

Tell Me a Mitzi, illustrated by Harriet Pincus, Farrar, Strauss (New York, NY), 1970.
All the Way Home, illustrated by James Marshall, Farrar, Strauss (New York, NY), 1973.
(Translator, with Randall Jarrell) Willem Grimm and Jacob Grimm, *The Juniper Tree, and Other Tales from Grimm,* illustrated by Maurice Sendak, Farrar, Strauss (New York, NY), 1974, revised edition, 2003.
The Church Mice Adrift, Macmillan (New York, NY), 1976.
Tell Me a Trudy, illustrated by Rosemary Wells, Farrar, Strauss (New York, NY), 1978.
(Translator) Willem Grimm and Jacob Grimm, *The Bear and the Kingbird,* Farrar, Strauss (New York, NY), 1979.
The Story of Old Mrs. Brueback and How She Looked for Trouble and Where She Found Him, illustrated by Marcia Sewall, Pantheon (New York, NY), 1981.
The Story of Mrs. Lovewright and Purrless, Her Cat, illustrated by Paul O. Zelinsky, Knopf (New York, NY), 1985.
The Book of Adam to Moses, illustrated by Leonard Baskin, Knopf (New York, NY), 1987.
The Story of King Saul and King David, Schocken Books (New York, NY), 1991.
Morris the Artist, illustrated by Boris Kulikov, Farrar, Strauss (New York, NY), 2003.
Why Mole Shouted, and Other Stories, illustrated by Sergio Ruzzier, Farrar, Strauss (New York, NY), 2004.
More Mole Stories and Little Gopher, Too, illustrated by Sergio Ruzzier, Farrar, Strauss (New York, NY), 2005.

OTHER

Other People's Houses (autobiographical novel), Harcourt (New York, NY), 1964.
(Translator with W. D. Snodgrass) Christian Morgenstern, *Gallows Songs,* University of Michigan Press (Ann Arbor, MI), 1967.
Lucinella (novel), Farrar, Strauss (New York, NY), 1976.

Short stories anthologized in books, including *Best American Short Stories,* 1989; and *O. Henry Prize Stories,* 1990. Contributor of stories to periodicals, including *New Yorker, Saturday Evening Post, New Republic, Epoch, Commentary, New American Review,* and *Story.* Contributor of reviews to *New York Times Book Review* and *New Republic.* Contributor of translations of poetry to *Mademoiselle, Atlantic Monthly, Hudson Review, Poetry,* and *Tri-Quarterly.*

Adaptations

The Story of Mrs. Lovewright and Purrless, Her Cat was adapted for audio cassette by Random House/ Miller-Brody Productions, 1986; *Tell Me a Mitzi* was adapted for audio cassette by Scholastic, 1986; *Her First American* was adapted for audio cassette by New Letters, 1990.

Sidelights

Lore Segal was born in Austria in 1928, and by the time the Jewish girl reached age ten World War II was raging across her European homeland. Fearing that harm would come to their daughter, in 1928 her parents, Ignatz and Franzi Groszmann, made the difficult decision to join thousands of other parents in Austria, Germany, and Czechoslovakia and sent their child to England, a safe haven in wartime. Like 10,000 other European children, Segal boarded a train for Great Britain as part of the Kindertransport of the late 1930s, leaving her parents behind to endure the efforts of German Chancellor Adolf Hitler to rid the region of all persons of Jewish descent. After arriving at England's Dovercourt

In Why Mole Shouted *Lore Segal introduces a young mole and his grandmother, who live together happily except when monstrous complications arise. (Illustration by Sergio Ruzzier.)*

Camp, Segal wrote passionate letters to the London refugee committee, begging that her Jewish parents be rescued, and in response the Groszmanns were eventually brought to England. Ironically, due to his Austrian origins, Segal's father was interred in a Scottish prisoner-of-war camp after England entered World War II; he fell ill and died days before the war ended. While she has gone on to a successful career as an academic and has authored several highly praised books for young children, Segal is still haunted by her experiences growing up during war time. These memories shadow her books for adult readers, and her first novel, *Other People's Houses,* focuses on her memories of childhood and the aftershocks she experienced as an emigrée in England.

Segal's childhood world was a world of extremes. While she spent the first decade of her life as "the center of attention, admiration, and the focus of great expectations" as a much-loved child in a comfortably-off family living in Vienna, she explained in an essay for *Something about the Author Autobiography Series* (SAAS) that everything changed in 1938, when Hitler annexed Austria and sent the German Army to occupy Vienna. As she writes in *Other People's Houses:* "One day the first German regiment moved in. By noon the square outside our windows was black with tanks, armored cars, radio trucks. Our yard was requisitioned for the paymaster's headquarters. The soldiers borrowed one of our kitchen chairs and the card table. . . . Two helmeted guards stood on either side of the table while the German soldiers in the gray-green uniforms filed past to collect their money."

In keeping with Hitler's notorious Final Solution—a plan to purify the so-called Aryan race—the Nazi occupation government immediately ordered Jewish children such as Segal to attend a separate school. Ignatz Groszmann lost his job at a Vienna bank when Nazi leaders passed restrictions eliminating Jewish workers from mainstream commerce and industry. With no means of support, the family moved in with Segal's grandparents, who had a home in the country. Unfortunately, things were no better there; as Segal writes in *Other People's Houses,* formerly friendly neighbors now defaced the front of Segal's grandfather's store with anti-Semitic slogans. "At night they threw stones through the bedroom windows. One evening they brought ladders and stepped right through the living-room windows and carried away whatever they felt like taking."

After Segal, and then her parents, made their escape to England, they found themselves impoverished. Segal was forced to continue living as a refugee, and boarded with five different English families before reaching age eighteen. Attending Bedford College, London, she earned her B.A. in English with honors in 1948, the same year the war ended. At the urging of her mother, she moved to the Dominican Republic, joining her now-widowed mother and her grandparents, who had fled

Being a birthday-party guest is no fun when the gift you bring is something you really want yourself, as a young boy learns in **Morris the Artist.** *(Illustration by Boris Kulikov.)*

there during wartime. Segal remained there for three years, teaching English at a business school and tutoring members of the diplomatic corps who desired to learn English.

In 1951 Segal and her mother immigrated to the United States and made their new home in New York City. Her first years in the United States were difficult ones; she worked as a filing clerk in a shoe factory, as a receptionist, and for a textile design studio. During this period she also began writing fiction, and was soon selling stories to such vaunted magazines as *Commentary* and the *New Yorker*. In 1961, at age thirty-three, she married David Segal, with whom she had two children; sadly, David passed away nine years later.

1964 saw the publication of her first novel, *Other People's Houses,* which traces Segal's own life as it follows its protagonist from war-torn Austria to the United States. The book was highly praised by critics, Elizabeth Thalman describing it in *Library Journal* as "a story of courage, endurance and humor."

In 1970, with *Tell Me a Mitzi,* Segal began to address a younger readership, inspired by her more upbeat experiences as the mother of young children. The book collects several tales about a little girl named Mitzie who gets into trouble with her baby brother Jacob. Each story is written as if it is being told by a parent to a child, and the children beg their parent to "tell me a Mitzi" when they want to hear another tale. The same technique is used in *Tell Me a Trudy,*; and Segal has noted that both the tales and the phrase requesting them are based on the bedtime traditions she enjoyed with her own children.

In addition to writing her own books for children, Segal has also adapted and translated two collections of fairy and folk tales collected by the Brothers Grimm. With its illustrations by noted artist Maurice Sendak, one of these books, *The Juniper Tree, and Other Tales from Grimm,* has become a childhood classic and has remained in print ever since its 1973 publication. Other books for children, such as *The Story of Old Mrs.*

Brubeck and How She Looked for Trouble and Where She Found Him, are written using classic fairy-tale techniques.

In contrast to her own experiences, in her fiction for young children Segal creates what *Horn Book* contributor Deirdre F. Baker described in a review of *More Mole Stories and Little Gopher Too* as "an idiosyncratic, comfortable world where affection rules." In the four tales contained in this book, as well those as its prequel, *Why Mole Shouted, and Other Stories,* Segal focuses on the close bond between a preschool-aged child and a grandparent, although in this case the "child" is in fact a mole. Navigating the childhood temptation of a cookie meant to be eaten AFTER chores are done, the difficulty in sharing favorite toys, and the desire for attention, Segal's text was praised by Baker as "perceptive" and "amusing," While a *Kirkus* reviewer referred to the author's "classically droll style." In *Why Mole Shouted, and Other Stories* Segal impressed a *Publishers Weekly* reviewer who remarked that the author "again proves she's in tune with a child's mindset," and in *School Library Journal* Linda M. Kenton wrote that "Segal captures the caprice and occasionally challenging nature of young children in a book featuring Italian-born artist Sergio Ruzzier's "dreamy, almost surreal" illustrations.

Other books for children include *Morris the Artist,* which *Booklist* contributor Gillian Engberg described as an "unusual, visually stimulating story" that illustrates the complex dynamics at play in children's relationships and "letting creativity loose." In the story a boy named Morris grudgingly takes time away from his favorite activity—painting—to attend friend Benjamin's birthday party. Finding the perfect gift is easy: paints, of course. However, when it comes time to relinquish the gift, he clings to the nice new paint box. Ultimately Morris finds a way to keep the gift and give at the same time when he turns the party into a painting frenzy, sparking his friends' creativity and entertaining them with his talent and enthusiasm for art. Praising Segal's text for its "empathy and imagination," a *Publishers Weekly* reviewer also noted Boris Kulikov's "extraordinary paintings," with their "off kilter, funhouse feeling." Within what Engberg described as Kulikov's "odd, fantastical world," Segal's story highlights a childhood situation that the critic dubbed "universal."

Biographical and Critical Sources

BOOKS

Lanes, Selma, *Down the Rabbit Hole,* Atheneum (New York, NY), 1971.

Segal, Lore, *Other People's Houses,* Harcourt (New York, NY), 1964.

Something about the Author Autobiography Series, Volume 11, Gale (Detroit, MI), 1991.

PERIODICALS

Booklist, August, 2003, Gillian Engberg, review of *Morris the Artist,* p. 1990; May 1, 2004, Hazel Rochman, review of *Why Mole Shouted, and Other Stories,* p. 1564.

Book Week, November 29, 1964.

Commentary, March, 1965, Cynthia Ozick, review of *Other People's Houses.*

Commonweal, March, 1965.

Contemporary Fiction, fall, 1993, Philip G. Cavanaugh, "The Present Is a Foreign Country: Lore Segal's Fiction," p. 475.

Horn Book, March-April, 2005, Deirdre F. Baker, review of *More Mole Stories and Little Gopher, Too,* p. 194.

Kirkus Reviews, May 1, 2003, review of *Morris the Artist,* p. 683; April 1, 2004, review of *Why Mole Shouted, and Other Stories,* p 337.

Library Journal, November 15, 1964, Elizabeth Thalman, review of *Other People's Houses.*

New Republic, December 12, 1964, Richard Gilman, review of *Other People's Houses;* August 15, 1985, Laura Obolensky, review of *Her First American,* p. 41.

New Statesman, March 19, 1965.

Newsweek, July 8, 1985.

New York Review of Books, November 19, 1964.

New York Times Book Review, May 17, 1970; October 24, 1976; May 19, 1985.

Publishers Weekly, April 7, 1003, review of *Morris the Artist,* p. 66; March 22, 2004, review of *Why Mole Shouted, and Other Stories,* p. 85.

Reporter, November 19, 1964.

Saturday Review, July 25, 1970; October 16, 1976.

School Library Journal, April, 2004, Linda M. Kenton, review of *Why Mole Shouted, and Other Stories,* p. 124.

Time, April 24, 1972.*

*   *   *

SHERMAN, Josepha

Personal

Born in New York, NY; daughter of Nat (a theatre manager) and Alice (a writer and teacher; maiden name, Altschuler) Sherman. *Education:* Hunter College of the City University of New York, B.A., M.A.

Addresses

Home—New York, NY. *Office*—Sherman Editorial Services, 500 E. 85th St., Suite 11F, New York, NY 10028. *E-mail*—jsherman@ses-ny.com.

Career

Writer, editor, and folklorist.

Member

Science Fiction and Fantasy Writers of America, Society of Children's Book Writers and Illustrators, Authors Guild, American Folklore Society, Sierra Club.

Awards, Honors

Compton Crook Award, 1990; Nebula Award nominee, 1991; Best Book citation, American Library Association, 1993, for *Child of Faerie, Child of Earth.*

Writings

JUVENILE NOVELS

The Invisibility Factor, Ballantine, 1986.

The Crystal of Doom, Ballantine (New York, NY), 1986.

(Reteller) *Vassilisa the Wise: A Tale of Medieval Russia,* illustrated by Daniel San Souci, Harcourt (New York, NY), 1988.

Gleaming Bright, Walker (New York, NY), 1994.

Orphans of the Night, Walker (New York, NY), 1995.

Vulcan's Forge (based on the *Star Trek* television series), Pocket Books (New York, NY), 1997.

Vulcan's Heart (based on the *Star Trek* television series), Pocket Books (New York, NY), 1999.

Deep Water, Pocket Pulse (New York, NY), 2000.

Vulcan's Soul. Book 1, Exodus (based on the *Star Trek* television series), Pocket Books (New York, NY), 2004.

Through the Looking Glass (based on the television series *Gene Roddenberry's Andromeda*), Tor (New York, NY), 2005.

FANTASY NOVELS

Song of the Dark Druid, (interactive novel), TSR, 1987.

Secret of the Unicorn Queen, Book 1: Swept Away!, Fawcett (New York, NY), 1988, reprinted, Ballantine (New York, NY), 2004.

Secret of the Unicorn Queen, Book 5: Sorcery of the Dark Gods, Fawcett (New York, NY), 1989.

The Shining Falcon, Avon (New York, NY), 1989.

The Horse of Flame, Avon (New York, NY), 1990.

Child of Faerie, Child of Earth, Walker (New York, NY), 1992.

(With Mercedes Lackey) *Castle of Deception,* Baen Books (New York, NY), 1992.

A Strange and Ancient Name, Baen Books (New York, NY), 1993.

Windleaf, Walker (New York, NY), 1993.

The Chaos Gate, Baen Books (New York, NY), 1993.

Gleaming Bright, Walker (New York, NY), 1993.

(With Mercedes Lackey) *A Cast of Corbies,* Baen Books (New York, NY), 1993.

OTHER

Indian Tribes of North America, Portland House, 1990.

Once upon a Galaxy: Folktales, Fantasy, and Science Fiction, August House (Little Rock, AR), 1994.

The First American: Spirit of the Land and the People, Smithmark (New York, NY), 1996.

Xena: All I Need to Know I Learned from the Warrior Princess, Pocket Books (New York, NY), 1998.

Puerto Rico, Benchmark Books (New York, NY), 1999.

Welcome to the Rodeo!, Heinemann Library (Chicago, IL), 2000.

Tricks and Optical Illusions Experiment Log, Scholastic (New York, NY), 2000.

Steer Wrestling, Heinemann Library (Chicago, IL), 2000.

Ropers and Riders, Heinemann Library (Chicago, IL), 2000.

Bull Riding, Heinemann Library (Chicago, IL), 2000.

Bronc Riding, Heinemann Library (Chicago, IL), 2000.

Bill Gates: Computer King, Millbrook Press (Brookfield, CT), 2000.

Barrel Racing, Heinemann Library (Chicago, IL), 2000.

Venus Williams, Heinemann Library (Chicago, IL), 2001.

Terrell Davis, Heinemann Library (Chicago, IL), 2001.

Stone Cold Steve Austin, Heinemann Library (Chicago, IL), 2001.

Jerry Yang and David Filo: Chief Yahoos of Yahoo!, Twenty-first Century Books (Brookfield, CT), 2001.

Jeff Gordon, Heinemann Library (Chicago, IL), 2001.

Jeff Bezos: King of Amazon, Twenty-first Century Books (Brookfield, CT), 2001.

Competitive Soccer for Girls, Rosen (New York, NY), 2001.

The Upper Limbs: Learning How We Use Our Arms, Elbows, Forearms, and Hands, Rosen (New York, NY), 2002.

The Ear: Learning How We Hear, Rosen (New York, NY), 2002.

Samuel de Champlain, Explorer of the Great Lakes Region and Founder of Quebec, Rosen (New York, NY), 2003.

Internet Safety, Franklin Watts (New York, NY), 2003.

The History of the Personal Computer, Franklin Watts (New York, NY), 2003.

The History of the Internet, Franklin Watts (New York, NY), 2003.

Henry Hudson: English Explorer of the Northwest Passage, Rosen (New York, NY), 2003.

Deep Space Observation Satellites, Rosen (New York, NY), 2003.

Nature's Fireworks: A Book about Lightening, Picture Window Books (Minneapolis, MN), 2004.

Hydroelectric Power, Capstone Press (Mankato, MN), 2004.

Gusts and Gales: A Book about Wind, Picture Window Books (Minneapolis, MN), 2004.

Geothermal Power, Capstone Press (Mankato, MN), 2004.

Fossil Fuel Power, Capstone Press (Mankato, MN), 2004.

Flakes and Flurries: A Book about Snow, Picture Window Books (Minneapolis, MN), 2004.

The Constitution, Rosen (New York, NY), 2004.

The Cold War, Lerner Publications (Minneapolis, MN), 2004.

The War against Germs, Rosen (New York, NY), 2004.

Sunshine: A Book about Sunlight, Picture Window Books (Minneapolis, MN), 2004.

Splish, Splash!: A Book about Rain, Picture Window Books (Minneapolis, MN), 2004.

Solar Power, Capstone Press (Mankato, MN), 2004.

Shapes in the Sky: A Book about Clouds, Picture Window Books (Minneapolis, MN), 2004.

Nuclear Power, Capstone Press (Mankato, MN), 2004.

Your Travel Guide to Ancient Israel, Lerner Publications (Minneapolis, MN), 2004.

Your Travel Guide to Ancient China, Lerner Publications (Minneapolis, MN), 2004.

Wind Power, Capstone Press (Mankato, MN), 2004.

J. J. Thomson and the Discovery of Electrons, Mitchell Lane Publishers (Hockessin, DE), 2005.

How Do We Know the Nature of Time?, Rosen (New York, NY), 2005.

How Do We Know the Nature of the Cell?, Rosen (New York, NY), 2005.

Henry Cavendish and the Discovery of Hydrogen, Mitchell Lane Publishers (Hockessin, DE), 2005.

Exploring the North Pole: The Story of Robert Edwin Peary and Matthew Henson, Mitchell Lane Publishers (Hockessin, DE), 2005.

Dale Earnhardt, Jr., Mitchell Lane Publishers (Hockenssin, DE), 2005.

Charles Babbage, Mitchell Lane Publishers (Newark, DE), 2005.

Barbara Park, Mitchell Lane Publishers (Hockessin, DE), 2005.

Syd Hoff, Mitchell Lane Publishers (Hockessin, DE), 2005.

The Story of Harley-Davidson, Mitchell Lane Publishers (Hockessin, DE), 2005.

Shaquille O'Neal, Mitchell Lane Publishers (Hockessin, DE), 2005.

Queen Lydia Liliuokalani, Last Ruler of Hawaii, Carolrhoda Books (Minneapolis, MN), 2005.

Pearl Harbor and the Story of World War II, Mitchell Lane Publishers (Hockessin, DE), 2005.

Mark Twain, Mitchell Lane Publishers (Hockessin, DE), 2005.

Johnny Gruelle, Mitchell Lane Publishers (Hockessin, DE), 2005.

Also author of "The Space Sorcerers," an episode for the television series *Adventures of the Galaxy Rangers.* Contributor of numerous short stories to anthologies, including *Sword and Sorceress IV,* DAW Books, 1987; *Vampires,* HarperCollins, 1991; *Horse Fantastic,* DAW, 1991; and *Sisters in Fantasy,* New American Library, 1993. Also contributor to periodicals, including *Cricket, Children's Digest, Jack and Jill, Highlights for Children,* and *Dragon.* Consulting editor for Baen Books; field editor for Walker & Company.

ANTHOLOGIES

(Reteller) *A Sampler of Jewish-American Folklore,* August House, 1992.

(Reteller) *Rachel the Clever and Other Jewish Folktales,* August House (Little Rock, AK), 1993.

(Reteller) *Told Tales: Nine Folktales from around the World,* Silver Moon Press (New York, NY), 1995.

(Editor) *Greasy Grimy Gopher Guts: The Subversive Folklore of Childhood,* August House (Little Rock, AR), 1995.

(Reteller) *Trickster Tales: Forty Folk Stories from around the World,* illustrated by David Boston, August House (Little Rock, AR), 1996.

(Reteller) *Merlin's Kin: World Tales of the Hero Magician,* August House (Little Rock, AR), 1998.

(Reteller) *Mythology for Storytellers: Themes and Tales from around the World,* Sharpe Reference (Armonk, NY), 2003.

(Reteller) *Magic Hoofbeats: Horse Tales from Many Lands,* illustrated by Linda Wingerter, Barefoot Books (Cambridge, MA), 2004.

(Editor with Tamora Pierce) *Young Warriors,* Random House (New York, NY), 2005.

Adaptations

Vulcan's Soul, Book 1: Exodus was adapted as an audio recording, Simon & Schuster Audio, 2004.

Sidelights

Josepha Sherman is a prolific writer whose works for children span a number of genres. In addition to creating folklore anthologies and fantasy novels for older readers, Sherman has produced a long list of nonfiction works, including biographies of sports stars, business leaders, and famous explorers as well as books on a variety of other topics. As Sherman once told *Something about the Author:* "I've led the usual checkered life of a writer, having been everything from an archaeologist to a scientific book indexer, and am right now a writer/editor/folklorist. Like many a fantasy writer, I came under the influence of J. R. R. Tolkien at an early age. But it was his essay 'On Fairy-Stories' that turned me on to the fascinating world that is comparative folklore. Many of my books and stories reflect my love of folklore."

One of Sherman's books inspired by folklore is *Vassilisa the Wise: A Tale of Medieval Russia,* a retelling of a twelfth-century Russian legend. The main character, Vassilisa, is, like most storybook heroines, very intelligent; she is also the most beautiful woman in the kingdom. Her proud husband foolishly boasts about his wife in front of royalty, claiming that Vassilia is lovelier than the princess and smarter than the prince; not surprisingly, he soon finds himself imprisoned in the royal dungeon. When Vassilisa learns that the prince now intends to abduct her, she cuts off her beautiful blonde hair, disguises herself as a man, and sets about to rescue her husband. Woven into the plot are three seemingly impossible tasks which the clever Vassilisa must accomplish during her quest. *Washington Post Book World* contributor Michael Dirda dubbed *Vassilisa the Wise* a "fine" retelling of the eastern European tale.

Sherman's volumes of collected folk tales include *Magic Hoofbeats: Horse Tales from Many Lands* and *Merlin's Kin: World Tales of the Hero Magician* both of which draw on her interest in fantasy. *Magic Hoofbeats,* which collects eight tales about talking horses, was praised by *School Library Journal* contributor Susan Hepler as a "rich combination of scholarly . . . historical information and well-told story." Sherman's *Mythology for Storytellers: Themes and Tales from around the World* takes a broad look at mythology as it has evolved within several cultures around the world. Sherman discusses the origins of myth, explaining that some form of mythology is woven into the cultural fabric of every human society on Earth. Ellen M. J. Keane, writing in *Reference & User Services Quarterly,* called Sherman's work a "handy reference tool," while Judy Sokoll wrote in *School Library Journal* that for storytellers who wish to "promote greater understanding" of a variety of cultures, *Mythology for Storytellers* will provide them with a "fascinating, demanding, and well-researched" resource.

Biographical and Critical Sources

PERIODICALS

Booklist, March 1, 1994, Carolyn Phelan, review of *Gleaming Bright,* p. 1253; October 1, 1994, Dennis Winters, review of *Once upon a Galaxy: Folktales and Science Fiction,* p. 245; June 1, 1995, Jeanne Triner, review of *Orphans of the Night,* p. 1753; February 1, 1996, Janice Del Negro, review of *Told Tales: Nine Folktales from around the World,* p. 928; April 15, 1996, Janice Del Negro, review of *Greasy Grimy Gopher Guts: The Subversive Folklore of Childhood,* p. 1448; June 1, 1996, Patricia Monaghan, review of *The First Americans: Spirit of the Land and the People,* p. 1672; April 15, 1999, Kay Weisman, review of *Merlin's Kin: World Tales of the Hero Magician,* p. 1527; June 1, 1999, Roland Green, review of *Vulcan's Heart,* p. 1743; April 1, 2004, Ed Sullivan, review of *The Korean War,* p. 1371; October 15, 2000, Stephanie Zvirin, review of *Welcome to the Rodeo!,* p. 463; March 15, 2001, Carolyn Phelan, review of *Jeff Bezos: King of Amazon,* p. 1396; March 1, 2004, Shauna Yusko, review of *Mythology for Storytellers: Themes and Tales from around the World,* p. 1231.

Entertainment Weekly, November 25, 1994, Michele Landsberg, review of *Once upon a Galaxy,* p. 100.

Library Journal, May 15, 1998, Jackie Cassada, review of *Son of Darkness,* p. 119; October 15, 1998, Jackie Cassada, review of *Merlin's Kin,* p. 104; January, 2004, Katherine K. Koenig, review of *Mythology for Storytellers,* p. 124.

New York Times Book Review, May 8, 1988, pp. 23, 34.

Publishers Weekly, May 19, 1997, review of *Vulcan's Forge,* p. 70; June 1, 1999, review of *Vulcan's Heart,* p. 59.

Reference & User Services Quarterly, summer, 2004, Ellen M. J. Keane, review of *Mythology for Storytellers,* p. 351.

School Library Journal, August, 2000, Time Wadham, review of *Bull Riding,* p. 207; August, 2000, Tim Wadham, review of *Bronc Riding,* p. 207; August, 2000, Tim Wadham, review of *Barrel Racing,* p. 207; September, 2000, Lana Miles, review of *Welcome to the Rodeo!,* p. 256; September, 2000, Lana Miles, review of *Steer Wrestling,* p. 256; September, 2000, Lana Miles, review of *Ropers and Riders,* p. 256; November, 2000, Sandra L. Doggett, review of *Bill Gates: Computer King,* p. 175; July, 2001, Mary Mueller, review of *Jeff Bezos: King of Amazon,* p. 122; December, 2001, Yapha Nussbaum Mason, review of *Jerry Yang and David Filo: Chief Yahoos of Yahoo!,* p. 153; March, 2002, p. 254; July, 2003, p. 119; September, 2003, Jennifer England, review of *Ferdinand Magellan: The First Voyage around the World,* p.227; February, 2004, Linda L. Walkins, review of *Shapes in the Sky: A Book about Clouds,* p. 140; April, 2004, Doris Losey, review of *Your Travel Guide to Ancient Rome,* p. 174; August, 2004, Judy Sokoll, review of *Mythology for Storytellers,* p. 150; February, 2005, Susan Hepler, review of *Magic Hoofbeats; Horse Tales from Many Lands,* p. 153.

Washington Post Book World, October 9, 1988, Michael Dirda, review of *Vassilisa the Wise,* p. 10.

ONLINE

Sherman Editorial Services Web site, http://www.ses-ny.com/ (July 6, 2005).

*   *   *

SNYDER, Zilpha Keatley 1927-

Personal

Born May 11, 1927, in Lemoore, CA; daughter of William Solon (a rancher and driller) and Dessa J. (Jepson) Keatley; married Larry Allan Snyder, June 18, 1950; children: Susan Melissa, Douglas; foster children: Ben. *Education:* Whittier College, B.A., 1948; additional study at University of California, Berkeley, 1958-60. *Politics:* Democrat. *Religion:* Episcopalian. *Hobbies and other interests:* "My hobbies seem to change from time to time, but reading and travel remain among the top favorites. And of course writing which, besides being my occupation, is still and always will be my all-time favorite hobby."

Addresses

Home—52 Miller Ave., Mill Valley, CA 94941.

Career

Writer. Public school teacher at Washington School, Berkeley, CA, and in New York, Washington, and Alaska, 1948-62; University of California, Berkeley, master teacher and demonstrator for education classes, 1959-61; lecturer.

Awards, Honors

Lewis Carroll Shelf Award, and Spring Book Festival first prize, both 1967, Newbery honor book, 1968, and George G. Stone Recognition of Merit, Claremont

Zilpha Keatley Snyder

Graduate School, 1973, all for *The Egypt Game;* Christopher Medal, 1970, for *The Changeling;* William Allen White Award, Newbery honor book, and Christopher Medal, all 1972, and Hans Christian Andersen International honor list, International Board on Books for Young People, 1974, all for *The Headless Cupid;* Outstanding Book, *New York Times,* 1972, and National Book Award finalist and Newbery honor book, both 1973, all for *The Witches of Worm;* Outstanding Book, *New York Times,* 1981, for *A Fabulous Creature;* PEN Literary Award, 1983, and Parents' Choice Award, Parents' Choice Foundation, both for *The Birds of Summer;* Bay Area Book Reviewers Award, 1988, William Allen White Master Reading List, 1989-90, and Georgia Children's Book Award Master List, 1990-91, all for *And Condors Danced;* New Mexico State Award, 1989-90, and Notable Trade Books in the Language Arts, National Council of Teachers of English, both for *The Changing Maze;* Notable Books, American Library Association, for *Season of Ponies, The Egypt Game, The Headless Cupid, The Witches of Worm, Libby on Wednesday,* and *A Fabulous Creature;* Honor Book designation, *Horn Book,* for *The Velvet Room* and *The Egypt Game; Blair's Nightmare* was included on state awards master lists in Missouri, Texas, Nebraska, the Pacific Northwest, and New Mexico; *Libby on Wednesday* was included on the Virginia state award master list; finalist, Mythopoeic Society Award, and state award master lists in Missouri, Illinois, and Utah, for *Song of the Gargoyle;* Best Books, New York Public Library and *School Library Journal,* CLA Beatty Award, and Book of the Year for Children, Child Study Children's Book Committee, all 1994, all for *Cat Running;* nomi-

nee, California Young Readers' Medal, 1994-95, for *Fool's Gold;* Texas Bluebonnet Award master list inclusion, 1996, for *The Trespassers;* honorary D.H.L., Whittier College, 1998; inclusion on state master lists in Texas, Nebraska, Vermont, New Mexico, and South Carolina, 1999-2000, for *Gib Rides Home;* Parents' Choice Foundation silver medal, 2004, for *The Unseen.*

Writings

FOR CHILDREN

Season of Ponies, illustrated by Alton Raible, Atheneum (New York, NY), 1964.

The Velvet Room, illustrated by Alton Raible, Atheneum (New York, NY), 1965.

Black and Blue Magic, illustrated by Gene Holtan, Atheneum (New York, NY), 1966.

The Egypt Game, illustrated by Alton Raible, Atheneum (New York, NY), 1967.

Eyes in the Fishbowl, illustrated by Alton Raible, Atheneum (New York, NY), 1968.

Today Is Saturday (poetry), photographs by John Arms, Atheneum (New York, NY), 1969.1969.

The Changeling, illustrated by Alton Raible, Atheneum (New York, NY), 1970.

The Headless Cupid, illustrated by Alton Raible, Atheneum (New York, NY), 1971.

The Witches of Worm, illustrated by Alton Raible, Atheneum (New York, NY), 1972.

The Princess and the Giants (picture book), illustrated by Beatrice Darwin, Atheneum (New York, NY), 1973.

The Truth about Stone Hollow, illustrated by Alton Raible, Atheneum (New York, NY), 1974, published in England as *The Ghosts of Stone Hollow,* Lutterworth, 1978.

Below the Root (first volume in the "Green-sky" trilogy), illustrated by Alton Raible, Atheneum (New York, NY), 1975.

And All Between (second volume in the "Green-sky" trilogy), illustrated by Alton Raible, Atheneum (New York, NY), 1976.

Until the Celebration (third volume in the "Green-sky" trilogy), illustrated by Alton Raible, Atheneum (New York, NY), 1977.

The Famous Stanley Kidnapping Case, illustrated by Alton Raible, Atheneum (New York, NY), 1979.

Come on, Patsy (picture book), illustrated by Margot Zemach, Atheneum (New York, NY), 1982.

Blair's Nightmare, Atheneum (New York, NY), 1984.

The Changing Maze (picture book), illustrated by Charles Mikolaycak, Macmillan (New York, NY), 1985.

The Three Men, Harper (New York, NY), 1986.

And Condors Danced, Delacorte (New York, NY), 1987.

Squeak Saves the Day and Other Tooley Tales, illustrated by Leslie Morrill, Delacorte (New York, NY), 1988.

Janie's Private Eyes, Delacorte (New York, NY), 1989.

Libby on Wednesday, Delacorte (New York, NY), 1990.

Song of the Gargoyle, Delacorte (New York, NY), 1991.

Fool's Gold, Delacorte (New York, NY), 1993.

Cat Running, Delacorte (New York, NY), 1994.

The Trespassers, Delacorte (New York, NY), 1994.

Castle Court Kids (series; including *The Diamond War, The Box and the Bone, Ghost Invasion,* and *Secret Weapons*), Yearling, 1995.

The Gypsy Game, Delacorte (New York, NY), 1997.

Gib Rides Home, Delacorte (New York, NY), 1998.

The Runaways, Delacorte (New York, NY), 1999.

Gib and the Gray Ghost, Delacorte (New York, NY), 2000.

Spyhole Secrets, Delacorte (New York, NY), 2001.

The Ghosts of Rathburn Park, Delacorte (New York, NY), 2002.

The Magic Nation Thing, Delacorte (New York, NY), 2005.

NOVELS; FOR YOUNG ADULTS

A Fabulous Creature, Atheneum (New York, NY), 1981.

The Birds of Summer, Atheneum (New York, NY), 1983.

The Unseen, Delacorte (New York, NY), 2004.

OTHER

Heirs of Darkness (adult novel), Atheneum (New York, NY), 1978.

Snyder's manuscripts are housed in the Kerlan Collection, University of Minnesota at Minneapolis. Her books have been translated into many languages, and her short stories have been anthologized in sixteen collections.

Adaptations

Black and Blue Magic was made into a filmstrip with audiotape, Pied Piper, 1975; *The Egypt Game* was recorded by Miller-Brody, 1975, and produced as a filmstrip and audiotape by Piped Piper; *The Headless Cupid* was recorded for *Newbery Award Cassette* stories by Miller-Brody, 1976, and made into a filmstrip with audiotape by Pied Piper, 1980; *The Witches of Worm* was recorded by Miller-Brody, 1978; *Below the Root* was made into a computer game by Spinnaker Software's Windham Classics, 1985; *Cat Running, The Egypt Game, Song of the Gargoyle, The Witches of Worm, The Headless Cupid, Gib Rides Home, Gib and the Gray Ghost, Spyhole Secrets,* and *The Ghosts of Rathburn Park* were adapted as audiobooks by Recorded Books (New York, NY).

Sidelights

Three-time Newbery Honor Book recipient Zilpha Keatley Snyder is noted for her novels for middle graders, books full of wonder, mystery, and suspense. Addressing topics from magic to dysfunctional families, from murder to witchcraft, her works range in genre from fantasy to mainstream fiction, and usually focus on a female protagonist. Snyder writes an elegant but no-nonsense, tightly plotted prose that appeals to readers of all ages. Indeed, in addition to the majority of her work written for juvenile readers, she has also written two young adult novels, an adult Gothic novel, and poetry. Newbery Honor books from Snyder include *The Egypt Game, The Headless Cupid,* and *The Witches of Worm,* while the list of her other award-winning titles is a lengthy one: *The Changeling, A Fabulous Creature, The Birds of Summer, And Condors Danced, The Changing Maze, Blair's Nightmare, Song of the Gargoyle, Cat Running,* and *Gib Rides Home,* among others.

Snyder was born in Lemoore, California, in 1927, the daughter of a rancher and oil driller. Growing up in the Depression era, she and her friends found entertainment in simple things, developing fantasy games and play. She also formed a love for books and for the fantasy worlds they create. Skipping a grade in elementary school, she found herself out of sync with the older children in her grade and retreated further into books and fantasy. From high school on, she determined to become a writer, and harbored romantic dreams of living in a New York garret after graduating from Whittier College. However, marriage and a family as well as her career teaching elementary school intervened until the publication of Snyder's first novel, *Season of Ponies,* in 1964.

This first title drew on Snyder's lifelong love for horses. The story of a young and lonely girl living with two aunts whose boredom is mitigated by the arrival of magical ponies, *Season of Ponies* had in place many of the trademark Snyder elements. Zena Sutherland, writing in *Bulletin of the Center for Children's Literature,* neatly summed up the Snyder effect: "A story that is written on two levels—realistic and fanciful." From that first novel, Snyder went on to develop her characteristic style, creating books heavily inspired and infused with her own childhood experiences, featuring lonely, reclusive young girls, and with a strong element of the supernatural or of mystery in an outwardly realistic tale.

One of Snyder's most highly regarded early books, *The Egypt Game,* was published in 1967. In this work, April and Melanie turn a vacant lot into a pretend ancient Egypt for their fantasy games, but play turns nasty when a child-killer stalks April. Using a multiracial cast of urban characters, Snyder created "one the controversial books of the decade" of the 1960s, in the opinion of *Bulletin of the Center for Children's Books* contributor Sutherland. "It is strong in characterization, the dialogue is superb, the plot is original. . . . *The Egypt Game* is a distinguished book," Sutherland concluded. This book found a sequel three decades later in *The Gypsy Game,* which continues the story of April and Melanie, and introduced Melanie's little brother, Marshall. This time out the children are playing gypsies, having grown weary with playing ancient Egyptians. In the process, they try to figure out why their friend Toby has disappeared. Deborah Stevenson noted in the *Bulletin of the Center for Children's Books* that "the multicultural and age-diverse gang of characters retains much of its original charm," while Jennifer M. Brabander commented in *Horn Book* that readers who responded to the exotic costumes and rites of *The Egypt Game* "will find themselves drawn to and intrigued by the jewelry, colorful clothes, and fortune-telling in this adventure."

Another pair of youthful protagonists appears in *The Changeling,* a book that traces the growth of Ivy and Martha from age seven to their early teens. "It will be comforting to children to hear they can grow up without necessarily turning into those dull creatures known as 'grown-ups,'" noted Jean Fritz in the *New York Times Book Review.* In *The Witches of Worm,* another lonely young girl finds solace in the company of animals; this time it is a cat she finds, until she becomes convinced that the cat is possessed by a witch. Elizabeth Minot Graves, writing in *Commonweal,* called this book "a haunting story of the mind and ritual, as well as of misunderstanding, anger, loneliness and friendship." Of Snyder's *The Headless Cupid,* Barbara Sherrard-Smith noted in *Children's Book Review* that "This most readable and enjoyable book races along absorbingly," while Graves commented in *Commonweal* that it "pokes fun in a discerning way at the current interest in the occult and its beaded young practitioners, at the same time leaving an avenue open to a belief in ghosts and poltergeist."

With *The Headless Cupid,* Snyder began a quartet of novels about the Stanley family, five stepbrothers and stepsisters who get involved in dangerous and often comic situations. All four novels are told from the character David's point of view. These children also make appearances in *The Famous Stanley Kidnapping Case, Blair's Nightmare,* and *Janie's Private Eyes.* In the award-winning *Blair's Nightmare,* the Stanley kids want to keep a dog that Blair has found and also try to discover if a group of escaped convicts have come to their locale. Felice Buckvar, writing in the *New York Times Book Review,* concluded that "There is enough mystery to keep the reader turning the pages and enough realism to illustrate the theme," while Kathleen Brachman wrote in *School Library Journal* that "this will delight Snyder's fans and earn her new ones."

Another group of interlocking books, this time a science-fiction series, is the "Green-Sky" trilogy, comprising *Below the Root, And All Between,* and *Until the Celebration.* The trio of books deals with themes from violence and human nature to the morality of actions governments take. Set in an arboreal world far above the forest floor, the books feature young Raamo and Genaa and their mission to liberate the Erdlings, long ago captured among the roots below. "This is intellectual fantasy in that the ideas are in complete control," noted a *Kirkus Reviews* critic of *Until the Celebration,* "but throughout the trilogy they always come embodied in well-paced action."

Of Snyder's young-adult novels, *Birds of Summer* remains the most popular, and "just as timely today as it

was in 1983," according to Hazel K. Davis, writing in the *St. James Guide to Young Adult Writers.* In this novel, fifteen-year-old Summer has to deal not only with her budding sexuality, but also with a mother, Oriole, still tripping from her days on a commune. Living in a run-down trailer while on welfare, the glory days of sex, drugs and rock and roll are gone for Oriole, while Summer must determine how to make her own way in the world. Writing in *Voice of Youth Advocates,* Eleanor Klopp concluded, "What a joy to find a truly heroic heroine in a book whose plot alone will endear it."

Not one to write the same book over and over, Snyder turned from contemporary novels to history with *And Condors Danced,* a novel set in turn-of-the-twentieth-century southern California. Young Carly's mother is dying and the family's citrus farm is threatened with a water-rights issue in this book that "vividly captures the daily life of the farming community of Santa Luisa . . . before the automobile superseded the horse and buggy," according to Wendy Martin in the *New York Times Book Review.* Snyder serves up "a mercurial, uncertain medieval time," in *Song of the Gargoyle,* according to *Booklist* reviewer Ilene Cooper. A blend of history and fantasy, the book tells the story of Tymmon, who vows to rescue his father, Kommus, from his kidnapper. Teaming up with the gargoyle, Troff, Tymmon sets out to learn news of Kommus by entertaining villagers in the region. "Snyder continues to be one of our best storytellers," Cooper commented, concluding that the novel "is deeply layered and affecting."

Sticking with historical settings, Snyder focuses on life in a small California town during the Depression years in *Cat Running,* on an orphanage at the turn of the twentieth century in *Gib Rides Home,* and on a lonely desert town in the 1950s in *The Runaways.* In *Cat Running,* eleven-year-old Cat Kinsey builds a secret hideaway to find refuge from her home life, and soon finds friendship with a family of "Okies" who have lost their home in the wide-scale drought known as the Dust Bowl. In so doing, Cat comes smack up against her family's intolerance and bigotry. *Booklist* critic Stephanie Zvirin felt that Snyder illustrates "Cat's change from self-absorbed child to caring young woman with energy and enough verisimilitude to keep readers pleasantly involved." Roger Sutton concluded in the *Bulletin of the Center for Children's Books* that "Cat's an honorable, prickly heroine in a girls'-book tradition that stretches from Alcott's Jo March to Cynthia Voigt's Dicey."

In *The Runaways,* Dani O'Donnell, twelve years old and bored, hates the desert town of Rattler Springs, Nevada, where she is now living. Her mother works at the local bookstore and Dani spends most of her time with Stormy, a troubled nine-year-old dyslexic boy. She dreams of running away, heading back to the coastal town where she used to live. But such flight plans are complicated with the arrival of young Pixie and her geologist parents. GraceAnne A. DeCandido, writing in *Booklist,* called Stormy "an unforgettable portrait of a child whose life is heartbreakingly complicated." *Publishers Weekly* observed that even "minor characters . . . seem to have lives off the page" in Snyder's atmospheric novel of longing and regret.

Drawing on her father's stories of his childhood in a Nebraska orphanage, Snyder tells the story of the plight of orphans a century ago in *Gib Rides Home* and *Gib and the Gray Ghost.* Gib Whittaker manages to keep an optimistic outlook despite harsh treatment at the Lovell House Home for Orphaned and Abandoned Boys. When adopted by the wealthy Thornton family, he thinks he has finally found a loving family, only to discover that he has actually been sent into a sort of bondage, "farmed out," as is the practice with orphans, to be another farm hand. Susan Dove Lempke wrote in *Booklist* that "deft pacing and characterization, along with a background rich in sensory detail . . . make this a touching, satisfying tribute to Snyder's father and to all children who face difficult lives with courage." *Gib and the Gray Ghost* continues the story of Gib Whittaker, finding him leaving the orphanage for good and returning to work with the Thornton family again. While working on the ranch, he attends school and makes new friends, including Livy Thornton, and trains the horse named Gray Ghost, who mysteriously showed up at the ranch during a snowstorm. Lauralyn Persson, writing in the *School Library Journal,* found Gib to be "a sympathetic and appealing character." Kay Weisman in *Booklist* praised "Snyder's strong characterizations, compelling story, and rich setting details."

Snyder introduces readers to a troubled eleven-year-old girl named Hallie in *Spyhole Secrets.* When Hallie's father is killed in a traffic accident, she and her mother move to a new house. Hallie misses her father and hates the new home she must live in and the new school she now attends. Lonely and bored, she discovers a peephole in the attic where she can look across at the teenaged girl next door. The girl fascinates her because she seems to be undergoing tragic events that Hallie cannot quite understand. She nicknames the girl "Rapunzel" because of her long blonde hair. When Hallie befriends "Rapunzel's" younger brother, Zachary, she begins to learn more about the enigmatic girl in the window, a process that takes her out of her own depressive state. Shelle Rosenfeld, writing in *Booklist,* called *Spyhole Secrets* "an absorbing book with many intriguing issues," while a critic for *Publishers Weekly* praised the "realism and power of Snyder's writing."

The strange and paranormal appear in Snyder's *The Ghosts of Rathburn Park* and *The Unseen.* In the first title, the Hamilton family has just moved to Timber City. At the town's Fourth of July picnic, young Matt hears about the great fire that consumed the town years before and about the ghosts that are said to still haunt the town's park. Later, he sees a dog in the woods that no one else is able to see. Then he meets a strange girl,

Amelia, who dresses in clothes from the nineteenth century. Together they explore an old church, the local swamp, and the Rathburn mansion, where the town's oldest family live. Kathryn Kosiorek, writing in *School Library Journal,* called *The Ghosts of Rathburn Park* a "skillfully told story," while a *Publishers Weekly* critic found that Snyder's "gifts for fashioning lifelike and sympathetic characters are as pronounced as ever."

The Unseen tells of Xandra Hobson, a twelve year old who enjoys exploring the woods and taking in orphaned animals. One day she rescues a bird that mysteriously disappears the next day, leaving only a white feather behind. Xandra's friend Belinda claims that the feather is magical and can lead the two of them into unknown worlds. As they explore the feather's potential for bestowing special powers, Xandra unwittingly betrays her friend. Saleena L. Davidson, writing in the *School Library Journal,* called *The Unseen* "a wonderful ride into fantasy." Carolyn Phelan wrote in *Booklist* that Snyder's "well-grounded fantasy" has a "satisfying conclusion."

Throughout her more than three decades of writing, Snyder has continued to grow as a writer and to entertain as well as inform. Her many works have spanned the timeline and bridged genres, blending fantasy and history, realism and the supernatural, suspense and humor. A primary ingredient in each Snyder story is a compelling plot. "I still begin a story by indulging in what has always been for me a form of self-entertainment," Snyder wrote in *The Writer.* "I look for a character or characters and a beginning situation that cries out to be explored and embellished. . . . This beginning situation must be something that connects directly to my long-established urge to find excitement, mystery, and high emotion in the midst of even the most prosaic circumstances."

Biographical and Critical Sources

BOOKS

American Women Writers, 2nd edition, St. James Press (Detroit, MI), 2000.
Authors and Artists for Young Adults, Volume 15, Gale (Detroit, MI), 1995.
Beacham's Guide to Literature for Young Adults, Volume 1, Beacham Publishing (Osprey, FL), 1990.
Carpenter, Humphrey and Prichard, Mari, *The Oxford Companion to Children's Literature,* Oxford University Press (Oxford, England), 1984.
Children's Literature Review, Volume 31, Gale (Detroit, MI), 1994.
Contemporary Literary Criticism, Volume 17, Gale (Detroit, MI), 1981.
Hopkins, Lee Bennett, *More Books by More People: Interviews with Sixty-five Authors of Books for Children,* Citation Press (New York, NY), 1974.

Legends in Their Own Time, Prentice Hall (New York, NY), 1994.

Reginald, Robert, *Science Fiction and Fantasy Literature, 1975-1991,* Gale (Detroit, MI), 1992.

Silvey, Anita, editor, *Children's Books and Their Creators,* Houghton (Boston, MA), 1995.

St. James Guide to Young-Adult Writers, 2nd edition, St. James Press (Detroit, MI), 1999.

Twentieth-Century Children's Writers, 3rd edition, St. James Press (Detroit, MI), 1989.

PERIODICALS

Booklist, February 1, 1991, Ilene Cooper, review of *Song of the Gargoyle,* p. 1127; September 1, 1994, Stephanie Zvirin, review of *Cat Running,* p. 44; June 1, 1995, p. 1773; February 1, 1997, Ilene Cooper, review of *The Gypsy Game,* p. 942; January 1, 1998, Susan Dove Lempke, review of *Gib Rides Home,* p. 816; January 1, 1999, GraceAnne A. DeCandido, review of *The Runaways,* p. 879; January 1, 2000, Kay Weisman, review of *Gib and the Gray Ghost,* p. 912; May 1, 2001, Shelle Rosenfeld, review of *Spyhole Secrets,* p. 1612; December 15, 2001, Patricia Austin, review of *Gib and the Gray Ghost* (audiobook), p. 745; March 1, 2004, Carolyn Phelan, review of *The Unseen,* p. 1190.

Booktalker, September, 1989, p. 9.

Bulletin of the Center for Children's Books, September, 1964, Zena Sutherland, review of *Season of Ponies,* p. 20; May 13, 1967, Zena Sutherland, review of *The Egypt Game,* pp. 55-56; June, 1974; December, 1979, p. 82; March, 1982; January, 1983; April, 1984; November, 1985; November, 1987; May, 1988; January, 1995, Roger Sutton, review of *Cat Running,* p. 178; October, 1995, pp. 70-71; February, 1997, Deborah Stevenson, review of *The Gypsy Game,* p. 223.

Catholic Literary World, October, 1976, p. 138.

Children's Book Review, October, 1973, Barbara Sherrard-Smith, review of *The Headless Cupid,* p. 146.

Christian Science Monitor, February 29, 1968.

Commonweal, November 19, 1971, Elizabeth Minot Graves, "The Year of the Witch," pp. 179-182; November 17, 1972, Elizabeth Minot Graves, review of *The Witches of Worm,* p. 157.

Dell Carousel, fall-winter, 1985-1986.

Growing Point, September, 1976, p. 2939.

Horn Book, June, 1964, p. 284; April, 1965, p. 173; April, 1967, pp. 209-210; April, 1968, pp. 182-183; October, 1970, p. 479; October, 1971; December, 1972; October, 1973, p. 459; August, 1974, p. 380; March-April, 1995, p. 196; March-April, 1997, Jennifer M. Brabander, review of *The Gypsy Game,* p. 204; March-April, 1998, Susan P. Bloom, review of *Gib Rides Home,* p. 224; May, 2000, review of *Gib and the Gray Ghost,* p. 321.

Junior Bookshelf, December, 1978, p. 324.

Junior Literary Guild, March, 1975; March, 1984; November 15, 1985, p. 57.

Kirkus Reviews, March 1, 1974, p. 245; March 1, 1975, p. 239; February 1, 1977, review of *Until the Celebration,* p. 95; February 1, 1977, p. 95; September 1, 1978, p. 973; June 15, 1995, p. 863; November 15, 1996, p. 1675; December 1, 1997, p. 1779; September 15, 2002, review of *The Ghosts of Rathburn Park,* p. 1401; March 15, 2004, review of *The Unseen,* p. 277.

New York Times Book Review, May 9, 1965; July 24, 1966, p. 22; July 23, 1967; May 26, 1968; December 13, 1970, Jean Fritz, review of *The Changeling,* p. 26; December 10, 1972, Jean Fritz, review of *The Witches of Worm,* pp. 8, 10; November 7, 1971, pp. 42-44; May 4, 1975, pp. 32, 34; May 23, 1976, p. 16; May 8, 1977, p. 41; July 8, 1984, Felice Buckvar, review of *Blair's Nightmare,* p. 15; December 27, 1987, Wendy Martin, review of *And Condors Danced,* p. 17; October 22, 1995, p. 41.

Publishers Weekly, February 7, 1972; February 27, 1977; February 1, 1991, p. 81; January 20, 1997, review of *The Gypsy Game,* p. 402; January 18, 1999, review of *The Runaways,* p. 340; August 30, 1999, review of *Gib Rides Home,* p. 86; July 2, 2001, review of *Spyhole Secrets,* p. 76; October 21, 2002, review of *The Ghosts of Rathburn Park,* p. 76.

Saturday Review, May 13, 1967, pp. 55-56.

School Library Journal, August, 1984, Kathleen Brachman, review of *Blair's Nightmare,* pp. 77-78; April, 1990, p. 124; November, 1994, pp. 108-109; August, 1995, pp. 144-145; February, 1997, Lisa Dennis, review of *The Gypsy Game,* p. 106; January, 1998, Janet Hilbun, review of *Gib Rides Home,* p. 114; March, 1999, Susan Oliver, review of *The Runaways,* p. 215; March, 2000, Lauralyn Persson, review of *Gib and the Gray Ghost,* p. 242; June, 2001, Ellen Fader, review of *Spyhole Secrets,* p. 156; October, 2001, Veronica Schwartz, review of *Gib and the Gray Ghost,* p. 89; September, 2002, Kathryn Kosiorek, review of *Ghosts of Rathburn Park,* p. 234; August, 2003, Cheryl Preisendorfer, review of *The Ghosts of Rathburn Park,* p. 70; April, 2004, Saleena L. Davidson, review of *The Unseen,* p. 162.

Voice of Youth Advocates, October, 1983, Eleanor Klopp, review of *Birds of Summer,* pp. 208-209; October, 1994, p. 218; August, 1995, p. 166.

Washington Post Book World, December 3, 1967.

World of Children's Books, fall, 1977, pp. 33-35.

Writer, July, 1993, Zilpha Keatley Snyder, "To Be a Storyteller."

Young Readers Review, May, 1966; May, 1967; May, 1968; October, 1969.

ONLINE

Zilpha Keatley Snyder Web site, http://www.zksnyder.com (May 8, 2005).

OTHER

A Talk with Zilpha Keatley Snyder (videotape), Tim Podell Productions, 1998.*

Autobiography Feature

Zilpha Keatley Snyder

Zilpha Keatley Snyder contributed the following autobiographical essay to *SATA:*

When I look back to the beginning, at least as far back as memory will take me, I see most vividly animals and games and books. People are there, too, my mother and father and older sister, but in those earliest memories they are much less distinct. I don't know what this says about my priorities at the time, but there it is.

There were lots of animals. Although my father worked for Shell Oil, he had grown up on cattle ranches, and by dream and desire he was always a rancher. So we lived in the country where he had room for a garden and as many animals as possible. Among my earliest acquaintances were cows, goats, ducks, chickens, rabbits, dogs, cats, and, a little later on, horses. I can recall in some detail the day we acquired a collie puppy and a young kitten. I was three years old. The kitten was nominally mine and from the mysterious depths of a three-year-old's mind I produced a name—Maryland. I can remember some of the ensuing argument—no one else thought it was a sensible name—but I can't remember the reason for my choice.

Neither the kitten nor I had ever been to Maryland, nor had either of us, as far as I know, ancestors from there. But Maryland she was, and she and her offspring play a prominent part in many of my early memories.

And then there were games. Some were secret, some less so, and most of them grew out of a compul-

Zilpha (right) with her parents, Dessa J. and William S. Keatley, and her sister, Elizabeth, about 1930

sion to endow everything animal, vegetable and mineral with human characteristics. I suspect that all very young children are naturally given to anthropomorphism, but with me it must have been almost a full-time occupation. Not only animals, but also trees, plants, toys, and many other inanimate objects had personalities, and sometimes complicated life histories. Often these creatures seemed to have been in need of a helping hand. I built leafy shelters for homeless insects, doctored ailing toys, and every morning I saved Orphan Annie from drowning.

Glazed on the bottom of my cereal bowl, Orphan Annie was daily threatened by a sea of milk and gummy oatmeal. It was necessary for me to eat the disgusting mess quickly to save her from drowning. But once her face was uncovered, and the milk dammed behind a dike of oatmeal, my duty was done. My mother may have wondered why I began so eagerly and then left that thick dam of oatmeal around the center of the bowl.

Other inhabitants of my world of secret games were not so helpless, or so innocuous. Knives and hammers could be intentionally cruel; wagons and roller skates and all their ilk were often sneakily vindictive; and at the foot of my bed there lived a permanent settlement of little black demons with pitchforks just waiting for me to carelessly straighten out my legs. But I fooled them. For years I slept curled in a ball.

There were many other demons, most of whom haunted closets and the dark corners of rooms. Although they really frightened me, I don't think I would have wanted to be talked out of them. They were *my* demons and we had a working relationship.

Books and reading must have had a beginning somewhere but it is beyond memory. I seemed to have been born reading. Actually my mother claimed I taught myself after eavesdropping on lessons she was giving my older sister. Then one day when she was sick and I was four years old, I offered to read to her. When I proceeded to do so she thought I had memorized the book until she began to ask me individual words. Later when I became, briefly, a kind of neighborhood oddity—I had not yet been to school and I could read the newspaper and was sometimes called into neighbors' homes to demonstrate to sceptical guests—my mother claimed to have had nothing to do with it. Actually I think she used two methods which are almost certain to produce an early reader. First of all, she read to us—a lot. And then, when I tried to horn in on my sister's reading lessons, she told me I was too young—a challenge that no self-respecting four-year-old is going to take lying down.

Of course the games and the reading merged. Little Orphan Annie and the demons were soon joined by the likes of Heidi, Dorothy and Dr. Dolittle, not to mention some of the more intriguing characters I met in the pages of a very fat book called *Hurlbut's Story of the Bible*. My favorites were the ones whose lives included episodes that played well, such as Noah, Daniel, and

Jonah. Jonah, in particular, was a role that adapted well when one had, as I often did, tonsillitis. Being forced to stay in bed was less of a handicap when the scene being enacted took place in a whale's stomach.

But something should be said about the real people who were an important part of those early years. My father, William Solon Keatley, was a tall slow-moving man, the memory of whose kindness, patient devotion and unfailing sense of humor is, to me, proof that it is possible to surmount the effects of an appalling childhood.

The first child of John William Keatley, a young Englishman who immigrated to America in the 1870s, and Zilpha Johnson his Nebraskan bride—my father's first few years of life were happy ones. But when he was five years old his mother died. Putting my father and his two younger brothers in an orphanage, my grandfather went to California, promising to send for the boys as soon as he was able. But for some reason the summons to a new life never came. The orphanage, losing patience, allowed the two younger boys to be adopted. But by then my father was too old to interest adoptive parents, and old enough to be of temporary interest to various people, some of them relatives of his mother, who needed an extra ranch hand. Forced to do a man's work at the age of eight, often beaten, punished by being sent out mittenless in freezing weather, so that his frozen hands very nearly had to be amputated, he survived to become a gentle man with crooked hands, who loved people almost as much as he loved horses, and who treated both with unfailing kindness.

As a young man he worked as a cowboy, in the days when many ranges were still unfenced; and in later years he told wonderful stories about broncobusting, roundups and stampedes, and above all—HORSES. He sometimes said that he might forget a man but never a horse, and I'm sure it was true. As a child I knew all his horses through his stories including Old Washboard, who had an iron mouth and a penchant for hunting wild horses and who, on spotting a herd of wild ones, took off, completely ignoring the desires of his helpless rider who willy-nilly accompanied him on a mad chase, leaping gulleys and plunging down almost vertical cliffs with wild abandon. Fearing that someday Old Washboard would tackle a cliff he couldn't handle—"the only horse that ever scared me spitless," my father would say—he chickened out and sold him to a gullible passerby, just as innumerable owners had surely done before.

It was not until my father was in his forties and the owner of a small horse ranch in Wyoming that he was contacted by his father. Warmly received by his father's second family in California, he decided to relocate there. And it was there that he met Dessa Jepson, a thirty-five-year-old spinster schoolteacher, a cousin of his stepmother.

The Jepsons were Quakers. They had lived for many generations in Maine, the first Jepson arriving there in 1720, but in the 1870s several branches of the family moved west. My mother was born in California, the youngest of six children. Several years younger than her nearest sibling, she was born when her parents were middle-aged, and on the death of her mother she became her father's housekeeper and companion.

I never knew my grandfather, Isaiah Clarkson Jepson, but he must have been a complicated and determined man. A farmer who had tried photography and teaching and who loved poetry, he doted on Dessa, his youngest daughter, and effectively discouraged her early suitors. She became a schoolteacher, attending UCLA when it was still Los Angeles Normal School, and devoted herself to teaching and to her father. His death when she was in her early thirties left her rudderless and she suffered what she later referred to as a nervous breakdown. On recovering she returned to work and was teaching in Yorba Linda, California when she met my father. It was a romance right out of Zane Grey—the bachelor rancher meets the lonely schoolteacher.

My parents were living in Lemoore, California when my older sister, Elisabeth, and I were born, my father having accepted what he thought of as a temporary job until he could get back to ranching. But the Depression deepened and, to support his growing family, he continued at a job he hated. It was after he was transferred to Ventura, California that my younger sister, Ruth, was born.

Like my father, my mother was a storyteller. Like his, her stories were true accounts of past events. Mother's childhood was always very close to her and she had a tremendous memory for detail. She made the people and events of rural California at the turn of the century as real to me as were those of my own childhood in the l930s.

So I came by my storytelling instincts honestly but, as it soon became apparent, their acquisition was all that was honest about them. It wasn't exactly that I was a liar. I don't think I told any more of the usual lies of childhood—those meant to get you out of trouble or get someone else into it—than most children. It was just that when I had something to tell I had an irresistible urge to make it worth telling, and without the rich and rather lengthy past that my parents had to draw on, I was forced to rely on the one commodity of which I had an adequate supply—imagination. Sometimes when I began an account of something I had heard or witnessed my mother would sigh deeply and say, "Just tell it. Don't embroider it."

*

At the age of eight I became, in my own eyes at least, a writer. I sometimes say that I decided on a writing career as soon as it dawned on me that there were people whose life's work consisted of making up stories. Up until then my tendency to "make things up" was one of the things that came to mind when I repeated that phrase about "trespasses" in our nightly prayers. The idea that there were people who were paid, even praised, for such activities was intriguing. I began

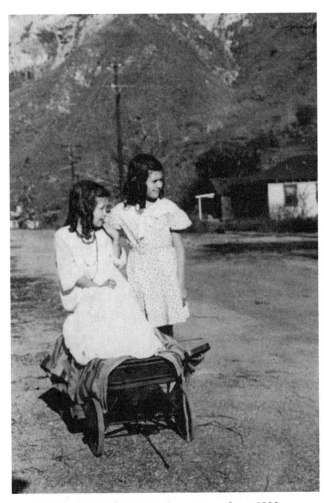

"Princess" Zilpha in the wagon, about 1933

as most children do with poems and very short stories, and I was fortunate to have a fourth-grade teacher who took an interest in what I was doing. She collected my works, typed them, and bound them into a book. I loved it—and her.

This early opus, while showing no great originality of thought or unique turns of phrase, does seem to exhibit a certain feeling for the rhythm and flow of words. The following excerpt owed its subject matter to a "social studies project" on China.

The Water Buffalo

Did you ever see a water buffalo,
Slowly around a rice field go,
Dragging a plow at every step?
To plow a rice field takes lots of pep,
So when the buffalo's work is done
He goes down to the river to have some fun.
He wallows down where the mud is deep,
And shuts his eyes and goes to sleep.

My memories of my first five years of school are pleasant ones. I was a good student, although my abilities were decidedly lopsided. I could memorize a poem in a flash, but the result of multiplying seven times eight eluded me for months, until my mother printed this slippery bit of information on a card and pinned it to the wall in front of the kitchen sink where I was forced to stare at it every evening while doing the dishes. It worked, I guess. I'm not sure whether my hatred of doing dishes spilled over onto the multiplication tables or vice versa, but I'm still not particularly fond of either.

Although there were times when I would have gladly traded my proficiency in reading and writing for a little skill at something that really mattered to my contemporaries such as running races or catching fly balls, I had few problems in the small country schools I attended until the end of sixth grade. But then came the seventh grade in the big city of Ventura. Too young for my grade, having been advanced by a first-grade teacher who didn't know what to do with me while she was teaching reading, and further handicapped by being raised by a mother who hadn't really faced up to the twentieth century, I was suddenly a terrible misfit. Still wearing long curls and playing secret games, I was too intimidated to make an effort to relate to girls who wore makeup and danced with boys. So I retreated further into books and daydreams.

Books! Books were the window from which I looked out of a rather meager and decidedly narrow room, onto a rich and wonderful universe. I loved the look and feel of them, even the smell. I'm still a book sniffer. That evocative mixture of paper and ink and glue and dust never fails to bring back the twinge of excitement that came with the opening of a new book. Libraries were treasure houses. I always entered them with a slight thrill of disbelief that all their endless riches were mine for the borrowing. And librarians I approached with reverent awe—guardians of the temple, keepers of the golden treasure.

It has occurred to me to wonder if I might not have faced up to life sooner if I had been deprived of books. (I know my father worried sometimes about the amount of time I spent reading. My father, not my mother. Her first priority was that we were safely and virtuously at home, with a book or without one.) Lacking a refuge in books, would I have been forced to confront my social inadequacies and set myself to learning the skills that would have made me acceptable to my peers? Perhaps. But then I wonder if it would really have been a fair trade. Would dances and parties and inexpert kisses by pimply contemporaries have made me happier than did Mr. Rochester, Heathcliff, the Knights of the Round Table and the many other heroes and heroic villains with whom I was intermittently in love? Who's to say? In any event, I went on reading—and suffering the daily agony of the preteen outcast.

Beyond my personal world of home and school and books and dreams, the Depression deepened. Although my father never lost his job, his salary was cut and cut again until he was finally unable to cover the mortgage payments and it was only the New Deal's mortgage relief legislation that enabled us to keep our home. Like so many other families, we lived constantly under that sword of Damocles called the "pink slip." My sisters and I, as well as many of our friends, knew about the slip of pink paper which might at any time be included in our father's pay envelope, and we knew that the result would be the disgrace of "relief lines" and perhaps actual hunger. Sometimes as I walked past the "Okie Camp" that had sprung up on a neighbor's vacant land—trying to pretend I wasn't staring at the cardboard shanties, broken down cars and ragged dirty children—I fantasized that I belonged there; that I would turn in on the dirt road and as I approached the first crumbling shanty I would see my mother in the doorway. It was a game that both intrigued and terrified me.

As the first decade of my life ended the times slowly began to get better. The Okie camps disappeared, people who had been laid off went back to work and salaries began to rise. And then one day when we turned into our driveway after a Sunday morning at church, a neighbor ran to meet us. The Japanese, she said, had attacked Pearl Harbor.

I was in my early teens during the war and I would *like* to report that I thought deeply about the issues involved and the terrible suffering that was going on around the world—but it wouldn't be true. In spite of the fact that a Japanese sub once shelled an empty field not far from where we lived, and we had occasional air raid drills in our classrooms, the war seemed distant and almost unreal. I wrote a few sentimental war poems and went on reading and dreaming. Years later when I visited Anne Frank's apartment in Amsterdam and saw the pictures of movie stars on her bedroom walls, familiar Hollywood faces of the forties, treasured by teenage girls in California as well as those in hiding in Amsterdam, I was deeply shaken. I cried not only with grief for Anne but with shame that I had known and cared so little.

By the time I was in high school my social skills had begun to improve, and I became a little less afraid of my peers. I had some good teachers and made some exciting new friends, such as Shakespeare and Emily Dickinson.

And college was wonderful. At Whittier College, a small private liberal arts school in Southern California, originally established by Quakers, I grew physically and socially as well as intellectually. I discovered contemporary authors, politics, social injustice, psychology—and boys; men, actually, as the time was the late forties and campuses were full of returned servicemen. It was a good time to be in college. I learned a lot at Whittier: facts, ideas, and essences. Many of the facts have faded, as elusive as seven times eight, but I remember that Whittier taught me how little I knew; a startling concept to any new high school graduate. And even more important—how little anyone knew. Until then I had been satisfied that all possible knowledge was pretty much in hand, and as a student my only job would be to commit it to memory. What a thrill to real-

Zilpha at Whittier College, about 1947

ize that a lot of so-called facts were actually still up for grabs, and that decision-making was a part of learning.

And one more thing I owe to Whittier—my husband, Larry Snyder. We met first in the Campus Inn where we both waited on tables, and when I first saw him he was playing the piano. Six-foot-five with curly black hair and blue eyes, Larry was a music major who was also an athlete, a charismatic extrovert who was—and still is—a natural scholar, and a small-town boy who was born with a Ulysses-like yearning for new horizons. I liked him a lot. I still do.

But I was planning to be a writer. I wanted to live in New York City, in an attic apartment, and write serious novels for serious people. It's a good thing I didn't try it. At barely twenty-one with a new college degree, I had a sketchy instinct for self-preservation and all the sophistication of a cocker spaniel puppy. New York City would have eaten me alive, and that's without even trying to guess what New York editors would have done to me. The pages that have survived from the period suggest that as a writer I still had the lively imagination of my childhood, and some feeling for the sound and sweep of a sentence. But style, theme, subject matter, and even handwriting (I still didn't own a typewriter) have a pronounced aura of puppy.

Facing up to the fact that I didn't even have the money for a ticket to New York City, I decided to be practical. So, "temporarily until I got back to ranching,"

I took another job—I decided to teach school. Only I was more fortunate than my poor dear father. I didn't hate my temporary job. In fact, I liked it a lot. After the first year, which was a bit traumatic until I stopped being surprised when I told the class to do something and they did it, I developed into what must have been a pretty good teacher. I taught in the upper elementary grades for a total of nine years, three of them as a master teacher for the University of California at Berkeley, during which time my classroom was almost constantly being observed by teachers in training. I found teaching to be as rewarding as it was demanding, and I would probably still be at it if I hadn't been lucky enough to have my dream-ranch become a reality when my first book was published—but that was later. And I also decided to accept Larry's offer of marriage, which was probably the best decision I ever made.

*

Larry and I were married in June of 1950, and the next ten years flew by. They were happy years for the most part, although I sometimes think that if they hadn't been I might not have had time to notice. During that time Larry was in graduate school at Eastman School of Music; taught for one year at Eastern Washington College in Cheney, Washington; and then, because of the Korean War, was in the air force in Texas, New York and Alaska, before returning to graduate school at UC Berkeley. In the period we moved fifteen times, I taught school in New York, Washington, Alaska and California, and we had three children. Our first child was born by emergency caesarian section in 1952 and died two days after his birth. Our daughter, Susan Melissa, was born in 1954 in Rome, New York and our son Douglas in Alaska in 1956. There were no further additions to our family until 1966 when our foster son, Ben, came to live with us. Ben was born in Kowboon, China and when he became a part of our family he was eleven years old and spoke no English. Three years later he was the valedictorian of his eighth-grade class. Ben is like that.

In the early sixties the dust began to settle a bit. Larry was out of school and teaching at the College of Mann north of San Francisco, and the children were in school, Doug, the youngest, in kindergarten. I was still teaching but there seemed to be a bit more time and I caught my breath and thought about writing. Writing for children hadn't occurred to me when I was younger, but nine years of teaching in the upper elementary grades had given me a deep appreciation of the gifts and graces that are specific to individuals with ten or eleven years of experience as human beings. It is, I think, a magical time—when so much has been learned, but not yet enough to entirely extinguish the magical reach and freedom of early childhood. Remembering a dream I'd had when I was twelve years old about some strange and wonderful horses, I sat down and began to write.

Now comes the hard part. I've always maintained that I would never write an autobiography. To me, writing anything other than fiction is a chore. Take away the marvelous incentive of a world yours-for-the-making, and the joy dies. Thus, I once answered when asked if I would write an autobiography, by saying, "Not unless they'd let me make it up as I went along."

But then I weakened and accepted the invitation to participate in the *Something about the Author Autobiography Series,* and up to this point I've found, to my surprise, that I've enjoyed it a great deal. But from here on it won't be so easy.

My husband says that all authors' autobiographies should be titled *And Then I Wrote.* This, of course, has put me on my mettle to avoid, not only that phrase, but also anything even remotely resembling it while, at the same time, covering twenty-one books and a computer game. After considerable thought I've decided to rely on the appended bibliography to provide chronology, while I deal with my years as a writer in a less structured way.

One of the questions most often asked of a writer concerns how he or she managed the giant step between being "would be" and "published." Everyone has heard about the difficulties involved in selling a first book; the closets full of unpublished manuscripts, and walls papered with rejection slips. I've been known to answer such questions by blandly announcing that I sold my first manuscript to the first publisher I sent it to. It's the truth, but not unfortunately, the whole truth; and I always go on to explain the less-glorious particulars. But once when I made the initial pronouncement in a gathering of writers and before I could qualify it, someone said quite justifiably, "Stand back, everyone. I'm going to shoot her."

The truth is that I did send my first attempt to write for young people to Atheneum and it was, indeed, published there some time later. The other part of the story is what happened in between.

I was still teaching school that year and I began to write at night after a day in the classroom. I was a lousy typist and at that time I was completely unable to compose at the typewriter, so I wrote on a tablet, and my husband, whose fingers move almost as well on a typewriter as they do on the piano, typed it for me. Later, when the book was accepted, he bought me an electric typewriter and told me to get busy and learn to type as he didn't intend to make a profession of typing manuscripts.

I didn't exactly pick Atheneum because it was at the beginning of the alphabet, but it was nearly that arbitrary. It was recommended to me by our school librarian as a house that had recently published some good fantasies. But what I received when I mailed in my manuscript—"over the transom," no agent, no introduction—was neither the rejection slip I fully expected, nor the enthusiastic acceptance of which I'd occasionally allowed myself to daydream. What I received was a long letter, two full pages, telling me what was wrong with my story. It was only at the very end that the editor, Jean Karl, stated that if I were going to be working on it some more she would like to see it again. I remember telling my husband that either she was slightly interested or I had just received the world's longest rejection slip.

Of course I was going to be working on it some more. It never occurred to me to reply, "Who the hell are you?" as one well-known author is reported to have done when an editor asked for changes in his first manuscript. It was my first attempt to write for young people, and almost the only writing I had done for ten years. I knew I had lots to learn and I was delighted that someone was willing to help.

My first version of *Season of Ponies* was, among other failings, much too short to be a book for the age level towards which it was aimed. Jean liked the ending but wanted me to lengthen and strengthen the body of the story. I did, and she liked it better, but still there were problems. It was after the third complete rewriting that the book was accepted, and I became a published writer.

Being published, I found, makes a difference. It makes a difference to all writers, but there are, I think, differences specific to the writer who is also a wife and mother. Almost no one feels called upon to honor the working hours of an unpublished wife and mother who insists on wasting large chunks of time in front of a typewriter. But once she is published, friends are some-

Larry A. and Zilpha K. Snyder, June 18, 1950

Melissa and Douglas Snyder, about 1960

what more hesitant about calling up for long midmorning chats, and recruiters for the United Fund, the PTA and Faculty Wives are a little less inclined to put her on the "readily available" list.

Within my own family, however, being published made very little difference. Larry had always been encouraging and supportive, and he continued to be.

And my mother, who often lived with us, continued to bring her reading or mending into my room. "Just for the company, I won't say a word." She would say, "Go right on with your writing." And I would try to, knowing that she was lonely and watching for the slightest sign that my attention was wavering and that I was, therefore, fair game. And, of course, published or unpublished, I was always fair game to the children. Rules concerning an off-limits area in the general vicinity of my typewriter during certain hours of the day were impossible to enforce in the face of such major crises as the need for financing an ice cream purchasing expedition, or the mysterious and momentous disappearance of a baseball, rollerskate, sneaker, or any one of numerous pets, including cats, dogs, hamsters, rats, snakes and one very large, very green iguana. The demand for my expertise as a pet finder was especially pressing when the snakes or iguana were involved, since grandmothers and other guests objected to coming across them suddenly in unexpected places.

But children do go to school, and after I stopped teaching there were the blessedly quiet hours of the school day in which to write, and the list of my published books began to grow, usually at the rate of one a year.

My second book evolved from the remains of a manuscript written when I was nineteen years old, a novel for adults set in a fictional town in Ventura County during the Depression. The story, lustily begun,

had run into plotting problems and had dwindled off in midsentence on about the forty-fifth page, but the setting and a few of the characters still intrigued me. Knocking a dozen years off the ages of the central characters I began the book again and the result was *The Velvet Room.*

*

I had not been a published writer for long when I discovered a new threat to my precious time at the typewriter, one which I had not counted on. I began to get invitations to speak or lecture. Many were requests that I speak in classrooms, and these, except for the loss of writing time involved, were never any problem. I was accustomed to the classroom situation, I enjoy interacting with children, and it was a thrill to learn about their reactions to my books. But a request that I speak to an adult group was a different matter. I accepted the first one because I was asked eight months ahead of time and I didn't think they'd believe me if I said I'd already booked the date. And then it was such a long time away—perhaps the world would come to an end, or some other fortuitous circumstance would prevent me from having to face up to my commitment. But the day did arrive, preceded by many sleepless nights during which I lay awake wondering what my hosts would do when I collapsed in a dead faint at the podium. But both I and my audience of several hundred librarians managed to survive that one, the requests continued to come, and my terror when facing large bodies of librarians, teachers or writers, gradually diminished.

The Egypt Game was my fourth book, and a good one to look at as an example of the complexity of the only possible answer to a simple, and very commonly asked question; "Where do you get your ideas?" Children ask it poised on tiptoe, ready to run off and get some of their own, and adults suspiciously, as if expect-

Ben and Doug (and Wotan), about 1966

ing one to either: 1) Admit to having personally experienced every event described in one's body of work, or 2) Own up to hereditary insanity. The only answer to the question is "everywhere," and without meaning to be facetious, because in any one book the idea roots are many and varied; some of them easily followed while others are fainter and more mysterious.

For example the beginning seeds of *The Egypt Game* were sown during my early childhood, as is true of a great many of my books. A fifth-grade project on ancient Egypt started me on my "Egyptian period," a school year in which I read, dreamed, and played Egyptian. But my dream of Egypt was private and it was my daughter, many years later, who actually played a game very like the one in the story, after I had turned her on to the fascinating game possibilities of a culture that includes pyramids, mummies, hieroglyphic writing, and an intriguing array of gods and goddesses. However the actual setting and all six of the main characters came from my years as a teacher in Berkeley. The neighborhood described in the story, the ethnic mix in the classroom, as well as the murder, were all taken from realities of our years in Berkeley. So, as I tell children who ask me if I ever write "true" stories, all of my stories have bits-and-pieces of truth—true events, true people, true facts, as well as true memories and even true dreams (the real sound-asleep kind). But the fun comes from what goes on in between and around and over the bits and pieces, tying them together and making them into a story. The in-between substance is woven of imagination and that is what makes fiction fascinating, to write as well as to read.

And then there is another element, a mysterious idea source which, it seems, many writers tap from time to time, and its unexpected and unpredictable gifts provide some of the most exciting and rewarding moments in writing. One might call such exciting moments a lateral-thinking breakthrough, serendipity, the light-bulb syndrome, or just sudden inspiration; an inspiration that seems to come from nowhere and to have no known roots. Whatever you call it, it's the kind of thing that makes you look up from the keyboard and say, "Hey. Thanks a lot."

The Egypt Game came out in 1967. We were still living in Mann County while across the bay to the east, Berkeley was leading the way in a world-wide explosion of protest. To the south, in San Francisco, the Flower Children were painting gracious old HaightAshbury Victorians purple and living on love and LSD. And in our own neighborhood Ken Kesey's psychedelic bus was parked not three blocks away, and Janis Joplin's west coast hangout was just up the street. Larry and I marched in anti-war parades but otherwise mostly watched in wonder from the sidelines while lifestyles changed, traditions crumbled, and protest, drugs and violence became a part of American life—and our children entered their teenage years. It was not an easy time to be a parent or a writer of books for young people. *Eyes in the Fishbowl, The Changeling, The Headless Cupid,* and *The Witches of Worm* came from those years.

Zilpha in France, 1968

Also during those years Larry became the dean at the San Francisco Conservatory of Music, and we began to make almost yearly trips to Europe. In 1970 we spent a month touring France with our three children, who were sixteen, fifteen, and thirteen at the time. Melissa chose the day we arrived in France to announce that she had just become a strict vegetarian; Ben, who had been working hard at being a typical American teenager, perfected an admirably authentic teenage griping technique; and Doug showed little interest in French culture other than *pâtisseries,* pigeons. and stray cats. With the five of us cooped up together daily in a small rental car Larry and I came to the conclusion that early teenagers, like fine wines, do not travel well.

It was not until some years later that all three of them began to tell us how much they enjoyed that summer in France and how much it had meant to them.

In 1971 Larry took a position at Sonoma State University in Sonoma County and we moved to a one-hundred-year-old-farmhouse in the country near Santa Rosa, California. Larry was anxious to get out of administration and back into music and teaching and we wanted to get our children into a quieter, more rural atmosphere. We were also eager to own horses, a goal that was quickly accomplished after the move. I was out horse shopping almost before we were unpacked.

In our old house, mysteriously like the one I'd described in *The Headless Cupid,* I finished *The Witches of Worm, The Princess and the Giants, The Truth about Stone Hollow,* and the three books of the Green-Sky Trilogy.

Like so many of my books the trilogy's deepest root goes back to my early childhood when I played a game that involved crossing a grove of oak trees by climbing from tree to tree, because something incredibly dangerous lived "below the root." Years later when

I was writing *The Changeling* I recalled the game, and in the course of embellishing it for that story, became intrigued with the idea of returning to the world of Green-sky for a longer stay. The return trip took three years and produced three more books. Initially published in 1975, 1976, and 1978, the trilogy has (1985) been reincarnated as a computer game, as well as in a paperback edition by Tor Books.

The computer game transpired when I was contacted by a young computer programmer named Dale Disharoon. After Dale introduced me to the world of computer games, I wrote and charted, Dale programmed, and a young artist named Bill Groetzinger made marvelous graphics for a game that takes off from where the third book of the trilogy ends.

In 1977–78, with our children grown and away from home, Larry and I spent his first sabbatical year in Europe. Larry, who is quite fluent in Russian and had done much of his graduate work on Russian music, had for some years been leading a UC Berkeley Extension tour to the Soviet Union during the summers. For his sabbatical project we traveled for seven weeks in Russia, the Baltic Republics, Poland, and Czechoslovakia while he did research on contemporary music. It was an incredible trip, sometimes uncomfortable and often a bit dismaying, but never less than fascinating, and very productive in terms of Larry's project.

When we finally reached Italy we were ready to settle down, which we did for four months in a lovely villa in the Tuscan countryside between Florence and Siena. During that time we alternated trips around Italy with long days of work, in which Larry compiled his collected data and practiced the piano, and I finished a novel for adults, *Heirs of Darkness,* and began a children's book set in Italy (a sequel to *The Headless Cupid* titled *The Famous Stanley Kidnapping Case*). "Just like Chopin and Georges Sand," Alton Raible, who has illustrated many of my books, wrote, and then added, "Without all the coughing and spitting, I hope." Our villa was part of a complex of rental units constructed from a country manor house and outlying farm buildings, and among the residents were writers, artists, and academics from various countries. It was an environment *molto simpatico* and friendships we made there have been important and lasting.

On returning to Sonoma County I began work on a novel for young adults. It was a story concerning a teenage boy and a magnificent buck deer, and when I began to write I had in mind a fantasy about mythical animals. But *A Fabulous Creature* turned out to be one of those novels that seem to take over and direct their own development and I soon found I was writing a story that was quite realistic and that had a bit to say about one of my pet antipathies—the whole mystique of the sport of hunting. As had happened many times before, I suddenly said, "Oh, so *that's* what I'm writing about."

That backdoor approach to themes or "messages" has been a part of the scene for me since my first book,

when I thought I was basing my story's antagonist on Greek mythology and only discovered after-the-fact that I'd been writing about someone I once knew—and feared; and my unconscious theme concerned the evil that arises when selfish and insensitive use is made of a naturally dominant personality.

It worried me for a while, this rather haphazard approach to thematic material, and now and then I tried it the other way, starting a few stories with the intention of addressing a given problem. But it never turned out well. Plots went lame and characters turned into caricatures. After a while I decided that, for me at least, "messages" were best left to their own devices. I would mind my own business, which was to tell a good story and let "messages" take care of themselves. They could, and would, I found, and in more subtle and interesting ways than when marshalled by my conscious mind. A case in point were some books of mine that were endorsed by the National Organization for Women. The stories in question had been written before my own consciousness had risen very far, and I'd not set out to say anything in particular about liberation or equality. But the message—that little girls can be vital and original and courageous people—found an appropriate opening, and there it was. Or when *Heirs of Darkness,* which I'd set out to write as a straightforward, one-dimensional Gothic horror story (not for children) turned into an ex-

Larry and Zilpha at a party celebrating the 100th year of their house, The Gables, 1977

ploration of guilt, and its relationship to the passive/masochistic personality.

*

As the eighties began we were still living in Sonoma County. Larry had been lured back into administration serving as dean of humanities and then of the School of Performing Arts at Sonoma State University—and the pendulum of American youth culture had begun a dramatic swing. Liberal arts departments were shrinking, while business management and computer sciences burgeoned. Watching this new breed of hard working, practical young people, it suddenly occurred to me that some of the present teenagers, were undoubtedly the offspring of the flower-child generation. The next step was to wonder where teenage rebellion might take a child who had grown up in the "hippie" milieu. The result was another young-adult novel called *The Birds of Summer.*

Blair's Nightmare, a third book about the Stanley family of *The Headless Cupid,* and *The Changing Maze,* a picture-book fantasy illustrated by Charles Mikolaycak, brings me up to the present, the spring of 1985—a present set in a garden flat near the Porta Romana in Florence, Italy, where Larry and I are again living, this time for a year in which he is serving as director of the California State University's foreign study program in Italy. Having transported a word processor to Italy, with no little difficulty, I am still writing while Larry deals with the Italian bureaucracy and sixty-nine California students of art, literature, and architecture. Among the side trips we've been able to make this year was a nine-day exploration of Egypt, a destination that has been high on my must-see list since I used to walk to school as Queen Nefertiti when I was ten years old. In the fall, after another trip to the Soviet Union for UC Berkeley, we plan to return to the San Francisco Bay area.

Larry and Zilpha and a camel named Moses, 1985

So there it is, the story of my life and work, and while sticking to the facts wasn't easy, or nearly as much fun as fiction, I've faithfully done so. "See Mom, no embroidering." But before I sign off there's just one more question I'd like to address. And that is *why?*

Once, some years ago during the question and answer period after a lecture, a man asked me why I wrote for children. "Do you do it for the pocketbook, or just for the ego?" was the way he put it. He didn't give me any other choices, but there is another answer. The ego and the pocketbook are affected, of course, at least minimally; much of the time only too minimally. But the maximum reward is simply—joy; the storyteller's joy in creating a story and sharing it with an audience.

So I write for joy, my own and my imagined audience's—but why for children? Unlike many writers who say that they are not aware of a particular audience as they write, I know that I am very conscious of mine. Sometimes I can almost see them, and they look very much like the classes I taught, and often read to. And, like those classes when the story was going well, they are wide-eyed and open-mouthed, rapt in the story and carried out of the constraining walls of reality into the spacious joys of the imagination.

I began to write for children by accident, through the fortunate accident of nine years in the classroom. But I've continued to do so because over the years I've come to realize that it's where I'm happiest. It is, I think, a matter of personal development (or lack of it, as the case may be). There are several peculiarities that I share with children which, like having no front teeth, are perhaps more acceptable in the very young, but which, for better or worse, seem to be a part of my makeup.

First of all, there is optimism. Since growth and hope are almost synonymous no one begrudges a child's natural optimism, but a writer's is another matter. It's not fashionable to write optimistically for adults, nor I must admit, even very sensible, given the world we live in today. But my own optimism seems to be organic, perhaps due to "a bad memory and a good digestion" (a quote that I can't attribute due to the aforementioned failing).

Secondly, there is curiosity. Mine is as intense as a three-year-old's, but where a three-year-old's most obnoxious trait might be asking "Why" several hundred times a day, I am given to eavesdropping on conversations, peering into backyards and lighted windows, and even reading other people's mail if I get a chance.

And thirdly there is a certain lack of reverence for factual limitations and a tendency to launch out into the far reaches of possibility.

So I enjoy writing for an audience that shares my optimism, curiosity, and freewheeling imagination. I intend to go on writing for some time, and though I may occasionally try something for adults, I will always come back to children's books, where I am happiest and most at home.

Zilpha Snyder and friends, 1983

Zilpha Keatley Snyder contributed the following update to *SATA* in 2005:

It has been forty one years since 1964 when my first book, *Season of Ponies,* was published by Atheneum. Since then I have continued to produce fiction for young readers at the rate of about one book a year. Forty-two at last count, and another, *The Magic Nation Thing,* published in August of 2005.

Over the years I have occasionally asked myself "why?" Why do I keep on writing? Especially in recent years when, on finishing a book, I often announce that I am considering retirement, or at least a long vacation from writing. But then, after a week or two, I invariably catch myself beginning the slow spin of interrelated ideas that gradually lead to the production of character sketches, beginning scenes, and plot ideas for a new book.

"Why write?" was a question that I attempted to answer in my first autobiographical essay written in 1985, during the year that my husband and I were living in Florence, Italy, while he served as director of the California State University foreign study program. And now, twenty years later, my answer would be very similar.

I would again touch on the fact that for me writing fiction is probably, more than anything else, a continuation of a childhood habit. The habit of amusing myself by taking bits and pieces of information about real events, people, places, etc., and building on them until I had produced something, a game or a story, that was more interesting and exciting than the bare facts had been. As before, I would have to admit that it was a behavior pattern that occasionally got me into trouble, most often with my mother for doing something she referred to as "embroidering." This talent for "embroidery" also seemed to bother one of my elementary schoolteachers who objected to my tendency to add new and original episodes to a well-known book on which I was giving an oral book report. So it almost seems, for better or worse, that turning facts into fiction is one of my inborn character traits.

Another answer I have at times given to the "why write?" question is to say, "Being involved in writing a piece of fiction is a lot like being in love." The similarity lies in the tendency of people truly in love to see everything not only through their own eyes, but also through the eyes of the person they love. As in, "What would he think of that?" or "How would she feel about that?" The fiction writer's reaction when witnessing an event, or overhearing a remark, is somewhat similar. You find yourself thinking, "Yes, that's exactly what Gib would have said," or, "That's the way April would have reacted." Like being in love, being intimately involved with fictional acquaintances simply adds an extra dimension to life.

So in recent years I have continued to produce characters that run into interesting and sometimes slightly supernatural problems that I have them solve in ways that I try to make intriguing and believable. Among these stories are *Song of the Gargoyle,* a tale set in the Middle Ages in which a boy makes friends with a creature who may be a gargoyle enchanted into life, or simply a very large, very ugly dog. As in many of my stories the ending gives the reader an opportunity to opt for a supernatural explanation for what has occurred or a more realistic one.

Another book that I feel especially good about is *Cat Running.* A story set in California during the Great Depression, it concerns a girl named Cat (Catherine) who is locally famous for her ability to win races. Her own family's problems and her interactions with a schoolmate whose family lives in a nearby "Okietown" lead to a footrace which turns out to be a matter of life or death. *Cat Running* won many tributes, among them the Patricia Beatty Award from the California Library Association, an award given to a distinguished children's book that best promotes an awareness of California and its people.

Other recent works include two books that were inspired by my father's early life. *Gib Rides Home* and *Gib and the Gray Ghost* tell the story of a boy's life in

Zilpha in Persopolis, 2004

Larry and Zilpha in Mohanpura, India, 2003

a Nebraskan orphanage in the early nineteen hundreds, and then with the family by whom he is adopted, or perhaps only "farmed out." Gib's story is a fictionalized version of my father's life, but it does portray a child who, like him, endured a terrible childhood but managed to keep a kind heart, an unquenchable sense of humor, and an amazing ability to communicate with horses ("Gray Ghost" is, of course, a horse).

The Unseen, published in 2004, is the story of Xandra who feels herself to be the only ungifted and unloved member of a large family, all the rest of whom are beautiful and talented. Animals, particularly ill or abandoned ones, have long been her friends and companions, and when a mysterious bird leaves her a strange feather, she soon realizes that it is a key: a key to a world in which emotions are turned into living creatures, love and sympathy into gentle, cuddly animals, and anger and jealousy into painful monsters.

The Unseen was on *School Library Journal*'s Best Books of the Year list, was a silver medalist for the Parents' Choice Foundation, and was a nominee for the Edgar Award.

The Magic Nation Thing, published in August 2005, concerns Abby, whose mother, Dorcas, is a San Francisco detective. Dorcas would like to think that she has inherited some of her Celtic ancestor's supernatural abilities, which could be useful in solving difficult cases. But actually, Abby is the one who has such talents. She can produce visions revealing the whereabouts of a per-

son by holding one of their belongings in her hand. As a young child, Abby had asked a baby-sitter about her disturbing visions and was told, "Don't worry about it. It's just your imagination." But what Abby heard was, "It's just your Magic Nation," and for a while she thought everyone had one. When she realized that wasn't true, she began to resent her "weird" ability. Abby wants to be like her school friends who lead "normal" lives, but circumstances often force her to make use of her strange talent in one way or another. It was a particularly fun book to write.

Other career-related information might include the fact that several more of my recent books have been recorded by Recorded Books Inc. Among these are the "Gib" books, *Spyhole Secrets,* and *The Ghosts of Rathburn Park.* I have been pleased with the quality of these recordings, all of which are unabridged and are read by talented actors.

Since the recent publication of *The Egypt Game* in Thai and Czech, I now have books translated into sixteen languages.

Along with writing, I have continued to travel. I have often said that I married a man who was born knowing he wanted to see the whole world, just as I was born knowing I wanted to write. In recent years my husband and I have made several trips inside the U.S. A., traveled to Cuba with a Global Exchange group, cruised around Tahiti, toured Thailand, Cambodia, Vietnam, and India, and in September 2004 we went to Iran and Lebanon, again with Global Exchange.

All travel is enlightening but the visit to Iran was particularly eye-opening. Before we left, friends and neighbors would ask if we weren't frightened and nervous about visiting Iran. And I guess I was, just a bit. However, we are now able to tell our doubtful friends that we have never been in a country where we were welcomed with such eager enthusiasm. The young people of Iran (and there are lots of them—fifty percent of the population is no more than twenty-five years old) are among the best educated in the Middle East. They are on the Internet, are surprisingly well informed about world affairs, and are curious about America. And, having grown up during their horrible war with Iraq, they tend to be less angry at us for what we are doing in that country than are the people of many other areas. Along with the friendly and engaging people, Iran also has many fabulous tourist sites, including the amazing ruins of Persepolis, the palace of Darius the Great, built more than 500 years B.C.

If I am to cover the most significant developments in my life since I last updated my *Something about the Author* material, I can't leave out the results of our first trip to India. While we were staying in the Bissau Palace Hotel in Jaipur we decided to join a group that was taking a trip, via bus and camel, to a village in the country. It was during that excursion that we visited a school: an elementary school with an enrollment of almost 150 children, that had no running water or electricity, desks, books, pens or paper, and where most of the students sat outdoors on the ground and copied on slates what the teachers wrote on portable blackboards.

When we returned home we decided to establish a fund at the Marin Community Foundation to provide support for the school and were able to locate an Indian couple in Jaipur, already active in non-governmental organization work, to act as our local administrators. Our fund was named the Mohanpura Education Project and several of our friends contributed to it. That was in 1998 and when we returned in March of 2003 we were welcomed with great ceremony and were able to see the many improvements that had been made possible by the modest funds we, and our friends, had been able to provide.

Where there had been only three teachers for five grades there are now five. The pupils now have texts and workbooks, pens and pencils, and a daily hot lunch. Scholarships have been awarded to a few older students

Zilpha and Larry, enjoying their travels in Tahiti, 2004

to travel to Jaipur for technical classes, and electric wiring has been provided for a new computer. Because a librarian friend donated a large number of discarded children's books, there is now a school library which contains many American picture books, and some slightly longer books in Hindi which our Jaipur representatives were able to acquire by trading with some of the private schools in Jaipur, where many of the older students speak and read English well.

One development that particularly delighted me was that the huge first-grade class now is largely made up of older girls who had never been allowed to go to school before, but whose parents now see school attendance as worthwhile for them. Where there had been a very small percentage of female students, there are now more girls than boys enrolled.

Our fund has also made it possible for some women to learn to use sewing machines, and for a self-help women's group to be established. Members of the group receive low interest loans that allow them to buy items that make it possible for them to contribute to their families' income—a development that also helps to improve women's status in the community. The women buy such things as sewing machines, goats, and—for the more ambitious—female water buffalos, which give milk as well as pull plows.

When someone asks, as a few have, why we chose to help these Indian children when there are so many people in our own country who could use some assistance, we can only say that the amount of money we were able to provide would not be enough to accomplish much of anything here at home. On the other hand, in a country where a teacher's salary is only about $250 per semester, we knew we could make an important difference in the lives of a great many children.

And so life and the written word goes on. My newest effort is set in an enormous crumbling palace that will someday be inherited by seriously undersized Harleigh IV, my central character. But then Harleigh, who has given up on believing that a recent operation will enable him to grow, meets Allegra, a strange girl who claims and at times really seems able to fly. Harleigh's growth, which has been stunted not only by his malformed heart but also by his strange impersonal family life, discovers and finally achieves several different ways to grow. As for the title? Don't ask. It's still being debated.

STEWART, Paul 1955-

Personal

Born June 4, 1955, in London, England; married Julie Stewart (a primary school teacher); children: Joseph, Anna. *Education:* Lancaster University, B.A., 1977; University of East Anglia, M.A., 1979; attended Heidelberg University, 1980-82.

Addresses

Agent—Philippa Milnes-Smith, Lucas, Alexander, Whitley, 14 Vernon St., London W14 0RJ, England.

Career

Author, 1989—. Teacher of English as a foreign language in Germany, 1979-82, in Sri Lanka, 1982-83, and in Brighton, England, 1983-90.

Awards, Honors

Smarties Gold Medal award in six-to-eight-year-old category, Youth Libraries Group, 2004, for *Fergus Crane.*

Writings

FICTION; FOR CHILDREN

The Thought Domain, illustrated by Jon Riley, Viking (London, England), 1988, Puffin (New York, NY), 1989.

The Weather Witch, illustrated by Jon Riley, Viking (London, England), 1989, Puffin (New York, NY), 1990.

Adam's Ark, illustrated by Kevin Jones, Viking (London, England), 1990, Puffin (New York, NY), 1992.

Giant Gutso and the Wacky Gang, Orchard (London, England), 1991.

Rory McCrory's Nightmare Machine, Viking (London, England), 1992, Puffin (New York, NY), 1993.

The Snowman Who Couldn't Melt, illustrated by Annabel Large, Viking (London, England), 1993, Puffin (New York, NY), 1994.

Bubble and Shriek, illustrated by Annabel Large, Viking (London, England), 1993, Puffin (New York, NY), 1995.

Castle of Intrigue, illustrated by Jane Gedye, Usborne Books (London, England), 1994.

Neighborhood Witch, illustrated by Annabel Large, Viking (London, England), 1994, Puffin (New York, NY), 1995.

Stage Fright, illustrated by Alan Marks, Usborne Books (London, England), 1995.

Brown Eyes, Penguin (London, England), 1996, new edition, Pearson Education (Harlow, England),1999.

The Diary, Penguin (London, England), 1996.

The Clock of Doom, Usborne Books (London, England), 1996.

The Wakening, Yearling Books (London, England), 1996.

Football Mad, Hippo (London, England), 1997.

The Midnight Hand, Yearling Books (London, England), 1997.

Dogbird, illustrated by Tony Ross, Corgi (London, England), 1998.

The Hanging Tree, Scholastic (London, England), 1998.

Football Mad II: Off-Side!, Hippo (London, England), 1998.

The Birthday Presents, illustrated by Chris Riddell, Andersen (London, England), 1998, HarperCollins (New York, NY), 2000.

A Little Bit of Winter, illustrated by Chris Riddell, Andersen (London, England), 1998.

(With Chris Riddell) *A Little Bit of Winter* (picture book), illustrated by Riddell, Andersen Press (London, England), 1998, HarperCollins (New York, NY), 1999.

Millie's Party (picture novel for beginning readers), illustrated by Bernard Lodge, Blue Bananas, 1999.

(With Chris Riddell) *The Birthday Presents* (picture book), illustrated by Riddell, Andersen Press (London, England), 1999, HarperCollins (New York, NY), 2000.

Millie's Party, illustrated by Bernard Lodge, Mammoth (London, England), 1999.

Football Mad III: Hat-Trick!, Hippo (London, England), 1999.

Football Mad IV: Teamwork!, Hippo (London, England), 2000.

Freight Train, Scholastic (London, England), 2000.

Rabbit's Wish, illustrated by Chris Riddell, HarperCollins (New York, NY), 2001.

Sausage, illustrated by Nick Ward, Oxford University Press (Oxford, England), 2002.

What Do You Remember?, illustrated by Chris Riddell, Andersen (London, England), 2002.

The Were-Pig, illustrated by Tony Ross, Corgi (London, England), 2002.

The Watch-Frog, illustrated by Tony Ross, Corgi (London, England), 2003.

(With Chris Riddell) *Fergus Crane* ("Far Flung Adventures" series), illustrated by Riddell, Doubleday (London, England), 2004.

The Curse of Magoria, Usborne (London, England), 2004.

(With Chris Riddell) *Corby Flood* ("Far Flung Adventures" series), illustrated by Riddell, Random House (London, England), 2005.

"THE EDGE CHRONICLES"; CO-AUTHOR WITH ILLUSTRATOR CHRIS RIDDELL

Beyond the Deepwoods, Doubleday (London, England), 1998, David Fickling Books (New York, NY), 2004.

Stormchaser, Doubleday (London, England), 1999, David Fickling Books (New York, NY) 2004.

Midnight over Sanctaphrax, Doubleday (London, England), 2000, David Fickling Books (New York, NY), 2004.

The Curse of the Gloamglozer, Doubleday (London, England), 2001, David Fickling Books (New York, NY), 2005.

Cloud Wolf, illustrated by Chris Riddell, Corgi (London, England), 2001.

The Last of the Sky Pirates, Doubleday (London, England), 2002, David Fickling Books (New York, NY), 2005.

Vox, Doubleday (London, England), 2003.

Freeglader, Doubleday (London, England), 2005.

Winter Knights, Doubleday (London, England), 2005.

"BLOBHEADS" SERIES; CO-AUTHOR WITH ILLUSTRATOR CHRIS RIDDELL

Invasion of the Blobs, Macmillan (London, England), 2000.

Talking Toasters, Macmillan (London, England), 2000.

School Stinks, Macmillan (London, England), 2000.

Beware of the Babysitter, Macmillan (London, England), 2000.

Garglejuice, Macmillan (London, England), 2000.

Silly Billy, Macmillan (London, England), 2000.

Naughty Gnomes, Macmillan (London, England), 2000.

Purple Alert!, Macmillan (London, England), 2000.

Blobheads (omnibus), Macmillan (London, England), 2003.

Blobheads Go Boing!, Macmillan (London, England), 2004.

"MUDDLE EARTH" SERIES; CO-AUTHOR WITH ILLUSTRATOR CHRIS RIDDELL

Muddle Earth, Macmillan (London, England), 2003.

Here Be Dragons, Macmillan (London, England), 2004.

Dr. Cuddles of Giggle Glade, Macmillan (London, England), 2004.

"KNIGHT'S STORY" SERIES; CO-AUTHOR WITH ILLUSTRATOR CHRIS RIDDELL

Free Lance and the Lake of Skulls, Hodder (London, England), 2003, Simon and Schuster (New York, NY), 2004.

Free Lance and the Field of Blood, Hodder (London, England), 2004.

Joust of Honor, Atheneum (New York, NY), 2005.

Free Lance and the Dragon's Hoard, Hodder (London, England), 2005, published as *Dragon's Hoard,* Atheneum (New York, NY), 2005.

OTHER

Trek (adult novel), Jonathan Cape (London, England), 1991.

Lucky Luke and Other Very Short Stories, Penguin (London, England), 1997.

Also author of numerous short stories published in magazines, including *Me* and *Mayfair,* anthologized in collections from Doubleday, and broadcast on BBC-TV. Author of "Australian Connection" series (graded readers for teens).

Author's works have been translated into over two dozen languages.

Adaptations

The Blobheads was turned into an animated television series by the Canadian Broadcasting Corporation. Film rights to the "Edge Chronicles" were sold to Jigsaw Films, 2004.

Sidelights

Paul Stewart is a British author of fantasy, time-travel and palpably realistic novels, all with a speculative edge that are targeted at an audience of middle-grade readers. Though they find their main audience in Great Britain, many of Stewart's books, such as *Adam's Ark, Bubble and Shriek,* and *The Wakening,* have found fans with readers in North America as well.

"Most of my books for children originate from a 'what if' question," Stewart once explained to *Something about the Author (SATA).* "'What if there was a machine that could record our nightmares?' 'What if there was a snowman that couldn't melt?' 'What if someone didn't know what winter felt like?' Then I play with the idea—researching the background and working on the plot—and decide the genre with which best to explore the story. Only when I am completely certain where the story is heading do I start writing."

Stewart, who was born in 1955 and grew up in southwest London, earned a master's degree in creative writing at the University of East Anglia. Stewart recalled his experience there to an interviewer for the *Achuka*

Paul Stewart joins illustrator and coauthor Chris Riddell in continuing the adventures of sixteen-year-old Twig and his company in the popular "Edge Chronicles."

Web site: "You learnt to become extremely thick-skinned, because you were surrounded by this little group of people who were ripping to shreds something you'd just written and . . . [it] was very good at pinpointing what was wrong with a piece."

Upon graduation Stewart produced short stories for adults, as well as some unpublished novels, while further studying and working as an English teacher in Germany and then Sri Lanka. Returning to England in 1983, he began casting about for a new project and went back to an early idea he had regarding a sister book to *The Phantom Tollbooth* by American writer Norton Juster; it was one of the books that informed his youth. This led to Stewart's first publication, *The Thought Domain,* a children's novel aimed at ten-to-thirteen year olds.

This initial title was followed the next year by *The Weather Witch,* a time-travel story about a village hidden under a lake for four hundred years. Two children from the present, Kerry and Joe, discover the hidden village when they are sent for the summer to stay with their Great Aunt Eleanor. A dull summer is suddenly filled with danger and excitement when the two are sucked into a time vortex while rowing on the lake. They end up in the ancient village of Cleedale, replete with villagers and resident weather witch Megwyn, an ancestor of Great Aunt Eleanor and the one who imprisoned the villagers under water four centuries earlier when ostensibly saving them from an invading Protestant army. In fact, Kerry and Joe turn out to be the long-prophesied duo who will save the villagers. "How they return to Great Aunt Eleanor, and bring into the present a girl and a boy from 400 years back makes exciting reading," a reviewer for *Junior Bookshelf* noted. "The whole story is fantastic in more ways than one," the same reviewer added, "but the author's skill renders it quite believable."

Adam's Ark is one of Stewart's most popular books. "It's about a boy who's been diagnosed as autistic," Stewart explained in his *Achuka* online interview, "but he isn't, he's just been born able to communicate with animals rather than humans. It's his cat who teaches him to speak and to act in a way in which he should act, in an appropriate way, so that people don't think he's round the bend." As he grows older, Adam begins to learn that he can communicate with animals of all sorts because he is a holdover from prehistoric times when mammals of all kinds could communicate in a language called Mammalogue. Working at the zoo, Adam can communicate with many animals. From a dolphin Adam learns it is to be his mission to protect animals from human aggression of the sort which his own father carries out in his research laboratory.

"This is an interesting book," commented Jo Goodman in a review of *Adam's Ark* for *Magpies,* "imperfect but, it its own way, compelling." Jane Inglish, writing in *School Librarian,* dubbed Stewart's story a "passionate teenage novel," while Linda Newbery commented in

Books for Keeps that this "moving story will find an appreciative audience in the growing numbers of young people concerned about animal welfare and environmental issues." A reviewer for *Junior Bookshelf* concluded that Stewart "has tackled this theme of some considerable grandeur in a down to earth, matter of fact style which renders easy the suspension of disbelief in so unusual a thesis. . . . Young readers will enjoy this cleverly constructed story."

Several more books followed, all published by Viking and edited by Morris Lyon. Next in line was *Rory Mc-Crory's Nightmare Machine,* about a scheme for recording nightmares that goes horribly awry. *The Snowman Who Couldn't Melt,* published in 1993, is a "strange mix of a story," according to Adrian Jackson in *Books for Keeps,* "part fairy tale, which eventually becomes a moving account of . . . attempts to rescue the snowman." Cruel Balthazar Grot has constructed the snowman in question, and has given him ice for a heart; thus, he is unable to melt. Young Amy arranges for the snowman to come to a summertime beach in hopes of helping the icy creature by showing him the better side of humans. Unfortunately, they encounter some of the worst examples of the human species, and finally it is Amy's own goodness that melts the snowman's heart and sets him free. Jocelyn Hanson noted in *School Librarian* that this "is a cheerful and fast-moving story . . . with a lively and determined girl as the main character."

An amazing bottle of bubbles that, when blown, contain those things most feared proves the catalyst for *Bubble and Shriek,* a "readable and clever story for smart readers," according to David Bennett, writing in *Books for Keeps.* Young Charlie does not like the continual limelight of being a star in advertisements, while Vinny despises the pressure his father puts on him to succeed. These two apparent enemies at school encounter one another at a fair, and with a little help from the mysterious Madame Tatania and her magic bubbles, Charlie is able to both neutralize the animosity from Vinny and reclaim his childhood from a television career. "Stewart has some wise things to say about the inner fears of childhood and the consequences of obsessive parenting," commented a reviewer for *Junior Bookshelf.* "He presents a fable in a style which will capture the interest of the primary school reader and may stimulate healthy discussion as a class experience."

Stewart soon changed pace and began writing for younger audiences, producing books such as the "Football Mad" series, *Dogbird,* and several picture books with author/illustrator Chris Riddell. In the soccer books, Gary, Danny, and Craig have adventures on and off the field; the series is developed for seven-to-nine year olds. Novels for young readers, such as *Dogbird* and *Millie's Party,* focus on small, generally humorous events to entice beginning readers. In *Dogbird,* for example, a barking parakeet proves to be the perfect pet for young Alice.

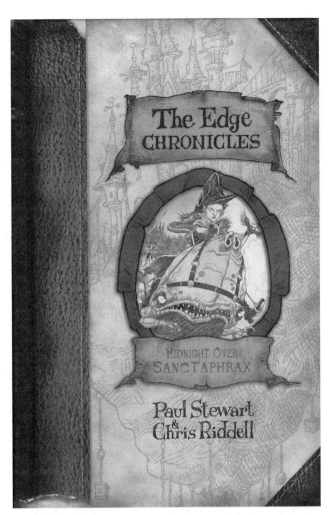

The "Edge Chronicles" continue as young sky pirate captain Twig attempts to save a floating city from an ominous storm. (Cover illustration by Chris Riddell.)

With frequent collaborator Riddell as illustrator, Stewart has also tried his hand at picture books. *A Little Bit of Winter* introduces Rabbit and Hedgehog. When spring reunites the two friends—Hedgehog has hibernated for the season—they share a little bit of the season they just missed together. A reviewer for *Publishers Weekly* commented that "This tale of friendship from a British team gently distills the elements of the winter season." The same reviewer concluded that "the emotional connection between the two [animals] emits warmth and wit." The two critters return in *Rabbit's Wish,* in which Rabbit wants the nocturnal Hedgehog to stay awake and have fun with him during the day. He gets his wish when a rainstorm floods the animals' burrows, forcing them to spend a day cavorting in the rain until their homes dry out.

More ambitious in scope is the collaboration of Riddell and Stewart on the fantasy series, the "Edge Chronicles." As Stewart noted in his *Achuka* interview, Riddell provides line drawings for the series, but also has editorial input on the story as well as planning the ftoryline with him; thus they share the credit for the books. The series was planned as a trilogy, but in the

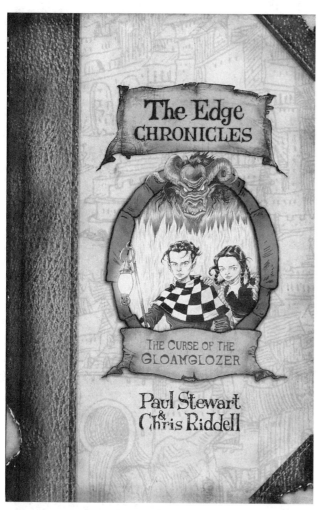

Quint and friend Maris find themselves in a terrifying situation when they go beneath the floating city and accidentally invoke an ancient curse unleashing an evil force. (Cover illustration by Chris Riddell.)

end went much longer. *Beyond the Deepwoods* starts things off when thirteen-year-old Twig is told that the Woodtrolls who raised him are not his real parents, and that he must venture into the Deepwoods to discover the truth about his parentage and himself. On his journey he stumbles off the path and into a frightening other world, a world full of magic, adventure, danger, and hordes of slimy, vicious, strange monsters.

A reviewer for *Interzone* praised *Beyond the Deepwoods* and wrote that "Stewart combines the horrific and the absurd to produce an atmosphere of sustained nightmare." The reviewer acknowledged that it is "strong stuff," but claimed "the writing is so full of zest, Stewart's imagination so fertile, his love of language so inventive" that "every child from [age] nine to eleven should be given a copy." A *Kirkus Reviews* critic also thought that "readers fond of nonstop adventures thickly stocked with . . . plug-uglies will be in hog heaven," and *Booklist* reviewer Carolyn Phelan likewise wrote that "those with hearty appetites for adventure (and strong stomachs) will find this a tremendously exciting fantasy."

In *Stormchaser,* the second volume of "The Edge Chronicles," Twig is reunited with his sky-pirate father aboard the flying sailship *Stormchaser.* With Twig as a stowaway, the ship undertakes a dangerous mission, sailing into the heart of a Great Storm to save the city of Sanctaphrax. This volume "is a rousing adventure tale," Phelan declared, "with a story that's more complex and satisfying than its predecessor," although another bloodthirsty villain means that this volume too is "not for the fainthearted." *Reviewers Bookwatch* critic Molly Martin similarly praised *Stormchaser* as "a thrilling yarn of conspiracy, conniving and complicity" with "often eerie and extraordinary characters," set in a world that is "elaborate]and] marvelously detailed."

Twig and his father's quest to save their world continues in *Midnight over Sanctaphrax,* which continues the progression of "The Edge Chronicles" towards deeper storylines. In this volume, Lisa Prolman noted in *School Library Journal,* "Stewart tackles issues of slavery and class structure while still maintaining a good adventure story."

The fourth volume, *The Curse of the Gloamglozer,* is an extended flashback to the youth of Twig's parents, Quint and Maris. Maris's father, Linux Pallitax, is a respected scholar in Sanctaphrax, a city composed almost entirely of scholars and built on a large floating rock. Quint is Linux's apprentice, both during the day when he is a student and at night when he goes on mysterious little missions for Linux. The more Quint learns about what Linux is doing, the more he comes to believe that the man's studies are leading to something very dangerous for the city.

The Curse of the Gloamglozer has several notable differences from the first three books in the series, Jenna Miller noted in *School Library Journal,* including less swashbuckling adventure and more intrigue, but "the primary charm of the series remains the imaginative settings and creatures."

The Last of the Sky Pirates brings a new main character: Rook, an apprentice librarian. He has been exiled from Sanctaphrax to a community of earth-scholars built in the sewers beneath Undertown. He dreams of being allowed to journey out into the Deepwoods and continue on his path to becoming a Librarian Knight, but when he gets his wish he finds the Deepwoods just as terrifying as Twig did in the first book of the series. Rook's "adventures pull readers along," Walter Minkel wrote in *School Library Journal,* "and the pages flip by in no time."

"Some children want to grow up to be a brain surgeon or an astronaut," Stewart once commented to *SATA.* "I always wanted to be an author. It took a long time but, in 1988—and after a lot of other jobs—my first novel for children was published. I am now a full-time author, writing books and short stories for children of all ages, as well as a novel for adults and several readers for foreign learners of English. . . . Writing has always been a compulsion for me, and I count myself so very lucky that I can earn a living from what I enjoy doing best in the world."

Biographical and Critical Sources

PERIODICALS

Booklist, March 1, 1999, Carolyn Phelan, review of *A Little Bit of Winter,* p. 1223; October 15, 2001, Helen Rosenberg, review of *Rabbit's Wish,* p. 402; July, 2004, Carolyn Phelan, review of *Beyond the Deepwoods,* p. 1844; August, 2004, Carolyn Phelan, review of *Stormchaser,* p. 1925; September 1, 2004, Carolyn Phelan, review of *Midnight over Sanctaphrax,* p. 125.

Bookseller, January 24, 2003, "In Search of a Lost Snuggly-Wuggly," p. 29; December 10, 2005, "Smarties for Random," p. 6.

Books for Keeps, July, 1992, Linda Newbery, review of *Adam's Ark,* p. 13; January, 1995, Adrian Jackson, review of *The Snowman Who Couldn't Melt,* p. 10; November, 1995, David Bennett, review of *Bubble and Shriek,* p. 12; January, 1997, Adrian Jackson, review of *The Wakening,* p. 25.

Daily Telegraph, December 12, 1998.

Interzone, January, 1999, review of *Beyond the Deepwoods.*

Junior Bookshelf, December, 1989, review of *The Weather Witch,* p. 303; April, 1991, review of *Adam's Ark,* p. 68; June, 1992, p. 125; June, 1993, p. 107; February, 1994, review of *Bubble and Shriek,* p. 27; December, 1996, p. 261.

Kirkus Reviews, July 1, 2004, review of *Beyond the Deepwoods,* p. 637.

Magpies, July, 1991, Jo Goodman, review of *Adam's Ark,* pp. 31-32; May, 1992, review of *Great Gutso and the Wacky Gang,* p. 30; July, 1993, review of *Rory Mc-Crory's Nightmare Machine,* p. 33.

Publishers Weekly, December 14, 1998, review of *A Little Bit of Winter,* p. 74; January 31, 2000, review of *The Birthday Presents,* p. 108; November 13, 2000, review of *A Little Bit of Winter,* p. 106; June 4, 2001, review of *Rabbit's Wish,* p. 82; May 17, 2004, p. 12; December 14, 1998, review of *A Little Bit of Winter,* p. 74; June 21, 2004, review of *Beyond the Deepwoods,* p. 63.

Reviewer's Bookwatch, August, 2004, Molly Martin, review of *Stormchaser.*

School Librarian, February, 1991, review of *Adam's Ark,* p. 32; August, 1991, Jane Inglish, review of *Adam's Ark,* p. 91; August, 1993, Jocelyn Hanson, review of *The Snowman Who Couldn't Melt,* p. 112; May, 1994, review of *Bubble and Shriek,* p. 62; February, 1997, review of *Clock of Doom,* p. 34.

School Library Journal, July, 2001, Ann Cook, review of *Rabbit's Wish,* p. 89; September, 2004, Erin Gray, review of *Lake of Skulls,* p. 218; October, 2004, Lisa Prolman, review of *Midnight over Sanctaphrax,* p. 178; February, 2005, Jenna Miller, review of *The Curse of the Gloamglozer,* p. 140; June, 2005, Walter Minkel, review of *The Last of the Sky Pirates,* p. 170.

Sunday Telegraph (London, England), November 22, 1998.

Times Educational Supplement, November 3, 1989, p. 32; November 8, 1991, p. 32; August 27, 1999.

ONLINE

Achuka Web site, http://www.achuka.co.uk/ (July 24, 2005), interview with Stewart.

Fantastic Fiction Web site, http://www.fantasticfiction.co.uk/ (July 6, 2005), "Paul Stewart."

Readingmatters.co.uk, http://www.readingmatters.co.uk/ (July 6, 2005), review of *The Curse of the Gloamglozer* and *The Curse of the Sky Pirates.*

T

TAKAHASHI, Rumiko 1957-

Personal
Born October 10, 1957, in Nigata, Japan. *Education:* Attended Nihon Josei-dai (Japan Women's University); attended Gekiga Sonjuko (manga school); studied with Kazuo Koike.

Addresses
Agent—c/o Author Mail, VIZ Communications, P.O. Box 77010, San Francisco, CA 94107.

Career
Manga artist and writer.

Member

Awards, Honors
New Comic Artist award, Shogakukan (publishers), 1977, for "Katte na Yatsuma"; Inkpot Award, 1994.

Writings

COLLECTED MANGA

Ranma 1/2, 32 volumes, VIZ Communications (San Francisco, CA), 1995–2005, 2nd edition, 2004—.

Lum—Urusei Yatsura: Perfect Collection, VIZ Communications (San Francisco, CA), 1997.

Return of Lum, 8 volumes, VIZ Communications (San Francisco, CA), 1997.

Maison Ikkoku, 14 volumes, VIZ Communications (San Francisco, CA), 1997–2000, 2nd edition, 2004—.

Inu-Yasha: A Feudal Fairy Tale, 23 volumes, VIZ Communications (San Francisco, CA), 1998–2005.

Contributor of short manga to *Bibitto* (magazine). Contributor of manga series "Urusei Yatsura" to *Shonen Sunday,* 1978-87; "Maison Ikkoku," to *Big Comic Spir-*

its, 1982-87; "Ranma 1/2," to *Shonen Sunday,* 1987-96; "Mermaid Saga," to *Shonen Sunday,* beginning 1987; "One-Pound Gospel," to *Young Sunday,* beginning 1987; and "Inu-Yasha Sengoku Otogi Zoushi," to *Shonen Sunday,* beginning 1996. Short stories also published in *Big Goro, Petit Comics,* and *Heibon Punch.*

"MERMAID SAGA"; COLLECTED MANGA

Mermaid Forest, VIZ Communications (San Francisco, CA), 1994.

Mermaid's Scar, VIZ Communications (San Francisco, CA), 1996.

Mermaid's Gaze, VIZ Communications (San Francisco, CA), 1997.

"RUMIC" STORIES; COLLECTED MANGA

Rumic Theater, VIZ Communications (San Francisco, CA), 1996.

Rumic World Trilogy, VIZ Communications (San Francisco, CA), 1996.

Rumic Theater: One of Double, VIZ Communications (San Francisco, CA), 1998.

"ONE-POUND GOSPEL" SERIES; COLLECTED MANGA

One-Pound Gospel, VIZ Communications (San Francisco, CA), 1996.

One-Pound Gospel: Hungry for Victory, VIZ Communications (San Francisco, CA), 1997.

One-Pound Gospel: Knuckle Sandwich, VIZ Communications (San Francisco, CA), 1998.

Adaptations
"Urusei Yatsura" was adapted as a Japanese television series, 1981-86, five animated feature films, and three original videos; "Maison Ikkoku" was adapted as a Japanese television series, 1986-88, as an animated feature, and as a live-action movie; several short stories

from "Rumic World" were adapted as original video animated movies; "Ranma 1/2" was adapted as a Japanese television series, 1989-92, and for several animated feature films; "Inu-Yasha" was adapted as an animated Japanese television series, beginning 2000, and as several animated feature films. Other television series based on Takahashi's works include *Takahashi Rumiko Gekijyou,* 2003, and *Ningyo no mori* (based on "Mermaid's Forest"), 2003.

Sidelights

Well known to fans of manga—Japanese comics—throughout the world, Rumiko Takahashi is also one of the planet's top-selling authors, with over one hundred-million books sold in her native Japan and internationally. Takahashi's four major manga series have been translated into English, and her work has been adapted for both anime—animated—television series and feature films. Her "Urusei Yatsura" series appeared between 1978 and 1987, and was followed from 1982 to 1987 by "Maison Ikkoku," a "romantic soap opera with comic elements," according to Charles Solomon writing in the *Los Angeles Times.* Takahashi's

The loves and life of residents of a Japanese apartment building are the focus of Takahashi's multi-volume manga written for older teen readers.

biggest success has been her offbeat martial arts-focused "Ranma 1/2" manga, which ran from 1987 to 1996. "Inu-Yasha Sengoku Otogi Zoushi," Takahashi's epic manga about a modern girl who suddenly finds herself thrust back in time to feudal Japan, known to English-speaking readers as *Inu-Yasha: A Feudal Fairy Tale;* the series extended over twenty volumes of approximately 200 pages each by 2005. In addition to the many books comprising her four major series, the prolific Takahashi has written and illustrated numerous short stories, making herself one of Japan's most published authors.

Born in 1957, Takahashi began her love affair with manga at a young age, and by high school she was publishing her own comic-strip in the newsletter of the school manga club she founded. Despite her obvious talent, manga remained a hobby while the studious Takahashi concentrated mainly on her academics.

Attending a women's college on a full-time basis, Takahashi also decided to enroll in evening classes at a Japanese manga school run by famous artist Kazuo Koike, author of "Crying Freeman." Because there were no Japanese women then creating manga, she did not consider manga as a possible career. However, the popularity of the manga she published through her university's manga club between 1976 and 1977 gained her a following. Word spread regarding Takahashi's talent, and she published her first professional story, "Katte na Yatsura" ("Those Selfish Aliens") in the boy's magazine *Shonen Sunday,* winning that magazine's new comic artist award in 1977. She also worked as an assistant to Kazuo Umezu, author of "Makoto-chan."

"Urusei Yatsura" began running in *Shonen Sunday* that same year, and that magazine has continued to publish most of Takahashi's major series. "Urusei Yatsura" follows Ataru Moroboshi, a young man who is chosen to compete against an alien princess named Lum. Their competition is a game of tag, but one with serious consequences: the fate of the world rests on its outcome. Ataru wins the contest, and the two opponents also fall in love during the course of their high-stakes game. A strong female character, Lum stands as a contrast to the typical portrait of the docile Japanese female seen in most manga. As Takahashi explained to Seiji Horibuchi in *Animerica,* she designed "Urusei Yatsura" as a "school comedy/romance with some science fiction and whatnot, based on a foundation of slapstick." The puns, metaphors, and other wordplay in the series, as well as the presence of strong female characters, have become characteristic of Takahashi's mangas.

It took a year for "Urusei Yatsura" to establish itself as a weekly series; Takahashi needed time to get used to the demands of producing a weekly strip, and the series did not generate a large income. In fact, early on her tiny apartment was filled with art supplies, and Takahashi slept in a closet. However, the manga's success was such that in 1981 "Urusei Yatsura" was adapted as an anime by filmmaker Mamoru Oshii. The series lasted five years and made Takahashi's name a household word throughout Japan. Fan clubs sprouted up all over the country, extolling the work of the twenty-something manga artist.

Because of its appeal to a young-adult audience, "Maison Ikkoku," Takahashi's second manga series, was published in *Big Comic Spirits;* she would return to *Shonen Sunday* for her subsequent work. In this manga Takahashi sets her tale in modern Japan, and focuses on a love triangle. College student Yusaku Godai is smitten by his older, beautiful, widowed landlady, Kyoko Otonashi, but for her part Kyoko must deal with both her qualms about dating a much younger man and the competing attentions of suave tennis coach Shun Mitaka. Geared for older readers, "Maison Ikkoku" "brims with slapstick hijinks, misunderstandings, and, possibly, love," according to a reviewer for *Publishers Weekly*. Writing in *Library Journal,* Steve Raiteri described the multi-volume published collection *Maison Ikkoku* as a "wonderful true-to-life romance" that ranks as one of Takahashi's "finest works." As with "Urusei Yatsura," "Maison Ikkoku" was adapted for both anime and feature film.

In 1987 Takahashi began her most popular manga, the martial-arts adventure "Ranma 1/2." Ranma Saotome is a young practitioner of martial arts who has a secret: due to a curse, if splashed with cold water, he turns into a girl. Splashed with hot, he becomes a man again. This condition creates problems when the female Ranma begins to attract attention from young men; meanwhile the original Ranma has fallen in love with a beautiful martial arts expert. Appealing to a wide readership, "Ranma 1/2" became an instant success, and ran until 1996. Re-released in book form, the series filled thirty-eight volumes and was adapted as both anime and feature films. Noting that with this series Takahashi had developed her writing and drawing abilities and truly established herself as a publishing phenomenon, Raiteri called "Ranma 1/2" "among [Takahashi's] best loved works."

In 1996 Takahashi's fans were introduced to Kagome Higurashi, a teen who falls down a well and into the world of feudal Japan. In "Inu-Yasha Sengoku Otogi Zoushi" Kagome encounters the half-demon Inu-Yasha. In love with a human woman named Kikyo many years before, Inu-Yasha is awakened from an enchanted sleep by the arrival of Kagome. While he believes Kagome is Kikyo, reincarnated, Kagome behaves as a modern teen, miniskirt and all, and fights the underworld's feudal traditions. As the reincarnation of Kikyo, she possesses the Jewel of Four Souls, a stone that caused Kikyo's death and Inu-Yasha's long slumber. When the jewel is broken, Kagome and Inu-Yasha must recover its lost pieces, battling the evil Naraku and finding love along the way. Their task is made more difficult when the real Kikyo returns from the dead and discovers that her

Cursed to transform into a girl when doused with water, a Japanese teen encounters a series of adventures narrated in Takahashi's characteristically sarcastic and humorous style.

place in Inu-Yasha's demon heart has been usurped by a modern teen.

Despite sharing the same plot framework as her previous manga—a love triangle—"Inu-Yasha Sengoku Otogi Zoushi" is less slapstick than her Takahashi's previous manga. As Takahashi told Horibuchi, "I wanted to draw a story-oriented manga. Also, I liked the idea of a historical piece. Something I could easily draw. That's the premise I start with." Despite its grounding in the history of feudal Japan—a history unfamiliar to American readers—the book-length collections of "Inu-Yasha" were as successful as Takahashi's previous manga, and by 2005 the series had filled over twenty volumes. Anime and feature films based on "Inu-Yasha" were also created, and Web surfers could find several sites devoted to the series.

In addition to her weekly manga, Takahashi includes a personal commentary in each issue of *Shonen Sunday,* continueing to foster her bond with her many readers. A baseball fan when she is not working, she is a supporter of the Hanshin Tigers and also enjoys music. To many manga fans, she truly lives up to her title as the "Princess of Manga."

Biographical and Critical Sources

PERIODICALS

Animerica, February, 1993, Seiji Horibuchi, interview with Takahashi; May, 1997, Seiji Horibuchi, interview with Takahashi.
Kliatt, January, 2005, George Galuschak, review of *Mermaid Saga,* p. 25.
Library Journal, September 1, 2003, Steve Raiteri, review of *Ranma 1/2, Volume 1: Action Edition,* p. 144; January, 2004, Steve Raiteri, review of *Maison Ikkoku, Volume 1,* p. 82.
Los Angeles Times, August 17, 2000, Charles Solomon, "A Worldwide Comic Book Success Story," p. 54.
New York Times, September 17, 1995, Andrew Pollack, "Japan, a Superpower among Superheroes," section 2, p. 32.
Publishers Weekly, March 22, 2004, review of *Maison Ikkoku: Book One,* p. 65.
Virginian Pilot, May 23, 1997, F. Daniel Valentini, "Forget the Flintstones! Japanese Animation Has Verve, Vision, and Variety," p. E1.

ONLINE

Rumic World Online, http://www.furinkan.com/ (October 24, 2004), "Rumiko Takahashi: The Princess of Manga."
Shogakukan Web site, http://www.shogakukan.co.jp/ (October 24, 2004).
VIZ Communications Web site, http://www.viz.com/ (October 24, 2004), "Rumiko Takahashi."*

* * *

THOMPSON, Colin (Edward) 1942-

Personal

Born 1942, in London, England; married and divorced twice; married, 1999; third wife's name Anne (a librarian); children: (first marriage) Charlotte; (second marriage) Hannah, Alice. *Education:* Attended art school in London, England.

Addresses

Home—Bellingen, New South Wales, Australia. *Agent*—c/o Author Mail, Lothian Books, Level 5, 132-136 Albert Rd., South Melbourne, Victoria 3205, Australia. *E-mail*—colin@colinthompson.com.

Career

Writer and illustrator of children's books, beginning 1990. Worked as a silkscreen printer, graphic designer, stage manager, documentary filmmaker for British Broadcasting Corp., and ceramicist.

Awards, Honors

Primary English Best Picture Book Award, 1994, for *Ruby;* Aurealis Award, for *How to Live Forever;* Picture Book of the Year Award, English Association, for *Falling Angels;* Honor Book citation, Australian Children's Book Council, 2004, for *The Violin Man;* Astrid Lindgren Memorial Award nomination (Sweden), 2005.

Writings

SELF-ILLUSTRATED PICTURE BOOKS

Ethel the Chicken, Hodder & Stoughton (London, England), 1990.
A Giant Called Norman Mary, Hodder & Stoughton (London, England), 1991.
The Paperbag Prince, Julia MacRae (London, England), 1992, published as *The Paper Bag Prince,* Knopf (New York, NY), 1992.
Pictures of Home, Julia MacRae (London, England), 1992, Green Tiger Press (New York, NY), 1993.

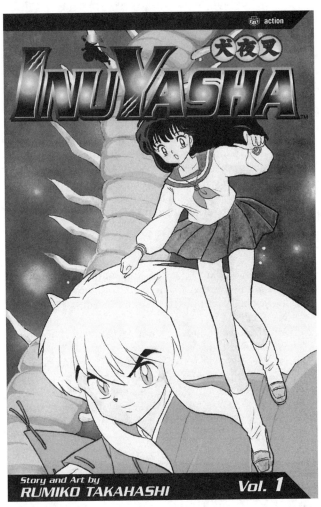

In Takahashi's manga series "Inu-Yashi," the author/artist draws readers back to feudal Japan where a magical dog-boy searches for a power-giving jewel and eventually comes face to face with a modern Japanese teen.

Colin Thompson

Looking for Atlantis, Julia MacRae (London, England), 1993, Knopf (New York, NY), 1994.

Sid the Mosquito and Other Wild Stories, Knight (London, England), 1993.

Ruby, Knopf (New York, NY), 1994.

Attila the Bluebottle and More Wild Stories, Hodder & Stoughton (London, England), 1995.

How to Live Forever (also see below), Julia MacRae (London, England), 1995, Knopf (New York, NY), 1996.

Venus the Caterpillar and Further Wild Stories, Hodder & Stoughton (London, England), 1996.

The Haunted Suitcase and Other Stories, Hodder & Stoughton (London, England), 1996.

The Tower to the Sun, Julia MacRae (London, England), 1996, Knopf (New York, NY), 1997.

Castle Twilight and Other Stories, Hodder & Stoughton (London, England), 1997.

The Paradise Garden, Knopf (New York, NY), 1998.

The Last Alchemist, Hutchinson (London, England), 1999.

Falling Angels, Hutchinson (London, England), 2001.

Violin Man, Hodder Headline (Sydney, New South Wales, Australia), 2003.

Castles, Hutchinson (London, England), 2006.

PICTURE BOOKS

Sailing Home, illustrated by Matt Ottley, Hodder Headline (London, England), 1996.

The Last Circus, illustrated by Kim Gamble, Hodder Headline (London, England), 1997.

The Staircase Cat, illustrated by Anna Pignataro, Hodder Headline (Sydney, New South Wales, Australia), 1998.

The Puzzle Duck, illustrated by Emma Quay, Random House (Milsons Point, New South Wales, Australia), 1999.

Unknown, illustrated by Anna Pignataro, Walker (New York, NY), 2000.

The Last Clown, illustrated by Penelope Gamble, Hodder Headline (Sydney, New South Wales, Australia), 2001.

No Place like Home, illustrated by Anna Pignataro, Hodder Headline (Sydney, New South Wales, Australia), 2001.

One Big Happy Family, illustrated by Karen Carter, Hodder Headline (Sydney, New South Wales, Australia), 2002.

Round and Round and Round and Round, illustrated by Penelope Gamble, Hodder Headline (Sydney, New South Wales, Australia), 2002.

Gilbert, illustrated by Chris Mould, Lothian Books (South Melbourne, Victoria, Australia), 2003.

The Great Montefiasco, illustrated by Ben Redlich, Star Bright Books (New York, NY), 2005.

The Short and Incredibly Happy Life of Riley, illustrated by Amy Lissiat, Lothian Books (South Melbourne, Victoria, Australia), 2005.

Gilbert Goes Outside, illustrated by Chris Mould, Lothian Books (South Melbourne, Victoria, Australia), 2005.

POETRY; FOR CHILDREN

The Dog's Been Sick in the Honda, illustrated by Peter Viska, Hodder Headline (Sydney, New South Wales, Australia), 1999, revised as *Fish Are So Stupid,* illustrated by Chris Mould, Hodder & Stoughton (London, England), 2000.

My Brother Drinks out of the Toilet, illustrated by Peter Viska, Hodder Headline (Sydney, New South Wales, Australia), 2000.

There's Something Really Nasty on the Bottom of My Shoe, illustrated by Peter Viska, Hodder Headline (Sydney, New South Wales, Australia), 2003.

NOVELS; FOR CHILDREN AND YOUNG ADULTS

Future Eden, Walker (London, England), 1999, published as *Future Eden: A Brief History of Next Time,* Simon and Schuster Books for Young Readers (New York, NY), 2000.

Pepper Dreams, Hodder Headline (Sydney, New South Wales, Australia), 2003.

How to Live Forever (novel; based on Thompson's picture book of the same title), Random House (Milsons Point, New South Wales, Australia), 2004.

Space the Final Effrontery (sequel to *Future Eden*), Lothian (South Melbourne, Victoria, Australia), 2005.

"FLOODS" SERIES; SELF-ILLUSTRATED

Neighbors, Random House (Milsons Point, New South Wales, Australia), 2005.

Home and Away, Random House (Milsons Point, New South Wales, Australia), 2006.

Playschool, Random House (Milsons Point, New South Wales, Australia), in press.

OTHER

Laughing for Beginners (adult novel), Sceptre (Sydney, New South Wales, Australia), 2002.

Work in Progress

theshophalfwaydownthestreet.com, for Hodder Headline; *I Should Have Been Susan,* "a collection of strange and wonderful pictures from my grandmother's photograph albums"; a novel based on *The Paradise Garden; Enthusiasm Costs Extra,* a sequel to *Laughing for Beginners; Instructions,* a book of short stories; *The Mirrorball of the Gods,* an adult novel; the picture books *Love Is Sometimes under Your Foot* and *Norman and Betty,* both illustrated by Amy Lissiat; *Gilbert Goes Outside,* the sequel to *Gilbert.*

Sidelights

Regarded as a gifted author and illustrator, Colin Thompson is lauded as a particularly imaginative artist as well as a committed supporter of the environment. He is recognized for providing young readers with demanding, yet satisfying, books that are considered both thought-provoking and entertaining. As an illustrator, Thompson creates colorful, intricate pictures filled with both realistic and surrealistic images as well as visual jokes and intertextual references; his work has been compared to such artists as Graeme Base and M. C. Escher.

Thompson came relatively late to writing literature for young children and did not begin publishing his detailed and inventive picture books and fantasies until the early 1990s. Born in London, England in 1942, his early schooling in both Yorkshire and West London led to two years of art instruction in his hometown of Ealing and in Hammersmith, where, as Thompson admitted on his home page, "I met people who could draw much better than I could." This knowledge did not dissuade him from working in the visual arts, however. Employed for a period of time as a silkscreen painter and graphic designer, Thompson later studied film and worked for the British Broadcasting Corporation (BBC) creating television documentaries. In the late 1960s he moved to Scotland's Outer Hebrides islands and in 1975 to Cumbria. During this time, he began crafting ceramics while living in a remote farmhouse; he also spent a good deal of free time planting trees due to his concern for the environment, as well as raising his family and caring for his numerous adopted pets.

Thompson's first children's book, the easy-reader *Ethel the Chicken,* appeared in 1990. Heroine Ethel, who lives in a box labeled First Class Oranges, has been all but forgotten since the death of the old woman who used to feed her. A rat named Neville happens upon Ethel's home in the vacant house and the two become friends until Neville and his family move away. Briefly overcome with loneliness, Thompson's talking chicken finds happiness and companionship once again when a human family moves into the old woman's house. Written with care and childlike simplicity, *Ethel the Chicken* is designed to teach young children how to read, to appeal to their sense of humor, and to address their particular anxieties about friendship, love, and loneliness. *Growing Point* reviewer Margery Fisher lauded the work, noting that "When words and illustrations consort perfectly together, expressing both the warmth of humor and the tinge of wit, the result is a masterpiece and I think *Ethel the Chicken* is a masterpiece."

Thompson's second picture book, *The Paper Bag Prince,* is set in a town dump and expresses a pro-environmental message. The book's protagonist, an old man whose name has long since been forgotten, is known as the "Paper Bag Prince." He lives on the site, inhabiting a derelict railroad car and surviving off the town's refuse and junk. The arrival of Sarah from the city council and her announcement that the dump is to be shut down proves a welcome harbinger to the Paper Bag Prince: once the land on which the dump is located was his, and with the landfill closed nature can now begin to reclaim the soil so long abused by humans. A reviewer for *Kirkus Reviews* enthused, "In Thompson's lovely, intricate art . . . signs of life and renewal creep in everywhere. . . . More than just another ecological fantasy, this dump is a compelling symbol of the earth itself; it's to be hoped that, like the old man, humanity will be here to welcome nature back if the pollution ever abates." Writing in *School Library Journal,* Lori A. Janick commented that *The Paper Bag Prince* "effectively portrays the tenacity of nature as well as the resilience of the human spirit," while *Books for Keeps* critic Trevor Dickinson called the book one "which deserves to be widely popular through and beyond the school years."

Pictures of Home represents something of a departure for Thompson. The work consists of numerous detailed illustrations of houses along with several short, poetic texts composed by British schoolchildren. The texts describe each child's individual interpretation of home; for example, "Home is my parents./ You should have love in all homes./ Love is my parents." Although critics generally approved of Thompson's almost surreal paintings, many found *Pictures of Home* lacking a clear-cut connection between text and illustration. A *Kirkus Reviews* contributor found more to like, describing *Pictures of Home* as a "fascinating book, to pore over and share."

In *Looking for Atlantis* a man recalls his childhood and the return of his grandfather from an ocean voyage. Upon his arrival, the old man tells his grandson about a sea chest that contains the secret of a path to Atlantis. The rest of the story is a celebration of the joys of observation, accompanied by Thompson's detailed and engrossing drawings. Reviewing *Looking for Atlantis* in *School Library Journal,* Barbara Peklo Abrahams wrote that Thompson's "watercolor masterpieces . . . contain

A shy stray overlooked at the local dog pound suddenly gains fame during a tragic fire in Thompson's uplifting **Unknown.** *(Illustration by Anna Pignataro.)*

myriad images that are striking, mysterious, dreamlike, witty, and eternal, and the simple, spare prose holds transcendental truth." *Booklist* critic Mary Harris Veeder concluded that fans of *Where's Waldo?* will enjoy the book's illustrations due to their "combination of fine, realistic detailing and fantastical images"

In his award-winning picture-book mystery *Ruby* Thompson spins two interconnected tales involving an automobile: a red 1934 Austin Seven called Ruby. One tale evokes Ruby's travels around the world to exotic locations such as China's Great Wall and England's Stonehenge, while the other presents a tiny family lured from the safety of their tree-home by the arrival of the shiny red car. The miniature family members find themselves trapped in the vehicle, while their son Kevin is doubly so, having locked himself inside a briefcase. As Kevin's family attempts to find the combination to the case in order to free the boy, Thompson invites his readers to do the same, informing them that Ruby's license plate number and the combination are one and the same. Only by actively exploring the book's illustrations can the mystery be solved. A *Publishers Weekly* critic commented that, "Once again Thompson breaks barriers of narrative space and time with an ornately crafted, multilevel picture book," while a *Kirkus Reviews* contributor called *Ruby* "two wonderful picture books in one."

Thompson once again displays his cleverness and artistic virtuosity in *How to Live Forever.* The story's hero, Peter, finds himself in a vast library of a thousand rooms that is purported to contain every book ever written. Peter learns that one book, alluringly titled *How to Live Forever,* is missing. Eventually he happens upon the Ancient Child, a creature suspended in time, apparently because he has read the elusive book, and Peter wisely decides to give up his search. A *Junior Bookshelf* commentator praised the control exhibited in "Thompson's brief sentences and still more precise and exquisite drawings." While a *Publishers Weekly* critic warned that "many of the visual puns are too sophisticated for younger readers but will delight adults," the reviewer added that *How to Live Forever* "excites [reader] interest on several levels."

Set in the not-too-distant future, *The Tower of the Sun* presents a planet cloaked in a yellow fog of pollutants which permanently obscure the sun. Thompson's novel opens as the world's wealthiest man promises his grandson that he will one day show the boy a blue sky and a shining sun: "What use is all my money if I can't build dreams?" The man institutes an ambitious plan to construct a magnificent tower to achieve his goal, incorporating into his edifice such famous structures as the Guggenheim museum, the Taj Mahal, the Chrysler Building, and the Leaning Tower of Pisa. A *Publishers Weekly* critic mused that, "With its rich visual tapestry, a subtle message about what constitutes real wealth and an upbeat ending," Thompson's novel is "a crowd-pleaser," while a *Reading Time* contributor called *Tower of the Sun* an "extraordinary fantasy" that "challenges readers' moral insights and at the same time leaves those readers aesthetically satisfied."

In 1995 Thompson traveled from England to Sydney, Australia, to do a school visit, "and fell so much in love with the place that two weeks later I came back to live here," he wrote on his home page. Four years later, the divorced writer/illustrator married the librarian who first invited him to come to the school. Since moving to Australia he has collaborated with Australian artists on works such as *Sailing Home,* a collaboration with illustrator Matt Otley about a family who awakes one day and realizes that their house is no longer on firm land but instead is floating along in the middle of the sea.

Thompson collaborated with Aussie illustrator Anna Pignataro on *Unknown,* a book that teaches children an important lesson about pet ownership. The book takes its title from a shy little dog that has been abandoned at a local pound. All the animals in the shelter are named for the reasons why they wound up there: "Grown-Too-Large," "Owner-Died," "Unwanted-Christmas-Gift," and little "Unknown." None of the families who come to the pound looking for a pet take notice of the shy Unknown, hiding in the back of his cage, but the little dog proves his bravery when a fire threatens the shelter and its inhabitants. While there is a happy ending for

The worst magician in the world takes on an assistant and finds his popularity rising along with his trick-failure rate in **The Great Montefiasco.** *(Illustration by Ben Redlich.)*

the dogs, "Unknown's parting comment puts an edge on the sweetness," as John Peters noted in *Booklist.* "I got lucky," the little dog says. "But it would be good if we could put all the humans in cages and walk along with our noses in the air and choose the ones WE wanted." *Unknown* was deemed "a sure bet for any prospective young dog owner to stimulate discussion about owning a pet for life" by Holly Belli in her review for *School Library Journal.*

Thompson's other collaborative picture books include *The Staircase Cat,* about a cat who waits patiently in his long-time home after his caretaker disappears during a war; *The Puzzle Duck,* about an imaginative duck who makes up crazy stories and gives ill-thought-out advice; *Gilbert,* about a very skittish cat; *The Great Montefiasco,* about the most incompetent magician on earth; and *The Short and Incredibly Happy Life of Riley,* about a very contented rat.

Self-illustrated books written since Thompson's move to Australia include *The Paradise Garden,* in which, according to a *Publishers Weekly* reviewer, "Once again, . . . his intricate, fantastical illustrations lure readers to a parallel universe where nothing is quite as it seems." In the book, the parallel universe is located in a small garden in the middle of a large, dirty, noisy city that is home to a boy named Peter. Peter runs away from his chaotic home to live in the garden and enjoy the fresh air and peace and quiet for a summer. Although he must eventually return home, he takes home a new-found sense of peace along with a few seeds from the garden

plants. Thompson's illustrations of Peter's refuge show glimpses of tiny fairy-houses in the shrubbery and bamboo, along with many more of his trademark page-filling details.

The Last Alchemist is another solo effort by Thompson. A king who is determined to find an alchemist who can create gold is now on his nineteenth alchemist, Spiniflex. Spiniflex is highly motivated by the king's promises of treasure if he succeeds (and by a considerably worse fate if he fails), but he still cannot seem to find the correct formula. In the end the alchemist succeeds in turning the kingdom to gold, but not quite in the manner the king hoped. Critics particularly praised Thompson's illustrations for *The Last Alchemist,* wherein "each page is a treasure chest bursting with color, minute detail, wit, and surprise," according to Shelle Rosenfeld in *Booklist.* A *Publishers Weekly* contributor also pointed out "a running sight gag in Thompson's [more recent] oeuvre—the ubiquitous "Café Max," with its red-checked curtains, tucked in like a cheeky footnote."

Ethel the chicken, fresh from Thompson's first book, returns in a very different story in *Future Eden: A Brief History of Next Time.* This "wickedly barbed low fantasy," as *School Library Journal* contributor John Peters termed it, began life as a serial that ran on Thompson's Web site. The story is set in 2287, when human beings are nearly extinct. One of the few remaining humans, Jay, has been camping out in a penthouse with the thickly feathered Ethel, but he gets bored and decides to go out and explore the world. Ethel is more than she seems, however: she is in fact a higher life form, originally from the planet Megatron. Since she created humans—and every other living thing on earth—she feels responsible for all the pain, war, and suffering Earth's creatures have felt throughout history. Ethel the alien's quest to discover why Earth's humans were all happy for one brief hour in October of 2042 provides the plot of the story. Her companions on this quest include Jay, whom she declares the Chosen One; the Delphic Oracle reincarnated as a goldfish; and the wizard Merlin from the King Arthur legends.

A prolific author, Thompson continues to produce his own picture books and to develop collaborative stories. In each of his works, however, his overall philosophy remains constant. "I have always believed in the magic of childhood and think that if you get your life right that magic should never end. I feel that if a children's book cannot be enjoyed properly by adults there is something wrong with either the book or the adult reading it."

Biographical and Critical Sources

BOOKS

Thompson, Colin, *Unknown,* illustrated by Anna Pignataro, Walker (New York, NY), 2000.

PERIODICALS

Booklist, December 1, 1992, Hazel Rochman, review of *The Paper Bag Prince,* p. 678; April 1, 1994, Mary Harris Veeder, review of *Looking for Atlantis,* p. 1441; July, 1999, Shelle Rosenfeld, review of *The Last Alchemist,* p. 1974; May 1, 2000, John Peters, review of *Unknown,* p. 1680.

Books for Keeps, May, 1992, Trevor Dickinson, review of *The Paperbag Prince,* p. 28.

Growing Point, July, 1991, Margery Fisher, review of *Ethel the Chicken,* pp. 5537-38.

Junior Bookshelf, April, 1996, review of *How to Live Forever,* p. 63.

Kirkus Reviews, July 15, 1992, review of *The Paper Bag Prince,* p. 926; April 1, 1993, review of *Pictures of Home,* p. 465; November 11, 1994, review of *Ruby,* p. 1544; March 15, 1997, p. 469; September 1, 2001, review of *Falling Angels,* p. 1302; December 15, 2004, review of *The Great Montefiasco,* p. 1209.

New York Times Book Review, October 23, 1994, review of *Looking for Atlantis,* p. 30.

Publishers Weekly, August 31, 1992, review of *The Paper Bag Prince,* p. 79; April 19, 1993, review of *Pictures of Home,* p. 59; April 4, 1994, review of *Looking for Atlantis,* p. 77; October 24, 1994, review of *Ruby,* p. 60; May 13, 1996, review of *How to Live Forever,* p. 74; March 10, 1997, review of *The Tower to the Sun,* p. 65; March 16, 1998, review of *The Paradise Garden,* p. 64; June 14, 1999, review of *The Last Alchemist,* p. 70; December 17, 2001, review of *Falling Angels,* p. 94.

Reading Time, February, 1997, review of *The Tower to the Sun,* p. 15.

School Librarian, February, 1997, reviews of *The Haunted Suitcase* and *The Tower to the Sun,* p. 34.

School Library Journal, February, 1993, Lori A. Janick, review of *The Paper Bag Prince,* p. 80; July, 1993, JoAnn Rees, review of *Pictures of Home,* p. 82; May, 1994, Barbara Peklo Abrahams, review of *Looking for Atlantis,* p. 118; December, 1994, Steven Engelfried, review of *Ruby,* p. 87; July, 1996, Heide Piehler, review of *How to Live Forever,* p. 74; May, 1998, Heide Piehler, review of *The Paradise Garden,* p. 127; July, 2000, Holly Belli, review of *Unknown,* p. 88; November, 2000, John Peters, review of *Future Eden: A Brief History of Next Time,* p. 162.

Wilson Library Bulletin, November, 1992, Frances Bradburn, review of *The Paper Bag Prince,* p. 75.

ONLINE

Colin Thompson Home Page, http://www.colinthompson. com (July 6, 2005).

One Woman's Writing Retreat Web site, http://www.prairie den.com/ (July 19, 2005), interview with Thompson.

*   *   *

TORRES, John A(lbert) 1965-

Personal

Born August 18, 1965, in New York, NY; son of Americo, Jr. (a retail manager) and Carmen (Calderon)

Torres; married Julie Perry (a secretary), June 9, 1990; children: Daniel, Jacqueline. *Education:* Fordham University, B.A., 1987. *Politics:* "Independent." *Religion:* Roman Catholic.

Addresses

Agent—c/o Author Mail, Enslow Publishers, Box 398, 40 Industrial Road, Berkeley Heights, NJ 07922-0398. *E-mail*—JohnnyPitt@aol.com.

Career

Writer. Little league coach.

Writings

(With Michael J. Sullivan) *Sports Great Darryl Strawberry,* Enslow Publishers (Springfield, NJ), 1990.

(Self-illustrated) *Home-Run Hitters: Heroes of the Four Home-Run Game,* Simon & Schuster (New York, NY), 1995.

Sports Reports: Hakeem Olajuwon, Enslow Publishers (Springfield, NJ), 1997.

Sports Great Jason Kidd, Enslow Publishers (Springfield, NJ), 1997.

Greg Maddux, Lerner Publications (Minneapolis, MN), 1997.

Sports Great Jason Kidd, Enslow Publishers (Springfield, NJ), 1998.

Bobby Bonilla, Mitchell Lane Publishers (Childs, MD), 1999.

Top Ten Basketball Three-Point Shooters, Enslow Publishers (Springfield, NJ), 1999.

Tino Martinez, Mitchell Lane Publishers (Childs, MD), 1999.

Sports Great Oscar de la Hoya, Enslow Publishers (Springfield, NJ), 1999.

Kevin Garnett: "Da Kid", Lerner Sports (Minneapolis, MD), 2000.

Mia Hamm, Mitchell Lane Publishers (Childs, MD), 2000.

Sports Great Dikembe Mutombo, Enslow Publishers (Springfield, NJ), 2000.

Michelle Kwan, Mitchell Lane Publishers (Childs, MD), 2000.

Top Ten NBA Finals Most Valuable Players, Enslow Publishers (Springfield, NJ), 2000.

Top Ten Baseball Legends, Enslow Publishers (Springfield, NJ), 2000.

Sports Great Grant Hill, Enslow Publishers (Springfield, NJ), 2001.

Kobe Bryant, Mitchell Lane Publishers (Bear, DE), 2001.

Derek Jeter, Mitchell Lane Publishers (Bear, DE), 2001.

Fitness Stars of Bodybuilding: Featuring Profiles of Arnold Schwarzenegger, Lou Ferrigno, Ronnie Coleman, and Lenda Murray, Mitchell Lane Publishers (Bear, DE), 2001.

Fitness Stars of Pro Football: Featuring Profiles of Deion Sanders, Shannon Sharpe, Darrell Green, and Wayne Chrebet, Mitchell Lane Publishers (Bear, DE), 2001.

Marc Anthony, Mitchell Lane Publishers (Bear, DE), 2002.

Tiger Woods, Mitchell Lane Publishers (Bear, DE), 2002.

Careers in the Music Industry, Mitchell Lane Publishers (Bear, DE), 2002.

Sheryl Swoopes, Mitchell Lane Publishers (Bear, DE), 2002.

Sports Great Tim Duncan, Enslow Publishers Inc. (Berkeley Heights, NJ), 2002.

Sports Great Sammy Sosa, Enslow Publishers Inc. (Berkeley Heights, NJ), 2003.

Allen Iverson: Never Give Up, Enslow Publishers Inc. (Berkeley Heights, NJ), 2004.

The African Elephant, MyReportLinks.com Book (Berkeley Heights, NJ), 2004.

The Manatee, MyReportLinks.com Book (Berkeley Heights, NJ), 2004.

P. Diddy, Mitchell Lane Publishers (Hockessin, DE), 2004.

Shaquille O'Neal: Gentle Giant, Enslow Publishers Inc. (Berkeley Heights, NJ), 2004.

Vince Carter: Slam Dunk Artist, Enslow Publishers (Berkeley Heights, NJ), 2004.

Disaster in the Indian Ocean, Tsunami 2004, Mitchell Lane Publishers (Hockessin, DE), 2005.

Clay Aiken, Mitchell Lane Publishers (Hockessin, DE), 2005.

Tsunami Disaster in Indonesia, 2004, Mitchell Lane Publishers (Hockessin, DE), 2005.

Usher, Mitchell Lane Publishers (Hockessin, DE), 2005.

Sidelights

John A. Torres once told *Something about the Author:* "Ever since I can remember, I have wanted to be a writer. My idol as a child was Ernest Hemingway. Since I also love sports, I tried to combine my two loves: writing and sports. My ultimate dream is to have my novel published and to be able to become a full–time writer. The most important development in my evolution as a writer was when I read [Ernest] Hemingway's *The Old Man and the Sea* during the summer I spent interning at United Press International. That was truly a baptism by fire."

Biographical and Critical Sources

PERIODICALS

Booklist, April 1, 2004, Carlos Orellana, review of *Shaquille O'Neal: Gentle Giant,* p. 1384.

Horn Book Guide, July, 1990, p. 145; fall, 1995, p. 373.

School Library Journal, November, 1990, p. 124; May, 1995, p. 116.*

V

VAIL, Rachel 1966-

Personal

Born July 25, 1966, in New York, NY; married, husband's name Mitchell; children: Zachary. *Education:* Georgetown University, B.A., 1988.

Addresses

Home—New York, NY. *Office*—c/o Writers House, 21 W. 26th St., New York, NY 10010. *E mail*—rachel@ rachelvail.com.

Career

Writer.

Member

Authors Guild.

Awards, Honors

Editor's Choice designation, *Booklist,* 1991, for *Wonder,* and 1992, for *Do-Over;* Pick-of-the-List designation, American Booksellers Association, 1991, for *Wonder;* Blue Ribbon designation, *Bulletin of the Center for Children's Books,* 1992, for *Do-Over;* Books for the Teen Age selection, New York Public Library, 1992, for *Do-Over,* and 1994, for *Ever After;* Best Books designation, *School Library Journal,* 1996, for *Daring to Be Abigail.*

Writings

YOUNG-ADULT NOVELS

Wonder, Orchard Books (New York, NY), 1991.
Do-Over, Orchard Books (New York, NY), 1992.
Ever After, Orchard Books (New York, NY), 1994.

Rachel Vail

Daring to Be Abigail, Orchard Books (New York, NY), 1996.
(With Avi) *Never Mind!: A Twin Novel,* HarperCollins (New York, NY), 2004.
If We Kiss, HarperCollins (New York, NY), 2005.

"FRIENDSHIP RING" SERIES; YOUNG-ADULT NOVELS

Please, Please, Please, Scholastic (New York, NY), 1998.
Not That I Care, Scholastic (New York, NY), 1998.
If You Only Knew, Scholastic (New York, NY), 1998.
Fill in the Blank, Scholastic (New York, NY), 2000.
Popularity Contest, Scholastic (New York, NY), 2000.

"MAMA REX AND T" SERIES; PICTURE BOOKS

Mama Rex and T Shop for Shoes, illustrated by Steve Björkman, Scholastic (New York, NY), 2000.

Mama Rex and T Lose a Waffle, illustrated by Steve Björkman, Scholastic (New York, NY), 2000.

Mama Rex and T Run Out of Tape, illustrated by Steve Björkman, Scholastic (New York, NY), 2001.

The Horrible Play Date, illustrated by Steve Björkman, Scholastic (New York, NY), 2001.

The Sort-of-Super Snowman, illustrated by Steve Björkman, Scholastic (New York, NY), 2002.

Mama Rex and T Turn off the TV, illustrated by Steve Björkman, Scholastic (New York, NY), 2002.

Mama Rex and T Have Homework Trouble, illustrated by Steve Björkman, Scholastic (New York, NY), 2002.

The (Almost) Perfect Mother's Day, illustrated by Steve Björkman, Scholastic (New York, NY), 2002.

Halloween Knight, illustrated by Steve Björkman, Scholastic (New York, NY), 2003.

The Reading Champion, illustrated by Steve Björkman, Orchard Books (New York, NY), 2003.

The Prize, illustrated by Steve Björkman, Orchard Books (New York, NY), 2003.

Mama Rex and T Stay up Late, illustrated by Steve Björkman, Orchard Books (New York, NY), 2003.

PICTURE BOOKS

Over the Moon, Orchard Books (New York, NY), 1998.

Sometimes I'm Bombaloo, illustrated by Yumi Heo, Scholastic Press (New York, NY), 2002.

Sidelights

Born in New York City, children's book author Rachel Vail grew up in nearby New Rochelle, New York. In her youth she never intended to be a writer, but with the encouragement of various teachers, both in high school and later at Georgetown University, she worked to develop her talent. In an autobiographical sketch for *Horn Book*, Vail recalled one instructor in particular named Doc Murphy. A theater professor, Murphy encouraged her to focus on the essentials of character. Vail observed, "I think writing would be so much more exciting and less daunting to children if the emphasis were put on the details, the questions that propel the writer to create astonishing, unique characters who, by their juxtaposition with other astonishing, unique characters, make stories happen."

Vail's emphasis on character was apparent to readers of her first novel for children, the coming-of-age story *Wonder*. As twelve-year-old Jessica enters seventh grade, she finds that she has suddenly become unpopular. Sheila, her former best friend, and five other girls succeed in ostracizing Jessica, giving her the humiliating nickname "Wonder" after one of the girls describes Jessica's new polka-dot dress as "a Wonder Bread explosion." With determination, and with the welcome attentions of Conor O'Malley, the object of her first crush, Jessica perseveres.

Lauded by critics for its skillful rendering of character, *Wonder* proved to be a highly successful debut novel for its author. "Vail has the measure of this vulnerable age and its painful concern about identity within the group," noted a *Kirkus Reviews* commentator. *School Library Journal* contributor Debra S. Gold also spoke favorably of *Wonder*'s title character, commenting that "Jessica's first-person account reveals a three-dimensional character with whom readers will laugh and empathize." Deborah Abbott noted in *Booklist*: "Piercing and funny, Vail's breezy story describes the hazards of junior high, sketched with the emotional chasms universal to the age."

One of Jessica's schoolmates, Whitman Levy, becomes the hero of Vail's next story, *Do-Over*. Eighth-grader Whitman faces some severe family problems, including his parents' imminent break-up, while also struggling to deal with his first real crush and get a handle on his acting role in an upcoming school play. Vail balances the comical tale of the teen's various escapades with several thorny issues, including Whitman's discovery that his best friend Doug is a bigot. Eventually the self-conscious and somewhat bewildered Whitman comes to understand how to deal with all that confronts him in a moment of self-realization while on stage: "I could screw up or I could be amazing, and there's no turning back, no do-overs."

Reviewers noted that *Do-Over* again highlights Vail's skill in dealing with character and dialog. *School Library Journal* contributor Jacqueline Rose called the author "a master at portraying adolescent self-absorption, awkwardness, and fickleness, all with freshness and humor." In the *Bulletin of the Center for Children's Books*, Roger Sutton compared Vail favorably with popular children's book writer Judy Blume, noting that "Vail is funnier than Blume, and more moving, partly because of her natural ear for teenaged talk, and partly because she never, ever preaches. This is the real thing." Stephanie Zvirin, in *Booklist*, likewise spoke of the "sharp and genuine" dialog in *Do-Over*, commending Vail's "remarkable talent for capturing so perfectly the pleasure and pain of being thirteen—in a real kids' world."

In *Ever After* Vail employs a new narrative technique, presenting much of her story in the form of diary entries written by fourteen-year-old Molly. Best friends Molly and Vicky live year-round on a small Massachusetts island. The presence of a new friend, summer visitor Grace, causes Vicky to feel insecure and puts a strain on her relationship with Molly. Vicky's possessiveness begins to disturb Molly, and ultimately destroys the girls' friendship when Molly learns that Vicky has been reading her personal journal without permission. "That Vicky and Molly's rift is likely to be permanent . . . is just one hallmark of the authenticity of this carefully conceived story," noted a *Publishers Weekly* reviewer. A *Kirkus Reviews* commentator praised *Ever After* as "an unusually immediate portrayal of a thoughtful teen finding her balance among her peers while making peace with her own capabilities." *School Library Journal* contributor Ellen Fader characterized the book as "a breezy, smart-talking novel that explores the ever-fascinating arena of young teen friendship," while Hazel Rochman, in *Booklist,* expressed a common critical refrain when noting that "the contemporary teenage voice is exactly right."

Daring to Be Abigail features a narrative format similar to that which Vail employs in *Ever After.* The story unfolds through the letters of Abby Silverman, an eleven year old who has decided to "reinvent herself" while away at Camp Nashaquitsa for the summer. Abby's newly adopted boldness wins the acceptance of her fellow campers, but also seems to require that Abby—now Abigail—forsake Dana, an unpopular girl in her cabin. Although she likes Dana, Abigail succumbs to peer pressure by accepting a dare to urinate in Dana's mouthwash. Unable to stop Dana before she uses the rinse, Abigail is thrown out of the camp, and addresses a final, poignant letter to her dead father, whose apparent disappointment with his daughter was the central reason for her crisis of identity and her efforts at "reinvention."

Deborah Stevenson, writing in the *Bulletin of the Center for Children's Books,* noted that Abigail's "vulnerability and her poignantly, desperately upbeat letters home will engender reader sympathy and understanding." *Booklist* reviewer Stephanie Zvirin praised Vail for once again being "right on target when it comes to the reality of preadolescent girls, catching how they act and what they say, their nastiness and envy and sweetness, and how confusing it is to long for independence, yet be afraid of the freedom and responsibility that come with it." Lauren Adams, reviewing *Daring to Be Abigail* for *Horn Book,* commented: "As in her other books, Vail displays her talent for capturing the humor and angst of early adolescence; this latest novel . . . is her most sophisticated yet."

In 1998 Vail launched the unique "Friendship Ring" series. These small-format books (each volume is about the size of a compact disc case, with bright neon covers to match) chronicle the middle-school travails of a group of friends trying to cope with adolescence. "Each book is like an episode in a sitcom, told in the first person by a different member of the group," Rochman explained in a review of one book in the series, *If You Only Knew,* for *Booklist.* However, throughout the books "Vail backtracks over the same events, viewing them from a different character's perspective," Christine M. Heppermann wrote in a review of the series for *Horn Book.* "It's a technique designed to correct the misconceptions of any seventh-grader who regards her peers' apparently carefree lives with envy and feels totally alone at the bottom of 'the pit.'" Like all middle-schoolers, the characters have many insecurities. Are they popular enough? Are they pretty and feminine enough to get boyfriends? The characters also frequently

have family problems; one girl's son's father abandoned her family, leaving her mother bitter and depressed; another has an older sister and a father who fight constantly. Vail addresses these issues "with complexity and humor," Rochman noted in a review of *Not That I Care,* "in a quick-talking, immediate, sitcom mode that offers no formula happy ending."

Vail teamed up with fellow young-adult novelist Avi for *Never Mind!: A Twin Novel.* The book's perspective alternates between two fraternal twins. Meg, a hardworking student, will be attending a more prestigious school for seventh grade, while her twin brother Edward, does only as much schoolwork as is required. The popular and athletic Meg is worried that the girls at her new school will think less of her if they realize she has a scrawny "loser" brother, so she lies and tells them that he is a future rock star. Predictably, this one little lie quickly spirals into a giant, hilarious mess. "As screwball comedies go, this one is consistently entertaining," Heppermann commented of *Never Mind!* in a *Horn Book* review, "and the dual narrators remain sympathetic and genuine-sounding." Edward in particular "is hilarious—wry, touching, and very smart," declared *Booklist* reviewer Rochman.

If We Kiss is a story about a high school freshman named Charlie (short for Charlotte) and her attempts to understand grown-up feelings of love and lust. Charlie gets her long-awaited first kiss from Kevin Lazarus outside the school one day, but this quickly turns into much more than just a kiss. Charlie, shocked by Kevin's surprise move and unsure of how she feels about it, tells no one about the experience. Then her best friend, Tess, unaware of this complication, becomes involved with Kevin, and Charlie's mother begins dating Kevin's father.

"The author's frank representation of teen sentiments and razorsharp wit will keep readers turning pages to see how Charlie will handle her dilemmas," wrote a *Publishers Weekly* contributor. Several critics praised Vail's prose style in *If We Kiss; School Library Journal* reviewer Angela M. Boccuzzi-Reichert commented that "Charlie tells her story in a fresh voice," and a *Publishers Weekly* critic declared Charlie "much funnier and more knowing than any ninth-grader on the planet."

In addition to her young-adult novels, Vail has also written several picture books for younger readers. Many of these books feature Mama Rex and T, a mother-and-child dinosaur duo who face difficulties that will be familiar to young children and their parents. In *Homework Trouble,* T forgets about a diorama he has to make for school until the day before it is due; in *The Horrible Play Date,* he and friend Walter have trouble playing nicely together. The latter tale "will strike resonant chords among its readers, no doubt," predicted a *Kirkus Reviews* contributor, while another critic for the same magazine praised the "droll sense of humor" in *Homework Trouble.* Vail spins another picture-book tale about

Vail's Sometimes I'm Bombaloo *focuses on something young children—and their parents—know all too well: the terrible toddler temper tantrum. (Illustration by Yumi Heo.)*

childhood difficulties in *Sometimes I'm Bombaloo,* which finds a little girl named Katie struggles to control her temper tantrums with the help of her loving, caring parents. "Vail gets right inside a kid's psyche," Ilene Cooper noted in *Booklist,* "captures the intensity of emotion that children . . . feel when they are angry, and then distills it with laughter." A *Publishers Weekly* contributor also praised the book, nothing that Vail's "kid-friendly phrasing and language add immediacy and some humor to the proceedings."

Biographical and Critical Sources

BOOKS

Seventh Book of Junior Authors and Illustrators, H. W. Wilson (Bronx, NY), 1996.

PERIODICALS

Booklist, September 1, 1991, Deborah Abbott, review of *Wonder,* p. 54; August, 1992, Stephanie Zvirin, review of *Do-Over,* p. 2013; March 1, 1994, Hazel Rochman, review of *Ever After,* p. 1254; March 1, 1996, Stephanie Zvirin, review of *Daring to Be Abigail,* p. 1184; September 15, 1998, Kathleen Squires, review of *Over the Moon,* p. 241; October 15, 1998, Hazel Rochman, review of *If You Only Knew,* p. 422; November 15, 1998, Hazel Rochman, review of *Not That I Care,* p. 591; February 1, 2002, Ilene Cooper, review of *Sometimes I'm Bombaloo,* p. 940; March, 2002, Nina Lindsay, review of *Sometimes I'm Bomba-*

loo, p. 204; April 1, 2004, Hazel Rochman, review of *Never Mind!: A Twin Novel,* p. 1365; March 15, 2005, Ilene Cooper, review of *If We Kiss,* p. 1285.

Bulletin of the Center for Children's Books, September, 1991, review of *Wonder,* p. 24; December, 1992, Roger Sutton, review of *Do-Over,* pp. 125-126; February, 1996, Deborah Stevenson, review of *Daring to Be Abigail,* p. 207.

Horn Book, November-December, 1992, Ellen Fader, review of *Do-Over,* p. 731; May-June, 1994, Rachel Vail, "Making Stories Happen," pp. 301-304; May-June, 1996, Lauren Adams, review of *Daring to Be Abigail,* pp. 337-339; January-February, 1999, Christine M. Heppermann, review of *If You Only Knew* and *Not That I Care,* p. 71; May-June, 2004, Christine M. Heppermann, review of *Never Mind!,* p. 324.

Kirkus Reviews, August 8, 1991, review of *Wonder,* p. 1095; July 15, 1992, p. 927; April 1, 1994, review of *Ever After,* p. 486; January 1, 2002, review of *Sometimes I'm Bombaloo,* p. 53; July 1, 2002, review of *Mama Rex and T: The Horrible Play Date,* p. 964; July 15, 2002, review of *Mama Rex and T: Homework Trouble,* p. 1046; April 15, 2005, review of *If We Kiss,* p. 483.

Kliatt, May, 2004, Michele Winship, review of *Never Mind!,* p. 5; May, 2005, Heidi Hauser Green, review of *Ever After,* p. 31.

Publishers Weekly, August 9, 1991, review of *Wonder,* p. 58; December 20, 1991, "Flying Starts," p. 24; February 21, 1994, review of *Ever After,* pp. 255-256; June 8, 1998, review of *The Friendship Ring,* p. 61; July 20, 1998, review of *Over the Moon,* p. 218; December 24, 2001, review of *Sometimes I'm Bombaloo,* p. 63; May 10, 2004, review of *Never Mind!,* p. 60; April 11, 2005, review of *If We Kiss,* p. 56.

School Library Journal, August, 1991, Debra S. Gold, review of *Wonder,* p. 196; September, 1992, Jacqueline Rose, review of *Do-Over,* p. 282; May, 1994, Ellen Fader, review of *Ever After,* p. 136; March, 1996, Connie Tyrrell Burns, review of *Daring to Be Abigail,* p. 198; March, 2002, Nina Lindsay, review of *Sometimes I'm Bombaloo,* p. 204; May, 2005, Angela M. Boccuzzi-Reichert, review of *If We Kiss,* p. 140.

Voice of Youth Advocates, August, 2004, Pam Carlson, review of *Never Mind!,* p. 207.

Washington Post Book World, July 18, 2004, Elizabeth Ward, review of *Never Mind!,* p. 11.

ONLINE

BookPage.com, http://www.bookpage.com/ (July 18, 2005), Heidi Henneman, interview with Vail and Avi.

Rachel Vail Home Page, http://www.rachelvail.com (July 6, 2005).

Teenreads.com, http://www.teenreads.com/ (July 18, 2005), Kristi Olson, review of *If We Kiss;* "Rachel Vail."*

*   *   *

VAN KAMPEN, Vlasta 1943-

Personal

Born August 22, 1943, in Belleville, Ontario, Canada; daughter of Frank (an engineer) and Myriel (Bowman)

Rabel; married Jan Van Kampen (a graphic designer); children: Dimitri, Saskia. *Education:* Ontario College of Art and Design, diploma (with honors), 1966; studied at Gerritt Rietveld Akademie (Amsterdam, Netherlands), 1966-67.

Addresses

Home—258 Silver Heights Dr., R.R.#1 Hastings, Ontario KOL-140, Canada. *E-mail*—contact@vlasta.ca.

Career

Illustrator and author. McClelland & Stewart, Toronto, Ontario, Canada, staff artist, 1968-70; freelance graphic artist, beginning 1970; National Film Board of Canada, storyboard artist, 1986. Guest teacher and lecturer, 1982—.

Member

Canadian Society of Children's Authors, Illustrators, and Performers, Canadian Children's Book Centre.

Awards, Honors

Academic Award, Society of Illustrators, 1966; Amelia Francis Howard-Gibbon Award runner-up, 1979, for *Great Canadian Animal Stories;* Canada Council Award, 1982, for *A B C, 1 2 3: The Canadian Alphabet and Counting Book; Applied Arts* magazine award, 1997, for *Beetle Bedlam;* Parent's Guide to Children's Media Award, 1999, for *The Last Straw; Skipping Stones* Award, 2001, for *What's the Difference;* Storytelling Award, Storytelling World, 2001, for *Two Lazy Bears;* International Orders of the Daughters of England Award, 2002, for *A Drop of Gold;* Toy Council of Canada Award, 2003, for *Marigold's Wings.*

Writings

SELF-ILLUSTRATED

A B C, 1 2 3: The Canadian Alphabet and Counting Book, Hurtig (Edmonton, Alberta, Canada), 1982.
Beetle Bedlam, Charlesbridge (Watertown, MA), 1997.
(Reteller) *Bear Tales: Three Treasured Stories,* Annick Press (Toronto, Ontario, Canada), 2000.
A Drop of Gold, Annick Press (Toronto, Ontario, Canada), 2001.
It Couldn't Be Worse!, Annick Press (Toronto, Ontario, Canada), 2003.
Marigold's Wings, Gareth Stevens Pub. (Milwaukee, WI), 2005.

ILLUSTRATOR

Muriel Whitaker, editor, *Great Canadian Animal Stories,* Hurtig (Edmonton, Alberta, Canada), 1978.
Muriel Whitaker, editor, *Great Canadian Adventure Stories,* Hurtig (Edmonton, Alberta, Canada), 1979.

Muriel Whitaker, *The Princess, the Hockey Player, Magic, and Ghosts: Canadian Stories for Children,* Hurtig (Edmonton, Alberta, Canada), 1980.
Muriel Whitaker, editor, *Stories from the Canadian North,* (Edmonton, Alberta, Canada), 1980.
Kathy Corrigan, *Emily Umily,* Annick Press (Toronto, Ontario, Canada), 1984.
Patricia Quinlan, *My Dad Takes Care of Me,* Annick Press (Toronto, Ontario, Canada), 1987.
Dorothy Joan Harris, *Racing Stripes for William,* Three Trees Press (Toronto, Ontario, Canada), 1987.
Dorothy Joan Harris, *Four Seasons for Toby,* North Winds Press (Richmond Hill, Ontario, Canada), 1987.
Irene C. Eugen, *Orchestranimals,* Scholastic (New York, NY), 1989.
Linda Manning, *Animal Hours,* Oxford University Press (New York, NY), 1990.
Irene C. Eugen, *Rockanimals,* North Winds Press (Richmond Hill, Ontario, Canada), 1991.
Arthur Johnson, *King of Cats,* Stoddart (Toronto, Ontario, Canada), 1992.
Linda Manning, *Dinosaur Days,* BridgeWater Books (Mahwah, NJ), 1994.
Arnold Shapiro, *God Loves You,* Thomas Nelson Publishers (Nashville, TN), 1996.
Laurel Dee Gugler, *Muddle Cuddle,* Annick Press (Toronto, Ontario, Canada), 1997.
Laurel Dee Gugler, reteller, *Monkey Tales,* Annick Press (Toronto, Ontario, Canada), 1998.
Fredrick Thury, *The Last Straw,* Charlesbridge (Watertown, MA), 1999.
Judy Diehl and David Plumb, *What's the Difference?: Ten Animal Look-alikes,* Annick Press (Toronto, Ontario, Canada), 2000.

Sidelights

Canadian children's book illustrator, author, and artist Vlasta Van Kampen is a graduate of the Ontario College of Art who has illustrated dozens of books since beginning her career in the late 1970s. After spending several decades creating artwork to enhance the texts of picture-book authors, Van Kampen decided to add "author" to her resume, and *Beetle Bedlam* became one of her first self-illustrated books. This introduction to beetles of the world, which *Resource Links* reviewer Pam Mountain praised as "hilarious and highly informative," has been followed by such picture books as *It Couldn't Be Worse!* and *A Drop of Gold.*

It Couldn't Be Worse! is a "simple but hilarious retelling" of a familiar Yiddish folktale, according to *Resource Links* reviewer Denise Parrott. Calling Van Kampen "a gem in Canadian children's literature" Parrott added that in this book she spins "a compelling tale." In the story a farmer's wife complains to a fishmonger known for his wisdom that her family's house is too crowded. The thoughtful man responds by suggesting that the woman bring her goat inside. The next day, she returns with the same predicament, and the fishmonger dispenses similar advice, and with every passing day the house gets more and more crowded. Finally, with a house full of animals, the woman returns with the same complaint, and this time the fishmonger proves his wisdom by advising her to remove all the animals, whereupon the house seems far less crowded. In retelling the tale Van Kampen adds "a few twists," commented Susan Marie Pitard in *School Library Journal,* while Parrott noted that the book's "clean, large watercolour illustrations are charming." A *Kirkus Reviews* critic also had praise for the book, stating that the author/illustrator's "beautiful illustrations complementing a very satisfying retelling" make *It Couldn't Be Worse!* "a winner" for readers of all ages.

In the porquoi tale *A Drop of Gold* Van Kampen paints a colorful tale in vivid watercolor. In her story Mother Natures sets to work painting the world, but leaves the birds until last. When all the paint is gone there is one bird left, the nightingale. When a monkey finds a drop of gold paint, Mother Nature gives the little bird a very special gift. "Vibrant colors and rich detail celebrate the variety of species," commented Gillian Engberg in *Booklist,* while *School Library Journal* reviewer Susan Marie Pitard noted that Van Kampen's artwork, as the book's strength, is "imaginative, full of color and action."

Biographical and Critical Sources

PERIODICALS

Booklist, July, 1994, Denia Hester, review of *Dinosaur Days,* p. 1951; June 1, 2000, Hazel Rochman, review of *Bear Tales: Three Treasured Stories,* p. 1899; February 1, 2002, Gillian Engberg, review of *A Drop of Gold,* p. 944; March 1, 2003, GraceAnne A. DeCandido, review of *It Couldn't Be Worse!,* p. 1202.

Kirkus Reviews, February 1, 2003, review of *It Couldn't Be Worse!,* p. 241.

Publishers Weekly, February 23, 1990, review of *Orchestranimals,* p. 217; June 23, 1997, review of *Beetle Bedlam,* p. 90; September 27, 1999, review of *The Last Straw,* p. 61.

Resource Links, August, 1997, review of *Beetle Bedlam,* p. 255; October, 2001, Stephanie Olson, review of *A Drop of Gold,* p. 6; April, 2003, Liz Abercrombie, review of *Marigold's Wings,* p. 10; April, 2003, Denise Parrott, review of *It Couldn't Be Worse!,* p. 9.

School Library Journal, October, 2000, Denise E. Agosto, review of *Bear Tales: Three Treasured Stories,* p. 154; January, 2002, Susan Marie Pitard, review of *A Drop of Gold,* p. 111; April, 2003, Susan Marie Pitard, review of *It Couldn't Be Worse!,* p. 156.

Skipping Stones, October, 2001, Stephanie Olson, review of *A Drop of Gold,* p. 6.

ONLINE

Annick Press Web site, http://www.annickpress.com/ (July 6, 2005),"Vlasta Van Kampen."

Vlasta Van Kampen Home Page, http://www.vlasta.ca. (July 15, 2005).*

W

WAX, Wendy A. 1963-

Personal

Born October 9, 1963, in Detroit, MI; daughter of Harvey (an attorney) and Laney (a program director at Naropa University) Wax; married Jon Holderer (a commercial photographer), December 12, 1999; children: Jonah. *Education:* University of Michigan, B.F.A. (graphic design).

Addresses

Home—P.O. Box 218, Remsenburg, NY 11960. *E-mail*—wendyawax@yahoo.com.

Career

Collage artist and author and illustrator of children's books.

Awards, Honors

Artist of the Month, Grey Advertising, 1998.

Writings

FOR CHILDREN

(With Della Rowland) *Ten Things I Know about Kangaroos,* illustrated by Thomas Payne, Contemporary Books (Chicago, IL), 1989.

(With Della Rowland) *Ten Things I Know about Penguins,* illustrated by Thomas Payne, Contemporary Books (Chicago, IL), 1989.

Inside the Aquarium, illustrated by Joe Murray, Contemporary Books (Chicago, IL), 1989.

(With Della Rowland) *Ten Things I Know about Whales,* illustrated by Thomas Payne, Contemporary Books (Chicago, IL), 1989.

(With Della Rowland) *Ten Things I Know about Elephants,* illustrated by Thomas Payne, Contemporary Books (Chicago, IL), 1990.

(Compiler) *A Treasury of Christmas Carols, Poems, and Games to Share,* Dell (New York, NY), 1992.

Say No and Know Why: Kids Learn about Drugs, photographs by Toby McAfee, Walker (New York, NY), 1992.

(Compiler) *Hanukkah, Oh, Hanukkah!: A Treasury of Stories, Songs, and Games to Share,* illustrated by John Speirs, Bantam (New York, NY), 1993.

(Adaptor) *Tom and Jerry: Friends to the End,* Turner (Atlanta, GA), 1993.

The Hungry Bunny, McClanahan Book Company (New York, NY), 1996.

Molly's Loose Tooth, McClanahan Book Company (New York, NY), 1996.

Home, Sweep Home, HarperActive (New York, NY), 1998.

Do You See What I See?, HarperActive (New York, NY), 1998.

Passport to Paris, (novelization of *Mary-Kate and Ashley* television series), Parachute Press (New York, NY), 2000.

Empire Dreams, illustrated by Todd Doney, Silver Moon Press (New York, NY), 2000.

Watch out, Otto! (based on *Rocket Power* television series), illustrated by Pilar Newton-Mitchell, Simon & Schuster (New York, NY), 2002.

Bus to Booville, Grosset & Dunlap (New York, NY), 2003.

A Very Mice Christmas, HarperCollins (New York, NY), 2003.

Picture Day, Penguin (New York, NY), 2003.

You Can't Scare Me!, Grosset & Dunlap (New York, NY), 2003.

A Valentine for Tommy, illustrated by Robert Roper, Simon & Schuster (New York, NY), 2003.

The Runaway Turkey (based on *Rugrats* television series), illustrated by Larissa Marantz and Shannon Bergman, Simon & Schuster (New York, NY), 2003.

A Time to Climb (based on *Rocket Power* television series), Simon & Schuster (New York, NY), 2004.

Too Many Turners, Simon & Schuster (New York, NY), 2004.

Reggie's Secret Admirer (based on *Rocket Power* television series), Simon & Schuster (New York, NY), 2004.

Practice Makes Perfect (based on *Rocket Power* television series), Simon & Schuster (New York, NY), 2004.

The Night before Easter (based on *The Wild Thornberries* television series), Simon & Schuster (New York, NY), 2004.

Snowed Under: The Bobblesberg Winter Games (based on *Bob the Builder* television series), Simon Spotlight (New York, NY), 2004.

Coolest Girl in School (based on *All Grown Up* television series), illustrated by Chrissie Boehm, Simon Spotlight (New York, NY), 2005.

Piggley Makes a Pie (based on *Jakers! The Adventures of Piggley Winks* television series), Simon Spotlight (New York, NY), 2005.

Big Book of Clues from A to Z, Innovativekids (Norwalk, CT), 2005.

Top-Secret Handbook (based on *Totally Spies!* television series), Simon Spotlight (New York, NY), 2005.

Candy Chaos! (based on *Totally Spies!* television series), Simon Spotlight (New York, NY), 2005.

A Royal Valentine (based on *Backyardigans* television series), Simon Spotlight (New York, NY), 2006.

For Love or Money (based on *Fairly OddParents* television series), Simon Spotlight (New York, NY), 2006.

Secret Agents (based on *Backyardigans* television series), Simon Spotlight (New York, NY), 2006.

Picknic Day! (based on *LazyTown* television series), Simon Spotlight (New York, NY), 2006.

Five Curious Buddies: A Turn and Learn Counting Book (based on *Curious Buddies* television series), Simon Spotlight (New York, NY), 2006.

It's Friendship Day! (based on *Blues Clues* television series), Simon Spotlight (New York, NY), 2006.

Nautical Nonsense: A SpongeBob Joke Book (based on *SpongeBob* television series), Simon Spotlight (New York, NY), 2006.

Sticky Situations: A Totally Spies! Guide to Getting out in a Clutch! (based on *Totally Spies!* television series), Simon Spotlight (New York, NY), 2006.

Sidelights

A prolific children's book author, Wendy A. Wax has written picture books, penned stories based on popular television programs such as *SpongeBob* and *Totally Spies!*, and produced two holiday anthologies. Among her many book titles for children are *Empire Dreams, Hanukkah, Oh, Hanukkah!: A Treasury of Stories, Songs, and Games to Share,* and *A Very Mice Christmas.*

Part of Silver Moon Press's "Adventures in America" series, *Empire Dreams* takes place in New York City during the Great Depression of the 1930s, and focuses on a preteen who discovers that her father is secretly unemployed. In order to try and help her family financially, eleven-year-old Julie Singer convinces her uncle to allow her to work in his dress-collar factory to earn some extra money. Throughout the course of Wax's story the young heroine learns the importance of family love and support while growing stronger as an individual. According to *School Library Journal* contributor Carolyn Janssen, *Empire Dreams* features a

heroine with a "distinct personality" who would prove interesting to "reluctant readers who want a short, quick read" highlighted by illustrations.

Wax offers up a fun holiday story in *A Very Mice Christmas,* a touch-and-feel board book. In this toddler-time tale a family of mice prepare for the holiday season by engaging in all of the traditional Yuletide festivities, including hanging up their stockings, decorating a Christmas tree, and filling their home with colorful decorations. Susan Patron noted in *School Library Journal* that the "pictures and text work well together" and combine to bring young children a fun holiday story-time experience. In another perspective on the holiday season, Wax collects poems and stories about the Jewish celebration in *Hanukkah, Oh, Hanukkah!,* which was described as "appealing and versatile" by *Booklist* contributor Ellen Mandel.

Biographical and Critical Sources

PERIODICALS

Booklist, January 15, 1993, James Jeske, review of *Say No and Know Why: Kids Learn about Drugs,* p. 905; October 15, 1993, Ellen Mandel, review of *Hanukkah, Oh, Hanukkah! A Treasury of Stories, Songs, and Games to Share,* p. 447.

Entertainment Weekly, December 17, 1993, Jessica Shaw, review of *Hanukkah, Oh, Hanukkah!,* p. 79.

Publishers Weekly, August 11, 1989, review of *Ten Things I Know about Penguins* and *Ten Things I Know about Kangaroos,* p. 455.

School Library Journal, December, 1989, Ellen Dibener, review of *Inside the Aquarium,* p. 97; March, 1990, J. J. Votapka, review of *Ten Things I Know about Penguins* and *Ten Things I Know about Kangaroos,* p. 215; August, 1990, Ruth M. McConnell, review of *Ten Things I Know about Whales* and *Ten Things I Know about Elephants,* p. 144; October, 1992, Denise L. Moll, review of *Say No and Know Why,* p. 139; March, 2001, Carolyn Janssen, review of *Empire Dreams,* p. 258; October, 2003, Susan Patron, review of *A Very Mice Christmas,* p. 69.

*   *   *

WISE, William 1923-

Personal

Born July 21, 1923, in New York, NY. *Education:* Yale University, B.A., 1948.

Addresses

Home—New York, NY. *Agent*—Curtis Brown, Ltd., 575 Madison Ave., New York, NY 10022.

Career

Writer.

Writings

FOR CHILDREN

Jonathan Blake: The Life and Times of a Very Young Man, illustrated by Howard Simon, Knopf (New York, NY), 1956.

Silversmith of Old New York: Myer Myers, illustrated by Leonard Everett Fisher, Farrar, Straus & Cudahy (New York, NY), 1958.

Albert Einstein: Citizen of the World, Farrar, Straus & Cudahy (New York, NY), 1960.

The House with the Red Roof, illustrated by Jo Polseno, Putnam (New York, NY), 1961.

The Cowboy Surprise, illustrated by Paul Galdone, Putnam (New York, NY), 1961.

Alexander Hamilton, Putnam (New York, NY), 1963.

The Story of Mulberry Bend, illustrated by Hoot von Zitzewitz, Dutton (New York, NY), 1963.

In the Time of the Dinosaurs, illustrated by Lewis Zacks, Putnam (New York, NY), 1964.

Detective Pinkerton and Mr. Lincoln, illustrated by Hoot von Zitzewitz, Dutton (New York, NY), 1964.

The Two Reigns of Tutankhamen, Putnam (New York, NY), 1964.

The World of Giant Mammals, illustrated by Lewis Zacks, Putnam (New York, NY), 1965.

The Spy and General Washington, illustrated by Peter Burchard, Dutton (New York, NY), 1965.

The Terrible Trumpet, Hamish Hamilton (London, England), 1966, with illustrations by B. Biro, Norton (New York, NY) 1969.

Franklin Delano Roosevelt, illustrated by Paul Frame, Putnam (New York, NY), 1967.

Monsters of Today and Yesterday, illustrated by Lee Smith, Putnam (New York, NY), 1967.

When the Saboteurs Came: The Nazi Sabotage Plot against America in World War II, illustrated by Robert Shore, Dutton (New York, NY), 1967.

Sir Howard, the Coward, illustrated by Susan Perl, Putnam (New York, NY), 1967.

Monsters of the Ancient Seas, illustrated by Joseph Sibal, Putnam (New York, NY), 1968.

Aaron Burr, Putnam (New York, NY), 1968.

Booker T. Washington, illustrated by Paul Frame, Putnam (New York, NY), 1968.

Nanette: The Hungry Pelican, illustrated by Winifred Lubell, Rand McNally (Chicago, IL), 1969.

Giant Birds and Monsters of the Air, illustrated by Joseph Sibal, Putnam (New York, NY), 1969.

The Amazing Animals of Latin America, illustrated by Joseph Sibal, Putnam (New York, NY), 1969.

The Amazing Animals of Australia, illustrated by Joseph Sibal, Putnam (New York, NY), 1970.

The Lazy Young Duke of Dundee, illustrated by Barbara Cooney, Rand McNally (Chicago, IL), 1970.

Fresh as a Daisy, Neat as a Pin, illustrated by Dora Leder, Parents' Magazine Press (New York, NY), 1970.

From Scrolls to Satellites: The Story of Communication, illustrated by Hans Zander, Parents' Magazine Press (New York, NY), 1970.

Giant Snakes and Other Amazing Reptiles, illustrated by Joseph Sibal, Putnam (New York, NY), 1970.

Charles A. Lindbergh: Aviation Pioneer, illustrated by Paul Sagsoorian, Putnam (New York, NY), 1970.

Monsters of the Middle Ages, illustrated by Tomie de Paola, Putnam (New York, NY), 1971.

The Amazing Animals of North America, illustrated by Joseph Sibal, Putnam (New York, NY), 1971.

Fresh, Canned, and Frozen: Food from Past to Future, illustrated by Shelley Fink, Parents' Magazine Press (New York, NY), 1971.

All on a Summer's Day, illustrated by Bill Binzen, Pantheon (New York, NY), 1971.

Off We Go! A Book of Transportation, illustrated by Sue L. Anderson, Parents' Magazine Press (New York, NY), 1972.

Cities, Old and New, illustrated by Mila Lazarevich, Parents' Magazine Press (New York, NY), 1973.

Leaders, Laws, and Citizens: The Story of Democracy and Government, Parents' Magazine Press (New York, NY), 1973.

The Strange World of Sea Mammals, illustrated by Joseph Sibal, Putnam (New York, NY), 1973.

Monsters of the Deep, illustrated by Ben F. Stahl, Putnam (New York, NY), 1975.

American Freedom and the Bill of Rights, illustrated by Roland Rodegast, Parents' Magazine Press (New York, NY), 1975.

Monsters of North America, illustrated by Ben F. Stahl, Putnam (New York, NY), 1978.

Animal Rescue: Saving Our Endangered Wildlife, illustrated by Heidi Palmer, Putnam (New York, NY), 1978.

Monsters from Outer Space?, illustrated by Richard Cuffari, Putnam (New York, NY), 1978.

Monster Myths of Ancient Greece, illustrated by Jerry Pinkney, Putnam (New York, NY), 1981.

(Reteller) *The Black Falcon: A Tale from the Decameron,* illustrated by Gillian Barlow, Philomel (New York, NY), 1990.

Ten Sly Piranhas: A Counting Story in Reverse (a Tale of Wickedness—and Worse!), illustrated by Victoria Chess, Dial Books for Young Readers (New York, NY), 1993.

Perfect Pancakes, If You Please, illustrated by Richard Egielski, Dial Books for Young Readers (New York, NY), 1997.

Nell of Branford Hall, Dial (New York, NY), 1999.

Dinosaurs Forever, illustrated by Lynn Munsinger, Dial (New York, NY), 2000.

Christopher Mouse: The Tale of a Small Traveler, Bloomsbury (New York, NY), 2004.

Ten Sly Piranhas: A Counting Story in Reverse, Dial Books for Young Readers (New York, NY), 2004.

FOR ADULTS

Killer Smog: The World's Worst Air Pollution, (nonfiction), Rand McNally (Chicago, IL), 1968.

Secret Mission to the Philippines: The Story of the "Spyron" and the American-Filipino Guerrillas of World War II, Dutton (New York, NY), 1968.

Massacre at Mountain Meadows: An American Legend and a Monumental Crime, Crowell (New York, NY), 1976.

The Amazon Factor (mystery), Harlequin (New York, NY), 1981.

Also author of "Raven House" mysteries for Harlequin, 1980-82. Author of television scripts; contributor of fiction to *Harper's, Yale Review,* and other periodicals, and of reviews to *New York Times* and *Saturday Review.*

Sidelights

A prolific author of both fiction and nonfiction, William Wise has been writing books for children for nearly half a century. His work includes straight nonfiction books and whimsical titles on mythical monsters, as well as rhyming picture books for the very young. Among his many children's titles are the rambunctious *Ten Sly Piranhas: A Counting Story in Reverse (a Tale of Wickedness—and Worse!),* the historical novel *Nell of Brandford Hall,* and the humorous picture book *Dinosaurs Forever.* In a *Horn Book* review of *Ten Sly Piranhas,* Mary M. Burns termed Wise's tale "a triumph of the comic spirit" in its humorous treatment of the goings-on in a self-depleting gang of hungry piranhas.

The novel *Nell of Branford Hall* is based on a true story that took place in seventeenth-century England in a town called Eyam. Faced with an outbreak of the bubonic plague in their town, the citizens of Wise's fictional Branford decide to quarantine their entire village, allowing no one in or out and placing any citizens with symptoms of the black death under strict quarantine. Nell, part of a well-to-do family, lives beyond the village limits in a manor hall, and when Branford is barricaded, she faces isolation and anxiety as she worries about her friends inside the village proper and wonders whether the horrors of the plague will visit her unprotected home. Characters such as Isaac Newton and diarist Samuel Pepys also feature in the novel, and Nell's father, a scholar, educates his daughter in the medical science behind the dread disease. In *Booklist* Carolyn Phelan praised the "heroic" story, adding that Wise's tale "is enhanced by the contrasting backgrounds of city and village life."

Christopher Mouse: The Tale of a Small Traveler presents readers with a delightful tale about an adventuresome young mouse. Told in a first-person narrative, pet shop mouse Christopher recounts the adventures he has had throughout the course of his life and, while commonplace, meetings with hungry cats and troublemaking boys contain enough suspense to entertain a young audience. Ilene Cooper commented in *Booklist* that Wise's text is "very accessible, making the book not only a winner for reading aloud but also a delightful of-

fering for children moving past beginning readers." Vicki Arkoff, reviewing *Christopher Mouse* for *MBR Bookwatch,* also enjoyed Wise's story, writing that, "with the delightful feel of a lost classic," Wise introduces readers to "a rather extraordinary mouse who, through the force of will and good luck, finds his own small place in a very large world."

In *Dinosaurs Forever* Wise presents a quirky tale of that finds several prehistoric beasts—appropriately attired in modern clothing—inhabiting Manhattan. "Lilting, rhythmic rhymes will have the names of those ancient beasts rolling off readers' tongues, and scientific facts have never been so much fun" enthused Carolyn Janssen in *School Library Journal.* Wise includes over twenty rhyming poems that serve to both educate and entertain young dino-fans, and his poems are paired with illustrator Lynn Munsinger's "airy and cheerfully rendered" artwork, according to a *Publishers Weekly* critic. Ellen Mandel, reviewing the book for *Booklist,* called *Dinosaurs Forever* a "keenly imaginative" book in which "zippy" rhymes "humanize the extinct yet undyingly popular creatures."

A tiny but adventurous mouse-poet survives a series of negligent owners as well as a hungry cat before finding a secure home with a caring family in William Wise's engaging book. (Cover illustration by Patrick Benson.)

Biographical and Critical Sources

PERIODICALS

Booklist, December 1, 1996, Stephanie Zvirin, review of *Perfect Pancakes, If You Please,* p. 670; November 1, 1999, Carolyn Phelan, review of *Nell of Branford Hall,* p. 531; May 15, 2000, Elen Mandel, review of *Dinosaurs Forever,* p. 1746; April 1, 2004, Ilene Cooper, review of *Christopher Mouse: The Tale of a Small Traveler,* p. 1365.

Children's Bookwatch, August, 2004, review of *Christopher Mouse,* p. 2.

Horn Book, July-August, 1993, Mary M. Burns, review of *Ten Sly Piranhas: A Counting Story in Reverse (a Tale of Wickedness—and Worse!),* p. 452.

Kirkus Reviews, April 15, 2004, review of *Christopher Mouse,* p. 403.

Library Journal,.

MBR Bookwatch, January, 2005, Vicki Arkoff, review of *Christopher Mouse.*

New York Times Book Review, October 9, 1994, Kyoko Mori, review of *Ten Sly Piranhas,* p. 26; May 14, 2000, J. D. Biersdorfer, review of *Dinosaurs Forever,* p. 18.

People, March 26, 1990, Susan Toepfer, review of *The Black Falcon: A Tale from the Decameron,* p. 32.

Publishers Weekly, May 31, 1993, review of *Ten Sly Piranhas,* p. 54; December 9, 1996, review of *Perfect Pancakes, If You Please,* p. 67; September 20, 1999, review of *Nell of Branford Hall,* p. 88; June 3, 2002, review of *Dinosaurs Forever,* p. 91.

School Library Journal, October, 1999, Patricia B. McGee, review of *Nell of Branford Hall,* p. 162; July, 2000, Carolyn Janssen, review of *Dinosaurs Forever,* p. 99.

ONLINE

Bloomsbury USA Web site, http://www.bloomsburyusa.com/ (July 6, 2005), "William Wise."*

*   *   *

WOOLMAN, Steven 1969-2004

Personal

Born August 31, 1969, in Adelaide, South Australia, Australia; died April 30, 2004, in Australia; son of Dean (an aeroplane detailer) and Judith (a homemaker; maiden name, Robertson) Woolman. *Education:* University of South Australia, B. A. (graphic design), 1990.

Career

Illustrator. ERA Publications, Adelaide, South Australia, Australia, production staff member, 1990-2004.

Member

Awards, Honors

Picture Book of the Year citation, 1995, for *The Watertower,* and Notable Book selections, 1995, for *Peter and the Polar Bear,* 1996, for *The Lighthouse,* and 1997, for *Tagged,* all from Australian Children's Book Council; IBBY Ena Noel Award, 1997, for body of work.

Writings

SELF-ILLUSTRATED

Budgie, Omnibus Books (Norwood, South Australia, Australia), 2001.

ILLUSTRATOR

Janeen Brian and Gwen Pascoe, *There Was a Big Fish,* ERA Publications (Adelaide, South Australia, Australia), 1992.

Rodney Martin, *Wise and Wacky Works by Anonymous,* ERA Publications (Adelaide, South Australia, Australia), 1993.

Kath Lock and Francis Kelly, *Kuan Yin,* ERA Publications (Adelaide, South Australia, Australia), 1994.

Elizabeth Best, *Peter and the Polar Bear,* ERA Publications (Adelaide, South Australia, Australia), 1994.

Gary Crew, *The Watertower,* ERA Publications (Adelaide, South Australia, Australia), 1994.

Dyan Blacklock, *The Lighthouse,* ERA Publications (Adelaide, South Australia, Australia), 1995.

Gary Crew, *Caleb,* ERA Publications (Adelaide, South Australia, Australia), 1996.

Gary Crew, *Tagged,* ERA Publications (Adelaide, South Australia, Australia), 1997.

Gary Crew, *The Cave,* ERA Publications (Adelaide, South Australia, Australia), 1999,

Paul Collins, *Out of This World,* Koala Books (Mascot, New South Wales, Australia), 1999.

Taz Razzle, *Busybodies abc,* ERA Publications (Adelaide, South Australia, Australia), 2000.

Christopher Cheng, *One Child,* Crocodile Books (New York, NY), 2000.

Isobelle Carmody, *Dreamwalker,* Thomas C. Lothian (Port Melbourne, Victoria, Australia), 2001.

Isobelle Carmody, *Wildheart,* Omnibus Books (Norwood, South Australia, Australia), 2002.

Gary Crew, *Beneath the Surface!,* Hodder Headline (Sydney, New South Wales, Australia), 2004.

Mark Svendsen, *Kestrel,* Lothian Books (South Melbourne, Victoria, Australia), 2005.

Sidelights

Australian illustrator Steven Woolman was an author and illustrator of several award-winning children's picture books. He worked in a wide range of media and was influenced largely by the old movies he watched as a child while growing up. Woolman died on April 30, 2004 at the age of thirty-four.

Woolman once told *Something about the Author:* "I've always been interested in the macabre and been attracted to tales of horror and the supernatural. My teen years were filled with images from horror and black and white B-grade science fiction movies, TV shows and comics, and this has had a lasting influence on my work and the way I visualize stories. Looking back, I think the attraction to horror was not so much the thrill of being scared, but more the visual style with which these stories were told. Films such as *The Shining* and *Invasion of the Body Snatchers* (even schlock-horror splatter movies like *Evil Dead*) excited me through their use of closeups and strange angles, weird lighting, and cutaways. I find now when I begin illustrating manuscripts that my first step is to play out the action in my mind as though it were a movie, and the cinematic influence usually remains in the finished product. *The Watertower* was my first macabre book, and since it was aimed at an older audience I felt licensed to try a more sophisticated visual style and design. With its surreal photorealism, black borders, and wide-screen presentation, the book is very much a homage to those movies I watched in my teens. *Caleb,* the follow-up, also uses some of the same devices, with its unnatural viewpoints and manipulation of shadow and light.

"This is not to say all my work is horror-based and dark. I am after all a children's book illustrator and a large body of my work is humorous in nature and aimed at a younger age group. Books such as *Peter and the Polar Bear* and *The Lighthouse* are both complete diversions from my books for older readers, and I enjoyed the challenge of creating them just as much."

Biographical and Critical Sources

PERIODICALS

Horn Book, May-June, 1998, Kathleen T. Horning, review of *The Watertower,* p. 330.
Publishers Weekly, January 19, 1998, review of *The Watertower,* p. 378.
School Library Journal, August, 2000, Kathy Piehl, review of *One Child,* p. 146.

ONLINE

Steve Woolman Home Page, http://www.frontierisp.net/au/~woolman/ (July 6, 2005).

OBITUARIES

PERIODICALS

Horn Book, September-October, 2004, p. 621.

ONLINE

Adelaide Children's Library Web site, http://www.adelaide citycouncil.com/childrenslibrary/ (July 6, 2005), "Steven Woolman."*

Illustrations Index

(In the following index, the number of the *volume* in which an illustrator's work appears is given *before* the colon, and the *page number* on which it appears is given *after* the colon. For example, a drawing by Adams, Adrienne appears in Volume 2 on page 6, another drawing by her appears in Volume 3 on page 80, another drawing in Volume 8 on page 1, and so on and so on. . . .)

YABC

Index references to *YABC* refer to listings appearing in the two-volume *Yesterday's Authors of Books for Children,* also published by Thomson Gale. *YABC* covers prominent authors and illustrators who died prior to 1960.

Author Index

The following index gives the number of the volume in which an author's biographical sketch, Autobiography Feature, Brief Entry, or Obituary appears.

This index includes references to all entries in the following series, which are also published by The Gale Group.

YABC—*Yesterday's Authors of Books for Children: Facts and Pictures about Authors and Illustrators of Books for Young People from Early Times to 1960*

CLR—*Children's Literature Review: Excerpts from Reviews, Criticism, and Commentary on Books for Children*

SAAS—*Something about the Author Autobiography Series*

J

Author Index

Author Index

O'Hara, Kenneth
  See Morris, (Margaret) Jean
O'Hara, Mary
  See Alsop, Mary O'Hara
O'Hara (Alsop), Mary
  See Alsop, Mary O'Hara
O'Hare, Jeff(rey A.) 1958- 105
Ohi, Ruth 1964- 95
Ohiyesa
  See Eastman, Charles A(lexander)
Ohlsson, Ib 1935- 7
Ohmi, Ayano 1959- 115
Ohtomo, Yasuo 1946- 37
o huigin, sean 1942- 138
  See also CLR 75
Oiseau
  See Moseley, James W(illett)
Oke, Janette 1935- 97
O'Keefe, Susan Heyboer 133
O'Keeffe, Frank 1938- 99
O'Kelley, Mattie Lou 1908-1997 97
  Earlier sketch in SATA 36
Okimoto, Jean Davies 1942- 103
  Earlier sketch in SATA 34
Okomfo, Amasewa
  See Cousins, Linda
Olaleye, Isaac O. 1941- 96
  See also SAAS 23
Olcott, Frances Jenkins 1872(?)-1963 19
Old, Wendie C(orbin) 1943- 154
Old Boy
  See Hughes, Thomas
Oldenburg, E(gbert) William 1936-1974 35
Older, Effin 1942- 114
Older, Jules 1940- 156
  Earlier sketch in SATA 114
Oldfield, Jenny 1949- 140
Oldfield, Margaret J(ean) 1932- 56
Oldfield, Pamela 1931- 86
Oldham, June 70
Oldham, Mary 1944- 65
Olds, Elizabeth 1896-1991 3
  Obituary 66
Olds, Helen Diehl 1895-1981 9
  Obituary 25
Oldstyle, Jonathan
  See Irving, Washington
O'Leary, Brian (Todd) 1940- 6
O'Leary, Patsy B(aker) 1937- 97
Oliphant, B. J.
  See Tepper, Sheri S.
Oliver, Burton
  See Burt, Olive Woolley
Oliver, Chad
  See Oliver, Symmes C(hadwick)
Oliver, John Edward 1933- 21
Oliver, Marilyn Tower 1935- 89
Oliver, Narelle 1960- 152
Oliver, Shirley (Louise Dawkins) 1958- 74
Oliver, Symmes C(hadwick) 1928-1993 101
  See Oliver, Chad
Oliviero, Jamie 1950- 84
Olmsted, Lorena Ann 1890-1989 13
Olney, Ross R. 1929- 13
Olschewski, Alfred (Erich) 1920- 7
Olsen, Barbara 148
Olsen, Carol 1945- 89
Olsen, Ib Spang 1921- 81
  Earlier sketch in SATA 6
Olsen, Violet (Mae) 1922-1991 58
Olson, Arielle North 1932- 67
Olson, Gene 1922- 32
Olson, Helen Kronberg 48
Olson, Marianne
  See Mitchell, Marianne
Olugebefola, Ademole 1941- 15
Oluonye, Mary N(kechi) 1955- 111
Om
  See Gorey, Edward (St. John)
O'Malley, Kevin 1961- 157
Oman, Carola (Mary Anima) 1897-1978 35

O'Meara, Walter (Andrew) 1897-1989 65
Ommanney, F(rancis) D(ownes) 1903-1980 . 23
O Mude
  See Gorey, Edward (St. John)
Oneal, Elizabeth 1934- 82
  Earlier sketch in SATA 30
  See Oneal, Zibby
O'Neal, Reagan
  See Rigney, James Oliver, Jr.
Oneal, Zibby
  See CLR 13
  See Oneal, Elizabeth
O'Neill, Amanda 1951- 111
O'Neill, Gerard K(itchen) 1927-1992 65
O'Neill, Judith (Beatrice) 1930- 34
O'Neill, Mary L(e Duc) 1908(?)-1990 2
  Obituary 64
Onslow, Annette Rosemary MacArthur
  See MacArthur-Onslow, Annette Rosemary
Onyefulu, Ifeoma 1959- 157
  Earlier sketches in SATA 81, 115
Opie, Iona (Margaret Balfour) 1923- 118
  Earlier sketches in SATA 3, 63
  See also SAAS 6
Opie, Peter (Mason) 1918-1982 118
  Obituary 28
  Earlier sketch in SATA 3, 63
Oppel, Kenneth 1967- 153
  Earlier sketch in SATA 99
Oppenheim, Joanne 1934- 136
  Earlier sketches in SATA 5, 82
Oppenheimer, Joan L(etson) 1925- 28
Oppong, Joseph Ransford 1953- 160
Optic, Oliver
  See Adams, William Taylor
  and Stratemeyer, Edward L.
Oram, Hiawyn 1946- 101
  Earlier sketch in SATA 56
Orbach, Ruth Gary 1941- 21
Orczy, Emma
  See Orczy, Baroness Emmuska
Orczy, Emma Magdalena Rosalia Maria Josefa
  See Orczy, Baroness Emmuska
Orczy, Emmuska
  See Orczy, Baroness Emmuska
Orczy, Baroness Emmuska 1865-1947 40
  See Orczy, Emma
Orde, A. J.
  See Tepper, Sheri S.
O'Reilly, Jackson
  See Rigney, James Oliver, Jr.
Orenstein, Denise Gosliner 1950- 157
Orgel, Doris 1929- 148
  Earlier sketches in SATA 7, 85
  See also CLR 48
  See also SAAS 19
Orleans, Ilo 1897-1962 10
Orlev, Uri 1931- 135
  Earlier sketch in SATA 58
  See also CLR 30
  See also SAAS 19
Ormai, Stella 57
  Brief entry 48
Ormerod, Jan(ette Louise) 1946- 132
  Brief entry 44
  Earlier sketches in SATA 55, 70
  See also CLR 20
Ormondroyd, Edward 1925- 14
Ormsby, Virginia H(aire) 1906-1990 11
Orr, Katherine S(helley) 1950- 72
Orr, Wendy 1953- 141
  Earlier sketch in SATA 90
Orris
  See Ingelow, Jean
Orth, Richard
  See Gardner, Richard (M.)
Ortiz Cofer, Judith
  See Cofer, Judith Ortiz
Orwell, George
  See CLR 68
  See Blair, Eric (Arthur)

Orwin, Joanna 1944- 141
Osborn, Elinor 1939- 145
Osborn, Lois D(orothy) 1915- 61
Osborne, Charles 1927- 59
Osborne, Chester G(orham) 1915-1987 11
Osborne, David
  See Silverberg, Robert
Osborne, George
  See Silverberg, Robert
Osborne, Leone Neal 1914-1996 2
Osborne, Mary Pope 1949- 144
  Earlier sketches in SATA 41, 55, 98
  See also CLR 88
Osceola
  See Blixen, Karen (Christentze Dinesen)
Osgood, William E(dward) 1926- 37
O'Shaughnessy, Darren 1972- 129
  See Shan, Darren
O'Shaughnessy, Ellen Cassels 1937- 78
O'Shea, (Catherine) Pat(ricia Shiels) 1931- . 87
  See also CLR 18
Osmond, Edward 1900- 10
Ossoli, Sarah Margaret (Fuller) 1810-1850 .. 25
  See Fuller, Margaret
  and Fuller, Sarah Margaret
Ostendorf, (Arthur) Lloyd, (Jr.) 1921-2000 .. 65
  Obituary 125
Otfinoski, Steven 1949- 116
  Earlier sketch in SATA 56
Otis, James
  See Kaler, James Otis
O'Toole, Thomas 1941- 71
O'Trigger, Sir Lucius
  See Horne, Richard Henry Hengist
Otten, Charlotte F(ennema) 1926- 98
Ottley, Matt 1962- 102
Ottley, Reginald Leslie 1909-1985 26
  See also CLR 16
Otto, Svend
  See Soerensen, Svend Otto
Oughton, Jerrie (Preston) 1937- 131
  Earlier sketch in SATA 76
Oughton, (William) Taylor 1925- 104
Ouida
  See De la Ramee, Marie Louise (Ouida)
Ousley, Odille 1896-1976 10
Outcalt, Todd 1960- 123
Overmyer, James E. 1946- 88
Overton, Jenny (Margaret Mary) 1942- 52
  Brief entry 36
Owen, Annie 1949- 75
Owen, Caroline Dale
  See Snedeker, Caroline Dale (Parke)
Owen, Clifford
  See Hamilton, Charles (Harold St. John)
Owen, Dilys
  See Gater, Dilys
Owen, (Benjamin) Evan 1918-1984 38
Owen, (John) Gareth 1936-2002 162
  Earlier sketch in SATA 83
  See also CLR 31
  See also SAAS 14
Owens, Bryant 1968- 116
Owens, Gail 1939- 54
Owens, Thomas S(heldon) 1960- 86
Owens, Tom
  See Owens, Thomas S(heldon)
Oxenbury, Helen 1938- 149
  Earlier sketches in SATA 3, 68
  See also CLR 70
Oxendine, Bess Holland 1933- 90
Oz, Frank (Richard) 1944- 60
Ozer, Jerome S. 1927- 59

P

Pace, Lorenzo 1943- 131
Pace, Mildred Mastin 1907- 46
  Brief entry 29

Author Index